The
Encyclopaedia of
**FORMS
AND
PRECEDENTS**

Fifth Edition
2000 Reissue

Volume 38(2)

**UNITED KINGDOM**
Butterworths, a Division of Reed Elsevier (UK) Ltd,
Halsbury House, 35 Chancery Lane, London WC2A 1EL and
4 Hill Street, Edinburgh EH2 3JZ

**AUSTRALIA**
Butterworths, a Division of Reed International Books Australia Pty Ltd, Chatswood,
New South Wales

**CANADA**
Butterworths Canada Ltd, Markham, Ontario

**HONG KONG**
Butterworths Asia (Hong Kong), Hong Kong

**INDIA**
Butterworths India, New Delhi

**IRELAND**
Butterworth (Ireland) Ltd, Dublin

**MALAYSIA**
Malayan Law Journal Sdn Bhd, Kuala Lumpur

**NEW ZEALAND**
Butterworths of New Zealand Ltd, Wellington

**SINGAPORE**
Butterworths Asia, Singapore

**SOUTH AFRICA**
Butterworths Publishers (PTY) Ltd, Durban

**USA**
Lexis Law Publishing, Charlottesville, Virginia

# The
# Encyclopaedia of
# FORMS
# AND
# PRECEDENTS

Fifth Edition

2000 Reissue

The Rt. Hon. Lord Millett, P.C.

A Lord of Appeal in Ordinary

Editor–in–Chief

Volume 38(2)

Sale of Land (Commercial Property Development)
>       Residential development
>       Contracts
>       Infrastructure
>       Warranties

BUTTERWORTHS
LONDON
2000

**First Edition**
Published between 1902 and 1909

**Second Edition**
Published in 1925 and 1926

**Third Edition**
Published between 1939 and 1950

**Fourth Edition**
Published between 1964 and 1983

**Fifth Edition**
Publication of the Fifth Edition of this Work was commenced in 1985 under the Editorship-in-Chief of the late Sir Raymond Walton, M.A., B.C.L., one of Her Majesty's Justices of the High Court of Justice (Chancery Division) (1973–1988), an Hon. Fellow of the College of Estate Management, and a Bencher of Lincoln's Inn.

ISBN
*for complete set of volumes:*       0 406 02360 3
for this volume:                      0 406 91349 8

ISBN 0-406-91349-8

9 780406 913494

Set in 10 on 11 pt Bembo and printed in Great Britain by
Butler & Tanner Ltd, Frome and London

**Visit us at our website: http://www.butterworths.com**

# Editor–in–Chief

## THE RT. HON. LORD MILLETT, P.C.
A Lord of Appeal in Ordinary

# Consulting Editors

*For Land Registry matters:*

RICHARD FEARNLEY, B.A., Solicitor
District Land Registrar,
Her Majesty's Land Registry

*For Direct Taxation matters:*

JOHN JEFFREY-COOK, F.T.I.I., F.C.A., F.C.I.S.

*For Value Added Tax and Stamp Duty matters:*

IAN HYDE, B.A., Partner
Pinsent Curtis

# Contributors

**SALE OF LAND**

CAROLINE BAILEY, B.A., Solicitor
Horsham District Council

GODFREY BRUCE-RADCLIFFE, Solicitor
Hobson Audley

ROBIN COLE, Solicitor
Richards Butler

IAN DAVISON, M.A.
Chief Solicitor to Horsham District Council

TREVOR HELLAWELL, M.A. (Cantab)

NICHOLAS J. F. LIGHTBODY, B.A., FRSA, Solicitor
The Law Offices of Nicholas J. F. Lightbody

PAUL MATCHAM, Solicitor
Maples Teesdale

JOHN PEET, Solicitor
Shoosmiths

NICHOLAS RADCLIFFE, Solicitor

# Volume 38(2)
# 2000 Reissue

For current information on the titles published in the Encyclopaedia, subscribers should refer to the *List of Titles*, in the Information Binder of the Service, which will always represent the most recent position of titles.

This volume will be kept up to date by material in the Fifth Edition Service which is issued quarterly and which should be filed in the appropriate Fifth Edition Service Binders.

## Summary of Titles

(For full details of the contents of the volume see the Table of Contents to the title and the index to the volume)

*reference no*

SALE OF LAND . . . . . . . . . . . . . . . . . . . . . . . . . . . . . . . . . . . . . . . . . **[3001]**

Practitioners have for many years relied upon the huge scale and comprehensive coverage of the '**Sale of Land**' title in the Encyclopaedia. The subject matter is vast and over the past few years both property law and conveyancing practice have developed radically.

Legislative changes include the coming into force of the Law of Property (Miscellaneous Provisions) Act 1994, the Landlord and Tenant (Covenants) Act 1995, the Trusts of Land and Appointment of Trustees Act 1996, the Land Registration Act 1997, the Land Registration Rules 1997 and 1999, the Contracts (Rights of Third Parties) Act 1999 and the publication of Regulations and statutory guidance under the Environment Act 1990 relating to contaminated land. Also completely new versions of a number of the more important Land Registry application and disposition forms have been prescribed for use.

Over the same period unprecedented commercial pressures have developed for those carrying out conveyancing. The need for speedy retrieval of reliable information and precedents is now, therefore, greater than ever and the **SALE OF LAND** volumes have placed a heavy emphasis on laying out revised and updated material in a logical order with a view to allowing rapid access to the relevant areas of the work.

**Volume 35 (1997 Reissue)** contains the whole of the commentary relating to the conveyancing process, including the National Conveyancing Protocol (3rd Edition) and the various forms prescribed for use under it, and the Standard Conditions of Sale (3rd Edition).

**Volume 36 (1997 Reissue)** contains the forms which will be required up to and including exchange of contracts and investigation of title, and complete forms of contract for the sale of freehold and leasehold land.

**Volume 37 (1998 Reissue)** contains the forms which will be required after exchange of contracts and specimen prescribed forms of transfer.

**Volume 38(1) (2000 Reissue)** deals with the acquisition and disposal of vacant and let commercial property. It contains:
- commentary on issues affecting commercial property transactions including VAT, stamp duty and direct taxation, employment, public health, contaminated land, and transfers of rights against contractors and professionals;

- forms of general conditions of sale including the Standard Conditions of Sale (3rd Edition) and the Standard Commercial Property Conditions (1st Edition), and notices to complete;
- pre-contract matters including checklists, pre-contract enquiries, environmental and due diligence enquiries, exclusivity and confidentiality agreements, and certificates and reports on title;
- grant of options and rights of pre-emption;
- general and special conditions for sales by auctions and tender;
- comprehensive forms of unconditional contract for the sale and purchase of commercial properties, both vacant and subject to occupational leases, together with extensive schedules;
- documents relating to leasehold reversions.

**Volume 38(2) (2000 Reissue)** contains precedents relating to commercial property development and residential estate development including:
- contracts conditional on the grant of planning permission and removal of tenants;
- further option agreements, including an option conditional on the grant of planning permission;
- alternative pricing schedules;
- development claw-back (overage) terms;
- forward funding and forward sale and purchase agreements, and agreements for development leases;
- infrastructure agreements and planning obligations;
- residential estate development pre-contract documents, contracts, transfers and management documents;
- appointment of a professional, collateral warranties and assignment;
- additional clauses for contracts.

**The law stated in this volume is in general that in force on 1 May 2000 although later developments have been noted wherever possible.**

# TABLE OF STATUTES

*References are to the numbers in square brackets which appear
on the right-hand side of the pages of text*

# TABLE OF
# STATUTORY INSTRUMENTS

*References are to the numbers in square brackets which appear*
*on the right-hand side of the pages of text*

# TABLE OF CASES

*References are to the numbers in square brackets which appear*
*on the right-hand side of the pages of text*

reference no

# SALE OF LAND (COMMERCIAL PROPERTY DEVELOPMENT)

*References are to the numbers in square brackets which appear*
*on the right hand side of the pages of text*

## (4): DEVELOPMENT CLAW-BACK (OVERAGE)

# PART 7: DEVELOPMENT AGREEMENTS

## (1): THE PURPOSE OF A FORWARD FUNDING OR FORWARD SALE/ PURCHASE AGREEMENT

## Commentary

### A: INTRODUCTION

### B: CONTRACTUAL ELEMENTS OF FORWARD FUNDING AND FORWARD SALE/PURCHASE

### C: DISPUTES

### D: LETTING

### E: VAT

### 1: GENERAL

# Forms and Precedents

## (2): AGREEMENTS FOR LEASE IN DEVELOPMENT

# Commentary

## A: INTRODUCTION

## B: AGREEMENT FOR LEASE BETWEEN LANDOWNER AND DEVELOPER

## C: AGREEMENT FOR LEASE BETWEEN DEVELOPER AND TENANT

## D: TAXATION

# Forms and Precedents

# PART 8: INFRASTRUCTURE AND PLANNING OBLIGATIONS

# Forms and Precedents

# PART 9: RESIDENTIAL DEVELOPMENT

# Forms and Precedents

## (1): PRELIMINARY DOCUMENTS

## (2): AGREEMENTS FOR SALE

## (6): MANAGEMENT DOCUMENTS

## (7): COUNTRY HOUSE FREEHOLD DIVISION SCHEME

## (8): RELEASES FROM SECURITY

# PART 10: PROFESSIONALS: APPOINTMENT AND COLLATERAL WARRANTIES

## Forms and Precedents

## PART 11: ADDITIONAL AND ALTERNATIVE CONTRACT CLAUSES

## Forms and Precedents

### A: BUILDING SAFETY

### B: ASSIGNMENT OF COLLATERAL WARRANTIES

### C: CONFIDENTIALITY

### D: ENVIRONMENTAL MATTERS

### E: REVERSIONS AND GROUND RENT

*Material dealing with the acquisition and disposal of vacant and let commercial property may be found in vol 38(1) (2000 Reissue) SALE OF LAND (Commercial Property Sales). It contains:*

•   *commentary on issues affecting commercial property transactions including VAT, stamp duty and direct taxation, employment, public health, contaminated land, and transfers of rights against contractors and professionals;*

•   *forms of general conditions of sale including the Standard Conditions of Sale (3rd Edition) and the Standard Commercial Property Conditions (1st Edition), and notices to complete;*

•   *pre-contract matters including checklists, pre-contract enquiries, environmental and due diligence enquiries, exclusivity and confidentiality agreements, and certificates and reports on title;*

•   *grant of options and rights of pre-emption;*

•   *general and special conditions for sales by auctions and tender;*

•   *comprehensive forms of unconditional contract for the sale and purchase of commercial properties, both vacant and subject to occupational leases, together with extensive schedules;*

•   *documents relating to leasehold reversions.*

# PART 6: CONDITIONAL CONTRACTS AND OPTIONS

## *Commentary*

### 296    Introduction

Forms 67 [3021]–71 [3201] together with vol 38(1) (2000 Reissue) SALE OF LAND Forms 56 [2021]–59 [2321] comprise a series of agreements and options for the sale and purchase of land for a wide range of typical investment and development land sales. They can be divided into two series, with associated satellite or supplementary precedents, as follows[1].

1    For a chart showing how the precedents may be used together see Form 66 [3011] post.

**[3001]**

### 297    Series A: unconditional agreements and options

Series A comprises the following precedents:

2.1              Investment Portfolio Sale and Purchase[1];
2.2              Single Freehold Investment Sale and Purchase[2];
2.3              Single Leasehold Investment Sale and Purchase[3];
2.4              Single Freehold Sale and Purchase with Vacant Possession[4];
2.5              Call Option for Freehold Sale and Purchase with Vacant Possession[5].

These are all complete documents in respect of which satellite provisions provide options for variation or indexation adjustment to the purchase price.

The principal satellite provision comprises an overage liability on the buyer, based upon post-completion letting of initially void space[6]. In addition, as such provision is often encountered in a transaction by which the seller has guaranteed rent payments on the same void space, an associated rent guarantee arrangement is also provided[7]. This precedent can also be used on its own. Where both these precedents are used together, definitions common to both should be removed (as shown by footnotes) to the main body of the agreement.

In the case of the stand-alone option agreement[8], the practitioner will be required to complete the relevant sale and purchase agreement[9] to annex to that option. An alternative form of option agreement with sale and purchase provisions fully incorporated is also provided[10] and could be utilised, if preferred, with minimum adaptation in the transactional circumstances contemplated by Form 70 [3171] post.

**[3002]**

1    See vol 38(1) (2000 Reissue) SALE OF LAND Form 56 [2021].
2    See vol 38(1) (2000 Reissue) SALE OF LAND Form 57 [2131].
3    See vol 38(1) (2000 Reissue) SALE OF LAND Form 58 [2221].
4    See vol 38(1) (2000 Reissue) SALE OF LAND Form 59 [2321].
5    Form 70 [3171] post.
6    Form 74 [3261] post.

7    See vol 38(1) (2000 Reissue) SALE OF LAND Form 60 [2381].
8    Form 70 [3171] post.
9    Most commonly in the form of vol 38(1) (2000 Reissue) SALE OF LAND Form 59 [2321].
10   Form 71 [3201] post.

**[3003]**


**298    Series B: conditional agreements and options**
Series B comprises the following precedents:
3.1              Simple Form of Freehold Sale Agreement Conditional upon Planning and
                 Vacant Possession[1];
3.2              Complex Form of Sale of Freehold Land with Vacant Possession
                 conditional upon Planning (Seller's Perspective)[2];
3.3              Complex Form of Sale of Freehold Land with Vacant Possession
                 Conditional upon Planning (Buyer's Perspective)[3];
3.4              Call Option for Freehold Sale and Purchase with Vacant Possession
                 Conditional on Planning[4].
These all require the use of one of the relevant supplementary precedents.
     The principal use of the supplementary precedents is to enable the practitioner to
utilise a common form of conditional sale and purchase agreement or option whilst
incorporating the relevant 'stand alone' pricing schedule which is appropriate to that
transaction.
     These supplements are:
3.5              Residual Land Valuation[5];
3.6              Open Market Value[6]; and
3.7              Residential Density[7].
Each takes the form of a separate schedule to be incorporated as appropriate. In each case,
footnotes describe for the practitioner the nature of the pricing mechanism and its
application.

**[3004]**

1    Form 67 [3021] post.
2    Form 68 [3061] post.
3    Form 69 [3121] post.
4    Form 71 [3201] post.
5    Form 72 [3251] post.
6    Form 73 [3257] post.
7    Form 75 [3267] post.

**[3005]–[3010]**

# Forms and Precedents

## (1): CONDITIONAL CONTRACTS

## 66

**Use of precedents in Part 6**

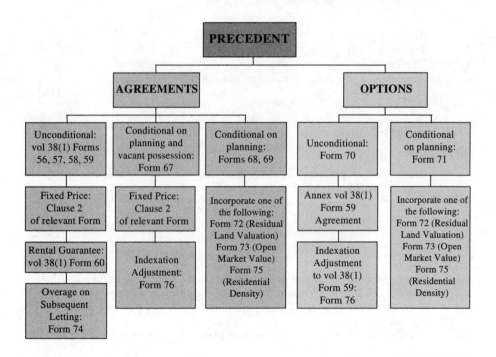

[3011]–[3020]

## 67

**Agreement for sale of a single freehold commercial property with vacant possession, conditional upon the grant of planning permission and the removal of existing tenants; purchase price fixed**[1]

### CONTENTS

**[3021]**

THIS AGREEMENT is made the ...... day of .........

BETWEEN:

(1)          *(name of seller)*[2] [company number *(number)*][3] [of *(address)* or whose registered office is at *(address)*] ('the Seller') and

(2)          *(name of buyer)* [company number *(number)*] [of *(address)* or whose registered office is at *(address)*] ('the Buyer')

## 1          Definitions and interpretation[4]

In this Agreement:

1.1          'this Agreement' means this document as varied by any subsequent documentation

1.2          'the Buyer's Solicitors' means *(insert name and address of person or firm)*

1.3          'Completion' means actual completion of the sale and purchase agreed in this Agreement

1.4          'the Completion Date'[5] means the date 20 working days after the Unconditional Date

1.5          'the Completion Moneys' means the Purchase Price (or any outstanding balance of it) as adjusted by all sums due between the parties at Completion

1.6          'the Contract Rate'[6] means *(insert interest rate or method of calculating the interest rate by reference eg to the base lending rate of a named bank)*

1.7          'the Deposit' means £... [which is [inclusive *or* exclusive] of VAT at the standard rate][7]

1.8          'the General Conditions'[8] means [the Standard Conditions of Sale (3rd Edn) *or* (specify)]

[1.9          'the Plan'[9] means the plan attached to this Agreement [and if numbered plans are attached any reference to a numbered plan is to the attached plan so numbered]]

1.10          'the Property'[10] means the freehold property described in Part I of the first schedule

**[3022]**

1.11    'the Purchase Price' means £...[11]
1.12    'the Seller's Solicitors' means *(insert name and address of person or firm)*
1.13    'the Tenancies' means the tenancies leases licenses and other occupational rights (if any) set out in the third schedule[12]
1.14    'the Transfer' means the transfer of the Property
1.15    'the Unconditional Date' means the date upon which both of the conditions set out in clause 2.2 have been satisfied or waived in accordance with clause 2
1.16    'VAT' means an amount equal to the value added tax as charged in accordance with VATA[13] or any equivalent or substituted tax
1.17    'VATA' means the Value Added Tax Act 1994 or any equivalent tax Act
1.18    'VAT invoice' means an invoice complying with the provisions of regulations 13 and 14 of the VAT Regulations 1995[14]
1.19    where the context so admits the expression[s] 'the Seller' [and 'the Buyer'] include[s] their respective personal representatives [and 'the Buyer' shall include any permitted successors in title of the Buyer][15]
1.20    words importing one gender shall be construed as importing any other gender
1.21    words importing the singular shall be construed as importing the plural and vice versa
1.22    words importing persons shall be construed as importing a corporate body and/ or a partnership and vice versa
1.23    where any party comprises more than one person the obligations and liabilities of that party under this Agreement shall be joint and several obligations and liabilities of those persons[16]
1.24    the clause headings do not form part of this Agreement and shall not be taken into account in its construction or interpretation
1.25    any reference to a clause or a paragraph or a schedule is to one in this Agreement so numbered
1.26    any reference to a colour or letter is to one on the [Plan *or* Plans]
1.27    in the absence of any contrary provision any reference to a statute includes any statutory modification or re-enactment of it and any and every order instrument regulation direction or plan made or issued under the statute or deriving validity from it

**[3023]**

## 2      Conditional agreement for sale

2.1     The Seller shall sell and the Buyer shall buy the Property for the Purchase Price
2.2     The sale and purchase is conditional upon:
        2.2.1    the grant of planning permission[17] for which application has already been made to the *(local planning authority)* under application reference number *(number)* with such amendments and variations as the Seller shall approve [in its absolute discretion *or* such approval not to be unreasonably withheld or delayed] by not later than *(date)* and
        2.2.2    the Seller obtaining (without limiting its completion obligations under clause 6) vacant possession of each part of the Property which at the date of this Agreement is affected by or subject to the Tenancies by not later than *(date)*
2.3     Upon any relevant condition being satisfied the party satisfying the condition shall promptly notify the other party in writing that the relevant condition has been satisfied such notification to be accompanied by appropriate written evidence showing how the condition has been satisfied
2.4     The Buyer has the sole benefit of each condition referred to in clause 2.2 and may by written notice given at any time prior to the date by which the relevant condition is to have been satisfied unilaterally waive that condition[18]

**3      Deposit[19]**

3.1     The Deposit [and the VAT on it][20] shall be paid[21] to the Seller's Solicitors [as agents for the Seller *or* to hold as stakeholders][22] [on the Unconditional Date][23]

3.2     The Law of Property Act 1925 Section 49(2) shall not have effect

[3.3    The Seller shall issue a valid VAT invoice in respect of the Deposit within [7] days of its payment to the Seller's Solicitors[24]]

**4      Completion**

4.1     Completion of the sale and purchase and payment of the Completion Moneys [and of the VAT] shall take place on the Completion Date[25] on or before [1.00 pm] [at the offices of the Seller's Solicitors or where they may reasonably direct[26]]

4.2     If the Completion Moneys are received after [1.00 pm][27] on the Completion Date or on a day which is not a working day Completion shall be deemed for the purposes of the General Conditions to have taken place on the next working day

**[3024]**

**[5      Title guarantee[28]** *(where the form of the assurance is not annexed)*

5.1     The Seller sells the Property [with [full *or* limited] *or* without any] title guarantee [with the modifications set out below]

[5.2    Where the Transfer is made with full title guarantee the Law of Property (Miscellaneous Provisions) Act 1994 Section 6(2)(a) shall have effect as though all matters now recorded in all registers open to or capable of public inspection are to be considered to be within the actual knowledge of the Buyer]

[5.3    Where the transfer is made with limited title guarantee the Law of Property (Miscellaneous Provisions) Act 1994 Section 3(3) shall not apply and instead the Seller will covenant that it has not since the transfer to it:

     5.3.1    charged or encumbered the Property by means of any charge or encumbrance which subsists at the date of the Transfer or granted third party rights in relation to the Property which so subsist or

     5.3.2    knowingly suffered the Property to be so charged or encumbered or subjected to any such rights]

[5.4    The Transfer shall contain the modifications set out above and include an application to the Registrar to enter on the register in an appropriate manner a note that the implied covenants are modified in the manner set out above]

*or*

**5      Title guarantee** *(where the form of Transfer is annexed)*

The Property is sold [with [the title guarantee set out in the annexed form of draft Transfer [with the modifications included in it] *or* without any title guarantee]]

**[3025]**

**6      Vacant Possession[29]**

6.1     Subject to clause 6.2 the Property is sold with vacant possession subject to the presence of any third party chattels

6.2     In the event of the Buyer waiving the condition set out in clause 2.2.2 the Property is sold subject to such [right title interest and estate of any third party existing and disclosed to the Buyer on or before the date of this Agreement or created after the date of this Agreement with the written consent of the Buyer *or* of the Tenancies] which affect[s] the Property as at the Unconditional Date but otherwise with vacant possession

**7      Title**[30]

[7.1     The title to the Property is unregistered and title shall commence with the
         document described as the root of title in Part II of the first schedule[31]
         *or*
         The title to the Property is registered at HM Land Registry and title shall be
         deduced in accordance with the Land Registration Act 1925 Section 110 [save
         that copies of the entries on the register the filed plan and any documents
         referred to shall be office copies[32]]]

7.2      Title having been deduced prior to the date of this Agreement the Buyer
         accepts the Seller's title to the Property and shall be deemed to purchase with
         full knowledge of the title in all respects and shall not raise any requisitions or
         make any objection in relation to the title[33] [but the Buyer may raise requisitions
         arising out of:

         7.2.1    events occurring after the date of this Agreement
         7.2.2    matters revealed by pre-completion searches which are not registered
                  at the date of this Agreement
         7.2.3    matters which a prudent buyer could not be aware of at the date of
                  this Agreement]

[7.3     The Seller does not have the documents (if any) noted as missing in Part II of
         the first schedule and the Buyer may not raise any requisition or objection on
         that account and no acknowledgement for production or undertaking for safe
         custody will be given nor copies produced][34]

                                                                                    **[3026]**

[8      **Encumbrances**[35] *(where the form of the assurance is not annexed)*

[8.1     The Property is sold subject to and (where appropriate) with the benefit of:
         8.1.1    the    matters    contained    or    referred    to    in    the    property
                  [proprietorship][36] and charges[37] registers of the title to the Property
                  [other than any subsisting financial charges]
         [8.1.2   the documents described in Part II of the first schedule] [and]
         [8.1.3   the matters set out in the second schedule]][38]

8.2      The Buyer or the Buyer's Solicitors having been supplied with copies of the
         documents referred to in clause 8.1 the Buyer shall be deemed to purchase with
         full notice and knowledge of the same and shall not raise any requisition or make
         any objection in relation to them

8.3      The Transfer shall contain a covenant by the Buyer that the Buyer will (by way
         of indemnity only) observe and perform the covenants conditions and other
         matters contained or referred to in the documents referred to in clause 8.1 and
         will indemnify and keep the Seller and its successors in title fully and effectually
         indemnified against all actions proceedings damages costs claims and expenses
         which may be suffered or incurred by the Seller or its successors in title in
         respect of [future] breach or non-observance or non-performance of those
         covenants and conditions [and obligations][39]

8.4      The Transfer shall be engrossed [in duplicate] by the Buyer's Solicitors and [the
         *or* both] engrossment[s] shall be executed by the Buyer before the Completion
         Date

[8.5     Immediately after Completion the Buyer shall at its own expense procure the
         proper stamping of the duplicate Transfer as a duplicate (including but not
         limited to the affixing of a particulars delivered stamp) and shall immediately
         after such stamping deliver the duly stamped duplicate to the Seller's Solicitors]

                                                                                    **[3027]**

*or*

**8      Encumbrances**[40] *(where the form of Transfer is annexed)*[41]

8.1     The Transfer shall be in the form of the annexed draft

[8.2    The Property is sold subject to and (where appropriate) with the benefit of:

    8.2.1     the matters contained or referred to in the annexed draft Transfer and the property [proprietorship][42] and charges[43] registers of the title to the Property [other than any subsisting financial charges]

    [8.2.2     the documents described in Part II of the first schedule] [and]

    [8.2.3     the matters set out in the second schedule]][44]

8.3     The Buyer or the Buyer's Solicitors having been supplied with copies of the matters (if any) referred to in clause 8.2 prior to the date of this Agreement the Buyer shall be deemed to purchase with full notice and knowledge of them and shall not raise any requisition or make any objection in relation to them

8.4     The Transfer shall be engrossed [in duplicate] by the Seller's Solicitors and [the *or* both] engrossment[s] shall be executed by the Buyer before the Completion Date

[8.5    Immediately after Completion the Buyer shall at its own expense procure the proper stamping of the duplicate Transfer as a duplicate (including but not limited to the affixing of a particulars delivered stamp) and shall immediately after such stamping deliver the duly stamped duplicate to the Seller's Solicitors]]

[3028]

**9      Matters affecting the Property**

The Property is sold subject to the following matters:

9.1     all local land charges whether registered or not before the date of this Agreement and all matters capable of registration as local land charges whether or not actually so registered[45]

9.2     all notices served and orders demands proposals or requirements made by any local public or other competent authority whether before or after the date of this Agreement

9.3     all actual or proposed charges notices orders restrictions agreements conditions contraventions or other matters arising under any statute

9.4     all easements quasi-easements rights exceptions or other similar matters including rights of way drainage water watercourses light rights of adjoining owners affecting the Property and liability to repair or covenants to repair roads pavements paths ways passages sewers drains gutters fences and other like matters whether or not apparent on inspection or disclosed in any of the documents referred to in this Agreement and without any obligation on the Seller to provide evidence of the creation of or to define or apportion any such liability

9.5     matters discoverable by inspection of the Property before the date of this Agreement

9.6     matters relating to the Property about which the Seller does not know

9.7     matters disclosed or which would be disclosed by any searches or as a result of enquiries (formal or informal and made in person in writing or orally) made by or for the Buyer or which a prudent buyer ought to make and

9.8     overriding interests as defined in the Land Registration Act 1925 Section 70(1) or matters which would be overriding interests if the title were registered

[3029]

**10    Disclaimer**[46]

10.1     The Buyer admits that:

        10.1.1     it has inspected the Property and purchases it with full knowledge of its actual state and condition and shall take the Property as it stands

        10.1.2     it enters into this Agreement solely as a result of its own inspection and on the basis of the terms of this Agreement and not in reliance upon any advertisement statement representation or warranty either written or oral or implied made by or on behalf of the Seller except as stated in clause 10.2

        10.1.3     no warranty statement or representation has been made or given to the Buyer that the Property can be used or developed in any particular way or for any particular purpose and the Seller shall not be liable to the Buyer if the Property cannot for any reason whatsoever be so used or developed

10.2     The Buyer may rely on factual representations and warranties made or given by the Seller's Solicitors to the Buyer's Solicitor's pre-contract enquiries but only in so far as such statements are not capable of independent verification by appropriate searches enquiries inspection survey of the Property or by inspection of the documents and information supplied to the Buyer's Solicitors

10.3     This Agreement contains the entire agreement between the parties and incorporates all the terms agreed between them for the purposes of the Law of Property (Miscellaneous Provisions) Act 1989 Section 2 and there are no other terms or provisions agreed prior to the date of this Agreement which have not been incorporated into this Agreement

                                                                    **[3030]**

**11    Incorporation of conditions of sale and documents**

11.1     The General Conditions [as amended by the [fourth] schedule][47] shall apply to this Agreement and are incorporated in it in so far as they are applicable to a sale by private treaty and are not varied by or inconsistent with the terms of this Agreement

11.2     If there is any conflict between the General Conditions [as amended] and the terms of this Agreement the terms of this Agreement prevail

11.3     All express agreements made or undertakings given by one party to the other [in *(set out list of letters and documents including relevant inter solicitor correspondence)*] are incorporated in this Agreement

**[12    Restriction on assignment and sub-sale**[48]

12.1     This Agreement is personal to the Buyer and is not capable of being assigned charged or mortgaged [except by way of floating charge]

[12.2     The Seller shall not be required to transfer the Property [to anyone other than the Buyer named in this Agreement *or* at a price greater than the Purchase Price *or* except by one Transfer at the Purchase Price]]]

**13    Merger on completion**[49]

The provisions of this Agreement shall not merge on completion of the Transfer so far as they remain to be performed

                                                                    **[3031]**

**14      VAT provisions**[50]

14.1     The Purchase Price is [inclusive *or* exclusive] of VAT at the standard rate as at Completion

14.2     All VAT payable by the Buyer shall be paid at the same time as the payment on which it is chargeable

14.3     The Seller shall provide the Buyer with a receipted VAT Invoice for any VAT paid by the Buyer under this Agreement

[14.4    The Seller warrants that it has not made an election to waive exemption from VAT and will not make any such election][51]

**[15     Insolvency of Buyer**

15.1     If the Buyer:

15.1.1       enters into voluntary liquidation (other than for the purpose of reconstruction or amalgamation not involving a realisation of assets) or has a winding-up order made against it by the court or has a receiver appointed over all or any part of its assets or an administration order is made pursuant to the Insolvency Act 1986 or

15.1.2       becomes insolvent or enters into any composition with its or his creditors or enters into a voluntary arrangement (within the meaning of the Insolvency Act 1986 Sections 1 or 253[52]) or distress sequestration or execution is levied on its goods

then and in any such case the Seller may rescind this Agreement by notice to the Buyer

15.2     Condition 7.2 of the General Conditions shall apply save that in this instance the Seller shall not be obliged to pay any interest which has accrued on the deposit]

**16      Jurisdiction and Governing Law**

This Agreement shall be governed by and construed in accordance with English law and the parties submit to the [non-exclusive] jurisdiction of the English courts[53]

**[3032]**

**17      Nature of this Agreement**

This Agreement [is *or* is not] a deed and [has *or* has not] been executed by the parties to it as a deed[54]

**18      Notices**[55]

18.1     Any notice to be given under or in connection with this Agreement shall be in writing and may be delivered personally or sent by first class post telex or fax to the party due to receive the notice at its address set out in this Agreement or the address of its solicitor or such other address as previously specified (by written notice) by such party

18.2     A notice may be given by either party's solicitor to the other party's solicitor provided it conforms to the provisions of clause 18.1

18.3     In the absence of evidence of earlier receipt a notice is deemed received:

18.3.1       if delivered personally when left at the address referred to in clause 18.1

18.3.2       if sent by post two working days after posting it

18.3.3       if sent by telex when the proper answerback is received

18.3.4       if sent by fax on completion of its transmission

18.4     In the case of a notice given pursuant to clauses 18.3.1 18.3.3 or 18.3.4 where this occurs after 5 pm on a working day or on a day which is not a working day the date of service shall be deemed to be the next working day

[18.5    The [Seller *or* Buyer] irrevocably appoints *(name and address)* as its agent for service to receive on its behalf service of proceedings in the English Courts or in any other court or courts of competent jurisdiction][56]

## [19     Contracts (Rights of Third Parties) Act 1999

For the purposes of the Contracts (Rights of Third Parties) Act 1999 it is agreed that [with the exception only of *(specify clauses)*] nothing in this Agreement shall confer on any third party any right to enforce or any benefit of any term of this Agreement]

[AS *or* IN] WITNESS etc

                                                                              **[3033]**

### [FIRST] SCHEDULE
The Property
Part I
Description of the Property

*(Describe the Property: eg)*
[All that freehold property situate at and known as *(address)* registered with title [absolute] at HM Land Registry under title number *(number)*
*or*
All that unregistered freehold property situate at and known as *(address)* which is shown for identification purposes only on the plan annexed to this Agreement and numbered '1']

### [Part II
Title Documents affecting the Property
*(commencing where applicable with the root of title)*

| Number | Date | Nature | Parties | Remarks |
|---|---|---|---|---|
| *(number)* | *(date)* | *(details)* | *(details)* | *(eg root of title; missing)]* |

### [SECOND SCHEDULE
The Subjections[57]
*(set out any other matters to which the Property is subject not specified or mentioned elsewhere)]*

### [[THIRD] SCHEDULE
The Tenancies
*(insert details)]*

                                                                              **[3034]**

### [[FOURTH] SCHEDULE
Amendments to the Standard Conditions of Sale (3rd Edition)

1        Standard Conditions 3.4, 4.3.2, 4.5.2, 4.5.5, 5.1.1, 5.1.2, 5.2.2(b), 5.2.2(e), 5.2.2(g), 5.2.3 and 5.2.7 shall not apply
2        The Standard Conditions shall be varied as follows:
    2.1      in Standard Condition 1.1.1(a) sub-paragraphs (i) and (ii) shall be deleted and the words 'the interest actually earned on money less any proper charges for handling the money' shall be inserted

2.2      in Standard Condition 1.1.1(g) the contract rate shall be 4% per annum above the base rate current from time to time of *(name of bank etc)*

2.3      in Standard Condition 3.1.2(c) the word 'reasonably' shall be inserted after the words 'could not'

2.4      in Standard Condition 5.2.2(f) the words 'nor change its use and is to comply with all statutory obligations relating to the property and indemnify the seller against all liability arising as a result of any breach of such obligation' shall be added at the end

2.5      in Standard Conditions 6.1.2 and 6.1.3 '1 pm' shall be substituted for '2 pm'[58]

2.6      in Standard Condition 6.5.1 the words 'actual completion' shall be added after the word 'after' and the remainder of that Standard Condition shall be deleted

2.7      in Standard Condition 6.8.2(b) the words 'or if reasonable evidence is produced that the property would be released from all such mortgages' shall be added immediately after the words 'free of all mortgages'

2.8      in Standard Condition 7.1.1 the words 'or in negotiations leading to it' and 'or was' shall be deleted

2.9      Standard Conditions 7.3.1 and 7.3.2 shall be deleted and the following substituted:

         '7.3.1      if the purchase shall not be completed on the completion date the buyer shall pay compensation to the seller but no such compensation shall be payable for so long as the seller is not ready able and willing to complete as contemplated by Standard Condition 6.8

         7.3.2      compensation is calculated at the contract rate on all sums payable under the agreement (other than pursuant to Standard Condition 6.3) for the period between the completion date and actual completion']

*(signatures (or common seals) of the parties)*[59]
[*(signatures of witnesses)*]
**[3035]**

---

1      No stamp duty. See Information Binder: Stamp Duties [172] (Agreement).

     This Form differs from vol 38(1) (2000 Reissue) SALE OF LAND Form 59 [2321] to the extent only that the performance of the sale and purchase agreement is pre-conditional upon the buyer obtaining planning permission and the seller obtaining vacant possession.

     In the case of unregistered land the agreement is capable of being registered by the buyer against the seller's name as an estate contract (see vol 25(1) (1999 Reissue) LAND CHARGES Paragraph 40.5 [75]). Registration should be effected against the estate owner rather than the seller where the seller is a contracting buyer who has agreed to sub-sell or a mortgagee exercising its power of sale. In addition, the agreement may be protected by way of caution against first registration (see vol 25(1) (1999 Reissue) LAND REGISTRATION Paragraph 204 [2661]).

     In the case of registered land, the agreement may be noted on the register as an estate contract if the land certificate is placed on deposit or deemed to be on deposit, or it could be the subject of a caution in other cases: see vol 25(1) (1999 Reissue) LAND REGISTRATION Paragraph 178 [2489]. Strictly, all contracts for the sale of land should be protected by registration as land charges irrespective of whether the seller is in practice likely to resell, but the vast majority of such contracts are not so registered unless, eg, as in this case, completion is likely to be delayed. A buyer is not under a duty to register a contract: *Wright v Dean* [1948] Ch 686, [1948] 2 All ER 415. However, it seems that in certain circumstances a solicitor might be held to be negligent for failing to protect his client by registering his interest as buyer under a contract: see, eg, *Midland Bank Trust Co Ltd v Hett, Stubbs & Kemp* [1979] Ch 384, [1978] 3 All ER 571.

The planning condition is designed for the very simplest cases such as an application for change of use or for the carrying out of relatively minor building operations where the following circumstances apply:
(a)  the application is not likely to be varied;
(b)  it is unlikely that the grant of the planning permission would be challenged by third parties by way of judicial review; and
(c)  it is unlikely that the planning authority would require a planning agreement or obligation to be entered into under, eg, the Town and Country Planning Act 1990 s 106 (46 Halsbury's Statutes (4th Edn) TOWN AND COUNTRY PLANNING) or any highway agreements.
        For forms suitable for more complex planning situations see Forms 68 [3061] and 69 [3121] post.

2    The Standard Conditions of Sale (3rd Edn) (for which see vol 38(1) (2000 Reissue) SALE OF LAND Form 1 [1011]), like the Standard Commercial Property Conditions (1st Edn) (for which see vol 38(1) (2000 Reissue) SALE OF LAND Form 2 [1071]), use the terminology 'seller' and 'buyer' in place of the traditional 'vendor' and 'purchaser'. If this Form is to be used in conjunction with general conditions other than the Standard Conditions of Sale or the Standard Commercial Property Conditions it is recommended that the expressions 'vendor' and 'purchaser' are used in place of 'seller' and 'buyer' in order to present a uniform approach to the definitions used in such other general conditions.

3    If any party is a company it is desirable to include the company registration number before the address of the registered office. This avoids any problems arising when a company has been wound up and a new company formed with the same name, or when the name of a company is changed, or if companies swap names, eg on a reconstruction of a group of companies. In addition the company registration number will be required by HM Land Registry under the provisions of the Land Registration Rules 1996, SI 1996/2975 r 2, Schedule para 18.

4    One view would add the words 'unless the context otherwise admits' or 'where the context admits' and this may be implied (see *Meux v Jacobs* (1875) LR 7 HL 481 at 493; *Law Society v United Services Bureau Ltd* [1934] 1 KB 343, DC). However, the better course is to use whenever practicable defined terms in such a way that there are no circumstances where the defined meanings do not apply.
        Definitions of terms used only in schedules are contained in the relevant schedule.
        Clauses 1.20–22 are not strictly necessary as the Law of Property Act 1925 s 61 (37 Halsbury's Statutes (4th Edn) REAL PROPERTY) provides such definitions but such definitions are usually inserted for the convenience of the parties.

5    If no date is specifically agreed for completion under a contract incorporating one of the sets of standard conditions the fall-back provisions of the relevant conditions will apply. See, eg, the Standard Conditions of Sale (3rd Edn) condition 6.1 (for which see vol 38(1) (2000 Reissue) SALE OF LAND Form 1 [1045]) and the Standard Commercial Property Conditions (1st Edn) condition 6.1 (for which see vol 38(1) (2000 Reissue) SALE OF LAND Form 2 [1103]). As to the Law Society's General Conditions of Sale (1984 Revision) condition 21 (for which see vol 38(1) (2000 Reissue) SALE OF LAND Form 3 [1146]) and the National Conditions of Sale (20th Edn) condition 5(1) (for which see vol 38(1) (2000 Reissue) SALE OF LAND Form 4 [1164]), which Conditions were replaced by the Standard Conditions of Sale as from March 1990, see vol 38(1) (2000 Reissue) SALE OF LAND Paragraph 290 [1001] et seq.

6    Note that certain conditions in the Standard Conditions of Sale (3rd Edn) (see eg conditions 5.2.6, 7.3.2 (for which see vol 38(1) (2000 Reissue) SALE OF LAND Form 1 [1042] and [1051])) provide for compensation payable at the 'contract rate' ie the Law Society's interest rate from time to time in force (see vol 38(1) (2000 Reissue) SALE OF LAND Form 1 condition 1.1.1(g) [1012]); there are also conditions (see eg conditions 2.2.3, 7.2(a), 7.5.2(a)(i), 7.6.2(a)) which provide for payment of 'accrued interest' (see vol 38(1) (2000 Reissue) SALE OF LAND Form 1 condition 1.1.1(a) [1011]).

7    As to VAT, see notes 11 and 20 post. Omit the words in square brackets if no VAT is payable or it is payable but the deposit is held as stakeholder.

8    In preparing this form of sale and purchase agreement, it was decided that it would be helpful to practitioners if incorporation of the Standard Conditions of Sale (3rd Edn) (for which see vol 38(1) (2000 Reissue) SALE OF LAND Form 1 [1011]) was retained in the short term notwithstanding the issue of the Standard Commercial Property Conditions (1st Edn) (for which see vol 38(1) (2000 Reissue) SALE OF LAND Form 2 [1071]) which have yet to be fully adopted and used. Differences between the two sets of conditions (which are highly similar in many respects) are discussed and summarised in vol 38(1) (2000 Reissue) SALE OF LAND Form 5 [1201].
        Other sets of standard conditions which might be referred to are the Statutory Form of Conditions of Sale 1925, SR&O 1925/779, which applies to contracts made by correspondence, and may, but only by express reference, be made to apply to any other cases (see the Law of Property Act 1925 s 46) and the Standard Commercial Property Conditions (1st Edn) (for which see vol 38(1) (2000 Reissue) SALE OF LAND Form 2 [1071]). As to the National Conditions of Sale (20th Edn) (for which see vol 38(1) (2000 Reissue) SALE OF LAND Form 4 [1161]) and the Law Society's General Conditions of Sale (1984 Revision) (for which see vol 38(1) (2000 Reissue) SALE OF LAND Form 3 [1131]), which Conditions were replaced by the Standard Conditions of Sale as from March 1990, see vol 38(1) (2000 Reissue) SALE OF LAND Paragraph 290 [1001] et seq. A contract by correspondence can still be made in relation to a short lease, or the creation or operation of a resulting, implied or constructive trust: see the Law of

Property (Miscellaneous Provisions) Act 1989 s 2 as amended by the Trusts of Land and Appointment of Trustees Act 1996 s 25(2), Sch 4 (37 Halsbury's Statutes (4th Edn) REAL PROPERTY).

9   The size and scale of the plan should be sufficiently large to enable all salient features to be readily identified: see *Scarfe v Adams* [1981] 1 All ER 843, CA. If many plans are required it may be convenient to bind them in a separate bundle, suitably referred to in the contract. Each plan should be individually numbered if there is more than one. As to plans generally see vol 35 (1997 Reissue) SALE OF LAND Paragraph 623 [816].

10  As to the identity of the property to be sold see vol 35 (1997 Reissue) SALE OF LAND Paragraph 346 [453] et seq.

**[3036]**

11  As to circumstances in which VAT is payable, see vol 38(1) (2000 Reissue) SALE OF LAND Paragraph 6 [18] et seq and vol 35 (1997 Reissue) SALE OF LAND Paragraph 136 [173] et seq and see the Information Binder: Property [1] (VAT and Property). The sale of a fee simple is exempt unless it is one of an incomplete commercial building, a commercial building completed less than three years from the time of supply, or is a commercial building subject to an election to waive exemption of the seller or a relevant associate of the seller: see the Value Added Tax Act 1994 Sch 9 Group 1 (48 Halsbury's Statutes (4th Edn) VALUE ADDED TAX). It should be noted that VAT forms part of the stampable consideration for the purposes of calculating stamp duty and land registration fees.

If VAT is or may be chargeable in respect of any part of the purchase price, and the price is to be exclusive of the tax, a comprehensive clause dealing with all aspects of the tax should be included. For an example of such a clause see clause 14 of this Form and see further vol 36 (1997 Reissue) SALE OF LAND Forms 351 [2521] and 352 [2522]. The VAT provisions in this Form expand those in the Standard Conditions of Sale (3rd Edn) condition 1.4 (for which see vol 38(1) (2000 Reissue) SALE OF LAND Form 1 [1013]) and are inserted to act as a reminder to the parties of the importance of considering VAT aspects at an early stage.

If the Value Added Tax Act 1994 s 89 is excluded or the purchase price is expressed to be inclusive of VAT any changes in the rate or incidence of VAT between contract and completion cannot be added to the price.

12  This definition incorporates all of the tenancies in relation to which the Property is subject at the date of the agreement. However, the practitioner must consider whether:

(a) it is desirable or necessary for the seller to create new interests whilst the contract remains conditional, and if so, on what terms. Certainly, it would be possible for the seller to create new short term tenancies/leases/licences and other occupational rights without the consent of the buyer and care should then be taken to ensure that such tenancies are capable of being terminated to meet any requirement by the buyer to complete with vacant possession other than in respect of the tenancies (as defined), eg by waiving the vacant possession and planning pre-conditions. Effectively, this would require the creation of tenancies at will or tenancies containing suitable termination provisions and security of tenure exclusions.

(b) it is practicable for the buyer's solicitors to have formally assessed the seller's ability to procure vacant possession. As the property is to be released for development purposes, it is always advisable to consider carefully before entering into this form of contract what rights, title, interest and estate of any third party may affect the property and the seller's ability to deliver vacant possession.

13  See note 11 above.

14  Ie the Value Added Tax Regulations 1995, SI 1995/2518.

**[3037]**

15  In the absence of any specific provision in the contract both seller and buyer are free to assign the benefit of the whole contract or a part of it (eg a charge of the benefit of the contract, or a sub-sale of part of the property). It may be thought desirable to limit these rights, whether because of the importance of the personality or standing of the buyer, or to avoid an immediate sub-sale of the whole or part of the property for tax or other reasons. For an example of such a provision allowing restricted assignment, see Form 68 clause 13.2 [3082] post and the definitions in clauses 1.2 and 1.5 [3062] of that Form. For clauses preventing sub-sales by the buyer see clause 12 of this Form and the Law Society's General Conditions of Sale (1984 Revision) condition 17(6) (for which see vol 38(1) (2000 Reissue) SALE OF LAND Form 3 [1143]). The Standard Conditions of Sale (3rd Edn) conditions 8.2.5 and 8.3.3 (for which see vol 38(1) (2000 Reissue) SALE OF LAND Form 1 [1055]), which prevent the buyer from transferring the benefit of the contract, apply only to the grant of a new lease.

16  Where the Standard Conditions of Sale (3rd Edn) are incorporated, this provision is rendered superfluous by condition 1.2 (for which see vol 38(1) (2000 Reissue) SALE OF LAND Form 1 [1013]). However, such words are commonly included for the convenience of the parties.

17  See note 1 above. This form of conditional obligation ignores the fact that planning permissions once granted remain capable of challenge. For a provision protecting the buyer from obligations to complete whilst the risk of challenge remains, see Form 68 [3061] post.

18  With this form of right to waive, there is no mechanism for the adjustment of the purchase price to take account of the uncertainty of obtaining planning permission or of the cost of obtaining vacant

possession. The buyer may wish to consider whether to install provisions for the reduction of the purchase price by the amount of statutory compensation (if any) to which each relevant tenant would become entitled on enforced repossession.

If it is considered likely that the buyer may wish to exercise the right to waive the requirements for vacant possession (see clause 2.2.2) the practitioner may wish to expand the clause to include a provision that the seller will provide such information from time to time as the buyer may reasonably require to identify what tenancies at the date of enquiry then affect the property.

The principal purpose of clause 2.4 is to enable the buyer to accelerate the completion of the purchase, essentially in circumstances where it is confident of the subsequent satisfaction of the conditions. The waiver mechanism in this clause permits this to happen and is particularly useful where either pre-condition would not or might not occur before the date prescribed for the formal satisfaction of the pre-condition.

For capital gains tax purposes the time of disposal and acquisition is when the conditions are satisfied or waived: Taxation of Chargeable Gains Act 1992 s 28(2) (42–44 Halsbury's Statutes (4th Edn) TAXATION). As to time of disposal, see *Simon's Direct Tax Service* C1.322.

**[3038]**

19    As to the deposit generally see vol 35 (1997 Reissue) SALE OF LAND Paragraph 331 [432] et seq. For alternative clauses relating to the deposit see vol 36 (1997 Reissue) SALE OF LAND Forms 197 [2239]–204 [2246].

      As to the capacity in which the deposit is held see vol 35 (1997 Reissue) SALE OF LAND Paragraph 332 [433] et seq. As to the position when the deposit is held by an estate agent see vol 35 (1997 Reissue) SALE OF LAND Paragraph 334 [438].

      As to the position of a stakeholder generally see 9(1) Halsbury's Laws (4th Edn Reissue) CONTRACT para 1143. It should be remembered that VAT considerations may have a bearing on the capacity in which the deposit is to be held: see note 11 above and note 20 below.

20    As to VAT, see note 11 above. Omit the words in square brackets if no VAT is payable or it is payable but the deposit is held as stakeholder. If the deposit is paid to anyone as agent for the seller, and VAT is payable on the purchase price, the seller must account to HM Customs and Excise for VAT on the deposit and the buyer is entitled to a VAT invoice for the deposit as well as a separate one for the balance on completion.

21    Except on a sale by auction the deposit is to be paid by banker's draft or cheque drawn on a solicitor's clearing bank account: see the Standard Conditions of Sale (3rd Edn) condition 2.2.1 (for which see vol 38(1) (2000 Reissue) SALE OF LAND Form 1 [1016]). The Standard Commercial Property Conditions (1st Edn) condition 2.2.2 (for which see vol 38(1) (2000 Reissue) SALE OF LAND Form 2 [1076]) requires the deposit to be paid by direct credit transfer of cleared funds except on a sale by auction. The National Conditions of Sale (20th Edition) (for which see vol 38(1) (2000 Reissue) SALE OF LAND Form 4 [1161]), which were replaced as from March 1990 with the Standard Conditions of Sale and have therefore not subsequently been updated, do not cover the point, although, where these are incorporated, express provisions may be inserted.

22    It is suggested that the deposit payment should equal the agreed percentage (typically 10% but frequently less) of the entire price for the property.

23    It is not envisaged that the buyer will have paid any deposit before satisfaction of the relevant conditions. If this is not the case, condition 7.2 of the Standard Conditions of Sale (3rd Edn) (for which see vol 38(1) (2000 Reissue) SALE OF LAND Form 1 [1051]) or condition 7.2 of the Standard Commercial Property Conditions (1st Edn) (for which see vol 38(1) (2000 Reissue) SALE OF LAND Form 2 [1108]), should be made to apply: an alternative interest-bearing deposit arrangement appears at Form 68 clause 3.2 [3069] post.

24    Omit this clause if no VAT is payable or it is payable but the deposit is held as stakeholder.

**[3039]**

25    As to the completion date, delay and notice to complete generally, see vol 35 (1997 Reissue) SALE OF LAND Paragraph 694 [902] et seq. For the provisions relating to payment of interest for late completion see the Standard Conditions of Sale (3rd Edn) condition 7.3 (for which see vol 38(1) (2000 Reissue) SALE OF LAND Form 1 [1051]) and the Standard Commercial Property Conditions (1st Edn) condition 7.3 (for which see vol 38(1) (2000 Reissue) SALE OF LAND Form 2 [1108]). As to the Law Society's General Conditions of Sale (1984 Revision) condition 22 (for which see vol 38(1) (2000 Reissue) SALE OF LAND Form 3 [1147]) and the National Conditions of Sale (20th Edn) condition 7 (for which see vol 38(1) (2000 Reissue) SALE OF LAND Form 4 [1161]), which Conditions were replaced by the Standard Conditions of Sale as from March 1990, see vol 38(1) (2000 Reissue) SALE OF LAND Paragraph 290 [1001] et seq. The differences between the various sets of conditions are great and should be carefully noted. For tables of comparison, see vol 38(1) (2000 Reissue) SALE OF LAND Form 5 [1201] et seq.

26    The inclusion of these words is not strictly necessary since the Standard Conditions of Sale (3rd Edn) condition 6.2 (for which see vol 38(1) (2000 Reissue) SALE OF LAND Form 1 [1045]) provides for completion to take place either at the seller's solicitor's office or at some other place which the seller reasonably specifies.

27    The Standard Conditions of Sale (3rd Edn) condition 6.1.2 (for which see vol 38(1) (2000 Reissue) SALE OF LAND Form 1 [1045]) states that if the money due on completion is received after 2.00 pm, completion is to be treated, for the purposes of apportionments and the provisions regarding late completion, as taking place on the next working day. Any amendments to this condition should be included in the fourth schedule.

28    As to implied covenants for title and the words importing them generally, see vol 35 (1997 Reissue) SALE OF LAND Paragraph 472 [597] et seq.

      Covenants for title are implied by the Law of Property (Miscellaneous Provisions) Act 1994 (37 Halsbury's Statutes (4th Edn) REAL PROPERTY) and (additionally in the case of registered land the Land Registration Rules 1925, SR&O 1925/1093 rr 76A–77A as inserted, substituted and amended by SI 1995/337) provide that key words are included in the assurance. Although under the Act and Rules no covenants are implied unless such key words are used, condition 4.5.2 of the Standard Conditions of Sale (3rd Edn) (for which see vol 38(1) (2000 Reissue) SALE OF LAND Form 1 [1025]) provides that if the contract for sale makes no provision as to title guarantee then subject to condition 4.5.3 the seller is to transfer the property with full title guarantee. Accordingly in cases where it is inappropriate for any covenants for title to be given a clause must be inserted expressly stating that no covenants for title will be given.

      For a form varying the implied covenants for title see vol 36 (1997 Reissue) SALE OF LAND Form 190 [2226].

**[3040]**

29    In the absence of any indication to the contrary, it is an implied term that vacant possession will be given: see vol 35 (1997 Reissue) SALE OF LAND Paragraph 328 [429].

30    As to deduction of title to unregistered property see vol 35 (1997 Reissue) SALE OF LAND Paragraph 400 [515] and as to deduction of title to registered property see vol 35 (1997 Reissue) SALE OF LAND Paragraph 399 [510]. As to the seller's duty to disclose defects in the title see vol 35 (1997 Reissue) SALE OF LAND Paragraph 295 [391] et seq. It is clearly in the interests of the seller to disclose any defects of which he is aware before exchange of contracts; therefore it is now common for title to be deduced in its entirety before exchange and for restrictions to be placed on the right to raise requisitions.

31    As to the proving and investigation of title generally see vol 35 (1997 Reissue) SALE OF LAND Paragraph 398 [509] et seq. As to instruments which may form a good root of title see vol 35 (1997 Reissue) SALE OF LAND Paragraph 400.2 [516].

32    The Standard Conditions of Sale (3rd Edn) condition 4.2.1 (for which see vol 38(1) (2000 Reissue) SALE OF LAND Form 1 [1024]) and the Standard Commercial Property Conditions (1st Edn) condition 4.2.1 (for which see vol 38(1) (2000 Reissue) SALE OF LAND Form 2 [1083]) provide that the evidence of registered title is to be office copies of the items required to be furnished by the Land Registration Act 1925 s 110(2). However it is still advisable to include the words in square brackets because the Standard Conditions of Sale are incorporated only in so far as they are not varied by or inconsistent with the terms of the agreement, and it is arguable that the provisions of clause 7 without the words in square brackets form a complete provision replacing the equivalent provision in the Standard Conditions of Sale. As to the deduction of title using HM Land Registry's direct access system see vol 35 (1997 Reissue) SALE OF LAND Paragraph 399.3 [512].

      The words in square brackets are required when the contract is made by reference to the National Conditions of Sale (20th Edn) (for which see vol 38(1) (2000 Reissue) SALE OF LAND Form 4 [1161]), which do not include this provision. These were replaced by the Standard Conditions of Sale as from March 1990 and have not been updated subsequently: see vol 38(1) (2000 Reissue) SALE OF LAND Paragraph 290 [1001] et seq. As to the desirability of providing office copies see vol 35 (1997 Reissue) SALE OF LAND Paragraph 399.3 [512].

**[3041]**

33    This clause should be included if it is desired to exclude requisitions on the title. Both the Standard Conditions of Sale (3rd Edn) (for which see vol 38(1) (2000 Reissue) SALE OF LAND Form 1 [1011]) and the Standard Commercial Property Conditions (1st Edn) (for which see vol 38(1) (2000 Reissue) SALE OF LAND Form 2 [1071]) omit the provision contained in the Standard Conditions of Sale (1st Edn) condition 4.5, which allowed the seller to rescind the contract if the buyer refused to withdraw a requisition which the seller was unable to satisfy.

34    The buyer should be wary of this clause. If important documents are missing then there may be difficulties in registering the title following completion where the land is unregistered. Of course, if a document is genuinely missing, the original cannot be produced. However, as much evidence as possible should be called for as to the contents of the document and the circumstances of its loss, and statutory declarations obtained (see, eg, vol 25(1) (1999 Reissue) LAND REGISTRATION Form 108 [3851]) so as to give the best possible chance of avoiding registration difficulties. If the land is already registered then, unless the missing document relates to an overriding interest (eg the counterpart of a lease for a term not exceeding 21 years), either:

(a)   the title is likely to be less than absolute (eg possessory or qualified) where the missing document is important to the seller's own title; or

(b)   there is likely to be a protective entry on the register (eg as to restrictive covenants where no copy of the deed creating them was supplied on first registration).

In either case the buyer will need to obtain as much information as possible about the missing document and the effect of this on quality of the title in order to assess the risk of accepting the defect. Various options may be open to the buyer, ranging from simply accepting the risk, if judged to be small, through negotiating a suitable adjustment to the price or obtaining defective title insurance cover to, in extreme cases, withdrawing from the transaction before exchanging contracts.

35   As to the seller's duty to disclose encumbrances generally see vol 35 (1997 Reissue) SALE OF LAND Paragraph 295 [391]. Where registered land is concerned, the rights of any person in actual occupation of the land will be overriding interests to which any disposition of the land will be subject unless enquiry has been made of that person and the rights were not disclosed: see the Land Registration Act 1925 s 70(1)(g). The same qualification does not apply in relation to other overriding interests listed in the Land Registration Act 1925 s 70(1) as amended.

36   The proprietorship register may need to be included if, eg, there is a restriction controlling dispositions of land which will remain on the register following sale.

37   Where certain charges, eg financial charges, are specifically excluded, a buyer may wish to ensure that any matters entered on the register before completion are also excluded. It might be argued that reference to exclusion of specific entries is to be interpreted as making the property subject to all other entries including new entries. It may be preferable to specify the entries to which the property is positively to be subject so that the position is clear.

38   Matters to be included in the second schedule are matters not recorded in the registers of title or property documents eg, rights created orally, wayleave agreements and short term or informal arrangements.

39   This sub-clause should be omitted if there are no matters affecting the property in respect of which the seller will remain liable notwithstanding the completion of the transfer of the property to the buyer. It may also be omitted in reliance upon the Standard Conditions of Sale (3rd Edn) condition 4.5.4 (for which see vol 38(1) (2000 Reissue) SALE OF LAND Form 1 [1025]) if incorporated. It should be omitted if the alternative sub-clauses 8.1 and 8.2 are used as the indemnity covenant will be set out in full in the draft assurance.

It may be preferred to set out the indemnity covenant the seller will require, rather than rely on standard conditions of sale, particularly if the contract is made by reference to the Law Society's General Conditions of Sale (1984 Revision) (for which see vol 38(1) (2000 Reissue) SALE OF LAND Form 3 [1131]) which do not require the buyer to covenant to observe and perform the covenants and conditions. See also the Standard Commercial Property Conditions (1st Edn) condition 4.5.4 (for which see vol 38(1) (2000 Reissue) SALE OF LAND Form 2 [1084]) and the Standard Conditions of Sale (3rd Edn) condition 4.5.4 (for which see vol 38(1) (2000 Reissue) SALE OF LAND Form 1 [1025]).

**[3042]**

40   As to encumbrances, see note 35 above.

41   Whilst the annexation of a draft assurance is more usual on a sale of part of the seller's property it may be appropriate also on a sale of the whole of a property where there are numerous or complex encumbrances to be referred to in the assurance or covenants to be imposed.

42   As to the proprietorship register, see note 36 above.

43   As to the charges register, see note 37 above.

44   As to matters to be included in the second schedule, see note 38 above.

45   A buyer should bear in mind that certain financial charges in respect of costs incurred by a local authority are registrable as local land charges. If these relate to expenditure arising before the date of the contract the buyer may wish to ensure that they are borne by the seller.

46   As an exclusion clause, this clause is subject to the test of reasonableness under the Unfair Contract Terms Act 1977 s 11 (11 Halsbury's Statutes (4th Edn) CONTRACT): see *Smith v Eric S Bush, Harris v Wyre Forest District Council* [1990] 1 AC 831, [1989] 2 All ER 514, HL. The seller cannot rely on a general disclaimer to avoid disclosing matters specifically known to him prior to sale: *Rignall Developments Ltd v Halil* [1988] Ch 190, [1987] 3 All ER 170. For further discussion on this issue see *Thomas Witter Ltd v TBP Industries Ltd* [1996] 2 All ER 573.

47   Consideration should be given to whether the conditions of sale incorporated require amendment in any way to suit the circumstances of the transaction or to ensure consistency with this agreement. As to possible modifications where the Standard Conditions of Sale (3rd Edn) are incorporated (for which see vol 38(1) (2000 Reissue) SALE OF LAND Form 1 [1011]), see vol 35 (1997 Reissue) SALE OF LAND Form 18 [1547]. Many of the suggested amendments are now incorporated in the Standard Commercial Property Conditions (1st Edn) (for which see vol 38(1) (2000 Reissue) SALE OF LAND Form 2 [1071]). The fourth schedule contains amendments to the Standard Conditions of Sale (3rd Edn) appropriate to this agreement.

**[3043]**

48    As to restriction on assignment and sub-sale, see note 15 above.

49    Where the Standard Conditions of Sale (3rd Edn) or the Standard Commercial Property Conditions (1st Edn) are being incorporated this clause can be omitted, although it is commonly included for the convenience of the parties: see the Standard Conditions of Sale (3rd Edn) condition 7.4 (for which see vol 38(1) (2000 Reissue) SALE OF LAND Form 1 [1052]) and the Standard Commercial Property Conditions (1st Edn) condition 7.4 (for which see vol 38(1) (2000 Reissue) SALE OF LAND Form 2 [1109]).

50    As to VAT, see note 11 above.

51    Whilst an exempt supply is frequently encountered with the release of land for development purposes, see vol 38(1) (2000 Reissue) SALE OF LAND Form 59 clause 15.4 [2333] if the seller has already elected to waive exemption.

52    Insolvency Act 1986 s 1 (4 Halsbury's Statutes (4th Edn) BANKRUPTCY AND INSOLVENCY) applies to composition; the Insolvency Act 1986 s 253 applies to voluntary arrangement.

53    The agreement is drawn up on the assumption that each party is resident in the United Kingdom, and accordingly, in the case of UK companies, has its own UK registered office. The words 'non-exclusive' are mostly used where either the seller or the buyer is an overseas party. The effect is to enable legal action or proceedings to enforce the agreement and/or judgment in an overseas jurisdiction. Although the subject matter of the agreement relates to UK real estate, in some circumstances it is advantageous to have access to courts in the jurisdiction local to that party, and, for example, to other non-domestic assets of the relevant party for the purposes of enforcing judgment. The practitioner should be aware that the law and practice in relation to the recognition of judgments and enforcement differs according to jurisdiction. Accordingly, the precise nature and extent of this provision should be the subject of a legal opinion obtained from lawyers in the relevant jurisdiction.

54    It is essential to state on the face of a document that it is a deed if it is to be one: see the Law of Property (Miscellaneous Provisions) Act 1989 s 1(2)(a) (37 Halsbury's Statutes (4th Edn) REAL PROPERTY).

**[3044]**

55    A notice provision is incorporated in clause 18 for use in two circumstances. The first is where the National Conditions of Sale (20th Edn) (for which see vol 38(1) (2000 Reissue) SALE OF LAND Form 4 [1161]) are incorporated in the agreement as such conditions do not have any express notification provisions. The National Conditions were replaced by the Standard Conditions of Sale as from March 1990 and have not been updated subsequently: see vol 38(1) (2000 Reissue) SALE OF LAND Paragraph 290 [1001] et seq. By contrast the Standard Conditions of Sale (3rd Edn) (for which see vol 38(1) (2000 Reissue) SALE OF LAND Form 1 [1011]) and the Standard Commercial Property Conditions (1st Edn) (for which see vol 38(1) (2000 Reissue) SALE OF LAND Form 2 [1071]) make detailed provision for the service of notices. Secondly, where either party is non-resident in the UK, provision would need to be made for the appointment of an agent for service and accordingly clause 18.5 would be required. Additionally, the practitioner would need to ensure that the arrangements referred to in clause 18.5 have actually been complied with, by sight of the appointment properly counter-signed by the appointed agent.

56    For longer form clauses relating to notices, see vol 4(3) (1997 Reissue) BOILERPLATE CLAUSES Forms 3.3 [171]–3.5 [173] and Paragraph 3.1 [22] et seq.

57    As to the subjections, see note 38 above. Insert here details of any matters (if any) subject to which the property is sold which are not mentioned in the registers of title nor in any documents listed in Part II of the first schedule.

58    The time to be stated here should accord with the time stated in clause 4.1 of this Form.

59    It is not usually necessary to have the contract executed as a deed unless the contract contains recitals which are intended to be binding or there are other special considerations (eg, there is a lack of valuable consideration or it is desired to extend the period set by the Limitation Act 1980 s 8 (24 Halsbury's Statutes (4th Edn) LIMITATION OF ACTIONS) for bringing claims).

Where a contract is to be executed as a deed sealing is not necessary either in the case of an individual or in the case of a company, but all parties must sign either on the same document or each on one of two identical parts which are exchanged and the signatures of all individuals must be witnessed: see the Law of Property (Miscellaneous Provisions) Act 1989 s 1(3). As to the execution of a deed by an individual and by a corporation, see vol 12 (1994 Reissue) DEEDS, AGREEMENTS AND DECLARATIONS Paragraphs 16 [1525] and 28 [1554]–30 [1560] respectively.

It is unnecessary for a contract by a corporate body to be under seal unless it would need to be a deed if made by private persons: see the Corporate Bodies' Contracts Act 1960 s 1 (11 Halsbury's Statutes (4th Edn) CONTRACT). A contract may be made by a company incorporated under the Companies Acts by writing under its common seal or on its behalf by any person acting under its authority, express or implied: Companies Act 1985 s 36 as substituted by the Companies Act 1989 s 130(1) (8 Halsbury's Statutes (4th Edn) COMPANIES).

**[3045]–[3060]**

## 68

**Agreement for sale of a single freehold commercial property with vacant possession, conditional upon the buyer obtaining planning permission: drafted in favour of the seller; purchase price fixed or ascertained by a method set out in one or other of Forms 72–76[1]**

### CONTENTS

**[3061]**

THIS AGREEMENT is made the ...... day of .........

BETWEEN:

(1)      *(name of seller)*[2] [company number *(number)*][3] [of *(address) or* whose registered office is at *(address)*] ('the Seller') and

(2)      *(name of buyer)* [company number *(number)*] [of *(address) or* whose registered office is at *(address)*] ('the Buyer') [and

[(3)     *(name of guarantor)* [company number *(number)*] [of *(address) or* whose registered office is at *(address)*] ('the Guarantor')]

## 1    Definitions and interpretation[4]

In this Agreement:

1.1     'the Act' means the Town and Country Planning Act 1990 and any act for the time being in force amending or replacing the same and all regulations and orders made thereunder [and any other legislation relating to town and country planning in force from time to time] [including the Planning (Listed Buildings and Conservation Areas) Act 1990]

1.2     'Affiliate' means in relation to any party a Subsidiary or a holding company (as defined by the Companies Act 1985 Section 736) of that party or any other Subsidiary of that holding company

1.3     'this Agreement' means this document as varied by any subsequent documentation

1.4     'Appeal' means:

    1.4.1     an appeal in the joint names of the Buyer and the Seller in a form previously approved by the Seller's Solicitors in writing:

        1.4.1.1     to the Secretary of State under Section 78 of the Act against a refusal of a Planning Application or the grant of a Planning Permission which is not a Satisfactory Planning Permission or

        1.4.1.2     to the Secretary of State under Section 78 of the Act against the non-determination of a Planning Application or

    1.4.2     a Call-in

1.5     'Authorised Transferee' means any Affiliate of the Buyer or such other legal entity as shall be previously approved in writing by the Seller such approval not to be unreasonably withheld or delayed [in the case of a publicly-quoted company or a company guaranteed by a publicly-quoted company and in determining what is a reasonable ground for withholding such approval the Seller shall be entitled where relevant to have regard to the consequent release of any guarantee it may already hold]

**[3062]**

1.6     'the Buyer's Solicitors' means *(insert name and address of person or firm)*

1.7     a 'Call-in' means the reference of a Planning Application to the Secretary of State under Section 77 of the Act

1.8     'Completion' means actual completion of the sale and purchase agreed in this Agreement

1.9     'the Completion Date'[5] means the date *(number)* days after the Unconditional Date[6]

1.10     'the Completion Moneys' means the Purchase Price (or any outstanding balance of it) as adjusted by all sums due between the parties at Completion

1.11     'the Contract Rate'[7] means *(insert interest rate or method of calculating the interest rate by reference eg to the base lending rate of a named bank)*

1.12     'the Deposit' means £... [which is [inclusive *or* exclusive] of VAT at the standard rate][8]

1.13     'Development' means the development on the Property or on some part thereof [for *(define use) or* for use within Class *(insert class number)* of the Town and Country Planning (Use Classes) Order 1987] [together with car parking and access roads and *(insert details)*]

1.14     'the General Conditions'[9] means [the Standard Conditions of Sale (3rd Edn) *or (specify)*]

**[3063]**

1.15       'the Local Planning Authority' means the local planning authority for the area
           in which the Property is situated
[1.16      'the Plan'[10] means the plan attached to this Agreement [and if numbered plans are
           attached any reference to a numbered plan is to the attached plan so numbered]]
1.17       'Planning Application' means [the [outline] planning application for the
           Development submitted on *(date)* and annexed to this Agreement and] any
           application for [outline] planning permission for the Development submitted by
           the Buyer in accordance with this Agreement [in the joint names of the Buyer
           and the Seller] in a form previously approved in writing by the Seller's Solicitors
1.18       'Planning Counsel' means [counsel experienced in town and country planning
           law of not less than ten years call *or* one of the planning counsel listed in the
           sixth schedule]
1.19       'Planning Obligation' means all or any of the following as the case may be:
           1.19.1       an agreement in respect of and affecting the Property (whether or
                        not also affecting other property) pursuant to the Local Government
                        (Miscellaneous Provisions) Act 1982 Section 33 and/or the Local
                        Government Act 1972 Section 111 and/or the Highways Act 1980
                        Sections 38 and/or 278 and/or the Water Industry Act 1991 Section
                        104 or any provision to similar intent or an agreement with a water
                        undertaker or a drainage undertaker (within the meaning of the
                        Water Industry Act 1991) or the Environment Agency or an Internal
                        Drainage Board (within the meaning of the Water Resources Act
                        1991 or the Land Drainage Act 1991) or other appropriate authority
                        as to water supply or drainage of surface and/or foul water from the
                        Property or an agreement with any competent authority or body
                        relating to other services and/or
           1.19.2       a planning obligation (whether entered into by agreement or
                        otherwise) in respect of and affecting the Property (whether or not
                        also affecting other property) pursuant to Section 106 of the Act
1.20       'Planning Permission' means a planning permission granted pursuant to a
           Planning Application

**[3064]**

1.21       'Proceedings' means either:
           1.21.1       an application for judicial review under the Civil Procedure Rules,
                        Schedule 1, RSC Ord 53 or an application pursuant to Section 288
                        of the Act including in each case any appeals to a higher court
                        following a judgment of a lower court or
           1.21.2       an application pursuant to Section 288 of the Act arising from the
                        grant of a Satisfactory Planning Permission or a Refusal by the
                        Secretary of State and in the latter case [made in the joint names of
                        the Buyer and the Seller] in a form previously approved in writing
                        by the Seller's Solicitors including in each case any appeals to a higher
                        court following a judgment of a lower court or
           1.21.3       any reconsideration by the Local Planning Authority or the Secretary
                        of State of an Appeal (as the case may be) following a previous
                        Satisfactory Planning Permission or Refusal being quashed pursuant
                        to an application within the meaning of clause 1.21.1 above and the
                        matter being remitted to the Local Planning Authority or the
                        Secretary of State (as the case may be) or
           1.21.4       an application (within the meaning of clauses 1.21.1 or 1.21.2)
                        arising from the grant of a Satisfactory Planning Permission or a
                        Refusal following a reconsideration of a Planning Application by the
                        Local Planning Authority or an Appeal to the Secretary of State
                        pursuant to clause 1.21.3

1.22 'the Property'[11] means the freehold property described in Part I of the second schedule

1.23 'the Purchase Price' means the purchase price[12] [stated in *or* ascertained in accordance with] the first schedule

1.24 'Refusal' means a refusal of a Planning Application by the Local Planning Authority or the refusal of an Appeal by the Secretary of State or the grant of a Planning Permission by the Local Planning Authority or the Secretary of State which is not a Satisfactory Planning Permission

**[3065]**

1.25 'Satisfactory Planning Permission' means a Planning Permission:
   1.25.1 which does not contain an Unreasonable Condition or
   1.25.2 which is deemed to be a Satisfactory Planning Permission pursuant to the proviso in clause 4.6.2.2 or
   1.25.3 which contains an Unreasonable Condition which the Buyer by notice in writing served on the Seller within [14] working days of receipt of the Planning Permission elects to waive

1.26 'Secretary of State' means the Secretary of State for the Environment Transport and the Regions (or other minister of the Crown to whom his relevant power or duty may from time to time be transferred) or any appropriate officer having authority to act on his behalf

1.27 'the Seller's Solicitors' means *(insert name and address of person or firm)*

1.28 'Subsidiary' means either:
   1.28.1 a subsidiary within the meaning of Section 736 of the Companies Act 1985[13] or
   1.28.2 unless the context requires otherwise a subsidiary undertaking within the meaning of Section 21 of the Companies Act 1989

1.29 'Termination Date' means the date which is *(number)* years from the date of this Agreement unless on that date:
   1.29.1 an Appeal made prior to such date has not been determined by the Secretary of State or
   1.29.2 a Satisfactory Planning Permission has been issued or
   1.29.3 Proceedings have been instituted
when in each case the Termination Date shall be extended until *(number)* days after the earlier of:
   1.29.4 the expiry of six weeks from the issue of a Refusal by the Secretary of State unless Proceedings have been instituted and
   1.29.5 the date on which a Satisfactory Planning Permission is not granted or upheld following the exhaustion of Proceedings (whenever instituted) which shall occur on the withdrawal of such Proceedings or when the time for appealing against the decision of any court has expired and no such appeal has been lodged
PROVIDED that in no circumstances shall the Termination Date extend beyond the date which is *(number)* years from the date of this Agreement

1.30 'the Transfer' means the transfer of the Property

**[3066]**

1.31 'Unconditional Date' means the first of the following to occur:
   1.31.1 in the event of the grant of a Satisfactory Planning Permission by the Local Planning Authority (whether or not this follows any reconsideration by the Local Planning Authority) the date which is [three months] from (but excluding) the date of the Satisfactory Planning Permission provided that no Proceedings have been instituted before this date

1.31.2   in the event of the grant of a Satisfactory Planning Permission by the Secretary of State (whether or not this follows any reconsideration by the Secretary of State) the date which is six weeks from (but excluding) the date of the Satisfactory Planning Permission provided that no Proceedings have been instituted before this date

1.31.3   in the event that following the grant of a Satisfactory Planning Permission Proceedings are instituted the date on which the Satisfactory Planning Permission is finally upheld following the exhaustion of Proceedings which shall occur on the withdrawal of such Proceedings or when the time for appealing against the decision of any court has expired and no such appeal has been lodged

1.32   'Unreasonable Condition' means a condition subject to which a Planning Permission is issued which has the effect of either:

1.32.1   making the Planning Permission personal to the Buyer or

1.32.2   granting a temporary planning permission

PROVIDED that a condition (or a condition which is not materially different to a condition) which the Buyer:

(i)      has at any time agreed in writing to accept (whether with the Seller or any third party) or

(ii)     has not specified as being an Unreasonable Condition in any notice served pursuant to clause 4.6.2.2

shall be deemed not to be an Unreasonable Condition

**[3067]**

1.33   'VAT' means an amount equal to the value added tax as charged in accordance with VATA[14] or any equivalent or substituted tax

1.34   'VATA' means the Value Added Tax Act 1994 or any equivalent tax Act

1.35   'VAT Invoice' means an invoice complying with the provisions of regulations 13 and 14 of the VAT Regulations 1995[15]

1.36   where the context so admits the expression[s] 'the Seller' [and 'the Buyer'] [and the Guarantor] include[s] their respective personal representatives [and 'the Buyer' shall include any permitted successors in title of the Buyer][16]

1.37   words importing one gender shall be construed as importing any other gender

1.38   words importing the singular shall be construed as importing the plural and vice versa

1.39   words importing persons shall be construed as importing a corporate body and/or a partnership and vice versa

1.40   where any party comprises more than one person the obligations and liabilities of that party under this Agreement shall be joint and several obligations and liabilities of those persons[17]

1.41   the clause headings do not form part of this Agreement and shall not be taken into account in its construction or interpretation

1.42   any reference to a clause or a paragraph or a schedule is to one in this Agreement so numbered

1.43   any reference to a colour or letter is to one on the [Plan *or* Plans]

1.44   in the absence of any contrary provision any reference to a statute includes any statutory modification or re-enactment of it and any and every order instrument regulation direction or plan made or issued under the statute or deriving validity from it

**[3068]**

## 2    Agreement for sale

2.1    Subject to clause 2.2 below the Seller shall sell and the Buyer shall buy the Property for the Purchase Price

2.2    The sale and purchase of the Property is conditional upon the Unconditional Date occurring prior to the Termination Date

2.3    The Buyer has the sole benefit of the condition referred to in clause 2.2 above and may by written notice given at any time prior to the Termination Date unilaterally waive the condition and upon the giving of notice to that effect the Unconditional Date shall be deemed to have occurred[18]

2.4    Unless the Unconditional Date has occurred this Agreement shall automatically determine upon the Termination Date but without prejudice to the accrued rights and liabilities of either party against the other party and the parties shall not (without prejudice to clause 3.2 below) be entitled to be paid any costs or compensation whatsoever

## 3    Deposit[19]

3.1    The Deposit shall be paid[20] [on the Unconditional Date] to the Seller's Solicitors to hold as stakeholders[21]

3.2    The Deposit shall be placed to the credit of an interest bearing deposit account until the date of Completion and the interest earned on the Deposit shall accrue to the Buyer and shall be paid to the Buyer on Completion or on determination pursuant to clause 2.4 above without any withholding or set off but net of such tax as the law may from time to time require to be deducted (for which the Seller shall account to the proper Revenue authorities unless such tax is deducted at source) PROVIDED that in the event of:

3.2.1    any delay in Completion (through no fault of the Seller) the interest earned on the Deposit shall accrue as from the Completion Date to and be paid to the Seller and

3.2.2    the Seller lawfully forfeiting the Deposit the interest earned on the Deposit shall as from the date it was deposited accrue to and be paid to the Seller

3.3    The Law of Property Act 1925 Section 49(2) shall not have effect

[3.4    The Seller shall issue a valid VAT invoice in respect of the Deposit within [7] working days of its payment to the Seller's Solicitors[22]]

**[3069]**

## 4    Obtaining Satisfactory Planning Permission

4.1    The Buyer shall use [all reasonable *or* its best] endeavours[23] at its own expense to procure that Satisfactory Planning Permission is obtained as soon as practicable and for that purpose the Buyer shall at its own expense:

4.1.1    as soon as practicable [and in any event within *(number of days)*] submit a Planning Application to the Local Planning Authority

4.1.2    enter into any Planning Obligation (in a form previously approved in writing by the Seller) reasonably required by the Local Planning Authority or other competent authority as a condition of granting a Satisfactory Planning Permission unless the Planning Obligation contains a provision having the same effect as an Unreasonable Condition

[4.1.3    lodge an objection (within any relevant time period prescribed in the Act) to any provision of a development plan or any alteration or replacement of any provision of a development plan which is not adopted by the Local Planning Authority and which materially affects the chances of obtaining Satisfactory Planning Permission]

4.2     [Unless Planning Counsel shall advise in writing that the same is necessary to facilitate the grant of a Satisfactory Planning Permission] the Buyer may not withdraw a Planning Application or an Appeal or Proceedings or amend or modify a Planning Application or an Appeal or Proceedings in any material respect [or submit further planning applications (other than duplicates of a Planning Application)] without the prior written consent of the Seller

**[3070]**

4.3     If a Planning Application is refused by the Local Planning Authority or is not determined within either the period prescribed in the Act during which the Local Planning Authority may determine a Planning Application or within such extended period as the Buyer may agree with the Local Planning Authority (PROVIDED that the Buyer shall not extend the period prescribed in the Act beyond a further period of one month without the written consent of the Seller) the Buyer shall at its own expense as soon as practicable lodge an Appeal with the Secretary of State and prosecute the Appeal with all reasonable speed and diligence

4.4     If the Local Planning Authority issues a Planning Permission which is not a Satisfactory Planning Permission and the Buyer has served notice accordingly under clause 4.6.2.2 the Buyer shall at its own expense as soon as practicable either:

4.4.1   submit an application for planning permission pursuant to Section 73 of the Act for development of the Property without complying with the Unreasonable Condition subject to which the Planning Permission was granted [in the joint names of the Buyer and the Seller] in a form previously approved in writing by the Seller's Solicitors (and in the event that such an application is made it shall for the purposes of this Agreement be treated as a Planning Application) or

4.4.2   (with the prior written consent of the Seller) lodge an Appeal with the Secretary of State

and prosecute the Appeal or the Planning Application (as the case may be) with all reasonable speed and diligence

4.5     The Buyer shall unless otherwise agreed in writing with the Seller:

4.5.1   prosecute an Appeal by way of a public inquiry

4.5.2   use all reasonable endeavours to secure the earliest available date for a public inquiry into an Appeal accepting the first date offered by the Secretary of State for a public inquiry into the Appeal

4.5.3   obtain the prior written approval of the Seller to the appointment of Planning Counsel proposed to be instructed in connection with an Appeal or Proceedings [Planning Counsel being instructed in the joint names of the Seller and the Buyer]

**[3071]**

4.5.4   keep the Seller fully informed of the progress of a Planning Application or an Appeal or Proceedings and in particular:

4.5.4.1   keep the Seller advised of the Buyer's progress in securing a date for a public inquiry into an Appeal and the date of that public inquiry

4.5.4.2   keep the Seller advised of all meetings discussions and negotiations in connection with a Planning Application or an Appeal or Proceedings with the Local Planning Authority or any authority body or person consulted in connection with a Planning Application pursuant to the requirements of the Act or with any third party (giving the Seller as much notice as reasonably possible of all such meetings) and permit the Seller and/or its professional advisers to attend and participate at all such meetings and send to the Seller and to such of its professional advisers as it shall direct copies of the minutes of all such meetings and copies of all correspondence with all such parties

4.5.4.3  permit the Seller and/or its professional advisers to attend and participate at all conferences (or as the case may be consultations) with Planning Counsel and at all meetings between the Buyer and its professional advisers in connection with a Planning Application or an Appeal or Proceedings and to supply to the Seller and the Seller's Solicitors a draft of all instructions to Planning Counsel and copies of all documents referred to therein (including the Buyer's experts' proofs of evidence) and permit the Seller and the Seller's Solicitors an opportunity to comment thereon prior to sending the papers to Planning Counsel

**[3072]**

4.5.4.4  supply to the Seller and to such of its professional advisers as it shall direct copies of all Planning Applications and Appeals and all documents relevant to a Planning Application or an Appeal or Proceedings including any statements or reports accompanying a Planning Application or an Appeal or Proceedings and statements served pursuant to any inquiries procedure rules and all proofs of evidence (whether in draft or otherwise) produced by or on behalf of the Buyer or supplied by the Local Planning Authority or any third party and all applications affidavits judgments and other relevant documents in connection with Proceedings and all heads of terms or draft heads of terms relating to any proposed Planning Obligation and all drafts of any proposed Planning Obligation

4.6  The Buyer shall:

4.6.1  within 14 days of receipt of a Refusal send a copy of the Refusal to the Seller's Solicitors

4.6.2  within 14 days of receipt of a Planning Permission:

4.6.2.1  send a copy of the Planning Permission to the Seller's Solicitors and

4.6.2.2  give notice in writing to the Seller's Solicitors whether the Planning Permission is a Satisfactory Planning Permission or whether in the Buyer's opinion it is subject to an Unreasonable Condition and give the reason why the Buyer considers that it constitutes an Unreasonable Condition PROVIDED that if the Buyer does not notify the Seller in writing within 14 days of receipt of a Planning Permission that it considers that any condition is an Unreasonable Condition and the reason for this then the Planning Permission shall be deemed to be a Satisfactory Planning Permission

**[3073]**

4.7     The Seller shall:
        4.7.1      at the request and cost of the Buyer support the Buyer in making and
                   pursuing a Planning Application and/or an Appeal and/or
                   Proceedings
        4.7.2      at the request and cost of the Buyer and if required by the Local
                   Planning Authority or other competent authority enter into any
                   Planning Obligation in a form previously approved in writing by the
                   Seller which the Buyer shall reasonably require to secure a
                   Satisfactory Planning Permission
                   PROVIDED that:
                   4.7.2.1      a Planning Obligation shall not require the carrying out
                                of any works on or restrict or regulate or otherwise
                                impose any obligation (whether of a financial nature or
                                otherwise) on either the development and/or the use or
                                enjoyment of the Property prior to the date when for
                                the purposes of Section 56 of the Act the Development
                                is taken to be begun or any land (other than the
                                Property) owned by the Seller
                   4.7.2.2      a Planning Obligation shall not impose any obligation
                                on the Seller after the Seller ceases to have any interest
                                in the Property
                   4.7.2.3      the Buyer will indemnify and keep indemnified the
                                Seller against all liabilities whatsoever arising out of or
                                in relation to a Planning Obligation and the Buyer will
                                if so required by the Seller covenant in this respect in a
                                deed of covenant entered into prior to or
                                contemporaneously with the execution of a Planning
                                Obligation
        4.7.3      permit the Buyer its agents and surveyors at all reasonable times and
                   after prior written notice of not less than seven days to the Seller to
                   enter the Property for the purpose of inspection and for the purpose
                   of general site investigation on the Buyer making good as soon as
                   possible any damage occasioned by the exercise of such right

                                                                                **[3074]**
        4.7.4      not whilst this Agreement remains in force submit any application to
                   the Local Planning Authority for planning permission nor (except
                   pursuant to clause 4.7.2) enter into any Planning Obligation in
                   respect of the Property or any part of it with or without any other
                   property [except *(specify)*]
4.8     The [Seller and the] Buyer shall not submit or cause to be submitted or pursue
        or assist in pursuing any application for planning permission [which will have
        a[n] [materially] adverse effect on the chances of obtaining Satisfactory
        Planning Permission] [for a competing development being a development
        within *(number)* miles of the Property for *(specify)* having a gross floor area in
        excess of *(specify)*]
4.9     Following the determination of this Agreement:
        4.9.1      the Seller shall have the right to prosecute any Planning Application
                   and/or Appeal and/or Proceedings which has not been finally
                   determined on the Termination Date (and the Buyer will at the
                   request of the Seller give written confirmation of such authority in
                   such form as the Seller shall reasonably require) [by serving notice to
                   that effect on the Buyer within 14 days of the Termination Date] and

4.9.2　　　the Buyer shall make no further representations on any such Planning Application and/or Appeal and/or Proceedings without the written consent of the Seller [and

4.9.3　　　if the Seller shall fail to service such notice the Buyer shall [join with the Seller] in withdrawing any Planning Application and/or Appeal and/or Proceedings and the Buyer shall be liable for all costs arising out of or in connection with such withdrawal]

4.10　　The Buyer will indemnify and keep indemnified the Seller against all liabilities whatsoever arising out of or in connection with a Planning Application and/or an Appeal and/or Proceedings and in particular (but without prejudice to the generality of this obligation) the Buyer will indemnify and keep indemnified the Seller against any award of costs made in respect of an Appeal and/or Proceedings

**[3075]**

## 5　　Completion

5.1　　Completion of the sale and purchase and payment of the Completion Moneys [and of the VAT] shall take place on the Completion Date[24] on or before [1.00 pm] [at the offices of the Seller's Solicitors or where they may reasonably direct][25]

5.2　　If the Completion Moneys are received after [1.00 pm][26] on the Completion Date or on a day which is not a working day Completion shall be deemed for the purposes of the General Conditions to have taken place on the next working day

## [6　　Title guarantee[27] *(where the form of the assurance is not annexed)*

6.1　　The Seller sells the Property [with [full *or* limited] *or* without any] title guarantee [with the modifications set out below]

[6.2　　Where the Transfer is made with full title guarantee the Law of Property (Miscellaneous Provisions) Act 1994 Section 6(2)(a) shall have effect as though all matters now recorded in all registers open to or capable of public inspection are to be considered to be within the actual knowledge of the Buyer]

[6.3　　Where the transfer is made with limited title guarantee the Law of Property (Miscellaneous Provisions) Act 1994 Section 3(3) shall not apply and instead the Seller will covenant that it has not since the transfer to it:

6.3.1　　charged or encumbered the Property by means of any charge or encumbrance which subsists at the date of the Transfer or granted third party rights in relation to the Property which so subsist or

6.3.2　　knowingly suffered the Property to be so charged or encumbered or subjected to any such rights]

[6.4　　The Transfer shall contain the modifications set out above and include an application to the Registrar to enter on the register in an appropriate manner a note that the implied covenants are modified in the manner set out above]

*or*

## 6　　Title guarantee *(where the form of Transfer is annexed)*

The Property is sold [with the title guarantee set out in the annexed form of draft Transfer [with the modifications included in it] *or* without any title guarantee]]

**[3076]**

## 7　　Vacant Possession[28]

The Property is sold with vacant possession subject to the presence of any third party chattels

**8      Title**[29]

[8.1      The title to the Property is unregistered and title shall commence with the document described as the root of title in Part II of the second schedule[30]
*or*
The title to the Property is registered at HM Land Registry and title shall be deduced in accordance with the Land Registration Act 1925 Section 110 [save that copies of the entries on the register the filed plan and any documents referred to shall be office copies[31]]]

8.2      Title having been deduced prior to the date of this Agreement the Buyer accepts the Seller's title to the Property and shall be deemed to purchase with full knowledge of the title in all respects and shall not raise any requisitions or make any objection in relation to the title[32] [but the Buyer may raise requisitions arising out of:

8.2.1      events occurring after the date of this Agreement

8.2.2      matters revealed by pre-completion searches which are not registered at the date of this Agreement

8.2.3      matters which a prudent buyer could not be aware of at the date of this Agreement]

[8.3      The Seller does not have the documents (if any) noted as missing in Part II of the second schedule and the Buyer may not raise any requisition or objection on that account and no acknowledgement for production or undertaking for safe custody will be given nor copies produced][33]

**[3077]**

**[9      Encumbrances**[34] *(where the form of the assurance is not annexed)*

[9.1      The Property is sold subject to and (where appropriate) with the benefit of:

9.1.1      the matters contained or referred to in the property [proprietorship][35] and charges[36] registers of the title to the Property [other than any subsisting financial charges]

[9.1.2      the documents described in Part II of the second schedule] [and]

[9.1.3      the matters set out in the third schedule]][37]

9.2      The Buyer or the Buyer's Solicitors having been supplied with copies of the documents referred to in clause 9.1 the Buyer shall be deemed to purchase with full notice and knowledge of the same and shall not raise any requisition or make any objection in relation to them

9.3      The Transfer shall contain a covenant by the Buyer that the Buyer will (by way of indemnity only) observe and perform the covenants conditions and other matters contained or referred to in the documents referred to in clause 9.1 and will indemnify and keep the Seller and its successors in title fully and effectually indemnified against all actions proceedings damages costs claims and expenses which may be suffered or incurred by the Seller or its successors in title in respect of [future] breach or non-observance or non-performance of those covenants and conditions [and obligations][38]

9.4      The Transfer shall be engrossed [in duplicate] by the Buyer's Solicitors and [the *or* both] engrossment[s] shall be executed by the Buyer before the Completion Date

[9.5      Immediately after Completion the Buyer shall at its own expense procure the proper stamping of the duplicate Transfer as a duplicate (including but not limited to the affixing of a particulars delivered stamp) and shall immediately after such stamping deliver the duly stamped duplicate to the Seller's Solicitors]

**[3078]**

*or*
## 9     Encumbrances[39] *(where the form of Transfer is annexed)*[40]

9.1     The Transfer shall be in the form of the annexed draft

[9.2     The Property is sold subject to and (where appropriate) with the benefit of:

    9.2.1     the matters contained or referred to in the annexed draft Transfer and the property [proprietorship][41] and charges[42] registers of the title to the Property [other than any subsisting financial charges]

    [9.2.2     the documents described in Part II of the second schedule] [and]

    [9.2.3     the matters set out in the third schedule]][43]

9.3     The Buyer or the Buyer's Solicitors having been supplied with copies of the matters (if any) referred to in clause 9.2 prior to the date of this Agreement the Buyer shall be deemed to purchase with full notice and knowledge of them and shall not raise any requisition or make any objection in relation to them

9.4     The Transfer shall be engrossed [in duplicate] by the Seller's Solicitors and [the *or* both] engrossment[s] shall be executed by the Buyer before the Completion Date

[9.5     Immediately after Completion the Buyer shall at its own expense procure the proper stamping of the duplicate Transfer as a duplicate (including but not limited to the affixing of a particulars delivered stamp) and shall immediately after such stamping deliver the duly stamped duplicate to the Seller's Solicitors]]

**[3079]**

## 10     Matters affecting the Property

The Property is sold subject to the following matters:

10.1     all local land charges whether registered or not before the date of this Agreement and all matters capable of registration as local land charges whether or not actually so registered[44]

10.2     all notices served and orders demands proposals or requirements made by any local public or other competent authority whether before or after the date of this Agreement

10.3     all actual or proposed charges notices orders restrictions agreements conditions contraventions or other matters arising under any statute

10.4     all easements quasi-easements rights exceptions or other similar matters including rights of way drainage water watercourses light rights of adjoining owners affecting the Property and liability to repair or covenants to repair roads pavements paths ways passages sewers drains gutters fences and other like matters whether or not apparent on inspection or disclosed in any of the documents referred to in this Agreement and without any obligation on the Seller to provide evidence of the creation of or to define or apportion any such liability

10.5     matters discoverable by inspection of the Property before the date of this Agreement

10.6     matters relating to the Property about which the Seller does not know

10.7     matters disclosed or which would be disclosed by any searches or as a result of enquiries (formal or informal and made in person in writing or orally) made by or for the Buyer or which a prudent buyer ought to make and

10.8     overriding interests as defined in the Land Registration Act 1925 Section 70(1) or matters which would be overriding interests if the title were registered

**[3080]**

**11      Disclaimer**[45]

11.1      The Buyer admits that:

11.1.1      it has inspected the Property and purchases it with full knowledge of its actual state and condition and shall take the Property as it stands

11.1.2      it enters into this Agreement solely as a result of its own inspection and on the basis of the terms of this Agreement and not in reliance upon any advertisement statement representation or warranty either written or oral or implied made by or on behalf of the Seller except as stated in clause 11.2

11.1.3      no warranty statement or representation has been made or given to the Buyer that the Property can be used or developed in any particular way or for any particular purpose and the Seller shall not be liable to the Buyer if the Property cannot for any reason whatsoever be so used or developed

11.2      The Buyer may rely on factual representations and warranties made or given by the Seller's Solicitors to the Buyer's Solicitors' pre-contract enquiries but only in so far as such statements are not capable of independent verification by appropriate searches enquiries inspection survey of the Property or by inspection of the documents and information supplied to the Buyer's Solicitors

11.3      This Agreement contains the entire agreement between the parties and incorporates all the terms agreed between them for the purposes of the Law of Property (Miscellaneous Provisions) Act 1989 Section 2 and there are no other terms or provisions agreed prior to the date of this Agreement which have not been incorporated into this Agreement

**[3081]**

**12      Incorporation of conditions of sale and documents**

12.1      The General Conditions [as amended by the [fourth] schedule][46] shall apply to this Agreement and are incorporated in it in so far as they are applicable to a sale by private treaty and are not varied by or inconsistent with the terms of this Agreement

12.2      If there is any conflict between the General Conditions [as amended] and the terms of this Agreement the terms of this Agreement prevail

12.3      All express agreements made or undertakings given by one party to the other [in *(set out list of letters and documents including relevant inter solicitor correspondence)*] are incorporated in this Agreement

**[13      Restriction on assignment and sub-sale**[47]

13.1      This Agreement is personal to the Buyer and is not capable of being assigned charged or mortgaged [except by way of floating charge]

[13.2      The Seller shall not be required to transfer the Property to anyone other than the Buyer named in this Agreement or an Authorised Transferee]]

**14      Merger on completion**[48]

The provisions of this Agreement shall not merge on completion of the Transfer so far as they remain to be performed

**[3082]**

## 15      VAT provisions[49]

15.1    The Purchase Price is [inclusive *or* exclusive] of VAT at the standard rate as at Completion

15.2    All VAT payable by the Buyer shall be paid at the same time as the payment on which it is chargeable

15.3    The Seller shall provide the Buyer with a receipted VAT invoice for any VAT paid by the Buyer under this Agreement

15.4    [The Seller warrants that it [has validly made *or* is bound by] an effective[50] election to waive exemption from VAT pursuant to VATA Schedule 10 paragraph 2 in respect of the Property *or* The Seller warrants that it has not made an election to waive exemption from VAT in respect of the Property and will not make any such election]

## [16     Guarantee

The Guarantor agrees with the Seller in the terms of the [fifth] schedule]

## [17     Insolvency of Buyer

17.1    If the Buyer:

   17.1.1    enters into voluntary liquidation (other than for the purpose of reconstruction or amalgamation not involving a realisation of assets) or has a winding-up order made against it by the court or has a receiver appointed over all or any part of its assets or an administration order is made pursuant to the Insolvency Act 1986 or

   17.1.2    becomes insolvent or enters into any composition with its or his creditors or enters into a voluntary arrangement (within the meaning of the Insolvency Act 1986 Sections 1 or 253[51]) or distress sequestration or execution is levied on its goods

then and in any such case the Seller may rescind this Agreement by notice to the Buyer

17.2    Condition 7.2 of the General Conditions shall apply save that in this instance the Seller shall not be obliged to pay any interest which has accrued on the deposit]

**[3083]**

## 18     Jurisdiction and Governing Law

This Agreement shall be governed by and construed in accordance with English law and the parties submit to the [non-exclusive] jurisdiction of the English courts[52]

## 19     Nature of this Agreement

This Agreement [is *or* is not] a deed and [has *or* has not] been executed by the parties to it as a deed[53]

## 20     Notices[54]

20.1    Any notice to be given under or in connection with this Agreement shall be in writing and may be delivered personally or sent by first class post telex or fax to the party due to receive the notice at its address set out in this Agreement or the address of its solicitor or such other address as previously specified (by written notice) by such party

20.2    A notice may be given by either party's solicitor to the other party's solicitor provided it conforms to the provisions of clause 20.1

20.3     In the absence of evidence of earlier receipt a notice is deemed received:
     20.3.1      if delivered personally when left at the address referred to in clause 20.1
     20.3.2      if sent by post two working days after posting it
     20.3.3      if sent by telex when the proper answerback is received
     20.3.4      if sent by fax on completion of its transmission
20.4     In the case of a notice given pursuant to clauses 20.3.1 20.3.3 or 20.3.4 where this occurs after 5 pm on a working day or on a day which is not a working day the date of service shall be deemed to be the next working day
[20.5    The [Seller *or* Buyer] irrevocably appoints *(name and address)* as its agent for service to receive on its behalf service of proceedings in the English Courts or in any other court or courts of competent jurisdiction][55]

**[21     Contracts (Rights of Third Parties) Act 1999**

For the purposes of the Contracts (Rights of Third Parties) Act 1999 it is agreed that [with the exception only of *(specify clauses)*] nothing in this Agreement shall confer on any third party any right to enforce or any benefit of any term of this Agreement]

[AS *or* IN] WITNESS etc

**[3084]**

FIRST SCHEDULE
The Purchase Price
*(Incorporate relevant form from Forms 72 [3251]–76 [3270] or insert fixed price)*

SECOND SCHEDULE
The Property
[Part I]
Description of the Property

*(Describe the Property: eg)*
[All that freehold property situate at and known as *(address)* registered with title [absolute] at HM Land Registry under title number *(number)*
*or*
All that unregistered freehold property situate at and known as *(address)* which is shown for identification purposes only on the plan annexed to this Agreement and numbered '1']

[Part II
Title Documents affecting the Property
*(commencing where applicable with the root of title)*

| **Number** | **Date** | **Nature** | **Parties** | **Remarks** |
|---|---|---|---|---|
| *(number)* | *(date)* | *(details)* | *(details)* | *(eg root of title; missing)]* |

[THIRD SCHEDULE
The Subjections[56]
*(set out any other matters to which the Property is subject not specified or mentioned elsewhere)]*

**[3085]**

[[FOURTH] SCHEDULE
Amendments to the Standard Conditions of Sale (3rd Edition)

1          Standard Conditions 3.4, 4.3.2, 4.5.2, 4.5.5, 5.1.1, 5.1.2, 5.2.2(b), 5.2.2(e), 5.2.2(g), 5.2.3 and 5.2.7 shall not apply
2          The Standard Conditions shall be varied as follows:
           2.1          in Standard Condition 1.1.1(a) sub-paragraphs (i) and (ii) shall be deleted and the words 'the interest actually earned on money less any proper charges for handling the money' shall be inserted
           2.2          in Standard Condition 1.1.1(g) the contract rate shall be 4% per annum above the base rate current from time to time of *(name of bank etc)*
           2.3          in Standard Condition 3.1.2(c) the word 'reasonably' shall be inserted after the words 'could not'
           2.4          in Standard Condition 5.2.2(f) the words 'nor change its use and is to comply with all statutory obligations relating to the property and indemnify the seller against all liability arising as a result of any breach of such obligation' shall be added at the end
           2.5          in Standard Conditions 6.1.2 and 6.1.3 '1 pm' shall be substituted for '2 pm'[57]
           2.6          in Standard Condition 6.5.1 the words 'actual completion' shall be added after the word 'after' and the remainder of that Standard Condition shall be deleted
           2.7          in Standard Condition 6.8.2(b) the words 'or if reasonable evidence is produced that the property would be released from all such mortgages' shall be added immediately after the words 'free of all mortgages'
           2.8          in Standard Condition 7.1.1 the words 'or in negotiations leading to it' and 'or was' shall be deleted
           2.9          Standard Conditions 7.3.1 and 7.3.2 shall be deleted and the following substituted:
                         '7.3.1          if the purchase shall not be completed on the completion date the buyer shall pay compensation to the seller but no such compensation shall be payable for so long as the seller is not ready able and willing to complete as contemplated by Standard Condition 6.8
                         7.3.2          compensation is calculated at the contract rate on all sums payable under the agreement (other than pursuant to Standard Condition 6.3) for the period between the completion date and actual completion']

                                                                                      **[3086]**

[[FIFTH] SCHEDULE
Guarantee[58]

In consideration of the Seller entering into this Agreement at the Guarantor's request the Guarantor agrees with the Seller as a primary obligation that:
1          the Buyer or the Guarantor will perform all the Buyer's obligations in this Agreement
2          if the Buyer defaults in performing its obligations the Guarantor will perform them and without prejudice to the generality of the foregoing will pay the Completion Monies and pay and make good to the Seller all costs losses and damages suffered by the Seller and will indemnify the Seller against all liability incurred or to be incurred arising from the Buyer's default

3     if this Agreement has been disclaimed following the insolvency of the Buyer the Seller may serve notice in writing on the Guarantor ('the Guarantor Notice') requiring the Guarantor to complete the purchase of the Property in accordance with this Agreement with the following modifications:

3.1     all obligations of the Buyer shall be deemed to have been entered into by the Guarantor as though it were named as buyer in place of the party defined as the Buyer in this Agreement

3.2     if a notice to complete served by the Seller on the Buyer has expired at the date of service of the Guarantor Notice the Completion Date shall be **[5]** working days after the date of service of the Guarantor Notice

3.3     the Guarantor is to pay interest on the balance of the Purchase Price from the contractual Completion Date specified in clause 1.9 until the date of Completion inclusive of both days and all moneys expended by the Seller in consequence of the Buyer's default from the date of expenditure until Completion inclusive of both days

**[3087]**

4     The liability of the Guarantor shall not be affected reduced or extinguished by

4.1     any time or indulgence granted by the Seller to the Buyer

4.2     any neglect or forbearance of the Seller in enforcing its rights under this Agreement

4.3     any variation of this Agreement between the Seller and the Buyer [provided that no variation is to bind the Guarantor to the extent that it is materially prejudicial to it]

4.4     the exercise by the Seller of any right duty or obligation under the General Conditions or this Agreement in relation to the management of the Property without obtaining the consent of the Buyer

4.5     anything else by which apart from this paragraph 4 the Guarantor would be released other than a release under seal]

**[SIXTH] SCHEDULE**
Planning Counsel
*(Give details of Planning Counsel)*

*(signatures (or common seals) of the parties)*[59]
*[(signatures of witnesses)]*
**[3088]**

1   No stamp duty. See Information Binder: Stamp Duties [172] (Agreement).

This Form differs from vol 38(1) (2000 Reissue) SALE OF LAND Form 59 [2321] to the extent only that the performance of the agreement is pre-conditional upon the Buyer obtaining planning permission.

The contract is capable of being protected by registration. In the case of unregistered land the agreement is capable of being registered by the buyer against the seller's name as an estate contract (see vol 25(1) (1999 Reissue) LAND CHARGES Paragraph 40.5 [75]). Registration should be effected against the estate owner rather than the seller where the seller is a contracting buyer who has agreed to sub-sell or a mortgagee exercising its power of sale. In addition, the agreement may be protected by way of caution against first registration (see vol 25(1) (1999 Reissue) LAND REGISTRATION Paragraph 204 [2661]).

In the case of registered land, the agreement may be noted on the register as an estate contract if the land certificate is placed on deposit or deemed to be on deposit, or it could be the subject of a caution in other cases: see vol 25(1) (1999 Reissue) LAND REGISTRATION Paragraph 178 [2489]. Strictly, all contracts for the sale of land should be protected by registration as land charges irrespective of whether the seller is in practice likely to resell, but the vast majority of such contracts are not so registered unless, eg, as in this case, completion is likely to be delayed. A buyer is not under a duty to register a contract: *Wright v Dean* [1948] Ch 686, [1948] 2 All ER 415. However, it seems that in certain circumstances a solicitor might be held to be negligent for failing to protect his client by registering his interest as buyer under a contract: see, eg, *Midland Bank Trust Co Ltd v Hett, Stubbs & Kemp* [1979] Ch 384, [1978] 3 All ER 571.

**[3089]**

The planning provisions in this Form and in Form 69 [3121] post are designed for more complex and lengthy planning applications than those envisaged in Form 67 [3021] ante, including those involving a significant prospect of challenge or appeal. Each precedent is likely to be suitable for use in a wide range of circumstances and planning ambitions. However, the precedents have been developed to reflect two distinctly different approaches to the process of obtaining planning permission. Broadly speaking, the key differences are:

(a)   in this Form planning applications are joint and made only after the prior written approval of the seller; in Form 69 [3121] post an application is prepared and submitted by the buyer without the seller's approval;

(b)   in this Form the process of appeal is joint and mandatory (subject to counsel's opinion of success); in Form 69 [3121] post the buyer is under no obligation to appeal but may do so. Under this Form the buyer may not withdraw any application, appeal or proceeding without the consent of the seller; under Form 69 [3121] post the buyer is free to do so;

(c)   in this Form there is an ultimate cut-off date ('the Termination Date': see clause 1.29) by which the agreement must have become unconditional, regardless of the status of any then current proceedings or appeals. This is a long-stop date for automatic rescission and provision is made for an initial termination date with an interim extension if at the initial termination date an appeal or proceedings are outstanding or a satisfactory planning permission has been issued. In Form 69 [3121] post the extension is indefinite to allow for the exhaustion of all relevant proceedings and appeals;

(d)   in this Form the buyer accepts wide-ranging obligations to endeavour to obtain the requisite planning permission and seller control.

For simple planning situations Form 67 [3021] ante should be used.

**[3090]**

This Form provides for the property to be sold with vacant possession on completion. It is not made conditional on the removal of existing tenants. If the practitioner is concerned about the removal of existing tenants he should import the condition in Form 67 clause 2.2.2 [3024] ante. Where there are existing tenants the buyer should satisfy himself that the seller will be able to procure their removal so as to deliver with vacant possession. Where the property is not vacant at the date of the agreement, or if the circumstances suggest the potential for a lengthy planning process, consideration should be given to the terms and basis upon which tenancies and other interests might be created or preserved during the pre-conditional planning period.

Certainly, it would be possible for the seller to create new short term tenancies/leases/licences and other occupational rights without the consent of the buyer, but great care should then be taken to ensure that such tenancies are capable of being terminated to meet any requirement by the buyer to complete with vacant possession eg by waiving the planning pre-condition (see clause 2.3 of this Form). Effectively, this would require the creation of tenancies at will or tenancies containing suitable termination provisions and security of tenure exclusions.

This Form is not likely to be capable of use without amendment to reflect the detailed terms negotiated. Every deal is different and this Form is purely one example of a contract conditional on the grant of planning permission.

**[3091]**

2     The Standard Conditions of Sale (3rd Edn) (for which see vol 38(1) (2000 Reissue) SALE OF LAND Form 1 [1011]), like the Standard Commercial Property Conditions (1st Edn) (for which see vol 38(1) (2000 Reissue) SALE OF LAND Form 2 [1071]), use the terminology 'seller' and 'buyer' in place of the traditional 'vendor' and 'purchaser'. If this Form is to be used in conjunction with general conditions other than the Standard Conditions of Sale or the Standard Commercial Property Conditions it is recommended that the expressions 'vendor' and 'purchaser' are used in place of 'seller' and 'buyer' in order to present a uniform approach to the definitions used in such other general conditions.

3     If any party is a company it is desirable to include the company registration number before the address of the registered office. This avoids any problems arising when a company has been wound up and a new company formed with the same name, or when the name of a company is changed, or if companies swap names, eg on a reconstruction of a group of companies. In addition the company registration number will be required by HM Land Registry under the provisions of the Land Registration Rules 1996, SI 1996/2975 r 2, Schedule para 18.

4     One view would add the words 'unless the context otherwise admits' or 'where the context admits' and this may be implied (see *Meux v Jacobs* (1875) LR 7 HL 481 at 493; *Law Society v United Services Bureau*

*Ltd* [1934] 1 KB 343, DC). However, the better course is to use whenever practicable defined terms in such a way that there are no circumstances where the defined meanings do not apply.

Definitions of terms used only in schedules are contained in the relevant schedule.

Clauses 1.37–39 are not strictly necessary as the Law of Property Act 1925 s 61 (37 Halsbury's Statutes (4th Edn) REAL PROPERTY) provides such definitions but such definitions are usually inserted for the convenience of the parties.

5    If no date is specifically agreed for completion under a contract incorporating one of the sets of standard conditions the fall-back provisions of the relevant conditions will apply. See, eg, the Standard Conditions of Sale (3rd Edn) condition 6.1 (for which see vol 38(1) (2000 Reissue) SALE OF LAND Form 1 [1045]) and the Standard Commercial Property Conditions (1st Edn) condition 6.1 (for which see vol 38(1) (2000 Reissue) SALE OF LAND Form 2 [1103]). As to the Law Society's General Conditions of Sale (1984 Revision) condition 21(1) (for which see vol 38(1) (2000 Reissue) SALE OF LAND Form 3 [1131]) and the National Conditions of Sale (20th Edn) condition 5(1) (for which see vol 38(1) (2000 Reissue) SALE OF LAND Form 4 [1161]), which Conditions were replaced by the Standard Conditions of Sale in March 1990, see vol 38(1) (2000 Reissue) SALE OF LAND Paragraph 290 [1001] et seq. None of the fall-back provisions is appropriate to this agreement.

6    This wording is appropriate to a circumstance where the purchase price is fixed, or is a liquidated calculation. If the purchase price is to be ascertained or agreed by some other method, the completion date could be fixed by reference to the date of ascertainment (eg *(number)* days after the date on which the purchase price has been ascertained in accordance with the *(number)* schedule). However, depending upon the circumstances of each case, consideration should be given to whether completion should take place on the payment of a fixed interim minimum amount, with provision for further payment, with interest, of the amount by which the price as ascertained exceeds the interim amount.

**[3092]**

7    Note that certain conditions in the Standard Conditions of Sale (3rd Edn) (see eg conditions 5.2.6, 7.3.2) provide for compensation payable at the 'contract rate' ie the Law Society's interest rate from time to time in force (see vol 38(1) (2000 Reissue) SALE OF LAND Form 1 condition 1.1.1(g) [1012]); there are also conditions (see eg conditions 2.2.3, 7.2(a), 7.5.2(a)(i), 7.6.2(a)) which provide for payment of 'accrued interest' (see vol 38(1) (2000 Reissue) SALE OF LAND Form 1 condition 1.1.1(a) [1011]).

8    As to VAT, see note 12 post. Omit the words in square brackets if no VAT is payable or it is payable but the deposit is held as stakeholder.

9    In preparing this form of sale and purchase agreement, it was decided that it would be helpful to practitioners if incorporation of the Standard Conditions of Sale (3rd Edn) (for which see vol 38(1) (2000 Reissue) SALE OF LAND Form 1 [1011]) was retained in the short term notwithstanding the issue of the Standard Commercial Property Conditions (1st Edn) (for which see vol 38(1) (2000 Reissue) SALE OF LAND Form 2 [1071]) which have yet to be fully adopted and used. Differences between the two sets of conditions (which are highly similar in many respects) are discussed and summarised in vol 38(1) (2000 Reissue) SALE OF LAND Form 5 [1201].

Other sets of standard conditions which might be referred to are the Statutory Form of Conditions of Sale 1925, SR&O 1925/779, which applies to contracts made by correspondence, and may, but only by express reference, be made to apply to any other cases (see the Law of Property Act 1925 s 46) and the Standard Commercial Property Conditions (1st Edn) (for which see vol 38(1) (2000 Reissue) SALE OF LAND Form 2 [1071]). As to the National Conditions of Sale (20th Edn) (for which see vol 38(1) (2000 Reissue) SALE OF LAND Form 4 [1161]) and the Law Society's General Conditions of Sale (1984 Revision) (for which see vol 38(1) (2000 Reissue) SALE OF LAND Form 3 [1131]), which Conditions were replaced by the Standard Conditions of Sale as from March 1990, see vol 38(1) (2000 Reissue) SALE OF LAND Paragraph 290 [1001] et seq. A contract by correspondence can still be made in relation to a short lease, or the creation or operation of a resulting, implied or constructive trust: see the Law of Property (Miscellaneous Provisions) Act 1989 s 2 as amended by the Trusts of Land and Appointment of Trustees Act 1996 s 25(2), Sch 4 (37 Halsbury's Statutes (4th Edn) REAL PROPERTY).

10    The size and scale of the plan should be sufficiently large to enable all salient features to be readily identified: see *Scarfe v Adams* [1981] 1 All ER 843, CA. If many plans are required it may be convenient to bind them in a separate bundle, suitably referred to in the contract. Each plan should be individually numbered if there is more than one. As to plans generally see vol 35 (1997 Reissue) SALE OF LAND Paragraph 623 [816].

**[3093]**

11    As to the identity of the property to be sold see vol 35 (1997 Reissue) SALE OF LAND Paragraph 346 [453] et seq.

12    As to circumstances in which VAT is payable see vol 38(1) (2000 Reissue) SALE OF LAND Paragraph 6 [18] et seq and vol 35 (1997 Reissue) SALE OF LAND Paragraph 136 [173] et seq and see the Information Binder: Property [1] (VAT and Property). The sale of a fee simple is exempt unless it is one of an incomplete commercial building, a commercial building completed less than three years from the time of supply, or is a commercial building subject to an election to waive exemption of the seller

or a relevant associate of the seller: see the Value Added Tax Act 1994 Sch 9 Group 1 (48 Halsbury's Statutes (4th Edn) VALUE ADDED TAX). It should be noted that VAT forms part of the stampable consideration for the purposes of calculating stamp duty and land registration fees.

If VAT is or may be chargeable in respect of any part of the purchase price, and the price is to be exclusive of the tax, a comprehensive clause dealing with all aspects of the tax should be included. For an example of such a clause see clause 15 of this Form and see further vol 36 (1997 Reissue) SALE OF LAND Forms 351 [2521] and 352 [2522]. The VAT provisions in this Form expand those in the Standard Conditions of Sale (3rd Edn) condition 1.4 (for which see vol 38(1) (2000 Reissue) SALE OF LAND Form 1 [1013]) and are inserted to act as a reminder to the parties of the importance of considering VAT aspects at an early stage.

If the Value Added Tax Act 1994 s 89 (48 Halsbury's Statutes (4th Edn) VALUE ADDED TAX) is excluded or the purchase price is expressed to be inclusive of VAT any changes in the rate or incidence of VAT between contract and completion cannot be added to the price.

13   Ie the Companies Act 1985 s 736 as amended by the Companies Act 1989 s 144 (8 Halsbury's Statutes (4th Edn) COMPANIES).

14   See note 12 above.

15   Ie the Value Added Tax Regulations 1995, SI 1995/2518.

16   In the absence of any specific provision in the contract both seller and buyer are free to assign the benefit of the whole contract or a part of it (eg a charge of the benefit of the contract, or a sub-sale of part of the property). It may be thought desirable to limit these rights, whether because of the importance of the personality or standing of the buyer, or to avoid an immediate sub-sale of the whole or part of the property for tax or other reasons. For clauses preventing sub-sales by the buyer see clause 13 of this Form and the Law Society's General Conditions of Sale (1984 Revision) condition 17(6) (see vol 38(1) (2000 Reissue) SALE OF LAND Form 3 [1131]). The Standard Conditions of Sale (3rd Edn) conditions 8.2.5 and 8.3.3 (for which see vol 38(1) (2000 Reissue) SALE OF LAND Form 1 [1011]), which prevent the buyer from transferring the benefit of the contract, apply only to the grant of a new lease.

**[3094]**

17   Where the Standard Conditions of Sale (3rd Edn) are incorporated, this provision is rendered superfluous by condition 1.2 (for which see vol 38(1) (2000 Reissue) SALE OF LAND Form 1 [1013]). However, such words are commonly included for the convenience of the parties.

18   The principal purpose of clause 2.3 is to enable the buyer to accelerate the completion of the purchase, essentially in circumstances where it is confident of the subsequent satisfaction of the conditions. The waiver mechanism in this clause permits this to happen and is particularly useful where the pre-condition would not or might not be satisfied before the unconditional date. However, as the planning condition is not solely for the benefit of the buyer, the clause can only be included where the purchase price could be established to the satisfaction of the seller without planning permission. It would therefore be necessary to make specific provision for a fixed price in this instance or if use is made of Form 72 [3251] post (residual land valuation) or Form 73 [3257] post (open market value) by amending such forms to include suitable assumptions as to the state of planning. An obvious solution would be to add an explicit assumption that if the buyer waives pursuant to clause 2.3 of this Form, planning permission would be assumed to have been granted on the terms originally applied for. See also note 1 above.

For capital gains tax purposes the time of disposal and acquisition is when the conditions are satisfied or waived: Taxation of Chargeable Gains Act 1992 s 28(2) (42–44 Halsbury's Statutes (4th Edn) TAXATION). As to time of disposal, see *Simon's Direct Tax Service* C1.322.

19   It is not envisaged that the buyer will have paid any deposit before satisfaction of the relevant conditions. If this is not the case, condition 7.2(a) of the Standard Conditions of Sale (3rd Edn) (for which see vol 38(1) (2000 Reissue) SALE OF LAND Form 1 [1051]) or condition 7.2(a) of the Standard Commercial Property Conditions (1st Edn) (for which see vol 38(1) (2000 Reissue) SALE OF LAND Form 2 [1108]), should be made to apply.

20   Except on a sale by auction the deposit is to be paid by banker's draft or cheque drawn on a solicitor's clearing bank account: see the Standard Conditions of Sale (3rd Edn) condition 2.2.1 (for which see vol 38(1) (2000 Reissue) SALE OF LAND Form 1 [1016]). The Standard Commercial Property Conditions (1st Edn) condition 2.2.2 (for which see vol 38(1) (2000 Reissue) SALE OF LAND Form 2 [1076]) requires the deposit to be paid by direct credit transfer of cleared funds except on a sale by auction. The National Conditions of Sale (20th Edition) (for which see vol 38(1) (2000 Reissue) SALE OF LAND Form 4 [1161]), which were replaced as from March 1990 with the Standard Conditions of Sale and have therefore not subsequently been updated, do not cover the point, although, where these are incorporated, express provisions may be inserted.

**[3095]**

21   It is suggested that the deposit payment should equal the agreed percentage (typically 10% but frequently less) of the entire price for the property. When the purchase price is to be ascertained by valuation after the unconditional date, the deposit should be specified as a fixed sum, being the appropriate proportion (usually 10%) of the estimated purchase price or minimum purchase price (if any).

22    Omit this clause if no VAT is payable or it is payable but the deposit is held as stakeholder.

23    As to the distinction between 'all reasonable', 'reasonable' and 'best' endeavours, see *UBH (Mechanical Services) Ltd v Standard Life Assurance Co* (1986) Times 13 November. The use of expressions such as 'best endeavours' or 'all reasonable endeavours' can give rise to problems. The former expression has (in the context of trying to obtain the landlord's consent to assign a lease) been held to mean 'something less than efforts which go beyond the bounds of reason but are considerably more than casual and intermittent activities': see *Pips (Leisure Productions) Ltd v Walton* (1982) 43 P & CR 415 at 420, per Megarry V-C. This would seem to entail the seller doing what a reasonable person would do in the circumstances. 'All reasonable endeavours' is probably seen generally as a lesser obligation than 'best endeavours', but in the light of the above definition it is not clear how much less. It may be preferable for the seller to omit both expressions, though a buyer may wish to see some definition of the degree of obligation on the seller.

24    As to the completion date, delay and notice to complete generally, see vol 35 (1997 Reissue) SALE OF LAND Paragraph 694 [902] et seq. For the provisions relating to payment of interest for late completion see the Standard Conditions of Sale (3rd Edn) condition 7.3 (for which see vol 38(1) (2000 Reissue) SALE OF LAND Form 1 [1051]) and the Standard Commercial Property Conditions (1st Edn) condition 7.3 (for which see vol 38(1) (2000 Reissue) SALE OF LAND Form 2 [1108]). As to the Law Society's General Conditions of Sale (1984 Revision) condition 22 (for which see vol 38(1) (2000 Reissue) SALE OF LAND Form 3 [1147]) and the National Conditions of Sale (20th Edn) condition 7 (for which see vol 38(1) (2000 Reissue) SALE OF LAND Form 4 [1161]), which Conditions were replaced by the Standard Conditions of Sale as from March 1990, see vol 38(1) (2000 Reissue) SALE OF LAND Paragraph 290 [1001] et seq. The differences between the various sets of conditions are great and should be carefully noted. For tables of comparison, see vol 38(1) (2000 Reissue) SALE OF LAND Form 5 [1201] et seq ante.

25    The inclusion of these words is not strictly necessary since the Standard Conditions of Sale (3rd Edn) condition 6.2 (for which see vol 38(1) (2000 Reissue) SALE OF LAND Form 1 [1045]) provides for completion to take place either at the seller's solicitor's office or at some other place which the seller reasonably specifies.

**[3096]**

26    The Standard Conditions of Sale (3rd Edn) condition 6.1.2 (for which see vol 38(1) (2000 Reissue) SALE OF LAND Form 1 [1045]) states that if the money due on completion is received after 2.00 pm, completion is to be treated, for the purposes of apportionments and the provisions regarding late completion, as taking place on the next working day. Any amendments to this condition should be included in the fourth schedule.

27    As to implied covenants for title and the words importing them generally, see vol 35 (1997 Reissue) SALE OF LAND Paragraph 472 [597] et seq.

      Covenants for title are implied by the Law of Property (Miscellaneous Provisions) Act 1994 (37 Halsbury's Statutes (4th Edn) REAL PROPERTY) and (additionally in the case of registered land the Land Registration Rules 1925, SR&O 1925/1093 rr 76A–77A as inserted, substituted and amended by SI 1995/337) provide that key words are included in the assurance. Although under the Act and Rules no covenants are implied unless such key words are used, condition 4.5.2 of the Standard Conditions of Sale (3rd Edn) (for which see vol 38(1) (2000 Reissue) SALE OF LAND Form 1 [1025]) provides that if the contract for sale makes no provision as to title guarantee then subject to condition 4.5.3 the seller is to transfer the property with full title guarantee. Accordingly in cases where it is inappropriate for any covenants for title to be given a clause must be inserted expressly stating that no covenants for title will be given.

      For a form varying the implied covenants for title see vol 36 (1997 Reissue) SALE OF LAND Form 190 [2226].

28    In the absence of any indication to the contrary, it is an implied term that vacant possession will be given: see vol 35 (1997 Reissue) SALE OF LAND Paragraph 328 [429]. See further note 1 above.

**[3097]**

29    As to deduction of title to unregistered property, see vol 35 (1997 Reissue) SALE OF LAND Paragraph 400 [515] and as to deduction of title to registered property see vol 35 (1997 Reissue) SALE OF LAND Paragraph 399 [510]. As to the seller's duty to disclose defects in the title see vol 35 (1997 Reissue) SALE OF LAND Paragraph 295 [391] et seq. It is clearly in the interests of the seller to disclose any defects of which he is aware before exchange of contracts; therefore it is now common for title to be deduced in its entirety before exchange and for restrictions to be placed on the right to raise requisitions.

30    As to the proving and investigation of title generally see vol 35 (1997 Reissue) SALE OF LAND Paragraph 398 [509] et seq. As to instruments which may form a good root of title see vol 35 (1997 Reissue) SALE OF LAND Paragraph 400.2 [516].

31    The Standard Conditions of Sale (3rd Edn) condition 4.2.1 (for which see vol 38(1) (2000 Reissue) SALE OF LAND Form 1 [1024]) and the Standard Commercial Property Conditions (1st Edn) condition 4.2.1 (for which see vol 38(1) (2000 Reissue) SALE OF LAND Form 2 [1083]) provide that the evidence of registered title is to be office copies of the items required to be furnished by the Land Registration Act 1925 s 110(2). However it is still advisable to include the words in square brackets

because the Standard Conditions of Sale are incorporated only in so far as they are not varied by or inconsistent with the terms of the agreement, and it is arguable that the provisions of clause 8 without the words in square brackets form a complete provision replacing the equivalent provision in the Standard Conditions of Sale. As to the deduction of title using HM Land Registry's direct access system see vol 35 (1997 Reissue) SALE OF LAND Paragraph 399.3 [512].

The words in square brackets are required when the contract is made by reference to the National Conditions of Sale (20th Edn) (for which see vol 38(1) (2000 Reissue) SALE OF LAND Form 4 [1161]), which do not include this provision. These were replaced by the Standard Conditions of Sale as from March 1990 and have not been updated subsequently: see vol 38(1) (2000 Reissue) SALE OF LAND Paragraph 290 [1001] et seq. As to the desirability of providing office copies see vol 35 (1997 Reissue) SALE OF LAND Paragraph 399.3 [512].

32  This clause should be included if it is desired to exclude requisitions on the title. Both the Standard Conditions of Sale (3rd Edn) (for which see vol 38(1) (2000 Reissue) SALE OF LAND Form 1 [1011]) and the Standard Commercial Property Conditions (1st Edn) (for which see vol 38(1) (2000 Reissue) SALE OF LAND Form 2 [1071]) omit the provision contained in the Standard Conditions of Sale (1st Edn) condition 4.5, which allowed the seller to rescind the contract if the buyer refused to withdraw a requisition which the seller was unable to satisfy.

33  The buyer should be wary of this clause. If important documents are missing then there may be difficulties in registering the title following completion where the land is unregistered. Of course, if a document is genuinely missing, the original cannot be produced. However, as much evidence as possible should be called for as to the contents of the document and the circumstances of its loss, and statutory declarations obtained (see, eg, vol 25(1) (1999 Reissue) LAND REGISTRATION Form 108 [3851]) so as to give the best possible chance of avoiding registration difficulties. If the land is already registered then, unless the missing document relates to an overriding interest (eg the counterpart of a lease for a term not exceeding 21 years), either:

(a)  the title is likely to be less than absolute (eg possessory or qualified) where the missing document is important to the seller's own title; or

(b)  there is likely to be a protective entry on the register (eg as to restrictive covenants where no copy of the deed creating them was supplied on first registration).

In either case the buyer will need to obtain as much information as possible about the missing document and the effect of this on quality of the title in order to assess the risk of accepting the defect. Various options may be open to the buyer, ranging from simply accepting the risk, if judged to be small, through negotiating a suitable adjustment to the price or obtaining defective title insurance cover to, in extreme cases, withdrawing from the transaction before exchanging contracts.

**[3098]**

34  As to the seller's duty to disclose encumbrances generally see vol 35 (1997 Reissue) SALE OF LAND Paragraph 295 [391]. Where registered land is concerned, the rights of any person in actual occupation of the land will be overriding interests to which any disposition of the land will be subject unless enquiry has been made of that person and the rights were not disclosed: see the Land Registration Act 1925 s 70(1)(g). The same qualification does not apply in relation to other overriding interests listed in the Land Registration Act 1925 s 70(1) as amended.

35  The proprietorship register may need to be included if, eg, there is a restriction controlling dispositions of land which will remain on the register following sale.

36  Where certain charges, eg financial charges, are specifically excluded, a buyer may wish to ensure that any matters entered on the register before completion are also excluded. It might be argued that reference to exclusion of specific entries is to be interpreted as making the property subject to all other entries including new entries. It may be preferable to specify the entries to which the property is positively to be subject so that the position is clear.

37  Matters to be included in the third schedule are matters not recorded in the registers of title or property documents eg, rights created orally, wayleave agreements and short term or informal arrangements.

38  This sub-clause should be omitted if there are no matters affecting the property in respect of which the seller will remain liable notwithstanding the completion of the transfer of the property to the buyer. It may also be omitted in reliance upon the Standard Conditions of Sale (3rd Edn) condition 4.5.4 (for which see vol 38(1) (2000 Reissue) SALE OF LAND Form 1 [1025]) if incorporated. It should be omitted if the alternative sub-clauses 9.1 and 9.2 are used as the indemnity covenant will be set out in full in the draft assurance.

It may be preferred to set out the indemnity covenant the seller will require, rather than rely on standard conditions of sale, particularly if the contract is made by reference to the Law Society's General Conditions of Sale (1984 Revision) (for which see vol 38(1) (2000 Reissue) SALE OF LAND Form 3 [1131]) which do not require the buyer to covenant to observe and perform the covenants and conditions. See also the Standard Commercial Property Conditions (1st Edn) condition 4.5.4 (for which see vol 38(1) (2000 Reissue) SALE OF LAND Form 2 [1084]) and the Standard Conditions of Sale (3rd Edn) condition 4.5.4 (for which see vol 38(1) (2000 Reissue) SALE OF LAND Form 1 [1025]).

**[3099]**

39    As to encumbrances, see note 34 above.

40    Whilst the annexation of a draft assurance is more usual on a sale of part of the seller's property it may be appropriate also on a sale of the whole of a property where there are numerous or complex encumbrances to be referred to in the assurance or covenants to be imposed.

41    As to the proprietorship register, see note 35 above.

42    As to the charges register, see note 36 above.

43    As to matters to be included in the third schedule, see note 37 above.

44    A buyer should bear in mind that certain financial charges in respect of costs incurred by a local authority are registrable as local land charges. If these relate to expenditure arising before the date of the contract the buyer may wish to ensure that they are borne by the seller.

45    As an exclusion clause, this clause is subject to the test of reasonableness under the Unfair Contract Terms Act 1977 s 11 (11 Halsbury's Statutes (4th Edn) CONTRACT): see *Smith v Eric S Bush, Harris v Wyre Forest District Council* [1990] 1 AC 831, [1989] 2 All ER 514, HL. The seller cannot rely on a general disclaimer to avoid disclosing matters specifically known to him prior to sale: *Rignall Developments Ltd v Halil* [1988] Ch 190, [1987] 3 All ER 170. For further discussion on this issue see *Thomas Witter Ltd v TBP Industries Ltd* [1996] 2 All ER 573.

46    Consideration should be given to whether the conditions of sale incorporated require amendment in any way to suit the circumstances of the transaction or to ensure consistency with this agreement. As to possible modifications where the Standard Conditions of Sale (3rd Edn) are incorporated (for which see vol 38(1) (2000 Reissue) SALE OF LAND Form 1 [1011]), see vol 35 (1997 Reissue) SALE OF LAND Form 18 [1547]. Many of the suggested amendments are now incorporated in the Standard Commercial Property Conditions (1st Edn) (for which see vol 38(1) (2000 Reissue) SALE OF LAND Form 2 [1071]). The fourth schedule contains amendments to the Standard Conditions of Sale (3rd Edn) appropriate to this agreement.

**[3100]**

47    As to restriction on assignment and sub-sale see note 16 above.

48    Where the Standard Conditions of Sale (3rd Edn) or the Standard Commercial Property Conditions (1st Edn) are being incorporated this clause can be omitted, although it is commonly included for the convenience of the parties: see the Standard Conditions of Sale (3rd Edn) condition 7.4 (for which see vol 38(1) (2000 Reissue) SALE OF LAND Form 1 [1052]) and the Standard Commercial Property Conditions (1st Edn) condition 7.4 (for which see vol 38(1) (2000 Reissue) SALE OF LAND Form 2 [1109]).

49    As to VAT, see note 12 above.

50    Where the election is made on or after 1 March 1995 it is only effective if written notification is given to HM Customs and Excise not later than the end of the period of 30 days beginning on the date on which the election is made, subject to certain exceptions: see the Value Added Tax Act 1994, Sch 10 para 3(6)(b) as substituted by SI 1995/279 (48 Halsbury's Statutes (4th Edn) VALUE ADDED TAX).

51    Insolvency Act 1986 s 1 (4 Halsbury's Statutes (4th Edn) BANKRUPTCY AND INSOLVENCY) applies to composition; the Insolvency Act 1986 s 253 applies to voluntary arrangement.

52    The agreement is drawn up on the assumption that each party is resident in the United Kingdom, and accordingly, in the case of UK companies, has its own UK registered office. The words 'non-exclusive' are mostly used where either the seller or the buyer is an overseas party. The effect is to enable legal action or proceedings to enforce the agreement and/or judgment in an overseas jurisdiction. Although the subject matter of the agreement relates to UK real estate, in some circumstances it is advantageous to have access to courts in the jurisdiction local to that party, and, for example, to other non-domestic assets of the relevant party for the purposes of enforcing judgment. The practitioner should be aware that the law and practice in relation to the recognition of judgments and enforcement differs according to jurisdiction. Accordingly, the precise nature and extent of this provision should be the subject of a legal opinion obtained from lawyers in the relevant jurisdiction.

**[3101]**

53    It is essential to state on the face of a document that it is a deed if it is to be one: see the Law of Property (Miscellaneous Provisions) Act 1989 s 1(2)(a) (37 Halsbury's Statutes (4th Edn) REAL PROPERTY).

54    A notice provision is incorporated in clause 20 for use in two circumstances. The first is where the National Conditions of Sale (20th Edn) (for which see vol 38(1) (2000 Reissue) SALE OF LAND Form 4 [1161]) are incorporated in the agreement as such conditions do not have any express notification provisions. The National Conditions were replaced by the Standard Conditions of Sale as from March 1990 and have not been updated subsequently: see vol 38(1) (2000 Reissue) SALE OF LAND Paragraph 290 [1001] et seq. By contrast the Standard Conditions of Sale (3rd Edn) (for which see vol 38(1) (2000 Reissue) SALE OF LAND Form 1 [1011]) and the Standard Commercial Property Conditions (1st Edn) (for which see vol 38(1) (2000 Reissue) SALE OF LAND Form 2 [1071]) make detailed provision for the service of notices. Secondly, where either party is non-resident in the UK, provision would need to be made for the appointment of an agent for service and accordingly clause 20.5 would be required; but as the identity of the buyer is not known when the conditions are drafted, the condition cannot

deal also with the buyer appointing an agent. Additionally, the practitioner would need to ensure that the arrangements referred to in clause 20.5 have actually been complied with, by sight of the appointment properly counter-signed by the appointed agent.

55    For longer form clauses relating to notices see vol 4(3) (1997 Reissue) BOILERPLATE CLAUSES Forms 3.3 [171]–3.5 [173] and Paragraph 3.1 [22] et seq.

56    As to the subjections, see note 37 above. Insert here details of any matters (if any) subject to which the property is sold which are not mentioned in the register of title nor in any documents listed in Part II of the second schedule.

57    The time to be stated here should accord with the time stated in clause 5.1 of this Form.

58    As to guarantees generally see vol 17(2) (1995 Reissue) GUARANTEES AND INDEMNITIES.

59    It is not usually necessary to have the contract executed as a deed unless the contract contains recitals which are intended to be binding or there are other special considerations (eg, there is a lack of valuable consideration or it is desired to extend the period set by the Limitation Act 1980 s 8 (24 Halsbury's Statutes (4th Edn) LIMITATION OF ACTIONS) for bringing claims).

Where a contract is to be executed as a deed sealing is not necessary either in the case of an individual or in the case of a company, but all parties must sign either on the same document or each on one of two identical parts which are exchanged and the signatures of all individuals must be witnessed: see the Law of Property (Miscellaneous Provisions) Act 1989 s 1(3). As to the execution of a deed by an individual and by a corporation, see vol 12 (1994 Reissue) DEEDS, AGREEMENTS AND DECLARATIONS Paragraphs 16 [1525] and 28 [1554]–30 [1560] respectively.

It is unnecessary for a contract by a corporate body to be under seal unless it would need to be a deed if made by private persons: see the Corporate Bodies' Contracts Act 1960 s 1 (11 Halsbury's Statutes (4th Edn) CONTRACT). A contract may be made by a company incorporated under the Companies Acts by writing under its common seal or on its behalf by any person acting under its authority, express or implied: Companies Act 1985 s 36 as substituted by the Companies Act 1989 s 130(1) (8 Halsbury's Statutes (4th Edn) COMPANIES).

**[3102]–[3120]**

# 69

## Agreement for sale of a single freehold commercial property with vacant possession, conditional upon the buyer obtaining planning permission— drafted in favour of the buyer; purchase price fixed or ascertained by a method set out in one or other of Forms 72–76[1]

### CONTENTS

Schedules

1        The Purchase Price
2        The Property
3        The Subjections
4        Amendments to the Standard Conditions of Sale (3rd Edn)
5        Guarantee
6        Planning Counsel

[3121]


THIS AGREEMENT is made the …… day of ………

BETWEEN:

(1)      *(name of seller)*² **[**company number *(number)***)]**³ **[**of *(address)* or whose registered
         office is at *(address)***]** ('the Seller') and

(2)      *(name of buyer)* **[**company number *(number)***]** **[**of *(address)* or whose registered
         office is at *(address)***]** ('the Buyer') **[**and

**[**(3)    *(name of guarantor)* **[**company number *(number)***]** **[**of *(address)* or whose registered
         office is at *(address)***]** ('the Guarantor')**]**


1        **Definitions and interpretation**⁴

In this Agreement:

1.1      'the Act' means the Town and Country Planning Act 1990 and any act for the
         time being in force amending or replacing the same and all regulations and
         orders made thereunder **[**and any other legislation relating to town and country
         planning in force from time to time**]** **[**including the Planning (Listed Buildings
         and Conservation Areas) Act 1990**]**

1.2      'Affiliate' means in relation to any party a Subsidiary or a holding company (as
         defined by the Companies Act 1985 Section 736) of that party or any other
         Subsidiary of that holding company

1.3      'this Agreement' means this document as varied by any subsequent
         documentation

1.4      'Appeal' means all or any of the following as the case may be:
         1.4.1    an appeal to the Secretary of State under Section 78 of the Act
                  against a refusal of a Planning Application or the grant of a Planning
                  Permission which is not a Satisfactory Planning Permission or
         1.4.2    an appeal to the Secretary of State under Section 78 of the Act
                  against the non-determination of a Planning Application or
         1.4.3    a Call-in

1.5      'Authorised Transferee' means any Affiliate of the Buyer or such other legal
         entity as shall be previously approved in writing by the Seller such approval not
         to be unreasonably withheld or delayed **[**in the case of a publicly-quoted
         company or a company guaranteed by a publicly-quoted company and in
         determining what is a reasonable ground for withholding such approval the
         Seller shall be entitled where relevant to have regard to the consequent release
         of any guarantee it may already hold**]**

[3122]

1.6      'the Buyer's Solicitors' means *(insert name and address of person or firm)*

1.7      a 'Call-in' means the reference of a Planning Application to the Secretary of
         State under Section 77 of the Act

1.8      'Completion' means actual completion of the sale and purchase agreed in this
         Agreement

1.9     'the Completion Date'[5] means the date *(number)* days after the Unconditional
        Date[6]

1.10    'the Completion Moneys' means the Purchase Price (or any outstanding
        balance of it) as adjusted by all sums due between the parties at Completion

1.11    'the Contract Rate'[7] means *(insert interest rate or method of calculating the interest rate
        by reference eg to the base lending rate of a named bank)*

1.12    'the Deposit' means £... [which is [inclusive *or* exclusive] of VAT at the
        standard rate][8]

1.13    'Development' means the development on the Property or on some part thereof
        [for *(define use)* or for use within Class *(insert class number)* of the Town and
        Country Planning (Use Classes) Order 1987] [together with car parking and
        access roads and *(insert details)*]

1.14    'the General Conditions'[9] means [the Standard Conditions of Sale (3rd Edn) *or
        (specify)*]

1.15    'the Local Planning Authority' means the local planning authority for the area
        in which the Property is situated

[1.16   'the Plan'[10] means the plan attached to this Agreement [and if numbered plans
        are attached any reference to a numbered plan is to the attached plan so
        numbered]]

**[3123]**

1.17    a 'Planning Application' means [the [outline] planning application for the
        Development submitted on *(date)* and appended to this Agreement and] any
        application for [outline] planning permission for the Development submitted
        by the Buyer in accordance with this Agreement

1.18    'Planning Counsel' means [counsel experienced in town and country planning
        law of not less than ten years call *or* one of the planning counsel listed in the
        sixth schedule]

1.19    'Planning Obligation' means all or any of the following as the case may be:

        1.19.1    an agreement in respect of and affecting the Property (whether or
                  not also affecting other property) pursuant to the Local Government
                  (Miscellaneous Provisions) Act 1982 Section 33 and/or the Local
                  Government Act 1972 Section 111 and/or the Highways Act 1980
                  Section(s) 38 and/or 278 and/or the Water Industry Act 1991
                  Section 104 or any provision to similar intent or an agreement with
                  a water undertaker or a drainage undertaker (within the meaning of
                  the Water Industry Act 1991) or the Environment Agency or an
                  Internal Drainage Board (within the meaning of the Water
                  Resources Act 1991 or the Land Drainage Act 1991) or other
                  appropriate authority as to water supply or drainage of surface and/
                  or foul water from the Property or an agreement with any competent
                  authority or body relating to other services and/or

        1.19.2    a planning obligation (whether entered into by agreement or
                  otherwise) in respect of and affecting the Property (whether or not
                  also affecting other property) pursuant to Section 106 of the Act

1.20    'Planning Permission' means a planning permission granted pursuant to a
        Planning Application

**[3124]**

1.21    'Proceedings' means either:

        1.21.1    an application for judicial review under the Civil Procedure Rules,
                  Schedule 1, RSC Ord 53 or an application pursuant to Section 288
                  of the Act including in each case any appeals to a higher court
                  following a judgment of a lower court or

1.21.2      any reconsideration by the Local Planning Authority or the Secretary of State of an Appeal (as the case may be) following a previous Satisfactory Planning Permission or Refusal being quashed pursuant to an application within the meaning of clause 1.21.1 above and the matter being remitted to the Local Planning Authority or the Secretary of State (as the case may be) or

1.21.3      an application (within the meaning of clause 1.21.1) arising from the grant of a Satisfactory Planning Permission or a Refusal following a reconsideration of a Planning Application by the Local Planning Authority or an Appeal to the Secretary of State pursuant to clause 1.21.2

1.22      'the Property'[11] means the freehold property described in Part I of the second schedule

1.23      'the Purchase Price' means the purchase price[12] [stated in *or* ascertained in accordance with] the first schedule

1.24      'Refusal' means a refusal of a Planning Application by the Local Planning Authority or the refusal of an Appeal by the Secretary of State or the grant of a Planning Permission by the Local Planning Authority or the Secretary of State which is not a Satisfactory Planning Permission

1.25      'Satisfactory Planning Permission' means a Planning Permission which does not contain an Unreasonable Condition

1.26      'the Secretary of State' means the Secretary of State for the Environment (or other minister of the Crown to whom his relevant power or duty may from time to time be transferred) or any appropriate officer having authority to act on his behalf

1.27      'the Seller's Solicitors' means *(insert name and address of person or firm)*

**[3125]**

1.28      'Subsidiary' means either:

1.28.1      a subsidiary within the meaning of the Companies Act 1985[13] Section 736 or

1.28.2      unless the context requires otherwise a subsidiary undertaking within the meaning of the Companies Act 1989 Section 21

1.29      'Termination Date' means the date which is *(number)* year[s] from the date of this Agreement unless on that date:

1.29.1      an Appeal made prior to such date has not been determined by the Secretary of State or

1.29.2      a Satisfactory Planning Permission has been issued or

1.29.3      Proceedings have been instituted

when in each case the Termination Date shall be extended until the expiry of three months from the issue of a Refusal by the Secretary of State unless Proceedings (or further Proceedings) have been instituted

1.30      'the Transfer' means the transfer of the Property

1.31      'Unconditional Date' means the date which is the earlier of:

1.31.1      [four] months from (but excluding) the date of the Satisfactory Planning Permission provided that no Proceedings have been instituted before or within this period

1.31.2      the date of the giving of any notice under clause 2.3 whether or not any Proceedings have been instituted

1.31.3      the date upon which the result of Proceedings in relation to a Satisfactory Planning Permission result in the validation or grant of a Satisfactory Planning Permission which is incapable of challenge by way of Proceedings

1.32     'Unreasonable Condition' means a condition subject to which a Planning Permission is issued which has the effect of either:

1.32.1     making the Planning Permission personal to the Buyer or

1.32.2     granting a temporary planning permission or

1.32.3     being materially detrimental to the operation use occupation or economic viability of the Development

**[3126]**

1.33     'VAT' means an amount equal to the value added tax as charged in accordance with VATA[14] or any equivalent or substituted tax

1.34     'VATA' means the Value Added Tax Act 1994 or any equivalent tax Act

1.35     'VAT Invoice' means an invoice complying with the provisions of regulations 13 and 14 of the VAT Regulations 1995[15]

1.36     where the context so admits the expression[s] 'the Seller' [and 'the Buyer'] [and 'the Guarantor'] include[s] their respective personal representatives [and 'the Buyer' shall include any permitted successors in title of the Buyer][16]

1.37     words importing one gender shall be construed as importing any other gender

1.38     words importing the singular shall be construed as importing the plural and vice versa

1.39     words importing persons shall be construed as importing a corporate body and/ or a partnership and vice versa

1.40     where any party comprises more than one person the obligations and liabilities of that party under this Agreement shall be joint and several obligations and liabilities of those persons[17]

1.41     the clause headings do not form part of this Agreement and shall not be taken into account in its construction or interpretation

1.42     any reference to a clause or a paragraph or a schedule is to one in this Agreement so numbered

1.43     any reference to a colour or letter is to one on the [Plan *or* Plans]

1.44     in the absence of any contrary provision any reference to a statute includes any statutory modification or re-enactment of it and any and every order instrument regulation direction or plan made or issued under the statute or deriving validity from it

**[3127]**

## 2     Agreement for sale

2.1     Subject to clause 2.2 below the Seller shall sell and the Buyer shall buy the Property for the Purchase Price

2.2     The sale and purchase of the Property is conditional upon the Unconditional Date occurring prior to the Termination Date

2.3     The Buyer has the sole benefit of the condition referred to in clause 2.2 above and may by written notice given at any time prior to the Termination Date unilaterally waive the condition and upon the giving of the notice to that effect the Unconditional Date shall be deemed to have occurred[18]

2.4     Unless the Unconditional Date has occurred this Agreement shall automatically determine upon the Termination Date but without prejudice to the accrued rights and liabilities of either party against the other party and the parties shall not (without prejudice to clause 3.2 below) be entitled to be paid any costs or compensation whatsoever

## 3     Deposit[19]

3.1     The Deposit shall be paid[20] [on the Unconditional Date] to the Seller's Solicitors to hold as stakeholders[21]

3.2    The Deposit shall be placed to the credit of an interest bearing deposit account
       until the date of Completion and the interest earned on the Deposit shall accrue
       to the Buyer and shall be paid to the Buyer on Completion or on determination
       pursuant to clause 2.4 above without any withholding or set off but net of such
       tax as the law may from time to time require to be deducted (for which the
       Seller shall account to the proper Revenue authorities unless such tax is
       deducted at source) PROVIDED that in the event of:
       3.2.1     any delay in Completion (through no fault of the Seller) the interest
                 earned on the Deposit shall accrue as from the Completion Date to
                 and be paid to the Seller and
       3.2.2     the Seller lawfully forfeiting the Deposit the interest earned on the
                 Deposit shall as from the date it was deposited accrue to and be paid
                 to the Seller
3.3    The Law of Property Act 1925 Section 49(2) shall not have effect
[3.4   The Seller shall issue a valid VAT invoice in respect of the Deposit within [7]
       working days of its payment to the Seller's Solicitors[22]]

                                                                              **[3128]**

**4      Obtaining Satisfactory Planning Permission**

4.1    The Buyer shall as soon as reasonably practicable [and in any event within
       *(number of days)*] submit a Planning Application to the Local Planning Authority
4.2    The Buyer may withdraw and resubmit a Planning Application or amend or
       modify a Planning Application or an Appeal or Proceedings and submit further
       planning applications (including duplicates of a Planning Application)
4.3    If a Planning Application is refused by the Local Planning Authority or is not
       determined within either the period prescribed in the Act during which the
       Local Planning Authority may determine a Planning Application or within such
       extended period as the Buyer may agree with the Local Planning Authority the
       Buyer may lodge and prosecute an Appeal with the Secretary of State
4.4    If the Local Planning Authority issues a Planning Permission which is not a
       Satisfactory Planning Permission the Buyer may either:
       4.4.1     submit an application for planning permission pursuant to Section 73
                 of the Act for development of the Property without complying with
                 the conditions subject to which the Planning Permission was granted
                 (and in the event that such an application is made it shall for the
                 purposes of this Agreement be treated as a Planning Application) or
       4.4.2     lodge an Appeal with the Secretary of State
4.5    The Buyer shall within 28 days of receipt of either a Refusal or a Planning
       Permission send a copy of it to the Seller's Solicitors
[4.6   The Buyer may issue Proceedings in respect of any Refusal by the Secretary of
       State but shall not be obliged to pursue any Planning Application or Appeal or
       Proceedings and may withdraw the same if Planning Counsel advises that there
       is less that a *(specify)*% chance of obtaining a Satisfactory Planning Permission
       provided that the Buyer shall not be limited in the number of times it may seek
       counsel's advice]

                                                                              **[3129]**

4.7    The Seller shall:
       4.7.1     support the Buyer in making and pursuing a Planning Application
                 and/or an Appeal and/or Proceedings
       4.7.2     at the request of the Buyer and if required by the Local Planning
                 Authority or other competent authority enter into any Planning
                 Obligation which the Buyer shall require to secure a Satisfactory

Planning Permission within [10] working days of service of such Planning Obligation upon the Seller [and the Seller shall use its best endeavours[23] to procure that any other person with an interest in the Property shall enter into any such Planning Obligation]

4.7.3 permit the Buyer its agents and surveyors at all reasonable times to enter the Property for the purpose of inspection and for the purpose of general site investigation the Buyer making good as soon as possible any damage occasioned by the exercise of such right

4.7.4 not whilst this Agreement remains in force submit any application to the Local Planning Authority for planning permission nor (except pursuant to sub-clause 4.7.2 above) enter into any Planning Obligation in respect of the Property or any part of it with or without any other property without the written consent of the Buyer

4.7.5 not whilst this Agreement remains in force carry out any works to or change the use of the Property [and for the avoidance of doubt the Seller shall not begin the Development (within the meaning of Section 56 of the Act) authorised by any Planning Permission]

4.7.6 not submit or cause to be submitted or pursue or assist in pursuing any application for planning permission [which will have a[n] [materially] adverse effect on the chances of obtaining Satisfactory Planning Permission] [for a competing development being a development within *(number)* miles of the Property for *(details)* having a gross floor area in excess of *(details)*]

**[3130]**

## 5 Completion

5.1 Completion of the sale and purchase and payment of the Completion Moneys [and of the VAT] shall take place on the Completion Date[24] on or before [1.00pm] [at the offices of the Seller's Solicitors or where they may reasonably direct][25]

5.2 If the Completion Moneys are received after [1.00 pm][26] on the Completion Date or on a day which is not a working day Completion shall be deemed for the purposes of the General Conditions to have taken place on the next working day

## [6 Title guarantee[27] *(where the form of the assurance is not annexed)*

6.1 The Seller sells the Property [with [full *or* limited] *or* without any] title guarantee [with the modifications set out below]

[6.2 Where the Transfer is made with full title guarantee the Law of Property (Miscellaneous Provisions) Act 1994 Section 6(2)(a) shall have effect as though all matters now recorded in all registers open to or capable of public inspection are to be considered to be within the actual knowledge of the Buyer]

[6.3 Where the transfer is made with limited title guarantee the Law of Property (Miscellaneous Provisions) Act 1994 Section 3(3) shall not apply and instead the Seller will covenant that it has not since the transfer to it:

6.3.1 charged or encumbered the Property by means of any charge or encumbrance which subsists at the date of the Transfer or granted third party rights in relation to the Property which so subsist or

6.3.2 knowingly suffered the Property to be so charged or encumbered or subjected to any such rights]

[6.4 The Transfer shall contain the modifications set out above and include an application to the Registrar to enter on the register in an appropriate manner a note that the implied covenants are modified in the manner set out above]

*or*

**6     Title guarantee** *(where the form of Transfer is annexed)*

The Property is sold [with the title guarantee set out in the annexed form of draft
Transfer [with the modifications included in it] *or* without any title guarantee]]

[3131]

**7     Vacant Possession**[28]

The Property is sold with vacant possession subject to the presence of any third party
chattels

**8     Title**[29]

[8.1     The title to the Property is unregistered and title shall commence with the
         document described as the root of title in Part II of the second schedule[30]
         *or*
         The title to the Property is registered at HM Land Registry and title shall be
         deduced in accordance with the Land Registration Act 1925 Section 110 [save
         that copies of the entries on the register the filed plan and any documents
         referred to shall be office copies[31]]]

8.2      Title having been deduced prior to the date of this Agreement the Buyer
         accepts the Seller's title to the Property and shall be deemed to purchase with
         full knowledge of the title in all respects and shall not raise any requisitions or
         make any objection in relation to the title[32] [but the Buyer may raise requisitions
         arising out of:

         8.2.1     events occurring after the date of this Agreement

         8.2.2     matters revealed by pre-completion searches which are not registered
                   at the date of this Agreement

         8.2.3     matters which a prudent buyer could not be aware of at the date of
                   this Agreement]

[8.3     The Seller does not have the documents (if any) noted as missing in Part II of
         the second schedule and the Buyer may not raise any requisition or objection
         on that account and no acknowledgement for production or undertaking for
         safe custody will be given nor copies produced][33]

[3132]

[**9     Encumbrances**[34] *(where the form of the assurance is not annexed)*

[9.1     The Property is sold subject to and (where appropriate) with the benefit of:

         9.1.1     the matters contained or referred to in the property
                   [proprietorship][35] and charges[36] registers of the title to the Property
                   [other than any subsisting financial charges]

         [9.1.2    the documents described in Part II of the second schedule] [and]

         [9.1.3    the matters set out in the third schedule]][37]

9.2      The Buyer or the Buyer's Solicitors having been supplied with copies of the
         documents referred to in clause 9.1 the Buyer shall be deemed to purchase with
         full notice and knowledge of the same and shall not raise any requisition or make
         any objection in relation to them

9.3      The Transfer shall contain a covenant by the Buyer that the Buyer will (by way
         of indemnity only) observe and perform the covenants conditions and other
         matters contained or referred to in the documents referred to in clause 9.1 and
         will indemnify and keep the Seller and its successors in title fully and effectually
         indemnified against all actions proceedings damages costs claims and expenses

which may be suffered or incurred by the Seller or its successors in title in respect of [future] breach or non-observance or non-performance of those covenants and conditions [and obligations][38]

9.4     The Transfer shall be engrossed [in duplicate] by the Buyer's Solicitors and [the *or* both] engrossment[s] shall be executed by the Buyer before the Completion Date

[9.5    Immediately after Completion the Buyer shall at its own expense procure the proper stamping of the duplicate Transfer as a duplicate (including but not limited to the affixing of a particulars delivered stamp) and shall immediately after such stamping deliver the duly stamped duplicate to the Seller's Solicitors]

**[3133]**

*or*

**9      Encumbrances**[39] *(where the form of Transfer is annexed)*[40]

9.1     The Transfer shall be in the form of the annexed draft

[9.2    The Property is sold subject to and (where appropriate) with the benefit of:
        9.2.1     the matters contained or referred to in the annexed draft Transfer and the property [proprietorship][41] and charges[42] registers of the title to the Property [other than any subsisting financial charges]
        [9.2.2    the documents described in Part II of the second schedule] [and]
        [9.2.3    the matters set out in the third schedule]][43]

9.3     The Buyer or the Buyer's Solicitors having been supplied with copies of the matters (if any) referred to in clause 9.2 prior to the date of this Agreement the Buyer shall be deemed to purchase with full notice and knowledge of them and shall not raise any requisition or make any objection in relation to them

9.4     The Transfer shall be engrossed [in duplicate] by the Seller's Solicitors and [the *or* both] engrossment[s] shall be executed by the Buyer before the Completion Date

[9.5    Immediately after Completion the Buyer shall at its own expense procure the proper stamping of the duplicate Transfer as a duplicate (including but not limited to the affixing of a particulars delivered stamp) and shall immediately after such stamping deliver the duly stamped duplicate to the Seller's Solicitors]]

**[3134]**

**10     Matters affecting the Property**

The Property is sold subject to the following matters:

10.1    all local land charges whether registered or not before the date of this Agreement and all matters capable of registration as local land charges whether or not actually so registered[44]

10.2    all notices served and orders demands proposals or requirements made by any local public or other competent authority whether before or after the date of this Agreement

10.3    all actual or proposed charges notices orders restrictions agreements conditions contraventions or other matters arising under any statute

10.4    all easements quasi-easements rights exceptions or other similar matters including rights of way drainage water watercourses light rights of adjoining owners affecting the Property and liability to repair or covenants to repair roads pavements paths ways passages sewers drains gutters fences and other like matters whether or not apparent on inspection or disclosed in any of the documents referred to in this Agreement and without any obligation on the Seller to provide evidence of the creation of or to define or apportion any such liability

10.5    matters discoverable by inspection of the Property before the date of this Agreement

10.6     matters relating to the Property about which the Seller does not know
10.7     matters disclosed or which would be disclosed by any searches or as a result of
         enquiries (formal or informal and made in person in writing or orally) made by
         or for the Buyer or which a prudent buyer ought to make and
10.8     overriding interests as defined in the Land Registration Act 1925 Section 70(1)
         or matters which would be overriding interests if the title were registered

                                                                                    **[3135]**

## 11     Disclaimer[45]

11.1     The Buyer admits that:

         11.1.1     it has inspected the Property and purchases it with full knowledge of
                    its actual state and condition and shall take the Property as it stands

         11.1.2     it enters into this Agreement solely as a result of its own inspection
                    and on the basis of the terms of this Agreement and not in reliance
                    upon any advertisement statement representation or warranty either
                    written or oral or implied made by or on behalf of the Seller except
                    as stated in clause 11.2

         11.1.3     no warranty statement or representation has been made or given to
                    the Buyer that the Property can be used or developed in any
                    particular way or for any particular purpose and the Seller shall not
                    be liable to the Buyer if the Property cannot for any reason
                    whatsoever be so used or developed

11.2     The Buyer may rely on factual representations and warranties made or given by
         the Seller's Solicitors to the Buyer's Solicitors' pre-contract enquiries but only
         in so far as such statements are not capable of independent verification by
         appropriate searches enquiries inspection survey of the Property or by
         inspection of the documents and information supplied to the Buyer's Solicitors

11.3     This Agreement contains the entire agreement between the parties and
         incorporates all the terms agreed between them for the purposes of the Law of
         Property (Miscellaneous Provisions) Act 1989 Section 2 and there are no other
         terms or provisions agreed prior to the date of this Agreement which have not
         been incorporated into this Agreement

                                                                                    **[3136]**

## 12     Incorporation of conditions of sale and documents

12.1     The General Conditions [as amended by the [fourth] schedule][46] shall apply to
         this Agreement and are incorporated in it in so far as they are applicable to a sale
         by private treaty and are not varied by or inconsistent with the terms of this
         Agreement

12.2     If there is any conflict between the General Conditions [as amended] and the
         terms of this Agreement the terms of this Agreement prevail

12.3     All express agreements made or undertakings given by one party to the other
         [in *(set out list of letters and documents including relevant inter solicitor correspondence)*]
         are incorporated in this Agreement

## [13     Restriction on assignment and sub-sale[47]

13.1     This Agreement is personal to the Buyer and is not capable of being assigned
         charged or mortgaged [except by way of floating charge]

[13.2    The Seller shall not be required to transfer the Property to anyone other than
         the Buyer named in this Agreement or an Authorised Transferee]]

**14      Merger on completion**[48]

The provisions of this Agreement shall not merge on completion of the Transfer so far as they remain to be performed

**15      VAT provisions**[49]

15.1    The Purchase Price is [inclusive *or* exclusive] of VAT at the standard rate as at Completion

15.2    All VAT payable by the Buyer shall be paid at the same time as the payment on which it is chargeable

15.3    The Seller shall provide the Buyer with a receipted VAT invoice for any VAT paid by the Buyer under this Agreement

15.4    [The Seller warrants that it [has validly made *or* is bound by] an effective[50] election to waive exemption from VAT pursuant to VATA Schedule 10 paragraph 2 in respect of the Property *or* The Seller warrants that it has not made an election to waive exemption from VAT in respect of the Property and will not make any such election]

                                                                          **[3137]**

**[16     Guarantee**

The Guarantor agrees with the Seller in the terms of the [fifth] schedule]

**[17     Insolvency of Buyer**

17.1    If the Buyer:

17.1.1    enters into voluntary liquidation (other than for the purpose of reconstruction or amalgamation not involving a realisation of assets) or has a winding-up order made against it by the court or has a receiver appointed over all or any part of its assets or an administration order is made pursuant to the Insolvency Act 1986 or

17.1.2    becomes insolvent or enters into any composition with its or his creditors or enters into a voluntary arrangement (within the meaning of the Insolvency Act 1986 Sections 1 or 253[51]) or distress sequestration or execution is levied on its goods

then and in any such case the Seller may rescind this Agreement by notice to the Buyer

17.2    Condition 7.2 of the General Conditions shall apply save that in this instance the Seller shall not be obliged to pay any interest which has accrued on the deposit]

**18      Jurisdiction and Governing Law**

This Agreement shall be governed by and construed in accordance with English law and the parties submit to the [non-exclusive] jurisdiction of the English courts[52]

**19      Nature of this Agreement**

This Agreement [is *or* is not] a deed and [has *or* has not] been executed by the parties to it as a deed[53]

                                                                          **[3138]**

**20      Notices**[54]

20.1    Any notice to be given under or in connection with this Agreement shall be in writing and may be delivered personally or sent by first class post telex or fax to the party due to receive the notice at its address set out in this Agreement or the address of its solicitor or such other address as previously specified (by written notice) by such party

20.2    A notice may be given by either party's solicitor to the other party's solicitor provided it conforms to the provisions of clause 20.1

20.3    In the absence of evidence of earlier receipt a notice is deemed received:

20.3.1    if delivered personally when left at the address referred to in clause 20.1

20.3.2    if sent by post two working days after posting it

20.3.3    if sent by telex when the proper answerback is received

20.3.4    if sent by fax on completion of its transmission

20.4    In the case of a notice given pursuant to clauses 20.3.1 20.3.3 or 20.3.4 where this occurs after 5 pm on a working day or on a day which is not a working day the date of service shall be deemed to be the next working day

[20.5    The [Seller *or* Buyer] irrevocably appoints *(name and address)* as its agent for service to receive on its behalf service of proceedings in the English Courts or in any other court or courts of competent jurisdiction][55]

**[21    Contracts (Rights of Third Parties) Act 1999**

For the purposes of the Contracts (Rights of Third Parties) Act 1999 it is agreed that [with the exception only of *(specify clauses)*] nothing in this Agreement shall confer on any third party any right to enforce or any benefit of any term of this Agreement]

[AS *or* IN] WITNESS etc

**[3139]**

FIRST SCHEDULE
The Purchase Price
*(Incorporate relevant form from Forms 72 [3251]–76 [3270] or insert fixed price)*

SECOND SCHEDULE
The Property
[Part I]
Description of the Property

*(Describe the Property: eg)*
[All that freehold property situate at and known as *(address)* registered with title [absolute] at HM Land Registry under title number *(number)*
*or*
All that unregistered freehold property situate at and known as *(address)* which is shown for identification purposes only on the plan annexed to this Agreement and numbered '1']

[Part II
Title Documents affecting the Property
*(commencing where applicable with the root of title)*

| Number | Date | Nature | Parties | Remarks |
|---|---|---|---|---|
| *(number)* | *(date)* | *(details)* | *(details)* | *(eg root of title; missing)]* |

**[THIRD SCHEDULE**
The Subjections[56]
*(set out any other matters to which the Property is subject not specified or mentioned elsewhere)*]
**[3140]**

**[[FOURTH] SCHEDULE**
Amendments to the Standard Conditions of Sale (3rd Edition)

1      Standard Conditions 3.4, 4.3.2, 4.5.2, 4.5.5, 5.1.1, 5.1.2, 5.2.2(b), 5.2.2(e), 5.2.2(g), 5.2.3 and 5.2.7 shall not apply

2      The Standard Conditions shall be varied as follows:

2.1      in Standard Condition 1.1.1(a) sub-paragraphs (i) and (ii) shall be deleted and the words 'the interest actually earned on money less any proper charges for handling the money' shall be inserted

2.2      in Standard Condition 1.1.1(g) the contract rate shall be 4% per annum above the base rate current from time to time of *(name of bank etc)*

2.3      in Standard Condition 3.1.2(c) the word 'reasonably' shall be inserted after the words 'could not'

2.4      in Standard Condition 5.2.2(f) the words 'nor change its use and is to comply with all statutory obligations relating to the property and indemnify the seller against all liability arising as a result of any breach of such obligation' shall be added at the end

2.5      in Standard Conditions 6.1.2 and 6.1.3 '1 pm' shall be substituted for '2 pm'[57]

2.6      in Standard Condition 6.5.1 the words 'actual completion' shall be added after the word 'after' and the remainder of that Standard Condition shall be deleted

2.7      in Standard Condition 6.8.2(b) the words 'or if reasonable evidence is produced that the property would be released from all such mortgages' shall be added immediately after the words 'free of all mortgages'

2.8      in Standard Condition 7.1.1 the words 'or in negotiations leading to it' and 'or was' shall be deleted

2.9      Standard Conditions 7.3.1 and 7.3.2 shall be deleted and the following substituted:

'7.3.1      if the purchase shall not be completed on the completion date the buyer shall pay compensation to the seller but no such compensation shall be payable for so long as the seller is not ready able and willing to complete as contemplated by Standard Condition 6.8

7.3.2      compensation is calculated at the contract rate on all sums payable under the agreement (other than pursuant to Standard Condition 6.3) for the period between the completion date and actual completion']
**[3141]**

**[[FIFTH] SCHEDULE**
Guarantee[58]

In consideration of the Seller entering into this Agreement at the Guarantor's request the Guarantor agrees with the Seller as a primary obligation that:

1         the Buyer or the Guarantor will perform all the Buyer's obligations in this
          Agreement
2         if the Buyer defaults in performing its obligations the Guarantor will perform
          them and without prejudice to the generality of the foregoing will pay the
          Completion Monies and pay and make good to the Seller all costs losses and
          damages suffered by the Seller and will indemnify the Seller against all liability
          incurred or to be incurred arising from the Buyer's default
3         if this Agreement has been disclaimed following the insolvency of the Buyer the
          Seller may serve notice in writing on the Guarantor ('the Guarantor Notice')
          requiring the Guarantor to complete the purchase of the Property in accordance
          with this Agreement with the following modifications:
          3.1      all obligations of the Buyer shall be deemed to have been entered into
                   by the Guarantor as though it were named as buyer in place of the
                   party defined as the Buyer in this Agreement
          3.2      if a notice to complete served by the Seller on the Buyer has expired
                   at the date of service of the Guarantor Notice the Completion Date
                   shall be [5] working days after the date of service of the Guarantor
                   Notice
          3.3      the Guarantor is to pay interest on the balance of the Purchase Price
                   from the contractual Completion Date specified in clause 1.9 until
                   the date of Completion inclusive of both days and all moneys
                   expended by the Seller in consequence of the Buyer's default from
                   the date of expenditure until Completion inclusive of both days
                                                                                   **[3142]**
4         The liability of the Guarantor shall not be affected reduced or extinguished by
          4.1      any time or indulgence granted by the Seller to the Buyer
          4.2      any neglect or forbearance of the Seller in enforcing its rights under
                   this Agreement
          4.3      any variation of this Agreement between the Seller and the Buyer
                   [provided that no variation is to bind the Guarantor to the extent
                   that it is materially prejudicial to it]
          4.4      the exercise by the Seller of any right duty or obligation under the
                   General Conditions or this Agreement in relation to the
                   management of the Property without obtaining the consent of the
                   Buyer
          4.5      anything else by which apart from this paragraph 4 the Guarantor
                   would be released other than a release under seal]

**[[SIXTH] SCHEDULE**
Planning Counsel
*(Insert details of Planning Counsel)]*

*(signatures (or common seals) of the parties)*[59]
*[(signatures of witnesses)]*
**[3143]**

1     No stamp duty. See Information Binder: Stamp Duties [172] (Agreement).
          This Form differs from vol 38(1) (2000 Reissue) SALE OF LAND Form 59 [2321] to the extent
      only that the performance of the agreement is pre-conditional upon the Buyer obtaining planning
      permission.
          The contract is capable of being protected by registration. In the case of unregistered land the
      agreement is capable of being registered by the buyer against the seller's name as an estate contract (see
      vol 25(1) (1999 Reissue) LAND CHARGES Paragraph 40.5 [75]). Registration should be effected against
      the estate owner rather than the seller where the seller is a contracting buyer who has agreed to sub-

sell or a mortgagee exercising its power of sale. In addition, the agreement may be protected by way of caution against first registration (see vol 25(1) (1999 Reissue) LAND REGISTRATION Paragraph 204 [2661]).

In the case of registered land, the agreement may be noted on the register as an estate contract if the land certificate is placed on deposit or deemed to be on deposit, or it could be the subject of a caution in other cases: see vol 25(1) (1999 Reissue) LAND REGISTRATION Paragraph 178 [2489]. Strictly, all contracts for the sale of land should be protected by registration as land charges irrespective of whether the seller is in practice likely to resell, but the vast majority of such contracts are not so registered unless, eg, as in this case, completion is likely to be delayed. A buyer is not under a duty to register a contract: *Wright v Dean* [1948] Ch 686, [1948] 2 All ER 415. However, it seems that in certain circumstances a solicitor might be held to be negligent for failing to protect his client by registering his interest as buyer under a contract: see, eg, *Midland Bank Trust Co Ltd v Hett, Stubbs & Kemp* [1979] Ch 384, [1978] 3 All ER 571.

The planning provisions in this Form and in Form 68 [3061] ante are designed for more complex and lengthy planning applications than those envisaged in Form 67 [3021] ante, including those involving a significant prospect of challenge or appeal. Each precedent is likely to be suitable for use in a wide range of circumstances and planning ambitions. However, the precedents have been developed to reflect two distinctly different approaches to the process of obtaining planning permission. Broadly speaking, the key differences are:

(a)   in Form 68 planning applications are joint and made only after the prior written approval of the seller; in this Form an application is prepared and submitted by the buyer without the seller's approval;

(b)   in Form 68 the process of appeal is joint and mandatory (subject to counsel's opinion of success); in this Form the buyer is under no obligation to appeal but may do so. Under Form 68 the buyer may not withdraw any application, appeal or proceeding without the consent of the seller; under this Form the buyer is free to do so;

(c)   in Form 68 there is an ultimate cut-off date ('the Termination Date': see Form 68 clause 1.29 [3066] ante by which the agreement must have become unconditional, regardless of the status of any then current proceedings or appeals. This is a long-stop date for automatic rescission and provision is made for an initial termination date with an interim extension if at the initial termination date an appeal or proceedings were outstanding or a satisfactory planning permission has been issued. In this Form the extension is indefinite to allow for the exhaustion of all relevant proceedings and appeals;

(d)   in Form 68 the buyer accepts wide-ranging obligations to endeavour to obtain the requisite planning permission and seller control.

For agreements suited to simple planning situations Form 67 [3021] ante should be used.

**[3144]**

This Form provides for the property to be sold with vacant possession on completion. It is not made conditional on the removal of existing tenants. If the practitioner is concerned about the removal of existing tenants he should import the condition in Form 67 clause 2.2.2 [3024] ante. Where there are existing tenants the buyer should satisfy himself that the seller will be able to procure their removal so as to deliver with vacant possession. Where the property is not vacant at the date of the agreement, or if the circumstances suggest the potential for a lengthy planning process, consideration should be given to the terms and basis upon which tenancies and other interests might be created or preserved during the pre-conditional planning period. Certainly, it would be possible for the seller to create new short term tenancies/leases/licences and other occupational rights without the consent of the buyer, but great care should then be taken to ensure that such tenancies are capable of being terminated to meet any requirement by the buyer to complete with vacant possession eg by waiving the planning pre-condition (see clause 2.3 of this Form). Effectively, this would require the creation of tenancies at will or tenancies containing suitable termination provisions and security of tenure exclusions.

This Form is not likely to be capable of use without amendment to reflect the detailed terms negotiated. Every deal is different and this Form is purely one example of a contract conditional on the grant of planning permission.

**[3145]**

2     The Standard Conditions of Sale (3rd Edn) (for which see vol 38(1) (2000 Reissue) SALE OF LAND Form 1 [1011]), like the Standard Commercial Property Conditions (1st Edn) (for which see vol 38(1) (2000 Reissue) SALE OF LAND Form 2 [1071]), use the terminology 'seller' and 'buyer' in place of the traditional 'vendor' and 'purchaser'. If this Form is to be used in conjunction with general conditions other than the Standard Conditions of Sale or the Standard Commercial Property Conditions it is recommended that the expressions 'vendor' and 'purchaser' are used in place of 'seller' and 'buyer' in order to present a uniform approach to the definitions used in such other general conditions.

3     If any party is a company it is desirable to include the company registration number before the address of the registered office. This avoids any problems arising when a company has been wound up and a

new company formed with the same name, or when the name of a company is changed, or if companies swap names, eg on a reconstruction of a group of companies. In addition the company registration number will be required by HM Land Registry under the provisions of the Land Registration Rules 1996, SI 1996/2975 r 2, Schedule para 18.

4    One view would add the words 'unless the context otherwise admits' or 'where the context admits' and this may be implied (see *Meux v Jacobs* (1875) LR 7 HL 481 at 493; *Law Society v United Services Bureau Ltd* [1934] 1 KB 343, DC). However, the better course is to use whenever practicable defined terms in such a way that there are no circumstances where the defined meanings do not apply.

Definitions of terms used only in schedules are contained in the relevant schedule.

Clauses 1.37–39 are not strictly necessary as the Law of Property Act 1925 s 61 (37 Halsbury's Statutes (4th Edn) REAL PROPERTY) provides such definitions but such definitions are usually inserted for the convenience of the parties.

5    If no date is specifically agreed for completion under a contract incorporating one of the sets of standard conditions the fall-back provisions of the relevant conditions will apply. See, eg, the Standard Conditions of Sale (3rd Edn) condition 6.1 (for which see vol 38(1) (2000 Reissue) SALE OF LAND Form 1 [1045]) and the Standard Commercial Property Conditions (1st Edn) condition 6.1 (for which see vol 38(1) (2000 Reissue) SALE OF LAND Form 2 [1103]). As to the Law Society's General Conditions of Sale (1984 Revision) condition 21(1) (for which see vol 38(1) (2000 Reissue) SALE OF LAND Form 3 [1131]) and the National Conditions of Sale (20th Edn) condition 5(1) (for which see vol 38(1) (2000 Reissue) SALE OF LAND Form 4 [1161]), which Conditions were replaced by the Standard Conditions of Sale in March 1990, see vol 38(1) (2000 Reissue) SALE OF LAND Paragraph 290 [1001] et seq. However, none of the fall-back provisions is appropriate to this agreement.

6    This wording is appropriate to a circumstance where the purchase price is fixed, or is a liquidated calculation. If the purchase price is to be ascertained or agreed by some other method, the completion date could be fixed by reference to the date of ascertainment (eg *(number)* days after the date on which the purchase price has been ascertained in accordance with the *(number)* schedule). However, depending upon the circumstances of each case, consideration should be given to whether completion should take place on the payment of a fixed interim minimum amount, with provision for further payment, with interest, of the amount by which the price as ascertained exceeds the interim amount.

**[3146]**

7    Note that certain conditions in the Standard Conditions of Sale (3rd Edn) (see eg conditions 5.2.6, 7.3.2) provide for compensation payable at the 'contract rate' ie the Law Society's interest rate from time to time in force (see vol 38(1) (2000 Reissue) SALE OF LAND Form 1 condition 1.1.1(g) [1012]); there are also conditions (see eg conditions 2.2.3, 7.2(a), 7.5.2(a)(i), 7.6.2(a)) which provide for payment of 'accrued interest' (see vol 38(1) (2000 Reissue) SALE OF LAND Form 1 condition 1.1.1(a) [1011]).

8    As to VAT, see note 12 below. Omit the words in square brackets if no VAT is payable or it is payable but the deposit is held as stakeholder.

9    In preparing this form of sale and purchase agreement, it was decided that it would be helpful to practitioners if incorporation of the Standard Conditions of Sale (3rd Edn) (for which see vol 38(1) (2000 Reissue) SALE OF LAND Form 1 [1011]) was retained in the short term notwithstanding the issue of the Standard Commercial Property Conditions (1st Edn) (for which see vol 38(1) (2000 Reissue) SALE OF LAND Form 2 [1071]) which have yet to be fully adopted and used. Differences between the two sets of conditions (which are highly similar in many respects) are discussed and summarised in vol 38(1) (2000 Reissue) SALE OF LAND Form 5 [1201].

Other sets of standard conditions which might be referred to are the Statutory Form of Conditions of Sale 1925, SR&O 1925/779, which applies to contracts made by correspondence, and may, but only by express reference, be made to apply to any other cases (see the Law of Property Act 1925 s 46) and the Standard Commercial Property Conditions (1st Edn) (for which see vol 38(1) (2000 Reissue) SALE OF LAND Form 2 [1071]). As to the National Conditions of Sale (20th Edn) (for which see vol 38(1) (2000 Reissue) SALE OF LAND Form 4 [1161]) and the Law Society's General Conditions of Sale (1984 Revision) (for which see vol 38(1) (2000 Reissue) SALE OF LAND Form 3 [1131]), which Conditions were replaced by the Standard Conditions of Sale as from March 1990, see vol 38(1) (2000 Reissue) SALE OF LAND Paragraph 290 [1001] et seq. A contract by correspondence can still be made in relation to a short lease, or the creation or operation of a resulting, implied or constructive trust: see the Law of Property (Miscellaneous Provisions) Act 1989 s 2 as amended by the Trusts of Land and Appointment of Trustees Act 1996 s 25(2), Sch 4 (37 Halsbury's Statutes (4th Edn) REAL PROPERTY).

10    The size and scale of the plan should be sufficiently large to enable all salient features to be readily identified: see *Scarfe v Adams* [1981] 1 All ER 843, CA. If many plans are required it may be convenient to bind them in a separate bundle, suitably referred to in the contract. Each plan should be individually numbered if there is more than one. As to plans generally see vol 35 (1997 Reissue) SALE OF LAND Paragraph 623 [816].

**[3147]**

11    As to the identity of the property to be sold see vol 35 (1997 Reissue) SALE OF LAND Paragraph 346 [453] et seq.

12    As to circumstances in which VAT is payable see vol 38(1) (2000 Reissue) SALE OF LAND Paragraph 6 [18] et seq and vol 35 (1997 Reissue) SALE OF LAND Paragraph 136 [173] et seq and see the Information Binder: Property [1] (VAT and Property). It should be noted that VAT forms part of the stampable consideration for the purposes of calculating stamp duty and land registration fees.

      If VAT is or may be chargeable in respect of any part of the purchase price, and the price is to be exclusive of the tax, a comprehensive clause dealing with all aspects of the tax should be included. For an example of such a clause see clause 15 of this Form and see further vol 36 (1997 Reissue) SALE OF LAND Forms 351 [2521] and 352 [2522]. The VAT provisions in this Form expand those in the Standard Conditions of Sale (3rd Edn) condition 1.4 (for which see vol 38(1) (2000 Reissue) SALE OF LAND Form 1 [1013]) and are inserted to act as a reminder to the parties of the importance of considering VAT aspects at an early stage.

      If the Value Added Tax Act 1994 s 89 (48 Halsbury's Statutes (4th Edn) VALUE ADDED TAX) is excluded or the purchase price is expressed to be inclusive of VAT any changes in the rate or incidence of VAT between contract and completion cannot be added to the price.

13    Ie the Companies Act 1985 s 736 as amended by the Companies Act 1989 s 144 (8 Halsbury's Statutes (4th Edn) COMPANIES).

14    As to VAT see note 12 above.

15    Ie the Value Added Tax Regulations 1995, SI 1995/2518.

16    In the absence of any specific provision in the contract both seller and buyer are free to assign the benefit of the whole contract or a part of it (eg a charge of the benefit of the contract, or a sub-sale of part of the property). It may be thought desirable to limit these rights, whether because of the importance of the personality or standing of the buyer, or to avoid an immediate sub-sale of the whole or part of the property for tax or other reasons. For clauses preventing sub-sales by the buyer, see clause 13 of this Form and the Law Society's General Conditions of Sale (1984 Revision) condition 17(6) (for which see vol 38(1) (2000 Reissue) SALE OF LAND Form 3 [1131]). The Standard Conditions of Sale (3rd Edn) conditions 8.2.5 and 8.3.3 (for which see vol 38(1) (2000 Reissue) SALE OF LAND Form 1 [1055]), which prevent the buyer from transferring the benefit of the contract, apply only to the grant of a new lease.

      Sometimes there is commercial sensitivity to the buyer sub-selling at a greater price than it contracted to pay but no particular sensitivity regarding the ultimate acquiring party. In this circumstance the words in clause 13.2 '... to anyone other than the Buyer named in this Agreement or an Authorised Transferee' should be replaced with '... to anyone for a consideration receivable by the Seller and/or the Buyer which exceeds the Purchase Price'.

**[3148]**

17    Where the Standard Conditions of Sale (3rd Edn) are incorporated, this provision is rendered superfluous by condition 1.2 (for which see vol 38(1) (2000 Reissue) SALE OF LAND Form 1 [1013]). However, such words are commonly included for the convenience of the parties.

18    The principal purpose of clause 2.3 is to enable the buyer to accelerate the completion of the purchase, essentially in circumstances where it is confident of the subsequent satisfaction of the conditions. The waiver mechanism in this clause permits this to happen and is particularly useful where the pre-condition would not or might not be satisfied prior to the Unconditional Date. However, as the planning condition is not solely for the benefit of the buyer, the clause can only be included where the purchase price could be established to the satisfaction of the seller without planning permission. It would therefore be necessary to make specific provision for a fixed price in this instance or if use is made of Form 72 [3251] (residual land valuation) or 73 [3257] (open market value) post by amending such forms to include suitable assumptions as to the state of planning. An obvious solution would be to add an explicit assumption that if the buyer waives pursuant to clause 2.3 of this Form, planning permission would be assumed to have been granted on the terms originally applied for. See also note 1 above.

      For capital gains tax purposes the time of disposal and acquisition is when the conditions are satisfied or waived: Taxation of Chargeable Gains Act 1992 s 28(2) (42–44 Halsbury's Statutes (4th Edn) TAXATION). As to time of disposal see *Simon's Direct Tax Service* C1.322.

19    It is not envisaged that the buyer will have paid any deposit prior to satisfaction of the relevant conditions. If this is not the case, condition 7.2(a) of the Standard Conditions of Sale (3rd Edn) (for which see vol 38(1) (2000 Reissue) SALE OF LAND Form 1 [1051]) or condition 7.2(a) of the Standard Commercial Property Conditions (1st Edn) (for which see vol 38(1) (2000 Reissue) SALE OF LAND Form 2 [1108]) should be made to apply.

20    Except on a sale by auction the deposit is to be paid by banker's draft or cheque drawn on a solicitor's clearing bank account: see the Standard Conditions of Sale (3rd Edn) condition 2.2.1 (for which see vol 38(1) (2000 Reissue) SALE OF LAND Form 1 [1016]). The Standard Commercial Property Conditions (1st Edn) condition 2.2.2 (for which see vol 38(1) (2000 Reissue) SALE OF LAND Form 2

[1076]) requires the deposit to be paid by direct credit transfer of cleared funds except on a sale by auction. The National Conditions of Sale (20th Edition) (for which see vol 38(1) (2000 Reissue) SALE OF LAND Form 4 [1161]), which were replaced as from March 1990 with the Standard Conditions of Sale and have therefore not subsequently been updated, do not cover the point, although, where these are incorporated, express provisions may be inserted.

**[3149]**

21    It is suggested that the deposit payment should equal the agreed percentage (typically 10% but frequently less) of the entire price for the property. When the purchase price is to be ascertained by valuation after the unconditional date, the deposit should be specified as a fixed sum, being the appropriate proportion (usually 10%) of the estimated purchase price or minimum purchase price (if any).

22    Omit this clause if no VAT is payable or it is payable but the deposit is held as stakeholder.

23    As to the distinction between 'all reasonable', 'reasonable' and 'best' endeavours, see *UBH (Mechanical Services) Ltd v Standard Life Assurance Co* (1986) Times 13 November. The use of expressions such as 'best endeavours' or 'all reasonable endeavours' can give rise to problems. The former expression has (in the context of trying to obtain the landlord's consent to assign a lease) been held to mean 'something less than efforts which go beyond the bounds of reason but are considerably more than casual and intermittent activities': see *Pips (Leisure Productions) Ltd v Walton* (1982) 43 P & CR 415 at 420, per Megarry V-C. This would seem to entail the seller doing what a reasonable person would do in the circumstances. 'All reasonable endeavours' is probably seen generally as a lesser obligation than 'best endeavours', but in the light of the above definition it is not clear how much less. It may be preferable for the seller to omit both expressions, though a buyer may wish to see some definition of the degree of obligation on the seller.

24    As to the completion date, delay and notice to complete generally, see vol 35 (1997 Reissue) SALE OF LAND Paragraph 694 [902] et seq. For the provisions relating to payment of interest for late completion see the Standard Conditions of Sale (3rd Edn) condition 7.3 (for which see vol 38(1) (2000 Reissue) SALE OF LAND Form 1 [1051]) and the Standard Commercial Property Conditions (1st Edn) condition 7.3 (for which see vol 38(1) (2000 Reissue) SALE OF LAND Form 2 [1108]). As to the Law Society's General Conditions of Sale (1984 Revision) condition 22 (for which see vol 38(1) (2000 Reissue) SALE OF LAND Form 3 [1147]) and the National Conditions of Sale (20th Edn) condition 7 (for which see vol 38(1) (2000 Reissue) SALE OF LAND Form 4 [1161]), which Conditions were replaced by the Standard Conditions of Sale as from March 1990, see vol 38(1) (2000 Reissue) SALE OF LAND Paragraph 290 [1001] et seq. The differences between the various sets of conditions are great and should be carefully noted. For tables of comparison, see vol 38(1) (2000 Reissue) SALE OF LAND Form 5 [1201] et seq.

**[3150]**

25    The inclusion of these words is not strictly necessary since the Standard Conditions of Sale (3rd Edn) condition 6.2 (for which see vol 38(1) (2000 Reissue) SALE OF LAND Form 1 [1045]) provides for completion to take place either at the seller's solicitor's office or at some other place which the seller reasonably specifies.

26    The Standard Conditions of Sale (3rd Edn) condition 6.1.2 (for which see vol 38(1) (2000 Reissue) SALE OF LAND Form 1 [1045]) states that if the money due on completion is received after 2.00 pm, completion is to be treated, for the purposes of apportionments and the provisions regarding late completion, as taking place on the next working day. Any amendments to this condition should be included in the fourth schedule.

27    As to implied covenants for title and the words importing them generally see vol 35 (1997 Reissue) SALE OF LAND Paragraph 472 [597] et seq.

      Covenants for title are implied by the Law of Property (Miscellaneous Provisions) Act 1994 (37 Halsbury's Statutes (4th Edn) REAL PROPERTY) and (additionally in the case of registered land the Land Registration Rules 1925, SR&O 1925/1093 rr 76A–77A as inserted, substituted and amended by SI 1995/337) provide that key words are included in the assurance. Although under the Act and Rules no covenants are implied unless such key words are used, condition 4.5.2 of the Standard Conditions of Sale (3rd Edn) (for which see vol 38(1) (2000 Reissue) SALE OF LAND Form 1 [1025]) provides that if the contract for sale makes no provision as to title guarantee then subject to condition 4.5.3 the seller is to transfer the property with full title guarantee. Accordingly in cases where it is inappropriate for any covenants for title to be given a clause must be inserted expressly stating that no covenants for title will be given.

      For a form varying the implied covenants for title see vol 36 (1997 Reissue) SALE OF LAND Form 190 [2226].

28    In the absence of any indication to the contrary, it is an implied term that vacant possession will be given: see vol 35 (1997 Reissue) SALE OF LAND Paragraph 328 [429]. See, further, note 1 above.

**[3151]**

29     As to deduction of title to unregistered property see vol 35 (1997 Reissue) SALE OF LAND Paragraph 400 [515] and as to deduction of title to registered property see vol 35 (1997 Reissue) SALE OF LAND Paragraph 399 [510]. As to the seller's duty to disclose defects in the title see vol 35 (1997 Reissue) SALE OF LAND Paragraph 295 [391] et seq. It is clearly in the interests of the seller to disclose any defects of which he is aware before exchange of contracts; therefore it is now common for title to be deduced in its entirety before exchange and for restrictions to be placed on the right to raise requisitions.

30     As to the proving and investigation of title generally see vol 35 (1997 Reissue) SALE OF LAND Paragraph 398 [509] et seq. As to instruments which may form a good root of title see vol 35 (1997 Reissue) SALE OF LAND Paragraph 400.2 [516].

31     The Standard Conditions of Sale (3rd Edn) condition 4.2.1 (for which see vol 38(1) (2000 Reissue) SALE OF LAND Form 1 [1024]) and the Standard Commercial Property Conditions (1st Edn) condition 4.2.1 (for which see vol 38(1) (2000 Reissue) SALE OF LAND Form 2 [1083]) provide that the evidence of registered title is to be office copies of the items required to be furnished by the Land Registration Act 1925 s 110(2). However it is still advisable to include the words in square brackets because the Standard Conditions of Sale are incorporated only in so far as they are not varied by or inconsistent with the terms of the agreement, and it is arguable that the provisions of clause 8 without the words in square brackets form a complete provision replacing the equivalent provision in the Standard Conditions of Sale. As to the deduction of title using HM Land Registry's direct access system see vol 35 (1997 Reissue) SALE OF LAND Paragraph 399.3 [512].

       The words in square brackets are required when the contract is made by reference to the National Conditions of Sale (20th Edn) (for which see vol 38(1) (2000 Reissue) SALE OF LAND Form 4 [1161]), which do not include this provision. These Conditions were replaced by the Standard Conditions of Sale as from March 1990 and have not been updated subsequently: see vol 38(1) (2000 Reissue) SALE OF LAND Paragraph 290 [1001] et seq. As to the desirability of providing office copies see vol 35 (1997 Reissue) SALE OF LAND Paragraph 399.3 [512].

32     This clause should be included if it is desired to exclude requisitions on the title. Both the Standard Conditions of Sale (3rd Edn) (for which see vol 38(1) (2000 Reissue) SALE OF LAND Form 1 [1011]) and the Standard Commercial Property Conditions (1st Edn) (for which see vol 38(1) (2000 Reissue) SALE OF LAND Form 2 [1071]) omit the provision contained in the Standard Conditions of Sale (1st Edn) condition 4.5, which allowed the seller to rescind the contract if the buyer refused to withdraw a requisition which the seller was unable to satisfy.

33     The buyer should be wary of this clause. If important documents are missing then there may be difficulties in registering the title following completion where the land is unregistered. Of course, if a document is genuinely missing, the original cannot be produced. However, as much evidence as possible should be called for as to the contents of the document and the circumstances of its loss, and statutory declarations obtained (see, eg, vol 25(1) (1999 Reissue) LAND REGISTRATION Form 108 [3851]) so as to give the best possible chance of avoiding registration difficulties. If the land is already registered then, unless the missing document relates to an overriding interest (eg the counterpart of a lease for a term not exceeding 21 years), either:

(a)     the title is likely to be less than absolute (eg possessory or qualified) where the missing document is important to the seller's own title; or

(b)     there is likely to be a protective entry on the register (eg as to restrictive covenants where no copy of the deed creating them was supplied on first registration).

In either case the buyer will need to obtain as much information as possible about the missing document and the effect of this on quality of the title in order to assess the risk of accepting the defect. Various options may be open to the buyer, ranging from simply accepting the risk, if judged to be small, through negotiating a suitable adjustment to the price or obtaining defective title insurance cover to, in extreme cases, withdrawing from the transaction before exchanging contracts.

**[3152]**

34     As to the seller's duty to disclose encumbrances generally see vol 35 (1997 Reissue) SALE OF LAND Paragraph 295 [391]. Where registered land is concerned, the rights of any person in actual occupation of the land will be overriding interests to which any disposition of the land will be subject unless enquiry has been made of that person and the rights were not disclosed: see the Land Registration Act 1925 s 70(1)(g). The same qualification does not apply in relation to other overriding interests listed in the Land Registration Act 1925 s 70(1) as amended.

35     The proprietorship register may need to be included if, eg, there is a restriction controlling dispositions of land which will remain on the register following sale.

36     Where certain charges, eg financial charges, are specifically excluded, a buyer may wish to ensure that any matters entered on the register before completion are also excluded. It might be argued that reference to exclusion of specific entries is to be interpreted as making the property subject to all other entries including new entries. It may be preferable to specify the entries to which the property is positively to be subject so that the position is clear.

37     Matters to be included in the third schedule are matters not recorded in the registers of title or property documents eg, rights created orally, wayleave agreements and short term or informal arrangements.

38    This sub-clause should be omitted if there are no matters affecting the property in respect of which the seller will remain liable notwithstanding the completion of the transfer of the property to the buyer. It may also be omitted in reliance upon the Standard Conditions of Sale (3rd Edn) condition 4.5.4 (for which see vol 38(1) (2000 Reissue) SALE OF LAND Form 1 [1025]) if incorporated. It should be omitted if the alternative sub-clauses 9.1 and 9.2 are used as the indemnity covenant will be set out in full in the draft assurance.

      It may be preferred to set out the indemnity covenant the seller will require, rather than rely on standard conditions of sale, particularly if the contract is made by reference to the Law Society's General Conditions of Sale (1984 Revision) (for which see vol 38(1) (2000 Reissue) SALE OF LAND Form 3 [1131]) which do not require the buyer to covenant to observe and perform the covenants and conditions. See also the Standard Commercial Property Conditions (1st Edn) condition 4.5.4 (for which see vol 38(1) (2000 Reissue) SALE OF LAND Form 2 [1084]) and the Standard Conditions of Sale (3rd Edn) condition 4.5.4 (for which see vol 38(1) (2000 Reissue) SALE OF LAND Form 1 [1025]).

**[3153]**

39    As to encumbrances, see note 34 above.
40    Whilst the annexation of a draft assurance is more usual on a sale of part of the seller's property it may be appropriate also on a sale of the whole of a property where there are numerous or complex encumbrances to be referred to in the assurance or covenants to be imposed.
41    As to the proprietorship register, see note 35 above.
42    As to the charges register, see note 36 above.
43    As to matters to be included in the third schedule, see note 37 above.
44    A buyer should bear in mind that certain financial charges in respect of costs incurred by a local authority are registrable as local land charges. If these relate to expenditure arising before the date of the contract the buyer may wish to ensure that they are borne by the seller.
45    As an exclusion clause, this condition is subject to the test of reasonableness under the Unfair Contract Terms Act 1977 s 11 (11 Halsbury's Statutes (4th Edn) CONTRACT): see *Smith v Eric S Bush, Harris v Wyre Forest District Council* [1990] 1 AC 831, [1989] 2 All ER 514, HL. The seller cannot rely on a general disclaimer to avoid disclosing matters specifically known to him prior to sale: *Rignall Developments Ltd v Halil* [1988] Ch 190, [1987] 3 All ER 170. For further discussion on this issue see *Thomas Witter Ltd v TBP Industries Ltd* [1996] 2 All ER 573.
46    Consideration should be given to whether the conditions of sale incorporated require amendment in any way to suit the circumstances of the transaction or to ensure consistency with this agreement. As to possible modifications where the Standard Conditions of Sale (3rd Edn) are incorporated (for which see vol 38(1) (2000 Reissue) SALE OF LAND Form 1 [1011]), see vol 35 (1997 Reissue) SALE OF LAND Form 18 [1547]. Many of the suggested amendments are now incorporated in the Standard Commercial Property Conditions (1st Edn) (for which see vol 38(1) (2000 Reissue) SALE OF LAND Form 2 [1071]). The fourth schedule contains amendments to the Standard Conditions of Sale (3rd Edn) appropriate to this agreement.
47    As to restriction on assignment and sub-sale, see note 16 above.
48    Where the Standard Conditions of Sale (3rd Edn) or the Standard Commercial Property Conditions (1st Edn) are being incorporated this clause can be omitted, although it is commonly included for the convenience of the parties: see the Standard Conditions of Sale (3rd Edn) condition 7.4 (for which see vol 38(1) (2000 Reissue) SALE OF LAND Form 1 [1052]) and the Standard Commercial Property Conditions (1st Edn) condition 7.4 (for which see vol 38(1) (2000 Reissue) SALE OF LAND Form 2 [1109]).
49    As to VAT, see note 12 above.

**[3154]**

50    Where the election is made on or after 1 March 1995 it is only effective if written notification is given to HM Customs and Excise not later than the end of the period of 30 days beginning on the date on which the election is made, subject to certain exceptions: see the Value Added Tax Act 1994, Sch 10 para 3(6)(b) as substituted by SI 1995/279 (48 Halsbury's Statutes (4th Edn) VALUE ADDED TAX).
51    Insolvency Act 1986 s 1 (4 Halsbury's Statutes (4th Edn) BANKRUPTCY AND INSOLVENCY) applies to composition; the Insolvency Act 1986 s 253 applies to voluntary arrangement.
52    The agreement is drawn up on the assumption that each party is resident in the United Kingdom, and accordingly, in the case of UK companies, has its own UK registered office. The words 'non-exclusive' are mostly used where either the seller or the buyer is an overseas party. The effect is to enable legal action or proceedings to enforce the agreement and/or judgment in an overseas jurisdiction. Although the subject matter of the agreement relates to UK real estate, in some circumstances it is advantageous to have access to courts in the jurisdiction local to that party, and, for example, to other non-domestic assets of the relevant party for the purposes of enforcing judgment. The practitioner should be aware that the law and practice in relation to the recognition of judgments and enforcement differs according to jurisdiction. Accordingly, the precise nature and extent of this provision should be the subject of a legal opinion obtained from lawyers in the relevant jurisdiction.

53    It is essential to state on the face of a document that it is a deed if it is to be one: see the Law of Property (Miscellaneous Provisions) Act 1989 s 1(2)(a) (37 Halsbury's Statutes (4th Edn) REAL PROPERTY).

54    A notice provision is incorporated in clause 20 for use in two circumstances. The first is where the National Conditions of Sale (20th Edn) (for which see vol 38(1) (2000 Reissue) SALE OF LAND Form 4 [1161]) are incorporated in the agreement as such conditions do not have any express notification provisions. The National Conditions were replaced by the Standard Conditions of Sale as from March 1990 and have not been updated subsequently: see vol 38(1) (2000 Reissue) SALE OF LAND Paragraph 290 [1001] et seq. By contrast the Standard Conditions of Sale (3rd Edn) (for which see vol 38(1) (2000 Reissue) SALE OF LAND Form 1 [1011]) and the Standard Commercial Property Conditions (1st Edn) (for which see vol 38(1) (2000 Reissue) SALE OF LAND Form 2 [1071]) make detailed provision for the service of notices. Secondly, where either party is non-resident in the UK, provision would need to be made for the appointment of an agent for service and accordingly clause 20.5 would be required; but as the identity of the buyer is not known when the conditions are drafted, the condition cannot deal also with the buyer appointing an agent. Additionally, the practitioner would need to ensure that the arrangements referred to in clause 20.5 have actually been complied with, by sight of the appointment properly counter-signed by the appointed agent.

**[3155]**

55    For longer form clauses relating to notices see vol 4(3) (1997 Reissue) BOILERPLATE CLAUSES Forms 3.3 [171]–3.5 [173] and Paragraph 3.1 [22] et seq.

56    As to the subjections, see note 37 above. Insert here details of any matters (if any) subject to which the property is sold which are not mentioned in the register of title nor in any documents listed in Part II of the second schedule.

57    The time to be stated here should accord with the time stated in clause 5.1 of this Form.

58    As to guarantees generally see vol 17(2) (1995 Reissue) GUARANTEES AND INDEMNITIES.

59    It is not usually necessary to have the contract executed as a deed unless the contract contains recitals which are intended to be binding or there are other special considerations (eg, there is a lack of valuable consideration or it is desired to extend the period set by the Limitation Act 1980 s 8 (24 Halsbury's Statutes (4th Edn) LIMITATION OF ACTIONS) for bringing claims).

Where a contract is to be executed as a deed sealing is not necessary either in the case of an individual or in the case of a company, but all parties must sign either on the same document or each on one of two identical parts which are exchanged, and the signatures of all individuals must be witnessed: see the Law of Property (Miscellaneous Provisions) Act 1989 s 1(3). As to the execution of a deed by an individual and by a corporation, see vol 12 (1994 Reissue) DEEDS, AGREEMENTS AND DECLARATIONS Paragraphs 16 [1525] and 28 [1554]–30 [1560] respectively.

It is unnecessary for a contract by a corporate body to be under seal unless it would need to be a deed if made by private persons: see the Corporate Bodies' Contracts Act 1960 s 1 (11 Halsbury's Statutes (4th Edn) CONTRACT). A contract may be made by a company incorporated under the Companies Acts by writing under its common seal or on its behalf by any person acting under its authority, express or implied: Companies Act 1985 s 36 as substituted by the Companies Act 1989 s 130(1) (8 Halsbury's Statutes (4th Edn) COMPANIES).

**[3156]–[3170]**

# (2): OPTIONS

# 70

### Call option agreement for purchase of the whole of a single freehold commercial property with vacant possession at a fixed price; full form of sale and purchase agreement to be incorporated by annexation[1]

THIS OPTION AGREEMENT is made the ...... day of .........

BETWEEN:

(1)    *(name of seller)*[2] [company number *(number)*][3] [of *(address)* or whose registered office is at *(address)*] ('the Seller') and

(2)    *(name of buyer)* [company number *(number)*] [of *(address)* or whose registered office is at *(address)*] ('the Buyer')

**1         Definitions and interpretation**[4]

In this option agreement:

1.1        'Agreement' means the settled form of sale and purchase agreement annexed
1.2        'the Buyer's Solicitors' means *(insert name and address of person or firm)*
1.3        'the Completion Date' has the meaning given to it in the Agreement
1.4        'the Option' means the option granted to the Buyer by clause 2
1.5        'the Option Notice' means the notice served by the Buyer pursuant to clause 3
1.6        'the Option Period' means the period of *(insert period during which the option is to be exercisable)* from the date of this option agreement
1.7        'the Property' means the property described in the first schedule to the Agreement
1.8        'the Purchase Price' has the meaning given to it in the Agreement
1.9        'the Seller's Solicitors' means *(insert name and address of person or firm)*
1.10       expressions defined in the Agreement shall have the same meanings in this option agreement
1.11       words importing one gender shall be construed as importing any other gender
1.12       words importing the singular shall be construed as importing the plural and vice versa
1.13       words importing persons shall be construed as importing a corporate body and/ or a partnership and vice versa
1.14       where any party comprises more than one person the obligations and liabilities of that party under this option agreement shall be joint and several obligations and liabilities of those persons
1.15       the clause headings do not form part of this option agreement and shall not be taken into account in its construction or interpretation
1.16       any reference to a clause or schedule is to one in this option agreement so numbered

**[3171]**

**2         Grant of the Option**

2.1        In consideration of £...[5] paid by the Buyer to the Seller (receipt of which is acknowledged) the Seller grants to the Buyer the option to buy the freehold interest in the Property on the terms and conditions of the Agreement
2.2        The consideration is not refundable to the Buyer in any circumstances [but will be deducted from the balance of the Purchase Price due on completion if the Buyer completes the purchase of the Property *or* and does not form part of the Purchase Price]

**3         Exercise of the Option**

3.1        Subject to clause 3.4 the Option shall be exercisable by the Buyer serving on the Seller at any time during the Option Period notice in writing in the form set out in the schedule[6] [accompanied by *or* preceded by] payment of the deposit in accordance with clause 3.4
3.2        On valid exercise of the Option a binding contract for the sale and purchase of the Property shall immediately come into effect on the terms and conditions of the Agreement
[3.3       The Seller by way of security appoints the Buyer its attorney for the sole purpose of signing the Option Notice for the Seller][7]
[3.4       The Option Notice when served shall be accompanied by the payment of the deposit referred to in clause 3 of the Agreement by banker's draft drawn by and on a Clearing Bank or by a cheque drawn on a solicitors' clearing bank account

unless remitted to the Seller's Solicitors beforehand by CHAPS or other payment method acceptable to the Seller's Solicitors (acting reasonably). The Option shall not be validly exercised unless payment is made in accordance with this clause 3.4 but subject thereto payment made under this clause 3.4 shall be treated as performance by the Buyer of the corresponding obligation in clause 3 of the Agreement][8]

[3172]

4    **Disclaimer**[9]

4.1    The Buyer admits that:

4.1.1    it has inspected the Property and enters into this option agreement with full knowledge of its actual state and condition and shall take the Property as it stands

4.1.2    it enters into this option agreement solely as a result of its own inspection and on the basis of the terms of this option agreement and not in reliance upon any representation or warranty either written or oral or implied made by or on behalf of the Seller (save for any representation or warranty contained in written replies given by the Seller's Solicitors to any preliminary inquiries raised by the Buyer or the Buyer's Solicitors)

4.2    This option agreement together with the Agreement contains the entire agreement between the parties

5    **Restriction on assignment**[10]

[The Option is personal to the Buyer and shall not capable of being assigned charged or mortgaged [except by way of floating charge]][11]
*or*
The Buyer may assign the benefit of the Option and the assignee may exercise the Option as though he were a party to it]

6    **Dealings by the Seller**[12]

The Seller shall not create any legal or equitable interest (including without limitation any easement right or covenant) in on over or under nor create any right or licence to occupy or use the Property or any part of it except in favour of the Buyer or with the Buyer's prior written consent (which shall not be unreasonably withheld or delayed)

[3173]

7    **Registration**

7.1    If the Option shall not be [protected by registration of a notice under the Land Registration Act 1925 Section 49(1) *or* registered as a Class C(iv) land charge under the Land Charges Act 1972 Section 2(4)] within [21] working days of the date of this option agreement then this option agreement and everything contained in it shall cease and determine and neither of the parties to it shall have any right of action whether for damages or otherwise against the other[13]

[7.2    The Seller shall within [3] working days after the date of this option agreement [deposit the Seller's land certificate *or* procure the deposit of the Seller's charge certificate] relating to his title to the Property in HM Land Registry

7.3    The Seller consents to registration of a notice of this option agreement in the charges register of the Seller's title to the Property and shall do all things necessary to enable a notice under the Land Registration Act 1925 Section 49(1) to be registered][14]

7.4 If the Option expires the Buyer shall forthwith cancel any registrations made by it in any registers to protect the option and by way of security appoints the Seller its attorney for the purpose of effecting such cancellations

## 8 Existing Mortgagees[15]

The Seller warrants that it has obtained the written consent to the grant of the Option of all mortgagees and holders of any security interest in the Property on or before the date of this option agreement

[3174]

## 9 Insurance pending exercise of the Option

9.1 Until the Option is exercised the Seller shall insure the Property against the risks listed in clause 9.2 with underwriters or insurers of repute in the full cost of rebuilding and reinstating the Property including VAT professional fees and shoring up site clearance and incidental expenses and shall lay out the proceeds of such insurance in rebuilding or reinstating the Property

9.2 The risks are fire storm tempest earthquake lightning explosion riot civil commotion malicious damage impact by vehicles and by aircraft and articles dropped from aircraft flood damage and bursting or overflowing of water pipes and tanks

## 10 VAT[16]

10.1 All VAT payable by the Buyer shall be paid at the same time as the payment on which it is chargeable

10.2 The Seller shall provide the Buyer with a receipted VAT invoice for any VAT paid by the Buyer under this option agreement

10.3 [The Seller warrants that it has validly made an election to waive exemption from VAT in respect of the Property *or* The Seller warrants that it has not made an election to waive exemption from VAT in respect of the Property and will not make any such election]

## 11 Jurisdiction and Governing Law

This option agreement shall be governed by and construed in accordance with English law and the parties submit to the [non-exclusive] jurisdiction of the English courts[17]

[3175]

## 12 Nature of this option agreement

This option agreement [is *or* is not] a deed and [has *or* has not] been executed by the parties to it as a deed[18]

## 13 Notices[19]

13.1 Any notice to be given under or in connection with this option agreement shall be in writing and may be delivered personally or sent by first class post telex or fax to the party due to receive the notice at its address set out in this option agreement or the address of its solicitor or such other address as previously specified (by written notice) by such party

13.2 A notice may be given by either party's solicitor to the other party's solicitor provided it conforms to the provisions of clause 13.1

13.3 In the absence of evidence of earlier receipt a notice is deemed received:

13.3.1     if delivered personally when left at the address referred to in clause 13.1

13.3.2     if sent by post [2] working days after posting it

13.3.3     if sent by telex when the proper answerback is received

13.3.4     if sent by fax on completion of its transmission

13.4     In the case of a notice given pursuant to clauses 13.3.1 13.3.3 or 13.3.4 where this occurs after 5 pm on a working day or on a day which is not a working day the date of service shall be deemed to be the next working day

[13.5     The [Seller *or* Buyer] irrevocably appoints *(name and address)* as its agent for service to receive on its behalf service of proceedings in the English Courts or in any other court or courts of competent jurisdiction][20]

**14     Certificate of value**

*(Insert if appropriate)*

[AS *or* IN] WITNESS etc[21]

**[3176]**

SCHEDULE
Form of Option Notice[22]

To:  *(seller's name and address)*
From:  *(buyer's name and address)*
Property:  *(insert details)*

In accordance with the terms of the option agreement dated *(date)* made between *(name and address of first party)* (1) and *(name and address of second party)* (2) relating to the Property described above I GIVE NOTICE to you that I exercise my option to buy the Property on the terms and conditions referred to in the Agreement attached to the option agreement

I [enclose the deposit of £... *(insert details of cheque draft or (as the case may be))* or have paid the deposit of £... to *(seller's solicitors)* by *(insert method of payment)*][23]

Signed [by *(buyer)* or by *(name or agent)* the duly authorised agent of *(buyer)* on its behalf]:
Date:

*(signatures (or common seals) of the parties)*[24]
[*(signatures of witnesses)*]
**[3177]**

1     As to stamp duty on the option consideration see Information Binder: Stamp Duties [1] (Conveyance or transfer) and *Wimpey (George) and Co Ltd v IRC* [1975] 2 All ER 45, [1975] 1 WLR 975, CA. If there is no consideration for the option it must be granted by deed.

As to options generally, see vol 38(1) (2000 Reissue) SALE OF LAND Paragraph 241 [611] et seq.

The contract is capable of being protected by registration. In the case of unregistered land the agreement is capable of being registered by the buyer against the seller's name as an estate contract (see vol 25(1) (1999 Reissue) LAND CHARGES Paragraph 40.5 [75]). Registration should be effected against the estate owner rather than the seller where the seller is a contracting buyer who has agreed to grant the option or a mortgagee is granting the option. In addition, the agreement may be protected by way of caution against first registration (see vol 25(1) (1999 Reissue) LAND REGISTRATION Paragraph 204 [2661]).

In the case of registered land, the agreement may be noted on the register as an estate contract if the land certificate is placed on deposit or deemed to be on deposit, or it could be the subject of a caution in other cases: see vol 25(1) (1999 Reissue) LAND REGISTRATION Paragraph 178 [2489]. Strictly, all contracts for the sale of land should be protected by registration as land charges irrespective of whether the seller is in practice likely to resell, but the vast majority of such contracts are not so registered unless, eg, as in this case, completion is likely to be delayed. A buyer is not under a duty to register a contract: *Wright v Dean* [1948] Ch 686, [1948] 2 All ER 415. However, it seems that in certain circumstances a solicitor might be held to be negligent for failing to protect his client by registering his interest as buyer under a contract: see, eg, *Midland Bank Trust Co Ltd v Hett, Stubbs & Kemp* [1979] Ch 384, [1978] 3 All ER 571.

2    The Standard Conditions of Sale (3rd Edn) (for which see vol 38(1) (2000 Reissue) SALE OF LAND Form 1 [1011]), like the Standard Commercial Property Conditions (1st Edn) (for which see vol 38(1) (2000 Reissue) SALE OF LAND Form 2 [1071]), use the terminology 'seller' and 'buyer' in place of the traditional 'vendor' and 'purchaser'. If this Form is to be used in conjunction with an agreement for sale incorporating general conditions other than the Standard Conditions of Sale or the Standard Commercial Property Conditions it is recommended that the expressions 'vendor' and 'purchaser' are used in place of 'seller' and 'buyer' in order to present a uniform approach to the definitions used in such other general conditions.

**[3178]**

3    If any party is a company it is desirable to include the company registration number before the address of the registered office. This avoids any problems arising when a company has been wound up and a new company formed with the same name, or when the name of a company is changed, or if companies swap names, eg on a reconstruction of a group of companies. In addition the company registration number will be required by HM Land Registry under the provisions of the Land Registration Rules 1996, SI 1996/2975 r 2, Schedule para 18.

4    One view would add the words 'unless the context otherwise admits' or 'where the context admits' and this may be implied (see *Meux v Jacobs* (1875) LR 7 HL 481 at 493; *Law Society v United Services Bureau Ltd* [1934] 1 KB 343, DC). However, the better course is to use whenever practicable defined terms in such a way that there are no circumstances where the defined meanings do not apply.

Clauses 1.11–1.13 are not strictly necessary as the Law of Property Act 1925 s 61 (37 Halsbury's Statutes (4th Edn) REAL PROPERTY) provides such definitions but such definitions are usually inserted for the convenience of the parties.

5    The sum to be inserted here is the consideration (if any) for the grant of the option. Care should be taken to ensure that VAT cannot become payable on the option fee if the property is not a 'new' property, eg by the seller electing to waive exemption; in this circumstance, the second alternative clause 10.3 should be utilised. If an election has taken place or the grant will involve a standard rated supply, care should be taken to explore whether VAT paid on the option fee would be recoverable depending upon the nature of the transaction and the buyer's circumstances, for example if the option is never exercised. Subject to the appropriate use of the certificate of value, the option fee is stampable ad valorem. Practitioners will note that there is a danger of stamp duty being paid twice on the option fee amount, ie if the credit for the option fee does not take effect as a reduction in the purchase price. An alternative to deducting the option fee from the balance payable on completion is simply to reduce the purchase price stated in or ascertained in accordance with the agreement by the amount of the option consideration.

As to capital gains tax on the grant of an option see Taxation of Chargeable Gains Act 1994 s 144 (42–44 Halsbury's Statutes (4th Edn) TAXATION) and see *Simon's Direct Tax Service* C2.1009, 1010.

**[3179]**

6    As to exercising the option generally see vol 38(1) (2000 Reissue) SALE OF LAND Paragraph 241 [611] et seq and vol 35 (1997 Reissue) SALE OF LAND Paragraph 928 [1223]. The clause is drafted on the assumption that the parties are satisfied that exercise of the option in the traditional manner with the option notice signed only by the buyer will be effective to create a binding contract in reliance on *Spiro v Glencrown Properties Ltd* [1991] Ch 537, [1991] 1 All ER 600. If the parties have concern on this point there are alternatives, as to which, see vol 38(1) (2000 Reissue) SALE OF LAND Form 40 note 6 [1666].

7    This optional clause is inserted for use by those who wish each party to hold a copy of the option notice signed by both parties so as to pre-empt the argument (rejected in *Spiro v Glencrown Properties Ltd* [1991] Ch 537, [1991] 1All ER 600) that the option notice must be so signed, as to which see note 6 above. It will be noted that the sale and purchase agreement is signed by both parties before exchange of the option agreement.

8    This provision is only appropriate where a deposit payment is to be made on exercise of the option; for the most part, this will arise in circumstances where the purchase price is fixed or has been ascertained before exercise of the option. If the purchase price is not so fixed or ascertained, a deposit would be appropriately payable within a given period, say, 10 working days, of the purchase price having been ascertained assuming the option has already been exercised. An alternative approach is to arrange for a fixed deposit, perhaps a fixed amount or an agreed percentage of a fixed minimum purchase price, to be paid on exercise regardless of whether the ultimate purchase price has been ascertained.

9    As an exclusion clause, this condition is subject to the test of reasonableness under the Unfair Contract Terms Act 1977 s 11 (11 Halsbury's Statutes (4th Edn) CONTRACT): see *Smith v Eric S Bush, Harris v Wyre Forest District Council* [1990] 1 AC 831, [1989] 2 All ER 514, HL. The seller cannot rely on a general disclaimer to avoid disclosing matters specifically known to him prior to sale: *Rignall Developments Ltd v Halil* [1988] Ch 190, [1987] 3 All ER 170. For further discussion on this issue see *Thomas Witter Ltd v TBP Industries Ltd* [1996] 2 All ER 573.

**[3180]**

10    In the absence of any specific provision in the contract both seller and buyer are free to assign the benefit of the option. It may be thought desirable to limit these rights, whether because of the importance of the personality or standing of the buyer, or for tax or other reasons. For a clause preventing sub-sales by the buyer see the Law Society's General Conditions of Sale (1984 Revision) condition 17(6) (for which see vol 38(1) (2000 Reissue) SALE OF LAND Form 3 [1143]). The Standard Conditions of Sale (3rd Edn) conditions 8.2.5 and 8.3.3 (for which see vol 38(1) (2000 Reissue) SALE OF LAND Form 1 [1055]), which prevent the buyer from transferring the benefit of the contract, apply only to the grant of a new lease.

11    An option is a chose in action and assignable by the buyer. To vest the benefit of an option in an assignee at law notice must be given to the seller under the Law of Property Act 1925 s 136(1). Failure to give notice results in the assignment being merely equitable, with the consequence that the assignee cannot enforce the benefit of the option at law in his own name against the seller. Failure to give notice does not prejudice the assignee's title against the assignor ie the original buyer.

12    From the buyer's perspective, it is worth considering whether the seller should be prevented or restricted from disposing of its interest in the property. Although the option agreement will be binding upon the seller's successors in title, if the decision in *Spiro v Glencrown Properties Ltd* [1991] Ch 537, [1991] 1 All ER 600 is incorrect, the buyer would then need the successor to countersign the form of option notice, but would not have an enforceable power of attorney to sign it for that successor; clause 3.3 is limited to an appointment by the seller itself. However, in some circumstances, commercial realities may suggest a strong need for a restriction on the disposal. An obvious example would be where the option agreement has been expanded to include provisions for liaison between the parties and/or approval of an agreed planning process. For an alternative method, but which is believed to be little used, see vol 38(1) (2000 Reissue) SALE OF LAND Form 40 clause 14.2 [1658] and fourth schedule [1663].

**[3181]**

13    The buyer owes no duty to the seller to register his option: *Wright v Dean* [1948] Ch 686, [1948] 2 All ER 415. The seller's contractual obligation to convey the property to the buyer is not discharged by conveyance of the property to a third party: the seller is liable in damages to the grantee of the option if the latter is unable to enforce the option specifically against a buyer of the seller's interest because of its non-registration, hence the need for this clause. On the question of whether a grantor who has paid damages to the grantee is entitled to indemnity from the buyer of the freehold who declines to give effect to the option see *Eagon v Dent* [1965] 3 All ER 334.

14    Clauses 7.2 and 7.3 should be added in the case of registered land.

15    The buyer must be advised to insist on deduction of title and on sight of all relevant consents to dealing prior to entering into the option agreement regardless of whether consideration is payable for the option.

      If the option is granted before the mortgage is created the option will be binding on the mortgagee and any buyer from it if the option is protected by registration: Law of Property Act 1925 s 104(1). For this reason mortgagees usually do not lend on the security of property which is already the subject of an option.

      If the property is already mortgaged at the date of grant of the option, the buyer is at risk of losing the benefit of the option as any sale by the mortgagee under his statutory power will overreach the option: Law of Property Act 1925 s 104(1). Exercise of other powers such as leasing, taking possession or foreclosure will also be prejudicial to the buyer. The buyer will accordingly need to ensure that the option will not be over-reached and that if the option is exercised the seller will be able to complete the sale. It is rare for mortgagees to join in an option agreement but for a clause for use in such a case, see vol 38(1) (2000 Reissue) SALE OF LAND Form 40 clause 14 [1658]. More commonly, the mortgagee will issue a written consent and, once issued, any sale, pursuant to any mortgagee remedy or by the company in receivership, would be subject to and with the benefit of the option.

**[3182]**

16    As to circumstances in which VAT is payable, see vol 38(1) (2000 Reissue) SALE OF LAND Paragraph 6 [18] et seq and vol 35 (1997 Reissue) SALE OF LAND Paragraph 136 [173] et seq and see the Information Binder: Property [1] (VAT and Property). It should be noted that VAT forms part of the stampable consideration for the purposes of calculating stamp duty and land registration fees.

      If VAT is or may be chargeable in respect of any part of the option price or the purchase price, and the price is to be exclusive of the tax, a comprehensive clause dealing with all aspects of the tax should be included. See further vol 36 (1997 Reissue) SALE OF LAND Forms 351 [2521] and 352 [2522]. The VAT provisions in the agreement for sale expand those in the Standard Conditions of Sale (3rd Edn) condition 1.4 (for which see vol 38(1) (2000 Reissue) SALE OF LAND Form 1 [1013]) and are inserted to act as a reminder to the parties of the importance of considering VAT aspects at an early stage.

      If the Value Added Tax Act 1994 s 89 (48 Halsbury's Statutes (4th Edn) VALUE ADDED TAX) is excluded or the purchase price is expressed to be inclusive of VAT any changes in the rate or incidence of VAT between contract and completion cannot be added to the price.

17      The option agreement is drawn up on the assumption that each party is resident in the United Kingdom, and accordingly, in the case of UK companies, has its own UK registered office. The words 'non-exclusive' are mostly used where either the seller or the buyer is an overseas party. The effect is to enable legal action or proceedings to enforce the agreement and/or judgment in an overseas jurisdiction. Although the subject matter of the agreement relates to UK real estate, in some circumstances it is advantageous to have access to courts in the jurisdiction local to that party, and, for example, to other non-domestic assets of the relevant party for the purposes of enforcing judgment. The practitioner should be aware that the law and practice in relation to the recognition of judgments and enforcement differs according to jurisdiction. Accordingly, the precise nature and extent of this provision should be the subject of a legal opinion obtained from lawyers in the relevant jurisdiction.

18      The option should be executed as a deed because of the grant of powers of attorney in clauses 3.3 and 7.4 and must be so executed if there is no consideration for the grant of the option.

**[3183]**

19      A notice provision is incorporated in clause 13 for use in two circumstances. The first is where the National Conditions of Sale (20th Edn) (for which see vol 38(1) (2000 Reissue) SALE OF LAND Form 4 [1161]) are incorporated in the agreement as such conditions do not have any express notification provisions. The National Conditions were replaced by the Standard Conditions of Sale as from March 1990 and have not been updated subsequently: see vol 38(1) (2000 Reissue) SALE OF LAND Paragraph 290 [1001] et seq. By contrast the Standard Conditions of Sale (3rd Edn) (for which see vol 38(1) (2000 Reissue) SALE OF LAND Form 1 [1011]) and the Standard Commercial Property Conditions (1st Edn) (for which see vol 38(1) (2000 Reissue) SALE OF LAND Form 2 [1071]) make detailed provision for the service of notices. Secondly, where either party is non-resident in the UK, provision would need to be made for the appointment of an agent for service and accordingly clause 13.5 would be required; but as the identity of the buyer is not known when the conditions are drafted, the condition cannot deal also with the buyer appointing an agent. Additionally, the practitioner would need to ensure that the arrangements referred to in clause 13.5 have actually been complied with, by sight of the appointment properly counter-signed by the appointed agent.

20      For longer form clauses relating to notices, see vol 4(3) (1997 Reissue) BOILERPLATE CLAUSES Forms 3.3 [171]–3.5 [173] and Paragraph 3.1 [22] et seq.

21      See note 18 above.

22      See note 6 above.

23      Where a contract is to be executed as a deed sealing is not necessary either in the case of an individual or in the case of a company, but all parties must sign either on the same document or each on one of two identical parts which are exchanged, and the signatures of all individuals must be witnessed: see the Law of Property (Miscellaneous Provisions) Act 1989 s 1(3). As to the execution of a deed by an individual and by a corporation, see vol 12 (1994 Reissue) DEEDS, AGREEMENTS AND DECLARATIONS Paragraphs 16 [1525] and 28 [1554]–30 [1560] respectively.

It is unnecessary for a contract by a corporate body to be under seal unless it would need to be a deed if made by private persons: see the Corporate Bodies' Contracts Act 1960 s 1 (11 Halsbury's Statutes (4th Edn) CONTRACT). A contract may be made by a company incorporated under the Companies Acts by writing under its common seal or on its behalf by any person acting under its authority, express or implied: Companies Act 1985 s 36 as substituted by the Companies Act 1989 s 130(1) (8 Halsbury's Statutes (4th Edn) COMPANIES).

**[3184]–[3200]**

# 71

**Call option for purchase of a single freehold commercial property with vacant possession conditional on the buyer obtaining planning permission; purchase price fixed or ascertained by a method set out in one or other of Forms 72–76 post[1]**

## CONTENTS

                                                                **[3201]**


THIS OPTION AGREEMENT is made the ...... day of .........

BETWEEN:

(1)      *(name of seller)*[2] [company number *(number)*][3] [of *(address)* *or* whose registered
         office is at *(address)*] ('the Seller') and
(2)      *(name of buyer)* [company number *(number)*] [of *(address)* *or* whose registered
         office is at *(address)*] ('the Buyer')


**1        Definitions and interpretation**[4]

In this Agreement:
1.1      'the Act' means the Town and Country Planning Act 1990 and any act for the
         time being in force amending or replacing the same and all regulations and
         orders made thereunder [and any other legislation relating to town and country
         planning in force from time to time] [including the Planning (Listed Buildings
         and Conservation Areas) Act 1990]
1.2      'this Agreement' means this document as varied by any subsequent
         documentation
1.3      'the Buyer's Solicitors' means *(insert name and address of person or firm)*
1.4      'Competing Development' means a development or proposed development of
         land any part of which is within *(number)* miles of the Property other than one
         which is the subject of a Planning Application
1.5      'Completion' means actual completion of the sale and purchase agreed in this
         Agreement

                                                                **[3202]**

1.6      'the Completion Date'[5] means the date *(number)* [weeks *or* months] after the
         Purchase Price has been agreed or ascertained in accordance with the first
         schedule

1.7      'the Completion Moneys' means the Purchase Price (or any outstanding
         balance of it) as adjusted by all sums due between the parties at Completion

1.8      'the Contract Rate'[6] means *(insert interest rate or method of calculating the interest rate
         by reference eg to the base lending rate of a named bank)*

1.9      'the Deposit' means [an amount equal to ...% of the Purchase Price [stated in
         *or* ascertained in accordance with] the [first] schedule *or* £...] [which is
         [inclusive *or* exclusive] of VAT at the standard rate][7]

1.10     'Development' means the erection of a building or buildings for use within
         Class *(number)* of the Town and Country Planning (Use Classes) Order 1987 or
         for [residential use] (excluding caravan parks or gypsy encampments) or for such
         other development as may first be approved in writing by the Seller (such
         approval not to be unreasonably withheld or delayed) in all cases with associated
         services and ancillary facilities

1.11     'the General Conditions'[8] means [the Standard Conditions of Sale (3rd Edn) *or*
         *(specify)*]

1.12     'the Option' means the option granted to the Buyer by clause 2

1.13     'the Option Notice' means the notice served by the Buyer pursuant to clause 3

1.14     'the Option Period' means the period of *(insert period during which the option is to
         be exercisable)* from the date of this Agreement

[1.15    'the Plan'[9] means the plan attached to this Agreement [and if numbered plans
         are attached any reference to a numbered plan is to the attached plan so
         numbered]]

                                                                              **[3203]**

1.16     'Planning Obligation' means all or any of the following as the case may be:

         1.16.1     an agreement in respect of and affecting the Property (whether or
                    not also affecting other property) pursuant to the Local Government
                    (Miscellaneous Provisions) Act 1982 Section 33 and/or the Local
                    Government Act 1972 Section 111 and/or the Highways Act 1980
                    Section(s) 38 and/or 278 and/or the Water Industry Act 1991
                    Section 104 or any provision to similar intent or an agreement with
                    a water undertaker or a drainage undertaker (within the meaning of
                    the Water Industry Act 1991) or the Environment Agency or an
                    Internal Drainage Board (within the meaning of the Water
                    Resources Act 1991 or the Land Drainage Act 1991) or other
                    appropriate authority as to water supply or drainage of surface and/
                    or foul water from the Property or an agreement with any competent
                    authority or body relating to other services and/or

         1.16.2     a planning obligation (whether entered into by agreement or
                    otherwise) in respect of and affecting the Property (whether or not
                    also affecting other property) pursuant to Section 106 of the Act

1.17     'Planning Permission' means [outline *or* detailed] planning permission for the
         Development of the Property issued by the local planning authority or other
         authorities responsible for the time being for controlling the development of
         land and/or on appeal by the Secretary of State

1.18     'the Property'[10] means the freehold property described in Part I of the second
         schedule

1.19     'the Purchase Price' means the purchase price[11] [stated in *or* ascertained in
         accordance with] the first schedule

1.20    'the Secretary of State' means the Secretary of State for the Environment Transport and the Regions (or other minister of the Crown to whom his relevant power or duty may from time to time be transferred) or any appropriate officer having authority to act on his behalf

**[3204]**

1.21    'the Seller's Solicitors' means *(insert name and address of person or firm)*

1.22    'the Transfer' means the transfer of the Property

1.23    'VAT' means an amount equal to the value added tax as charged in accordance with VATA[12] or any equivalent or substituted tax

1.24    'VATA' means the Value Added Tax Act 1994 or any equivalent tax Act

1.25    'VAT invoice' means an invoice complying with the provisions of regulations 13 and 14 of the VAT Regulations 1995[13]

1.26    where the context so admits the expression[s] 'the Seller' [and 'the Buyer'] include[s] their respective personal representatives [and 'the Buyer' shall include any permitted successors in title of the Buyer][14]

1.27    words importing one gender shall be construed as importing any other gender

1.28    words importing the singular shall be construed as importing the plural and vice versa

1.29    words importing persons shall be construed as importing a corporate body and/ or a partnership and vice versa

1.30    where any party comprises more than one person the obligations and liabilities of that party under this Agreement shall be joint and several obligations and liabilities of those persons[15]

1.31    the clause headings do not form part of this Agreement and shall not be taken into account in its construction or interpretation

1.32    any reference to a clause or a paragraph or a schedule is to one in this Agreement so numbered

1.33    any reference to a colour or letter is to one on the [Plan *or* Plans]

1.34    in the absence of any contrary provision any reference to a statute includes any statutory modification or re-enactment of it and any and every order instrument regulation direction or plan made or issued under the statute or deriving validity from it

**[3205]**

**2      Grant of the Option**

2.1     In consideration of £... [inclusive *or* exclusive of VAT at the standard rate][16] paid by the Buyer to the Seller (receipt of which is acknowledged) the Seller grants to the Buyer the option to buy the freehold interest in the Property on the terms and conditions of this Agreement

2.2     The consideration is not refundable to the Buyer in any circumstances [but will be deducted from the balance of the Purchase Price due on completion if the Buyer completes the purchase of the Property *or* and does not form part of the Purchase Price]

**3      Exercise of the Option and Deposit**

3.1     [Subject to clauses 3.4 and 3.5] the Option shall be exercisable by the Buyer serving on the Seller at any time during the Option Period notice in writing in the form set out in the [fifth] schedule[17] [[accompanied by *or* preceded by] payment of the Deposit in accordance with clause 3.4][18]

3.2     On valid exercise of the Option a binding contract for the sale and purchase of the Property shall immediately come into effect on the terms and conditions of this Agreement

3.3     The Seller by way of security appoints the Buyer its attorney for the sole
        purpose of signing the Option Notice for the Seller

[3.4    The Option Notice when served shall be accompanied by the payment of the
        Deposit by banker's draft drawn by and on a Clearing Bank or by a cheque
        drawn on a solicitors' clearing bank account unless remitted to the Seller's
        Solicitors beforehand by CHAPS or other payment method acceptable to the
        Seller's Solicitors (acting reasonably). The Option shall not be validly exercised
        unless payment is made in accordance with this clause 3.4][19]

3.5     The Buyer shall not be entitled to exercise the Option unless it has first obtained
        Planning Permission for the Development

                                                                                    [3206]

4       **Planning Application and other development related undertakings**

4.1     The Buyer agrees:
        4.1.1   not to submit any application for Planning Permission without firstly
                obtaining the Seller's prior written approval to the application which
                will not be unreasonably withheld or delayed
        4.1.2   within [14] days of the issue of each and every Planning Permission
                to provide a copy of it to the Seller
        4.1.3   having regard to the current strategic and local planning policy and
                the advice of its consultants to endeavour from time to time
                throughout the Option Period to obtain [outline or detailed]
                planning permission for Development but shall not be obliged to do
                so for the duration of any period which it is advised that it does not
                have a greater than (specify)% prospect of success
        4.1.4   if any application for Planning Permission submitted by or on behalf
                of the Buyer shall be refused (whether on an action or deemed basis)
                or shall be granted subject to conditions which are unacceptable to
                the Buyer the Buyer will if advised by counsel nominated by the
                Buyer and approved in writing by the Seller (such approval not to be
                unreasonably withheld or delayed) that the Buyer would have greater
                than a [50]% prospect of success on appeal submit and pursue an
                appeal to the Secretary of State
        4.1.5   in preparing any application for Planning Permission the Buyer shall
                endeavour to lay out the proposed development of the Property in
                an efficient and attractive manner and shall endeavour to obtain an
                occupational density which is consistent with maximising the
                economic value of the Property

                                                                                    [3207]

4.2     During the Option Period the Seller shall not:
        4.2.1   submit any planning application for Development of the whole or
                any part of the Property or for any Competing Development
                [PROVIDED THAT nothing contained in this clause shall prevent
                the Seller at any time during the Option Period from submitting a
                planning application or applications for development on the
                Property comprising [eg the refurbishment or conversion of existing
                buildings for residential or commercial use or the conversion or
                erection of a shooting or fishing lodge or any form of agricultural
                development of any kind including new agricultural buildings or
                new agricultural dwellings or (as the case may be)[20]]]
        4.2.2   in any way aid or incite to be made a planning application in respect of
                the whole or any part of the Property or any Competing Development
                by any third party (save as permitted under sub-clause 4.2.1 above) or

4.2.3    voluntarily do or permit to be done any acts or things which might in any way prejudice any planning application made by or on behalf of the Buyer or hinder delay or render more difficult costly or expensive the implementation of or subsequent use or Development of the Property

4.3    If it is necessary to do so for the obtaining of Planning Permission and the Buyer so requests at any time during the Option Period the Seller shall enter into any Planning Obligation with the local planning authority and/or any other relevant authority and/or the Secretary of State but at the cost in all respects of the Buyer and subject to the Seller approving the terms of the Planning Obligation such approval not to be unreasonably withheld or delayed

**[3208]**

4.4    The Buyer shall at the completion of any Planning Obligation give an indemnity to the Seller in respect of all matters arising under the Planning Obligation and discharge all payments to be made and expenses reasonably incurred under the Planning Obligation

4.5    The Seller will allow the Buyer and those acting on its behalf to have access to the Property during the Option Period upon reasonable notice for the purpose of carrying out soil tests site surveys and inspections and other things reasonably required by it (including trial bore holes) to satisfy the Buyer as to the extent of the Property and/or its fitness for the purpose of Development [and subject to obtaining the prior written approval of the Seller (which shall not be unreasonably withheld or delayed) and complying with any reasonable requirements or conditions of the Seller for the purpose of repositioning within the Property or removing or altering any overhead cables and associated supports situated within the Property in co-operation with the relevant service authority]²¹ the Buyer causing as little inconvenience to the Seller and causing as little damage to the Property as is practicable and forthwith making good any physical damage at its own expense or paying fair compensation for crop sowing and cultivating which is not practicable or reasonable to make good

[4.6    Subject to the prior written approval of the Buyer as to the route of such footpath which approval shall not be unreasonably withheld or delayed but which may be withheld (without prejudice to the generality of the foregoing) where the same would or might materially interfere with prospective Development of or access to the Property or any part thereof the Seller may utilise such part of the [Property] as may be necessary for the purpose of diverting from *(location)* the [public footpaths] coloured *(colour)* on the Plan²²]

**[3209]**

## 5    Completion

5.1    Completion of the sale and purchase and payment of the Completion Moneys [and of the VAT] shall take place on the Completion Date²³ on or before [1.00 pm] [at the offices of the Seller's Solicitors or where they may reasonably direct²⁴]

5.2    If the Completion Moneys are received after [1.00 pm]²⁵ on the Completion Date or on a day which is not a working day Completion shall be deemed for the purposes of the General Conditions to have taken place on the next working day

## [6    Title guarantee²⁶ *(where the form of the assurance is not annexed)*

6.1    The Seller sells the Property [with [full *or* limited] *or* without any] title guarantee [with the modifications set out below]

[6.2    Where the Transfer is made with full title guarantee the Law of Property (Miscellaneous Provisions) Act 1994 Section 6(2)(a) shall have effect as though all matters now recorded in all registers open to or capable of public inspection are to be considered to be within the actual knowledge of the Buyer]

[6.3    Where the transfer is made with limited title guarantee the Law of Property (Miscellaneous Provisions) Act 1994 Section 3(3) shall not apply and instead the Seller will covenant that it has not since the transfer to it:

6.3.1    charged or encumbered the Property by means of any charge or encumbrance which subsists at the date of the Transfer or granted third party rights in relation to the Property which so subsist or

6.3.2    knowingly suffered the Property to be so charged or encumbered or subjected to any such rights]

[6.4    The Transfer shall contain the modifications set out above and include an application to the Registrar to enter on the register in an appropriate manner a note that the implied covenants are modified in the manner set out above]

*or*

**6    Title guarantee** *(where the form of Transfer is annexed)*

The Property is sold [with the title guarantee set out in the annexed form of draft Transfer [with the modifications included in it] *or* without any title guarantee]]

**[3210]**

**7    Vacant Possession**[27]

The Property is sold with vacant possession subject to the presence of any third party chattels

**8    Title**[28]

[8.1    The title to the Property is unregistered and title shall commence with the document described as the root of title in Part II of the second schedule[29]

*or*

The title to the Property is registered at HM Land Registry and title shall be deduced in accordance with the Land Registration Act 1925 Section 110[30] [save that copies of the entries on the register the filed plan and any documents referred to shall be office copies[31]]]

8.2    Title having been deduced prior to the date of this Agreement the Buyer accepts the Seller's title to the Property and shall be deemed to purchase with full knowledge of the title in all respects and shall not raise any requisitions or make any objection in relation to the title[32] [but the Buyer may raise requisitions arising out of:

8.2.1    events occurring after the date of this Agreement

8.2.2    matters revealed by pre-completion searches which are not registered at the date of this Agreement

8.2.3    matters which a prudent buyer could not be aware of at the date of this Agreement]

[8.3    The Seller does not have the documents (if any) noted as missing in Part II of the second schedule and the Buyer may not raise any requisition or objection on that account and no acknowledgement for production or undertaking for safe custody will be given nor copies produced][33]

**[3211]**

**[9    Encumbrances**[34] *(where the form of the assurance is not annexed)*

[9.1    The Property is sold subject to and (where appropriate) with the benefit of:

9.1.1    the matters contained or referred to in the property [proprietorship][35] and charges[36] registers of the title to the Property [other than any subsisting financial charges]

[9.1.2    the documents described in Part II of the second schedule] [and]

[9.1.3    the matters set out in the third schedule]][37]

9.2    The Buyer or the Buyer's Solicitors having been supplied with copies of the documents referred to in clause 9.1 the Buyer shall be deemed to purchase with full notice and knowledge of the same and shall not raise any requisition or make any objection in relation to them

9.3    The Transfer shall contain a covenant by the Buyer that the Buyer will (by way of indemnity only) observe and perform the covenants conditions and other matters contained or referred to in the documents referred to in clause 9.1 and will indemnify and keep the Seller and its successors in title fully and effectually indemnified against all actions proceedings damages costs claims and expenses which may be suffered or incurred by the Seller or its successors in title in respect of [future] breach or non-observance or non-performance of those covenants and conditions [and obligations][38]

9.4    The Transfer shall be engrossed [in duplicate] by the Buyer's Solicitors and [the *or* both] engrossment[s] shall be executed by the Buyer before the Completion Date

[9.5    Immediately after Completion the Buyer shall at its own expense procure the proper stamping of the duplicate Transfer as a duplicate (including but not limited to the affixing of a particulars delivered stamp) and shall immediately after such stamping deliver the duly stamped duplicate to the Seller's Solicitors]

**[3212]**

*or*

**9    Encumbrances**[39] *(where the form of Transfer is annexed)*[40]

9.1    The Transfer shall be in the form of the annexed draft

[9.2    The Property is sold subject to and (where appropriate) with the benefit of:

9.2.1    the matters contained or referred to in the annexed draft Transfer and the property [proprietorship][41] and charges[42] registers of the title to the Property [other than any subsisting financial charges]

[9.2.2    the documents described in Part II of the second schedule] [and]

[9.2.3    the matters set out in the third schedule]][43]

9.3    The Buyer or the Buyer's Solicitors having been supplied with copies of the matters (if any) referred to in clause 9.2 prior to the date of this Agreement the Buyer shall be deemed to purchase with full notice and knowledge of them and shall not raise any requisition or make any objection in relation to them

9.4    The Transfer shall be engrossed [in duplicate] by the Seller's Solicitors and [the *or* both] engrossment[s] shall be executed by the Buyer before the Completion Date

[9.5    Immediately after Completion the Buyer shall at its own expense procure the proper stamping of the duplicate Transfer as a duplicate (including but not limited to the affixing of a particulars delivered stamp) and shall immediately after such stamping deliver the duly stamped duplicate to the Seller's Solicitors]]

**[3213]**

**10    Matters affecting the Property**

The Property is sold subject to the following matters:

10.1    all local land charges whether registered or not before the date of this Agreement and all matters capable of registration as local land charges whether or not actually so registered[44]

10.2    all notices served and orders demands proposals or requirements made by any local public or other competent authority whether before or after the date of this Agreement

10.3     all actual or proposed charges notices orders restrictions agreements conditions
         contraventions or other matters arising under any statute
10.4     all easements quasi-easements rights exceptions or other similar matters
         including rights of way drainage water watercourses light rights of adjoining
         owners affecting the Property and liability to repair or covenants to repair roads
         pavements paths ways passages sewers drains gutters fences and other like matters
         whether or not apparent on inspection or disclosed in any of the documents
         referred to in this Agreement and without any obligation on the Seller to
         provide evidence of the creation of or to define or apportion any such liability
10.5     matters discoverable by inspection of the Property before the date of this
         Agreement
10.6     matters relating to the Property about which the Seller does not know
10.7     matters disclosed or which would be disclosed by any searches or as a result of
         enquiries (formal or informal and made in person in writing or orally) made by
         or for the Buyer or which a prudent buyer ought to make and
10.8     overriding interests as defined in the Land Registration Act 1925 Section 70(1)
         or matters which would be overriding interests if the title were registered

**[3214]**

## 11     Disclaimer[45]

11.1     The Buyer admits that:
         11.1.1     it has inspected the Property and purchases it with full knowledge of
                    its actual state and condition and shall take the Property as it stands
         11.1.2     it enters into this Agreement solely as a result of its own inspection
                    and on the basis of the terms of this Agreement and not in reliance
                    upon any advertisement statement representation or warranty either
                    written or oral or implied made by or on behalf of the Seller except
                    as stated in clause 11.2
         11.1.3     no warranty statement or representation has been made or given to
                    the Buyer that the Property can be used or developed in any
                    particular way or for any particular purpose and the Seller shall not
                    be liable to the Buyer if the Property cannot for any reason
                    whatsoever be so used or developed
11.2     The Buyer may rely on factual representations and warranties made or given by
         the Seller's Solicitors to the Buyer's Solicitor's pre-contract enquiries but only
         in so far as such statements are not capable of independent verification by
         appropriate searches enquiries inspection survey of the Property or by
         inspection of the documents and information supplied to the Buyer's Solicitors
11.3     This Agreement contains the entire agreement between the parties and
         incorporates all the terms agreed between them for the purposes of the Law of
         Property (Miscellaneous Provisions) Act 1989 Section 2 and there are no other
         terms or provisions agreed prior to the date of this Agreement which have not
         been incorporated into this Agreement

**[3215]**

## 12     Incorporation of conditions of sale and documents

12.1     The General Conditions [as amended by the [fourth] schedule][46] shall apply to
         this Agreement and are incorporated in it in so far as they are applicable to a sale
         by private treaty and are not varied by or inconsistent with the terms of this
         Agreement
12.2     If there is any conflict between the General Conditions [as amended] and the
         terms of this Agreement the terms of this Agreement prevail

12.3     All express agreements made or undertakings given by one party to the other [in *(set out list of letters and documents including relevant inter solicitor correspondence)*] are incorporated in this Agreement

**[13     Restriction on dealings**[47]

13.1     This Agreement is personal to the Buyer and is not capable of being assigned charged or mortgaged [except by way of floating charge][48]

[13.2     The Seller shall not be required to transfer the Property[49] [to anyone other than the Buyer named in this Agreement *or* at a price greater than the Purchase Price *or* except by one Transfer at the Purchase Price]]

[13.3     The Seller shall not create any legal or equitable interest (including without limitation any easement right or covenant) in on over or under nor create any right or licence to occupy or use the Property or any part of it except in favour of the Buyer or with the Buyer's prior written consent (which shall not be unreasonably withheld or delayed)[50]]]

**14     Merger on completion**[51]

The provisions of this Agreement shall not merge on completion of the Transfer so far as they remain to be performed

**[3216]**

**15     VAT provisions**[52]

15.1     The Purchase Price is [inclusive *or* exclusive] of VAT at the standard rate as at Completion

15.2     All VAT payable by the Buyer shall be paid at the same time as the payment on which it is chargeable

15.3     The Seller shall provide the Buyer with a receipted VAT invoice for any VAT paid by the Buyer under this Agreement

15.4     [The Seller warrants that it [has validly made *or* is bound by] an effective[53] election to waive exemption from VAT pursuant to VATA Schedule 10 paragraph 2 *or* The Seller warrants that it has not made an election to waive exemption from VAT and will not make any such election]

**16     Registration**

16.1     If the Option shall not be [protected by registration of a notice under the Land Registration Act 1925 Section 49(1) *or* registered as a Class C(iv) land charge under the Land Charges Act 1972 Section 2(4)] within [21] working days of the date of this Agreement then this Agreement and everything contained in it shall cease and determine and neither of the parties to it shall have any right of action whether for damages or otherwise against the other[54]

[16.2     The Seller shall within [3] working days after the date of this Agreement [deposit the Seller's land certificate *or* procure the deposit of the Seller's charge certificate] relating to his title to the Property in HM Land Registry]

[16.3     The Seller consents to registration of a notice of this Agreement in the charges register of the Seller's title to the Property and shall do all things necessary to enable a notice under the Land Registration Act 1925 Section 49(1) to be registered][55]

16.4     If the Option expires the Buyer shall forthwith cancel any registrations made by it in any registers to protect this Agreement and by way of security appoints the Seller its attorney for the purpose of effecting such cancellations

**[3217]**

**17      Existing Mortgagees**[56]

The Seller warrants that it has obtained the written consent to the grant of the Option of all mortgagees and holders of any security interest in the Property on or before the date of this Agreement

**[18     Insolvency of Buyer**

18.1     If the Buyer:

> 18.1.1     enters into voluntary liquidation (other than for the purpose of reconstruction or amalgamation not involving a realisation of assets) or has a winding-up order made against it by the court or has a receiver appointed over all or any part of its assets or an administration order is made pursuant to the Insolvency Act 1986 or
>
> 18.1.2     becomes insolvent or enters into any composition with its or his creditors or enters into a voluntary arrangement (within the meaning of the Insolvency Act 1986 Sections 1 or 253[57]) or distress sequestration or execution is levied on its goods

then and in any such case the Seller may rescind this Agreement by notice to the Buyer

18.2     Condition 7.2 of the General Conditions shall apply save that in this instance the Seller shall not be obliged to pay any interest which has accrued on the deposit]

**19      Jurisdiction and Governing Law**

This Agreement shall be governed by and construed in accordance with English law and the parties submit to the [non-exclusive] jurisdiction of the English courts[58]

**20      Nature of this Agreement**

This Agreement [is *or* is not] a deed and [has *or* has not] been executed by the parties to it as a deed[59]

**[3218]**

**21      Notices**[60]

21.1     Any notice to be given under or in connection with this Agreement shall be in writing and may be delivered personally or sent by first class post telex or fax to the party due to receive the notice at its address set out in this Agreement or the address of its solicitor or such other address as previously specified (by written notice) by such party

21.2     A notice may be given by either party's solicitor to the other party's solicitor provided it conforms to the provisions of clause 21.1

21.3     In the absence of evidence of earlier receipt a notice is deemed received:

> 21.3.1     if delivered personally when left at the address referred to in clause 21.1
>
> 21.3.2     if sent by post two working days after posting it
>
> 21.3.3     if sent by telex when the proper answerback is received
>
> 21.3.4     if sent by fax on completion of its transmission

21.4     In the case of a notice given pursuant to clauses 21.3.1 21.3.3 or 21.3.4 where this occurs after 5 pm on a working day or on a day which is not a working day the date of service shall be deemed to be the next working day

[21.5     The [Seller *or* Buyer] irrevocably appoints *(name and address)* as its agent for service to receive on its behalf service of proceedings in the English Courts or in any other court or courts of competent jurisdiction][61]

**[22    Contracts (Rights of Third Parties) Act 1999**

For the purposes of the Contracts (Rights of Third Parties) Act 1999 it is agreed that [with the exception only of *(specify clauses)*] nothing in this Agreement shall confer on any third party any right to enforce or any benefit of any term of this Agreement]

**23    Certificate of value**

*(Insert if appropriate)*

[AS *or* IN] WITNESS etc[62]

[3219]

FIRST SCHEDULE
The Purchase Price
*(Incorporate relevant form from Forms 72 [3251]–76 [3270] post or insert fixed price)*

SECOND SCHEDULE
The Property
[Part I]
Description of the Property

*(Describe the Property: eg)*
[All that freehold property situate at and known as *(address)* registered with title [absolute] at HM Land Registry under title number *(number)*
*or*
All that unregistered freehold property situate at and known as *(address)* which is shown for identification purposes only on the plan annexed to this Agreement and numbered '1']

[Part II
Title Documents affecting the Property
*(commencing where applicable with the root of title)*

| **Number** | **Date** | **Nature** | **Parties** | **Remarks** |
|---|---|---|---|---|
| *(number)* | *(date)* | *(details)* | *(details)* | *(eg root of title; missing)]* |

[THIRD SCHEDULE
The Subjections[63]
*(set out any other matters to which the Property is subject not specified or mentioned elsewhere)]*

[3220]

[[FOURTH] SCHEDULE
Amendments to the Standard Conditions of Sale (3rd Edition)

1    Standard Conditions 3.4, 4.3.2, 4.5.2, 4.5.5, 5.1.1, 5.1.2, 5.2.2(b), 5.2.2(e), 5.2.2(g), 5.2.3 and 5.2.7 shall not apply
2    The Standard Conditions shall be varied as follows:
    2.1    in Standard Condition 1.1.1(a) sub-paragraphs (i) and (ii) shall be deleted and the words 'the interest actually earned on money less any proper charges for handling the money' shall be inserted
    2.2    in Standard Condition 1.1.1(g) the contract rate shall be 4% per annum above the base rate current from time to time of *(name of bank etc)*
    2.3    in Standard Condition 3.1.2(c) the word 'reasonably' shall be inserted after the words 'could not'

2.4       in Standard Condition 5.2.2(f) the words 'nor change its use and is to comply with all statutory obligations relating to the property and indemnify the seller against all liability arising as a result of any breach of such obligation' shall be added at the end

2.5       in Standard Conditions 6.1.2 and 6.1.3 '1 pm' shall be substituted for '2 pm'[64]

2.6       in Standard Condition 6.5.1 the words 'actual completion' shall be added after the word 'after' and the remainder of that Standard Condition shall be deleted

2.7       in Standard Condition 6.8.2(b) the words 'or if reasonable evidence is produced that the property would be released from all such mortgages' shall be added immediately after the words 'free of all mortgages'

2.8       in Standard Condition 7.1.1 the words 'or in negotiations leading to it' and 'or was' shall be deleted

2.9       Standard Conditions 7.3.1 and 7.3.2 shall be deleted and the following substituted:

    '7.3.1    if the purchase shall not be completed on the completion date the buyer shall pay compensation to the seller but no such compensation shall be payable for so long as the seller is not ready able and willing to complete as contemplated by Standard Condition 6.8

    7.3.2    compensation is calculated at the contract rate on all sums payable under the agreement (other than pursuant to Standard Condition 6.3) for the period between the completion date and actual completion']

**[3221]**

## [FIFTH] SCHEDULE
### Form of Option Notice[65]

To:  *(Seller's name and address)*
From:  *(Buyer's name and address)*
Property:  *(insert details)*

In accordance with the terms of the Option Agreement dated *(date)* made between *(name and address of first party)* (1) and *(name and address of second party)* (2) relating to the Property described above I GIVE NOTICE to you that I exercise my option to buy the Property [at the price of *(purchase price)*][66]

I [enclose the deposit of £… *(insert details of cheque draft or (as the case may be))* or have paid the deposit of £… to *(Seller's Solicitors)* by *(insert method of payment)*]

Signed [by the Buyer *or* by *(name or agent)* the duly authorised agent of *(Buyer)* on its behalf]:
Date:

*(signatures (or common seals) of the parties)*[67]
[*(signatures of witnesses)*]
**[3222]**

---

1    As to stamp duty on the option consideration see Information Binder: Stamp Duties [1] (Conveyance or transfer) and *George Wimpey & Co Ltd v IRC* [1975] 2 All ER 45, [1975] 1 WLR 975, CA. If there is no consideration for the option it must be granted by deed.

As to options generally, see vol 38(1) (2000 Reissue) SALE OF LAND Paragraph 241 [611] et seq.

The contract is capable of being protected by registration. In the case of unregistered land the agreement is capable of being registered by the buyer against the seller's name as an estate contract (see vol 25(1) (1999 Reissue) LAND CHARGES Paragraph 40.5 [75]). Registration should be effected against the estate owner rather than the seller where the seller is a contracting buyer who has agreed to grant the option or a mortgagee is granting the option. In addition, the agreement may be protected by way of caution against first registration (see vol 25(1) (1999 Reissue) LAND REGISTRATION Paragraph 204 [2661]).

In the case of registered land, the agreement may be noted on the register as an estate contract if the land certificate is placed on deposit or deemed to be on deposit, or it could be the subject of a caution in other cases: see vol 25(1) (1999 Reissue) LAND REGISTRATION Paragraph 178 [2489]. Strictly, all contracts for the sale of land should be protected by registration as land charges irrespective of whether the seller is in practice likely to resell, but the vast majority of such contracts are not so registered unless, eg, as in this case, completion is likely to be delayed. A buyer is not under a duty to register a contract: *Wright v Dean* [1948] Ch 686, [1948] 2 All ER 415. However, it seems that in certain circumstances a solicitor might be held to be negligent for failing to protect his client by registering his interest as buyer under a contract: see, eg, *Midland Bank Trust Co Ltd v Hett, Stubbs & Kemp* [1979] Ch 384, [1978] 3 All ER 571.

2      The Standard Conditions of Sale (3rd Edn) (for which see vol 38(1) (2000 Reissue) SALE OF LAND Form 1 [1011]), like the Standard Commercial Property Conditions (1st Edn) (for which see vol 38(1) (2000 Reissue) SALE OF LAND Form 2 [1071]), use the terminology 'seller' and 'buyer' in place of the traditional 'vendor' and 'purchaser'. If this Form is to be used in conjunction with general conditions other than the Standard Conditions of Sale or the Standard Commercial Property Conditions it is recommended that the expressions 'vendor' and 'purchaser' are used in place of 'seller' and 'buyer' in order to present a uniform approach to the definitions used in such other general conditions.

**[3223]**

3      If any party is a company it is desirable to include the company registration number before the address of the registered office. This avoids any problems arising when a company has been wound up and a new company formed with the same name, or when the name of a company is changed, or if companies swap names, eg on a reconstruction of a group of companies. In addition the company registration number will be required by HM Land Registry under the provisions of the Land Registration Rules 1996, SI 1996/2975 r 2, Schedule para 18.

4      One view would add the words 'unless the context otherwise admits' or 'where the context admits' and this may be implied (see *Meux v Jacobs* (1875) LR 7 HL 481 at 493; *Law Society v United Services Bureau Ltd* [1934] 1 KB 343, DC). However, the better course is to use whenever practicable defined terms in such a way that there are no circumstances where the defined meanings do not apply.

Definitions of terms used only in schedules are contained in the relevant schedule.

Clauses 1.27–29 are not strictly necessary as the Law of Property Act 1925 s 61 (37 Halsbury's Statutes (4th Edn) REAL PROPERTY) provides such definitions but such definitions are usually inserted for the convenience of the parties.

5      If no date is specifically agreed for completion under a contract incorporating one of the sets of standard conditions the fall-back provisions of the relevant conditions will apply. See, eg, the Standard Conditions of Sale (3rd Edn) condition 6.1 (for which see vol 38(1) (2000 Reissue) SALE OF LAND Form 1 [1045]) and the Standard Commercial Property Conditions (1st Edn) condition 6.1 (for which see vol 38(1) (2000 Reissue) SALE OF LAND Form 2 [1103]). As to the Law Society's General Conditions of Sale (1984 Revision) condition 21(1) (for which see vol 38(1) (2000 Reissue) SALE OF LAND Form 3 [1131]) and the National Conditions of Sale (20th Edn) condition 5(1) (for which see vol 38(1) (2000 Reissue) SALE OF LAND Form 4 [1161]), which Conditions were replaced by the Standard Conditions of Sale in March 1990, see vol 38(1) (2000 Reissue) SALE OF LAND Paragraph 290 [1001] et seq. However, none of the fall-back provisions is appropriate to this agreement.

6      Note that certain conditions in the Standard Conditions of Sale (3rd Edn) (see eg conditions 5.2.6, 7.3.2) provide for compensation payable at the 'contract rate' ie the Law Society's interest rate from time to time in force (see vol 38(1) (2000 Reissue) SALE OF LAND Form 1 condition 1.1.1(g) [1012]); there are also conditions (see eg conditions 2.2.3, 7.2(a), 7.5.2(a)(i), 7.6.2(a)) which provide for payment of 'accrued interest' (see vol 38(1) (2000 Reissue) SALE OF LAND Form 1 condition 1.1.1(a) [1011]).

**[3224]**

7      As to VAT, see note 11 below. Omit the last two sets of words in square brackets if no VAT is payable or it is payable in respect of the purchase price but the deposit is held as stakeholder. Where the purchase price is to be ascertained by valuation after service of the option notice any deposit then payable should be specified as a fixed sum being the appropriate percentage (usually 10%) of the estimated purchase price or minimum purchase price (if any).

8      In preparing this form of sale and purchase agreement, it was decided that it would be helpful to practitioners if incorporation of the Standard Conditions of Sale (3rd Edn) (for which see vol 38(1) (2000 Reissue) SALE OF LAND Form 1 [1011]) was retained in the short term notwithstanding the issue

of the Standard Commercial Property Conditions (1st Edn) (for which see vol 38(1) (2000 Reissue) SALE OF LAND Form 2 [1071]) which have yet to be fully adopted and used. Differences between the two sets of conditions (which are highly similar in many respects) are discussed and summarised in vol 38(1) (2000 Reissue) SALE OF LAND Form 5 [1201].

Other sets of standard conditions which might be referred to are the Statutory Form of Conditions of Sale 1925, SR&O 1925/779, which applies to contracts made by correspondence, and may, but only by express reference, be made to apply to any other cases (see the Law of Property Act 1925 s 46) and the Standard Commercial Property Conditions (1st Edn) (for which see vol 38(1) (2000 Reissue) SALE OF LAND Form 2 [1071]). As to the National Conditions of Sale (20th Edn) (for which see vol 38(1) (2000 Reissue) SALE OF LAND Form 4 [1161]) and the Law Society's General Conditions of Sale (1984 Revision) (for which see vol 38(1) (2000 Reissue) SALE OF LAND Form 3 [1131]), which Conditions were replaced by the Standard Conditions of Sale as from March 1990, see vol 38(1) (2000 Reissue) SALE OF LAND Paragraph 290 [1001] et seq. A contract by correspondence can still be made in relation to a short lease, or the creation or operation of a resulting, implied or constructive trust: see the Law of Property (Miscellaneous Provisions) Act 1989 s 2 as amended by the Trusts of Land and Appointment of Trustees Act 1996 s 25(2), Sch 4 (37 Halsbury's Statutes (4th Edn) REAL PROPERTY).

9     The size and scale of the plan should be sufficiently large to enable all salient features to be readily identified: see *Scarfe v Adams* [1981] 1 All ER 843, CA. If many plans are required it may be convenient to bind them in a separate bundle, suitably referred to in the contract. Each plan should be individually numbered if there is more than one. As to plans generally see vol 35 (1997 Reissue) SALE OF LAND Paragraph 623 [816].

**[3225]**

10    As to the identity of the property to be sold see vol 35 (1997 Reissue) SALE OF LAND Paragraph 346 [453] et seq.

11    As to circumstances in which VAT is payable, see vol 38(1) (2000 Reissue) SALE OF LAND Paragraph 6 [18] et seq and vol 35 (1997 Reissue) SALE OF LAND Paragraph 136 [173] et seq and see the Information Binder: Property [1] (VAT and Property). It should be noted that VAT forms part of the stampable consideration for the purposes of calculating stamp duty and land registration fees.

If VAT is or may be chargeable in respect of any part of the purchase price (which will only be the case if the grantor, or a relevant associate of the grantor, has made a valid election to waive the exemption in respect of the property), and the price is to be exclusive of the tax, a comprehensive clause dealing with all aspects of the tax should be included. For an example of such a clause see clause 15 of this Form and see further vol 36 (1997 Reissue) SALE OF LAND Forms 351 [2521] and 352 [2522]. The VAT provisions in this Form expand those in the Standard Conditions of Sale (3rd Edn) condition 1.4 (for which see vol 38(1) (2000 Reissue) SALE OF LAND Form 1 [1013]) and are inserted to act as a reminder to the parties of the importance of considering VAT aspects at an early stage.

If the Value Added Tax Act 1994 s 89 (48 Halsbury's Statutes (4th Edn) VALUE ADDED TAX) is excluded or the purchase price is expressed to be inclusive of VAT any changes in the rate or incidence of VAT between contract and completion cannot be added to the price.

12    As to VAT, see note 11 above.

13    Ie the Value Added Tax Regulations 1995, SI 1995/2518.

14    In the absence of any specific provision in the contract both seller and buyer are free to assign the benefit of the whole contract or a part of it (eg a charge of the benefit of the contract, or a sub-sale of part of the property). It may be thought desirable to limit these rights, whether because of the importance of the personality or standing of the buyer, or to avoid an immediate sub-sale of the whole or part of the property for tax or other reasons. For clauses preventing sub-sales by the buyer see clause 13 of this Form and the Law Society's General Conditions of Sale (1984 Revision) condition 17(6) (for which see vol 38(1) (2000 Reissue) SALE OF LAND Form 3 [1143]). The Standard Conditions of Sale (3rd Edn) conditions 8.2.5 and 8.3.3 (for which see vol 38(1) (2000 Reissue) SALE OF LAND Form 1 [1055]), which prevent the buyer from transferring the benefit of the contract, apply only to the grant of a new lease.

**[3226]**

15    Where the Standard Conditions of Sale (3rd Edn) are incorporated, this provision is rendered superfluous by condition 1.2 (for which see vol 38(1) (2000 Reissue) SALE OF LAND Form 1 [1013]). However, such words are commonly included for the convenience of the parties.

16    The sum to be inserted here is the consideration (if any) for the grant of the option. Care should be taken to ensure that VAT cannot become payable on the option fee if the property is not a 'new' property, eg by the seller electing to waive exemption; in this circumstance, the second alternative clause 15.4 should be used. If an election has taken place or the grant will involve a standard-rated supply, care should be taken to explore whether VAT paid on the option fee would be recoverable depending upon the nature of the transaction and the buyer's circumstances, for example if the option is never exercised. Subject to the appropriate use of the certificate of value, the option fee is stampable ad valorem. Practitioners will note that there is a danger of stamp duty being paid twice on the option fee amount, ie if the credit for the option fee does not take effect as a reduction in the purchase price. An alternative

to deducting the option fee from the balance payable on completion is simply to reduce the purchase price stated in or ascertained in accordance with the agreement by the amount of the option consideration.

As to capital gains tax on the grant of an option see Taxation of Chargeable Gains Act 1994 s 144 (42–44 Halsbury's Statutes (4th Edn) TAXATION) and see *Simon's Direct Tax Service* C2.1009, 1010.

17    As to exercising the option generally, see vol 38(1) (2000 Reissue) SALE OF LAND Paragraph 241 [611] et seq and vol 35 (1997 Reissue) SALE OF LAND Paragraph 928 [1223]. The clause is drafted on the assumption that the parties are satisfied that exercise of the option in the traditional manner with the option notice signed only by the buyer will be effective to create a binding contract in reliance on *Spiro v Glencrown Properties Ltd* [1991] Ch 537, [1991] 1 All ER 600. If the parties have concern on this point there are alternatives, as to which, see vol 38(1) (2000 Reissue) SALE OF LAND Form 40 note 6 [1666].

18    The payment of a deposit will only be possible in the circumstances where the purchase price is fixed and the deposit amount capable of quantification as a percentage of the purchase price. The words in square brackets should be omitted where the relevant pricing schedule (for which, see Forms 72 [3251]–76 [3270] post) contains provision for price ascertainment. Similarly, clause 3.4 of this Form should be omitted in the same circumstances. See note 7 above.

**[3227]**

19    This provision is only appropriate where a deposit payment is to be made on exercise of the option; for the most part, this will arise in circumstances where the purchase price is fixed or has been ascertained before exercise of the option. If the purchase price is not so fixed or ascertained, a deposit would be appropriately payable within a given period, say, 10 working days, of the purchase price having been ascertained assuming the option has already been exercised.

An alternative approach is to arrange for a fixed deposit, perhaps a fixed amount or an agreed percentage of a fixed minimum purchase price, to be paid on exercise regardless of whether the ultimate purchase price has been ascertained.

20    The permitted development is illustrative only and should be amended as required.

21    This provision is illustrative only and should be amended as required.

22    See note 21 above.

23    As to the completion date, delay and notice to complete generally, see vol 35 (1997 Reissue) SALE OF LAND Paragraph 694 [902] et seq. For the provisions relating to payment of interest for late completion see the Standard Conditions of Sale (3rd Edn) condition 7.3 (for which see vol 38(1) (2000 Reissue) SALE OF LAND Form 1 [1051]) and the Standard Commercial Property Conditions (1st Edn) condition 7.3 (for which see vol 38(1) (2000 Reissue) SALE OF LAND Form 2 [1108]). As to the Law Society's General Conditions of Sale (1984 Revision) condition 22 (for which see vol 38(1) (2000 Reissue) SALE OF LAND Form 3 [1147]) and the National Conditions of Sale (20th Edn) condition 7 (for which see vol 38(1) (2000 Reissue) SALE OF LAND Form 4 [1161]), which Conditions were replaced by the Standard Conditions of Sale as from March 1990, see vol 38(1) (2000 Reissue) SALE OF LAND Paragraph 290 [1001] et seq. The differences between the various sets of conditions are great and should be carefully noted. For tables of comparison, see vol 38(1) (2000 Reissue) SALE OF LAND Form 5 [1201] et seq.

24    The inclusion of these words is not strictly necessary since the Standard Conditions of Sale (3rd Edn) condition 6.2 (for which see vol 38(1) (2000 Reissue) SALE OF LAND Form 1 [1011]) provides for completion to take place either at the seller's solicitor's office or at some other place which the seller reasonably specifies.

**[3228]**

25    The Standard Conditions of Sale (3rd Edn) condition 6.1.2 (for which see vol 38(1) (2000 Reissue) SALE OF LAND Form 1 [1045]) states that if the money due on completion is received after 2.00 pm completion is to be treated, for the purposes of apportionments and the provisions regarding late completion, as taking place on the next working day. Any amendments to this condition should be included in the fourth schedule.

26    As to implied covenants for title and the words importing them generally see vol 35 (1997 Reissue) SALE OF LAND Paragraph 472 [597] et seq.

Covenants for title are implied by the Law of Property (Miscellaneous Provisions) Act 1994 (37 Halsbury's Statutes (4th Edn) REAL PROPERTY) and (additionally in the case of registered land the Land Registration Rules 1925, SR&O 1925/1093 rr 76A–77A as inserted, substituted and amended by SI 1995/337) provide that key words are included in the assurance. Although under the Act and Rules no covenants are implied unless such key words are used, condition 4.5.2 of the Standard Conditions of Sale (3rd Edn) (for which see vol 38(1) (2000 Reissue) SALE OF LAND Form 1 [1025]) provides that if the contract for sale makes no provision as to title guarantee then subject to condition 4.5.3 the seller is to transfer the property with full title guarantee. Accordingly in cases where it is inappropriate for any covenants for title to be given a clause must be inserted expressly stating that no covenants for title will be given.

For a form varying the implied covenants for title see vol 36 (1997 Reissue) SALE OF LAND Form 190 [2226].

27    In the absence of any indication to the contrary, it is an implied term that vacant possession will be given: see vol 35 (1997 Reissue) SALE OF LAND Paragraph 328 [429].

28    As to deduction of title to unregistered property see vol 35 (1997 Reissue) SALE OF LAND Paragraph 400 [515] and as to deduction of title to registered property see vol 35 (1997 Reissue) SALE OF LAND Paragraph 399 [510]. As to the seller's duty to disclose defects in the title see vol 35 (1997 Reissue) SALE OF LAND Paragraph 295 [391] et seq. It is clearly in the interests of the seller to disclose any defects of which he is aware before exchange of contracts; therefore it is now common for title to be deduced in its entirety before exchange and for restrictions to be placed on the right to raise requisitions.

**[3229]**

29    As to the proving and investigation of title generally see vol 35 (1997 Reissue) SALE OF LAND Paragraph 398 [509] et seq. As to instruments which may form a good root of title see vol 35 (1997 Reissue) SALE OF LAND Paragraph 400.2 [516].

30    Ie the Land Registration Act 1925 s 110 as amended by the Land Registration Act 1988 s 2, Schedule (37 Halsbury's Statutes (4th Edn) REAL PROPERTY).

31    The Standard Conditions of Sale (3rd Edn) condition 4.2.1 (for which see vol 38(1) (2000 Reissue) SALE OF LAND Form 1 [1024]) and the Standard Commercial Property Conditions (1st Edn) condition 4.2.1 (for which see vol 38(1) (2000 Reissue) SALE OF LAND Form 2 [1083]) provide that the evidence of registered title is to be office copies of the items required to be furnished by the Land Registration Act 1925 s 110(2). However it is still advisable to include the words in square brackets because the Standard Conditions of Sale are incorporated only in so far as they are not varied by or inconsistent with the terms of the agreement, and it is arguable that the provisions of clause 8 without the words in square brackets form a complete provision replacing the equivalent provision in the Standard Conditions of Sale. As to the deduction of title using HM Land Registry's direct access system see vol 35 (1997 Reissue) SALE OF LAND Paragraph 399.3 [512].

     The words in square brackets are required when the contract is made by reference to the National Conditions of Sale (20th Edn) (for which see vol 38(1) (2000 Reissue) SALE OF LAND Form 4 [1161] and Paragraph 290 [1001] et seq) which do not include this provision. As to the desirability of providing office copies see vol 35 (1997 Reissue) SALE OF LAND Paragraph 399.3 [512].

32    This clause should be included if it is desired to exclude requisitions on the title. Both the Standard Conditions of Sale (3rd Edn) (for which see vol 38(1) (2000 Reissue) SALE OF LAND Form 1 [1011]) and the Standard Commercial Property Conditions (1st Edn) (for which see vol 38(1) (2000 Reissue) SALE OF LAND Form 2 [1071]) omit the provision contained in the Standard Conditions of Sale (1st Edn) condition 4.5, which allowed the seller to rescind the contract if the buyer refused to withdraw a requisition which the seller was unable to satisfy.

33    The buyer should be wary of this clause. If important documents are missing then there may be difficulties in registering the title following completion where the land is unregistered. Of course, if a document is genuinely missing, the original cannot be produced. However, as much evidence as possible should be called for as to the contents of the document and the circumstances of its loss, and statutory declarations obtained (see, eg, vol 25(1) (1999 Reissue) LAND REGISTRATION Form 108 [3851]) so as to give the best possible chance of avoiding registration difficulties. If the land is already registered then, unless the missing document relates to an overriding interest (eg the counterpart of a lease for a term not exceeding 21 years), either:

(a)   the title is likely to be less than absolute (eg possessory or qualified) where the missing document is important to the seller's own title; or

(b)   there is likely to be a protective entry on the register (eg as to restrictive covenants where no copy of the deed creating them was supplied on first registration).

In either case the buyer will need to obtain as much information as possible about the missing document and the effect of this on quality of the title in order to assess the risk of accepting the defect. Various options may be open to the buyer, ranging from simply accepting the risk, if judged to be small, through negotiating a suitable adjustment to the price or obtaining defective title insurance cover to, in extreme cases, withdrawing from the transaction before exchanging contracts.

**[3230]**

34    As to the seller's duty to disclose encumbrances generally see vol 35 (1997 Reissue) SALE OF LAND Paragraph 295 [391]. Where registered land is concerned, the rights of any person in actual occupation of the land will be overriding interests to which any disposition of the land will be subject unless enquiry has been made of that person and the rights were not disclosed: see the Land Registration Act 1925 s 70(1)(g). The same qualification does not apply in relation to other overriding interests listed in the Land Registration Act 1925 s 70(1) as amended.

35    The proprietorship register may need to be included if, eg, there is a restriction controlling dispositions of land which will remain on the register following sale.

36    Where certain charges, eg financial charges, are specifically excluded, a buyer may wish to ensure that any matters entered on the register before completion are also excluded. It might be argued that reference to exclusion of specific entries is to be interpreted as making the property subject to all other entries including new entries. It may be preferable to specify the entries to which the property is positively to be subject so that the position is clear.

37   Matters to be included in the third schedule are matters not recorded in the registers of title or property documents eg, rights created orally, wayleave agreements and short term or informal arrangements.

38   This sub-clause should be omitted if there are no matters affecting the property in respect of which the seller will remain liable notwithstanding the completion of the transfer of the property to the buyer. It may also be omitted in reliance upon the Standard Conditions of Sale (3rd Edn) condition 4.5.4 (for which see vol 38(1) (2000 Reissue) SALE OF LAND Form 1 [1025]) if incorporated. It should be omitted if the alternative sub-clauses 9.1 and 9.2 are used as the indemnity covenant will be set out in full in the draft assurance.

It may be preferred to set out the indemnity covenant the seller will require, rather than rely on standard conditions of sale, particularly if the contract is made by reference to the Law Society's General Conditions of Sale (1984 Revision) (for which see vol 38(1) (2000 Reissue) SALE OF LAND Form 3 [1131]) which do not require the buyer to covenant to observe and perform the covenants and conditions. See also the Standard Commercial Property Conditions (1st Edn) condition 4.5.4 (for which see vol 38(1) (2000 Reissue) SALE OF LAND Form 2 [1084]) and the Standard Conditions of Sale (3rd Edn) condition 4.5.4 (for which see vol 38(1) (2000 Reissue) SALE OF LAND Form 1 [1025]).

**[3231]**

39   As to encumbrances see note 34 above.

40   Whilst the annexation of a draft assurance is more usual on a sale of part of the seller's property it may be appropriate also on a sale of the whole of a property where there are numerous or complex encumbrances to be referred to in the assurance or covenants to be imposed.

41   As to the proprietorship register see note 35 above.

42   As to the charges register see note 36 above.

43   As to matters to be included in the third schedule see note 37 above.

44   A buyer should bear in mind that certain financial charges in respect of costs incurred by a local authority are registrable as local land charges. If these relate to expenditure arising before the date of the contract the buyer may wish to ensure that they are borne by the seller.

45   As an exclusion clause, this condition is subject to the test of reasonableness under the Unfair Contract Terms Act 1977 s 11 (11 Halsbury's Statutes (4th Edn) CONTRACT): see *Smith v Eric S Bush, Harris v Wyre Forest District Council* [1990] 1 AC 831, [1989] 2 All ER 514, HL. The seller cannot rely on a general disclaimer to avoid disclosing matters specifically known to him prior to sale: *Rignall Developments Ltd v Halil* [1988] Ch 190, [1987] 3 All ER 170. For further discussion on this issue see *Thomas Witter Ltd v TBP Industries Ltd* [1996] 2 All ER 573.

46   Consideration should be given to whether the conditions of sale incorporated require amendment in any way to suit the circumstances of the transaction or to ensure consistency with this agreement. As to possible modifications where the Standard Conditions of Sale (3rd Edn) are incorporated (for which see vol 38(1) (2000 Reissue) SALE OF LAND Form 1 [1011]), see vol 35 (1997 Reissue) SALE OF LAND Form 18 [1547]. Many of the suggested amendments are now incorporated in the Standard Commercial Property Conditions (1st Edn) (for which see vol 38(1) (2000 Reissue) SALE OF LAND Form 2 [1071]). The fourth schedule contains amendments to the Standard Conditions of Sale (3rd Edn) appropriate to this agreement.

47   As to restriction on assignment and sub-sale see note 14 above.

48   An option is a chose in action and assignable by the buyer. To vest the benefit of an option in an assignee at law notice must be given to the seller under the Law of Property Act 1925 s 136(1). Failure to give notice results in the assignment being merely equitable, with the consequence that the assignee cannot enforce the benefit of the option at law in his own name against the seller. Failure to give notice does not prejudice the assignee's title against the assignor ie the original buyer.

**[3232]**

49   A less restrictive arrangement for sub-transfer in favour of affiliated companies and entities is set out in Form 68 [3061] ante.

50   From the buyer's perspective, it is worth considering whether the seller should be prevented or restricted from disposing of its interest in the property. Although the option agreement will be binding upon the seller's successors in title, if the decision in *Spiro v Glencrown Properties Ltd* [1991] Ch 537, [1991] 1 All ER 600 is incorrect, the buyer would then need the successor to countersign the form of option notice, but would not have an enforceable power of attorney to sign it for that successor; clause 3.3 is limited to an appointment by the seller itself. However, in some circumstances, commercial realities may suggest a strong need for a restriction on the disposal. An obvious example would be where the option agreement includes provisions for liaison between the parties and/or approval of an agreed planning process as in this Form.

51   Where the Standard Conditions of Sale (3rd Edn) or the Standard Commercial Property Conditions (1st Edn) are being incorporated this clause can be omitted, although it is commonly included for the convenience of the parties: see the Standard Conditions of Sale (3rd Edn) condition 7.4 (for which see vol 38(1) (2000 Reissue) SALE OF LAND Form 1 [1052]) and the Standard Commercial Property Conditions (1st Edn) condition 7.4 (for which see vol 38(1) (2000 Reissue) SALE OF LAND Form 2 [1109]).

52   As to VAT see note 11 above.

53     Where the election is made on or after 1 March 1995 it is only effective if written notification is given to HM Customs and Excise not later than the end of the period of 30 days beginning on the date on which the election is made, subject to certain exceptions: see the Value Added Tax Act 1994, Sch 10 para 3(6)(b) as substituted by SI 1995/279 (48 Halsbury's Statutes (4th Edn) VALUE ADDED TAX).

54     The buyer owes no duty to the seller to register his option: *Wright v Dean* [1948] Ch 686, [1948] 2 All ER 415. The seller's contractual obligation to convey the property to the buyer is not discharged by conveyance of the property to a third party; the seller is liable in damages to the grantee of the option if the latter is unable to enforce the option specifically against a buyer of the seller's interest because of its non-registration, hence the need for this clause. On the question of whether a grantor who has paid damages to the grantee is entitled to indemnity from the buyer of the freehold who declines to give effect to the option see *Eagon v Dent* [1965] 3 All ER 334.

**[3233]**

55     Clauses 16.2 and 16.3 should be added in the case of registered land.

56     The buyer must be advised to insist on deduction of title and on sight of all relevant consents to dealing prior to entering into the option regardless of whether consideration is payable for the option.

       If the option is granted before the mortgage is created the option will be binding on the mortgagee and any buyer from it if the option is protected by registration: Law of Property Act 1925 s 104(1). For this reason mortgagees usually do not lend on the security of property which is already the subject of an option. If the property is already mortgaged at the date of grant of the option, the grantee is at risk of losing the benefit of the option as any sale by the mortgagee under his statutory power will overreach the option: Law of Property Act 1925 s 104(1). Exercise of other powers such as leasing, taking possession or foreclosure will also be prejudicial to the buyer. The buyer will need to ensure that the option will not be over-reached and that if the option is exercised the seller will be able to complete the sale agreement. It is rare for mortgagees to join in an option agreement, but for a clause containing various provisions see vol 38(1) (2000 Reissue) SALE OF LAND Form 40 clause 14 [1658].

57     Insolvency Act 1986 s 1 (4 Halsbury's Statutes (4th Edn) BANKRUPTCY AND INSOLVENCY) applies to composition; the Insolvency Act 1986 s 253 applies to voluntary arrangement.

58     The agreement is drawn up on the assumption that each party is resident in the United Kingdom, and accordingly, in the case of UK companies, has its own UK registered office. The words 'non-exclusive' are mostly used where either the seller or the buyer is an overseas party. The effect is to enable legal action or proceedings to enforce the agreement and/or judgment in an overseas jurisdiction. Although the subject matter of the agreement relates to UK real estate, in some circumstances it is advantageous to have access to courts in the jurisdiction local to that party, and, for example, to other non-domestic assets of the relevant party for the purposes of enforcing judgment. The practitioner should be aware that the law and practice in relation to the recognition of judgments and enforcement differs according to jurisdiction. Accordingly, the precise nature and extent of this provision should be the subject of a legal opinion obtained from lawyers in the relevant jurisdiction.

59     The agreement should be executed as a deed because of the grant of powers of attorney in clauses 3.3 and 16.4 and must be so executed if there is no consideration for the grant of the option.

**[3234]**

60     A notice provision is incorporated in clause 21 for use in two circumstances. The first is where the National Conditions of Sale (20th Edn) (for which see vol 38(1) (2000 Reissue) SALE OF LAND Form 4 [1161]) are incorporated in the agreement as such conditions do not have any express notification provisions. The National Conditions were replaced by the Standard Conditions of Sale as from March 1990 and have not been updated subsequently: see vol 38(1) (2000 Reissue) SALE OF LAND Paragraph 290 [1001] et seq. By contrast the Standard Conditions of Sale (3rd Edn) (for which see vol 38(1) (2000 Reissue) SALE OF LAND Form 1 [1011]) and the Standard Commercial Property Conditions (1st Edn) (for which see vol 38(1) (2000 Reissue) SALE OF LAND Form 2 [1071]) make detailed provision for the service of notices. Secondly, where either party is non-resident in the UK, provision would need to be made for the appointment of an agent for service and accordingly clause 21.5 would be required. Additionally, the practitioner would need to ensure that the arrangements referred to in clause 21.5 have actually been complied with, by sight of the appointment properly counter-signed by the appointed agent.

61     For longer form clauses relating to notices, see vol 4(3) (1997 Reissue) BOILERPLATE CLAUSES Forms 3.3 [171]–3.5 [173] and Paragraph 3.1 [22] et seq.

62     See note 59 above.

63     As to the subjections, see note 37 above. Insert here details of any matters (if any) subject to which the property is sold which are not mentioned in the register of title nor in any documents listed in Part II of the second schedule.

64     The time to be stated here should accord with the time stated in clause 5.1 of this Form.

65     See note 17 above.

66     The words in square brackets should be omitted if the purchase price is not fixed or has not been ascertained at the date of service of the option notice.

67       Where a contract is to be executed as a deed sealing is not necessary either in the case of an individual or
         in the case of a company, but all parties must sign either on the same document or each on one of two
         identical parts which are exchanged, and the signatures of all individuals must be witnessed: see the Law
         of Property (Miscellaneous Provisions) Act 1989 s 1(3). As to the execution of a deed by an individual and
         by a corporation see vol 12 (1994 Reissue) DEEDS, AGREEMENTS AND DECLARATIONS Paragraphs 16
         [1525] and 28 [1554]–30 [1560] respectively.
              It is unnecessary for a contract by a corporate body to be under seal unless it would need to be a
         deed if made by private persons: see the Corporate Bodies' Contracts Act 1960 s 1 (11 Halsbury's Statutes
         (4th Edn) CONTRACT). A contract may be made by a company incorporated under the Companies
         Acts by writing under its common seal or on its behalf by any person acting under its authority, express
         or implied: Companies Act 1985 s 36 as substituted by the Companies Act 1989 s 130(1) (8 Halsbury's
         Statutes (4th Edn) COMPANIES).

**[3235]–[3250]**

# (3):  PRICING SCHEDULES

## 72

### Schedule—Purchase Price Ascertained by Residual Valuation

**1        Definitions**

In this schedule:

1.1      'Independent Valuer' means an independent chartered surveyor with not less
         than 10 years post qualification experience in the valuation of land and
         developments for use as permitted by the [Satisfactory] Planning Permission in
         *(state location)* who shall be appointed by the Seller and Buyer or in default of
         agreement within [14] working days of either party seeking the agreement of
         the other to an appointment at the request of the Buyer or the Seller by or on
         behalf of the President for the time being of the Royal Institution of Chartered
         Surveyors

1.2      'Permitted Development' means the development of the Property in
         accordance with the [Satisfactory] Planning Permission together with the
         performance of all Planning Obligations and the carrying out of all enabling and
         off-site works required to enable the Property to be brought into permanent
         occupation and use

1.3      'Residual Land Value'[1] means the best price at which the sale of the [freehold]
         interest in the Property (together with any rights easements provisions
         covenants and other matters benefiting it but subject to any encumbrances
         restrictions stipulations or covenants which may affect it and which still subsist
         and are capable of taking effect) would have been completed unconditionally
         for cash consideration by private treaty at the date of the Option Notice with
         vacant possession on completion of the sale assuming:[2]

**[3251]**

1.3.1        that the Property is undeveloped and that at the date of the Option
             Notice it is and always will be unlawful[3] to develop and use the
             Property otherwise than in accordance with the [Satisfactory]
             Planning Permission (and any conditions attaching to it) and any
             Planning Obligation or other agreement required or entered into for
             the purpose of obtaining or implementing the Permitted Development

1.3.2        a willing seller

1.3.3    that prior to the date of the Option Notice there had been a reasonable period (having regard to the nature of the Property and the state of the market) for the proper marketing of the interest the agreement of price and terms and the completion of the sale

1.3.4    that the state of the market levels of values and other circumstances were on any earlier assumed date of exchange of contracts the same as on the date of the Option Notice

1.3.5    that no account is taken of [any bid by a prospective owner occupier or of] any additional bid by a purchaser with a special interest[4]

[1.3.6    that each bidder would require a [minimum] development return on cost of *(specify)*[5]]

1.3.7    that both parties to the transaction had acted knowledgeably prudently and without compulsion

proper account being taken of the cost fees and expenses to be incurred in implementing the Permitted Development[6] and complying with any Planning Obligation and any other agreement required or entered into for the purpose of obtaining or implementing the Permitted Development on the date of the Option Notice and thereafter completing the Permitted Development including (without being limited to) the physical state and condition of the Property and site clearance

[3252]

## 2    Purchase Price

2.1    The Purchase Price for the Property shall be ascertained in accordance with this schedule and shall be the [greater of the] Residual Land Value as agreed or determined in accordance with this schedule [and £...]

2.2    In the event that any cost fees or expenses to be incurred in carrying out the Permitted Development are unquantifiable at the time the Residual Land Value falls due to be agreed or determined there shall be included a fair and reasonable allowance for that item to be calculated by the Buyer acting reasonably such calculations to be supported with evidence of the method of calculation and of the assumptions made in such calculations and in the event that the Seller shall dispute the amount of the allowance so calculated within [14] working days of the calculations being produced to the Seller either party shall be entitled to refer the determination of the matter to an Independent Valuer[7]

## 3    Residual Land Value

3.1    Immediately upon service of the Option Notice the Seller and the Buyer shall consult together and attempt in good faith to agree the Residual Land Value of the Property in accordance with this schedule

3.2    If the Seller and the Buyer have not agreed the Residual Land Value within [20] working days of the service of the Option Notice either party shall be entitled to refer the matter for determination to an Independent Valuer who shall act as an expert (and not as an arbitrator)

[3253]

3.3    The Independent Valuer shall have regard to any representations of the Seller and the Buyer made within [10] working days of notifying the Seller and the Buyer of his appointment. The Independent Valuer shall within [10] working days of receipt of any written representations from either party serve a copy of such representations on the other party and shall have regard to any written cross-representations made by that party in respect of the original representations of the other party within [10]

3.4  working days of service by the Independent Valuer of the copy of the original written representations. The Independent Valuer shall deliver a written and reasoned decision for his determination to both the Seller and the Buyer
3.4  The Independent Valuer's fee shall be within his award
3.5  It is the desire of the parties that a determination of the Residual Land Value shall be made by the Independent Valuer within [30] working days of his appointment
3.6  In the event of delays on the part of the Independent Valuer beyond the times specified above the Seller and the Buyer may make representations to the President for the time being of the Royal Institution of Chartered Surveyors and if in the opinion of the President there shall have been unreasonable delay the President shall be entitled to dismiss the Independent Valuer and appoint a new Independent Valuer as the case may require in his place and notwithstanding the foregoing the Seller and the Buyer shall in any event have a right to require such replacement if the decision of the Independent Valuer is not made within [3] months of the date of his appointment
3.7  If the Buyer or the Seller does not pay its due proportion of the fees payable to the Independent Valuer within [10] working days of the date of demand then the other party shall be entitled to make the payment and the amount paid shall be a debt due from the party in default to the other party and shall be payable by the party in default with interest from the date of expenditure until payment at the rate of 4% above the base rate of *(name)* Bank Plc from time to time in force
3.8  The determination of the Independent Valuer in relation to any matter or fact which he is appointed to determine shall be final and binding upon the parties except in the case of manifest error

**[3254]**

1  A residual land valuation involves the identification of a land value as the residual/remaining component of an entire set of forecast development costs, fees and expenses. Such costs, fees and expenses are deducted from the assumed completed development value, that value itself being established by capitalisation of estimated rental values by an appropriate investment yield. Full account is taken of the prospective length of the project and of the time it will take for the completed development value to be fully let and income producing.

2  The assumptions set out in paragraphs 1.3.1–1.3.7 of this Form comprise modified open market value assumptions appearing in Practice Statement 4.2 of the RICS Appraisal and Valuation Manual.

3  It is essential for residual land valuation purposes that a specific detailed planning permission is assessed. It is therefore necessary to ensure that no other attribution of value is given to the land and that the property must always be used for the purposes and in the way envisaged by the given planning permission.

4  It is not essential that owner-occupier bids are disregarded and the words 'any bid by a prospective owner/occupier or of' may be omitted. However, it is desirable from a developer's perspective to ensure that the valuation includes a reasonable development profit element. It is frequently suggested that an owner-occupier will increase its competing offer for the same property by up to the amount of the perceived developer profit requirement to secure the opportunity to acquire and develop the site for its own purposes.

**[3255]**

5  It being accepted that the residual land valuation will include an assumed developer profit requirement, this additional assumption attempts to fix as a percentage of cost the developer's profit requirement. Its inclusion is frequently controversial and it is by no means appropriate to use in all circumstances. If included to provide a minimum rather than an aspirational profit floor plate for the developer, it would at least give the developer some certainty of the profit element even in a competitive bidding environment. This would seem fair and balanced, particularly where the developer has taken on responsibility and considerable expense to acquire the planning permission in question. In other circumstances, for example where a developer is seeking to establish a fixed development return on cost and thereby avoid the impact of market conditions, the provision may not seem appropriate. It should be borne in mind that, if the developer's profit is a percentage of development cost, the developer's profit would increase as forecast costs escalated rather than increase by reduction of development cost—at the expense of the residual land value.

6       It will be noted that the <u>entire</u> development cost is taken into account, including the cost of off-site and enabling works and infrastructure. In circumstances where land is to be developed in phases, but requires heavy initial infrastructure investment for, for example, the whole scheme, a disproportionate weighting of infrastructure cost would be applied to the initial phase. If this is likely to occur, consideration should be given to spreading infrastructure and other appropriate cost components over the whole of the development project.

7       Consideration should be given to whether a further accounting should take place between buyer and seller in the event that there is a significant discrepancy between the allowance given for any unquantifiable costs, fees and expenses and the actual costs, fees and expenses when ascertained.

**[3256]**

# 73

## Schedule—Purchase Price Ascertained on an Open Market Value Basis

**1       Definitions**

In this schedule:

1.1       'Independent Valuer' means an independent chartered surveyor with not less than 10 years post qualification experience in the valuation of land and developments for use as permitted by the [Satisfactory] Planning Permission in *(state location)* who shall be appointed by the Seller and Buyer or in default of agreement within [14] working days of either party seeking the agreement of the other to an appointment at the request of the Buyer or the Seller by or on behalf of the President for the time being of the Royal Institution of Chartered Surveyors

1.2       'Open Market Value'[1] means the best price at which the sale of the [freehold] interest in the Property (together with any rights easements provisions covenants and other matters benefiting it but subject to any incumbrances restrictions stipulations or covenants which may affect it and which still subsist and are capable of taking effect) would have been completed unconditionally for cash consideration by private treaty at the date of the Option Notice with vacant possession on completion of the sale assuming:

1.2.1       a willing seller

1.2.2       that prior to the date of the Option Notice there had been a reasonable period (having regard to the nature of the Property and the state of the market) for the proper marketing of the interest the agreement of price and terms and the completion of the sale

1.2.3       that the state of the market levels of values and other circumstances were on any earlier assumed date of exchange of contracts the same as on the date of the Option Notice

1.2.4       that no account is taken of any additional bid by a buyer with a special interest

1.2.5       that both parties to the transaction had acted knowledgeably prudently and without compulsion

but disregarding the existence of the Buyer's rights under this Agreement

**[3257]**

**2       Purchase Price**

The Purchase Price for the Property shall be ascertained in accordance with this schedule and shall be the greater of [...% of] the Open Market Value as agreed or determined in accordance with this schedule and £...[2]

### 3        Open Market Value

3.1        Immediately upon service of the Option Notice the Seller and the Buyer shall consult together and attempt in good faith to agree in accordance with this schedule the Open Market Value of the Property

3.2        If the Seller and the Buyer have not agreed the Open Market Value within [20] working days of the service of the Option Notice either party shall be entitled to refer the matter for determination to an Independent Valuer who shall act as an expert (and not as an arbitrator)

3.3        The Independent Valuer shall have regard to any representations of the Seller and the Buyer made within [10] working days of notifying the Seller and the Buyer of his appointment. The Independent Valuer shall within [10] working days of receipt of any written representations from either party serve a copy of such representations on the other party and shall have regard to any written cross-representations made by that party in respect of the original representations of the other party within [10] working days of service by the Independent Valuer of the copy of the original written representations. The Independent Valuer shall deliver a written and reasoned decision for his determination to both the Seller and the Buyer

**[3258]**

3.4        The Independent Valuer's fee shall be within his award

3.5        It is the desire of the parties that a determination of the Open Market Value shall be made by the Independent Valuer within [30] working days of his appointment

3.6        In the event of delays on the part of the Independent Valuer beyond the times specified above the Seller and the Buyer may make representations to the President for the time being of the Royal Institution of Chartered Surveyors and if in the opinion of the President there shall have been unreasonable delay the President shall be entitled to dismiss the Independent Valuer and appoint a new Independent Valuer as the case may require in his place and notwithstanding the foregoing the Seller and the Buyer shall in any event have a right to require such replacement if the decision of the Independent Valuer is not made within [3] months of the date of his appointment

3.7        If the Buyer or the Seller does not pay its due proportion of the fees payable to the Independent Valuer within [10] working days of the date of demand then the other party shall be entitled to make the payment and the amount paid shall be a debt due from the party in default to the other party and shall be payable by the party in default with interest from the date of expenditure until payment at the rate of 4% above the base rate of *(name)* Bank Plc from time to time in force

3.8        The determination of the Independent Valuer in relation to any matter or fact which he is appointed to determine shall be final and binding upon the parties except in the case of manifest error

**[3259]**

---

1        This definition follows closely with the definition appearing in RICS *Appraisal and Valuation Manual* PS4.2. It is not necessary that a particular planning permission is taken into account. The valuation is an overall valuation of the land taking full account of actual use and hope value. According to PS4.2.7, in an open market valuation it should not be assumed that planning permission has been obtained for a development purpose unless the market would generally make that assumption. In the context of Forms 67 [3021]–69 [3121] ante, the definition is operated only when a particular planning permission has been granted. Nevertheless, it is not necessary that that permission is assumed to be the only planning permission which would be sought or could be obtained. Accordingly, if an alternative planning permission is to be taken into account (ie one which shows increased density or a more

valuable use), an allowance for risk of not obtaining that planning permission would be made if the market generally would do so.

　　The open market value basis is particularly useful in circumstances where an outline planning permission has already been granted or is to be obtained, since particular density or plot ratios may not be available. In such circumstances, the valuer will make assumptions about such density or plot ratios as would be made by prospective buyers in the market but without any deduction for risk.

2　　It is quite common to see a negotiation develop over whether the contract in question should include a minimum purchase price.

**[3260]**

# 74

## Schedule—Purchase Price adjusted according to rents reserved on the subsequent letting of vacant space[1]

## 1　　Definitions

In this schedule:

1.1　　'Approved Criteria'[2] means the criteria set out in paragraph 4 below

1.2　　'Approved Letting'[3] means a letting of the Vacant Floor Area approved in writing by the Buyer

1.3　　'Cut Off Date'[4] means a date *(number)* years after the date of Completion

1.4　　'Minimum Net Annual Rent'[5] means £... a year

1.5　　'Net Annual Rent'[6] means the yearly rent or aggregate of the yearly rents reserved and made payable under Approved Lettings[7] (or any such payable in lieu of such rent pursuant to any agreement or undertaking for an Approved Letting) disregarding:

　　　[1.5.1　　any rent free or rent reduced periods (except to the extent that such periods falls after the Cut Off Date) and assuming instead that the yearly rent payable on the expiration of such periods was also payable throughout such periods[8]]

　　　1.5.2　　any sum by way of service charge interest or insurance premiums or otherwise not for such occupation which are expressed in any Approved Letting to be payable as rent

　　　1.5.3　　any VAT chargeable as rent

**[3261]**

1.6　　'Notional Value'[9] means the product of[10]:

　　[*(relevant multiplier)* and the amount (if any) by which the Net Annual Rent exceeds the Minimum Net Annual Rent [but does not exceed £... a year[11]]
　　*or*
　　*(relevant multiplier)* and the amount (if any) by which the Net Annual Rent exceeds the Minimum Net Annual Rent up to and including £A plus *(relevant multiplier)* and the amount (if any) by which the Net Annual Rent exceeds £A but does not exceed £B plus *(relevant multiplier)* and the amount (if any) by which the Net Annual Rent exceeds £B [but does not exceed £C][12]

1.7　　'Purchase Price' means £... subject to adjustment in accordance with paragraph 2 of this schedule

1.8　　'Qualifying Tenant'[13] means a tenant [who is neither the Buyer nor any subsidiary or associated company (as defined in the Companies Act 1985) of the Buyer and] who[14]:

　　　1.8.1　　does not enjoy diplomatic or state immunity [but this circumstance shall not apply where the prospective tenant is the Government of the United Kingdom of Great Britain and Northern Ireland or any of its departments]

[1.8.2      is resident in the EU]

[1.8.3      (*continue with subparagraphs on, eg, credit rating, pre-tax profits test or net assets; non-competing use; excluded occupiers, etc)*]

1.9      'Standard Form Lease'[15] means the draft leases of the whole and of part of the Property in the forms attached hereto

1.10     'Vacant Floor Area'[16] means the net internal areas in square metres of that part of the Property shown edged [red] on the floor plans annexed hereto [and the gross internal areas in square metres of the areas shown edged [blue] on the said floor plans each] calculated in accordance with the Code of Measuring Practice of the Royal Institution of Chartered Surveyors/Incorporated Society of Valuers and Auctioneers in force at the date of this Agreement

**[3262]**

**2      Purchase Price adjustment**

2.1      The Purchase Price of the Property shall be subject to adjustment by payment of the Notional Value (if any) calculated in accordance with this schedule

2.2      If the date on which the Vacant Floor Area is entirely let occurs before the Cut Off Date and the Net Annual Rent reserved and made payable under the terms of Approved Lettings exceeds the Minimum Net Annual Rent the Buyer shall pay to the Seller an amount equal to the Notional Value excluding VAT

**3      Letting procedure**

3.1      Subject to paragraph 3.6 the Seller will[17]:

3.1.1      use its best endeavours (without obligation to expend monies on more than the usual fees and usual marketing expenses) until the Cut Off Date to agree lettings of the Vacant Floor Area in accordance with the Approved Criteria with such departures therefrom as the Buyer may in its absolute discretion approve and

3.1.2      will seek the written approval of the Buyer to each proposed letting and shall provide to the Buyer all relevant details of the proposed tenant and the proposed letting and shall use all reasonable endeavours to supply to the Buyer such additional information concerning the proposed tenant as the Buyer shall reasonably require

3.2      The Buyer will notify the Seller of its approval (such approval not to be unreasonably withheld or delayed in the case of a Qualifying Tenant willing to accept a lease which accords with the Approved Criteria) or rejection of any proposed letting as soon as is reasonably practicable

3.3      Subject to paragraph 3.6 the Seller shall have the conduct of the marketing and negotiations of lettings of the Vacant Floor Area

**[3263]**

3.4      Subject to paragraph 3.6 the Seller shall keep the Buyer fully informed of the progress of marketing and the negotiations for lettings and the Buyer shall be entitled to be represented at all marketing meetings with letting agents

3.5      Subject to paragraph 3.6 the Buyer shall:

3.5.1      give prompt consideration and response to any application for amendment to the draft Standard Form Lease proposed by a prospective tenant for a letting which the Buyer has approved in principle (approval to such proposed amendments not to be unreasonably withheld or delayed having regard to reasonable sound institutional investment practice)

3.5.2      render such assistance to the Seller as it may reasonably require for the purpose of securing and approving lettings and

3.5.3       not grant any lease (or enter into any agreement therefor) of the Vacant Floor Area or any part of it or occupy or permit anyone else to occupy the Vacant Floor Area without the prior written approval of the Seller such approval not to be unreasonably withheld or delayed

3.6       If the Seller is in breach of paragraph 3.1 and after reasonable written notice from the Buyer requiring it to comply remains in breach the Buyer may by further written notice to the Seller elect to determine paragraph 3.1 of this Schedule. For the avoidance of doubt any termination under this paragraph 3.6 will not affect or negate the obligations of the Seller under any other paragraph

## 4       Letting terms

Each letting[18] shall be:

4.1       to a Qualifying Tenant

4.2       for a term certain of not less than *(number)* years commencing on *(date)*

4.3       at an open market rent obtained without any fine premium or other consideration or any inducement exceeding in value the inducement permitted by sub-paragraph 4.4 [provided that the Buyer shall not be obliged to permit or approve a letting at less than £... per net square metre]

4.4       made without the giving of any inducement however characterised (and including the value of any period of permitted occupation prior to the lease being granted) which exceeds in aggregate value an amount equal to *(number)* months rent calculated at the rate initially reserved under the lease as granted

4.5       on the terms of the Standard Form Lease

**[3264]**

1       This schedule is intended for use where the purchase price is later increased by an amount equal to the capital value of rents achieved on the letting of vacant space after completion but before an agreed cut-off date. It is capable of use whether the whole or merely a part of the lettable space is vacant at the completion date, and whether a rental guarantee (vol 38(1) (2000 Reissue) SALE OF LAND Form 60 [2381]) in respect of lettable space has been provided by the seller to the buyer.
         As to the capital gains tax treatment of contingent consideration see *Simon's Direct Tax Service* C2.107.

2       This definition is common to Form 74 and vol 38(1) (2000 Reissue) SALE OF LAND Form 60 [2381]; where these forms are used together, it should be moved to the front of the agreement to enable the incorporation of both forms as separate schedules without inappropriate duplication.

3       This definition is common to Form 74 and vol 38(1) (2000 Reissue) SALE OF LAND Form 60 [2381]; where these forms are used together, it should be moved to the front of the agreement to enable the incorporation of both forms as separate schedules without inappropriate duplication.

4       This definition is common to Form 74 and vol 38(1) (2000 Reissue) SALE OF LAND Form 60 [2381]; where these forms are used together, it should be moved to the front of the agreement to enable the incorporation of both forms as separate schedules without inappropriate duplication.

5       This definition is common to Form 74 and vol 38(1) (2000 Reissue) SALE OF LAND Form 60 [2381]; where these forms are used together, it should be moved to the front of the agreement to enable the incorporation of both forms as separate schedules without inappropriate duplication.

6       This definition is common to Form 74 and vol 38(1) (2000 Reissue) SALE OF LAND Form 60 [2381]; where these forms are used together, it should be moved to the front of the agreement to enable the incorporation of both forms as separate schedules without inappropriate duplication.

7       The buyer should consider, in appropriate circumstances, widening the definition of 'Net Annual Rent' to ensure that all income derived from the Property is taken into the calculation, for example advertising hoarding and licensing income.

8       It will be noted that in this Form rent free and rent reduced periods are disregarded for the purpose of calculating net annual rent; accordingly, if the annual rent reserved under a lease with a six month rent free period is, say, £50,000, it is assumed for drafting purposes in this schedule that rent is payable at that rate as soon as the lease is granted. However, in practice, a value of £25,000 is not received by the buyer from either the seller (under the guarantee) or the tenant. The effective cost of the rent free period is absorbed at the cost of the buyer. Whether this is appropriate will depend on the particular

circumstances and care should be taken to ensure that the purpose and burden of the rent free period is correctly identified and agreed at the outset. In this respect, frequently, the letting criteria to be set out at paragraph 4 will include a maximum rent free period on any prospective letting.

**[3265]**

9        Notional value is the product of capitalising the whole or an agreed part of the rent reserved by an agreed yield. Depending on the agreement between the parties, it is possible that the <u>whole</u> of the rent achieved on the letting would be capitalised. In other instances, it may be the <u>excess</u> over an agreed minimum net annual rent; this is likely to be the case where the initial Purchase Price already includes an element of capitalised value in respect of the unlet space.

10       It is sometimes the case that different capitalisation rates are applied to elements of the rent achieved in respect of the void space. The drafting alternatives are set out in the paragraph.

11       It is sometimes the case that a ceiling is imposed on the capitalisation arrangements, so that a part of the rent achieved after completion in respect of lettable space is disregarded for capitalisation purposes.

12       Eg, where the minimum annual rent is £100,000 and the rent achieved is £150,000, the excess rent will be £50,000; and where A = £115,000; B = £135,000 and C = £145,000 and the relevant multipliers are 8%, 7.75% and 7.5% respectively, the notional value will be:

| | | |
|---|---|---|
| 8% | x £15,000 | = £187,500 |
| 7.75% | x £20,000 | = £258,060 |
| 7.5% | x £10,000 | = £133,330 |
| 0% | x £ 5,000 | = £0 |
| | £50,000 | £578,890 |

13       This definition is common to Form 74 and vol 38(1) (2000 Reissue) SALE OF LAND Form 60 [2381]; where these forms are used together, it should be moved to the front of the agreement to enable the incorporation of both forms as separate schedules without inappropriate duplication.

14       This paragraph should prescribe the qualification of the tenants in terms of covenant strength or required credit rating, minimum term and rental parameters and any other specific qualifications, eg non-competitive use.

15       This definition is common to Form 74 and vol 38(1) (2000 Reissue) SALE OF LAND Form 60 [2381]; where these forms are used together, it should be moved to the front of the agreement to enable the incorporation of both forms as separate schedules without inappropriate duplication.

16       This definition is common to Form 74 and vol 38(1) (2000 Reissue) SALE OF LAND Form 60 [2381]; where these forms are used together, it should be moved to the front of the agreement to enable the incorporation of both forms as separate schedules without inappropriate duplication.

17       Paragraph 3 is common to Form 74 and vol 38(1) (2000 Reissue) SALE OF LAND Form 60 [2381].

18       Paragraph 4 is common to Form 74 and vol 38(1) (2000 Reissue) SALE OF LAND Form 60 [2381].

**[3266]**

# 75

### Schedule—Purchase Price ascertained according to residential density

## 1        Definitions

In this schedule:

1.1      'Habitable Rooms' means all rooms intended to provide living accommodation excluding kitchens bathrooms water closets lobbies halls stairways passages landings storage spaces and garages

1.2      'Net Developable [Hectarage]' means the Property excluding[1]:

1.2.1           any land which pursuant to the terms of the [Satisfactory] Planning Permission or any Planning Obligation is to be transferred to a third party

1.2.2           the roadways pedestrian footpaths cycle ways and verges giving public access to the residential accommodation to be erected on the Property which it is intended shall either be maintained by the Developer or at the cost of some or all of the occupiers of the residential accommodation or shall be dedicated to the public

1.2.3    any areas of landscaping open space amenity land play areas required or approved pursuant to the [Satisfactory] Planning Permission or any Planning Obligation and which are to be maintained at the cost of some or all of the occupiers of the residential accommodation or by the local authority

## 2    Purchase Price

The Purchase Price for the Property shall be ascertained in accordance with this schedule and shall be the greater of[2]:

2.1    £... multiplied by the total Net Developable [Hectarage]
2.2    £... multiplied by the total number of Habitable Rooms or *(number)* Habitable Rooms whichever is the higher and
2.3    £...

[3267]

## 3    Residential density

3.1    Immediately upon service of the Option Notice the Seller and the Buyer shall consult together and attempt to agree in good faith in accordance with this schedule the Net Developable Hectarage [and the relevant number of Habitable Rooms in each case] calculated by reference to or permitted by the [Satisfactory] Planning Permission

3.2    If the Seller and the Buyer have not agreed the Net Developable Hectarage [and the relevant number of Habitable Rooms] within [20] working days of the service of the Option Notice either party shall be entitled to refer the matter for determination to an Independent Valuer who shall act as an expert (and not as an arbitrator)

3.3    The Independent Valuer shall have regard to any representations of the Seller and the Buyer made within [10] working days of notifying the Seller and the Buyer of his appointment. The Independent Valuer shall within [10] working days of receipt of any written representations from either party serve a copy of such representations on the other party and shall have regard to any written cross-representations made by that party in respect of the original representations of the other party within [10] working days of service by the Independent Valuer of the copy of the original written representations. The Independent Valuer shall deliver a written and reasoned decision for his determination to both the Seller and the Buyer

3.4    The Independent Valuer's fee shall be within his award

3.5    It is the desire of the parties that a determination of any matter referred to the Independent Valuer shall be made by him within [30] working days of his appointment

3.6    In the event of delays on the part of the Independent Valuer beyond the times specified above the Seller and the Buyer may make representations to the President for the time being of the Royal Institution of Chartered Surveyors and if in the opinion of the President there shall have been unreasonable delay the President shall be entitled to dismiss the Independent Valuer and appoint a new Independent Valuer as the case may require in his place and notwithstanding the foregoing the Seller and the Buyer shall in any event have a right to require such replacement if the decision of the Independent Valuer is not made within [3] months of the date of his appointment

3.7    If the Buyer or the Seller does not pay its due proportion of the fees payable to the Independent Valuer within [10] working days of the date of demand then the other party shall be entitled to make the payment and the amount paid shall be a debt due from the party in default to the other party and shall be payable by the party in default with interest from the date of expenditure until payment at the rate of 4% above the base rate of *(name)* Bank Plc from time to time in force

3.8    The determination of the Independent Valuer in relation to any matter or fact which he is appointed to determine shall be final and binding upon the parties except in the case of manifest error

[3268]

1    The exclusions stated in this paragraph are not exhaustive.
2    Paragraphs 2.1–2.3 are alternatives. A minimum purchase price is achieved by including paragraph 2.3 whilst a minimum density is achieved by including paragraph 2.2.

[3269]

# 76

## Schedule—Purchase Price adjusted by reference to indexation

**1    Definitions**

In this schedule:

1.1    'Additional Sum' means the amount that bears the same proportion to the Original Amount as the Increase bears to the Base Figure

1.2    'Base Figure' means *(insert the Index figure for the month preceding the date of the Agreement or otherwise as has been agreed)*

1.3    'Calculation Date' means the Completion Date[1]

1.4    'Increase' means the amount if any by which the Index figure for the month preceding the Calculation Date exceeds the Base Figure

1.5    'Index' means the ['all Items'] index figure of the Index of Retail Prices published by the Office for National Statistics or any successor ministry or department

1.6    'Original Amount' means £...

1.7    'Purchase Price' means the aggregate of the Original Amount and the Additional Sum

[3270]

**2    Calculation of the Additional Sum**

2.1    On the Calculation Date a calculation shall be made to determine the amount (if any) of the Additional Sum

2.2    If the reference base used to compile the Index changes after the date of this Agreement the figure taken to be shown in the Index after the change is to be the figure that would have been shown in the Index if the reference base current at the date of this Agreement had been retained

2.3    If it becomes impossible to calculate the Additional Sum by reference to the Index because of any change in the methods used to compile the Index after the date of this Agreement or for any other reason whatever or if any dispute or question whatever arises between the parties as to the amount of the Additional Sum or the construction or effect of this schedule then the calculation of the Additional Sum or the disputed matter is to be determined by an arbitrator to be appointed either by agreement between the parties or in the absence of agreement by the President for the time being of The Royal Institution of Chartered Surveyors or any person authorised by him to make appointments on his behalf on the application of the Seller or the Buyer. This provision is deemed to be a submission to arbitration within the meaning of the Arbitration Act 1996. The arbitrator is to have full power to determine on such date as he considers appropriate what the increase in the Index would have been had it been continued on the basis assumed for the operation of this schedule and in view of the information assumed to be available for it

2.4    In the event that at the Calculation Date any relevant figure appears in the Index marked as a provisional average or estimated figure or marked as uncertain subject to revision or not finally ascertained (each a 'reservation') such figure ('the Provisional Figure') shall (subject to paragraph 2.5) be treated nonetheless as the relevant figure for the purpose of the initial calculation of the Additional Sum by this Schedule

2.5    If within *(number)* months after the Additional Sum has been initially calculated the Provisional Figure in the Index is replaced by a figure which is not subject to a reservation ('the Replacement Figure') the Seller shall be entitled to recalculate the Additional Sum by reference to the Replacement Figure. In the event that the Additional Sum as recalculated is greater than the Additional Sum as calculated by reference to the Provisional Figure the Seller shall upon notification of a written claim to the Buyer within *(number)* months of the first publication of the Replacement Figure (as to which notification time shall be of the essence) accompanied by a proper recalculation of the Additional Sum and proper evidence of the change in the Index and the date of its first publication be entitled to receive a further payment equal to the difference between the Additional Sum initially so calculated and the Additional Sum as recalculated such amount to be paid within [15] working days of the date of proper notification

**[3271]**

1    Care should be taken with the wording of the completion mechanism, for example, to avoid circularity where the completion date is dependent upon the agreement or determination of the purchase price.

**[3272]–[3290]**

# (4):  DEVELOPMENT CLAW-BACK (OVERAGE)

# 77

**Agreement supplemental to a sale or option agreement for the disposal of agricultural land, providing for payment of additional consideration based on residual land value**

CONTENTS

Schedule
1        Ascertainment of Further Consideration


THIS SUPPLEMENTAL DEED is made the ...day of ......

BETWEEN:

(1)     *(name of seller)* [company number *(number)*] [of *(address) or* whose registered
        office is at *(address)*] ('the Seller') and
(2)     *(name of buyer)* [company number *(number)*] [of *(address) or* whose registered
        office is at *(address)*] ('the Buyer')

WHEREAS:

(A)     By [an option agreement *or* sale and purchase agreement]¹ ('the Contract')
        bearing the same date as this Supplemental Deed the Seller has agreed [to grant
        an option] to sell the Property to the Buyer at the Initial Price
(B)     [If the option is exercised the *or* The] transfer to the Buyer ('the Transfer') is to
        be in the form [referred to in *or* annexed to] the Contract and shall contain
        various covenants in favour of the Seller
(C)     It was further agreed in the course of negotiations leading to the Contract that
        the parties should enter into this Supplemental Deed the provisions of which
        shall [if the option is exercised] be supplemental to both the Contract and the
        Transfer

                                                                              **[3291]**


**1        Definitions and interpretation**

In this Agreement:
1.1     'Buyer's Request' has the meaning given to it in clause 2.2
1.2     'Cut-Off Period' has the meaning given to it in clause 7.1
1.3     'Deed of Variation' has the meaning given to it in clause 2.2 and includes any
        deed of variation if more than one of them shall be required pursuant to that
        clause
1.4     'Further Consideration' means the additional consideration calculated in
        accordance with the schedule
1.5     'Initial Price' means *(the purchase price stated in the option agreement or sale and
        purchase agreement)*
1.6     'Intended Use' means *(details)* or other use within Class *(number)* of the Town
        and Country Planning (Use Classes) Order 1987 [with ancillary *(specify: eg roads,
        services)*] and other associated activities
1.7     'Relevant Planning Consent' has the meaning given to it in clause 2.2
[1.8    'Residual Land Value' has the meaning given to it in the schedule]²
1.9     'Planning Obligation' means in relation to the Property or any relevant part of
        it all or any of the following as the case may be:
        1.9.1     an agreement (whether or not also affecting other property) pursuant
                  to the Local Government (Miscellaneous Provisions) Act 1982 Section
                  33 and/or the Local Government Act 1972 Section 111 and/or the
                  Highways Act 1980 Sections 38 and/or 278 and/or the Water Industry
                  Act 1991 Section 104 or any provision to similar intent or an
                  agreement with a water undertaker or a drainage undertaker (within
                  the meaning of the Water Industry Act 1991) or the Environment
                  Agency or an Internal Drainage Board (within the meaning of the
                  Water Resources Act 1991 or the Land Drainage Act 1991) or other

appropriate authority as to water supply or drainage of surface and/or foul water or an agreement with any competent authority or body relating to other services and/or

1.9.2      a planning obligation (whether entered into by agreement or otherwise and whether or not also affecting other property) pursuant to the Town and Country Planning Act 1990 Section 106

1.10      'Property' means the property more particularly described in the Contract

**[3292]**

## 2    Agreement[3]

2.1      The Transfer will prohibit the use of the Property otherwise than as agricultural land and by reason of the covenants limiting development the amount of the consideration to be paid for the initial acquisition of the Property was limited to the Initial Price

2.2      It is the common intention of the parties that the Buyer shall if practicable obtain planning permission for the use of the Property[4] for the Intended Use and if at any time within the Cut-Off Period the Buyer shall obtain planning consent whether outline or detailed (a 'Relevant Planning Consent') permitting the development of the Property for the Intended Use the Seller[5] at the request in writing of the Buyer ('the Buyer's Request') and upon prior payment of the Further Consideration will enter into a deed varying the covenants imposed by [and the right of re-entry vested in the Seller[6] by] the Transfer [and the legal charge granted by the Buyer][7] (a 'Deed of Variation') to such extent only as shall be:

2.2.1      necessary to enable the Relevant Planning Consent to be implemented and the Property be brought into permanent occupation and use

2.2.2      in accordance with the terms of this Agreement and

2.2.3      necessary to accord with the Relevant Planning Consent

**[3293]**

## 3    Deed of Variation

The Deed of Variation shall:

3.1      be in such form as may be agreed upon by the parties at the time and in default of such agreement shall be settled by leading conveyancing counsel to be appointed by agreement between the parties or in default of such agreement selected by the President for the time being of the Law Society upon the application of either party

3.2      not be required to be entered into at any time prior to the completion of the Transfer

3.3      be completed only on or on prior payment of the Further Consideration

3.4      not be required to be entered into unless the Seller shall first reasonably be satisfied that development use and other operations proposed to be permitted by the Deed of Variation shall be in accordance in all respects with the provisions of the Transfer

## 4    Further consideration

4.1      The Further Consideration payable shall be ascertained and calculated in a manner set out in the schedule to this Agreement and shall become due and payable to the Seller:

4.1.1      on the date [4] calendar months after the date of the Buyer's Request[8] or

4.1.2     in the event that determination of the amount of the Further Consideration is referred to an Independent Valuer in accordance with the schedule then on the date one calendar month after the Independent Valuer's determination

4.2     If for any reason the Further Consideration is not paid on the due date it shall carry interest from the due date until the date of actual receipt by the Seller at the rate of 4% per annum above the base rate of *(name)* Bank Plc from time to time in force

**[3294]**

## 5      Buyer Obligations

During the subsistence of this Agreement the Buyer shall in relation to the Property:

5.1     keep the Seller informed of:

5.1.1     any and all planning applications and decisions relating to the Property or any property within [2] miles thereof if the scheme proposed in respect of such property is relevant to the Intended Use of the Property in respect of which the Buyer (or anyone acting on behalf of or in co-operation with the Buyer) has made a planning application and shall if required supply to the Seller free of charge a copy of the planning application made by it or on its behalf and shall upon reasonable request inform the Seller of all relevant facts concerning the progress of such applications and/or associated appeals

5.1.2     any Planning Obligations being negotiated by the Buyer in respect of the Property

[5.1.3     its progress in obtaining vacant possession of the Property and in conducting negotiations for possession the Buyer shall seek to agree that payment to the occupiers of the Property shall be limited to the amount (if any) of statutory compensation to which such occupiers would be entitled on the expiry or contractual termination of that occupier's right of occupation subject to the Buyer's discretion to pay such further compensation as may reasonably be considered appropriate in the circumstances to obtain vacant possession][9]

5.2     not assign sub-contract charge or otherwise attempt or purport to part with the benefit of this Agreement except by way of charge to secure finance for the development contemplated by the Contract or by the sale of the whole of the Property to a buyer who covenants in a form satisfactory to the Seller to observe and perform the Buyer's obligations set out in this Supplemental Deed and the Seller shall be bound on the Buyer's successors in title and any mortgagee of the Buyer or such successor complying with the conditions in this Deed and in the Contract and the Transfer to enter into the Deed of Variation with such mortgagee or successor in title to the Buyer in either case only if such mortgagee or successor in title shall be entitled in respect of the whole of the Property

**[3295]**

## 6      Receipt

Upon payment to the Seller of any sum or sums due hereunder by way of Further Consideration the Seller shall give a good and sufficient receipt for all such sum or sums and (if the same shall not be recorded in the Deed of Variation) execute such document or form as may be necessary to evidence the payment

## 7    Cut-Off Period

7.1    This Agreement shall endure for a period from the date hereof until *(date)*[10] ('the Cut-Off Period') (which shall for the purpose of this Supplemental Deed be the applicable perpetuity period) and on the expiration of the said period all the provisions of this Agreement shall cease to operate and be of no effect but without prejudice to the rights and liabilities of the parties which shall have accrued before the expiration of the Cut-Off Period[11]

7.2    If called upon to do so the Seller will at the Buyer's expense at the end of the Cut-Off Period do and execute all such things deeds and documents as may reasonably be required by the Buyer to discharge the Property or such part or parts of the Property as may still be subject to this Deed from all the provisions of this Deed immediately before the end of the Cut-Off Period (subject to prior payment of all outstanding sums due to the Seller by way of Further Consideration accrued due at that time) and without prejudice to the continuing effect of all the provisions contained or referred to in the Transfer[12]

## 8    Joint and Several Liability

All covenants made by any party in this Deed shall be deemed to be made jointly and severally

IN WITNESS etc

[3296]

SCHEDULE
Ascertainment of Further Consideration

## 1    Definitions

In this schedule:

1.1    'Independent Valuer' means an independent chartered surveyor with not less than 10 years post qualification experience in the valuation of land and developments for use as permitted by the Relevant Planning Consent in *(state location)* who shall be appointed by the Seller and Buyer or in default of agreement within [14] working days of either party seeking the agreement of the other to an appointment appointed at the request of the Buyer or the Seller by or on behalf of the President for the time being of the Royal Institution of Chartered Surveyors

1.2    'Residual Land Value' means the best price at which the sale of the [freehold] interest in the Property[13] (together with any rights easements provisions covenants and other matters benefiting it but subject to any encumbrances restrictions stipulations or covenants which may affect it and which still subsist and are capable of taking effect) would have been completed unconditionally for cash consideration by private treaty at the date of the [Option Notice *or* sale and purchase agreement] with vacant possession on completion of the sale assuming:

    1.2.1    that the Property[14] is undeveloped and that at the date of the Buyer's Request it is and always will be unlawful to develop and use the Property otherwise than in accordance with the Relevant Planning Consent (and any conditions attaching to it) and any Planning Obligation or other agreement required or entered into for the purpose of obtaining or implementing the Relevant Planning Consent

    1.2.2    a willing seller

1.2.3    that prior to the date of the Buyer's Request there had been a reasonable period (having regard to the nature of the Property and the state of the market) for the proper marketing of the interest the agreement of price and terms and the completion of the sale

1.2.4    that the state of the market levels of values and other circumstances were on any earlier assumed date of exchange of contracts the same as on the date of the Buyer's Request

1.2.5    that no account is taken of any [bid by a prospective owner occupier or of any] additional bid by a buyer with a special interest

[1.2.6    that each bidder would require a minimum development return on cost of *(specify)*]

1.2.7    that both parties to the transaction had acted knowledgeably prudently and without compulsion

1.2.8    the relevant Deed of Variation has already been entered into

proper account being taken of the cost fees and expenses to be incurred in implementing the Relevant Planning Consent and complying with any Planning Obligation and other agreement required or entered into for the purpose of obtaining or implementing the Relevant Planning Consent on the date of the Buyer's Request and thereafter carrying out and completing the development permitted thereby including (without being limited to) the physical state and condition of the Property and site clearance

**[3297]**

## 2    Further Consideration

2.1    The Further Consideration for the Property shall be ascertained in accordance with this schedule and shall be an amount equal to the difference between Residual Land Value as agreed or determined in accordance with this schedule and the aggregate of the Initial Price and any Further Consideration already paid or payable by the Buyer to the Seller

2.2    In the event that any cost fees or expenses to be incurred in carrying out the Relevant Planning Consent and complying with any Planning Obligation and other agreement required or entered into for the purpose of obtaining or implementing the Relevant Planning Consent are unquantifiable at the time the Residual Land Value falls due to be agreed or determined there shall be included a fair and reasonable allowance for that item to be calculated by the Buyer acting reasonably such calculations to be supported with evidence of the method of calculation and of the assumptions made in such calculations and in the event that the Seller shall dispute the amount of the allowance so calculated within [14] working days of the calculations being produced to the Seller either party shall be entitled to refer the determination of the matter to an Independent Valuer

**[3298]**

## 3    Residual Land Value

3.1    Immediately upon service of the Buyer's Request the Seller and the Buyer shall consult together and attempt in good faith to agree the Residual Land Value of the Property in accordance with this Schedule

3.2    If the Seller and the Buyer have not agreed the Residual Land Value within [20] working days of the service of the Buyer's Request either party shall be entitled to refer the matter for determination to an Independent Valuer who shall act as an expert (and not as an arbitrator)

3.3     The Independent Valuer shall have regard to any representations of the Seller and the Buyer made within [10] working days of notifying the Seller and the Buyer of his appointment. The Independent Valuer shall within [10] working days of receipt of any written representations from either party serve a copy of such representations on the other party and shall have regard to any written cross-representations made by that party in respect of the original representations of the other party within [10] working days of service by the Independent Valuer of the copy of the original written representations. The Independent Valuer shall deliver a written and reasoned decision for his determination to both the Seller and the Buyer

3.4     The Independent Valuer's fee shall be within his award

3.5     It is the desire of the parties that a determination of the Residual Land Value shall be made by the Independent Valuer within [30] working days of his appointment

3.6     In the event of delays on the part of the Independent Valuer beyond the times specified above the Seller and the Buyer may make representations to the President for the time being of the Royal Institution of Chartered Surveyors and if in the opinion of the President there shall have been unreasonable delay the President shall be entitled to dismiss the Independent Valuer and appoint a new Independent Valuer as the case may require in his place and notwithstanding the foregoing the Seller and the Buyer shall in any event have a right to require such replacement if the decision of the Independent Valuer is not made within *(number)* months of the date of his appointment

3.7     If the Buyer or the Seller does not pay its due proportion of the fees payable to the Independent Valuer within [10] working days of the date of demand then the other party shall be entitled to make the payment and the amount paid shall be a debt due from the party in default to the other party and shall be payable by the party in default with interest from the date of expenditure until payment at the rate of 4% above the base rate of *(name)* Bank Plc from time to time in force

3.8     The determination of the Independent Valuer in relation to any matter or fact which he is appointed to determine shall be final and binding upon the parties except in the case of manifest error

> *(signatures (or common seals) of the parties)*
> [*(signatures of witnesses)*]
> **[3299]**

1       See Form 70 [3171] ante and see vol 38(1) (2000 Reissue) SALE OF LAND Form 59 [2321].

2       A residual land value definition is incorporated in the schedule by which the value of the developable land is calculated by reference to the planning permission which has been obtained. In some circumstances it may be more appropriate to incorporate an open market value definition, particularly if the development contemplated by the planning permission which triggers the buyer's request is outline planning permission for a use which may not be implemented.

        As to the capital gains tax treatment of contingent consideration see *Simon's Direct Tax Service* C2.107.

3       In accepting this clause the buyer will need to distinguish between those cases where the seller retains land capable of benefiting from the covenant and those where the seller does not. In the former case the covenant referred to will be a restrictive covenant benefiting the seller's retained land whereas in the latter case it will simply be a personal covenant in favour of the seller. An important point about this distinction, at least in cases where (as here) it is intended that the covenant should be released or varied in certain circumstances, is that, where the covenant is a restrictive covenant benefiting the land of the seller, the buyer will need to ensure that the seller retains the capacity to release or vary the covenants at the appropriate time. In particular, either the seller will need to retain all the benefiting land at the

time of the release or variation, or the seller will need to have ensured that, in relation to any part of the land disposed of, the seller retains the power to release or vary the covenants in relation to the land disposed of or the buyer's right to a release or variation remains enforceable against the disponee and successors in title. In either case, it seems desirable from the buyer's point of view to ensure that, if the seller's retained land is registered, the seller agrees to apply for a consent restriction on the register of the retained land in the buyer's favour (so that the buyer has a say in the process whereby any part of the land is disposed of) and/or the seller covenants not to dispose of any part of the retained land until the release or variation has been effected.

4      Detailed consideration must be given to the position which will arise if planning permission is only to be sought for part of the property.

5      It will be noted that the payment obligation is triggered only by service at a buyer's request. Sometimes the mere obtaining of planning permission is considered to be sufficient to trigger the quantification and subsequent payment obligations. Whilst each transaction depends on its circumstances, in a long term contract the receipt of planning permission may not occur at an opportune moment in the development or occupational demand cycle. It is equally arguable that to leave the timing of the request to the buyer would enable the buyer to take full advantage of depressed pricing conditions.

**[3300]**

6      In all cases involving the sale of agricultural land for development purposes a restrictive covenant (in the form of Forms 78 [3331] or 79 [3332] post) should be incorporated in the sale and purchase agreement (for which see vol 38(1) (2000 Reissue) SALE OF LAND Form 59 [2321]) if the purchase price is calculated on an agricultural land value basis. Where the payment of further consideration is sought over a relatively short timescale, the nature of the covenant will usually be sufficient, provided there is retained land which is capable of benefiting from the restrictive covenant, to prevent development of the land without payment of the further consideration as envisaged by this form. However, care must be taken to consider what additional protection the seller would need and can conveniently obtain where there is no retained land. In these circumstances, the restrictive covenant is of contractual benefit between the original parties and could be supplemented by a provision requiring that no disposal of the land take place without a fresh covenant in terms mutatis mutandis from the direct disponee; however, the protection afforded is weak. Therefore, where there is no retained land or a long term enforceability is envisaged, it is usual for the seller to include a right of re-entry or to take a charge to secure payment of the further consideration. In almost all circumstances a right of re-entry is preferable to the seller; however, problems will be encountered with rights of re-entry if and to the extent that the buyer requires secured third party debt to raise the funds required to complete the purchase of the land itself. Similarly where legal charges are granted to both the seller and the buyer's own mortgagee, a deed of priority and/or postponement defining the rights of the competing securities would be required.

The words in square brackets should be omitted if a legal charge is granted by the buyer instead.

7      The words in square brackets should be omitted if the seller obtains a right of re-entry rather than a legal charge.

8      The period of four calendar months is suggested for two reasons. Firstly, it will be possible in that period to determine whether a challenge is to be made to the planning permission. Secondly, the period should be sufficient to enable a residual land valuation to be undertaken. It will be noted that paragraph 2.2 of the schedule enables interim assessment to be made of any unquantifiable cost.

9      The purpose of this provision is to recognise the prospective costs to the buyer of obtaining vacant possession in respect of premises which it may be favourable to continue letting whilst development proposals are considered and planning permission obtained; a balance according to each transaction must be struck between allowing the buyer freedom to negotiate suitable compensation arrangements for vacant possession and ensuring that the quantum level, which will form part of development costs for residual land value calculations, is not excessive.

10     A suitable period will be required according to the planning character of the proposal and current local policy affecting the property and the area generally.

11     Given the potentially arbitrary impact of the cut off date, it is considered essential that accrued rights and liabilities remain unaffected.

12     Consideration should be given to whether the valuation is in respect of the whole of the property or whether a phased planning arrangement suggests the need for valuation only of that part which is the subject of planning permission. If part only, the impact of initial infrastructure costs, if benefiting the whole site, may need to be spread across the phased project.

13     See note 12 above.

14     See note 12 above.

**[3301]–[3330]**

## 78

### Restrictive covenant benefiting retained land preventing use of the property except for agricultural purposes for insertion into vol 38(1) Form 59[1]

[8.4]     The Transfer shall contain covenants by the Buyer that the Buyer will to the intent that the burden of this covenant may (so far as possible) run with and bind the Property and each and every part thereof and to the intent that the benefit thereof may (so far as possible) be annexed to and run with the Retained Land and each and every part thereof not in any circumstances use or cause or permit or suffer the Property during a period of seventy-nine years from and including the date of the Transfer (which for the purposes of the Transfer shall be the applicable perpetuity period ('the Perpetuity Period')) to be used otherwise than as agricultural land and not during the Perpetuity Period make any change of use of nor carry out any development in on or under the Property within the meaning of planning legislation except as it exists at the date of the Transfer (save for such development (if any) as is consistent with the use and occupation of the Property as agricultural land) it being specifically hereby recorded that by reason of the imposition of the restrictions contained in this clause the amount of consideration paid for the acquisition of the Property was thereby limited

1        This Form provides additional provisions to be inserted into vol 38(1) (2000 Reissue) SALE OF LAND Form 59 [2321] and is for use in conjunction with Form 77 [3291] ante. As to security by way of a legal charge or right of re-entry see Form 77 note 6 [3301] ante.

**[3331]**

## 79

### Restrictive covenants preventing use of the property except for agricultural purposes and seller's right of re-entry (no retained land) for insertion into vol 38(1) Form 59[1]

[8.4]     The Transfer shall contain covenants that the Buyer will not to the intent that the burden of this covenant may (so far as possible) bind the Property and each and every part thereof and all persons who at any time own any estate or interest in the Property or occupy it or any part of it in any circumstances use or cause or permit or suffer the Property during a period of seventy-nine years from and including the date of the Transfer (which for the purposes of the Transfer shall be the applicable perpetuity period ('the Perpetuity Period')) to be used otherwise than as agricultural land and not during the Perpetuity Period make any change of use of nor carry out any development in on or under the Property within the meaning of planning legislation except as it exists at the date of the Transfer (save for such development (if any) as is consistent with the use and occupation of the Property as agricultural land) it being specifically hereby recorded that by reason of the imposition of the restrictions contained in this clause the amount of consideration paid for the acquisition of the Property was thereby limited

[8.5]     The Transfer to the Buyer shall include a right in favour of the Seller[2] to the intent that the burden of this covenant may (so far as possible) bind the Property and each and every part thereof and all persons who at any time own any estate or interest in the Property or occupy it or any part of it that:

[8.5.1] if at any time before the expiry of the Perpetuity Period the Property or any part or parts of it shall be used or occupied otherwise than in accordance with clause [8.4] then the Seller or any other person in whom the benefit of the right conferred by this clause shall from time to time be vested may give written notice identifying the use or occupation which breaches the provision of clause [8.4] and requiring that the unlawful use occupation or development (as the case may be) shall be discontinued [and in the case of development the Property restored to the physical state and condition which but for such unlawful development would comply with clause [8.4]] within a period of *(specify)* and if the period specified in such notice expires without the unlawful use occupation or development having been discontinued or removed as required by this clause or if a breach of clause [8.6] or of any equivalent covenant given pursuant to that provision occurs then and in every such case it shall be lawful for the person in whom the benefit of the rights and interest hereby conferred shall then be vested to enter upon the Property or any part of it in the name of the whole and with effect from the event of such entry to hold and enjoy the Property in fee simple in possession free from encumbrances or any estate or interest arising thereunder

[8.5.2] that upon any lawful exercise of the right set forth in clause [8.5.1] the Seller or other person in whom the benefit of such covenant or equivalent covenant given as contemplated by clause [8.6] is vested shall be entitled to delivery of the land or charge certificate and all other title deeds and documents

**[3332]**

[8.6] The Transfer shall contain a covenant by the Buyer to the intent that the burden of this covenant may (so far as possible) bind the Property and each and every part thereof and all persons who at any time own any estate or interest in the Property or occupy it or any part of it that the Buyer will not create or dispose of any interest in the whole or any part of the Property unless:

[8.6.1] such a transaction is expressly made subject to the terms of the Transfer

[8.6.2] the relevant document contains a covenant by the disponee in favour of the Seller or other person in whom the benefit of the covenants referred to in clause [8.4] and clause [8.5] shall from time to time be vested to observe and perform all the covenants and obligations on the part of the Buyer contained in clause [8.4] and clause [8.6] of the Transfer (including this paragraph but limited to the part of the Property thereby affected if such transaction does not relate to the whole of the Property)

[8.7] The Transfer shall contain a provision by which the Buyer agrees to apply upon registration of this Transfer at HM Land Registry for the provisions of the Transfer to be noted on the registered title of the Property (including the new registered title to be allotted on registration)

1   This Form provides additional provisions to be inserted into vol 38(1) (2000 Reissue) SALE OF LAND Form 59 [2321] and is for use in conjunction with Form 77 [3291] ante.

2   As to security by way of legal charge or right of re-entry, see Form 77 note 6 [3301] ante.

**[3333]–[3400]**

# PART 7: DEVELOPMENT AGREEMENTS

## (1): FORWARD FUNDING OR FORWARD SALE/ PURCHASE AGREEMENTS

## Commentary

### A: INTRODUCTION

**299    Nature of forward funding**

An investor ('fund') may look beyond acquiring a standing investment to direct investment in new development. To enter into a contract to buy land conditional upon development first being carried out (by or through the immediate seller) is generally known as 'forward sale' or 'forward purchase'[1] (although the terminology, having no generic meaning, is sometimes attributed to forward funding). It is implicit in such arrangements that neither purchase money is paid (save perhaps for a deposit) nor is title transferred until the development, or the relevant phase of it, is complete. If the development is not, by then, let, but the fund is nevertheless contractually committed to complete the acquisition, the purchase is said to be speculative. In these circumstances, the inference is that either the seller (usually 'the developer') will be required to sustain an income commitment until first letting and/or may receive further remuneration as and when lettings are achieved, combined with an obligation to seek lettings.

The implementation of the development and the procuration of lettings will be contractually controlled under forward funding. The fund acquires a site at the outset, usually directly from or through the developer (immediate seller). This sets in train a relationship under which, against payments made to the developer (or as the case may be directly to the contractor and/or others who are engaged upon the development), the developer is financed to procure the development for the benefit of the fund. In addition, the developer is required to seek lettings and so turn this outlay into an investment. That is not to say that funds do not themselves engage in direct development, or employ project managers to assist them. The engagement of a developer usually results from the developer having identified and assembled a site, obtained planning permission, had appropriate site and soil surveys carried out, appointed his professional team and generally packaged the prospective result (including, as the case may be, the procurement of pre-letting, whether of whole or part) in a way which is attractive to a fund.

---

1    In this commentary the term 'forward sale/purchase' is used.

**300      Fund's financial outlay**

Under forward funding, the fund's financial outlay will include not only the cost to it of acquiring the site but of meeting, within defined parameters, the development cost incurred by the developer. This outlay will include such costs as the fund will itself incur in safeguarding its interests throughout the development process[1]. A fund in this case will be concerned not only with timing of the exercise overall but, particularly, with the extent of its financial exposure, and will therefore impose a maximum commitment. Against its outlay, a fund will apply a notional accumulation (finance charge) which will be rolled up against the development cost (project costs), being debited periodically to the development account, until the maximum commitment is reached. Thereafter, the developer may itself be required, until practical completion, and until the development has been fully let for the first time, to make payment to the fund in lieu of rental income from the whole or part of the development as the case may be.

Sometimes this particular outlay is deferred to be set against the developer's remuneration. Forward funding on this basis is said to be by way of 'profit erosion'. Profit erosion funding is particularly attractive to a developer who, unless the fund's maximum commitment is reached before the entirety of the substantive development cost has been expended (or it was not authorised in any case under the forward funding agreement), may consequently either recoup or avoid personal payment of the entirety of the cost of procuring the development. Perhaps understandably, amongst developers, forward funding has been described as 'the perfect off-balance sheet funding medium'.

**[3402]**

---

1    Judgment must be exercised by a fund in appointing an adviser whose functions may duplicate that of a developer's appointee and in every case an issue arises as to whether it is more practical and cost effective to rely instead solely upon a warranty from the developer's appointee instead (or statutorily prescribed third party rights as the case may be).

**[3403]**

# B: CONTRACTUAL ELEMENTS OF FORWARD FUNDING AND FORWARD SALE/PURCHASE

**301      Main documents**

Traditionally, two main documents drive the contractual relationship between developer and fund in forward funding. The first is the sale and purchase contract. The second is the forwarding funding agreement itself, usually expressed to be effective upon completion of the sale and purchase[1]. Conveniently, the two agreements may be combined. However, consequent upon the Housing Grants, Construction and Regeneration Act 1996, dispute resolution under the construction provisions of an apparently independent forward funding agreement entered into on or after 1 May 1998 may be subject to adjudication in manner prescribed by the Act, unless the agreement is combined with the contract for sale and purchase[2].

The essence of the development provisions, whether of a forward funding or of a forward sale/purchase agreement is nonetheless, in practical terms, a construction agreement under which the developer adopts the role of a contractor charged with the procuration and delivery of the project[3]. The developer's own contractor and professional team may thus be seen as effectively subcontracted and it is therefore to be expected that the contractor and professional team will, subject to the Contracts (Rights of Third Parties) Act 1999, be required to provide warranties to the fund as well as to prospective tenants.

**[3404]**

1        See Forms 80 [3441] and 81 [3521] post. The forward funding agreement (Form 80 [3441]) is expressed
         as a separate agreement with provision for an enabling sale and purchase if desired. In so far as it does
         not include a conveyancing contract, provision has been made for adoption of the Technology and
         Construction Solicitors Association ('TeCSA') Adjudication Rules to apply to any dispute in so far as
         the agreement comprises a construction contract. However, the precedent for forward sale/purchase
         (Form 81 [3521] post) is set up as a basic contract for sale and purchase, but with separate development
         provisions to include such definitions and other mechanisms to keep that part of the agreement largely
         self-contained. The draftsman should take care to ensure that no part of the principal contract is so
         drawn as to set up a conflict between its operative provisions and the schedule.
             A forward sale/purchase agreement (Form 81 [3521] post), by contrast, is essentially expressed as a
         contract for sale and purchase, conditional not upon the developer's purchase but upon delivery of the
         completed development.
2        See the Construction Contracts (England and Wales) Exclusion Order 1998, SI 1998/648 reg 6 and see
         Paragraph 306 [3410] et seq post.
3        The developer is thereby prospectively liable (under the former) as a contractor for the purpose of the
         construction industry tax scheme: see the Income Tax (Sub-contractors in the Construction Industry)
         Regulations 1993, SI 1993/743 as amended by SI 1998/2622 and by SI 1999/2159. See Paragraph 306
         [3410] et seq post.

**[3405]**

### 302    Contracts (Rights of Third Parties) Act 1999

The difference of principle between a pure construction contract and the development
provisions of a forward funding or forward sale/purchase agreement is slight in that, in
the case of the latter, in perhaps surrendering discretion as to the appointment and terms
of engagement of sub-contractors and professionals to express nomination, the developer
will be subjected to scrutiny and approval of all of those appointments and commitments,
their remuneration, conduct and enforcement. The Contracts (Rights of Third Parties)
Act 1999 has yet to be seen to be given full effect in construction and development
generally. For the moment, it appears that the construction and development industries
have preferred to avoid implementing the Act, but there is no reason why this cannot
change. Accordingly, none of the four precedents[1], forward funding, forward sale/
purchase, agreement for lease (landowner/developer) or agreement for lease (landlord/
developer/tenant) is expressed to avail a third party, or class of third party, of the benefit
of the Act in relation to the agreement in question or part of it. It will be apparent,
however, that if construction contracts, these kinds of agreement, or any other contract
were so drafted, the need for warranties might evaporate in the face of appropriate
contractual provisions designed to bring about the same result.

1        See Forms 80 [3441]–83 [3711] post.

**[3406]**

### 303    Appointment of professional to monitor expenditure

Whether under forward funding or forward sale/purchase, the fund will engage some
suitably qualified professional to act on its own behalf in a monitoring role analogous to
an employer's agent under a JCT design and build contract, and also to oversee and
approve, on behalf of the fund, the outlay of expenditure and other matters.

**[3407]**

### 304    Measures of performance

One of the lessons of the recession of the early 1990s is that not only funds, but also the
draftsmen of some forward funding and forward sale/purchase agreements, failed to
recognise that stringent conditions alone are not sufficient to deliver the desired measure
of performance. The fund must assess both the skill and the resources of the developer,
resources being particularly important where the development is speculative, and if an

independent income stream is to be relied upon until first letting. Moreover, in the case of forward sale/purchase, where the developer must meanwhile resource the project himself, too rigid conditions, particularly those affording any discretion to the fund in approvals, certification and so on, may serve only to make the particular arrangement potentially unbankable in the meantime. A lending bank must in such circumstances look only to the development itself in the light of lettings actually achieved.

[3408]

## 305    Consequences of breach of development

Breach of any development agreement brings with it the prospect of a series of related failures, including for the developer who, in the case of forward funding, may lose his licence from the fund to be on site, thus setting in train a series of claims for loss of profit from his contractors and professionals, quite apart from any claims from the fund. For the fund owning a site under forward funding, the dilemma is whether to novate these arrangements and continue the development and, for both fund and developer, an issue is to what extent the developer should be remunerated, which will depend not least on the progress the developer has made. For example, where an event of default is triggered by, say, the insolvency of a guarantor, but the progress of the development is not impaired; should the fund profit from the developer's technical default in completing and letting the development for itself, having first discharged the developer? These are entirely commercial issues, on which only guidance on drafting can be given. Unless the fund as landowner wishes to be rigorous in its exclusion of the developer from the site (under forward funding), however innocent the default, it is suggested that the fund should consider providing a payment, after the fund's own additional expenditure, so that the fund is no worse off than if the developer had concluded the entirety of the project itself.

Under forward sale/purchase, however, the fund has a choice: whether to walk away or to persevere. If the former applies, the developer is left with the property (and no doubt with an unsatisfied commitment to its bankers), but it at least has a continuing interest, as well as its ongoing commitments to its contractor and professionals, which may yet be salvaged.

[3409]

# C:  DISPUTES

## 306    Introduction

Although an allegation of breach may give rise to dispute, a fund's unwillingness to approve a certificate, or authorise a draw down, for example, may also give rise to a dispute. All disputes signal a prospect of delay, perhaps a lost letting, and it is perhaps only a practical and pragmatic relationship which, however the documentation is drafted, will help the parties to a formal dispute while allowing the agreement to continue to operate[1].

Alternative dispute resolution (ADR) procedures[2] are to be encouraged. It is debatable whether they need to be catered for expressly. The rationale for ADR is often stated to be the need for a practical mechanism to preserve an otherwise good, and possibly continuing, working relationship between the protagonists.

1    Eg, in the case of forward funding, for draw downs to continue to be made.
2    See vol 3(1) (1999 Reissue) ARBITRATION AND ALTERNATIVE DISPUTE RESOLUTION Paragraph 38 [71] et seq.

[3410]

**307     Statutory scheme for construction contracts**
Construction disputes between employer and contractor under a building contract can be extremely complex. Moreover, development documentation of all kinds, unless shown to be statutorily excluded, is now susceptible along with pure construction contracts to the imposition of a further, compulsory, tier of adjudication.

The Housing Grants, Construction and Regeneration Act 1996, Sections 104–117 came into force in relation to constructions contracts[1] entered into on or after 1 May 1998. Under these provisions, inter alia, there is imposed upon construction disputes a statutory scheme for construction contracts unless the parties devise their own scheme in accordance with the criteria set out in Section 108 of the Act. The arrangements prescribe a procedure for adjudication of disputes without prejudice to underlying prescribed procedures, the intention of which is to speed the continued implementation (and by implication enforcement) of the construction contract. The term 'construction contract' is defined at Section 104 subject to express exclusions prescribed by regulations[2]. Amongst such exclusions are a contract for the grant whether freehold or leasehold (for not less than 12 months) of development land, so that such portion of that contract as comprises a construction contract is not subject to the scheme[2].

A forward sale/purchase is, accordingly, excluded. By contrast, unless a forward funding agreement also incorporates a contract for the sale and purchase of relevant land, those provisions of it comprising a construction contract may be subject to the Act. The parties may consider that this is not, in fact, a hardship on the basis that it may help avoid a prolonged dispute albeit indirectly, and aid the prospects of letting (or of not losing lettings). It should be borne in mind at all times that the imposition of adjudication applies solely to those elements of an agreement comprising a construction contract as defined and does not, for example, apply to other matters such as letting policy. In so far as adjudication is imposed, the parties are at liberty to make provision for it to be binding as for formal resolution of disputes, and thus replace or override other disputes procedures contained in the agreement.

There is room for a view that adoption of adjudication, as for a pure construction contract, may ameliorate some of the hardship of disputes in development. These precedents[3] do not, however, speculate on the value of such an approach, and make no special provision.

**[3411]**

1    Construction Contracts (England and Wales) Exclusion Order 1998, SI 1998/648.
2    There are other express exclusions but the definitions are narrow. It is therefore essential to apply SI 1998/648 carefully to every contract with a construction element, however remote, to determine whether those provisions apply. The relevant sections of the Act also provide for regulation of remuneration, again applying the statutory scheme if certain criteria are not met: Housing Grants, Construction and Regeneration Act 1996 ss 109–113 (11 Halsbury's Statutes (4th Edn) CONTRACT).
3    Forms 80 [3441]–83 [3711] post.

**[3412]**

# D:  LETTING

**308     Letting opportunities**
At the heart of forward funding and forward sale/purchase is the letting of the completed development. Whilst the developer's interest may be seen as transient, in the sense that his commitment is effectively ended once the premises are first let and he has been remunerated, the raison d'être for the fund is the resultant investment. For this reason, the fund having concerned itself with delivery of the project to a certain standard and within a certain time frame, the criteria for letting determine the developer's ability to derive his remuneration.

As the recession of the early 1990s has highlighted, an unexpected shift in market conditions may mean that the developer's prospects of receiving remuneration will evaporate in the face of letting criteria eg minimum permitted rent levels which cannot in the event be applied. Where a profit erosion formula applies, the worst consequence for the developer may be no more than the ability to retreat from the scene, none the worse off. Where however its prospective remuneration is formula-based on lettings achieved, in turn governed by a minimum permitted rent, the result may be that the fund will (if the developer is sufficiently resourced) elect to rely on an income stream from the developer (or his surety) until market conditions are more propitious. It is therefore important for both draftsmen and legal opponents to be alive to the possible consequences of imposition of financial formulae and letting criteria of whatever kind. Where market conditions produce unexpected results, the only exit route for a defensive party may be a fresh bargain. The financial consequences of letting apart, the criteria for choosing tenants, allocation of lettable accommodation, user and so on is an area which is fraught with difficulty. Every development is different and paves the way for conflicting views on letting criteria. If letting opportunities are lost through a dispute between fund and developer, the weaknesses of the financial structure of the particular funding agreement are quickly felt.

**[3413]**

# E: VAT

## 1: GENERAL

**309　Introduction**

With the demise of the developer's self supply rules from 1 March 1995, and consequent upon the abolition of zero rating except in the case of buildings used for a 'relevant residential purpose' or a 'relevant charitable purpose', a measure of certainty now applies to all new (commercial) development. In appraising the economic viability of a development scheme it is essential that both the developer and the fund pay due regard to the chargeability and recoverability of VAT within the supply chain which results from the development process; the economic burden of irrecoverable VAT can, in certain cases, seriously prejudice the profitability of some schemes.

The changes in the treatment of most supplies affecting property and the construction industry, which were introduced by the Finance Act 1989 and which are now contained in the Value Added Tax Act 1994[1], make VAT a major consideration which needs to be taken into account in negotiating and settling the documentation necessary to implement a development scheme.

The following paragraphs summarise the more important features of the VAT rules which are of specific relevance to funding agreements.

1　See the Value Added Tax Act 1994 (48 Halsbury's Statutes (4th Edn) VALUE ADDED TAX). As to VAT in relation to land and property generally see vol 38(1) (2000 Reissue) SALE OF LAND Paragraph 8 [16] et seq and see the Information Binder: Property [1] (VAT and Property), *Scott and McLellan: VAT and Property* and *De Voil Indirect Tax Service*.

**[3414]**

**310　Zero rated supplies**

The pre-1989 zero rate treatments which applied to all buildings now only apply to the first grant of a major interest in, or supplies of building materials and certain services in relation to the construction of (or, in limited circumstances, the conversion of nonresidential buildings to) buildings designed as dwellings and buildings which are to be used solely for a 'relevant residential purpose' or a 'relevant charitable purpose'[1] (as such terms are specifically defined[2]).

1     See the Value Added Tax Act 1994 s 30, Sch 8 Group 5 Items 1–4 as substituted by SI 1995/280 and by SI 1997/50 (48 Halsbury's Statutes (4th Edn) VALUE ADDED TAX). As to zero rating see generally HM Customs and Excise Notice 708 'Buildings and Construction' (August 1997).
2     See the Value Added Tax Act 1994 Sch 8 Group 5 Notes (4), (6) as substituted by SI 1995/280.

**[3415]**

### 311     Exempt supplies

Subject to various exceptions[1], the grant[2] of any interest in or right over land, or of any licence to occupy land, is an exempt supply[3].

1     See the Value Added Tax Act 1994 s 31, Sch 9 Group 1 Item 1 (a)–(n) (48 Halsbury's Statutes (4th Edn) VALUE ADDED TAX) and Paragraph 313 [3420] post.
2     As to the meaning of 'grant' see the Value Added Tax Act 1994 s 31 Sch 9 Group 1 Note (1) as substituted by SI 1995/282.
3     As to the VAT liability of land transactions generally see HM Customs and Excise Notice 742 'Land and Property' (December 1995) with updates 2 (August 1999) and 3 (October 1999).

**[3416]**

### 312     Election to waive exemption

312.1     A landowner has the right to waive exemption[1] (commonly referred to as the 'option to tax') upon making a suitable election in relation to the following categories of supply[2]:

312.1.1     the sale of an interest in land, industrial or commercial buildings or works of civil engineering, other than on the grant of a fee simple in a 'new' or uncompleted (as defined) building or work of civil engineering (which will be chargeable at the standard rate in any event)[3];

312.1.2     a lease of land and/or industrial or commercial buildings (ie not buildings which otherwise qualify for a zero rate treatment)[4];

312.1.3     the surrender or reverse surrender of such a lease[5].

312.2     The effect of exercising the option to tax is to convert a supply which would otherwise be an exempt supply for VAT purposes into a taxable supply at the standard rate. An election once made applies to all supplies made by the landowner of interests in the land. Where land is subject to a lease, there is a separate supply of land each time rent becomes payable under the terms of the lease. Therefore if the landlord makes an election part way through the term of a lease, all payments of rent after the date of the election are treated as being made in respect of supplies taxable at the standard rate.

**[3417]**

312.3     An election to waive exemption applies to the whole of the landowner's/landlord's interest in the building in respect of which it is made. For this purpose, there is an extended meaning of the word 'building' which includes buildings linked internally or by a covered walkway, and complexes consisting of a number of units grouped round a fully enclosed concourse[6].

312.4     After 1 March 1995 an election has been revocable within three months, provided that no input tax has been recovered and no taxable supply has been made, or after 20 years[7].

312.5       There are special provisions which deal with the application of the option to tax in the context of VAT groups[8]. Where an election to waive exemption is made by a company, the election will apply to any grant made by a 'relevant associate'[9] of the company as well.

312.6       The exercise of the option must be notified in writing to HM Customs and Excise within 30 days[10]. Consent is normally required before the option can be exercised in circumstances where the person wishing to opt has already made exempt supplies in relation to the building[11].

312.7       In certain circumstances the option to tax may be disapplied, consequent upon the Finance Act 1997 Section 37[12]. Only property within the capital goods scheme is affected and where the relevant grant is made within ten years of the development being brought into use. However, forward sale/purchase may be affected where the development becomes exempt land occupied by the grantor, the financier (given a wide definition[13]) or someone connected with either, with such occupation not being wholly or mainly for eligible purposes. Such purposes comprise a business carried on by the relevant person providing supplies the input tax from which would entitle him to a related tax credit. A bank is a clear example. If the supply is ineligible, the grantor's option to tax is disapplied and the entirety of the recovery to which he was entitled from the outset in relation to the particular property (including all development cost) will be lost. The essential test is one of intention, and a developer undertaking forward sale/purchase or any disposal within the capital goods scheme is on enquiry accordingly. Where the occupier is unconnected, and is not treated as the financier of the development or a person connected with the financier, the position is as before, ie the grantor exercises his option to tax in the usual way and the resultant VAT is an absolute cost to the occupier.

**[3418]**

1       As to exempt supplies, see Paragraph 311 [3416] ante.
2       See the Value Added Tax Act 1994 Sch 10 para 2 as amended (48 Halsbury's Statutes (4th Edn) VALUE ADDED TAX).
3       See Paragraph 313 note 1 [3420] post.
4       See Paragraph 310 note 1 [3415] ante.
5       See the Value Added Tax Act 1994 s 31, Sch 9 Group 1 Item 1 Notes (1), (1A) as substituted and inserted by SI 1995/282.
6       See the Value Added Tax Act 1994 Sch 10 para 3(3) as amended by SI 1995/279.
7       See the Value Added Tax Act 1994 Sch 10 para 3(4), (5) as substituted by SI 1995/279.
8       See the Value Added Tax Act 1994 Sch 10 para 2(1), as amended by SI 1994/3013.
9       For the definition of 'relevant associate' see the Value Added Tax Act 1994 Sch 10 para 3(7).
10      Value Added Tax Act 1994 Sch 10 para 3(6) as substituted by SI 1995/279. There is otherwise no formality to an election, although suitable evidence of the decision may be prudent. See also para 8.6 of HM Customs and Excise Notice 742 'Land and property' (December 1995) with updates 2 (August 1999) and 3 (October 1999).
11      See the Value Added Tax Act 1994 Sch 10 para 3(9).
12      The Finance Act 1997 s 37 (48 Halsbury's Statutes (4th Edn) VALUE ADDED TAX) made changes to the Value Added Tax Act 1994 Sch 10 in relation to supplies to non-taxable persons. The VAT position of the developer in forward funding is not normally affected by these changes: a sale of land (in itself a properly taxable supply) is effected before development is commenced, although it may affect the grantee's position if it is making amended supplies relying on an election being effective.
13      See the Value Added Tax Act 1994 Sch 10 para 3A(3) as inserted by the Finance Act 1997 s 37.

**[3419]**

**313     Standard rated supplies**

VAT at the standard rate is imposed upon the following:

313.1          the grant of the fee simple in a 'new' or uncompleted 'commercial' building or work of civil engineering[1];

313.2          the supply of goods and services which do not constitute supplies of land, for example, on the construction and reconstruction of buildings which do not qualify for zero rating[2];

313.3          the supply of goods and services on the construction of a work of civil engineering;

313.4          the supply of certain short term licences, for example car parking licences, and the right to fell and remove timber[3].

1     See the Value Added Tax Act 1994 s 31, Sch 9 Group 1 Item 1(a) (48 Halsbury's Statutes (4th Edn) VALUE ADDED TAX). A building or work of civil engineering will be treated as 'new' if it was completed within three years before the date of grant: see the Value Added Tax Act 1994 Sch 9 Group 1 Notes (4)–(6). As to 'completed' see the Value Added Tax Act 1994 Sch 9 Group 1 Note (2). As to the meaning of 'grant' see the Value Added Tax Act 1994 Sch 9 Group 1 Note (1) as substituted by SI 1995/282.
2     As to zero rating see Paragraph 310 [3415] ante.
3     Value Added Tax Act 1994 Sch 9 Group 1 Item 1(b)–(n).

**[3420]**


**314     VAT provisions in contracts**

Unless a contract[1] provides that any consideration is exclusive of VAT, the consideration payable will be treated as being a VAT inclusive sum[2]. However, if after a contract or lease has been entered into the rate of VAT changes, then, unless the contract specifies otherwise, any increase or decrease in the rate must be added to or deducted from the consideration payable under the contract or lease[3]. This also applies to changes attributable to an election to waive exemption[4]; therefore, if a landlord waives exemption during the term of a lease, the tenant will normally be liable to account for VAT in addition to the rent to the landlord.

1     Including any implied terms.
2     See the Value Added Tax Act 1994 s 19(2) (48 Halsbury's Statutes (4th Edn) VALUE ADDED TAX).
3     See the Value Added Tax Act 1994 s 89.
4     See the Value Added Tax Act 1994 s 89(3).

**[3421]**


## 2: FORWARD FUNDING AGREEMENTS AND VAT

**315     Structure of forward funding agreements**

Conventionally, forward funding agreements are structured in the following way:

315.1          the developer sells his assembled interest in the development site to the fund (probably but not necessarily) at cost;

315.2          the fund employs the developer to carry out the development and, unless prelet, then usually to let the completed site; and

315.3          as consideration for the foregoing the fund agrees to pay the developer a sum calculated by reference to a formula often reflecting the capital value of the rents achieved on letting the completed development. The general term for the developer's profit or added value is 'overage'.

**[3422]**

**316    Application of the VAT rules**

Under the current rules (assuming that the building to be constructed is a 'commercial' building), the position is as follows.

**316.1    Sale of the site**

The sale by the developer to the fund of an undeveloped site gives rise to an exempt supply, subject always to the developer's right to waive exemption and charge the supply to VAT at the standard rate[1]. If at the time of sale the whole site has been partially developed, then the developer's supply is automatically chargeable to VAT at the standard rate if the sale is of a freehold interest[2]; if only part of the site has been developed then it is understood that HM Customs and Excise will accept a reasonable apportionment. If the sale is of a leasehold interest in a partially developed site, the supply remains exempt subject to the developer's option to tax[3]. It follows that in the case of a freehold forward sale/purchase the developer, having completed the sale, will have made supplies automatically chargeable plus VAT, and in the case of a leasehold interest will have needed to waive election in order to benefit in relation to its development cost.

1    See the Value Added Tax Act 1994 s 31, Sch 9 Group 1 Item 1 (48 Halsbury's Statutes (4th Edn) VALUE ADDED TAX) and Paragraphs 311 [3416] and 312 [3417] ante.
2    Value Added Tax Act 1994 s 31 Sch 9 Group 1 Item 1(a).
3    The mandatory charge at the standard rate on the supply of a freehold interest in a partially developed site applies where the building in question is above foundation level at the time of sale.

**[3423]**

**316.2    Developer's supply of construction and letting services**

The developer's supplies to the fund on the construction of a new commercial or industrial building[1] and on the supply of the service of procuring tenants for the completed building is chargeable to VAT at the standard rate.

1    See Paragraph 313 [3420] ante.

**[3424]**

**316.3    Fund's supply to tenant**

The fund's onward supply of the completed building to an occupational tenant is an exempt supply subject to the fund's exercise of the option to tax[1]. It will almost invariably wish to do so in order to recover VAT charged by the developer[2].

1    See Paragraphs 311 [3416] and 312 [3417] ante.
2    See Paragraph 317.4 [3429] post.

**[3425]**

**317    Effect of VAT on the supply chain**

The following is a summary, in general terms, of the effect of these rules on the conventional supply chain for the development of a commercial building.

**317.1    Developer's option to tax supply of undeveloped land**

The developer's supply of undeveloped land to the fund is exempt, subject to the developer's option to waive exemption and render the supply standard rated[1]. It is probable that in most cases the developer will exercise the option so as to enable it to recover any input tax which is attributable to its supply. In this respect, the developer may have incurred attributable input tax in relation to professional fees and/or on the cost to it of acquiring its interest in the land where it purchased the land from a seller who had itself exercised its option to tax.

1    See the Value Added Tax Act 1994 s 31, Sch 9 Group 1 Item 1 (48 Halsbury's Statutes (4th Edn) VALUE ADDED TAX) and Paragraphs 311 [3416], 312.1 [3417] ante.

**[3426]**

**317.2    Standard rate VAT on supply of partially completed building**
As already noted[1], to the extent that the developer's sale to the fund is of the freehold
interest in a partially completed building the sale is automatically standard rated.

1     See Paragraph 313.1 [3420] ante.

[3427]

**317.3    Standard rate VAT on supply of construction and letting services**
The developer's supply of construction and letting services under a forward funding
agreement to the fund is chargeable to VAT at the standard rate[1] with the consequence
that it is able to recover any input tax charged to it in relation to goods and services
supplied to it by the contractor and/or by members of its professional team. Under
forward sale/purchase, construction services are not separately identified as only the
completed building will be sold, thus giving rise to an automatic standard rated supply
in the case of a freehold. In so far as let, the same applies to that letting.

1     See Paragraphs 313.1 and 313.2 [3420] ante.

[3428]

**317.4    Fund's option to tax supply on letting to tenant**
The position is the same whether the financing was by way of forward funding or forward
sale/purchase. It is implicit that if the fund grants a lease it has an appropriate interest in
the completed building to enable it to do so. Conventionally, the fund will let the
property under the terms of what is commonly known as an 'institutional lease' (ie a lease
which is traditionally, but perhaps no longer 'usually', for a 25-year term at a rack rent
with periodic upward-only rent reviews and with full repairing covenants on the part of
the tenant). Provided that the fund elects to waive exemption[1], the fund is able to recover
any input tax charged to it by the developer in relation to the supply of land (where
appropriate) and supplies of construction and 'letting' services. Although, in practice, the
fund's decision as to whether or not it should elect will depend upon a variety of factors
including (inter alia) its perception of the market and its future intentions in relation to
the property, as a basic premise, if the tenant is a fully taxable trader and is able to recover
all input tax charged to it, the fund is able to charge VAT in relation to the rent without
that charge resulting in irrecoverable input tax for the tenant.

1     See Paragraph 312.1 [3417] ante.

[3429]

**317.5    Exempt or partially exempt tenants**
It is possible, however, that the fund will not want to exercise the option to tax either, for
example, because the tenant is in any case an exempt or partially exempt trader with a good
covenant and a strong bargaining position or because the property is located in an area in
which there is a high density of exempt or partially exempt traders who are likely to be resistant
to paying VAT in addition to rent. In this respect, it is conceivable that in certain localities there
may be a 'dual market' in commercial properties with differing capital values being attributed
to similar properties depending upon whether the owner or landlord of them has exercised its
option to tax in relation to the building. The ability to revoke an election after 20 years[1] is
probably unlikely to affect the fund's decision as to whether or not to exercise the option to tax.

1     See the Value Added Tax Act 1994 Sch 10 para 3(5) as substituted by SI 1995/279.

[3430]

### 317.6   Recovery of input tax by the fund

On the face of it (tax consequences for the developer apart), if the fund does not elect in relation to its supplies on letting the completed building or if it occupies the building for its own exempt use, it will not be able to recover any VAT on its own costs relating to the land purchase and the subsequent development. However, if the fund either occupies the building itself for a taxable purpose, or leases or sells the building subject to VAT (by exercising the option), within ten years of the building first being brought into use, the capital goods scheme[1] allows at least some of the VAT input tax to be recovered. Basically, the sooner the building is brought into taxable use or leased or sold subject to VAT (by occupation or exercising the option) the more VAT input tax is recoverable. If the 'going concern' rules[2] apply to the sale by the fund, the capital goods scheme rules operate so as to pass any future VAT input tax recovery on to the buyer[3].

**[3431]**

1     The capital goods scheme applies to developments costing more than £250,000: see the Value Added Tax Regulations 1995, SI 1995/2518 regs 112–116. As to the scheme generally, see vol 38(1) (2000 Reissue) SALE OF LAND Paragraph 27 [56]. As to capital items generally see *Scott and McLellan: VAT and Property* para [8.191] et seq.

2     Value Added Tax (Special Provisions) Order 1995, SI 1995/1268 art 5 as amended by SI 1998/760. As to the 'going concern' rules generally see vol 38(1) (2000 Reissue) SALE OF LAND Paragraph 28 [57] et seq. As to the interaction of the 'going concern' rules and the capital goods scheme see *Scott and McLellan: VAT and Property* para [2.384].

3     SI 1995/2518 reg 114(7) as substituted by SI 1997/1614.

**[3432]**

### 318   Essential VAT differences between forward funding and forward sale/purchase

In VAT terms, it should be noted that there are certain VAT consequences upon the distinction between forward funding and forward sale/purchase. Attention has been drawn to the changes made by the Finance Act 1997 Section 37 whereby land may be deemed exempt land, giving rise to a disapplication of the developer's election[1]. Because, under forward funding, the developer sells the land to the fund before commencement of the development, the developer's election ceases to be relevant in context. It has no continuing interest in the land and both pays and charges VAT in the course of its business of providing the building. Contrast the developer under a forward sale/purchase agreement who is providing the land with the completed building upon it.

1     As to which see Paragraph 312.7 [3418] ante.

**[3433]**

### 319   Summary

The foregoing commentary is not intended to be a complete analysis of the various VAT aspects which arise in relation to the funding of a property development: every case is different and it is important in negotiating the terms of any forward funding or forward sale/purchase agreement that full consideration is given to both the developer's and the fund's VAT positions having regard to prevailing law and the individual characteristics of the transaction under review.

**[3434]–[3440]**

# *Forms and Precedents*

## 80
### Forward funding agreement[1]

**DATE:** *(insert date)*

## PARTIES

(1)    The Fund: *(name)* [company number *(number)*] [of *(address) or* whose registered office is at *(address)*]

(2)    The Developer: *(name)* [company number *(number)*] [of *(address) or* whose registered office is at *(address)*]

[(3)    The Surety: *(name)* [company number *(number)*] [of *(address) or* whose registered office is at *(address)*]]

## CONTENTS

**[3441]**

## A    DEFINITIONS AND INTERPRETATION

### 1    Definitions

In this Agreement unless the context otherwise requires the following expressions (listed in alphabetical order) shall have the following meanings:

**1.1    'Agreement for Lease'**
any agreement entered into (inter alia) by the Developer for the grant of a Lease

**1.2    'Approved Scheme'**
as defined in clause 9

**1.3    'Architect'**
*(name and address)* or such other firm as may be approved by the Fund[2]

**1.4    'Balancing Payment'**
as defined in clause 47

1.5     **'Building Contract'**
[the contract dated *(date)* or] such [other] contract with the Contractor for
carrying out the Works as may be approved by the Fund

[1.6     **'Capital Value'**
the value of the Project as calculated under clause 48]

1.7     **'Charge Dates'**
[1 January 1 April 1 July and 1 October in each year]

1.8     **'clause'**
a clause of this Agreement

1.9     **'Code'**
the Code of Measuring Practice of the Royal Institution of Chartered Surveyors
and Incorporated Society of Valuers and Auctioneers [Edition 4, 1993]

1.10     **'Communication'**
any notice application approval certificate or other communication from or on
behalf of one Party to another pursuant to this Agreement

1.11     **'Consents'**
all the planning permissions listed building consents building regulations
consents fire officer approvals and other permissions approvals licences and
similar consents (including any modifications from time to time) which are
necessary to enable the Approved Scheme to be implemented without breach
of any statute or lawful requirement of any competent authority

**[3442]**

1.12     **'Consultants'**[3]
the Architect Environmental Consultant Mechanical and Electrical Engineer
Planning Supervisor Quantity Surveyor and Structural Engineer [*(add titles of
any other consultants already appointed and include relevant definitions of those titles in
alphabetical order as appropriate)*] and such other professional advisers as may be
approved by the Fund

1.13     **'Consultants' Warranty'**[4]
a deed to be entered into by each Consultant with the Fund and/or any Tenant
[substantially] in one or other as the case may be of the forms annexed

1.14     **'Contractor'**
*(name company number and address)* or such other building contractor as may be
approved by the Fund

1.15     **'Contractor's Warranty'**
a deed to be entered into by the Contractor with the Fund and/or any Tenant
[substantially] in one or other as the case may be of the forms annexed

1.16     **'Defects Liability Period'**
[12 months] from the [Practical Completion Date][5]

1.17     **'Deleterious Materials'**
materials not in accordance with British Standards or which are generally
known to be deleterious at the time of incorporation in the Works [and any
materials specifically mentioned in any Consultant's Warranty or Contractor's
Warranty][6]

**[3443]**

[1.18     **'Development'**
*(number)* square metres [Gross [External *or* Internal] *or* Net Internal] Area of
[industrial *or* warehouse *or* office] premises][7]

1.19     **'Documents'**
the documents listed in the First Schedule[8]

1.20     **'End Date'**
*(insert date)*[9]

**1.21**   **'Environmental Consultant'**
*(name and address)* or such other firm as may be approved by the Fund

**1.22**   **'Event of Default'**
as defined in clause 52

**1.23**   **'Excepted Risks'**

1.23.1   ionising radiations or contamination by radioactivity from any nuclear fuel or from any nuclear waste from the combustion of nuclear fuel

1.23.2   radioactive toxic explosive or other hazardous properties of any explosive nuclear assembly or nuclear component

1.23.3   pressure waves caused by aircraft or other aerial devices travelling at sonic or supersonic speeds

1.23.4   any other risks excepted by the insurance provisions of the Building Contract[10]

**1.24**   **'Fees'**
all fees referred to together with reasonable disbursements

**1.25**   **'Finance Charge'**
as defined in clause 45[11]

**1.26**   **'Full Reinstatement Value'**
the cost of complete reinstatement (assuming total destruction) allowing for inflation during the period of reinstatement the costs of demolition and site clearance and professional Fees including VAT where applicable on all such costs[12]

**[1.27**   **'Fund'**
includes the successors in title to the Fund of the Site [or any phase] and its assigns]

**1.28**   **'Gross [External *or* Internal] Area'**
The Gross [External *or* Internal] Area of the Development [or the relevant phase] as measured in accordance with the Code[13]

[3444]

**1.29**   **'Insolvent'**

1.29.1   in relation to a company that:

1.29.1.1   it is deemed unable to pay its debts as defined in the Insolvency Act 1986 Section 123 (referred to as 'the Act' in the remainder of this definition)

1.29.1.2   a proposal is made for a voluntary arrangement under Part I of the Act

1.29.1.3   a petition is presented for an administration order under Part II of the Act

1.29.1.4   a receiver or manager is appointed whether under Part III of the Act (including an administrative receiver) or otherwise

1.29.1.5   it goes into liquidation as defined in Section 247(2) of the Act (other than a voluntary winding up which is first approved by the Fund and is for the sole purpose of amalgamation or reconstruction while solvent)

1.29.1.6   a provisional liquidator is appointed under Section 135 of the Act

1.29.1.7   a proposal is made for a scheme of arrangement under the Companies Act 1985 Section 425 as amended

1.29.2 and in relation to an individual that:

  1.29.2.1 an application is made for an interim order or a proposal is made for a voluntary arrangement under Part VIII of the Act

  1.29.2.2 a bankruptcy petition is presented to the court or his circumstances are such that a bankruptcy petition could be presented under Part IX of the Act

  1.29.2.3 he enters into a deed of arrangement[14]

**1.30** **'Insured Risks'**

 1.30.1 fire lightning explosion storm tempest flood

 1.30.2 bursting or overflowing of water tanks apparatus or pipes

 1.30.3 earthquake

 1.30.4 aircraft and other aerial devices or articles dropped from them

 1.30.5 riot and civil commotion

  but excluding Excepted Risks

**1.31** **'Interest Rate'**

[4%] above the base lending rate from time to time of *(name of bank)* [compounded with rests at each Charge Date]

**[3445]**

**1.32** **'Lease'**

as defined in clause 37.1

**1.33** **'Letter of Appointment'**

the written terms under which a Consultant is appointed[15]

**1.34** **'Letting Agents'**

*(name and address)* or such other firm as may be approved by the Fund[16]

**1.35** **'Letting Policy'**

the letting policy so titled annexed to this Agreement[17]

**1.36** **'Maximum Commitment'**[18]

*(insert amount)*

**[1.37** **'Net Internal Area'**

the Net Internal Area of the Development [or the relevant phase] as measured in accordance with the Code[19]]

**1.38** **'Net Rental Income'**

[the initial annual rent[s] exclusive of VAT payable under [the *or* each] Lease[s] *or* the [average *or* highest] annual rent exclusive of VAT payable under [the *or* each] Lease[s] during the first [5] years of the term] disregarding any rent payable to reimburse the cost of insurance or services provided by the landlord

**1.39** **'Parties'**

the Developer and the Fund [and the Surety]

**1.40** **'Planning Supervisor'**

*(name and address)* or such other [person *or* firm] as may be approved by the Fund and appointed for the purpose the Construction (Design and Management) Regulations 1994[20]

**1.41** **'Plans'**

the plans and drawings for the Development referred to in clause 9.1 comprising the Approved Scheme

**1.42** **'Practical Completion'**

practical completion of the whole of the Works pursuant to the Building Contract

**1.43** **'Practical Completion Date'**

the date of Practical Completion as certified under the Building Contract[21]

**[1.44** **'Programme'**

as defined in clause 11]

**1.45** **'Project'**
all aspects of Site acquisition demolition site preparation (including remediation of contamination) design carrying out completion and letting of the Development as contemplated by this Agreement

**1.46** **'Project Costs'**
as defined in clause 41

**1.47** **'Project Account'**
as defined in clause 46[22]

[3446]

**1.48** **'Quantity Surveyor'**
*(name and address)* or such other firm as may be approved by the Fund

**1.49** **'Relevant Event'**[23]

1.49.1    force majeure

1.49.2    exceptionally adverse weather conditions

1.49.3    loss or damage occasioned by Insured Risks

1.49.4    civil commotion local combination of workmen strike or lockout affecting any of the trades engaged in the Works or in the preparation manufacture or transportation of goods or materials required for the Works or in the preparation of the design of the Works

1.49.5    the exercise after the date of this Agreement of any statutory power which restricts the availability or use of labour essential to the proper carrying out of the Works or prevents or delays goods materials fuel or energy essential to the proper carrying out of the Works

1.49.6    the carrying out by a local authority or statutory or other undertaking of work pursuant to its statutory obligations in relation to the Works or failure to carry out such work

1.49.7    delay (which both the Developer and Contractor have taken all practicable steps to avoid or reduce) consequent upon a change in statutory requirements since the date of this Agreement

[1.49.8    unreasonable delay on the part of the Surveyor in carrying out his functions under this Agreement]

1.49.9    delay in receipt of any necessary permission or approval of any statutory body which the Developer and the Contractor have taken all practicable steps to avoid or reduce

1.49.10   the use or threat of terrorism and/or the activity of the relevant authorities in dealing with such use or threat

**1.50** **'Schedule'**
a schedule to this Agreement

**1.51** **'Services'**
facilities such as water gas electricity drainage and telecommunications which are in or pass through over or under the Development and the relevant pipes wires ducts and other conduits

**1.52** **'Settlement Date'**
the date when [a Lease has *or* Leases have] been granted in respect of the whole of the Development (or all parts of it designed for letting) [and the full initial rent reserved has become payable][24]

[3447]

**1.53** **'Site'**
*(insert a short description of the land)*

**1.54** **'Site Completion Date'**
as defined in clause 4

1.55    **'Specification'**
the specification annexed including the bills of quantities [intended to be] comprised in the Building Contract

1.56    **'Structural Engineer'**
*(name and address)* or such other firm as may be approved by the Fund

1.57    **'Sub-contractor'**
a sub-contractor to the main contractor under the Building Contract having a design responsibility[25]

1.58    **'Sub-contractor's Warranty'**
a deed to be entered into by a Sub-Contractor with the Fund and/or any tenant [substantially] in one or other as the case may be of the forms annexed

1.59    **'Surveyor'**
*(name and address)* or such other [firm *or* surveyor] [of similar standing *or* suitably qualified and] nominated by the Fund

1.60    **'Target Completion Date'**
*(insert date)*

1.61    **'Target Rent'**
[*(amount)* a year *or* *(amount)* per square metre per annum of [Gross [External *or* Internal] *or* Net Internal] Area exclusive of VAT[26]

1.62    **'Total Project Costs'**
the final debit balance on the Project Account when all Project Costs due from or payable by the Fund have been debited to the Project Account including VAT which is in the [reasonable] opinion of the Fund irrecoverable and after all credits have been made to the Project Account (including recoveries of VAT) which are [reasonably] anticipated [subject nevertheless to clause 49]

1.63    **'VAT'**
value added tax

1.64    **'Working Day'**
any day except Saturdays Sundays and Bank or other Public Holidays

1.65    **'Works'**
the works of [demolition site preparation (including remediation of contamination) and] construction of the Development

1.66    **'Works Completion Certificate'**
as defined in clause 30[27]

1.67    **'Works Completion Date'**
as defined in clause 30

2       **Interpretation**
[2.1    The Law of Property Act 1925 Section 61 applies to this Agreement]
2.2     Reference to a statute includes any amendment modification consolidation or re-enactment of that statute and any statutory instrument regulation or order made under that statute and for the time being in force

[3448]

**B      SALE AND PURCHASE**

**3      Contract for sale**[28]

[The Developer will sell and the Fund will purchase the Site [on the conditions of sale set out in the Second Schedule] *or* The Developer and the Fund have entered into a sale contract of even date in relation to the Site made between (1) the Developer and (2) the Fund]

**4      Site Completion Date**

The date upon which the Site is transferred to the Fund will be the Site Completion Date

**5      Conditionality**

Clauses 6–53 of this Agreement do not come into force until the Site Completion Date[29]

**[3449]**

**C      PRELIMINARIES**

**6      Approvals**

6.1        All and any applications for any consents or approvals made by the Developer
           to the Fund shall
           6.1.1        be in writing
           6.1.2        be made to the Surveyor
[6.2       Every such consent or approval shall not be unreasonably withheld save where
           expressed to the contrary in this Agreement]
[6.3       Notwithstanding clause 6.2 where the Fund considers that to grant any consent
           or approval would have effect to materially alter the appearance restrict the user
           increase the cost diminish the lettable area or reduce the value of the Project the
           Fund may refuse such consent or approval]

**7      Consultants[30]**

7.1        The Consultants named in this Agreement are approved by the Fund
7.2        The Developer will not appoint any other professional adviser as a Consultant
           without the Fund's prior approval but will appoint such further Consultants as
           the Fund may reasonably require
7.3        The Developer will not dismiss a Consultant without the Fund's prior approval
7.4        The Developer will appoint each Consultant under a Letter of Appointment in
           a form first approved by the Fund at the same time obtaining from him in favour
           of the Fund a Consultant's Warranty

**8      Contractor**

8.1        The Contractor named in this Agreement is approved by the Fund
8.2        The Developer will not dismiss the Contractor nor engage any other building
           contractor or nominate any sub-contractor without the Fund's prior approval
8.3        The Developer will engage the Contractor under [the Building Contract *or* a
           building contract in a form first approved by the Fund[31]] at the same time
           obtaining from the Contractor in favour of the Fund a Contractor's Warranty

**9      Approved Scheme[32]**

9.1        The plans and drawings for the Development and the Specification [annexed to
           this Agreement *or* identified by the following numbers *(numbers)* or initialled by
           the Parties] have been approved by the Fund and comprise the Approved
           Scheme
9.2        To the extent that the designs for the Development are not described in full in
           the Approved Scheme such designs will be submitted to the Fund for the Fund's
           approval before construction of the relevant part of the Development is
           commenced provided that no such approval will in any way affect the
           responsibilities of the Developer under this Agreement

9.3 The Approved Scheme will not be varied without the Fund's approval [(which may be refused at the Fund's discretion)] and the expression 'Approved Scheme' means from time to time the Approved Scheme as originally approved incorporating all approved variations (if any)

**[3450]**

**10 Consents**[33]

10.1 The Developer will use all reasonable endeavours to obtain the Consents as soon as practicable submitting each application to the Fund for approval and obtaining such approval before application is made and promptly notifying the Fund of the outcome of each application supplying copies of any documents issued

10.2 The Developer will not implement any Consent until it has been approved by the Fund

**[11 The Programme**[34]

11.1 [The Programme is the [bar chart] programme annexed to this Agreement showing the estimated duration of each stage of the Works and when each stage including Practical Completion is due to be achieved

*or*

The Developer will prepare as soon as practicable [and in any event within *(time limit)*] a programme [in bar chart form] which will be the Programme for the purposes of this Agreement showing the estimated duration of each stage of the Works and when each stage including Practical Completion is due to be achieved]

11.2 The Developer will not vary the Programme except as provided in this Agreement and the expression 'the Programme' means the Programme as from time to time so varied]

**[3451]**

**D WORKS**

**12 Licence**[35]

12.1 The Fund grants to the Developer and those working for or on behalf of the Developer in relation to the Project a non-exclusive licence to enter the Site to enable the Developer to perform its obligations under this Agreement

12.2 Legal possession of the Site remains vested in the Fund

**13 General requirements**[36]

The Developer will carry out the Works:

13.1 in a proper and workmanlike manner

13.2 with good quality and suitable materials

13.3 in accordance with the Approved Scheme

13.4 in compliance with the Consents

13.5 diligently and expeditiously [in accordance with the Programme] in order to achieve Practical Completion by the Target Completion Date

13.6 in compliance with all requirements of statute and all lawful requirements of local authorities and other competent authorities

[13.7 in accordance with all relevant codes of practice and British Standards]

13.8 in compliance with the Building Contract [and the Documents]

13.9    without infringement of any rights reservations covenants restrictions stipulations or other incumbrances binding upon or affecting the Site

[13.10   to the [reasonable] satisfaction of the Fund]

## [14    Contaminated Land[37]

The [Third] Schedule shall have effect in relation to environmental matters [and] contaminated land [and remediation]]

## 15    Delay[38]

15.1    If by reason of a Relevant Event the Developer considers that delay will be caused to [the Programme or to] the Target Completion Date the Fund will upon application by the Developer supported by such evidence as the Fund may [reasonably] require [and the advice of the appropriate Consultant] allow such amendment to [the Programme or] the Target Completion Date as may [in its opinion be appropriate *or* be reasonable] after taking into account any extent to which such delay has been caused by any act default or omission of the Developer but under no circumstances will the Target Completion Date be postponed beyond the End Date

15.2    If the Developer fails to complete the Works by the Target Completion Date as extended by clause 15.1 the Developer will pay or allow to the Fund specified (or liquidated and ascertained) damages[39] at the rate of *(amount)* per [day *or* week] for the period between the Target Completion Date as so extended and the Works Completion Date

**[3452]**

## 16    Insurance[40]

### 16.1    General requirements

16.1.1   The Developer will effect or secure and maintain the insurance mentioned in this clause:

    16.1.1.1   with an insurance office [and on terms *or* under policies whose terms exclusions and conditions have first been] approved by the Fund

    16.1.1.2   naming the Fund as one of the joint insured parties

    16.1.1.3   from Site Completion Date until the End Date or (if earlier) until the Practical Completion Date

    16.1.1.4   under policies [copies of] which are to be produced to the Fund [on demand *or* within 7 days of issue] together with evidence that current premiums have been paid

and the Developer will not permit any variation of insurance cover without the Fund's prior approval and will immediately notify the Fund of any endorsements or other amendments to the relevant policies received from the insurers and will from time to time effect any further insurance which may in the Fund's [reasonable] opinion be prudent

16.1.2   For so long as the insurance prescribed by the Building Contract remains in force and to the extent that it complies with clause 16.1.1 (including both the Developer and the Fund as the named insured) then such insurance shall suffice for the purposes of clause 16.1.1

### 16.2    The Development

The Works all materials structures and buildings on Site and (when completed) the Development will be insured for Full Reinstatement Value against loss damage or destruction by any of the Insured Risks [and in an amount [of not less than £... million *or* first approved by the Fund]]

**16.3     Reinstatement**

In the event of any loss damage or destruction to the Works materials structures or buildings on Site or the completed Development:

16.3.1     the Developer will continue to carry out the Works unless the loss or damage is so extensive or of such a nature as to make this impossible or inadvisable

16.3.2     the Fund and the Developer will use all reasonable endeavours promptly to obtain the maximum payment of insurance moneys

16.3.3     all such insurance moneys will be paid to the Fund and credited by the Fund to the Project Account immediately upon receipt

16.3.4     the Developer will proceed diligently and expeditiously to reinstate the loss damage or destruction and to complete the Works in accordance with this Agreement

**16.4     Public liability**

Without prejudice to its liability to indemnify the Fund in accordance with clause 17 the Developer will take out and maintain insurance with a limit of indemnity of less than [£... million] for any one occurrence or series of occurrences arising out of the carrying out of the Works and in respect of damage to any property real or personal other than the Works arising out of the carrying out of the Works and caused by the negligence of the Developer the Contractor or any sub-contractor of the Contractor

**16.5     Failure**

If the Developer does not insure as required by this clause or fails to produce adequate evidence that such insurance is in force the Fund may itself effect such insurance cover as it may consider prudent and the cost of so doing will be a Project Cost

**16.6**     As and from the Practical Completion Date and notwithstanding that the Works Completion Date may not have arisen the Fund will insure the Development in accordance with the terms of the Lease the Developer indemnifying the Fund for the cost of so doing until the Works Completion Date[41]

**[3453]**

**17     Indemnity**

In addition to any claims which the Fund may have in relation to a breach of this Agreement the Developer will to the extent that moneys are not recovered from insurers indemnify the Fund in respect of any liability for the following matters in relation to the Project from Site Completion Date until the Practical Completion Date except to the extent that a lessee under a Lease is responsible to the Fund for such matters:

17.1     death or personal injury to any person arising out of the carrying out of the Works save to the extent that the same is due to any act or neglect of the Fund or any person for whom the Fund is responsible

17.2     injury or damage to any property real or personal other than the Works in so far as such injury or damage arises out of the carrying out of the Works and to the extent that the same is due to any negligence breach of statutory duty omission or default of the Developer the Contractor or a sub-contractor of the Developer

17.3     any liability in respect of and any fees or charges legally demandable under any Act of Parliament or any regulation or bye-law of any local authority or of any statutory undertaker in respect of the Works

17.4     the infringement of the rights of any third party in connection with the Site

17.5    all outgoings in connection with the Site

17.6    observing and performing all provisions contained or referred to in the
        Documents[42]

## 18    Third party rights[43]

18.1    The Developer will ensure that the rights and interests of third parties are not
        infringed by the Project and will with the prior approval of the Fund enter into
        such agreements relating to rights of light and other easements and party
        structures and pay such compensation as may be necessary (and the Fund will
        join in such agreements so far as necessary as owner of the Site)

18.2    Where the London Building Acts 1930–1939 the Party Wall, etc Act 1996 (or
        any re-enactment of them) apply the Developer will comply with (and issue all
        notices required under) those Acts in connection with the Development and
        will comply with the terms of any awards made pursuant to those Acts

                                                                              **[3454]**

## 19    Services

The Developer will with the Fund's prior approval negotiate such agreements with statutory
undertakers and others as may be required to secure for the Development all Services
required and the diversion in a satisfactory manner of all Services which are at Site
Completion Date located in a position which would interfere with the Project (and the Fund
will join in such agreements as are approved by it and so far as necessary as owner of the Site)

## 20    Site management[44]

The Developer will secure that:

20.1    the Site is at all times secured as fully as may be reasonably practicable against
        unauthorised entry

20.2    no material goods or equipment is brought deposited or stored on the Site
        except that from time to time properly required for the Works

20.3    all material stored on the Site is kept in a secure compound and adequately
        protected

20.4    all surplus material rubble rubbish and waste is properly cleared and removed
        from the Site when it is no longer required

20.5    the Site is maintained in a tidy condition and free from rubbish

20.6    there is no excavation of the Site or extraction of soil earth clay gravel sand or
        minerals except as required for the Works

20.7    proper precautions are taken for the safety of all persons upon or in the vicinity
        of the Site

20.8    there are no advertisements posters placards or signs affixed to displayed from on
        the boundaries of or on the Site except (with the prior approval of the Fund)
        those connected with the Project

20.9    the Works are carried out in a manner which does not cause a nuisance and
        causes the minimum of annoyance inconvenience and disturbance to owners or
        occupiers of neighbouring properties or members of the public [and in
        particular no work will be carried out except [between the hours of 8 am and
        6 pm Mondays to Fridays] [and 8 am and 1 pm on Saturdays]]

20.10   proper provision is made for the support and use of land walls roads footpaths
        and buildings adjoining adjacent or near to the Site and for the protection of all
        Services

20.11   all debris is removed from such roads and footpaths and the proper requirements
        of the highways and other competent authorities are observed and performed

20.12    hoardings of sufficient height are erected around the Site
20.13    good efficient and well maintained plant and equipment are used on the Site
20.14    proper arrangements are made with the relevant authorities for the provision of
         water gas electricity telephone and other services required for the Works
20.15    the requirements of highways and other competent authorities are duly met
20.16    the Works are maintained in good repair and condition

[3455]

## 21    Deleterious materials

The Developer will [use all reasonable endeavours to] ensure that no Deleterious
Materials are used in the Works

## 22    Deduction scheme[45]

22.1     In this clause 22 'the Act' means the Income and Corporation Taxes Act 1988
         and any amendment or any re-enactment of that Act and 'the Regulations'
         means the Income Tax (Sub-contractors in the Construction Industry)
         Regulations 1993[46] and any amendment or any replacement of those regulations

22.2     Not later than 21 days before the first or next payment is due from the Fund to
         the Developer the Developer will produce to the Fund:
         22.2.1    evidence satisfactory to the Fund that the payments under clause 43
                   (Claims for payment) and the Developer fall within regulations made
                   under Section 559(3A) of the Act or
         22.2.2    the Developer's current tax certificate issued under Section 561 of
                   the Act
         and the Fund will within 7 days of the date of such production confirm to the
         Developer in writing such production and the Developer's satisfaction or non-
         satisfaction of the Regulations or
         22.2.3    (where the Developer is a company which is the user of a tax
                   certificate as prescribed by the Regulations) a document as referred to
                   in those Regulations referable to the Developer's current tax certificate
         and the Fund will within 7 days of such production confirm to the Developer
         in writing such production and that the Developer has or has not reason to
         doubt the correctness of the information shown on the said document

22.3     Subject to the foregoing the Fund shall be entitled to make payment without
         the statutory deduction under Section 559(4) of the Act

22.4     The Developer shall forthwith notify the Fund of any changes in circumstances
         including the withdrawal or cancellation of the Developer's tax certificate

22.5     The Fund shall be entitled to make the statutory deduction under Section
         559(4) if it is of the view (acting reasonably) that it should be made

22.6     The Developer shall indemnify the Fund against any loss or expense arising
         from any inaccurate statement or information provided to the Fund in relation
         to any of the matters covered by this clause

[22.7    The Developer will ensure that the Building Contract incorporates proper
         provision for the operation of the deduction scheme for contractors and sub-
         contractors contained in the Act and the Regulations]

[3456]

## [23    Archaeological antiquities[47]

Subject always to the provisions of the Ancient Monuments and Archaeological Areas
Act 1979:
23.1     Any article of value or antiquity or remains of geological historical or
         archaeological interest on the Site will (as between the Developer and the Fund)
         belong to the Fund

23.2      If any such article is or remains are discovered the Developer will immediately inform the Fund and comply with the Fund's directions as to inspection protection and disposal of such article or remains]

**[3457]**

## E        ADMINISTRATION

### 24      The Surveyor[48]

The Fund has appointed the Surveyor to act as the agent of the Fund under this Agreement (unless otherwise expressly provided):

24.1      to consider and respond to applications for the Fund's approval
24.2      to monitor the performance of the Developer the Contractor and the Consultants
24.3      to issue certificates or otherwise indicate whether or not the Fund is satisfied with any matter
24.4      to issue and receive Communications on behalf of the Fund
24.5      to open and maintain the Project Account

and until notice is given to the contrary by the Fund the Developer is authorised and required to deal with and rely upon the Surveyor as the agent of the Fund in all such matters

### 25      Consultation

The Developer will in relation to the Project:

25.1      regularly inform consult report to and liaise with the Surveyor on all matters including all material measures taken and stages reached the general progress of the Works and any material problems or delays which have arisen or are likely to do so
25.2      promptly supply to the Surveyor copies of all relevant written material when it is received or produced by or on behalf of the Developer

**[3458]**

### 26      Information[49]

The following illustrate (but do not limit) the types of information to be supplied to the Surveyor under clause 25.2:

26.1      all plans and drawings the Specification structural calculations and other material from time to time comprising the Approved Scheme
26.2      applications for and correspondence relating to Consents and the outcome of such applications
26.3      Letters of Appointment
26.4      the Building Contract
26.5      lists of sub-contractors and suppliers
26.6      test certificates and specialist reports and surveys
26.7      valuations by the Quantity Surveyor
[26.8     Any written advice on contamination provided by the Environmental Consultant]
26.9      architect's instructions
26.10    minutes of all formal meetings (including site meetings design team meetings working party or project meetings)
26.11    [monthly] financial statements showing actual costs and updated forecasts of costs and cash flow

**27     Meetings**[50]

The Surveyor is entitled although not obliged to attend all formal meetings relating to the Project whether or not the Contractor or a Consultant or a Letting Agent is entitled to attend and will be given not less than [2] Working Days' notice (or in emergency as much notice as possible) of such meetings

**[3459]**

**28     Control**[51]

28.1     The Surveyor [and any duly authorised representative of the Fund] may upon reasonable notice (where practicable) at [any time *or* all reasonable times] enter the Site to carry out any inspection [test] or survey [or for any other [reasonable] purpose] connected with the Project but [he *or* they] will cause as little interference as practicable

28.2     If prior to Practical Completion the Surveyor gives notice to the Developer [on reasonable grounds] that any works or materials are not in accordance with the Approved Scheme or are not to the standard or the quality required by this Agreement the Developer will commence appropriate action to remove the defective works or materials and make good the defects as soon as practicable

28.3     The Surveyor will not issue any direct instructions to the Contractor or to any of the Consultants and will not communicate with the Contractor or with any of the Consultants except in an emergency or in a meeting where the Developer is represented but will (without prejudice to any Contractor's or Consultant's Warranty) address all other communications to the Developer

**29     Responsibility**

29.1     The Fund is relying on the Developer properly to carry out and complete the Project and the Developer warrants that it has the skill and experience required to carry out the Project[52]

29.2     No involvement by the Fund (whether through its Surveyor or otherwise) in considering whether or not to grant any consent or approval or issue certificates or in attending (or failing to attend) meetings or otherwise in supervising or omitting to supervise the Project in any way relieves or affects the duties of the Developer the Contractor or the Consultants in relation to the Project [except to the extent that the Fund or the Surveyor causes loss by imposing a requirement with which the Developer must under the terms of this Agreement comply but which is inconsistent with the recommendations of the Contractor or a Consultant][53]

29.3     The Developer will duly observe and perform all provisions of the Building Contract and of all Letters of Appointment and other agreements relating to the Project on the part of the Developer as employer to be observed or performed and (save with the approval of the Fund) secure the observance and performance by the other parties to such agreements of the provisions on their part to be observed or performed[54]

29.4     None of the provisions of the Building Contract or of any Letter of Appointment shall be varied or waived nor will any action to secure the compliance with such provisions be discharged settled or compromised without the approval of the Fund [which may be withheld in any such case at the Fund's discretion]

**[3460]**

**F     COMPLETION**

**30     Works completion**[55]

30.1     When the Works have reached Practical Completion in accordance with the terms of this Agreement and the Building Contract the Surveyor will issue a Works Completion Certificate to that effect and the date stated in the Works Completion Certificate is the Works Completion Date

[30.2     The Surveyor will not refuse to issue a Works Completion Certificate if minor defects in the Works exist of such a nature and number that they would not prevent the issue by the Architect of a certificate of Practical Completion under the Building Contract]

**31     Procedure**

31.1     The Parties will use their reasonable endeavours to ensure that the Works Completion Date and the Practical Completion Date are contemporaneous[56]

31.2     If the Developer gives to the Fund not less than [10] Working Days' notice of the date of the Site meeting at which the Architect is expected to decide whether Practical Completion has occurred the Surveyor will attend such meeting and endeavour to agree with the Architect whether or not it is appropriate to issue a certificate of Practical Completion under the Building Contract (but without prejudice to the Architect's professional discretion and duties under the Building Contract)

31.3     If he considers that the Works are not substantially complete in accordance with this Agreement the Surveyor will give his reasons orally at the relevant Site meeting and confirm these reasons in writing to the Developer within [3] Working Days stating what further Works are required

31.4     The Developer will carry out such further Works as soon as possible and then give to the Surveyor reasonable notice of a further Site meeting so that the procedure set out in this clause may be repeated (save as regards Practical Completion under the Building Contract if a Certificate of Practical Completion has been issued) as often as necessary until the Works Completion Certificate is issued

31.5     If the Works are substantially complete in accordance with this Agreement the Surveyor will issue the Works Completion Certificate within [5] Working Days of the relevant Site meeting

**[3461]**

**32     Defects**

Without prejudice to all other rights and remedies of the Fund the Developer will make good as soon as practicable all defects which may appear in the Development and are notified to the Developer before the end of the Defects Liability Period and which are due to the failure of the Developer to comply with its obligations under this Agreement or to frost occurring before the Practical Completion Date (or the Works Completion Date if later) and which (if inconsistent with the foregoing) the Architect has notified the Contractor should be carried out under the defects liability provisions of the Building Contract

**33     Completion documents**

Within [one month] following the Works Completion Date the Developer will supply to the Fund:

33.1     three sets of 'as built' Plans of the Development

33.2     maintenance manuals and manufacturer's warranties in relation to all plant and equipment installed in the Development

33.3    such confirmations as the Fund may reasonably require that no Deleterious Materials have been used in the Development

33.4    the health and safety file

**[34    Plans**

Within [one month] following the Works Completion Date the Developer will either:

34.1    procure the assignment absolutely to the Fund of the full copyright of the Plans to which the Developer may be entitled or

34.2    take such other steps effectually to procure for the Fund the full right and entitlement to use on licence without further payment or liability for further payment the Plans for the purposes only of maintaining repairing and renewing the Development and execute all such deeds and documents as the Fund may reasonably require effectually to vest such rights in the Fund]

**35    Proceedings[57]**

35.1    The Fund may at any time following expiry of the Defects Liability Period and the completion of all related remedial works require the Developer to assign to the Fund (in a form approved by the Fund) such rights as the Developer may have against the Contractor or any Consultant and in so far as necessary the Developer shall make application to the Contractor and/or any such Consultant as the case may be for any requisite consent and the Developer shall use all reasonable endeavours to obtain the same

35.2    In so far as assignment is not permitted or consent is not forthcoming the Fund may in the alternative commence prosecute or defend as the case may be any relevant proceedings in the name and on behalf of the Developer and in so far as the Developer is already entitled thereto shall pay to the Developer any costs and/or damages received to which the Developer may be entitled after counterclaim or set-off in relation to the Fund and in priority only after the interests of the Fund

**[3462]**

**G    LETTING**

**[36    Letting[58]**

36.1    The Developer shall in consultation with the Fund [use all reasonable endeavours to] negotiate the letting of the Development [as quickly as possible] and for this purpose will instruct the Letting Agents

36.2    The Developer shall [(except in so far as the Letting Agents expressly advise in writing or as the Fund may otherwise approve)] comply with the Letting Policy

36.3    The Developer shall not vary the Letting Policy except upon the written advice of the Letting Agents and with the approval of the Fund [which may be withheld at the Fund's discretion]

36.4    The Development is if possible to be let as a whole but if that is not achieved [6 months] after the Works Completion Date the Fund will permit the letting of the Development in not more than [3] parts [but under no circumstances will a Lease of less than one complete floor (excluding common parts) be allowed]

[36.5   Nothing will prevent the Fund from negotiating in its own right a Lease or Leases]]

**37      Lease**[59]

37.1    A Lease is to be [substantially] on the terms of the form of lease annexed [and
        as specified by the Fund] and will:

        37.1.1     be for a term of [not less than] [25] years [and comprising [the
                whole *or* a lettable [portion *or* portions] of the] [Development]]

        37.1.2     be at a rent to be first approved in writing by the Fund as the best
                rent reasonably obtainable without taking a fine or premium [[and
                with the view to achieving *or* at not less than] the Target Rent]

        37.1.3     provide for upward only rent reviews at intervals of not more than
                [5] years

        [37.1.4    be exclusive of outgoings insurance premiums and service charges]

        [37.1.5    be subject to a full repairing liability covenant]

        [37.1.6    contain such other provisions as are consistent in all material respects
                in so far as reasonably practicable with the covenants conditions and
                provisions contained in the lease annexed]

        [37.1.7    be consistent [in all respects] with the Letting Policy]

[37.2   The Fund will be under no obligation to enter into a Lease the terms of which
        fetter its discretion whether or not to make an election to waive exemption for
        the purposes of VAT or which shall or may result in disapplication of an election
        to waive exemption or which may otherwise adversely affect the Fund's ability
        to recover input tax]

                                                                              **[3463]**


**38      Approval**[60]

The Developer must not enter into any Agreement for Lease nor will the Fund be
required to enter into any Lease or (for the purpose of granting the Lease) Agreement
for Lease until the Fund has [in its absolute discretion] approved:

38.1    the proposed tenant and any guarantors required by the Fund and

38.2    the terms of the Lease or Agreement for Lease


**39      The Fund's obligations**

39.1    Where the Developer has before the date of this Agreement entered into an
        Agreement for Lease approved by the Fund the Fund will execute and grant the
        Lease in accordance with the terms of that Agreement for Lease

39.2    Where the Developer has otherwise negotiated an Agreement for Lease
        approved by the Fund the Fund will at the request of the Developer enter into
        the same (the Developer doing likewise as developer) and thereafter execute and
        grant the Lease in accordance with the terms of that Agreement for Lease

39.3    Where the Developer has negotiated a Lease which is approved by the Fund and
        the tenant is entitled to grant of the same the Fund will execute and grant the
        Lease by the latest of the following dates:

        39.3.1     Works Completion Date

        39.3.2     [14] days after receipt of the engrossed Lease for execution

        39.3.3     [3 Working Days after] the date upon which the Fund receives the
                counterpart Lease executed by the tenant together with any initial
                payment of rent or other money due upon the grant of the Lease


**40      Unlet premises**[61]

The Developer will at its own expense maintain each part of the Development not let at
Works Completion Date in good and substantial repair and condition and pay all rates

insurance premiums and other outgoings relating to it in accordance with the terms of a Lease until such liabilities are assumed by a tenant under a Lease [or until the End Date whichever is earlier]

**[3464]**

## H     PROJECT COSTS

### 41     Types of Project Cost[62]

Project Costs comprise the following costs related to the Project [up to the limits shown (which are exclusive of any VAT charged in respect of them)]:

41.1     the cost to the Fund of acquiring the Site (including the purchase price stamp duty [any arrangement fees] and Land Registry fees) [not exceeding *(amount)*] [plus *(amount)* representing costs incurred by the Developer prior to Site Completion Date]

[41.2     the cost of demolition works [not exceeding *(amount)*]]

[41.3     the cost of decontamination of the Site [not exceeding *(amount)*]]

41.4     all payments to the Contractor under the Building Contract [not exceeding *(amount)* plus a retention of *(amount)*]

41.5     Consultants' Fees [not exceeding *(amount)*]

41.6     the Developer's legal Fees in relation to [the sale of the Site to the Fund and] the negotiation of this Agreement [not exceeding *(amount)*]

41.7     the Fund's legal Fees in relation to the acquisition of the Site [and the negotiation of this Agreement] [not exceeding *(amount)*]

[41.8     the Developer's surveyor's Fees in relation to the sale of the Site to the Fund [not exceeding *(amount)*]]

41.9     the Surveyor's [funding and/*or* acquisition] Fees [equal to …% of Capital Value]

41.10     the Surveyor's [monitoring and supervision] Fees [equal to …% of all sums payable under the Building Contract]

[41.11     the Developer's project management Fees [equal to …% of all sums payable under the Building Contract]]

41.12     Letting Agents' Fees on the grant of Leases

41.13     legal Fees of both the Developer and the Fund in relation to Agreements for Lease and Leases in so far as these are not recovered from tenants

[41.14     Legal fees of both the Developer and the Fund in relation to implementation of this Agreement and not otherwise provided for in this clause except as arising out of any dispute between the Developer and the Fund]

41.15     the cost of insurance as required under this Agreement whether effected by the Developer or the Fund

[41.16     the cost of entering into any agreements required pursuant to clauses 18 and 19]

[41.17     all outgoings payable in relation to the Site [including but not restricted to rates and other annual recurring and capital outgoings whether parliamentary parochial or otherwise]]

41.18     the costs of extinguishment or variation of any interests or rights in over or against the Site held by a person who by the lawful exercise of his powers could prevent or impede the carrying out or progress of the Works or the use and enjoyment of the Development

41.19     the costs of obtaining the Consents and dealing with the other matters set out in clause 10

41.20     the costs of repair maintenance and upkeep and the provision of Services

41.21     such other costs of the Developer properly incurred in relation to the Works as the Fund may [reasonably] allow [but not exceeding *(amount)*]

41.22    all moneys which the Fund expends [whether] following an Event of Default [or otherwise as permitted under this Agreement]

[41.23   Finance Charge but not exceeding *(amount)*]

41.24    VAT on costs listed in this clause 41 to the extent that it is not recovered by the Fund

**[3465]**

## 42    Treatment of Project Costs[63]

Project Costs will be treated in accordance with the following provisions:

42.1    Any expenditure attributable to the breach non-observance or non-performance of the obligations on the part of the Developer under this Agreement may at the discretion of the Fund be included

42.2    References to costs include incidental costs expenses and fees incurred

42.3    References to Fees include incidental disbursements incurred

42.4    Items of Project Costs will be allowable to the extent only that they are reasonably and properly incurred and of reasonable amount and all claims by the Developer for payment of items of Project Costs shall first be submitted to and approved by the Surveyor accordingly

**[3466]**

## 43    Claims for payment[64]

The Fund will pay or reimburse to the Developer as consideration for the Works items of Project Costs incurred or paid by the Developer together with VAT on those items only on the following basis:

43.1    That they are first approved by the Fund upon application by the Developer

43.2    No payment will be due after service of a notice of default under clause 53

43.3    Payment will not be made at less than [monthly] intervals nor (prior to Settlement Date) for amounts totalling less than [£5,000][65]

43.4    The Fund will make all payments by cheque sent by first class post [or by direct bank transfer] and the date of posting [or the date of transfer] will be the date of payment for the purposes of this Agreement

43.5    Unless the Fund otherwise agrees all payments will be made:

    43.5.1    direct to any creditor where the Developer has not paid that creditor's account and

    43.5.2    to the Developer [in respect of the purchase price of the Site and] to reimburse expenditure by the Developer

43.6    Payment of items of Project Costs properly due under this clause will if approved by the Surveyor be notified to the Developer (including the basis of calculation) and made not later than 5 days after application is made to the Surveyor for payment accompanied by:

    43.6.1    a duly completed VAT invoice for an amount equal to the payment or reimbursement claimed plus VAT showing the Developer as supplier to the Fund

    43.6.2    details of the net cost to the Developer of each item of Project Costs in respect of which payment or reimbursement is claimed and of any VAT on such items

    43.6.3    [copies of] all VAT and other invoices statements receipts or such other evidence of entitlement on the part of the Developer as the Surveyor may [reasonably] require

If not approved immediately the Surveyor shall nevertheless give notice to the Developer within such period of 5 days as to his reasons and the procedure shall be repeated as necessary

43.7     In relation to payments under the Building Contract the Surveyor may require production of the relevant interim certificate [and evidence that the Contractor has received all previous payments from the Fund to the Developer in respect of sums due under the Building Contract]

[43.8    The Fund will retain from all sums payable to the Contractor against the production of Architect's interim certificates the amount shown in the relevant interim certificate as a retention [or [5%] of the value of the relevant interim certificate if greater] and in so far as the Building Contract prescribes place the same on deposit one half of such retention will be paid to the Contractor upon Practical Completion and the balance 12 months after Practical Completion Date or when (if later) all defects in the Works have been made good to the Fund's reasonable satisfaction][66]

[3467]

## 44     Maximum commitment

44.1     The Fund is not required to make any further payment in so far as the debit balance on the Project Account exceeds the Maximum Commitment [nor in respect of any specific item of Project Costs when the limit for items of that nature has been reached]

44.2     The Developer will perform all obligations under this Agreement at its own expense where the Fund is not required to make a payment in respect of such obligations

## 45     Finance charge[67]

45.1     The Fund will levy a charge (a 'Finance Charge') for each day that the Project Account shows a debit balance such charge being [10/365% per day] of such debit balance

45.2     On each Charge Date and (if it is not a Charge Date) on the Settlement Date the Finance Charge levied for each day from but excluding the preceding Charge Date (if any) up to and including the current Charge Date (or Settlement Date if appropriate) will be aggregated and such aggregate will:

45.2.1     [if within the limit set by clause 41.23 and] subject to clauses 43.2 and 44.1 be debited to the Project Account and

45.2.2     in so far as the Maximum Commitment may be exceeded be paid by the Developer immediately on demand and will if not so paid carry interest from the relevant Charge Date until so paid at the Interest Rate (as well after as before any judgment)

[3468]

## 46     Project account[68]

46.1     The Fund will operate and maintain until the liability of the Fund to make a payment under this Agreement has ceased an account ('the Project Account') to which all payments (except any Balancing Payments) by the Fund under this Agreement (including VAT paid by the Fund) and (if appropriate) the Finance Charge will be debited and to which will be credited all VAT recovered by the Fund which is directly attributable to the Project [and] any insurance moneys received in respect of insured loss to the Development [and income arising from the [Site *or* Development]] received by the Fund (but net of any income or corporation tax on such amount payable by the Fund) in respect of any period between Site Completion Date and Settlement Date

[46.2    The Fund shall also credit to the Project Account any rent received under a Lease [and any other income arising from the Development] [and whether or not any Settlement Date has meanwhile arisen in respect of any phase] to the extent of any Finance Charge arising for or within similar period the excess over (if any) belonging to the Fund absolutely][69]

46.3     The Fund will be entitled to pay and debit directly to the Project Account all Project Costs (including any VAT) which would otherwise be the liability of the Fund (such as stamp duty and Fees payable to the Fund's advisers) but will as soon as practicable notify the Developer of any such payments and produce copies of any relevant invoices

46.4     in so far as the Maximum Commitment has been exceeded the Developer shall indemnify the Fund for all such items of Project Costs mentioned in the last foregoing clause (together with interest (if any) arising under clause 45.2.2)

[46.5    The Fund will submit to the Developer a statement of the Project Account as at each [Charge Date] within [10] Working Days after each [Charge Date]][70]

**[3469]**


**I       PROFIT**

**47      Entitlement**[71]

If the Settlement Date precedes the End Date the Developer may be entitled to a further payment from the Fund ('Balancing Payment') as further consideration for the Works

**48      Calculation**[72]

48.1     [The Balancing Payment is the amount (if any) by which the Net Rental Income multiplied by [16] exceeds the Total Project Costs

*or*

The Balancing Payment is the amount (if any) by which Capital Value exceeds Total Project Costs where 'Capital Value' means:

48.1.1        [16] times the Net Rental Income (if Net Rental Income does not exceed the Target Rent) or

48.1.2        if the Net Rental Income does exceed the Target Rent the amount calculated by the following formula:

$16T + 8(R - T)$

where 'T' is the Target Rent and 'R' is Net Rental Income

*or*

A Balancing Payment calculated as follows is due to the Developer only if the following formula provides a figure greater than zero:

$(16R_1 + 8R_2) - C$

where:

'$R_1$'       is [£50,000] or (if less) Net Rental Income

'$R_2$'       is zero if Net Rental Income does not exceed [£50,000] and otherwise is [£20,000] or (if less) the amount by which Net Rental Income exceeds [£50,000]

'C'        is Total Project Costs]

[this procedure being repeated until the Development is fully let for the first time allowance being made for every previous Balancing Payment]

**[3470]**

**49     Payment**[73]

49.1     Subject to clause 49.2 any Balancing Payment due to the Developer from the Fund will be made together with VAT by bank transfer to the Developer's bank account previously advised in writing to the Fund within [20] Working Days after the later of:

49.1.1     the Settlement Date and

49.1.2     the date the Developer produces a duly completed VAT invoice showing the amount of the Balancing Payment the VAT due and the Developer as supplier to the Fund

[the Fund notifying the Developer not later than 5 days after the Developer's entitlement if any has arisen of the amount of the Balancing Payment and if any amount of the Balancing Payment is to be withheld for any reason including but not limited to a consequence of default the notice shall so state specifying (inter alia) the amount proposed to be withheld and the grounds for withholding payment or if there is more than one ground each ground and the amount attributable to it]

[and if not so paid the Fund will pay interest on the amount (exclusive of VAT) at *(specify interest rate)* for the period from [[20] Working Days after] the date it was due to be paid until the date of payment]

49.2     The Fund will be entitled (without prejudice to any other remedies which may be available to the Fund and subject to clause 49.3) to deduct from any Balancing Payment due to the Developer a sum equal to the amount of any lawful claim the Fund may have against the Developer so that only the balance (if any) of the amount due will be payable

49.3     The Fund will not be entitled to deduct any sums pursuant to clause 49.2 unless it represents an excess of Project Costs and any related interest arising under clause 46.3 or such sum has been:

49.3.1     agreed in writing by the Developer or

49.3.2     finally adjudged by a court of competent jurisdiction to be payable in respect of such claim or claims or

49.3.3     supported by counsel of at least [10] years' call stating that the chance of success of such claim or claims in the High Court of Justice in England and Wales is more likely than not

[49.4     The Fund shall not be required to make any Balancing Payment in so far as entitlement to the same may arise after the End Date]

                                                                        **[3471]**

**50     Unascertained Expenditure**[74]

If the Total Project Costs cannot be ascertained at the Settlement Date because further items of Project Costs remain to be paid [and it is not possible for the Fund to make a retention for such Project Costs because their amount is uncertain]:

50.1     the Surveyor will make a reasonable estimate of the amount of the Total Project Costs

50.2     a calculation to ascertain whether any Balancing Payment is due will be made at the Settlement Date on the basis of such estimated Total Project Costs and [95%] of any Balancing Payment so calculated will be paid in accordance with clause 49 and

50.3     within [28] days of the amount of the Total Project Costs being ascertained the calculation as at the Settlement Date will be repeated and any necessary monetary adjustments made

**51      [Gross [External *or* Internal] Area *or* Net Internal] Area**[75]

The [Gross [External *or* Internal] *or* Net Internal] Area will if not agreed between the Developer and the Fund within [5] Working Days after Works Completion Date be the amount determined by a Chartered Surveyor agreed upon by the Developer and the Fund and in the absence of agreement by a Chartered Surveyor appointed on the application of either of them by the President for the time being of the Royal Institution of Chartered Surveyors. If his decision is not communicated to the Parties by a date [10] Working Days after the Settlement Date the obligation of the Fund to pay any Balancing Payment to the Developer will be postponed until [10] Working Days after the date of such Communication

**[3472]**

**J      DEFAULT**

**52      Event of default**[76]

Each of the events specified in clauses 52.1–52.7 inclusive is an Event of Default:

52.1      The Developer becomes Insolvent

[52.2      The Developer fails to pay any moneys due from it to the Fund in cleared funds on the due date]

52.3      Any representation warranty or statement made by the Developer in this Agreement or in any notice or other document report certificate or statement delivered by it pursuant to or in connection with this Agreement proves to have been incorrect or misleading in any material respect when made or deemed to have been made

52.4      The Developer fails duly to perform or comply with any other obligation expressed to be assumed by it in this Agreement and

     52.4.1      (if in the opinion of the Fund such default is capable of remedy) the Developer fails to remedy the default within [10] Working Days after the Fund has given notice to the Developer specifying the default and the required remedy and

     52.4.2      such failure may in the reasonable opinion of the Fund prejudice to a material extent the ability of the Developer to complete the Works

52.5      The Developer repudiates this Agreement or does or allows to be done or omitted any act or thing which the Fund reasonably considers to evidence an intention to repudiate this Agreement

52.6      Any event or series of events occurs which in the reasonable opinion of the Fund may materially and adversely affect the business assets or financial condition of the Developer so that it may be unable to comply with any of its obligations under this Agreement

52.7      The Works are not completed by [a date [6] months after the Target Completion Date *or (specify)*] [or by the End Date if later]

**[3473]**

**53      Consequences of default**

Where an Event of Default occurs the Fund (without prejudice to any other available remedy) may serve notice of default on the Developer whereupon:

53.1      the Fund will not be obliged to make any further payment under this Agreement

53.2      the Developer's licence to enter the Site will cease and the Developer will immediately vacate the Site but will leave all Works and materials and plant and equipment on the Site

53.3      the Fund may (but is not obliged to) carry out and complete the Project

53.4     the Fund may (but is not obliged to) exercise its right to take an assignment of the Building Contract pursuant to the Contractor's Warranty and/or of any Letter of Appointment pursuant to a Consultant's Warranty

53.5     the Fund may dispose of the Site or carry out some other development or choose to retain the Site without completing the Works at its absolute discretion

53.6     If the Fund elects to carry out and complete the Development and if it does so before the End Date and otherwise in circumstances in which any Balancing Payment would have become due to the Developer the Fund may (but shall not be obliged to) make a Payment to the Developer in lieu of Balancing Payment together with VAT on it and clause 54 shall apply according [(and in any event and without prejudice to the foregoing clause 49.3 shall not apply)][77]

**54      Excess costs**[78]

If [within [6] months] after service of a notice under clause 53 the Fund [commences and then] proceeds to carry out and complete the Project (whether or not under the same Building Contract or using the same Contractor as the Developer):

54.1     the Fund will continue to maintain the Project Account until the Settlement Date (save that the Finance Charge will be increased with effect from the date the notice is served to [15/365]% per day)

54.2     if at the Settlement Date the debit balance on the Project Account plus any further costs (such as retentions) which the Fund is due to pay in order to complete the Project exceeds the Capital Value the excess will be paid by the Developer to the Fund together with VAT if applicable immediately upon demand and if not paid will carry interest from the date of demand to the date of payment at the Interest Rate (as well after as before any judgment)

                                                                                              **[3474]**

**55      Definition**[79]

For the purposes of clauses 55–61:

55.1 '    'Dispute' means a dispute issue difference question or claim as between the Fund and the Developer relating to or arising out of this Agreement

55.2     'Party' means a party to the Dispute

55.3     'Specialist' means a person qualified to act as an independent expert or an arbitrator in relation to the Dispute having experience in the profession in which he practises for the period of at least [10] years immediately preceding the date of referral

**56      Dispute Notice**

Either Party may give to the other notice ('Dispute Notice') requiring a Dispute to be referred to a Specialist and proposing an appropriate Specialist

**57      Counter Notice**

The Party served will be deemed to accept the proposals made in the Dispute Notice unless that Party within [10] Working Days of service of the Dispute Notice gives notice rejecting one or more of the proposals or unless each Party serves a Dispute Notice on the other contemporaneously

**58      Type of Specialist**[80]

Unless the Parties agree or are deemed to agree the appropriate Specialist:

58.1     if the Parties do not agree which type of Specialist is appropriate to resolve the Dispute either Party may refer that question to the President or next most senior available officer of the Royal Institution of Chartered Surveyors who will (with the right to take such further advice as he may require) determine that question and nominate or arrange to have nominated the appropriate Specialist

58.2    if the Parties do agree the appropriate type of Specialist but do not agree the identity of the Specialist he will be nominated on the application of either Party by the President or other most senior available officer of the organisation generally recognised as being responsible for the relevant type of Specialist but if no such organisation exists then by the President or next most senior available officer of the Royal Institution of Chartered Surveyors

[3475]

## 59    Arbitration

Unless the parties otherwise agree the reference to a Specialist shall be made to him as an arbitrator under the Arbitration Act 1996 but if the parties agree to the Specialist acting as an expert his decision shall be final and binding upon the parties

## 60    Adjudication[81]

In so far as any part of this Agreement shall constitute a construction contract for the purposes of the Housing Grants, Construction and Regeneration Act 1996 Part II and any orders issued under it for the time being in force then without prejudice to clauses 55–59 above the TeCSA Adjudication Rules shall apply to any dispute arising under it

## 61    Costs

The liability for paying all costs of referring a Dispute to a Specialist including costs connected with the appointment of the Specialist will be decided by the Specialist

## [L    SURETY

## 62    Surety[82]

62.1    This Agreement has been entered into with the consent and at the request of the Surety

62.2    The Surety guarantees the due performance by the Developer of all of the Developer's obligations under this Agreement and will perform them or otherwise indemnify the Fund in respect of any non-performance of such obligations including (for the avoidance of doubt) any obligation of the Developer which is agreed or determined under clauses 55–61

62.3    The obligations of the Surety will not be affected by:

62.3.1    any variation of this Agreement to which the Surety is not a party

62.3.2    any other agreement entered into by the Developer

62.3.3    any time or indulgence given by the Fund

62.3.4    the Developer becoming Insolvent

62.3.5    any other act deed or thing except an express release of the Surety or variation to the Surety's liability given in writing by the Fund]

[3476]

## M    MISCELLANEOUS

## 63    Communication[83]

63.1    All Communications shall be in writing

63.2    A Communication from any party ('the Sender') to any other ('the Recipient') will be duly made if in writing and either delivered to the Recipient (including in a manner provided at clause 63.5) or sent within the United Kingdom by [first class prepaid or] registered or recorded delivery post addressed to the Recipient at his address as stated in this Agreement or as the Recipient may from time to time notify the Sender

63.3 While the Surveyor is acting as agent of the Fund as specified in this Agreement a Communication duly made to the Surveyor will constitute a Communication duly made to the Fund

63.4 A Communication sent by post will be deemed to have been made on the second Working Day next following the day of posting [and it will be sufficient proof of posting for first class prepaid post to show that a prepaid envelope containing the Communication was properly addressed and either delivered to or collected by the Post Office or placed in a Post Office letterbox]

63.5 In this clause 63 'writing' includes telex facsimile or other electronic means of communication (except e-mail) and 'delivered' includes transmission by such means in which event the Communication will be deemed to have been made when the Sender has finished its transmission without having any reasonable grounds for suspecting that the transmission has failed or was incomplete (except that if such transmission takes place outside normal business hours the Communication will be deemed to have been made when normal business hours next commence)

63.6 In this clause 63 'normal business hours' are [9.30 am to 5.30 pm] on Working Days

**[3477]**

## 64 Duration

All provisions of this Agreement remain in force to the extent that and so long as they remain to be performed or observed

## 65 Personal[84]

This Agreement is strictly personal to the Developer which shall not be entitled to assign or otherwise deal in any way with its interest under this Agreement

## 66 Partnership and agency[85]

Neither the Developer nor the Fund has any intention of carrying on business in partnership with the other concerning the Project or any related matter

## 67 Waiver

No failure or delay by the Fund to exercise any right power or remedy under this Agreement will operate as a waiver of it in whole or in part nor will any partial exercise preclude any further exercise of the same or of some other right power or remedy

## 68 Headings

The clause and sub-clause headings do not affect the meaning of this Agreement

[AS *or* IN] WITNESS etc[86]

[FIRST] SCHEDULE
Documents[87]
*(insert details)*

[SECOND SCHEDULE
Conditions of Sale[88]
*(insert details)*]

[[THIRD] SCHEDULE
Contaminated Land[89]
*(insert appropriate provisions)*]

*(signatures (or common seals) of the parties)*
[*(signatures of witnesses)*]
**[3478]–[3488]**

1 No stamp duty is payable on a forward funding agreement as such (see Information Binder: Stamp Duties [1] (Agreement: Deed of any kind not otherwise described). As to forward funding agreements generally see Paragraph 299 [3401] et seq ante. As to VAT see Paragraph 309 [3414] ante and see vol 38(1) (2000 Reissue) SALE OF LAND Paragraph 8 [16] et seq.

As to stamp duty on the transfer to the fund, the Inland Revenue Statement of Practice SP8/93 'Stamp Duty: New Buildings' issued in the light of the decision in *Prudential Assurance Co Ltd v IRC* [1993] 1 WLR 211, [1992] STC 863 may apply to limit the stamp duty payable to the consideration expressed to be payable for the property where the conveyancing contract and forward funding agreement are separate and independent of each other. See also Inland Revenue Statement Practice SP11/91 'Stamp Duty and Value Added Tax—Interaction'.

However, there is a risk that the Finance Act 1994 s 242 (41 Halsbury's Statutes (4th Edn) STAMP DUTIES) applies in relation to unascertained consideration. This section may bring into charge to stamp duty any balancing payment or any other consideration payable to the developer under the forward funding agreement. Specifically, if the land is transferred together with the benefit of an agreement for lease or lease of the resultant development or part of it (ie a pre-let), and even if conditional upon the development being carried out it is arguable that the Finance Act 1994 s 242(3)(a) applies to the extent that any fixed remuneration (balancing payment) could also be taken into account for stamp duty purposes. Where a formula otherwise applies (as in this precedent) the amount remains unascertainable. Accordingly, in order to avoid the risk of an additional charge to stamp duty, the fund should avoid any financial mechanism in the event of a pre-let, whereby the developer's remuneration is ascertained and fixed.

Because this Form includes an agreement for sale and purchase, the agreement is capable of registration as an estate contract (either as a class C(iv) land charge under the Land Charges Act 1972 (37 Halsbury's Statutes (4th Edn) REAL PROPERTY) where the land is unregistered, or by way of notice (or caution) in the case of registered land).

2 For the purposes of this agreement the various professional appointments are not necessarily all those of the developer. For example, in the case of a JCT Design and Build Contract 1998 the professional team will largely be the appointees of the contractor. The terms of their engagement will still be of interest to both the developer and the fund as reflecting the value of any warranties which may be required of them and/or the impact of the Contracts (Rights of Third Parties) Act 1999. If the developer is, at the point when the forward funding agreement is entered into, uncertain of the form of building contract likely to be used, it may be helpful to add a further definition of, say, employers' agent, such a person being the administrator of the building contract rather than the architect, or combine the present definition with available alternatives.

From the fund's point of view, it should be borne in mind that the JCT Design and Build form places the onus on the employer (developer) to issue a statement of practical completion. In order for the employer's agent to have a more meaningful role, upon which the fund can particularly rely in relation to practical completion, an amendment to the building contract is helpful placing the employer's agent in the role of certifying practical completion in the same way as would an architect under a conventional building contract.

**[3489]**

3 A wide variety of professionals is now habitually employed in the development process. The planning supervisor referred to will be employed (as the relevant definition indicates) specifically for the purpose of compliance with regulations. An environmental consultant is likely to be employed, particularly where there is known contamination and where remedial works are required, possibly as a condition of any relevant planning permission.

4 Consultants' warranties are habitually required by both a fund and prospective tenants. Moreover, if the building contract is in a design and build or other managed form, then all parties will require a series of warranties both from consultants and any sub-contractors. It is helpful to include in all warranties a

clause making clear that the benefit of the warranty is in addition to and not in substitution for rights arising under the Contracts (Rights of Third Parties) Act 1999 (see note 2 above), but this depends on how the Act is applied.

5     This precedent associates defects liability with practical completion alone on the basis that works completion contemplates compliance with other provisions but defects liability is largely associated with the building contract. Some funds will take a more robust view on defects liability, suggesting further personal cost to the developer.

6     Traditionally, development documentation has proscribed deleterious materials in some detail. Often, use of standardisation of documentation leads to discrepancies between construction and development documentation. There is, however, a perceptible retreat from specifics towards British Standards in general and the proscription of materials which are generally considered deleterious. That said, all well drawn construction and development documentation should also cater for specific deleterious materials, where appropriate, in the context of the development in question.

7     The agreement provides definitions of 'Site' (the land itself) on which a 'Development' is to take place (of which a brief description should appear here). In accordance with an 'Approved Scheme' the plans and other documents describe the development in detail. 'Works' are the actual physical processes involved in carrying-out the development and 'Project' is the whole concept comprehended by the agreement from site assembly to completion of lettings. It follows that the description of the development which should feature here will usually be restricted in the main to the kind of information which appears on a planning permission as the permitted development.

8     The definition should none the less have regard to all legal inhibitions to include restrictive covenants, third party rights and so on affecting title to the site.

**[3490]**

9     End date is a long stop date. It may serve to create an ultimate event of default in case of non-performance in carrying-out the development. It may also serve as a date after which no balancing payment can arise. It will have been preceded by the target completion date. Depending upon the financial formula giving rise to a prospective balancing payment, it may not be necessary to impose the end date as a date after which no balancing payment can become due, leaving the economics of the situation to dictate the prospects. Under a profit erosion deal, eg unless inflationary pressures outstrip the prescribed rates of finance charge and interest, the point may well arise naturally when any prospect of a balancing payment will have evaporated. An end date provides certainty however.

10    The insurance market evolves. Accordingly, excepted risks should be drawn in the light of current practice and with the benefit of insurance advice.

11    The finance charge is effectively an accumulation of notional interest, not interest per se.

12    Recoverability of VAT is not contemplated by any related policy of insurance. The circumstances of recoverability are in each case perceived as unique.

13    The code as defined (in clause 1.9) may alter at any time. Not only must the code be redefined as necessary, but also the precise nature and definition of the area to which it must be applied.

14    The term 'insolvent' (as defined in clause 1.29) is applied to certain events of financial distress. Insolvency, however arising, may be innocent in the context of the observance and performance of the developer's obligations in the agreement. For this reason, including other factors such as substantial completion of the development, a dilemma may arise as to whether, for example, a receiver or an administrator of the developer should be permitted to complete the development and in particular, those elements of the project which include the obtaining of lettings giving rise to a prospective balancing payment.

      What is fair in context may be hard to determine. Hence clauses 53 and 54 which go some way towards avoiding an unexpected windfall for the fund. These matters are, essentially, of the essence of commercial negotiation and will colour the judgement of any developer as to whether or not to deal with a particular fund.

15    For the fund (or indeed any prospective tenants) the terms of any appointment are critical unless any shortcomings are addressed in a corresponding warranty. At all events, any appointee must be required, under the terms of a letter of appointment, to provide warranties as appropriate.

**[3491]**

16    The letting agents are the appointees of the developer. Sometimes letting agents are also appointed as the fund's surveyor. The roles are different and may thus avoid a conflict of interest. The practice of appointing joint letting agents, the second effectively the nominee of the fund, may produce a conflict, particularly in the area of letting policy.

17    Letting policy is one of the most overlooked provisions of development documentation where financial interests are dependent upon the success of letting. Whilst letting agents must determine what the letting criteria are to be in practice, the incorporation of a letting policy must nevertheless be susceptible to legal interpretation however extreme or unexpected the prevailing market conditions. Particularly, where the underlying loyalties of two or more letting agents are not identical, even though ostensibly the appointees of the developer, the prospect arises of conflict and recrimination, and the possibility of lost lettings to the detriment of the developer and fund alike, according to their respective interests.

18    Omission of a maximum commitment implies an unlimited financial commitment on the part of a fund. A maximum commitment must, therefore, be applied and if market conditions should change during the course of the project, any inherent weaknesses in the financial arrangements between the parties will no doubt come to light. The project costs by implication include irrecoverable VAT.

19    See note 13 above.

20    Construction (Design and Management) Regulations 1994, SI 1994/3140. As a result of statute, a planning supervisor is now an essential figure in all substantial development, although the role can be performed by the contractor (see JCT forms). As to the Regulations see vol 38(1) (2000 Reissue) SALE OF LAND Paragraph 118 [241] et seq.

21    Whilst practical completion and works completion are distinguished, the distinction also implies liabilities on the developer beyond the obligations of the contractor and an additional cost to the developer which the fund may choose, contractually, to disallow as a project cost. If this is done (this precedent does not make so fine a distinction) this becomes an absolute cost to the developer.

**[3492]**

22    The project account is the yardstick for determining the entitlement to the balancing payment if any (the project costs being subject to a maximum commitment). The maximum commitment determines the amount of project costs which can be reimbursed to the developer in the course of the development (after debiting of funds costs). The ultimate accounting treatment for the developer and fund respectively is separate and distinct. If the developer is, for example, a joint venture vehicle, it follows that the shares of profit from the project will reflect, but by no means necessarily equate to, any balancing payment.

23    Regard should be had to the terms of the building contract and such matters as are relevant events under it. However, just as the developer may be excused from the consequences of unreasonable delay on the part of the surveyor in carrying out his functions under this agreement, a fund may not allow any factor in such relevant events attributable to delay or default on the part of the developer.

24    The impact of the words in square brackets should be considered. If there are stepped rents, or a rent free period, the fund may wish to take into account the full initial rent before it pays any balancing payment to the developer. This is a matter of negotiation.

25    It is not usual to require warranties from a sub-contractor other than a sub-contractor as defined, ie having a design responsibility. In terms of practical implementation, that is simply a function delegated by the contractor. However, the developer should beware of the consequences of the fund taking to itself a discretion in the nomination of any sub-contractor whether with a design responsibility or not, and make appropriate provision in the building contract.

26    Target rent is referred to only obliquely at clause 37. If market conditions dictate that anything less than the target rent may be achieved, a fund properly refusing to enter into a letting (if the agreement in question so provides) may not only deprive the developer of a balancing payment but also its investors of income. This precedent seeks to avoid that particular conflict by offering alternatives. Unless special provision is made, the imposition of minimum rental criteria may deprive the fund of the ability to let at a lower rate until the end date.

27    See note 5 above.

28    An agreement for sale and purchase may be incorporated. The purchase price and any VAT thereon paid by the fund (except in so far as recovered by the fund) will form part of the project costs, so also will the costs to the fund of acquiring the site together with all related disbursements, stamp duty and land registration fees. If the agreement does not incorporate (actually or by supplemental association) a conveyancing contract, it prospectively stands alone as a construction contract as defined in the Housing Grants, Construction and Regeneration Act 1996 Part II without exclusion, by virtue of the Construction Contracts (England and Wales) Exclusion Order 1998, SI 1998/648. The effect of this distinction is to bring the agreement prospectively into the scheme for construction contracts regulating both the terms of the remuneration and also imposing a scheme for adjudication of disputes unless such matters are prescribed for in the agreement in the manner provided by the Housing Grants, Construction and Regeneration Act 1996 Act ss 104–117, and regulations for the time being made under it.

**[3493]**

29    Unless the sale and purchase contract has prescribed that the agreement will be entered into on the site completion date and is itself a condition of completion, other conditions may preclude operation of the agreement until they are satisfied. For example, the fund may not wish to be bound to complete the purchase until a satisfactory planning permission has been obtained. The sale and purchase agreement will also likely govern VAT albeit that in the context of prospective development, the developer, whether as seller of a freehold or of leasehold, will be likely to have waived exemption in any event. The fund will elect in order to make recoveries against development costs invoiced by the developer.

30    The consultants and contractor are defined. Depending upon the form of the building contract, some or all of the consultants (excepting in the case of design and build, for example, the quantity surveyor or the employer's agent) will be the appointees of the contractor. In that event, in so far as the fund wishes to influence those appointments, it follows that the building contract must make provision for this to be facilitated.

The terms of appointment of consultants and of any contractor are themselves 'construction contracts' as defined and must in turn, subject to regulations for the time being in force, be drawn so as to reflect statutory requirements. With the widespread requirement of warranties from consultants and contractors, it is essential that there be a consequential interaction with any relevant development documentation, or at least that conflict should be avoided.

31 Precisely when the building contract is to be entered into may be reflected here. In forward funding the inference is that the project will have been substantially costed before the fund is contractually committed. In other kinds of development agreement, where the development cost is not intended to be met directly by the landowner (eg a development agreement with the local authority granting a major interest but, perhaps, retaining some significant interest in the resultant development in lieu of premium) one may expect to see prescribed provision for approval of tenders, both in terms of identity and suitability of the prospective building contractor and also in terms of prospective building costs, to ensure that the developer can meet his commitments. If any of these elements are present, and the developer and fund have agreed to be committed to a forward funding agreement, notwithstanding, then these elements should be catered for in addition.

**[3494]**

32 The approved scheme is of the essence of the arrangement. The extent of departure from this may be contained at the fund's discretion: see clause 9.3. The approved scheme is also of the essence of the prospective investment. In a particular context however, variations may be seen as possible, but criteria beyond what is reasonable in context may be hard to define and be a likely source of dispute.

33 It is to be expected that most consents fundamental to the efficacy of the project, eg planning permission, including environmental requirements, will have been previously obtained or been a condition of site purchase, this agreement coming into effect only thereafter.

Approval of plans for building control purposes habitually follows the event. In that case, reliance must be placed upon the advice of appropriate consultants, as to compliance of the approved scheme with building regulations.

34 Whilst a method statement may also be part of the approved scheme, the programme may be dictated by the nature of the approved scheme and will, in turn, influence the target completion date and the end date. If the programme has not been ascertained at the outset, judgement must also be exercised with the assistance of consultants as necessary as to the timing of events overall. The programme may, of course, be extended by a relevant event, but the end date is intended as a constant (it does not have to be, but this is an obvious factor in the prospect of the project becoming income producing later than first expected).

35 Having sold the site to the fund, the developer has no continuing interest in land. A licence to go on site is therefore required. If the developer should be in breach of the agreement, and if in consequence his licence is terminated, the developer's commitments to the contractor and consultants are by implication impaired, and because the licence is terminated by reason of the developer's default, the implication is that the developer will be in breach of his contractual commitments and thus prospectively liable in damages to them except in so far as arising through the default of the consultant or contractor in question. Indeed in such circumstances the developer may himself be able to show loss. On the other hand, default on the part of any contractor or consultant may give rise to a relevant event and thus should not, on its own, be contractually allowed to give rise to termination of the developer's licence. It is in the nature of a licence that it is non-exclusive and that the fund should, at all times, have legal possession.

**[3495]**

36 The general requirements comprise a variety of matters including title elements, third party rights and so on. The developer should ensure that such matters are also reflected in the building contract.

37 As to contaminated land generally see vol 38(1) (2000 Reissue) SALE OF LAND Paragraph 147 [341] et seq. For environmental and due diligence enquiries and definitions and interpretation for use with those enquiries see vol 38(1) (2000 Reissue) SALE OF LAND Forms 35 [1585] and 36 [1592]. For a schedule of environmental warranties and indemnities see vol 38(1) (2000 Reissue) SALE OF LAND Form 61 [2401]. For alternative shorter warranty clauses see Forms 144 [4587] and 145 [4588] post. Practitioners should consider what provisions are appropriate to be included in the third schedule to this Form having regard to the actual state of the site the subject of this agreement and draft appropriate provisions which may be based on the above mentioned Forms, ensuring that the definitions and wording used is compatible with those used in this Form.

38 'Relevant Events' as defined are intended to make an allowance for all those things which are essentially beyond the developer's control. This being so they must include relevant events arising under the building contract, excepting those which would entitle the contractor to an extension of time by reason of his employers' default.

39 Whilst the Woolf reforms have redefined liquidated damages as being 'specified', construction parlance (and practice) is inherently conservative. As and when JCT forms of contract so redefine liquidated damages, then these provisions can be altered to suit.

40    Insurance requirements vary according to contractual commitments. As a first step, the insurance
      obligations in the building contract are likely to suffice for most practical purposes as also the insurance
      obligations imposed upon consultants under their letters of appointment.

41    There has been a practice of requiring developers to continue to insure after practical completion until,
      say, first letting or, where works completion is not synonymous with practical completion, until that
      time. Given that in practice the principal insurances will be those undertaken by the contractor, thus
      rendering double insurance pointless, a more pragmatic solution is suggested whereby, following practical
      completion, the fund insures immediately. The fund can instead, therefore, require the developer to
      indemnify it from practical completion to whatever date is considered appropriate. For example, if as part
      of the financial arrangements the developer is required in effect to observe and perform all the provisions
      of an occupational lease until first letting (or indeed to enter into such a stop-gap lease as some funds
      require) the fund is thereby covered for the cost of insurance from practical completion.

42    The fund is not only employing the developer, it is also the landowner, possibly having encumbrances
      upon its title and also the burden of positive as well as negative covenants. The manner of
      implementation of the development may infringe positive covenants the performance of which may, in
      context, require to form part of the works, eg the construction of a boundary wall and so on and, in
      the case of statutory agreements, off-site works maybe encountered as well.

                                                                                                    **[3496]**

43    Third party rights often include those the existence of which may not have been apparent at the outset:
      eg long hidden infrastructure the presence of which suggests acquisition of rights by prescription. Such
      contingencies are usually contemplated as part of the programme but may also give rise to a relevant
      event and permitted delay.

44    Proper and effective site management should guard against the possibility of nuisance or offence to third
      parties. In any case, statutory agreements often prescribe for conduct both on and off-site, eg,
      requirements of the highway authority for access and egress by construction traffic and so on. Where
      crane over-sailing is necessary then, inevitably, an express licence will be required.

45    The fund may be a 'contractor' for the purposes of the deduction scheme contained in the Income and
      Corporation Taxes Act 1988 ss 559–567 (as amended) (42-44 Halsbury's Statutes (4th Edn) TAXATION),
      the developer being a 'sub-contractor' accordingly. Current (ie SI 1993/743) (and any further)
      regulations should be considered and in the absence of an appropriate tax certificate the developer may
      be required to accept certain payments subject to deduction of tax at the relevant percentage (18% from
      6 April 2000). The developer should therefore ensure that all necessary tax certificates are in place.

46    SI 1993/743.

47    The presence of archaeological finds may trigger the intervention of the local authority and the
      imposition of delay to the programme. Moreover, even if there are no archaeological finds, in so far as
      the site lies within a scheduled ancient monument, the consent of English Heritage will be required
      and will, therefore, number among the consents as defined.

                                                                                                    **[3497]**

48    The surveyor being defined, the developer has only itself to blame if the person or firm so appointed
      at the outset is inadequate for the task. If the fund should be entitled to appoint a new surveyor at any
      time, then the criteria for appointment should be considered with care, although it is unlikely that a
      fund will allow the developer a say in the appointment. Given that the surveyor speaks for the fund as
      its agent particularly in granting consents, authorising expenditure and so on, his is a critical role on
      which the developer depends for the smooth operation of the project.

          (Not infrequently, the same firm will be appointed by the fund as the surveyor whilst, under a separate
      letter of appointment, it will be appointed by the developer as one of the letting agents (less likely, but
      possibly, the sole letting agent). Whilst the roles are essentially different, and thus the terms of engagement
      should not of themselves disclose any underlying conflict of interests, it is suggested that if the developer
      employs the same firm as the fund's surveyor in a letting agent role, the possibility arises of conflict of loyalties
      between that appointee and the developer's own appointee in matters of letting. A conflict may arise, for
      example, when a letting is negotiated and is put to the fund for approval. If there is conflict between the
      letting agents in that capacity, the prospect of the fund's approval per se is perhaps the more problematical.)
          The surveyor is also expressed to be the agent of the fund. Any other capacity suggests an
      adjudication role of some kind and by implication a duty of care. Whilst he is the agent of the fund,
      however, the duty of care is owed by the surveyor to the fund unless (unlikely) the contrary is expressed.

49    The surveyor depends upon a flow of information and personal attendances in order to perform his role
      effectively. The balance to be struck is between the provision of information on the one hand and the
      consequential judgement of the surveyor on the other. The matter in question requiring approval may be
      inherently reasonable or necessary but still justify a refusal if he is not presented with appropriate information.

50    The extent of meetings which the surveyor may be entitled to attend needs some parameters. The
      surveyor should not be obliged to attend meetings and the need to do so is alleviated by the proper
      provision of information. Formality of meetings, although in itself imprecise, is more readily
      understood, whether or not key professionals are invited to attend.

                                                                                                    **[3498]**

51   The taking of tests may cause delay and give rise to a relevant event (as to which see clause 15 of this Form). The developer should therefore be afforded a measure of protection in this respect (see clause 28.1 of this Form). Moreover, it should be emphasised that in so far as the agreement places a burden on the developer greater than that prescribed by the building contract, the interference caused to progress may unwittingly place the developer in breach of obligation to the contractor.

52   The extent of the developer's duty of care may, upon analysis, depend on the nature of its role. The inference is that the developer should be suitably insured. The developer's obligations are otherwise confined by its obligations to carry-out the works, say, in accordance with the building contract and so on. If the fund insists on this provision, as it normally will, the developer's insurance provision should be considered carefully. Fitness for purpose is not included, but may have a role in specific circumstances.

53   Exclusion clauses may be seen as prospectively ineffective to the extent that a duty of care is owed by the person relying on the exclusion. If the developer has elected to go along with the fund's requirement, but could notwithstanding have objected, the exclusion of liability on the part of the fund is perhaps more likely to stand.

54   This effectively underpins clause 13.

55   in so far as the agreement at large has not been complied with, the possibility arises of a works completion certificate not being issued, notwithstanding that practical completion has arisen. If some element of the approvals process, for example, has not been met, then possibly the practical completion certificate will be out of kilter with the fund's expectations. To the extent that performance of the building contract may otherwise fall outside compliance with the agreement, a differentiation between works completion and practical completion may be considered appropriate. A developer may, however, consider that the two should be made indistinguishable in so far as the terms of the building contract are consistent in all respects with the agreement, eg as to the specification. Note that where a design and build form of building contract is contemplated, references in this Form to a certificate of practical completion should be expanded to include a statement of practical completion.

56   The nub of the matter lies within the obligation to bring practical completion and works completion together. If works completion were left to the entire discretion of the fund, the developer would be at risk, both financially under this agreement and also, indirectly, in having to perform further works in order to satisfy the requirements of the fund. The view is taken, however, in this Form that once works completion has taken place then defects liability should be geared to the building contract as it is by then implicit that the building contract is consistent, or its operation has been made consistent, with the terms of the agreement (see clause 32).

**[3499]**

57   The need for clauses such as this may be seen as less critical following enactment of the Contracts (Rights of Third Parties) Act 1999. However, the benefit of the Act depends upon the extent afforded by the terms of the building contract and any letters of appointment, and provisions such as these are best incorporated at the very least until expectations of what other documents should contain are so commonplace as to go without saying, particularly any further printed amendments to the JCT forms.

The developer should note, however, that in so far as assignment of contractual rights is effected, his ability to meet outstanding or deemed continuing obligations to the fund may be impaired. It is a matter of negotiation whether to qualify this clause accordingly.

58   In so far as the fund is not buying together with the benefit of an agreement, or agreements, for lease of the whole of the lettable portions of the development, provision is required for the creation of lettings. These lie at the heart of the fund's investment.

The letting policy should contain all the essential criteria which the fund and the developer have agreed should be met for the creation of the investment (for example, in the case of a retail development, the mix of tenants may be critical). The lead tenant, particularly if already subject to an agreement for lease, may have already prescribed in that agreement for an absence of competition and this will be reflected in the letting policy. Again, in its negotiations with the developer, the fund may have prescribed that certain kinds of occupier are not welcome. Time was when public sector bodies in particular were avoided: not so much so today, although questions of financial accountability may arise, and the enabling legislation for public bodies should not be relied upon to deliver financial security. Statutory constitutions should be considered with care. Practical and commercial criteria should apply.

Depending upon the nature of the development, this precedent suggests a number of fallbacks. The practicality is that both aims and fallbacks should be incorporated as far as possible within the letting policy.

59   A form of lease will have been prescribed for the development. That form should be created so as to accommodate all the characteristics of the development including, eg the service charge regime if any which will be applied to the resultant investment. There is no reason at all why provisions such as those in clause 37 should not form part of the letting policy particularly in relation to achieving the target rent.

At clause 37.1.2 provision is made for the rent to be not less than the target rent. Such a provision has potentially a direct effect upon the financial provisions of the agreement. If market conditions are not propitious, the inference is that part or whole of the development may be unlettable if the strict criteria of the agreement are adhered to. If the developer presents a strong covenant, it may be in the interests of the fund instead to prescribe a minimum rent upon the basis of the developer being required either to meet the income requirements by way of interest post practical completion, by itself entering into a lease, or by enhancing the rental income until a certain threshold is reached. There is an inevitable interaction between income and the developer's remuneration and so the rental criteria and the criteria for determination of any balancing payment are directly connected.

**[3500]**

60    Provision has been made for the fund, in its discretion, to approve agreements for lease. The obvious drawback for the developer is that any such discretion imperils his ability to derive a balancing payment.

In the case of a pre-let, a fund should have particular regard to the development obligations in any agreement for lease. Particularly, the fund can avoid the effect of such development provisions, upon acquiring the site, if the agreement provides expressly that the obligations of the developer are personal to the developer and do not devolve upon the fund or any other successor in title of the developer. Whilst appropriate drafting has always had the potential to make this distinction, it is facilitated by the Landlord and Tenant (Covenants) Act 1995 s 3(6).

Again, where an agreement for lease is to be entered into after the fund has acquired the site, a fund's inherent reluctance to enter into development obligations may again be accommodated by the developer itself entering into such arrangements. The fund will be keen to ensure that the development obligations to the tenant are not inconsistent with the forward funding agreement. Sometimes, the tenant's negotiating position may have a fundamental effect on the efficacy of the forward funding agreement in which case, if a deal is to be struck with the particular tenant, some modification to the contractual relationship between developer and fund may be required.

61    The fund will be unlikely to want to see a diminution in its true income whilst service charges or, in the absence of a full repairing lease, tenant's obligations at large, are not met for the duration of any period whilst the development or part of it is not let. For that reason, the fund will usually wish to impose upon the developer a direct obligation to meet these.

Reference to the end date has been placed in square brackets. Under some forward funding agreements the fund will acquiesce in an effective release of the developer from all such obligations after a certain period. Where the investment assumes a strong developer covenant as its raison d'être, the developer's commitment may be expected to last until first letting, however long that may take.

62    The items of project costs are suggested but not unlimited. Nevertheless, they are prospectively all subject to a notional accumulation (finance charge) and the totality is a fundamental factor in determining the developer's remuneration. Costs arising under a dispute however, should not normally form part of project costs although some funds will seek to make them so. In case of default, additional costs to the fund are recognised under clause 54 in conjunction with clause 53.6 although a developer's amendments may seek to preclude unnecessary costs depriving him yet further of the possibility of the balancing payment or some payment in lieu. Under clause 61, the costs of dispute will be decided by the specialist. Under clause 49.2, the imposition of any such costs upon the developer may result in a corresponding deduction from the balancing payment.

The more closely costed the project, the more it will be possible to put clear maximum parameters on individual items of profits costs, capped overall by a maximum commitment. Items of project costs will be considered net of VAT but advanced together with VAT (see clause 41.24 and note 64 below).

A frequent difficulty for a developer is those costs which the fund itself incurs and which, in turn it debits to the project costs. It is important for the developer that these be incurred within set criteria and, more particularly, that they are notified to the developer. Although the surveyor will run the project account, in the hands of the fund, the developer will also be running a project account of its own, not least for audit and tax purposes. Moreover, failure to track the fund's expenditure may give rise to a false sense of security.

A further difficulty for the developer lies in the criteria to be applied to any fund's expenditure. The fund's surveyor has an essential role on behalf of the fund. The question also arises as to whether any other consultants should be employed to assist the surveyor or otherwise track the performance of the several appointees of the developer.

**[3501]**

63    The developer may wish to consider expressly excluding the fund's costs of any dispute until adjudication (if applicable) or otherwise until final judgment in the funds favour, in its amendments. See also note 62 above.

64    In paying the developer for items of project costs, the fund will expect to pay VAT. This is provided for at clause 41.24. The developer will be concerned with recoveries and the developer may wish to amend to provide that the fund shall seek recoveries expeditiously.

An argument frequently arises in negotiation concerning to whom payments should be made. Firstly, costs incurred directly by the fund will be payable directly by the fund in any event. However, if the developer is not being paid by way of reimbursement, the practice is often for the fund to make, against the developer's invoices, payment direct to those suppliers to whom the developer is obligated direct. This is particularly so in the case of the building contract, which, in the nature of things, makes up the major portion of the on-going expenditure after site acquisition. The developer on the other hand, will naturally seek payment of all items of project costs direct to itself on the basis of its need for overall control.

Such matters may be considered to fall within the remuneration requirements of the Housing Grants, Construction and Regeneration Act 1996 ss 109–113 if applicable (see note 28 above) although, as between the developer and its suppliers, this is likely to be the case in many cases. The provisions will only affect the developer if the agreement is a construction contract as defined, by standing apart in all respects from a conveyancing contract.

65    It will be impractical to make payments of small amounts, save in order to make a calculation upon a settlement date. An appropriate minimum drawn down meanwhile, should be negotiated, as also the manner of payment, and also provision for notification to the developer where payment is not received by him in the first instance.

(Note particularly clause 43.6, the first two lines of which are drawn particularly to comply with the Housing Grants, Construction and Regeneration Act 1996 s 110(2), if that Act applies in context. Reference to not less than five days is required, otherwise payments will be subjected to the scheme for construction contracts.)

66    A retention is to be expected under the terms of the building contract. There is little point in providing a retention against expenditure other than that of the building contract, or any other contractual commitment in respect of which a retention is made, as simply impacting upon the cashflow for the developer which relies, usually, solely on the fund.

**[3502]**

67    In some forward funding documents, the finance charge is defined as a notional accumulation or notional interest. It is not interest per se but represents, until income is actually derived, a cushion in lieu of income. Once the maximum commitment is reached, and unless a profit erosion formula is applied, a tangible income commitment may thereupon be imposed upon the developer.

68    Although the project account is nominally maintained by the surveyor, it is the fund's own account relating to expenditure, or deemed expenditure by it. Insurance monies will, as well as VAT recovered, be credited to it albeit that whilst the building contract is in force and, if the insurance arrangements under the agreement rely upon the efficacy of the contractor's insurance, the practicality is that to such extent insurance monies will be applied direct by the contractor in remedial works without passing through the project account.

69    It is not necessarily the case, depending upon the financial arrangements, that rental income will be credited to the project account. As lettings are achieved, this may be a convenient way to proceed: the fund may, for example, only credit back income equivalent to the target rent leaving the enhancement in rental income over as, perhaps, a factor in ultimate derivation of the developer's profit. There is no wholly predictable financial mechanism in forward funding: it is always a matter of negotiation, agreement and incorporation into the documentation.

70    Regularity of statements of accounts is fundamental to effective project management by the developer. As suggested above, depending on the frequency of statements (quarterly may be too infrequent in particular circumstances) a developer may wish to amend to provide that all items of project costs incurred by the fund on its own account should be notified more immediately.

71    As a matter of negotiation, a project management fee may find its way into project costs. If so, this represents remuneration for the developer as the project proceeds, and whether or not any balancing payment ultimately accrues (as remuneration, it may be covered by the scheme for construction contracts unless clothed with compliance with the Housing Grants, Construction and Regeneration Act 1996 ss 110, 111, but only where that Act applies). A balancing payment, however, is the more usual measure of the developer's input, depending fundamentally on the interaction between project costs and ultimate letting of the scheme.

72    Only simple examples are given in this precedent of the kinds of formula which may be applied, basically identifying the capital value and deducting from this the fund's expenditure, however derived. If there is to be more than one settlement date, the developer's remuneration may be influenced by the scope of the project itself, for example the need to construct infra-structure for all sections with the result that, however successful the letting, profit is not derived until letting of the development as a whole is substantially achieved.

The formulae offered include an incentive to achieve the target rent, while not necessarily depriving the developer of a profit. The third example, however, avails the fund of a cap on rents for the purposes of calculating the payment.

**[3503]**

73    Usually, no question should arise of the balancing payment being inclusive of VAT, both the developer and the fund being able to make recoveries. Provision is made at clause 49.2 for the fund to make deductions by way of counterclaim or set off. Clause 49.1, and in particular the bracketed section requiring that the fund notify the developer, not later than five days after the developer's entitlement if any has arisen to the balancing payment, is drawn in particular to meet the remuneration requirements of the Housing Grants, Construction and Regeneration Act 1996 ss 109–113, if applicable.

74    It should be recognised in all cases that a precise final figure may not be ascertainable when a balancing payment becomes due and that any doubt arising could otherwise postpone a balancing payment indefinitely. Accordingly, some mechanism must be applied to reflect the need for consequential adjustments.

75    Apart from whether or not the development complies with the specification, relevant areas of the development are only of importance in so far as they bear directly upon calculation of rental levels achieved and, in consequence, upon any balancing payment. They are also relevant to building obligations and compliance with the agreement at large, particularly where areas are described as being 'not less than …'. This clause is placed in this part of the agreement only because of its relevance to the calculation arising under clause 48 but can be placed elsewhere if thought more convenient in context.

76    Events of default trigger cessation of a fund's obligation to the developer, whether to advance items of project costs or to make any balancing payment. The consequences for the developer are, therefore, serious.

       An event of insolvency should not necessarily be viewed as giving rise automatically to a cessation of entitlement. Granted that it impacts directly upon the developer's ability to perform its contractual obligations, the possibility arises that the insolvency event is not one arising out of inherent default (but see note 77 below as to clause 53.6).

       The underlying consequence of an event of default is that the developer's licence to go on site is determined and, with it, its ability to perform both its obligations to the fund and also to meet its commitments to those whom it has engaged upon the development, the contractor, consultants and so on. Relevant events ameliorate the impact of delay but these, in their nature, exclude culpable delay.

77    There is always a dilemma in determining what the consequences of default may be. As a general principle, those administering the insolvency of the developer will not wish to see the fund profiting from default of any kind, and a developer in negotiating the agreement should seek to avoid such an eventuality. A developer's amendment to clause 53.6 may likely acknowledge the incurring of additional costs by the fund, as a direct consequence of the developer's default. Beyond this, (and this is an instance in which the fund may be justified in including in-house costs in its calculations) the developer should seek to allow for any residual balancing payment to be made so as to place the fund in neither a better nor worse position than if there had been no default on the part of the developer whilst affording to the developer's insolvency representatives the prospect, perhaps small, of deriving profit from the development. However, all these matters are subject to negotiation and this precedent adopts what is, in essence, an ex gratia basis for making a payment to the developer.

       The point is, however, worthy of careful thought given that the further the development progresses, and the greater the prospects of a balancing payment arising, the less the justification on the part of the fund for withholding wholly the remuneration otherwise accruing to the developer.

**[3504]**

78    Clause 54 simply recognises the fact of additional cost to the fund.

79    Consequent upon the Arbitration Act 1996, the devolvement of a technical dispute upon an expert for determination is less of an obvious choice. If the dispute is a complex one, it signals immediately a prospect of delay and of loss of remuneration for the developer. Unless an event of default has arisen, loss of letting income is also of concern. Arbitration today avails the arbitrator of the use of experts but, unlike, say, rent review under a lease, the impact of a dispute on forward funding is severe for all concerned.

80    A clause identifying an appropriate person to conduct the disputes procedure may be seen as helpful although, again, if arbitration is the chosen route, the provision of appropriate expertise from other disciplines is now readily obtainable. Where sureties are involved the emphasis is perhaps more greatly upon legal issues and the court may be seen as an appropriate tribunal.

81    If the agreement, or the relevant portion of it, is a construction contract as defined by the Housing Grants, Construction and Regeneration Act 1996 s 104 and relevant statutory instruments thereunder, there is imposed the scheme for construction contracts unless certain criteria laid down by s 108 of the Act are met. 'TeCSA' Adjudication rules, inter alia, meet these requirements. The imposition of adjudication procedures upon construction contracts is intended to facilitate resolution of disputes and continued implementation of the contract, but without prejudice to underlying disputes procedures. Arguably, any form of alternative dispute resolution is initially to be preferred to arbitration or determination by an expert where timing is critical. Adjudication under the Housing Grants, Construction and Regeneration Act 1996, however being only applicable to those parts of the agreement (if any) comprising a construction contract as defined would not, however, be useful in determining, disputes over implementation of letting policy, approval of tenancies and so on. There is, accordingly, room for development of these ideas into an appropriate form of fast track determination, perhaps like adjudication, so as not to impair underlying disputes procedures, to unlock difficulties of interpretation and so on.

**[3505]**

82    The surety is cast as a legal guarantor, and not merely as an indemnifier, affording the fund the ability to require the surety itself to perform the developer's obligation in their substance. Although this precedent does not provide, there is nothing to prevent the fund from prescribing that, in the case of developer default, a surety may be required to continue to carry out the development in the developer's stead. It is also open to the fund to include, as an event of default, insolvency of the surety whilst the agreement is in force in the hands of the developer.

Substitution of the surety in the developer role is not something which need be automatically offered. The surety having entered into his commitments in that capacity will be concerned to ensure that nothing befalls the developer which will give rise to an event of default. This will be particularly so where, for example, the developer is a wholly owned subsidiary of the surety or, again, the surety (perhaps a contractor in a joint venture with the developer) is providing the financial strength to support the developer's covenant as a rationale for the fund being willing to enter into the agreement at all.

83    Many agreements confine requirements for notices to those specified in Law of Property Act 1925 s 196 as amended. Modern means of communication, particularly when operated between solicitors, have their place although (at clause 63.5) e-mail is still considered unreliable as requiring viewing by an individual e-mail addressee. Whilst telex is rarely used nowadays, it still exists and facsimile is the established medium for rapid communication.

84    The agreement is expressed to be expressly personal to the developer. The developer has no continuing interest in land and is essentially a contracting party with whom the fund expects to deal at all times. By contrast the fund, as landowner, may for any reason wish to dispose of its holding. Under this precedent its contractual obligations are not undermined as a result of a disposal, but if any provision for release of the fund's obligations were incorporated, a developer would be rightly concerned as to the ability of the fund's successor to perform. These matters are, accordingly, left for negotiation and incorporation as appropriate.

85    In any agreement, a denial of partnership will not succeed in law unless the substance of the agreement shows this to be so. The surveyor is not a party to the agreement and is expressed to be an agent of the fund. The developer is cast as an independent contracting party whose expenditure, particularly for VAT purposes, is its own; the fund's expenditure, for VAT purposes, being the fund's alone. In terms of income and corporation tax, the absence of partnership will preserve the separate identities of the parties for tax purposes.

86    It is not usually necessary to have the contract executed as a deed unless the contract contains recitals which are intended to be binding or there are other special considerations (eg, there is a lack of valuable consideration or it is desired to extend the period set by the Limitation Act 1980 s 8 (24 Halsbury's Statutes (4th Edn) LIMITATION OF ACTIONS) for bringing claims).

Where a contract is to be executed as a deed sealing is not necessary either in the case of an individual or in the case of a company, but all parties must sign either on the same document or each on one of two identical parts which are exchanged and the signatures of all individuals must be witnessed: see the Law of Property (Miscellaneous Provisions) Act 1989 s 1(3) (37 Halsbury's Statutes (4th Edn) REAL PROPERTY). As to the execution of a deed by an individual and by a corporation, see vol 12 (1994 Reissue) DEEDS, AGREEMENTS AND DECLARATIONS Paragraphs 16 [1525] and 28 [1554]-30 [1560] respectively.

It is unnecessary for a contract by a corporate body to be under seal unless it would need to be a deed if made by private persons: see the Corporate Bodies' Contracts Act 1960 s 1 (11 Halsbury's Statutes (4th Edn) CONTRACT). A contract may be made by a company incorporated under the Companies Acts by writing under its common seal or on its behalf by any person acting under its authority, express or implied: Companies Act 1985 s 36 as substituted by the Companies Act 1989 s 130(1) (8 Halsbury's Statutes (4th Edn) COMPANIES).

87    See clause 1.19 and note 8 above. The documents should be as wide ranging as would be the case if the developer were proceeding unfunded. Firstly, everything relating to the title and third parties, including any pre-existing agreement for lease, is likely to be relevant. Moreover, the documents are, in turn, likely to be reflected in the building contract, via the specification or otherwise.

88    See clause 3 and note 28 above. The incorporation of conditions of sale, subject to which the operative provisions of the agreement will apply, will signal prospective exclusion of the agreement as a construction contract for the purposes of the Housing Grants, Construction and Regeneration Act 1996 s 104. (See note 28 above.) Whilst exclusion may also follow if the agreement is made expressly supplemental to a conveyancing contract, it would not follow if the agreement is independent. Neither will it necessarily follow if, for example, it is entered into as a condition of completion of a sale and purchase contract under which all the terms and conditions of the sale and purchase have been fulfilled so that the sale and purchase is, in all respects, a past and unrelated event. However, it is particularly important not to rely on general principles but to look to the exact circumstances and apply the Act accordingly. If the agreement is a construction contract in context then the relevant provisions of the Act relating both to adjudication and to remuneration will apply.

89    See note 37 above.

# 81
## Forward sale/purchase agreement[1]

**DATE:** *(insert date)*

## PARTIES

1       The Fund: *(name)* [company number *(number)*] [of *(address)* *or* whose registered office is at *(address)*]

2       The Developer: *(name)* [company number *(number)*] [of *(address)* *or* whose registered office is at *(address)*]

[3      The Surety: *(name)* [company number *(number)*] [of *(address)* *or* whose registered office is at *(address)*]]

## CONTENTS

[3521]

## A       DEFINITIONS AND INTERPRETATION
### 1       Definitions

In this Agreement unless the context otherwise requires the following expressions shall have the following meanings:

1.1       **'Communication'**
         any notice application approval certificate or other communication from or on behalf of one party to another pursuant to this Agreement

1.2       **'Completion Date'**
         the date so prescribed by paragraph 1.4 of the [Third] Schedule

1.3       **'Contract Rate'**
         *(insert interest rate or method of calculating the interest rate by reference eg to the base lending rate of a named bank)*

1.4       **'Developer's Solicitors'**
         *(insert name and address of person or firm)*

1.5       **'Development'**
         the Development as defined in paragraph 1.12 of the [Third] Schedule

[1.6       **'Documents'**
         the documents (if any) particulars of which are set out in the Second Schedule]

1.7       **'Fund'**
         includes the successors in title to the Fund of the Property and its assigns

1.8       **'Fund's Solicitors'**
         *(insert name and address of person or firm)*

1.9       **'General Conditions'**
         [the Standard Commercial Property Conditions (1st Edn) *or (specify)*]

[3522]

**1.10**     **'Insolvent'**

1.10.1     in relation to a company that:

   1.10.1.1 it is deemed unable to pay its debts as defined in the Insolvency Act 1986 Section 123 (referred to as 'the Act' in the remainder of this definition)

   1.10.1.2 a proposal is made for a voluntary arrangement under Part I of the Act

   1.10.1.3 a petition is presented for an administration order under Part II of the Act

   1.10.1.4 a receiver or manager is appointed whether under Part III of the Act (including an administrative receiver) or otherwise

   1.10.1.5 it goes into liquidation as defined in Section 247(2) of the Act (other than a voluntary winding up which is first approved by the Fund and is for the sole purpose of amalgamation or reconstruction while solvent)

   1.10.1.6 a provisional liquidator is appointed under Section 135 of the Act

   1.10.1.7 a proposal is made for a scheme of arrangement under the Companies Act 1985 Section 425 as amended

1.10.2     and in relation to an individual that:

   1.10.2.1 an application is made for an interim order or a proposal is made for a voluntary arrangement under Part VIII of the Act

   1.10.2.2 a bankruptcy petition is presented to the court or his circumstances are such that a bankruptcy petition could be presented under Part IX of the Act

   1.10.2.3 he enters into a deed of arrangement

**1.11**     **'paragraph'**

a paragraph of a Schedule

**1.12**     **'Property'**

the property described in the First Schedule

**1.13**     **'Purchase Price'**

the sum of £...... increased or decreased (if at all) as the case may be by paragraph 9 of the [Fourth] Schedule and/or paragraph 9.2 of the [Third] Schedule

**1.14**     **'VAT'**

value added tax[2]

**1.15**     **'Working Day'**

any day except Saturdays Sundays and Bank or other public holidays

**[3523]**

## 2     Interpretation

2.1     Words importing one gender shall be construed as importing any other gender

2.2     Words importing the singular shall be construed as importing the plural and vice versa

2.3     Words importing persons shall be construed as importing a corporate body and/or a partnership and vice versa

2.4     Where any party comprises more than one person the obligations and liabilities of that party under this Agreement shall be joint and several obligations and liabilities of those persons

2.5     The clause headings do not form part of this Agreement and shall not be taken into account in its construction or interpretation

2.6     Any reference to a clause or a paragraph or a schedule is to one in this Agreement so numbered

2.7     Reference to a statute includes any amendment modification consolidation or re-enactment of that statute and any statutory instrument regulation or order made under that statute and for the time being in force

2.8     In case of any inconsistency between the General Conditions and the provisions of this Agreement the latter shall prevail

[3524]


**B**       **SALE AND PURCHASE**
**3**       **Agreement for sale**[3]
3.1     The Developer shall sell and the Fund shall buy the Property at the Purchase Price

3.2     The sale and purchase hereby agreed is conditional upon the Developer observing and performing its several obligations contained in the [Third] Schedule and the Developer shall observe and perform them accordingly

3.3     The Purchase Price shall be increased (if at all) and the Developer shall be entitled to such further remuneration if any so far as arising under the [Fourth] Schedule

3.4     Notwithstanding the foregoing the Purchase Price may be reduced in accordance with paragraph 9.2 of the [Third] Schedule

3.5     The Developer and Fund shall also observe and perform the several obligations on their respective parts contained in the [Fourth] Schedule

[3.6    The [Fifth] Schedule shall have effect in relation to environmental matters [and] contaminated land [and remediation]][4]


**4      Deposit**[5]

The Fund shall on or before the date of this Agreement pay a deposit of [10%] of the Purchase Price [and of the VAT upon it][6] to the Developer's Solicitors as [stakeholders *or* agents for the Developer] [by means of cash or telegraphic or other direct transfer banker's draft or a building society or bank guaranteed cheque or a cheque drawn on a solicitor's clients' account]


**5      Completion**

Completion of the sale and purchase and payment of the balance of the Purchase Price [and of VAT [on the whole of the Purchase Price]] shall take place on the Completion Date [at the offices of the Developer's Solicitors or where they may direct]


**6      Title guarantee**

The Developer sells with [full *or* limited] title guarantee


**7      Possession**

The Property is sold with vacant possession on completion


**8      Title**

[Title shall commence with *(description of instrument)* dated *(date)* and made between *(parties)* [and the Fund or the Fund's Solicitors having been supplied with an epitome of the title prior to the date of this Agreement the Fund shall be deemed to purchase with full knowledge of the title in all respects and shall not raise any requisitions or make any objection in relation to the title]
*or*

Title to the Property is registered at HM Land Registry with [absolute] title under title number *(number)* and title shall be deduced in accordance with the Land Registration Act 1925 Section 110 [save that copies of the entries on the register the filed plan and any documents referred to shall be office copies] [and the Fund or the Fund's Solicitors having been supplied with such copies prior to the date of this Agreement the Fund shall be deemed to purchase with full knowledge of the title in all respects and shall not raise any requisitions or make any objection in relation to the title]]

[3525]

**9     Developer not registered proprietor**[7]

9.1     If at the date of this Agreement the Property is the subject of an application for first registration or the title to the property has not been registered at HM Land Registry but will require registration on behalf of the Developer the Fund shall raise no objection or requisition in that respect so long as:

    9.1.1     The Developer's Solicitors shall have prior to completion deduced title in accordance with clause 8 and have provided the Fund's Solicitors with certified copies of the application (if any) for first registration of title to the Property and/or any conveyance or transfer from the person or persons applying for first registration to the Developer and

    9.1.2     Such conveyance or transfer is duly stamped and all appropriate applications have been made to enable the Developer (or as the case may be its predecessors in title) to become registered

    9.1.3     Upon completion of any related acquisition or purchase by the Developer the Developer shall forthwith make an expedited application for first registration to HM Land Registry and shall provide certified copies of the application and of all related documents to the Fund

9.2     The Fund shall not be required to complete the sale and purchase hereby agreed before completion of registration of the Developer's title nor until it is [reasonably] satisfied that the Developer's registered title fairly reflects the title and all other documents deduced to it

9.3     If completion shall be delayed by reason of non-registration of the Developer's title then without prejudice to any decrease in the Purchase Price allowed under paragraph 9.2.1 of the [Third] Schedule there shall be deducted from the Purchase Price on completion the greater of interest at the Contract Rate on the Purchase Price and any income for the time being receivable from the Property during such period of whatever nature

9.4     At any time during which completion shall be delayed by reason of non-registration of title the Fund may by notice at any time rescind this Agreement and the Deposit shall be returned to the Fund together with interest from such date until payment at *(insert rate)*

[3526]

**10     Encumbrances**

10.1     The Property is sold subject to and (where appropriate) with the benefit of the matters contained or referred to in the [Documents *or* the property [proprietorship] and charges registers of title number *(number)* [save for the Developer's subsisting mortgage]]

10.2     The Fund or the Fund's Solicitors having been supplied with copies of the [Documents *or* the property [proprietorship] and charges registers and the matters contained or referred to in the registers] prior to the date of this

Agreement the Fund shall be deemed to purchase with full notice and knowledge of the same and shall not raise any requisition or make any objection in relation to them

[10.3    The [transfer *or* conveyance] of the Property shall contain a covenant by the Fund that the Fund will observe and perform the covenants and conditions [contained or referred to in the Documents *or* contained or referred to in the property [proprietorship] and charges registers of title number *(number)*] and will indemnify and keep the Developer and its successors in title fully and effectually indemnified against all actions proceedings damages costs claims and expenses which may be suffered or incurred by the Developer or its successors in title in respect of any future breach or non-observance or non-performance of those covenants and conditions]

## 11    Matters affecting the Property

The Property is sold subject to the following matters:

11.1    all local land charges whether registered or not before the date of this Agreement and all matters capable of registration as local land charges whether or not actually so registered

11.2    all notices served and orders demands proposals or requirements made by any local public or other competent authority whether before or after the date of this Agreement

11.3    all actual or proposed charges notices orders restrictions agreements conditions contraventions or other matters arising under the enactments relating to town and country planning and environmental law

11.4    all easements quasi-easements rights exceptions or other similar matters whether or not apparent on inspection or disclosed in any of the documents referred to in this Agreement

**[3527]**

## 12    Disclaimer[8]

The Fund admits that:

12.1    it enters into this Agreement solely as a result of its own inspection and on the basis of the terms of this Agreement and not in reliance upon any representation or warranty either written or oral or implied made by or on behalf of the Developer (save for any representation or warranty contained in written replies given by the Developer's Solicitors to any preliminary inquiries raised by the Fund or the Fund's Solicitors)

12.2    the disclaimer contained in clause 12.1 does not apply to any matter relating to or concerning either the [Third] Schedule or the [Fourth] Schedule or any part or parts of those Schedules

12.3    this Agreement contains the entire agreement between the parties

## 13    Incorporation of conditions of sale[9]

The General Conditions shall apply to this Agreement in so far as they are applicable to a sale by private treaty and are not varied by or inconsistent with the terms of this Agreement [and shall be amended as follows: *(insert details of amendments required)*]

## [14    Restrictions on assignment[10]

14.1    This Agreement is personal to the Fund and shall not be capable of assignment

[14.2    The Developer shall not be required to transfer the Property to anyone other than the Fund as named in this Agreement]]

## 15    Merger on completion[11]

The provisions of this Agreement shall not merge on completion of the [transfer *or* conveyance] of the Property so far as they remain to be performed

## 16    VAT[12]

16.1    On the Completion Date the Fund shall pay to the Developer VAT in respect of the Purchase Price [less any VAT paid in respect of the deposit] and the Developer shall provide to the Fund a receipted VAT invoice addressed to the Fund for the amount of the VAT paid by the Fund

16.2    The Fund declares that it has no intention of using the Property or of allowing it to be used whether by letting or otherwise in such a way as to give rise to the disapplication of any election to waive exemption to tax made by the Developer

16.3    The Fund shall indemnify and keep indemnified the Developer against all VAT which the Developer has to repay to HM Customs and Excise including any under the capital goods scheme and against all VAT which is irrecoverable by the Developer (together in each case with interest penalties and costs) due to the disapplication of any election to waive exemption to tax made by the Developer arising in any way from the use of the property or part or parts of it for an exempt purpose

## [17    Nature of this agreement[13]

This Agreement is a deed and has been executed by the parties to it as a deed]

**[3528]**

## C    DEFAULT

## 18    Events of default[14]

Each of the events specified in clauses 18.1–18.6 inclusive is an Event of Default:

18.1    The Developer becomes Insolvent

18.2    Any representation warranty or statement made by the Developer in this Agreement or in any notice or other document report certificate or statement delivered by it pursuant to or in connection with this Agreement proves to have been incorrect or misleading in any material respect when made or deemed to have been made

18.3    The Developer fails duly to perform or comply with any other obligation expressed to be assumed by it in this Agreement and

18.3.1    (if in the opinion of the Fund such default is capable of remedy) the Developer fails to remedy the default within [10] Working Days after the Fund has given notice to the Developer specifying the default and the required remedy and

18.3.2    such failure may in the reasonable opinion of the Fund prejudice to a material extent the ability of the Developer to complete the Works

18.4    The Developer repudiates this Agreement or does or allows to be done or omitted any act or thing which the Fund reasonably considers to evidence an intention to repudiate this Agreement

18.5    Any event or series of events occurs which in the reasonable opinion of the Fund may materially and adversely affect the business assets or financial condition of the Developer so that it may be unable to comply with any of its obligations under this Agreement

18.6    The Works are not completed by a date [6] months after the Target Completion Date (as such terms are defined in the [Third] Schedule) [or by the End Date (as defined in the [Third] Schedule) if later]

**19      Consequences of Default**

Where an Event of Default occurs the Fund (without prejudice to any other available remedy) may serve notice of default on the Developer whereupon:

19.1     If completion has taken place the Fund will not be obliged to make any further payment under this Agreement

19.2     If completion has not taken place the Fund may by notice at any time rescind this Agreement [and the deposit shall be returned to the Fund together with interest from such date until payment at the Contract Rate]

                                                                                          **[3529]**


**D       DISPUTES**

**20      Definition**

For the purposes of clauses 20–25:

20.1     'Dispute' means a dispute issue difference question or claim as between the Fund and the Developer relating to or arising at any time out of either or both of the [Third] Schedule and the [Fourth] Schedule in this Agreement[15]

20.2     'Party' means a party to the Dispute

20.3     'Specialist' means a person qualified to act as an independent expert or an arbitrator in relation to the Dispute having experience in the profession in which he practises for the period of at least [10] years immediately preceding the date of referral

**21      Dispute Notice**

Either Party may give to the other notice ('Dispute Notice') requiring a Dispute to be referred to a Specialist and proposing an appropriate Specialist

**22      Counter Notice**

The Party served will be deemed to accept the proposals made in the Dispute Notice unless that Party within [10] Working Days of service of the Dispute Notice gives notice rejecting one or more of the proposals or unless each Party serves a Dispute Notice on the other contemporaneously

**23      Type of Specialist**

Unless the Parties agree or are deemed to agree the appropriate Specialist:

23.1     if the Parties do not agree which type of Specialist is appropriate to resolve the Dispute either Party may refer that question to the President or next most senior available officer of the Royal Institution of Chartered Surveyors who will (with the right to take such further advice as he may require) determine that question and nominate or arrange to have nominated the appropriate Specialist

23.2     if the Parties do agree the appropriate type of Specialist but do not agree the identity of the Specialist he will be nominated on the application of either Party by the President or other most senior available officer of the organisation generally recognised as being responsible for the relevant type of Specialist but if no such organisation exists then by the President or next most senior available officer of the Royal Institution of Chartered Surveyors

**24      Arbitration**

Unless the Parties otherwise agree the reference to a Specialist shall be made to him as an arbitrator under the Arbitration Act 1996 but if the Parties agree to the Specialist acting as an expert his decisions shall be final and binding upon the Parties

**25     Costs**

The liability for paying all costs of referring a Dispute to a Specialist including costs connected with the appointment of the Specialist will be decided by the Specialist

**[3530]**

**[E     SURETY**

**26     Surety**

26.1     This Agreement has been entered into with the consent and at the request of the Surety

26.2     The Surety guarantees the due performance by the Developer of all of the Developer's obligations under this Agreement and will perform them or otherwise indemnify the Fund in respect of any non-performance of such obligations including (for the avoidance of doubt) any obligation of the Developer which is agreed or determined under clauses 20–25

26.3     The obligations of the Surety will not be affected by:

26.3.1     any variation of this Agreement to which the Surety is not a party

26.3.2     any other agreement entered into by the Developer

26.3.3     any time or indulgence given by the Fund

26.3.4     the Developer becoming Insolvent

26.3.5     any other act deed or thing except an express release of the Surety or variation to the Surety's liability given in writing by the Fund]

**[3531]**

**F     MISCELLANEOUS**

**27     Communication**

27.1     All Communications shall be in writing

27.2     A Communication from any party ('the Sender') to any other ('the Recipient') will be duly made if in writing and either delivered to the Recipient (including in a manner provided at clause 27.5) or sent within the United Kingdom by [first class prepaid or] registered or recorded delivery post addressed to the Recipient at its address as stated in this Agreement or as the Recipient may from time to time notify the Sender

27.3     While the Surveyor (as defined in the [Third] Schedule) is acting as agent of the Fund as specified in this Agreement a Communication duly made to the Surveyor will constitute a Communication duly made to the Fund

27.4     A Communication sent by post will be deemed to have been made on the second Working Day next following the day of posting [and it will be sufficient proof of posting for first class prepaid post to show that a prepaid envelope containing the Communication was properly addressed and either delivered to or collected by the Post Office or placed in a Post Office letterbox]

27.5     In this clause 27 'writing' includes telex facsimile or other electronic means of communication (except e-mail) and 'delivered' includes transmission by such means in which event the Communication will be deemed to have been made when the Sender has finished its transmission without having any reasonable grounds for suspecting that the transmission has failed or was incomplete (except that if such transmission takes place outside normal business hours the Communication will be deemed to have been made when normal business hours next commence)

27.6     In this clause 27 'normal business hours' are [9.30 am to 5.30 pm] on Working Days

**[3532]**

## 28    Partnership and agency

Neither the Developer nor the Fund has any intention of carrying on business in partnership with the other concerning the Project (as defined in the [Third] Schedule) or any related matter

## 29    Waiver

No failure or delay by the Fund to exercise any right power or remedy under this Agreement will operate as a waiver of it in whole or in part nor will any partial exercise preclude any further exercise of the same or of some other right power or remedy

## 30    Headings

The clause and sub-clause and schedule headings do not affect the meaning of this Agreement

FIRST SCHEDULE
The Property
*(describe the Property)*


[SECOND SCHEDULE
Documents
*(insert details)*]


[THIRD] SCHEDULE
Development Obligations

| I | Definitions and Interpretation |
| II | Preliminaries |
| III | Works |
| IV | Administration |
| V | Completion |

[3533]

## I    DEFINITIONS AND INTERPRETATION

In this Schedule unless the context otherwise requires the following further expressions shall have the following meanings:

**1.1    'Approved Scheme'**
As defined in paragraph 5 of this Schedule

**1.2    'Architect'**
*(name)* [company number *(number)*] [of *(address)* or whose registered office is at *(address)*] or such other firm as may be approved by the Fund[16]

**1.3    'Building Contract'**
[The contract dated *(date)* or] such [other] contract with the Contractor for carrying out the Works as may be approved by the Fund pursuant to paragraph 4 of this Schedule

**1.4    'Completion Date'**
The Completion Date as referred to at clause 1.2 of this Agreement as more particularly mentioned at paragraph 23.3 of this Schedule

**1.5   'Consents'**
All the planning permissions listed building consents building regulations consents fire officer approvals and other permissions approvals licences and similar consents (including any modifications from time to time) which are necessary to enable the Approved Scheme to be implemented without breach of any statute or lawful requirement of any competent authority

**1.6   'Consultants'**
The Architect Environmental Consultant Mechanical and Electrical Engineer Planning Supervisor Quantity Surveyor and Structural Engineer [*(add titles of any other consultants already appointed and include relevant definitions of those titles in alphabetical order as appropriate)*] and such other professional advisers as may be approved by the Fund

**1.7   'Consultant's Warranty'**
A deed to be entered into by each Consultant with the Fund and/or any tenant [substantially] in one or other as the case may be of the forms annexed

**1.8   'Contractor'**
*(name)* [company number *(number)*] [of *(address)* or whose registered office is at *(address)*] or such other building contractor as may be approved by the Fund pursuant to paragraph 4 of this Schedule

**1.9   'Contractor's Warranty'**
A deed to be entered into by the Contractor with the Fund and/or any tenant [substantially] in one or other as the case may be of the forms annexed[17]

[3534]

**1.10   'Defects Liability Period'**
[12 months] from the [Practical Completion Date][18]

**1.11   'Deleterious Materials'**
Materials not in accordance with British Standards or which are generally known to be deleterious at the time of incorporation in the Works [and any materials specifically mentioned in any Consultant's Warranty or Contractor's Warranty][19]

**1.12   'Development'**
*(number)* square metres [Gross [External *or* Internal] *or* Net Internal] Area as the term is defined in the [Fourth] Schedule of [industrial *or* warehouse *or* office] premises[20]

**1.13   'End Date'[21]**
*(insert date)*

**1.14   'Environmental Consultant'**
*(name and address)* or such other firm as may be approved by the Fund

**1.15   'Excepted Risks'**
1.15.1   Ionising radiations or contamination by radioactivity from any nuclear fuel or from any nuclear waste from the combustion of nuclear fuel
1.15.2   Radioactive toxic explosive or other hazardous properties of any explosive nuclear assembly or nuclear component
1.15.3   Pressure waves caused by aircraft or other aerial devices travelling at sonic or supersonic speeds
1.15.4   Any other risks excepted by the insurance provisions of the Building Contract[22]

**1.16   'Full Reinstatement Value'**
The cost of complete reinstatement (assuming total destruction) allowing for inflation during the period of reinstatement the costs of demolition and site clearance and professional fees including VAT where applicable on all such costs

[3535]

**1.17    'Insured Risks'**
1.17.1   Fire lightning explosion storm tempest flood
1.17.2   Bursting or overflowing of water tanks apparatus or pipes
1.17.3   Earthquake
1.17.4   Aircraft and other aerial devices or articles dropped from them
1.17.5   Riot and civil commotion
but excluding Excepted Risks

**1.18    'Letter of appointment'[23]**
The written terms under which a Consultant is appointed

**1.19    'Parties'**
The Developer and the Fund [and the Surety]

**1.20    'Planning Supervisor'**
*(name and address)* or such other [person *or* firm] as may be approved by the Fund and appointed for the purpose the Construction (Design and Management) Regulations 1994

**1.21    'Plans'**
The plans and drawings for the Development referred to in paragraph 5.1 of this Schedule comprising the Approved Scheme

**1.22    'Practical Completion'**
Practical completion of the Works pursuant to the Building Contract

**1.23    'Practical Completion Date'**
The date of Practical Completion as certified under the Building Contract[24]

**1.24    Programme**
As defined in paragraph 7 of this Schedule

**1.25    'Project'**
All aspects of [site acquisition] demolition site preparation (including remediation of contamination) design carrying out completion and letting of the Development as contemplated by this Agreement

**1.26    'Quantity Surveyor'**
*(name and address)* or such other firm as may be approved by the Fund

**[3536]**

**1.27    'Relevant Event'[25]**
1.27.1   Force majeure
1.27.2   Exceptionally adverse weather conditions
1.27.3   Loss or damage occasioned by Insured Risks
1.27.4   Civil commotion local combination of workmen strike or lockout affecting any of the trades engaged in the Works or in the preparation manufacture or transportation of goods or materials required for the Works or in the preparation of the design of the Works
1.27.5   The exercise after the date of this Agreement of any statutory power which restricts the availability or use of labour essential to the proper carrying out of the Works or prevents or delays goods materials fuel or energy essential to the proper carrying out of the Works
1.27.6   The carrying out by a local authority or statutory or other undertaking of work pursuant to its statutory obligations in relation to the Works or failure to carry out such work
1.27.7   Delay (which both the Developer and Contractor have taken all practicable steps to avoid or reduce) consequent upon a change in statutory requirements since the date of this Agreement

[1.27.8   Unreasonable delay on the part of the Surveyor in carrying out his functions under this Agreement]

1.27.9   Delay in receipt of any necessary permission or approval of any statutory body which the Developer and the Contractor have taken all practicable steps to avoid or reduce

1.27.10  The use or threat of terrorism and/or the activity of the relevant authorities in dealing with such use or threat

**1.28   'Services'**
Facilities such as water gas electricity drainage and telecommunications which are in or pass through over or under the Development and the relevant pipes wires ducts and other conduits

**1.29   'Specification'**
The specification annexed including the bills of quantities [intended to be] comprised in the Building Contract

[3537]

**1.30   'Structural Engineer'**
*(name and address)* or such other firm as may be approved by the Fund

**1.31   'Sub-contractor'**
A sub-contractor to the main contractor under the Building Contract having a design responsibility

**1.32   'Sub-contractor's Warranty'**
A deed to be entered into by a Sub-Contractor with the Fund and/or any tenant [substantially] in one or other as the case may be of the forms annexed[26]

**1.33   'Surveyor'**
*(name and address)* or such other [firm *or* surveyor] [of similar standing or suitably qualified and] nominated by the Fund

**1.34   'Target Completion Date'**
*(insert date)*

**1.35   'Works'**
The works of [demolition site preparation (including remediation of contamination) and] construction of the Development

**1.36   'Works Completion Certificate'**
As defined in paragraph 23

**1.37   'Works Completion Date'**
As defined in paragraph 23

[3538]–[3539]

**II   PRELIMINARIES**

**2   Approvals**

2.1   All and any applications for any consents or approvals made by the Developer to the Fund shall:
    2.1.1   be in writing and
    2.1.2   be made to the Surveyor
[2.2   Every such consent or approval shall not be unreasonably withheld save where expressed to the contrary in this Schedule]

[2.3    Notwithstanding paragraph 2.2 where the Fund considers that to grant any
        consent or approval under this Schedule would have effect to materially alter the
        appearance restrict the user increase the cost diminish the lettable area or reduce
        the value of the Project the Fund may refuse such consent or approval]

3       **Consultants**[27]

3.1     The Consultants named in this Schedule are approved by the Fund
3.2     The Developer will not appoint any other professional adviser as a Consultant
        without the Fund's prior approval but will appoint such further Consultants as
        the Fund may reasonably require
3.3     The Developer will not dismiss a Consultant without the Fund's prior approval
3.4     The Developer will appoint each Consultant under a Letter of Appointment in
        a form first approved by the Fund obtaining from him in favour of the Fund not
        later than the date of actual completion of the sale and purchase (time being of
        the essence) a Consultant's Warranty

4       **Contractor**

4.1     [The Contractor named in this Schedule is approved by the Fund
        *or*
        The Developer shall not appoint a contractor except as approved by the Fund
        and from a list of not less than [6] prospective contractors first submitted to and
        approved by the Fund]
4.2     The Developer will not dismiss the Contractor nor engage any other building
        contractor or nominate any sub-contractor without the Fund's prior approval
4.3     The Developer will engage the Contractor under the Building Contract or a
        building contract in a form first approved by the Fund [at the same time]
        obtaining from the Contractor in favour of the Fund [not later than the date of
        actual completion of the sale and purchase (time being of the essence)] a
        Contractor's Warranty

                                                                          **[3540]**

5       **Approved Scheme**[28]

5.1     The plans and drawings for the Development and the Specification [annexed to
        this Agreement or identified by the following numbers *(numbers)* or initialled by
        the Parties] have been approved by the Fund and comprise the Approved Scheme
5.2     To the extent that the designs for the Development are not described in full in
        the Approved Scheme such designs will be submitted to the Fund for the Fund's
        approval before construction of the Development is commenced provided that
        no such approval will in any way affect the responsibilities of the Developer
        under this Schedule
5.3     The Approved Scheme will not be varied without the Fund's approval [(which
        may be refused at the Fund's discretion)] and the expression 'Approved Scheme'
        means from time to time the Approved Scheme as originally approved
        incorporating all approved variations (if any)

6       **Consents**[29]

6.1     The Developer will use all reasonable endeavours to obtain the Consents as soon
        as practicable submitting each application to the Fund for approval and obtaining
        such approval before application is made and promptly notifying the Fund of the
        outcome of each application supplying copies of any documents issued
6.2     The Developer will not implement any Consent until it has been approved by the
        Fund

**7       The Programme**[30]

7.1      [The Programme is the [bar chart] programme annexed to this Agreement
         showing the estimated duration of each stage of the Works and when each stage
         including Practical Completion is due to be achieved
         *or*
         The Developer will prepare as soon as practicable [and in any event within *(time
         limit)*] a programme [in bar chart form] which will be the Programme for the
         purposes of this Schedule showing the estimated duration of each stage of the
         Works and when each stage including Practical Completion is due to be achieved]

7.2      The Developer will not vary the Programme except as provided in this
         Schedule and the expression 'the Programme' means the Programme as from
         time to time so varied

                                                                                    **[3541]**


**III     WORKS**

**8       General Requirements**[31]

The Developer will carry out the Works:

8.1      in a proper and workmanlike manner

8.2      with good quality and suitable materials

8.3      in accordance with the Approved Scheme

8.4      in compliance with the Consents

8.5      diligently and expeditiously [in accordance with the Programme] in order to
         achieve Practical Completion by the Target Completion Date

8.6      in compliance with all requirements of statute and all lawful requirements of
         local authorities and other competent authorities

8.7      [in accordance with all relevant codes of practice and British Standards]

8.8      in compliance with the Building Contract [and the Documents]

8.9      without infringement of any rights reservations covenants restrictions
         stipulations or other encumbrances binding upon or affecting the Property

[8.10    to the [reasonable] satisfaction of the Fund]


**9       Delay**[32]

9.1      If by reason of a Relevant Event the Developer considers that delay will be
         caused to [the Programme or to] the Target Completion Date the Fund will
         upon application by the Developer supported by such evidence as the Fund may
         [reasonably] require [and the advice of the appropriate Consultant] allow such
         amendment to [the Programme or] the Target Completion Date as may [in its
         opinion be appropriate or be reasonable] after taking into account any extent to
         which such delay has been caused by any act default or omission of the
         Developer but under no circumstances will the Target Completion Date be
         postponed beyond the End Date

9.2      If the Developer fails to complete the Works by the Target Completion Date as
         extended by paragraph 9.1 then at the option of the Fund:

         9.2.1     the Purchase Price shall be reduced by (amount) per [day *or* week]
                   for the period between the Target Completion Date as so extended
                   and the Works Completion Date [or] [and without prejudice to the
                   foregoing]

         9.2.2     The Fund may [notwithstanding] at any time rescind this Agreement
                   by notice [and the Deposit shall be returned to the Fund together
                   with interest from such date until payment at *(insert rate)*]

                                                                                    **[3542]**

## 10    Insurance[33]

### 10.1    General requirements

10.1.1    The Developer will at its own expense effect or secure and maintain the insurance mentioned in this Schedule:

    10.1.1.1    with an insurance office [and on terms or under policies whose terms exclusions and conditions have first been] approved by the Fund

    10.1.1.2    naming the Fund as one of the joint insured parties

    10.1.1.3    until the End Date or (if earlier) until the date of actual completion

    10.1.1.4    under policies [copies of] which are to be produced to the Fund [on demand or within 7 days of issue] together with evidence that current premiums have been paid

and the Developer will not permit any variation of insurance cover without the Fund's prior approval and will immediately notify the Fund of any endorsements or other amendments to the relevant policies received from the insurers and will from time to time effect any further insurance which may in the Fund's [reasonable] opinion be prudent

[10.1.2    For so long as the insurance prescribed by the Building Contract remains in force and to the extent that it complies with paragraph 10.1.1 (including both the Developer and the Fund as the named insured) then such insurance shall suffice for the purposes of paragraph 10.1.1]

### 10.2    The Development

The Works all materials structures and buildings upon the Property and (when completed) the Development will be insured for Full Reinstatement Value against loss damage or destruction by any of the Insured Risks [and in an amount [of not less than £... million *or* first approved by the Fund]]

### 10.3    Reinstatement

In the event of any loss damage or destruction to the Works materials structures or buildings on Site or the completed Development:

10.3.1    the Developer will continue to carry out the Works unless the loss or damage is so extensive or of such a nature as to make this impossible or inadvisable

10.3.2    the Developer will use all reasonable endeavours promptly to obtain the maximum payment of insurance moneys

10.3.3    the Developer will proceed diligently and expeditiously to reinstate the loss damage or destruction and to complete the Works in accordance with this Schedule

**[3543]**

### 10.4    Public liability

Without prejudice to its liability to indemnify the Fund in accordance with paragraph 11 of this Schedule the Developer will take out and maintain insurance with a limit of indemnity of not less than £... million for any one occurrence or series of occurrences arising out of the carrying out of the Works and in respect of damage to any property real or personal other than the Works arising out of the carrying out of the Works and caused by the negligence of the Developer the Contractor or any sub-contractor of the Contractor

### 10.5    Failure

If the Developer does not insure as required by this paragraph or fails to produce adequate evidence that such insurance is in force the Fund may:

10.5.1    itself effect such insurance cover as it may consider prudent and the Developer shall indemnify the Fund accordingly or

10.5.2    at any time rescind this Agreement in accordance with clause 18.3

**10.6      Development at risk of the Developer**

Notwithstanding the foregoing the Works the Development and the Property shall be at the risk in all respects of the Developer until the date of actual completion

**10.7      Insurance by the Fund**

Upon and from the date of actual completion the Fund will insure the Development in accordance with the terms of the Lease

[3544]

**11      Indemnity**[34]

In addition to any claims which the Fund may have in relation to a breach of this Agreement and this Schedule the Developer will to the extent that moneys are not recovered from insurers indemnify the Fund in respect of any liability for the following matters in relation to the Project until the date of actual completion except to the extent that a lessee under a Lease (as defined in the [Fourth] Schedule) is responsible to the Fund for such matters:

11.1      death or personal injury to any person arising out of the carrying out of the Works save any person for whom the Fund is responsible

11.2      injury or damage to any property real or personal other than the Works in so far as such injury or damage arises out of the carrying out of the Works and to the extent that the same is due to any negligence breach of statutory duty omission or default of the Developer the Contractor or a sub-contractor of the Developer

11.3      any liability in respect of and any fees or charges legally demandable under any Act of Parliament or any regulation or bye-law of any local authority or of any statutory undertaker in respect of the Works

11.4      the infringement of the rights of any third party in connection with the Property

11.5      observing and performing all provisions contained or referred to in the Documents

**12      Third party rights**[35]

12.1      The Developer will ensure that the rights and interests of third parties are not infringed by the Project and will with the prior approval of the Fund enter into such agreements relating to rights of light and other easements and party structures and pay such compensation as may be necessary (and the Fund will join in such agreements so far as necessary as contractual purchaser subject to the completion of the purchase and thereafter as owner of the Property)

12.2      Where the London Building Acts 1930–1939 the Party Wall, etc Act 1996 (or any re-enactment of them) apply the Developer will comply with (and issue all notices required under) those Acts in connection with the Development and will comply with the terms of any awards made pursuant to those Acts

**13      Services**

The Developer will with the Fund's prior approval negotiate such agreements with statutory undertakers and others as may be required to secure for the Development all Services required and the diversion in a satisfactory manner of all Services which are located in a position which would interfere with the Project (and the Fund will join in such agreements as are approved by it and so far as necessary as contractual purchaser subject to the completion of the purchase and thereafter as owner of the Property)

[3545]

**14      Site management**[36]

The Developer will secure that:

14.1     the Property is at all times secured as fully as may be reasonably practicable against unauthorised entry

14.2     no material goods or equipment is brought deposited or stored on the Property except that from time to time properly required for the Works

14.3     all material stored on the Property is kept in a secure compound and adequately protected

14.4     all surplus material rubble rubbish and waste is properly cleared and removed from the Property when it is no longer required

14.5     the Property is maintained in a tidy condition and free from rubbish

14.6     there is no excavation of the Property or extraction of soil earth clay gravel sand or minerals except as required for the Works

14.7     proper precautions are taken for the safety of all persons upon or in the vicinity of the Property

14.8     there are no advertisements posters placards or signs affixed to displayed from on the boundaries of or on the Property except (with the prior approval of the Fund) those connected with the Project

14.9     the Works are carried out in a manner which does not cause a nuisance and causes the minimum of annoyance inconvenience and disturbance to owners or occupiers of neighbouring properties or members of the public [and in particular no work will be carried out except [between the hours of 8 am and 6 pm Mondays to Fridays] [and 8 am and 1 pm on Saturdays]]

14.10    proper provision is made for the support and use of land walls roads footpaths and buildings adjoining adjacent or near to the Property and for the protection of all Services

14.11    all debris is removed from such roads and footpaths and the proper requirements of the highways and other competent authorities are observed and performed

14.12    hoardings of sufficient height are erected around the Property

14.13    good efficient and well-maintained plant and equipment are used on the Property

14.14    proper arrangements are made with the relevant authorities for the provision of water gas electricity telephone and other services required for the Works

14.15    the requirements of highways and other competent authorities are duly met

14.16    the Works are maintained in good repair and condition

                                                                                          **[3546]**

**15      Deleterious materials**

The Developer will [use all reasonable endeavours to] ensure that no Deleterious Materials are used in the Works

**16      Archaeological antiquities**[37]

Subject always to the provisions of the Ancient Monuments and Archaeological Areas Act 1979:

16.1     any article of value or antiquity or remains of geological historical or archaeological interest on the Property will (as between the Developer and the Fund and subject to completion of the sale and purchase of the Property) belong to the Fund

16.2     if any such article is or remains are discovered the Developer will immediately inform the Fund and comply with the Fund's directions as to inspection protection and disposal of such article or remains

                                                                                          **[3547]**

## IV   ADMINISTRATION

### 17   The Surveyor[38]

The Fund has appointed the Surveyor to act as the agent of the Fund under this Agreement (unless otherwise expressly provided):

17.1   to consider and respond to applications for the Fund's approval

17.2   to monitor the performance of the Developer the Contractor and the Consultants

17.3   to issue certificates or otherwise indicate whether or not the Fund is satisfied with any matter

17.4   to issue and receive Communications on behalf of the Fund

and until notice is given to the contrary by the Fund the Developer is authorised and required to deal with and rely upon the Surveyor as the agent of the Fund in all such matters

### 18   Consultation

The Developer will in relation to the Project:

18.1   regularly inform consult report to and liaise with the Surveyor on all matters including all material measures taken and stages reached the general progress of the Works and any material problems or delays which have arisen or are likely to do so

18.2   promptly supply to the Surveyor copies of all relevant written material when it is received or produced by or on behalf of the Developer

### 19   Information[39]

The following illustrate (but do not limit) the types of information to be supplied to the Surveyor under paragraph 18.2 of this Schedule:

19.1   All plans and drawings the Specification structural calculations and other material from time to time comprising the Approved Scheme

19.2   Applications for and correspondence relating to Consents and the outcome of such applications

19.3   Letters of Appointment

19.4   The Building Contract

19.5   Lists of sub-contractors and suppliers

19.6   Test certificates and specialist reports and surveys

[19.7   Valuations by the Quantity Surveyor]

[19.8   Any written advice on contamination provided by the Environmental Consultant]

19.9   Architect's instructions

19.10   Minutes of all formal meetings (including site meetings design team meetings working party or project meetings)

### 20   Meetings[40]

The Surveyor is entitled although not obliged to attend all formal meetings relating to the Project whether or not the Contractor or a Consultant is entitled to attend and will be given not less than [2] Working Days' notice (or in emergency as much notice as possible) of such meetings

[3548]

**21    Control**[41]

21.1    The Surveyor [and any duly authorised representative of the Fund] may upon reasonable notice (where practicable) at [any time *or* all reasonable times] enter the Property to carry out any inspection [test] or survey [or for any other [reasonable] purpose] connected with the Project but [he *or* they] will cause as little interference as practicable

21.2    If prior to Practical Completion the Surveyor gives notice to the Developer [on reasonable grounds] that any works or materials are not in accordance with the Approved Scheme or are not to the standard or the quality required by this Agreement the Developer will commence appropriate action to remove the defective works or materials and make good the defects as soon as practicable

21.3    The Surveyor will not issue any direct instructions to the Contractor or to any of the Consultants and will not communicate with the Contractor or with any of the Consultants except in an emergency or in a meeting where the Developer is represented but will (without prejudice to any Contractor's or Consultant's Warranty) address all other communications to the Developer

**[3549]**

**22    Responsibility**

22.1    The Fund is relying on the Developer properly to carry out and complete the Project and the Developer warrants that it has the skill and experience required to carry out the Project[42]

22.2    No involvement by the Fund (whether through its Surveyor or otherwise) in considering whether or not to grant any consent or approval or issue certificates or in attending (or failing to attend) meetings or otherwise in supervising or omitting to supervise the Project in any way relieves or affects the duties of the Developer the Contractor or the Consultants in relation to the Project [except to the extent that the Fund or the Surveyor causes loss by imposing a requirement with which the Developer must under the terms of this Agreement comply but which is inconsistent with the recommendations of the Contractor or a Consultant][43]

22.3    The Developer will duly observe and perform all provisions of the Building Contract and of all Letters of Appointment and other agreements relating to the Project on the part of the Developer as employer to be observed or performed and (save with the approval of the Fund) secure the observance and performance by the other parties to such agreements of the provisions on their part to be observed or performed[44]

22.4    None of the provisions of the Building Contract or of any Letter of Appointment shall be varied or waived nor will any action to secure the compliance with such provisions be discharged settled or compromised without the approval of the Fund [which may be withheld in any such case at the Fund's discretion]

**[3550]**

**V    COMPLETION**

**23    Works completion**[45]

23.1    When the Works have reached Practical Completion in accordance with the terms of this Agreement the Surveyor will issue a Works Completion Certificate to that effect and the date stated in the Works Completion Certificate is the Works Completion Date

[23.2    The Surveyor will not refuse to issue a Works Completion Certificate if minor defects in the Works exist of such a nature and number that they would not prevent the issue by the Architect of a certificate of Practical Completion under the Building Contract]

23.3    Subject to clause 18.6 of this Agreement the Completion Date shall be [10] Working Days after the Works Completion Date

## 24    Procedure[46]

24.1    The Parties will use their reasonable endeavours to ensure that the Works Completion Date and Practical Completion Date are contemporaneous

24.2    If the Developer gives to the Fund not less than [10] Working Days' notice of the date of the site meeting at which the Architect is expected to decide whether Practical Completion has occurred the Surveyor will attend such meeting and endeavour to agree with the Architect whether or not it is appropriate to issue a certificate of Practical Completion under the Building Contract (but without prejudice to the Architect's professional discretion and duties under the Building Contract)

24.3    If he considers that the Works are not substantially complete in accordance with this Agreement the Surveyor will give his reasons orally at the relevant site meeting and confirm these reasons in writing to the Developer within [3] Working Days stating what further Works are required

24.4    The Developer will carry out such further Works as soon as possible and then give to the Surveyor reasonable notice of a further site meeting so that the procedure set out in this paragraph may be repeated (save as regards Practical Completion under the Building Contract if a certificate of Practical Completion has been issued) as often as necessary until the Works Completion Certificate is issued

24.5    If the Works are substantially complete in accordance with this Agreement the Surveyor will issue the Works Completion Certificate within [5] Working Days of the relevant site meeting

**[3551]**

## 25    Defects

Without prejudice to all other rights and remedies of the Fund the Developer will at its own expense make good as soon as practicable all defects which may appear in the Development and are notified to the Developer before the end of the Defects Liability Period and which are due to the failure of the Developer to comply with its obligations under this Agreement or to frost occurring before the Practical Completion Date (or the Works Completion Date if later) and which (if inconsistent with the foregoing) the Architect has notified the Contractor should be carried out under the defects liability provisions of the Building Contract

## 26    Completion Documents

Within one month following the Completion Date the Developer will supply to the Fund:

26.1    three sets of 'as built' Plans of the Development

26.2    maintenance manuals and manufacturer's warranties in relation to all plant and equipment installed in the Development

26.3    such confirmations as the Fund may reasonably require that no Deleterious Materials have been used in the Development

26.4    the health and safety file

**[3552]**

**27     Plans**

Within one month following the Completion Date the Developer will either:

27.1      procure assignment absolutely to the Fund of the full copyright of the Plans to which the Developer may be entitled or

27.2      take such other steps effectually to procure for the Fund the full right and entitlement to use on licence without further payment or liability for further payment the Plans for the purposes only of maintaining repairing and renewing the Development and execute all such deeds and documents as the Fund may reasonably require effectually to vest such rights in the Fund

**28     Proceedings**[47]

28.1      The Fund may at any time following the latest of the date of actual completion the expiry of the Defects Liability Period and the completion of all related remedial works require the Developer to assign to the Fund (in a form approved by the Fund) such rights as the Developer may have against the Contractor or any Consultant and in so far as necessary the Developer shall make application to the Contractor and/or any such Consultant as the case may be for any requisite consent and the Developer shall use all reasonable endeavours to obtain the same

28.2      In so far as assignment is not permitted or consent is not forthcoming the Fund may in the alternative commence prosecute or defend as the case may be any relevant proceedings in the name and on behalf of the Developer and in so far as the Developer is already entitled thereto shall pay to the Developer any costs and/or damages received to which the Developer may be entitled after counterclaim or set-off in relation to the Fund and in priority only after the interests of the Fund

**[3553]**

[FOURTH] SCHEDULE[48]
LETTING PURCHASE PRICE AND FURTHER REMUNERATION

I        Definitions
II       Letting
III      Increase in Purchase Price and Further Remuneration

Part I: Definitions

**1     Definitions**

In this Schedule unless the context otherwise requires the following further expressions have the following meanings:

**1.1      'Agreement for Lease'**

Any agreement entered into (inter alia) by the Developer for the grant of a Lease

**1.2      'Code'**

The Code of Measuring Practice of The Royal Institution of Chartered Surveyors and Incorporated Society of Valuers and Auctioneers [Edition 4, 1993]

**1.3      'Gross [External *or* Internal] Area'**

The Gross [External *or* Internal] Area of the Development as measured in accordance with the Code

**1.4      'Interest Rate'**
*(insert interest rate or method of calculating the interest rate by reference eg to the base lending rate of a named bank)*

**[3554]**

**1.5      'Lease'**[49]
As defined in paragraph 3.1 of this Schedule

**1.6      'Letting Agents'**
*(name and address)* or such other firm as may be approved by the Fund

**1.7      'Letting Policy'**
The letting policy so entitled annexed to this Agreement

**[1.8      'Net Internal Area'**
The Net Internal Area of the Project as measured in accordance with the Code]

**1.9      'Net Rental Income'**
[The [aggregate] initial annual rent[s] exclusive of VAT payable under the Lease[s] *or* the [average *or* highest] annual rent exclusive of VAT payable under [the *or* each] Lease during the first [5] years of the term] disregarding any rent payable to reimburse the cost of insurance or services provided by the landlord

**1.10      'Settlement Date'**
The date when a Lease has [or Leases have] been granted in respect of the whole of the Development (or all parts of it designed for letting) [and the full initial rent reserved has become payable]

**1.11      'Target Rent'**
[*(amount)* per annum *or (amount)* per square metre per annum] of the [Gross [External *or* Internal] *or* Net Internal] Area exclusive of VAT

**[3555]**


Part II: Letting

**2      Letting**

2.1      The Developer shall in consultation with the Fund [use all reasonable endeavours to] negotiate the letting of the Development [as quickly as possible] and for this purpose will instruct the Letting Agents

2.2      The Developer shall [(except in so far as the Letting Agents expressly advise in writing or as the Fund may otherwise approve)] comply with the Letting Policy

2.3      The Developer shall not vary the Letting Policy except upon the written advice of the Letting Agents and with the approval of the Fund [which may be withheld at the Fund's discretion]

2.4      The Development is if possible to be let as a whole but if that is not achieved [6 months] after the Works Completion Date the Fund will permit the letting of the Development in not more than [3] parts [but under no circumstances will a Lease of less than one complete floor (excluding common parts) be allowed]

2.5      Subject to paragraph 2.6 nothing will prevent the Fund from negotiating in its own right and entering into a Lease or Leases or an Agreement or Agreements for the same

2.6      The Fund shall not (save with the consent of the Developer which may be withheld at the Developer's discretion) enter into any Agreement for Lease or Lease which would have effect to disapply the Developer's election to waive exemption in respect of VAT

**[3556]**

**3          Lease**

3.1      A Lease is to be [substantially] on the terms of the form of lease annexed [and
         as specified by the Fund] and will:
        3.1.1      be for a term of [not less than] [25] years and comprising [the whole
                *or* a lettable portion or portions] of the Development
        3.1.2      be at a rent to be first approved in writing by the Fund as the best
                rent reasonably obtainable without taking a fine or premium [[and
                with the view to achieving *or* at not less than] the Target Rent]
        3.1.3      provide for upward only rent reviews at intervals of not more than
                [5] years
        3.1.4      be exclusive of outgoings insurance premiums and service charges
        3.1.5      be subject to a full repairing liability covenant
        3.1.6      contain such other provisions as are consistent in all material respects
                in so far as reasonably practicable with the covenants conditions and
                provisions contained in the lease annexed
        [3.1.7      be consistent [in all respects] with the Letting Policy]
3.2      The Fund will be under no obligation to enter into a Lease or an Agreement
         for Lease the terms of which fetter its discretion whether or not to make an
         election to waive exemption for the purposes of VAT or which shall or may
         result in disapplication of an election to waive exemption or which may
         otherwise adversely affect the Fund's ability to recover input tax

                                                        **[3557]**

**4          Approval**

The Developer must not enter into any Agreement for Lease nor will the Fund be
required to enter into any Lease or (for the purpose of granting the Lease) any Agreement
for Lease until the Fund has [in its absolute discretion] approved:
4.1      the proposed tenant and any guarantors required by the Fund and
4.2      the terms of the Lease or Agreement for Lease

**5          The Fund's obligations**

5.1      Where the Developer has before the date of this Agreement entered into an
         Agreement for Lease approved by the Fund the Fund will (subject to
         completion of the sale and purchase of the Property) execute and grant the
         Lease in accordance with the terms of that Agreement for Lease
5.2      Where the Developer has otherwise negotiated an Agreement for Lease
         approved by the Fund the Fund will (subject to completion of the sale and
         purchase of the Property) at the request of the Developer enter into the same
         (the Developer doing likewise as developer) and thereafter execute and grant the
         Lease in accordance with the terms of that Agreement for Lease [but nothing
         shall preclude the Developer from itself completing a Lease to which the Fund
         has otherwise consented prior to completion of the sale to the Fund if the
         tenant is entitled to demand it]
5.3      [Subject to the foregoing] where the Developer has negotiated a Lease which
         is approved by the Fund and the tenant is entitled to grant of the same the Fund
         will (subject to completion of the sale and purchase of the Property) execute and
         grant the Lease by the latest of the following dates:
        5.3.1      [14] days after receipt of the engrossed Lease for execution
        5.3.2      [3 Working Days after] the date upon which the Fund receives the
                counterpart Lease executed by the tenant together with any initial
                payment of rent or other money due upon the grant of the Lease

                                                         **[3558]**

**6      Unlet premises[50]**

The Developer will at its own expense maintain each part of the Development not let at Works Completion Date in good and substantial repair and condition and pay all rates insurance premiums and other outgoings relating to it in accordance with the terms of a Lease until such liabilities are assumed by a tenant under a Lease [or until the End Date whichever is earlier]

**7      Interest**

[In so far as [the whole of the lettable parts of] the Development shall not be [or not have been for the first time] the subject of a Lease [or Leases] as at the date of actual completion] the Developer will pay interest on the amount of the Purchase Price (excluding any increase or decrease provided for under this Agreement) by equal quarterly payments in advance (and so proportionately for any part of a year commencing with the Completion Date) [on the usual quarter days *or* on 1st January 1st April 1st July and 1st October in each year] until the End Date or until [the whole of] the Development shall have been let under a Lease [or Leases] [for the first time] [less in every such case all income (including from Leases) for the time being receivable by the Fund from letting of the Property (excluding service charges and insurance premiums) [in case of any Lease which has been determined prior to determination of the contractual term and where the premises in question remain vacant as if it were still subsisting]]

**8      Completion and Leases**

8.1      If by the Completion Date the Development shall have been fully let under an Agreement or Agreements for Lease (or shall have been let in part) and the tenant in each case is entitled to the immediate grant of a Lease and has executed a counterpart of the same (or is entitled to call for a counterpart Lease but the Developer has failed to provide it) the Completion Date shall be postponed (subject to paragraph 5.3 of this Schedule) until the Lease [or Leases in question] [has *or* have] been executed the Fund entering into [the *or* every such] Lease as landlord so far as properly required to do

8.2      If notwithstanding earlier provisions of this Schedule the Developer fails to engross any Lease the Fund shall be entitled (but not obliged) to do so on its own account and submit it to [the *or* any such] tenant for execution accordingly

**[3559]**

Part III:  Increase in Purchase Price and Further Remuneration
**9      Increase in Purchase Price**

For every Lease completed contemporaneously with actual completion of this Agreement the Purchase Price shall be increased and for every Lease subsequently completed a further sum may become payable (if at all) in either case in accordance with the formula appearing at paragraph 10 of this Schedule

**10     Calculation[51]**

[The sum payable (whether by increase in the Purchase Price on completion or by way of further sum thereafter) is the amount (if any) by which the Net Rental Income multiplied by [16] exceeds the Purchase Price (excluding any decrease arising under this Agreement and in the case of more than one letting any other increase under this paragraph 10)

*or*

The sum payable (whether by increase in the Purchase Price on completion or by way of further sum thereafter (excluding any decrease arising under this Agreement and in the case of more than one letting any other increase under this paragraph 10)) is the amount (if any) by which Capital Value exceeds the Purchase Price where 'Capital Value' means either:

10.1    [16] times the Net Rental Income (if Net Rental Income does not exceed the Target Rent) in respect of which a like calculation can or has been made or

10.2    (if the Net Rental Income does exceed the Target Rent) the amount calculated by the following formula:

$$16T + 8(R - T)$$

where 'T' is the Target Rent and 'R' is Net Rental Income

*or*

A Sum calculated as follows is due to the Developer only if the following formula provides a figure greater than zero:

$$(16R_1 + 8R_2) - C$$

where:

'$R_1$'    is [£50,000] or (if less) Net Rental Income

'$R_2$'    is zero if [such] Net Rental Income does not exceed [£50,000] and otherwise is [£20,000] or (if less) the amount by which [such] Net Rental Income exceeds [£50,000] and

'C'    is Purchase Price (excluding any decrease arising under this Agreement and in the case of more than one letting any other increase under this paragraph 10

[this procedure being repeated until the Development is fully let for the first time allowance being made for every previous payment made]]

## 11    Payment

11.1    Any increase in the Purchase Price shall be paid on the date of actual completion

11.2    Any further sum becoming payable shall be paid within 5 Working Days after completion of the grant of the [relevant] Lease together with VAT thereon

11.3    Any payment made under paragraph 11.2 shall be made in like manner as for completion of the sale and purchase under this Agreement

[11.4    The Fund shall not be required to pay any further sum under this Schedule in so far as entitlement to the same may arise after the End Date]

[[FIFTH] SCHEDULE
Contaminated Land[52]
*(insert appropriate provisions)*]

*(signatures (or common seals) of the parties)*[53]
[*(signatures of witnesses)*]
**[3560]**

---

1    Although no stamp duty is payable on a forward sale/purchase agreement, stamp duty is payable on the resultant transfer/conveyance referable to the purchase price. There is no difference in principle between completion under such an agreement and under an open contract. However, a charge to additional stamp duty may arise where the development, or part of it, is prelet, conditional say on the development being carried out and in circumstances where a developer's further payment may arise,

even though, for some reason, the lease is not granted actually on completion or the payment is not actually made on that date: Finance Act 1994 s 242 (41 Halsbury's Statutes (4th Edn) STAMP DUTIES). Care is required in considering the value of the transaction because there may be additional events whereby the true consideration for the transfer is effectively ascertained albeit not wholly payable until a later date. Each case should, therefore, be considered on its merits.

As to forward sale and purchase agreements generally see Paragraph 299 [3401] et seq ante.

Because this Form includes an agreement for sale and purchase, the agreement is capable of registration as an estate contract (either as a class C(iv) land charge under the Land Charges Act 1972 (37 Halsbury's Statutes (4th Edn) REAL PROPERTY) where the land is unregistered, or by way of notice (or caution) in the case of registered land).

2    Because the developer will be commencing development and completing it prior to completion of the sale to the fund, inevitably the sale price will attract VAT. If it is the intention of the purchaser to occupy, or to let or otherwise allow the development to be occupied, wholly or mainly for an ineligible purpose then, by the Finance Act 1997 s 37 (48 Halsbury's Statutes (4th Edn) VALUE ADDED TAX), the developer's election to waive exemption from VAT will be disapplied. Note in particular clause 16.2 of this Form. As to VAT generally see Paragraph 309 [3414] et seq ante and see vol 38(1) (2000 Reissue) SALE OF LAND Paragraph 8 [16] et seq.

3    The transaction is essentially a sale and purchase conditional upon the carrying out of development. However, certain conditions, such as those contained in the fourth schedule of the draft ('letting') may give rise to ongoing obligations. Note that the definition 'Property' is thus used instead of 'Site' (cf Form 80 [3441] ante) for consistency throughout this Form.

4    As to contaminated land generally see vol 38(1) (2000 Reissue) SALE OF LAND Paragraph 147 [341] et seq. For environmental and due diligence enquiries and definitions and interpretation for use with those enquiries see vol 38(1) (2000 Reissue) SALE OF LAND Forms 35 [1585] and 36 [1592]. For a schedule of environmental warranties and indemnities see vol 38(1) (2000 Reissue) SALE OF LAND Form 61 [2401]. For alternative shorter warranty clauses see Forms 144 [4587] and 145 [4588] post. Practitioners should consider what provisions are appropriate to be included in the fifth schedule to this Form having regard to the actual state of the site the subject of this agreement and draft appropriate provisions which may be based on the above mentioned Forms, ensuring that the definitions and wording used is compatible with those used in this Form.

5    As with any other sale and purchase, a deposit may be required. However, given the duration of the period between exchange of contracts and completion, an investing institutional purchaser may be reluctant to allow a deposit at all, or will offer rather less than 'the usual 10%'.

6    Only where the deposit is held as agent for the seller should VAT be paid on the deposit at the time when the deposit is paid.

7    Although less likely now that compulsory registration is universal, it is still possible that the developer will be able to offer only an unregistered title. However, the prospect arises that in entering into a forward sale and purchase agreement with a fund, the developer will have bought the property quite possibly under a contemporaneous contract and may have only an unregistered title to offer in the first instance. Given the duration of the development period, the developer should have plenty of time in which to resolve any title issues (not least to satisfy his bankers).

The clause in this precedent is intended to satisfy institutional concerns. However, if all the developer has is an agreement for lease from a landowner leading to grant of a major interest in due course, the prospect is that there will be no further action for the developer to take save registration of his agreement for lease against the landowner's title (or registration of a land charge Class C(iv) as the case may be). Completion will in that event be effected by grant of the lease, and it is to be hoped that the developer will have negotiated his agreement for lease in such a way that the grant may be direct to the fund. Draft clauses for this kind of eventuality are not offered in this precedent because of the variety of circumstances which may arise. For other forms dealing with non-completion of registration see vol 38(1) (2000 Reissue) SALE OF LAND Form 57 schedule 8 [2163] and vol 36 (1997 Reissue) SALE OF LAND Forms 174 [2188]–176 [2190].

8    Given the nature of this particular form of agreement, a disclaimer clause of the kind commonly found in conveyancing clauses has particular significance. Accordingly, a fund may be advised to dissociate itself from such provisions to the extent of the Third and Fourth Schedules.

9    As this is a conveyancing contract, first and foremost, albeit conditional on development, the draftsman must consider what amendments may be required to suit the circumstances of the transaction or to ensure consistency with this agreement.

**[3561]**

10    An institutional purchaser may require greater flexibility than is suggested by clause 14.1, in order to deal with portfolio disposals. However, it must be considered rare for such an event to apply to unbuilt development, although that possibility must be contemplated. By contrast, however, so long as the fund's interest is registered at HM Land Registry, little may turn on a disposal elsewhere of the developer's legal estate in the meantime. Indeed, this may be necessary to raise interim development finance.

11    Again, in context, the non-merger clause is of greater significance than under an ordinary conveyancing contract because, specifically, outstanding building obligations may arise eg under defects liability, and the developer may remain under an obligation to seek lettings (see the third and fourth schedules of this Form).

12    Upon new commercial development, VAT must be paid. (See also note 2 above).

13    From all parties' points of view, the limitation period of twelve years implied by execution of the agreement is desirable given the nature of the obligations, particularly those of the developer in relation to construction of the development.

14    Events of default and consequences of default are placed in the main body of the agreement rather than, for example, in the development provisions at the third schedule. Essentially, these clauses operate so as to govern all aspects of the agreement.

15    It is, however, considered that the disputes provisions should be applied principally to the third and fourth schedules rather than to the conveyancing aspects of the contract.

16    The professionals are not necessarily those of the developer, particularly if they are appointed by a contractor under a JCT form of design and build contract. In such a case the contract administrator will need to be defined as well, eg 'Employer's Agent' and references elsewhere in the Form to the architect (where relevant) amended accordingly.

17    It is anticipated that the need for warranties, whether from consultants or contractors, may not · necessarily die with the advent of the Contracts (Rights of Third Parties) Act 1999. The need for such documents relies entirely on the form of the particular contract or appointment in question.

18    In practice, it is difficult to attach defects liability other than to defects liability arising under the building contract, otherwise the developer is prospectively exposed to additional expenditure beyond that contemplated by the building contract. However, funds may have their own criteria, and if imposed, the additional burden upon the developer must be clearly understood.

19    Traditionally, development documentation has proscribed deleterious materials in some detail. Often, use of standardised documentation leads to discrepancies between construction and development documentation. There is, however, a perceptible retreat from specifics towards British Standards in general and the proscription of materials which are generally considered deleterious. That said, all well drawn construction and development documentation should cater for specific deleterious materials, where appropriate, in the context of the development in question.

20    Development is the generic term for the works and the land. These are to be carried out in accordance with the approved scheme, as defined, the project as defined being the whole concept comprehended by the development from site assembly to completion of lettings. The definition here is likely to be restricted to the kind of information appearing on a planning permission as the permitted development. Note: the development will be carried out also in accordance with the documents so far as they go (these being defined in the main body of the agreement) the sale being subject to these as much as the development itself.

**[3562]**

21    End date is a long stop date which may serve a number of purposes, for example, a date by which the fund is no longer required to complete the purchase, or the date upon which no further sum can become due to the developer on account of lettings, or however the fund or purchaser decides to confine its exposure to the project and the financial consequences of it.

22    The insurance market evolves. Accordingly, excepted risks should be drawn in the light of current practice and with the benefit of insurance advice. It should be noted, under this precedent, that the risk in the development remains entirely with the developer until the completion date. However, the fund is concerned to see delivery of the project and that the developer should take all necessary steps (including under the building contract) to effect appropriate insurance. (See also paragraph 1.16 ('full reinstatement value') of the third schedule of this Form and paragraph 1.17 ('insured risks')).

23    For the fund (or indeed any interim financier or prospective tenant) the terms of an appointment are critical unless shortcomings are addressed in a corresponding warranty. All appointees must be required under the terms of their letters of appointment to provide warranties as appropriate (except in so far as the need for warranties is effectively displaced by the provisions of the Contracts (Rights of Third Parties) Act 1999).

24    Note that if works completion is distinguished from practical completion, the prospects of completion of the sale and purchase may be delayed whilst either further remedial works or other aspects of compliance with the agreement are complied with by the developer, at his own expense. See paragraphs 1.36 and 23 of the third schedule of this Form as to the works completion certificate.

25    Regard should be had to the terms of the building contract and such matters as are relevant under it. However, just as the developer may be excused from the consequences of unreasonable delay on the part of the surveyor in carrying out his functions under this agreement, a fund may not allow any factor in such relevant events which is attributable to delay or default on the part of the developer.

26    It is not usual to require warranties from a subcontractor other than a subcontractor as defined ie having a design responsibility.

27    The consultants and contractor are defined. Depending on the form of the building contract, some or all of the consultants (in the case of design and build, for example, except the quantity surveyor or the employer's agent) will be the appointees of the developer (or contractor). In that event, in so far as the contractor is to create and implement those appointments, it follows that the building contract must make provision for this to be facilitated and to reflect any particular requirements of the fund.

28    The approved scheme is of the essence of the arrangement. The extent of departure from this may be contained at the fund's discretion (see paragraph 5.3 of the third schedule).

29    It is to be accepted that most consents fundamental to the efficacy of the project, eg planning permission, including environmental requirements, will have been previously obtained or will, as here, be a condition of the contract. Approval of plans by the local authority for building control purposes habitually follows the event. In that case, reliance must be placed upon the advice of appropriate consultants, as to compliance of the approved scheme with building regulations.

30    Whilst a method statement may be part and parcel of the approved scheme, the necessity of a programme may be dictated by the nature of the approved scheme and will, in turn, influence the target completion date and the end date. If the programme has not been ascertained at the outset, judgement must also be exercised with the assistance of consultants as necessary as to the timing of events overall. The programme may, of course, be extended by a relevant event, but the end date is intended as a constraint (it does not have to be, but this is an obvious factor in the prospect of completion of the sale and purchase and/or of the project becoming income producing later than first expected).

**[3563]**

31    Unlike other kinds of development agreement, under a forward sale and purchase the developer is likely to be occupying the site in his own right as owner (unless, for example, he is a contractual lessee from a landowner under an agreement for (long) lease).

    The general requirements comprise a variety of matters including title elements, third party rights and so on. The developer should ensure that such matters are also reflected in the building contract.

32    Relevant events as defined are intended to make allowance for all those things which are beyond the developer's control. This being so they must include relevant events arising under the building contract, excepting those which will entitle the contractor to an extension of time by reason of his employer's default.

33    Insurance requirements vary according to contractual commitments. Until practical completion the insurance obligations in the building contract are likely to suffice for practical purposes as also the insurance obligations imposed upon professionals in their letters of appointment.

    Professional indemnity insurance on the part of the developer should also be considered particularly if he is managing the project. Otherwise, the professional indemnity cover of an appointed manager under his letter of appointment, or that prescribed by the design and build contract, may suffice.

34    Whilst not as extensive as a similar provision under Form 80 clause 17 [3454] ante, an indemnity may be required to the extent of the fund's contractual interest in the site. See also note 42 [3496] to that Form. A developer may wish to amend to make clear that the indemnity cannot operate to cover matters arising after completion of the sale and purchase and unconnected to implementation of the development. Before completion of the sale and purchase, breach of any of the documents will the more likely give rise to a direct liability from the developer to, eg, another landowner having the benefit of a restrictive covenant.

35    Third party rights often include those the existence of which may not have been apparent at the outset eg long hidden infrastructure the presence of which suggests acquisition of rights by prescription. Such contingencies are usually contemplated as part of the programme but may also give rise to a relevant event and permitted delay.

36    Proper and effective site management guards against the possibility of nuisance or offence to third parties. In any case, statutory agreements will often prescribe for conduct both on and off site eg requirements of the highway authority for access and egress by construction traffic and so on. Where crane oversailing is necessary then, inevitably, an express licence will be required.

37    The presence of archaeological finds may trigger the intervention of the local authority and the imposition of delay to the programme. Moreover, even if there are no archaeological finds, in so far as the property lies within a scheduled ancient monument, the consent of English Heritage will be required and will, therefore, number among the consents as defined.

**[3564]**

38    The surveyor being defined, the developer has only himself to blame if the person or firm so appointed at the outset is inadequate for the task. If the fund should be entitled to appoint a new surveyor at any time, then the criteria for appointment should be considered with care although it is also unlikely that a fund will allow the developer a say in the appointment.

    Given that the surveyor speaks for the fund particularly in granting consents, his is a critical role on which the developer depends for the smooth operation of the project. Not infrequently, the same firm will be appointed by the fund as the surveyor whilst, under a separate letter of appointment, it will be appointed by the developer as one of the letting agents (less likely, but possibly, the sole letting agent). Whilst the roles are essentially different, and thus the terms of engagement should not of themselves disclose any underlying conflict of interests, it is suggested that if the developer employs the same firm as the fund's surveyor in a letting agent's role, the possibility arises of conflict between that appointee and the developer's own appointee if acting jointly. A conflict may arise, for example, when a letting is negotiated and is put to the fund for approval. If there is conflict between the letting agents in that capacity, the prospect of the fund's approval per se is perhaps the more problematical.

     Any other capacity suggests an adjudication role of some kind and by implication a duty of care. Whilst the surveyor is the agent of the fund, however, the duty of care is owed by the surveyor to the fund, unless (unlikely) the contrary is expressed.

39     The surveyor depends upon a flow of information and personal attendances in order to perform his role effectively. The balance to be struck is between the provision of information on the one hand and the consequential judgement of the surveyor on the other. The matter in question requiring approval may be inherently reasonable or necessary but still justify a refusal if he is not presented with the appropriate information.

40     The extent of meetings which the surveyor may be entitled to attend needs some parameters. The surveyor should not be obliged to attend meetings and the need to do so is alleviated by the proper provision of information. Formality of meetings, although in itself imprecise, is more readily understood, whether or not key professionals are invited to attend.

41     The taking of tests may cause delay and give rise to a relevant event. The developer should therefore be afforded a measure of protection in this respect. Moreover, it should be emphasised that in so far as the agreement places a burden on the developer greater than that prescribed by the building contract, the interference caused to progress may unwittingly place the developer in breach of obligation to his contractor.

42     Reliance by the fund upon the developer is slightly different from that placed in the case of forward funding. There, the fund already owns the site and the developer's failure is therefore the more critical. Here, if there is a delay or the works are not carried out within the terms of the agreement, the fund can walk away (but may also suffer loss). Ideally, professional indemnity insurance should be carried (see note 33 above), and the fund may insist upon it.

43     Exclusion clauses may be seen as prospectively ineffective to the extent that a duty of care is owed by the person relying on the exclusion. If the developer has elected to go along with the fund's requirement but could notwithstanding have objected, the exclusion of liability on the part of the fund is perhaps more likely to stand.

**[3565]**

44     This effectively underpins paragraph 8 of the third schedule.

45     The need for a distinction between works completion and practical completion may arise in so far as other provisions of the agreement have not been complied with. See Form 80 note 55 [3499] ante as to the procedure relating to the certificate of practical completion (paragraph 24 of the third schedule to this Form).

46     As with the related provision in the forward funding precedent (Form 80 clause 31 [3461] ante), any outstanding works (save arising through later identified breach or forfeiture) once works completion has been declared, are deferred to the defects liability provisions of the building contract: see paragraph 25 of the third schedule.

47     The need for clauses such as this may be seen as less critical following enactment of the Contracts (Rights of Third Parties) Act 1999. However, the benefit of the Act depends upon the extent of reliance afforded by the terms of the building contract and any letters of appointment, and such provisions as these are best incorporated at the very least until expectations of what other documents should contain are so common place as to go without saying, particularly any further printed amendments to the JCT forms. The developer should note, however, that in so far as assignment of contractual rights is effected, his ability to meet outstanding or deemed continuing obligations to the fund may be impaired. It is a matter of negotiation whether to qualify this clause accordingly.

48     If the forward sale/purchase is for own occupation or is for intended investment unrelated to the developer's remuneration, letting and occupation may be seen, in financial terms, as of no concern to the developer. The developer's concerns regarding such matters will thus be confined essentially to the VAT consequences (see note 12 above). (Contrast forward funding where the land is purchased by the fund, with completion of the purchase effected before development commences. Under forward funding, the developer is not concerned, as here, with the impact of Finance Act 1997 s 37).

49     Similar considerations apply to the grant of leases whether under forward funding or forward sale and purchase. The criteria for institutional letting, for example, are essentially identical whichever investment medium is used. Hence, the same comments apply as to the form of lease and to any agreement for lease, including a prelet, as apply to forward funding (see Form 80 notes 59 [3500] and 60 [3501] ante). The obvious procedural difference is that, however long completion of the sale and purchase is delayed following practical completion of the development, the fund cannot in practice

grant a lease with title being vested in it. By contrast, if the criteria in any related agreement for lease have been satisfied, it is the developer who may be bound to grant and, unless some express mechanism provides otherwise, it is the developer who, until completion, will be entitled to the income from that letting. (See the words in square bracketed at the end of paragraph 5.2 of the third schedule to this Form).

Note that if the fund allows the developer to complete a letting (there may be no alternative if it is in the nature of the package which the fund is buying), the developer should be advised to incorporate in his letting documents, if possible, an express release of obligation as landlord (although a tenant would be unlikely to grant such release so far as concerns the developer's obligations as developer, under the related agreement for lease).

50   There is another analogy here with forward funding: once premises are subject to outgoings, those outgoings need to be paid for. Prior to completion of the sale and purchase, they will similarly be for the account of the developer in any case unless devolved upon a lessee. Once completion has taken place, they will be similarly for the account of the fund as landowner unless, contractually, the fund requires the developer to do so. The same comments accordingly apply as under Form 80 note 61 [3501] ante.

51   The prospective criteria for further remuneration are limitless. Moreover, circumstances may arise in which stamp duty ramifications should be considered. By contrast, these will not usually apply to forward funding (but see Form 80 note 1 [3489] ante).

The formulae chosen (as examples only) for both precedents are the same, save that in the case of forward sale/purchase the capital value factor is the basic purchase price whereas, under forward funding, the capital value essentially represents the fund's outlay. The further remuneration will be as much subject to VAT as the basic purchase price. Note that under the third alternative calculation suggested, a capped rental is catered for.

52   See note 4 above.

53   It is not usually necessary to have the contract executed as a deed unless the contract contains recitals which are intended to be binding or there are other special considerations (eg, there is a lack of valuable consideration or it is desired to extend the period set by the Limitation Act 1980 s 8 (24 Halsbury's Statutes (4th Edn) LIMITATION OF ACTIONS) for bringing claims: see note 13 above).

Where a contract is to be executed as a deed sealing is not necessary either in the case of an individual or in the case of a company, but all parties must sign either on the same document or each on one of two identical parts which are exchanged and the signatures of all individuals must be witnessed: see the Law of Property (Miscellaneous Provisions) Act 1989 s 1(3) (37 Halsbury's Statutes (4th Edn) REAL PROPERTY). As to the execution of a deed by an individual and by a corporation, see vol 12 (1994 Reissue) DEEDS, AGREEMENTS AND DECLARATIONS Paragraphs 16 [1525] and 28 [1554]–30 [1560] respectively.

It is unnecessary for a contract by a corporate body to be under seal unless it would need to be a deed if made by private persons: see the Corporate Bodies' Contracts Act 1960 s 1 (11 Halsbury's Statutes (4th Edn) CONTRACT). A contract may be made by a company incorporated under the Companies Acts by writing under its common seal or on its behalf by any person acting under its authority, express or implied: Companies Act 1985 s 36 as substituted by the Companies Act 1989 s 130(1) (8 Halsbury's Statutes (4th Edn) COMPANIES).

**[3566]–[3600]**

# (2): AGREEMENTS FOR LEASE IN DEVELOPMENT

## *Commentary*

### A: INTRODUCTION

**320    Purpose of an agreement for lease in development**

For a variety of reasons, the grant of a lease may be conditional on certain events. One such event may be the carrying out of development, whether by way of construction of new premises, refurbishment of others or the provision of facilities. A lease creates an estate in land and an agreement for lease, like a contract for sale and purchase, creates an equitable interest which can be enlarged into an estate upon grant of the lease.

Two principal kinds of transaction are illustrated in this volume: an agreement leading to the grant of a long lease (major interest), with potential as an investment vehicle[1], and an agreement leading to an occupational lease[2]. Beyond the basic characteristics of an agreement conditional upon development, each is entirely distinct from the other while recognising the existence, where the development is prelet to occupational tenants, of the other. That recognition, or interaction, is a crucial factor in the creation of an investment and in inducing financiers, whether bankers or investors or both, to participate.

Accordingly, the aim must be to achieve a bankable security; one which a lending institution can safely lend upon and realise its security if required, whilst at the same time being available for forward sale/purchase to an investor (or in the alternative being available for forward funding without the need for bank finance). The essence of development is an interaction between the widely differing interests of the participators through contract terms. Thus, an agreement for lease, say between a local authority land owner and a developer, should be so drawn as to constitute bankable security, and also provide a basis for the developer to enter into agreements for lease with occupational tenants. Just as any discretion afforded to an institutional buyer under a forward sale/purchase agreement may affect the bankability of a project in the hands of the developer, so also may an agreement for long lease, if it provides discretion to the landowner, or sets up criteria for default which do not enable a banker or investor to effect a remedy and thus preserve the security or potential investment.

**[3601]**

Interaction is thus a key principle in these relationships, and so also in relation to an agreement for lease with an occupational tenant. An occupational tenant under an agreement for, say, an institutional rack-rented lease, shares with an investing buyer under a forward sale/purchase agreement the peculiar characteristic that one of the consequences of the developer's breach is that it can simply walk away. From a developer's point of view, the issue in each case is to what extent it finds itself bound to a contract which affords its buyer or tenant the ability to rescind on discretionary grounds. Accordingly, subjective tests of compliance with development and other obligations are to be avoided and the impact of any such tests on related transactions, not least within the development scenario, must be analysed with care.

It should be noted that an agreement for lease containing development obligations does not comprise a construction contract for the purpose of Part II of the Housing Grants, Construction and Regeneration Act 1996. An agreement for lease is expressly excluded by the Construction Contracts (England and Wales) Exclusion Order 1998[3] so long as the resultant leasehold interest is for a period which is to expire no earlier than 12 months after the completion of the construction operations under the contract.

1    See Form 82 [3651] post.
2    See Form 83 [3711] post.
3    Construction Contracts (England and Wales) Exclusion Order 1998, SI 1998/648 reg 6.

**[3602]**


## 321    Contaminated land[1]

It will be noted from both forms of agreement for lease (and other development precedents in this volume) that there is recognition of the practicalities of dealing with contaminated land. Contaminated land is an increasing feature of development. The reforms introduced by the Environment Act 1995 assist that practical recognition. The basic principle that recognition needs to be given to acceptance by a tenant or buyer of the possible existence of contamination should not, on its own, avail it of a remedy against its grantor merely because of the grantor's capacity as such. Disclosure having been made, and recognition afforded, that should be an end to the matter subject to reliance upon the advice of professional consultants whose opinions are sought and in reliance upon which judgements are made. In case of entirely new build, however, a tenant properly advised would expect to insert provisions to leave environmental concerns wholly with its immediate landlord.

1    As to contaminated land generally see vol 38(1) (2000 Reissue) SALE OF LAND Paragraph 147 [341] et seq. For environmental and due diligence enquiries and definitions and interpretation for use with those enquiries see vol 38(1) (2000 Reissue) SALE OF LAND Forms 35 [1585] and 36 [1592]. For a schedule or environmental warranties and indemnities see vol 38(1) (2000 Reissue) SALE OF LAND Form 56 Sch 14 [2029] and for a schedule apportioning costs of remediation of contaminated land see vol 38(1) (2000 Reissue) SALE OF LAND Form 61 [2401]. For alternative shorter warranty clauses see Forms 144 [4587] and 145 [4588] post.

**[3603]**


# B:  AGREEMENT FOR LEASE BETWEEN LANDOWNER AND DEVELOPER


## 322    Nature of agreement

Although the proposed form of lease[1] is not here prescribed, an agreement for lease between a landowner and a developer largely presupposes the grant of a long lease intended to attract a capital value (and whose proviso for re-entry will accordingly exclude reference to any event of insolvency). As a long lease, its reversion is inherently remote and it is suggested that only those matters which affect the reversion, or which justify the use of a lease rather than transfer of a freehold, will be relevant in this context.

1    For forms of lease see Forms 82 [3651] and 83 [3711] post and for other building agreements and related documents see vol 22(4) (1997 Reissue) LANDLORD AND TENANT (BUSINESS TENANCIES) Forms 420 [7751]–430 [8096]. For commentary on agreements for lease see vol 22(1) (1996 Reissue) LANDLORD AND TENANT (BUSINESS TENANCIES) Paragraph 101 [201] et seq.

**[3604]**

### 323    Town centre developments

In the case of a town centre development, a local authority may wish to impose a measure of management to enhance its role as local authority. The development may be seen as a flagship and so controls may extend as far as types of use and tenant mix, which may then be carried into the alienation provisions of the lease. One of the characteristics of leases of town centre developments, particularly those granted since the 1960s, has been that when redevelopment has been considered, in some cases, the structure of the lease (particularly where income producing, and even where reserving only a share of occupational income), has practically precluded redevelopment or change of use. Thus, although the lease represents an investment in the standing bricks and mortar, as a vehicle for new investment upon redevelopment, the ransom nature of its terms may result in a dwindling capital value, except upon a renegotiation with an unsympathetic local authority landlord.

**[3605]**

### 324    Elements of agreement for lease
#### 324.1    Landowner's considerations

The form of lease which may be prescribed as the subject of a grant of a major interest is likely to be the result of a detailed commercial negotiation. So also is its enabling agreement, but in order to achieve that essential interaction with other elements of the development process, the agreement for lease should be characterised by a number of principal elements.

First, the landowner's underlying interest in the development process should be assessed. For a variety of reasons it may be interested in the identity of the contractor and of the professional team; it will certainly be interested in the development period and also the likely out-turn. The out-turn is, in turn, likely to be determined by the identity of the developer. In very large scale development, in some ways analogous to a bank loan agreement, even the shareholdings in or the key employees of the developer may be relevant, and the prospects of change may be drafted as a potential event of default. A lending bank, by contrast, needs to have the ability to realise its security on the agreement for lease. Banks are lenders, not developers, and in the case of developer default under a bank loan agreement, the bank needs to be able to assign the agreement for lease, in its capacity as chargee, to a new developer. This implies the need for a measure of permitted alienation under controlled conditions and particularly a degree of flexibility to allow a new developer to take up the reins.

**[3606]**

#### 324.2    Developer's licence

The developer will be granted licence to go on site by the landowner in order to carry out the development. This is somewhat analogous to a developer's licence to go on site afforded by an institution under a forward funding agreement. Termination of the developer's licence, however arising, will impact directly upon the developer's contractual responsibilities to his contractor and professionals, fund, buyer, and tenants under their respective agreements. To the extent, if at all, that the developer is to be subjected to any purely subjective tests in determining whether there has been an event of default depriving him of licence to go on site, it is advisable for all of the developer's other agreements to be ring-fenced by an appropriate exclusion. However, this implies that the particular agreement for lease may be seen as unbankable. Accordingly, although it may suit a landowner to impose discretionary controls, an unworkable agreement may ensue which, in the event, cannot be entered into, and an appropriate balance must be achieved. As a simple example, if a local authority prescribes that completion of the lease will be triggered only upon its unqualified acceptance of the certificate of practical completion under the building contract, the prospect arises that the lease may never be granted at all or at least only when, at the landowner's whim, the developer has carried out such further work as to satisfy it. This, it is suggested, is an inherently unbankable proposition.

**[3607]**

### 324.3   Criteria for termination

In case of breach of a developer's obligations, not only must a bank have the ability, through the medium of permitted alienation, to arrange for step-in, but also care should be exercised in determining the criteria for termination of the agreement. If there is a developer's breach, then it is helpful to incorporate a provision availing the developer of the benefit of the Law of Property Act 1925 Section 146 so that it is ultimately for the court's discretion whether or not to grant forfeiture of the agreement. If the breach is remediable, then the prospects of the developer obtaining relief from forfeiture seem favourable.

An agreement may contain certain events of default which are irremediable, for example, an end date. An end date should be chosen with care and either linked to relevant events (delaying factors) or placed at the limits of commercial tolerance. Insolvency of the developer, by contrast, is of equal concern to a bank lender or institutional buyer of the headlease in due course, and should properly trigger the ability to assign the benefit of the agreement, under controlled conditions, to a new developer. If the agreement has been used as the basis of forward funding (it being implied that the grant of the lease in due course will be to the fund direct), the implication is that it will have been assigned at the outset to the investor who will re-employ the developer as his own developer. Alienation of the agreement for lease should, therefore, also be contemplated in favour of a financial partner by way of forward funding. A local authority land owner should look favourably upon this in commercial terms although it is likely that the fund, if an institution, will qualify any covenant to the local authority with a limitation imposed by its trustee capacity. Since the Landlord and Tenant (Covenants) Act 1995, however, an authorised guarantee agreement should allay the landowner's concerns, and if one takes the usual denial of the existence of a tenancy in the agreement at face value, such a covenant can in any case be made an express condition[1].

---

1    Contrast development obligations in an agreement for lease with an occupational tenant, which an investor will seek to avoid. See Paragraph 325 [3609] et seq post.

**[3608]**

## C:  AGREEMENT FOR LEASE BETWEEN DEVELOPER AND TENANT

### 325    Interaction with other agreements

Depending upon the interests of the landowner, an agreement for lease with an occupational tenant may have to meet the requirements of the principal agreement for lease (between the landowner and developer) if any. Alternatively, if created out of a freehold (or out of a leasehold having no restrictions on underletting), it may still have to meet the criteria of a lender or of an investing (institutional) buyer, for example pursuant to a forward funding or forward sale/purchase agreement. Accordingly, the developer in negotiating an agreement for lease needs to have regard to the terms of other documentation including, for example, in the case of forward funding, the agreed letting policy. If the developer enters into an agreement for lease in breach of his other commitments, the agreement itself may be perfectly valid as a contract between the developer and the prospective tenant, but lead only to failure of grant and an action for damages if the developer cannot deliver.

Where the developer will be passing on the resultant development to an investor, the implication is that the investor may also be a party to the enabling agreement for lease. It is particularly important for the buyer from the developer, ie the investor, that the development obligations contained in any agreement for lease do not fall upon it. Although it has long been possible to make that distinction contractually, the Landlord and Tenant (Covenants) Act 1995 Section 3(6) enables the distinction to be more finely made and for the developer's obligations to be made expressly personal to the developer without being passed down. If a developer has developed in its own right, perhaps with bank finance, and even if the prospective investor is not also a party to the enabling agreement for lease, perhaps because it simply has not been identified at the time it was entered into, it is still essential that the developer makes all of its development obligations completely personal so that the resultant investment is confined solely to the landlord and tenant relationship. Otherwise, the transaction may be seen as unacceptably burdensome by a purchasing institution.

If the agreement for lease flows from an agreement with a landowner (superior landlord), by implication, compliance with the superior agreement and the grant of the major interest is a natural precursor to grant of the occupational lease. An agreement for an occupational lease must not be written so as to conflict with the superior agreement, whilst the superior agreement should seek to avoid characteristics of its own unattractive to an occupational tenant. Funders of whatever kind and, where relevant, even the superior landlord, will in any case be interested in the terms of such an agreement. The developer will, no doubt, be expected to offer development obligations but they should usually be confined to achieving what is necessary for that particular tenant in that part of the development. Apart from whatever criteria will lead to grant of the superior lease, there may be other criteria which are relevant to the underletting: for example, infrastructure and facilities on adjoining or neighbouring land, such as car parking.

**[3609]**

## 326    Timing

Like the other interested parties, the occupational tenant will be concerned with timing. Even if the development is not otherwise constrained by time, an occupying tenant will wish to open for trade. It cannot, therefore, have an open-ended commitment and it is likely that an end date will be required, whatever the developer's other commitments (or lack of them). Moreover, even if the unit or accommodation is itself practically complete, and meets the criteria of the tenant, ancillary facilities and parking may be equally critical and be subject to the overall time frame.

**[3610]**

# D: TAXATION

### 327     VAT

The circumstances in which an agreement for lease gives rise to a charge to VAT vary. In the case of a landowner entering into an agreement for lease conditional, say, upon development being carried out by the tenant (developer), only the circumstances appertaining to the landowner's interest apply. Thus, for example, if no election to waive exemption has been made and if the land is otherwise exempt land, then it will be received as such by the developer without charge to VAT. However, whereas the prospective development may be of no interest at all to the landowner, a developer entering into an agreement for lease with a prospective tenant of the built development will have necessarily had to elect for itself, in order to make appropriate recoveries in relation to its development costs.

A developer, while at liberty to make exempt supplies upon a grant of a lease, will in economic terms be discouraged from so doing. A developer should also have regard to the nature of the business or occupation of any prospective tenant. It should also be concerned as to the interests of a buyer of the development, concerned in any way with its funding, who intends to allow the development to be used wholly or mainly for an ineligible purpose as understood by the Finance Act 1997 Section 37. Accordingly, even though the developer may not itself enter into an agreement for lease direct with an occupational tenant, the circumstances surrounding the interests of a prospective buyer under a forward sale/purchase agreement should also be considered and contractual safeguards incorporated[1]. Otherwise, the developer's waiver of exemption may be disapplied.

1     See Form 81 [3521] ante.

**[3611]**

### 328     Stamp duty

The development provisions of an agreement for lease do not, to the extent that they comprise a condition of grant, affect the potential for liability of the tenant to stamp duty. However, the development provisions in the hands of a tenant under an agreement for lease in favour of, say, a developer, have such a potential. The agreement for lease may, for example, be granted for a premium which is readily ascertainable for stamp duty purposes. If the consideration includes other factors, such as (part of) the development itself, the value derived by the landlord may give rise to ad valorem stamp duty. The Finance Act 1994 Section 242[1] (consideration not ascertainable from conveyance or lease) should, however, be considered in any context where value is not certain at the time of the grant. The likelihood is that in the context of development and development obligations there will be limited scope for the benefit of this section to be gained. Note that for stamp duty purposes, stamp duty may be charged on the agreement, rather than on the lease, and must be paid before the agreement may be used in proceedings[2]. However, if the circumstances allow the agreement to be expressed as an option, the agreement is not stampable.

1     Ie the Finance Act 1994 s 242 as amended by the Finance Act 1999 s 112(4), Sch 14 (41 Halsbury's Statutes (4th Edn) STAMP DUTIES).
2     See the Information Binder: Stamp Duties [1] (Guide to Stamp Duties: Paragraph 19 [37]).

**[3612]–[3650]**

# Forms and Precedents

## 82
### Agreement for lease between landowner and developer[1]

DATE:   *(insert date)*

PARTIES:
1        The Landowner: *(name)* [company number *(number)*] [of *(address)* *or* whose registered office is at *(address)*]
2        The Developer: *(name)* [company number *(number)*] [of *(address)* *or* whose registered office is at *(address)*]
[3       The Surety: *(name)* [company number *(number)*] [of *(address)* *or* whose registered office is at *(address)*]]

CONTENTS:

[3651]

## A      DEFINITIONS AND INTERPRETATION
### 1      Definitions[2]

In this Agreement unless the context otherwise requires the following expressions shall have the following meanings:

**1.1      'Communication'**
any notice application approval certificate or other communication from or on behalf of one party to another pursuant to this Agreement

**1.2      'Completion Date'**
the date so prescribed by paragraph 1.4 of the [Third] Schedule

**1.3      'Contract Rate'**
*(insert interest rate or method of calculating the interest rate by reference, eg, to the base lending rate of a named bank)*

**1.4      'Developer's Solicitors'**
*(insert name and address of person or firm)*

**1.5    'Development'**
the Development as defined in paragraph 1.12 of the [Third] Schedule

**[1.6    'the Documents'**
the documents (if any) particulars of which are set out in the Second Schedule]

**1.7    'General Conditions'**
[the Standard Commercial Property Conditions of Sale (1st Edn) *or (specify)*]

[3652]

**1.8    'Insolvent'**
1.8.1    in relation to a company that:

      1.8.1.1    It is deemed unable to pay its debts as defined in the Insolvency Act 1986 Section 123 (referred to as 'the Act' in the remainder of this definition)

      1.8.1.2    A proposal is made for a voluntary arrangement under Part I of the Act

      1.8.1.3    A petition is presented for an administration order under Part II of the Act

      1.8.1.4    A receiver or manager is appointed whether under Part III of the Act (including an administrative receiver) or otherwise

      1.8.1.5    It goes into liquidation as defined in Section 247(2) of the Act (other than a voluntary winding up which is first approved by the Landowner and is for the sole purpose of amalgamation or reconstruction while solvent)

      1.8.1.6    A provisional liquidator is appointed under Section 135 of the Act

      1.8.1.7    A proposal is made for a scheme of arrangement under the Companies Act 1985 Section 425 as amended

1.8.2    and in relation to an individual that:

      1.8.2.1    An application is made for an interim order or a proposal is made for a voluntary arrangement under Part VIII of the Act

      1.8.2.2    A bankruptcy petition is presented to the court or his circumstances are such that a bankruptcy petition could be presented under Part IX of the Act

      1.8.2.3    He enters into a deed of arrangement

**1.9    'Landowner'**
includes the successors in title to the Landowner of its reversion to the Property and its assigns

**1.10    'Landowner's Solicitors'**
*(insert name and address of person or firm)*

**1.11    'Lease'**
a lease of the Property in the form annexed to this Agreement

[3653]

**1.12    'paragraph'**
a paragraph of a schedule

**1.13    'Premium'**
the sum of £......

**[1.14    'Premium Payment Date'**
*(if the agreement is conditional, eg on planning permission, insert date)*]

**1.15    'Property'**
the property described in the First Schedule

**1.16     'VAT'**[3]
value added tax

**1.17     'Working Day'**
any day except Saturdays Sundays and Bank or other public holidays

**2          Interpretation**

2.1     Words importing one gender shall be construed as importing any other gender

2.2     Words importing the singular shall be construed as importing the plural and vice versa

2.3     Words importing persons shall be construed as importing a corporate body and/or a partnership and vice versa

2.4     Where any party comprises more than one person the obligations and liabilities of that party under this Agreement shall be joint and several obligations and liabilities of those persons

2.5     The clause headings do not form part of this Agreement and shall not be taken into account in its construction or interpretation

2.6     Any reference to a clause or a paragraph or a schedule is to one in this Agreement so numbered

2.7     Reference to a statute includes any amendment modification consolidation or re-enactment of that statute and any statutory instrument regulation or order made under that statute and for the time being in force

2.8     In case of any inconsistency between the General Conditions and any provisions of this Agreement the latter shall prevail

[2.9    *(insert any appropriate statutory reference eg relevant power if local authority landowner)*][4]

**[3654]**

**B          GRANT OF LEASE**

**3          Agreement for grant of the Lease**[5]

3.1     The Landowner shall grant and the Developer shall take the Lease for the Premium

3.2     The grant of the Lease is conditional upon the Developer observing and performing its several obligations contained in the [Third] Schedule and the Landowner and the Developer shall observe and perform their respective obligations in that schedule accordingly

3.3     The Landowner and the Developer shall also observe and perform the several obligations on their respective parts contained in the [Fourth] Schedule

[3.4    The [Fifth] Schedule shall have effect in relation to environmental matters [and] contaminated land [and remediation]][6]

**4          Premium**[7]

4.1     [The Landlord acknowledges receipt of the Premium *or* the Developer shall pay the Premium to the Landlord on the Premium Payment Date]

[4.2    If the Premium shall not be paid on the Premium Payment Date the Developer shall pay interest upon it at the Contract Rate from the Premium Payment Date to the date of payment]

**5          Completion**

The original and counterpart respectively of the Lease shall be prepared by [and at the cost of] the Landlord who shall provide the counterpart to the Developer within [5] Working Days of being notified of Practical Completion as defined in and in accordance with the provisions of the [Third] Schedule. The Landowner and the Developer shall respectively execute the Lease and the counterpart of the Lease and completion shall take place on the Completion Date [at the offices of the Landowner's Solicitors or where they may direct]

## 6     Title guarantee

The Landowner grants the Lease with [full *or* limited] title guarantee

## 7     Possession[8]

Subject but without prejudice to the provisions of this Agreement the Lease shall be granted with vacant possession of the Property upon completion

**[3655]**

## 8     Title[9]

[Title shall commence with *(description of instrument)* dated *(date)* and made between *(parties)* [and the Developer or the Developer's Solicitors having been supplied with an epitome of the title prior to the date of this Agreement the Developer shall be deemed to purchase with full knowledge of the title in all respects and shall not raise any requisitions or make any objection in relation to the title]
*or*
Title to the Property is registered at HM Land Registry with [absolute] title under title number *(number)* and title shall be deduced in accordance with the Land Registration Act 1925 Section 110 [save that copies of the entries on the register the filed plan and any documents referred to shall be office copies] [and the Developer or the Developer's Solicitors having been supplied with such copies prior to the date of this Agreement the Developer shall be deemed to purchase with full knowledge of the title in all respects and shall not raise any requisitions or make any objection in relation to the title]]

## 9     Encumbrances

9.1     The Lease shall be granted subject to and (where appropriate) with the benefit of the matters contained or referred to in the [Documents *or* the property [proprietorship] and charges registers of title number *(number)*]

9.2     The Developer or the Developer's Solicitors having been supplied with copies of the [Documents *or* the property [proprietorship] and charges registers and the matters contained or referred to in the registers] prior to the date of this Agreement the Developer shall be deemed to take with full notice and knowledge of the same and shall not raise any requisition or make any objection in relation to them

## 10     Matters affecting the Property

The Lease shall be granted subject to the following matters:

10.1     all local land charges whether registered or not before the date of this Agreement and all matters capable of registration as local land charges whether or not actually so registered

10.2     all notices served and orders demands proposals or requirements made by any local public or other competent authority whether before or after the date of this Agreement

10.3     all actual or proposed charges notices orders restrictions agreements conditions conventions or other matters arising under the enactments relating to town and country planning and environmental law

10.4     all easements quasi-easements rights exceptions or other similar matters whether or not apparent on inspection or disclosed in any of the documents referred to in this Agreement

**[3656]**

## 11     Disclaimer[10]

11.1     The Developer admits that:

11.1.1     it enters into this Agreement solely as a result of its own inspection and on the basis of the terms of this Agreement and not in reliance upon any representation or warranty either written or oral or implied made by or on behalf of the Landowner (save for any representation or warranty contained in written replies given by the Landowner's Solicitors to any preliminary inquiries raised by the Developer or the Developer's Solicitors)

11.1.2     this Agreement contains the entire agreement between the parties

[11.2     The Landowner does not warrant that the Property may lawfully be used for any purpose authorised by the Lease]

## 12     Incorporation of conditions of sale[11]

The General Conditions shall apply to this Agreement in so far as they are applicable to the grant of a lease by private treaty and are not varied by or inconsistent with the terms of this Agreement [and shall be amended as follows: *(insert details of amendments required)*]

## 13     Assignment and other dealings[12]

13.1     This Agreement shall not be assigned or otherwise dealt with by the Developer save to the extent permitted by this clause 13

13.2     This Agreement may be assigned as a whole [by way of security] to a bank financial institution or other person (first approved by the Landowner whose approval shall not be unreasonably withheld) for the sole purpose of providing finance for the Development

13.3     Notwithstanding the foregoing there shall be no assignment of this Agreement save upon the prospective assignee [(unless a bank for the sole purpose of taking security for advances)] first entering into a covenant with the Landowner (upon terms [reasonably] acceptable to the Landowner) to observe and perform all the obligations on the part of the Developer under this Agreement

**[3657]**

13.4     Notwithstanding that an assignee of this Agreement shall be entitled as against the Developer to enforce its security no further assignment or other dealing whatsoever shall be permitted save:

13.4.1     a reassignment of the benefit of this Agreement to the Developer absolutely or

13.4.2     an assignment (otherwise than by way of security) in exercise of the powers constituted by its security and occasioned by the default of the Developer under them and in favour of a suitable person first approved by the Landowner (whose approval shall not be unreasonably withheld)

13.5     The Landowner shall not be obliged to grant the Lease other than to the Developer or to a person who [would be a permitted assignee under the Lease when granted and who] has first covenanted with the Landowner [in such manner as the Landowner shall reasonably require] to observe and perform all the outstanding obligations on the part of the Developer under this Agreement

**14     Merger on completion**[13]

The provisions of this Agreement shall not merge on grant of the Lease so far as they remain to be performed [and on the part of the Developer all outstanding or continuing obligations on its part under this Agreement shall bind the Developer (or other the tenant for the time being thereunder) as covenants on the part of the tenant under the Lease when granted] [but shall remain binding on the part of the Developer personally to the exclusion of the tenant thereunder if a person other than the Developer]

**15     VAT**[14]

15.1     On the [Completion Date *or* Premium Payment Date] the Developer shall pay to the Landowner VAT on the Premium and the Landowner shall provide to the Developer a receipted VAT invoice addressed to the Developer for the amount of the VAT paid by the Developer

15.2     The Developer declares that it has no intention of using the Property or of allowing it to be used whether by letting or otherwise in such a way as to give rise to the disapplication of any election to waive exemption to tax made by the Landowner

15.3     The Developer shall indemnify and keep indemnified the Landowner against all VAT which the Landowner has to repay to HM Customs and Excise including any under the capital goods scheme and against all VAT which is irrecoverable by the Landowner (together in each case with interest penalties and costs) due to the disapplication of any election to waive exemption to tax made by the Landowner arising in any way from the use of the Property or part or parts of it for an exempt purpose

**[16     Nature of this agreement**

This Agreement is a deed and has been executed by the parties to it as a deed]

**[3658]**

**C     DEFAULT**

**17     Events of Default**[15]

Each of the events specified in clauses 17.1–17.5 inclusive is an Event of Default:

17.1     The Developer becomes Insolvent

17.2     The Developer fails duly to perform or comply with any other obligation expressed to be assumed by it in this Agreement and

17.2.1     (if in the opinion of the Landowner such default is capable of remedy) the Developer fails to remedy the default within [10] Working Days after the Landowner has given notice to the Developer specifying the default and the required remedy and

17.2.2     such failure may in the reasonable opinion of the Landowner prejudice to a material extent the ability of the Developer to complete the Works

17.3     The Developer repudiates this Agreement or does or allows to be done or omitted any act or thing which the Landowner reasonably considers to evidence an intention to repudiate this Agreement

17.4     Any event or series of events occurs which in the reasonable opinion of the Landowner may materially and adversely affect the business assets or financial condition of the Developer so that it may be unable to comply with any of its obligations under this Agreement

17.5     The Works are not completed by [a date [six] months after the Target Completion Date (as such terms are defined in the [Third] Schedule)] [or by the End Date (as defined in the [Third] Schedule) if later]

**[3659]**

**18      Consequences of Default**[16]

18.1      Where an Event of Default occurs the Landowner (without prejudice to any other available remedy) may serve notice of default on the Developer whereupon:

    18.1.1      if completion of the Lease has not taken place the Landowner may by notice at any time rescind this Agreement [(and for the avoidance of doubt the Developer shall not be entitled to return of the Premium or any part of it)]

    18.1.2      the Developer's licence to enter upon the Property [and on the Retained Land (as defined in the [Third] Schedule)] will cease and the Developer will immediately vacate the Property [and the Retained Land] but will leave all Works and materials and plant and equipment on the Property [and as the case may be on the Retained Land]

    18.1.3      the Landlord may re-enter upon the Property [and the Retained Land] or any part of it in the name of the whole and the Property [the Retained Land] and all such works and materials and plant and equipment will be forfeit and will become the property of the Landowner and the Landowner shall not be liable to make any compensation or allowance to the Developer in that respect

    18.1.4      the Landowner may (but is not obliged to) take an assignment of the Building Contract pursuant to the Contractor's Warranty and/or of any Letter of Appointment pursuant to a Consultant's Warranty (as such terms are defined in the [Third] Schedule)

18.2      Any re-entry by the Landowner shall be without prejudice to the rights of either the Landowner or the Developer concerning any antecedent breach on the part of the other. Subject thereto this Agreement shall determine absolutely

[18.3      The right of re-entry and determination contained in this clause 18 shall be exercisable only in accordance with (and the Developer shall have the same rights of relief against forfeiture as are granted by) the Law of Property Act 1925 Section 146 the provisions of which are incorporated as if this Agreement were a lease for the purpose of giving effect to that section (but not otherwise)]

18.4      The Landowner shall not be entitled to re-enter the Property [or the Retained Land] nor shall this Agreement determine unless the Landowner shall have notified any permitted assignee of this Agreement that the Landowner's right to re-enter and determine has arisen and unless such assignee shall have failed to provide to the Landowner within [one month] a covenant in a form approved by the Landowner (such approval not to be unreasonably withheld) to observe and perform the outstanding obligations on the part of the Developer or itself assigns to a new developer as Developer so far as permitted under clause 13 above who within such a period enters into a deed of covenant with the Landowner as prescribed by that clause

**[3660]**

**D      DISPUTES**

**19      Definitions**[17]

For the purposes of clauses 19–22:

19.1      'Dispute' means a dispute issue difference question or claim as between the Landowner and the Developer relating to or arising at any time out of either or both of the [Third] Schedule and the [Fourth] Schedule to this Agreement

19.2      'Party' means a party to the Dispute

19.3     'Specialist' means a person qualified to act as an independent expert or an arbitrator in relation to the Dispute having experience in the profession in which he practises for the period of at least [10] years immediately preceding the date of referral

## 20     Dispute Notice and Counter Notice

20.1     Either Party may give to the other notice ('Dispute Notice') requiring a dispute to be referred to a Specialist and proposing an appropriate Specialist

20.2     The Party served will be deemed to accept the proposals made in the Dispute Notice unless that Party within [10] Working Days of service of the Dispute Notice gives notice rejecting one or more of the proposals or unless each Party serves a Dispute Notice on the other contemporaneously

## 21     Type of Specialist

Unless the Parties agree or are deemed to agree the appropriate Specialist:

21.1     if the Parties do not agree which type of Specialist is appropriate to resolve the Dispute either Party may refer that question to the President or next most senior available officer of the Royal Institution of Chartered Surveyors who will (with the right to take such further advice as he may require) determine that question and nominate or arrange to have nominated the appropriate Specialist

21.2     if the Parties do agree the appropriate type of Specialist but do not agree the identity of the Specialist he will be nominated on the application of either Party by the President or other most senior available officer of the organisation generally recognised as being responsible for the relevant type of Specialist but if no such organisation exists then by the President or next most senior available officer of the Royal Institution of Chartered Surveyors

## 22     Arbitration

Unless the Parties otherwise agree the reference to a Specialist shall be made to him as an arbitrator under the Arbitration Act 1996 but if the Parties agree to the Specialist acting as an expert his decision shall be final and binding on the Parties

## 23     Costs

The liability for paying all costs of referring a Dispute to a Specialist including costs connected with the appointment of the Specialist will be decided by the Specialist

**[3661]**

## [E     SURETY

## 24     Surety

24.1     This Agreement has been entered into with the consent and at the request of the Surety

24.2     The Surety guarantees the due performance by the Developer of all of the Developer's obligations under this Agreement and will perform them or otherwise indemnify the Landowner in respect of any non-performance of such obligations including (for the avoidance of doubt) any obligation of the Developer which is agreed or determined under clauses 19–23

24.3     The obligations of the Surety will not be affected by:

24.3.1     any variation of this Agreement to which the Surety is not a party

24.3.2     any other agreement entered into by the Developer

24.3.3    any time or indulgence given by the Landowner

24.3.4    the Developer becoming Insolvent

24.3.5    any other act deed or thing except an express release of the Surety or variation to the Surety's liability given in writing by the Landowner

24.4    If this Agreement shall in the hands of the Developer become forfeit the Landowner may (but shall not be obliged to) by notice at any time require the Surety to undertake all the obligations of the Developer under this Agreement and to take up the Lease as if it were the Developer whereupon this Agreement shall bind the Surety accordingly]

**[3662]**

## F    MISCELLANEOUS

## 25    Communication

25.1    All Communications shall be in writing

25.2    A Communication from any party ('the Sender') to any other ('the Recipient') will be duly made if in writing and either delivered to the Recipient (including in a manner provided at clause 25.5) or sent within the United Kingdom by [first class prepaid or] registered or recorded delivery post addressed to the Recipient at his address as stated in this Agreement or as the Recipient may from time to time notify the Sender

25.3    While the Surveyor (as defined in the [Third] Schedule) is acting as agent of the Landowner as specified in this Agreement a Communication duly made to the Surveyor will constitute a Communication duly made to the Landowner

25.4    A Communication sent by post will be deemed to have been made on the second Working Day next following the day of posting [and it will be sufficient proof of posting for first class prepaid post to show that a prepaid envelope containing the Communication was properly addressed and either delivered to or collected by the Post Office or placed in a Post Office letterbox]

25.5    In this clause 25 'writing' includes telex facsimile or other electronic means of communication (except e-mail) and 'delivered' includes transmission by such means in which event the Communication will be deemed to have been made when the Sender has finished its transmission without having any reasonable grounds for suspecting that the transmission has failed or was incomplete (except that if such transmission takes place outside normal business hours the Communication will be deemed to have been made when normal business hours next commence)

25.6    In this clause 25 'normal business hours' are [9.30 am to 5.30 pm] on Working Days

**[3663]**

## 26    Partnership and agency[18]

Neither the Landowner nor the Developer has any intention of carrying on business in partnership with the other concerning the Project (as defined in the [Third] Schedule) or any related matter

## 27    Waiver

No failure or delay by the Landowner to exercise any right power or remedy under this Agreement will operate as a waiver of it in whole or in part nor will any partial exercise preclude any further exercise of the same or of some other right power or remedy

## 28    Headings

The clause and sub-clause and schedule headings do not affect the meaning of this Agreement

[3664]

FIRST SCHEDULE
The Property
*(describe the property)*

[SECOND SCHEDULE
The Documents
*(insert details)*]

[THIRD] SCHEDULE
Development Obligations

| | |
|---|---|
| I | Definitions and Interpretation |
| II | Preliminaries |
| III | Works |
| IV | Administration |
| V | Completion |

Part I: Definitions and Interpretation

## 1    Definitions and Interpretation

In this Schedule unless the context otherwise requires the following further expressions have the following meanings:

### 1.1    'Approved Scheme'
As defined in paragraph 5 of this Schedule

### 1.2    'Architect'[19]
*(name and address)* or such other firm as may be approved by the Landowner

### 1.3    'Building Contract'
[The contract dated *(date)* or] such [other] contract with the Contractor for carrying out the Works as may be approved by the Landowner pursuant to paragraph 4 of this Schedule

### 1.4    'Completion Date'
The Completion Date as referred to at clause 1.2 of this Agreement as more particularly mentioned at paragraph 24.3 of this Schedule

### 1.5    'Consents'
All the planning permissions listed building consents building regulations consents fire officer approvals and other permissions approvals licenses and similar consents (including any modifications from time to time) which are necessary to enable the Approved Scheme to be implemented without breach of any statute or lawful requirement of any competent authority

[3665]

### 1.6    'Consultants'
The Architect Environmental Consultant Mechanical and Electrical Engineer Planning Supervisor Quantity Surveyor and Structural Engineer [*(add titles of any other consultants already appointed and include relevant definitions of those titles in alphabetical order as appropriate)*] and such other professional advisers as may be approved by the Landowner

**[1.7     'Consultants' Warranty'**[20]
A deed to be entered into by each Consultant with the Landowner and/or any tenant [substantially] in one or other as the case may be of the forms annexed]

**1.8     'Contractor'**
(name and address) or such other building contractor as may be approved by the Landowner pursuant to paragraph 4 of this Schedule

**[1.9     'Contractor's Warranty'**
A deed to be entered into by the Contractor with the Landowner and/or any tenant [substantially] in one or other as the case may be of the forms annexed]

**1.10     'Defects Liability Period'**[21]
[12 months] from the [Practical Completion Date]

**1.11     'Deleterious Materials'**[22]
Materials not in accordance with British Standards or which are generally known to be deleterious at the time of incorporation in the Works [and any materials specifically mentioned in any Consultant's Warranty or Contractor's Warranty]

**1.12     'Development'**[23]
(number) square metres [Gross [External or Internal] or Net Internal] Area as the term is defined in the [Fourth] Schedule of [industrial or warehouse or office] premises [including the Landowner's Works]

**1.13     'End Date'**[24]
(insert date)

**1.14     'Environmental Consultant'**
(name and address) or such other firm as may be approved by the Landowner

                                                              **[3666]**

**1.15     'Excepted Risks'**
1.15.1   Ionising radiations or contamination by radioactivity from any nuclear fuel or from any nuclear waste from the combustion of nuclear fuel
1.15.2   Radioactive toxic explosive or other hazardous properties of any explosive nuclear assembly or nuclear component
1.15.3   Pressure waves caused by aircraft or other aerial devices travelling at sonic or supersonic speeds
1.15.4   Any other risks excepted by the insurance provisions of the Building Contract

**1.16     'Full Reinstatement Value'**
The cost of complete reinstatement (assuming total destruction) allowing for inflation during the period of reinstatement the costs of demolition and site clearance and professional fees including VAT where applicable on all such costs

**1.17     'Insured Risks'**
1.17.1   Fire lightning explosion storm tempest flood
1.17.2   Bursting or overflowing of water tanks apparatus or pipes
1.17.3   Earthquake
1.17.4   Aircraft and other aerial devices or articles dropped from them
1.17.5   Riot and civil commotion
but excluding Excepted Risks

**[1.18     'Landowner's Works'**
(describe landowner's works) to be carried out by the Developer as part of the Works on the Retained Land]

**1.19      'Letter of Appointment'**[25]
The written terms under which a Consultant is appointed

**1.20      'Parties'**
The Landowner and the Developer [and the Surety]

**1.21      'Planning Supervisor'**
*(name and address)* or such other [person *or* firm] as may be approved by the Landowner
and appointed for the purpose the Construction (Design and Management) Regulations
1994

                                                                                    **[3667]**

**1.22      'Plans'**
The plans and drawings for the Development referred to in paragraph 5.1 of this
Schedule comprising the Approved Scheme

**1.23      'Practical Completion'**
Practical completion of the Works pursuant to the Building Contract

**1.24      'Practical Completion Date'**[26]
The date of Practical Completion as certified under the Building Contract

**[1.25      'Programme'**
As defined in paragraph 7 of this Schedule]

**1.26      'Project'**
All aspects of site acquisition demolition site preparation (including remediation of
contamination) design carrying out completion and letting of the Development as
contemplated by this Agreement

**1.27      'Quantity Surveyor'**
*(name and address)* or such other firm as may be approved by the Landowner

                                                                                    **[3668]**

**1.28      'Relevant Event'**[27]
1.28.1    Force majeure
1.28.2    Exceptionally adverse weather conditions
1.28.3    Loss or damage occasioned by Insured Risks
1.28.4    Civil commotion local combination of workmen strike or lockout affecting any
          of the trades engaged in the Works or in the preparation manufacture or
          transportation of goods or materials required for the Works or in the preparation
          of the design of the Works
1.28.5    The exercise after the date of this Agreement of any statutory power which
          restricts the availability or use of labour essential to the proper carrying out of
          the Works or prevents or delays goods materials fuel or energy essential to the
          proper carrying out of the Works
1.28.6    The carrying out by a local authority or statutory or other undertaking of work
          pursuant to its statutory obligations in relation to the Works or failure to carry
          out such work
1.28.7    Delay (which both the Developer and Contractor have taken all practicable
          steps to avoid or reduce) consequent upon a change in statutory requirements
          since the date of this Agreement
[1.28.8   Unreasonable delay on the part of the Surveyor in carrying out his functions
          under this Agreement]
1.28.9    Delay in receipt of any necessary permission or approval of any statutory body
          which the Developer and the Contractor have taken all practicable steps to avoid
          or reduce

1.28.10  The use or threat of terrorism and/or the activity of the relevant authorities in dealing with such use or threat

**[1.29    'Retained Land'**[28]
The land shown **[***(eg, edged red on the plan numbered (number) annexed)***)]]**

**1.30    'Services'**
Facilities such as water gas electricity drainage and telecommunications which are in or pass through over or under the Development and the relevant pipes wires ducts and other conduits

**[3669]**

**1.31    'Specification'**
The specification annexed including the bills of quantities [intended to be] comprised in the Building Contract

**1.32    'Structural Engineer'**
*(name and address)* or such other firm as may be approved by the Landowner

**1.33    'Sub-contractor'**
A sub-contractor to the main contractor under the Building Contract having a design responsibility

**[1.34    'Sub-contractor's Warranty'**[29]
A deed to be entered into by a Sub-Contractor with the Landowner and/or any Tenant [substantially] in one or other as the case may be of the forms annexed]

**1.35    'Surveyor'**[30]
*(name and address)* or such other [firm *or* surveyor] [of similar standing *or* suitably qualified and] nominated by the Landowner

**1.36    'Target Completion Date'**
*(insert date)*

**1.37    'Works'**
The works of [demolition site preparation (including remediation of contamination) and] construction of the Development

**1.38    'Works Completion Certificate'**
As defined in paragraph 24 of this Schedule

**1.39    'Works Completion Date'**
As defined in paragraph 24 of this Schedule

**[3670]**


Part II: Preliminaries

**2        Approvals**[31]
2.1      All and any applications for any consents or approvals made by the Developer to the Landowner shall
         2.1.1      be in writing and
         2.1.2      be made to the Surveyor
[2.2      Every such consent or approval shall not be unreasonably withheld save where expressed to the contrary in this Schedule]
[2.3      Notwithstanding paragraph 2.2 where the Landowner considers that to grant any consent or approval under this Schedule would have effect to materially alter the appearance restrict the user increase the cost diminish the lettable area or reduce the value of the Project the Landowner may refuse such consent or approval]

**3**        **Consultants**[32]
3.1        The Consultants named in this Schedule are approved by the Landowner
3.2        The Developer will not appoint any other professional adviser as a Consultant
           without the Landowner's prior approval but will appoint such further
           Consultants as the Landowner may reasonably require
3.3        The Developer will not dismiss a Consultant without the Landowner's prior
           approval
3.4        The Developer will appoint each Consultant under a Letter of Appointment in
           a form first approved by the Landowner [obtaining from him in favour of the
           Landowner not later than the date of actual completion of the grant of the Lease
           (time being of the essence) a Consultant's Warranty]

**4**        **Contractor**

4.1        [The Contractor named in this Schedule is approved by the Landowner
           *or*
           The Developer shall not appoint a contractor except as approved by the
           Landowner and from a list of not less than [6] prospective contractors first
           submitted to and approved by the Landowner]
4.2        The Developer will not dismiss the Contractor nor engage any other building
           contractor or nominate any sub-contractor without the Landowner's prior
           approval
4.3        The Developer will engage the Contractor under [the Building Contract *or* a
           building contract in a form first approved by the Landowner] [obtaining from
           the Contractor in favour of the Landowner [at the same time *or* not later than
           the date of actual completion of the grant of the Lease (time being of the
           essence)] a Contractor's Warranty]

                                                                              **[3671]**

**5**        **Approved Scheme**[33]
5.1        The plans and drawings for the Development and the Specification [annexed to
           this Agreement *or* identified by the following numbers *(numbers) or* initialled by
           the Parties] have been approved by the Landowner and comprise the Approved
           Scheme
5.2        To the extent that the designs for the Development are not described in full in
           the Approved Scheme such designs will be submitted to the Landowner for the
           Landowner's approval before construction of the Development is commenced
           provided that no such approval will in any way affect the responsibilities of the
           Developer under this Schedule
5.3        The Approved Scheme will not be varied without the Landowner's approval
           [(which may be refused at the Landowner's discretion)] and the expression
           'Approved Scheme' means from time to time the Approved Scheme as
           originally approved incorporating all approved variations (if any)

**6**        **Consents**[34]
6.1        The Developer will use all reasonable endeavours to obtain the Consents as soon
           as practicable submitting each application to the Landowner for approval and
           obtaining such approval before application is made and promptly notifying the
           Landowner of the outcome of each application supplying copies of any
           documents issued
6.2        The Developer will not implement any Consent until it has been approved by
           the Landowner

**[7      The Programme**

7.1      [The Programme is the [bar chart] programme annexed to this Agreement showing the estimated duration of each stage of the Works and when each stage including Practical Completion is due to be achieved

*or*

The Developer will prepare as soon as practicable [and in any event within *(time limit)*] a programme [in bar chart form] which will be the Programme for the purposes of this Schedule showing the estimated duration of each stage of the Works and when each stage including Practical Completion is due to be achieved]

7.2      The Developer will not vary the Programme except as provided in this Schedule and the expression 'the Programme' means the Programme as from time to time so varied]

**[3672]**


Part III: Works

**8      Licence**[35]

8.1      [Subject to payment of the Premium [on the Premium Payment Date]] the Landowner grants to the Developer and those working for or on behalf of the Developer in relation to the Project a non-exclusive licence to enter the Property [and upon the Retained Land] [on the Premium Payment Date] to enable the Developer to perform its obligations under this Agreement

8.2      Until completion of the Lease possession of the Property remains vested in the Landowner and this Agreement shall not operate as a demise of the Property

8.3      The Developer shall in all other respects as from [the date of this Agreement *or* the Premium Payment Date] observe and perform all the obligations on the part of the tenant to be contained in the Lease

**9      General Requirements**[36]

The Developer will carry out the Works:

9.1      in a proper and workmanlike manner

9.2      with good quality and suitable materials

9.3      in accordance with the Approved Scheme

9.4      in compliance with the Consents

9.5      diligently and expeditiously [in accordance with the Programme] in order to achieve Practical Completion by the Target Completion Date

9.6      in compliance with all requirements of statute and all lawful requirements of local authorities and other competent authorities

[9.7      in accordance with all relevant codes of practice and British Standards]

9.8      in compliance with the Building Contract [and the Documents]

9.9      without infringement of any rights reservations covenants restrictions stipulations or other encumbrances binding upon or affecting the Property

[9.10     to the [reasonable] satisfaction of the Landowner]

**10      Delay**[37]

10.1     If by reason of a Relevant Event the Developer considers that delay will be caused to [the Programme or to] the Target Completion Date the Landowner will upon application by the Developer supported by such evidence as the Landowner may [reasonably] require [and the advice of the appropriate Consultant] allow such amendment to [the Programme or] the Target Completion Date as may [in its opinion be appropriate *or* be reasonable] after taking into account any extent to which such delay has been caused by any act default or omission of the Developer but under no circumstances will the Target Completion Date be postponed beyond the End Date

10.2    If the Developer fails to complete the Works by the Target Completion Date as extended by paragraph 10.1 of this Schedule then without prejudice to clause 18 of this Agreement the Developer will pay or allow to the Landowner specified (or liquidated and ascertained) damages of *(amount)* per [day *or* week] for the period between the Target Completion Date as so extended and the Works Completion Date

**[3673]**

## 11    Insurance[38]

### 11.1    General Requirements

11.1.1    The Developer will at its own expense effect or secure and maintain the insurance mentioned in this paragraph:

    11.1.1.1    with an insurance office [and on terms *or* under policies whose terms exclusions and conditions have first been] approved by the Landowner

    11.1.1.2    naming the Landowner as the one of the joint insured parties

    11.1.1.3    until Practical Completion

    11.1.1.4    under policies [copies of] which are to be produced to the Landowner [on demand *or* within 7 days of issue] together with evidence that current premiums have been paid

and the Developer will not permit any variation of insurance cover without the Landowner's prior approval and will immediately notify the Landowner of any endorsements or other amendments to the relevant policies received from the insurers and will from time to time effect any further insurance which may in the Landowner's [reasonable] opinion be prudent

[11.1.2    For so long as the insurance prescribed by the Building Contract remains in force and to the extent that it complies with paragraph 11.1.1 (including both the Developer and the Landowner as the named insured) then such insurance shall suffice for the purposes of paragraph 11.1.1]

11.1.3    On and from the Practical Completion Date the [Landowner *or* Developer] shall insure the Property in accordance with the provisions of the Lease and the Developer shall [pay the premium and other sums payable and] observe and perform all the obligations on the part of the tenant under the lease

### 11.2    The Development

The Works all materials structures and buildings upon the Property [and the Retained Land] and (when completed) the Development will be insured for Full Reinstatement Value against loss damage or destruction by any of the Insured Risks [and in an amount [of not less than £... million] [first approved by the Landowner]]

**[3674]**

### 11.3    Reinstatement

In the event of any loss damage or destruction to the Works materials structures or buildings on Site or the completed Development:

11.3.1    the Developer will continue to carry out the Works unless the loss or damage is so extensive or of such a nature as to make this impossible or inadvisable

11.3.2    the Developer will use all reasonable endeavours promptly to obtain the maximum payment of insurance moneys

11.3.3    the Developer will proceed diligently and expeditiously to reinstate the loss damage or destruction and to complete the Works in accordance with this Schedule

**11.4     Public liability**
Without prejudice to its liability to indemnify the Landowner in accordance with paragraph 12 of this Schedule the Developer will take out and maintain insurance with a limit of indemnity of not less than £... million for any one occurrence or series of occurrences arising out of the carrying out of the Works and in respect of damage to any property real or personal other than the Works arising out of the carrying out of the Works and caused by the negligence of the Developer the Contractor or any sub-contractor of the Contractor

**11.5     Failure**
If the Developer does not insure as required by this paragraph or fails to produce adequate evidence that such insurance is in force the Landowner may:
11.5.1     itself effect such insurance cover as it may consider prudent and the Developer shall indemnify the Landowner accordingly or
11.5.2     at any time rescind this Agreement in accordance with clause 17.2 of this Agreement

**11.6     Development at risk of the Developer**
Notwithstanding the foregoing the Works the Development [and] the Property [and the Retained Land] shall be at the risk in all respects of the Developer until the Practical Completion Date

**[3675]**

**12     Indemnity**[39]

In addition to any claims which the Landowner may have in relation to a breach of this Agreement and this Schedule the Developer will to the extent that moneys are not recovered from insurers indemnify the Landowner in respect of any liability for the following matters in relation to the Project:
12.1     death or personal injury to any person arising out of the carrying out of the Works save any person for whom the Landowner is responsible
12.2     injury or damage to any property real or personal other than the Works in so far as such injury or damage arises out of the carrying out of the Works and to the extent that the same is due to any negligence breach of statutory duty omission or default of the Developer the Contractor or a sub-contractor of the Developer
12.3     any liability in respect of and any fees or charges legally demandable under any Act of Parliament or any regulation or bye-law of any local authority or of any statutory undertaker in respect of the Works
12.4     the infringement of the rights of any third party in connection with the Property
12.5     observing and performing all provisions contained or referred to in the Documents

**13     Third party rights**[40]

13.1     The Developer will ensure that the rights and interests of third parties are not infringed by the Project and will with the prior approval of the Landowner enter into such agreements relating to rights of light and other easements and party structures and pay such compensation as may be necessary (and the Landowner will join in such agreements so far as necessary as owner of the Property)

13.2     Where the London Building Acts 1930–1939 the Party Wall, etc Act 1996 (or
         any re-enactment of them) apply the Developer will comply with (and issue all
         notices required under) those Acts in connection with the Development and
         will comply with the terms of any awards made pursuant to those Acts

**14     Services**

The Developer will with the Landowner's prior approval negotiate such agreements with
statutory undertakers and others as may be required to secure for the Development all
Services required and the diversion in a satisfactory manner of all Services which are
located in a position which would interfere with the Project (and the Landowner will join
in such agreements as are approved by it and so far as necessary as owner of the Property)

**[3676]**

**15     Site Management**[41]

The Developer will secure that:
15.1     the Property [and the Retained Land] [is *or* are] at all times secured as fully as
         may be reasonably practicable against unauthorised entry
15.2     no material goods or equipment is brought deposited or stored on the Property
         [or the Retained Land] except that from time to time properly required for the
         Works
15.3     all material stored on the Property [or the Retained Land] is kept in a secure
         compound and adequately protected
15.4     all surplus material rubble rubbish and waste is properly cleared and removed
         from the Property [and the Retained Land] when it is no longer required
15.5     the Property [and the Retained Land] [is *or* are] maintained in a tidy condition
         and free from rubbish
15.6     there is no excavation of the Property [or the Retained Land] or extraction of
         soil earth clay gravel sand or minerals except as required for the Works
15.7     proper precautions are taken for the safety of all persons upon or in the vicinity
         of the Property [and the Retained Land]
15.8     there are no advertisements posters placards or signs affixed to displayed from on
         the boundaries of or on the Property [or the Retained Land] except (with the
         prior approval of the Landowner) those connected with the Project
15.9     the Works are carried out in a manner which does not cause a nuisance and
         causes the minimum of annoyance inconvenience and disturbance to owners or
         occupiers of neighbouring properties or members of the public [and in
         particular no work will be carried out except [between the hours of 8 am and
         6 pm Mondays to Fridays] [and 8 am and 1 pm on Saturdays]]

**[3677]**

15.10    proper provision is made for the support and use of land walls roads footpaths
         and buildings adjoining adjacent or near to the Property [and the Retained
         Land] and for the protection of all Services
15.11    all debris is removed from such roads and footpaths and the proper requirements
         of the highways and other competent authorities are observed and performed
15.12    hoardings of sufficient height are erected around the Property [and the
         Retained Land]
15.13    good efficient and well maintained plant and equipment are used on the
         Property [and the Retained Land]
15.14    proper arrangements are made with the relevant authorities for the provision of
         water gas electricity telephone and other services required for the Works
15.15    the requirements of highways and other competent authorities are duly met
15.16    the Works are maintained in good repair and condition

## 16     Deleterious Materials

The Developer will [use all reasonable endeavours to] ensure that no Deleterious Materials are used in the Works[42]

## 17     Archaeological antiquities[43]

Subject always to the provisions of the Ancient Monuments and Archaeological Areas Act 1979:

17.1     any article of value or antiquity or remains of geological historical or archaeological interest on the Property will (as between the Developer and the Landowner and subject to completion of the sale and purchase of the Property) belong to the Landowner

17.2     if any such article is or remains are discovered the Developer will immediately inform the Landowner and comply with the Landowner's directions as to inspection protection and disposal of such article or remains

**[3678]**

Part IV: Administration

## 18     The Surveyor[44]

The Landowner has appointed the Surveyor to act as the agent of the Landowner under this Agreement (unless otherwise expressly provided):

18.1     to consider and respond to applications for the Landowner's approval

18.2     to monitor the performance of the Developer the Contractor and the Consultants

18.3     to issue certificates or otherwise indicate whether or not the Landowner is satisfied with any matter

18.4     to issue and receive Communications on behalf of the Landowner

18.5     and until notice is given to the contrary by the Landowner the Developer is authorised and required to deal with and rely upon the Surveyor as the agent of the Landowner in all such matters

## 19     Consultation

The Developer will in relation to the Project:

19.1     regularly inform consult report to and liaise with the Surveyor on all matters including all material measures taken and stages reached the general progress of the Works and any material problems or delays which have arisen or are likely to do so

19.2     promptly supply to the Surveyor copies of all relevant written material when it is received or produced by or on behalf of the Developer

## 20     Information

The following illustrate (but do not limit) the types of information to be supplied to the Surveyor under paragraph 19.2 of this Schedule:

20.1     All plans and drawings the Specification structural calculations and other material from time to time comprising the Approved Scheme

20.2     Applications for and correspondence relating to Consents and the outcome of such applications

20.3     Letters of Appointment

20.4     The Building Contract

20.5     Lists of sub-contractors and suppliers

20.6      Test certificates and specialist reports and surveys
[20.7     Valuations by the Quantity Surveyor]
[20.8     Any written advice on contamination provided by the Environmental Consultant]
20.9      Architect's instructions
20.10     Minutes of all formal meetings (including site meetings design team meetings working party or project meetings)

**[3679]**

## 21      Meetings

The Surveyor is entitled although not obliged to attend all formal meetings relating to the Project whether or not the Contractor or a Consultant is entitled to attend and will be given not less than [2] Working Days' notice (or in emergency as much notice as possible) of such meetings

## 22      Control[45]

22.1      The Surveyor [and any duly authorised representative of the Landowner] may upon reasonable notice (where practicable) at [any time *or* all reasonable times] enter the Property [and the Retained Land] to carry out any inspection [test] or survey [or for any other [reasonable] purpose] connected with the Project but [he *or* they] will cause as little interference as practicable

22.2      If prior to Practical Completion the Surveyor gives notice to the Developer [on reasonable grounds] that any works or materials are not in accordance with the Approved Scheme or are not to the standard or the quality required by this Agreement the Developer will commence appropriate action to remove the defective works or materials and make good the defects as soon as practicable

22.3      The Surveyor will not issue any direct instructions to the Contractor or to any of the Consultants and will not communicate with the Contractor or with any of the Consultants except in an emergency or in a meeting where the Developer is represented but will [(without prejudice to any Contractor's or Consultant's Warranty)] address all other communications to the Developer

**[3680]**

## 23      Responsibility[46]

23.1      The Landowner is relying on the Developer properly to carry out and complete the Project and the Developer warrants that it has the skill and experience required to carry out the Project

23.2      No involvement by the Landowner (whether through its Surveyor or otherwise) in considering whether or not to grant any consent or approval or issue certificates or in attending (or failing to attend) meetings or otherwise in supervising or omitting to supervise the Project in any way relieves or affects the duties of the Developer the Contractor or the Consultants in relation to the Project [except to the extent that the Landowner or the Surveyor causes loss by imposing a requirement with which the Developer must under the terms of this Agreement comply but which is inconsistent with the recommendations of the Contractor or a Consultant]

23.3      The Developer will duly observe and perform all provisions of the Building Contract and of all Letters of Appointment and other agreements relating to the Project on the part of the Developer as employer to be observed or performed and (save with the approval of the Landowner) secure the observance and performance by the other parties to such agreements of the provisions on their part to be observed or performed

23.4    None of the provisions of the Building Contract or of any Letter of Appointment shall be varied or waived nor will any action to secure the compliance with such provisions be discharged settled or compromised without the approval of the Landowner [which may be withheld in any such case at the Landowner's discretion]

**[3681]**

Part V: Completion

**24      Works completion[47]**

24.1    When the Works have reached Practical Completion in accordance with the terms of this Agreement the Surveyor will issue a Works Completion Certificate to that effect and the date stated in the Works Completion Certificate is the Works Completion Date

[24.2    The Surveyor will not refuse to issue a Works Completion Certificate if minor defects in the Works exist of such a nature and number that they would not prevent the issue by the Architect of a certificate of Practical Completion under the Building Contract]

24.3    The Completion Date shall be [10] Working Days after the Works Completion Date

**25      Procedure**

25.1    The Parties will use their reasonable endeavours to ensure that the Works Completion Date and Practical Completion Date are contemporaneous

25.2    If the Developer gives to the Landowner not less than [10] Working Days' notice of the date of the site meeting at which the Architect is expected to decide whether Practical Completion has occurred the Surveyor will attend such meeting and endeavour to agree with the Architect whether or not it is appropriate to issue a certificate of Practical Completion under the Building Contract (but without prejudice to the Architect's professional discretion and duties under the Building Contract)

25.3    If he considers that the Works are not substantially complete in accordance with this Agreement the Surveyor will give his reasons orally at the relevant site meeting and confirm these reasons in writing to the Developer within [3] Working Days stating what further Works are required

25.4    The Developer will carry out such further Works as soon as possible and then give to the Surveyor reasonable notice of a further site meeting so that the procedure set out in this paragraph may be repeated (save as regards Practical Completion under the Building Contract if a certificate of Practical Completion has been issued) as often as necessary until the Works Completion Certificate is issued

25.5    If the Works are substantially complete in accordance with this Agreement the Surveyor will issue the Works Completion Certificate within [5] Working Days of the relevant site meeting

**[3682]**

**26      Defects**

Without prejudice to all other rights and remedies of the Landowner the Developer will at its own expense make good as soon as practicable all defects which may appear in the Development and are notified to the Developer before the end of the Defects Liability Period and which are due to the failure of the Developer to comply with its obligations under this Agreement or to frost occurring before the Practical Completion Date (or the Works Completion Date if later) and which (if inconsistent with the foregoing) the Architect has notified the Contractor should be carried out under the defects liability provisions of the Building Contract

**27    Completion Documents**

Within one month following the Completion Date the Developer will supply to the Landowner [but so far only as concerns the Retained Land]:

27.1    three sets of 'as built' Plans of the Development

27.2    maintenance manuals and manufacturer's warranties in relation to all plant and equipment installed in the Development

27.3    such confirmations as the Landowner may reasonably require that no Deleterious Materials have been used in the Development

27.4    the health and safety file

**[28    Plans**

Within one month following the Completion Date the Developer will so far only as concerns the Retained Land either:

28.1    procure assignment absolutely to the Landowner of the full copyright of the Plans to which the Developer may be entitled or

28.2    take such other steps effectually to procure for the Landowner the full right and entitlement to use on licence without further payment or liability for further payment the Plans for the purposes only of maintaining repairing and renewing the Development and execute all such deeds and documents as the Landowner may reasonably require effectually to vest such rights in the Landowner]

**[29    Proceedings[48]**

29.1    So far as concerns the Retained Land but not otherwise the Landowner may at any time following the latest of the date of actual completion the expiry of the Defects Liability Period and the completion of all related remedial works require the Developer to assign to the Landowner (in a form approved by the Landowner) such rights as the Developer may have against the Contractor or any Consultant and in so far as necessary the Developer shall make application to the Contractor and/or any such Consultant as the case may be for any requisite consent and the Developer shall use all reasonable endeavours to obtain the same

29.2    In so far as assignment is not permitted or consent is not forthcoming the Landowner may in the alternative commence prosecute or defend as the case may be any relevant proceedings in the name and on behalf of the Developer and in so far as the Developer is already entitled thereto shall pay to the Developer any costs and/or damages received to which the Developer may be entitled after counterclaim or set-off in relation to the Landowner and in priority only after the interests of the Landowner]

**[3683]**

[FOURTH] SCHEDULE[49]
LETTING AND FURTHER PAYMENTS

I       Definitions
II      Lettings
III     Further Payments

Part I: Definitions and Interpretation
## 1      Definitions

In this Schedule unless the context otherwise requires the following expressions shall have the following meanings:

**1.1      'Agreement for Underlease'**
Any agreement entered into (inter alia) by the Developer for the grant of an Underlease

**1.2      'Code'**
The Code of Measuring Practice of The Royal Institution of Chartered Surveyors and Incorporated Society of Valuers and Auctioneers [Edition 4, 1993]

**1.3      'Further Sum'**
A sum calculated in accordance with paragraph 7 of this Schedule

**1.4      'Gross [External *or* Internal] Area'**
The gross [external *or* internal] area of the Development as measured in accordance with the Code

**1.5      'Interest Rate'**
*(insert details)*

**[1.6      'Letting Agents'**
*(name and address)* or such other firm as may be approved by the Landowner]

**1.7      'Letting Policy'**
The letting policy so entitled annexed to this Agreement

**[1.8      'Net Internal Area'**
The Net Internal Area of the Project as measured in accordance with the Code]

**[1.9      'Target Rent'** *(insert only in so far as relevant to any calculations under this Schedule)*
[*(amount)* per annum *or (amount)* per square metre per annum of Gross [External *or* Internal] *or* Net Internal] Area exclusive of VAT]

**1.10      'Underlease'**
As defined in paragraph 3.1 of this Schedule

**[3684]**

Part II: Letting[50]
## 2      Letting

2.1      The Developer shall in consultation with the Landowner [use all reasonable endeavours to] negotiate the letting of the Development [other than the Retained Land] [as quickly as possible] [and for this purpose will instruct the Letting Agents]

2.2      The Developer shall [(except in so far as the Letting Agents expressly advise in writing or as the Developer may otherwise approve)] comply with the Letting Policy and the relevant provisions of the Lease

2.3      The Developer shall not vary the Letting Policy [except upon the written advice of the Letting Agents] and with the approval of the Landowner

2.4      [Subject to the relevant provisions of the Lease the *or* The] Development is if possible to be let as a whole but if that is not achieved [6 months] after the [relevant] Works Completion Date the Landowner will permit the letting of the Development in not more than [3] parts [but under no circumstances will an Underlease of less than one complete floor (excluding common parts) be allowed]

[2.5      This Part II of this Schedule applies only to letting(s) of the Development [or part of it] for the first time]

## 3    Underlease(s)

3.1    An agreement for Underlease shall be [substantially] in the form of Agreement for Underlease annexed [and otherwise approved by the Landowner]

3.2    An Underlease is to be [substantially] on the terms of the form of Underlease annexed [and otherwise as approved by the Landowner] and will:

    3.2.1    be for a term of [not less than] [25] years and comprising [the whole *or* a lettable portion or portions] of the Development

    [3.2.2    be at a rent to be first approved in writing by the Landowner as the best rent reasonably obtainable without taking a fine or premium [[and with the view to achieving *or* at] [not less than] the Target Rent]]

    3.2.3    be consistent [in all respects] with [the Letting Policy] and the terms of the Lease

3.3    The Developer shall not grant an Underlease or enter into an Agreement for Underlease which shall or may result in disapplication of an election by the Landowner to waive exemption or which may otherwise adversely affect the Landowner's ability to recover input tax

**[3685]**

## 4    Approval and Grant of Underlease

[Subject always to the terms of the Lease:]

4.1    The Developer must not enter into any Agreement for Underlease (or any Underlease as the case may be) until the Landowner has approved:

    4.1.1    the proposed tenant and any guarantors required by the Landowner and

    4.1.2    the terms of the Underlease or Agreement for Underlease

4.2    The Developer shall comply with and enforce [so far as practicable] every Agreement for Underlease

Part III: Further Payments[51]

## 5    Payment of Further Sum

Upon underletting [for the first time] of the Development [or part or parts of it] the Developer shall pay to the Landowner a Further Sum (exclusive of VAT)

## 6    Calculation

[The *or* Every] Further Sum *(insert formula(e))*

## 7    Payment

7.1    Any Further Sum becoming payable shall be paid within [5] Working Days after completion of the grant of the [relevant] Underlease together with VAT thereon

7.2    In the case of any payment made under paragraph 7.1 above it shall be made in like manner as for the Premium under this Agreement

[[FIFTH] SCHEDULE<br>Contaminated Land[52]<br>*(insert appropriate provisions)*]

*(signatures (or common seals) of the parties)*[53]<br>
[*(signatures of witnesses)*]<br>
**[3686]**

1      As to stamp duty see the Information Binder: Stamp Duties [1] (Lease; agreement for lease). Any stamp duty payable is payable on the agreement under the Finance Act 1999 s 112(3), Sch 13 para 14 (41 Halsbury's Statutes (4th Edn) STAMP DUTIES), and must be paid before this agreement may be used in civil proceedings. However, if entitlement to the lease is expressed as an option (not necessarily attractive to the landowner), liability to stamp duty is deferred to grant of the lease. As to agreements for lease between landowner and developer see Paragraph 322 [3604] et seq ante and for commentary on agreements for lease see vol 22(1) (1996 Reissue) LANDLORD AND TENANT (BUSINESS TENANCIES) Paragraph 101 [201] et seq.

         Because this Form includes an agreement for the grant of a lease, the agreement is capable of registration as an estate contract (either as a class C(iv) land charge under the Land Charges Act 1972 (37 Halsbury's Statutes (4th Edn) REAL PROPERTY) where the land is unregistered, or by way of notice (or caution) in the case of registered land).

2      Use of a capital letter identifies a word as a definition. In this precedent some definitions are to be found in its schedules as well as in the main body of the agreement.

3      Although development necessarily implies a VAT regime, the premium initially payable may be an exempt supply if no option to tax has been exercised appropriately. As to VAT see Paragraph 327 [3611] ante and see vol 38(1) (2000 Reissue) SALE OF LAND Paragraph 8 [16] et seq.

4      If the transaction is being carried out within a statutory regime, it is helpful to quote it here.

5      The transaction is essentially an agreement for lease conditional upon the carrying out of development. In this precedent, the conveyancing aspects are kept to the minimum to allow flexibility to the draftsman, but the development provisions (in the third schedule) are more comprehensive, to cater for a significant reversionary interest, if relevant.

6      As to contaminated land generally see vol 38(1) (2000 Reissue) SALE OF LAND Paragraph 147 [341] et seq. For environmental and due diligence enquiries and definitions and interpretation for use with those enquiries see vol 38(1) (2000 Reissue) SALE OF LAND Forms 35 [1585] and 36 [1592]. For a schedule of environmental warranties and indemnities see vol 38(1) (2000 Reissue) SALE OF LAND Form 61 [2401]. For alternative shorter warranty clauses see Forms 144 [4587] and 145 [4588] post. Practitioners should consider what provisions are appropriate to be included in the fifth schedule to this Form having regard to the actual state of the site the subject of this agreement and draft appropriate provisions which may be based on the above mentioned Forms, ensuring that the definitions and wording used is compatible with those used in this Form.

7      A premium may be required to be paid as a precursor to the developer being allowed on site (see paragraph 8 of the third schedule).

8      Distinguish this provision from the licence conferred by paragraph 8 of the third schedule.

9      It is still possible that an unregistered title may be offered and, if so, a land charge class C(iv) should be registered immediately on exchange of agreements (or, if the title is registered, a proper tenant's amendment would be for the landowner to acquiesce in a note of the agreement being made against the registered title, rather than for the developer to rely simply upon a caution).

10     The disclaimer clause, common to many conveyancing documents, also includes a warranty about the lawful use of the property. Such a disclaimer will usually be found in the corresponding lease.

11     The draftsman must consider his own conveyancing requirements.

12     Restrictions on dealing with an agreement for lease are to be expected. At the same time, to avoid being 'unbankable', the benefit of the agreement needs to be capable of being dealt with by any mortgagee in a responsible manner. Particular landowner requirements may suggest a harsher regime but the developer's representatives, in turn, must ensure that the finished result is not, upon analysis, an unbankable proposition.

13     Non-merger clauses are common to conveyancing contracts. However, where landlord and tenant issues are concerned, other issues arise. In the case of an agreement for lease between a developer and his occupational tenant, for example, (for which see Form 83 [3711] post) a buyer of the resultant investment will find any enabling agreements for lease unattractive in so far as, by implication of law, the developer's development obligations are passed to the investing buyer. In such a case, those obligations may remain solely with the developer upon making clear that the development obligations are personal (and by applying Landlord and Tenant (Covenants) Act 1995 s 3(6)).

         In the case of an agreement for lease between landowner and developer, the landowner naturally wishes to ensure that the development obligations, so far as they remain outstanding, are not personal but devolve upon the head lessee. A developer of substance either entering into or acting as surety under an agreement for lease may wish to shield its buyer (to whom the lease may in the event be granted direct), and, if the point is taken by the prospective investing buyer at a sufficiently early stage, the landowner's acquiescence will depend, amongst other things, on its residue, any prospective sharing in rents, its interests (if relevant) as a local authority and, as the case may be, its interest in development to be carried out by the developer on any retained land, in lieu of other consideration.

**[3687]**

14     See note 3 above and also the safeguards in clause 15.2 of this Form (Finance Act 1997 s 37 (48 Halsbury's Statutes (4th Edn) VALUE ADDED TAX)). It is helpful if both the headlease and underleases granted out of it contain similar provisions.

15     The events of default govern all aspects of the agreement and not just the development obligations.

16    The consequences of default go wider than, say, under a forward sale agreement. Once the lease has been granted agreements for lease are usually silent as to whether, upon analysis, forfeiture should be available in case of any outstanding developer obligations. In this precedent, the development is presumed to have been completed. If, as in some cases, the lease is granted before development is carried out then the right of forfeiture in the lease must also be made expressly exercisable in case of unremedied default.
      However, assuming that the lease has not been granted, a consequence of default is that the developer's licence terminates and the (perhaps part-built) development reverts to the landowner. Hence such provisions as those in clause 18.1 but note, for bankability, the provisions of clause 18.4. Indeed, because the developer is being put to the expense of carrying out the development, provisions such as that contained in clause 18.3 are helpful in the funding context.

17    The dispute provisions will in practice attach largely to the third and fourth schedules. As an agreement for lease, (and so long, as is assumed, as the resultant lease will be for not less than twelve months) the transaction is excluded by the Construction Contracts (England & Wales) Exclusion Order 1998, SI 1998/648 reg 6, but it is open to the parties to consider whether any dispute under this agreement should be subject to the effect for the time being of any adjudication arising under, say, the building contract or other construction contract within the meaning of the Act.

18    Arrangements between landowners and developers, and the whole fabric of property joint ventures in the widest sense, give rise to the possibility that a legal partnership exists, allowing one or more parties to bind the others, tax transparency and so on. Denial of such an arrangement does not alone suffice and, in all cases, it is a matter of substance.

19    Professionals are not necessarily those of the developer, particularly if they are appointed by a contractor under a JCT form of design and build contract. In such a case, the contract administrator will need to be defined as well (eg Employer's Agent) and references elsewhere in the document to the architect (where relevant) amended accordingly.

20    It is anticipated that the need for warranties, whether from consultants or contractors, may not necessarily die with the advent of the Contracts (Rights of Third Parties) Act 1999. Indeed, it is noted that as various forms of JCT construction contracts are from time to time revised, express provisions are being incorporated expressly denying the availability of the Act.

21    Under an agreement for lease, whether or not the landowner is interested in defects liability depends upon his reversionary interest and/or his interest in that part of the development (if any) carried out upon retained land. If grant of the lease is triggered simply by practical completion of the development, then this may not be relevant.

22    There is a perceptible retreat from defining deleterious materials at length. However, landowners may (again in terms of their reversion as before) be concerned with these and the developer, in turn, will be concerned with those restrictions on use of deleterious materials which are prescribed by its bankers/funders/tenants.

23    This is the general term, to be distinguished from the 'Works' as defined (see also paragraph 9 of the third schedule).

**[3688]**

24    The end date is a long-stop date which may signal forfeiture of the agreement.

25    The extent of control over the development clearly depends upon the landowner's interest. For the purpose of this precedent, it is assumed that the landowner has significant interests in the built outcome, and so there are parallels with the kinds of obligations which might, for example, be given by a developer to a fund under a forward sale and purchase agreement.

26    Note that if 'Works Completion' is distinguished from 'Practical Completion', the prospects for completion of the sale and purchase may be delayed whilst either further remedial works or other aspects of compliance with the agreement are complied with by the developer, at his own expense. See below as to the works completion certificate.

27    Regard should be had to the terms of the building contact and such matters as are relevant thereunder, also any other related development agreement. However, just as the developer may be excused from the consequences of unreasonable delay on the part of the landowner's surveyor in carrying out his functions under this agreement, neither the landlord nor, for example, a purchasing fund may allow any factor in such relevant events which is attributable to delay or default on the part of the developer.

28    It is not uncommon, particularly where public authorities are concerned, for the consideration to be expressed, in part or in whole, by a developer's obligation to carry out works on retained land. They may comprise more than accommodation works and be a substantive part of the development in their own right. Where accommodation works alone are required, then, with the consent of the appropriate public authority, those works may be carried out simply as an adjunct to the development obligations eg highway works.

29    It is not usual to require warranties from a sub-contractor other than a sub-contractor as defined (ie having a design responsibility).

30    The landowner will usually require representation if only to determine that the development has been sufficiently carried out to allow completion of the lease. Such a representative will have a wider ranging role in the case of any valuable reversion or works to be carried out on the retained land (if any).

31    If the agreement for lease is to be conditional upon, say, the obtaining of planning permission, then such provisions will appear in the main body of the agreement. For the substantive development, however, a wider range of consents may be considered, and the whole thrust of the development obligations is dependent upon the landowner's interests in the built outcome and may require to be adapted to suit.

32    The consultants and contractor are defined. Depending on the form of building contract, some or all of the consultants (in the case of design and build, for example, all except the quantity surveyor or the employer's agent) will be the appointees of the developer (or the contractor). In that event, in so far as the contractor is to create and implement those appointments, it follows that the building contract must make provision for this to be facilitated and to reflect any particular requirements of the landowner.

33    The approved scheme is of the essence of the arrangement. The extent of departure from this depends upon the landowner's interest in the built outcome. A fund, by contrast, may be interested in no departure at all.

34    Approval of plans for building control purposes habitually follows the event. In that case, reliance must be placed upon the advice of appropriate consultants as to compliance of the approved scheme with building regulations.

35    Much as with forward funding, as the land belongs to the landowner, a licence to go on site is required. Note clause 7 of the agreement, however, and that paragraph 8.2 of the third schedule declares that the agreement shall not operate as a demise of the property, albeit that a demise may still be implied in law.

36    The general requirements may be expanded to include particular characteristics, such as titles and so on. The agreement for lease may, in turn, need to be reflected in the employer's requirements under the building contract (and its observance and performance at large is likely to be reflected in all related development documents as well).

37    Relevant events as defined are intended to make allowance for all those things which are beyond the developer's control. This being so, they must include relevant events arising under the building contract, excepting those which will entitle the contractor to an extension of time by reason of his employer's default.

38    Insurance requirements vary according to contractual commitments. As a first step, the insurance obligations in the building contract are likely to suffice for practical purposes as also the insurance obligations imposed upon consultants in their letters of appointment. In this Form, the insurance provisions of the lease are expressed to operate from practical completion until grant.

39    Professional indemnity insurance on the part of the developer should also be considered, particularly if he is managing the project. Otherwise the professional indemnity cover of an appointed manager under his letter of appointment, or that prescribed by the design and build contract, may suffice.

      The interests of a landowner are fundamentally different from, say, those of a prospective buyer of or investor in the resultant development, save of course to the extent that there is a reversionary interest or the development is in part carried out upon retained land. However, the conduct of the development may yet expose the landowner to liability of some kind and an indemnity clause is, therefore, appropriate.

**[3689]**

40    Third party rights often include those the existence of which may not have been apparent at the outset: eg long hidden infrastructure the presence of which suggests acquisition of rights by prescription. Such contingencies are usually contemplated as part of the programme, but may also give rise to a relevant event and permitted delay.

41    Proper and effective site management guards against the possibility of nuisance or offence to third parties. In any case, (separate) statutory agreements will often prescribe the conduct both on and off site: eg requirements of the highway authority or access and egress by construction traffic and so on. Where crane oversailing is necessary then, inevitably, an express licence will be required. Site management will be of particular interest to a landowner with part of the development being carried out upon retained land.

42    Practitioners should take accountancy advice as to whether the tax deduction scheme is applicable. For a clause see Form 80 clause 22 [3456] ante.

43    The presence of archaeological finds may trigger the intervention of the local authority as local authority, and the imposition of delay to the programme. If the local authority is landowner, whatever the issues, whether planning, building control or whatever, its statutory functions must be distinguished clearly from that of landowner. (Some public authorities incorporate clauses expressly distancing themselves from their statutory functions).

44    A similar clause has been adopted as for forward funding and forward sale and purchase (for which we see Forms 80 [3441] and 81 [3521] respectively ante. However, the emphasis is different, given the interests of the landowner which may be remote or substantial. The approvals process, accordingly, needs to be considered in the same light, certification and also the whole area of administration.

45    The likelihood is, notwithstanding the above, that the landowner's surveyor will have an interest in ensuring the built outcome and a similar provision to that in the related funding documentation is appropriate.

46    The extent of reliance is measurable in relation to the interest of the landowner. Paragraph 23.1 of the third schedule is pivotal. The landowner's right to walk away essentially means forfeiture of the agreement on default, and much as with forward funding, and to the extent of the landowner's interest, the developer's

skills are in issue. Depending upon how such provisions are drafted, the general development obligations may be seen as confining the developer's role whereas paragraph 23.1 singles out the developer's professional skills. The need for professional indemnity cover should be considered in that light.

    Exclusion clauses (see paragraph 23.2) should be seen as prospectively ineffective to the extent that a duty of care is owed by the person relying on the exclusion. If the developer has elected to go along with the landowner's requirements but could notwithstanding have objected, the exclusion of liability on the part of the landowner is perhaps more likely to stand.

47    Distinguish works completion and practical completion, the former encapsulating compliance with the agreement whereas the latter, practical completion, may even be in breach of the agreement in some way. Again, the prospective interests of the landowner being so diverse, a full procedure has been adopted here as for funding agreements. See also Form 80 note 55 [3499] ante as to, inter alia, reference to the certificate of practical completion.

48    Paragraph 29 of the third schedule is optional. Unlike a funding scenario, it seems unlikely that a landowner will have sufficient interest to take an assignment of the entirety of the developer's interests in various construction related contracts. The paragraph otherwise follows similar paragraphs in the related funding documentation. The practical reality is that a major interest will be granted to the developer or its successor (perhaps a fund), and it is the fund which is the more likely to wish a provision such as this in its own documentation. Again, until the developer has exhausted the prospects of remuneration from its financing or disposals of the development, it may likely be advised to retain all its interests in construction related contracts for the time being.

49    If the agreement provides solely for the grant of a major interest without any further payment to the landowner then this schedule will not be required.

50    For the most part, alienation under the resultant lease will be governed if at all, under the provisions of that lease. The provisions of paragraphs 2–4 inclusive of the fourth schedule anticipate some wider interest on the part of the landowner, whether a share in rents, a desire to control tenant mix or so on. In connection with the latter, the letting policy may be of importance.

51    The possibilities are too wide to provide a standard clause. If the landowner is to be entitled, for example, to a share of occupational rents, the appropriate formula will be contained in the related lease. If it is to receive further payments (sometimes known as 'overage'), perhaps related to lettings, thus justifying imposing initial letting provisions under the agreement for lease, a formula may be required. Again, how this formula may be framed will depend, amongst other things, on whether a premium is to be paid initially by the developer, or whether such payments amount to a top-up.

52    See note 6 above.

53    It is not usually necessary to have the contract executed as a deed unless the contract contains recitals which are intended to be binding or there are other special considerations (eg, there is a lack of valuable consideration or it is desired to extend the period set by the Limitation Act 1980 s 8 (24 Halsbury's Statutes (4th Edn) LIMITATION OF ACTIONS) for bringing claims).

    Where a contract is to be executed as a deed sealing is not necessary either in the case of an individual or in the case of a company, but all parties must sign either on the same document or each on one of two identical parts which are exchanged and the signatures of all individuals must be witnessed: see the Law of Property (Miscellaneous Provisions) Act 1989 s 1(3) (37 Halsbury's Statutes (4th Edn) REAL PROPERTY). As to the execution of a deed by an individual and by a corporation, see vol 12 (1994 Reissue) DEEDS, AGREEMENTS AND DECLARATIONS Paragraphs 16 [1525] and 28 [1554]–30 [1560] respectively.

    It is unnecessary for a contract by a corporate body to be under seal unless it would need to be a deed if made by private persons: see the Corporate Bodies' Contracts Act 1960 s 1 (11 Halsbury's Statutes (4th Edn) CONTRACT). A contract may be made by a company incorporated under the Companies Acts by writing under its common seal or on its behalf by any person acting under its authority, express or implied: Companies Act 1985 s 36 as substituted by the Companies Act 1989 s 130(1) (8 Halsbury's Statutes (4th Edn) COMPANIES).

**[3690]–[3710]**

# 83

### Agreement for lease between landlord/developer/tenant[1]

DATE: *(insert date)*

PARTIES:

[1    The Landlord: *(name)* [company number *(number)*] [of *(address)* or whose registered office is at *(address)*]]

2    The Developer: *(name)* [company number *(number)*] [of *(address)* or whose registered office is at *(address)*]

3          The Tenant: *(name)* [company number *(number)*] [of *(address) or* whose registered
           office is at *(address)*]

[4         The Surety: *(name)* [company number *(number)*] [of *(address) or* whose registered
           office is at *(address)*]]

CONTENTS:

A          Definitions and Interpretation
B          Grant of Lease
C          Default
D          Surety
E          Miscellaneous

Schedule 1:  The Property
Schedule 2:  the Documents
Schedule 3:  Development Obligations
Schedule 4:  Contaminated Land

[3711]

## A       DEFINITIONS AND INTERPRETATION[2]

### 1       Definitions

In this Agreement unless the context otherwise requires the following expressions shall
have the following meanings:

**1.1      'Communication'**
any notice application approval certificate or other communication from or on behalf of
one party to another pursuant to this Agreement

**1.2      'Completion Date'**
[10] Working Days after the Practical Completion Date as defined in paragraph 1.17 of
the [Third] Schedule [or if later *(adapt as necessary to accommodate the grant of any superior
lease)*]

**1.3      'Contract Rate'**
*(insert interest rate or method of calculating the interest rate by reference, eg, to the base lending rate
of a named bank)*

**1.4      'Developer's Solicitors'**
*(insert name and address of person or firm)*

**[1.5      'the Documents'**
the documents (if any) particulars of which are set out in the Second Schedule]

**1.6      'General Conditions'**
[the Standard Commercial Property Conditions (1st Edn) *or (specify)*]

**[1.7      'Headlease'**
*(insert details)*]

**1.8      'Insolvent'**
1.8.1    in relation to a company that:
      1.8.1.1    it is deemed unable to pay its debts as defined in the Insolvency Act
               1986 Section 123 (referred to as 'the Act' in the remainder of this
               definition)
      1.8.1.2    a proposal is made for a voluntary arrangement under Part I of the
               Act

1.8.1.3   a petition is presented for an administration order under Part II of the Act

1.8.1.4   a receiver or manager is appointed whether under Part III of the Act (including an administrative receiver) or otherwise

1.8.1.5   it goes into liquidation as defined in Section 247(2) of the Act (other than a voluntary winding up which is first approved by the Landlord and is for the sole purpose of amalgamation or reconstruction while solvent)

1.8.1.6   a provisional liquidator is appointed under Section 135 of the Act

• 1.8.1.7   a proposal is made for a scheme of arrangement under the Companies Act 1985 Section 425 as amended

1.8.2   and in relation to an individual that:

1.8.2.1   an application is made for an interim order or a proposal is made for a voluntary arrangement under Part VIII of the Act

1.8.2.2   a bankruptcy petition is presented to the court or his circumstances are such that a bankruptcy petition could be presented under Part IX of the Act

1.8.2.3   he enters into a deed of arrangement

**[3712]**

## 1.9   'Landlord'
includes the successors in title to the Landlord of its reversion to the Property and its assigns

## [1.10   'Landlord's Solicitors'
*(insert name and address of person or firm)*]

## 1.11   'Lease'[3]
a lease [(or underlease)] of the Property in the form annexed to this Agreement

## 1.12   'paragraph'
a paragraph of a schedule

## 1.13   'Planning Acts'
the enactments from time to time in force relating to town and country planning

## 1.14   'Property'
the property described in the First Schedule

## 1.15   'Rent Commencement Date'
the Practical Completion Date as defined in paragraph 1.17 of the [Third] Schedule or if earlier the date of completion of the Tenant's Works (as also defined in the [Third] Schedule)

## 1.16   'Tenant'
includes the tenant for the time being under the Lease

## 1.17   'Tenant's Solicitors'
*(insert name and address of person or firm)*

## 1.18   'Term'
*(number)* years commencing on [the Practical Completion Date] [(subject as mentioned in the Lease)]

## 1.19   'VAT'
value added tax

## 1.20   'Working Day'
any day except Saturdays Sundays and Bank or other public holidays

**2          Interpretation**

2.1      Words importing one gender shall be construed as importing any other gender

2.2      Words importing the singular shall be construed as importing the plural and vice versa

2.3      Words importing persons shall be construed as importing a corporate body and/or a partnership and vice versa

2.4      Where any party comprises more than one person the obligations and liabilities of that party under this Agreement shall be joint and several obligations and liabilities of those persons

2.5      The clause headings do not form part of this Agreement and shall not be taken into account in its construction or interpretation

2.6      Any reference to a clause or a paragraph or a schedule is to one in this Agreement so numbered

2.7      Reference to a statute includes any amendment modification consolidation or re-enactment of that statute and any statutory instrument regulation or order made under that statute and for the time being in force

2.8      In case of any inconsistency between the General Conditions and the provisions of this Agreement the latter shall prevail

**[3713]**

**B          GRANT OF LEASE**

**3          Agreement for grant of the Lease[4]**

3.1      In consideration of the covenants and obligations on the part of the Tenant [(and of the Surety respectively)] to be contained in the Lease the [Landlord *or* Developer] shall grant and the Tenant shall take the Lease

3.2      The grant of the Lease is conditional upon the [Landlord and/*or* [the] Developer] and the Tenant observing and performing their respective several obligations contained in the [Third] Schedule and the [Landlord and/*or* [the] Developer] and the Tenant shall respectively observe and perform them accordingly

3.3      The Development Obligations (comprised in the [Third] Schedule) are on the part of the Developer expressly personal to the Developer as named in this Agreement and shall not have effect to bind [the Landlord any successor in title to the Landlord or] any other person

[3.4     The [Fourth] Schedule shall have effect in relation to environmental matters [and] contaminated land [and remediation]][5]

**4          Completion**

4.1      The original and counterpart respectively of the Lease shall be prepared by [and at the cost of] the [Landlord *or* Developer] who shall provide the counterpart to the Tenant within [5] Working Days of being notified of practical completion (as construed in accordance with paragraph 1.17 of the [Third] Schedule). The [Landlord *or* Developer] and the Tenant [together with the Surety] shall respectively execute the Lease and the counterpart of the Lease and completion shall take place on the Completion Date [at the offices of the [Developer's] [Landlord's] Solicitors or where they may direct]

[4.2     To facilitate the grant of the Lease the [Landlord *or* Developer] shall do all things [reasonably] necessary to procure the grant of the Headlease and thereupon shall do all things necessary to register the same at HM Land Registry]

**5      Title guarantee**

The [Landlord *or* Developer] grants the Lease with [full *or* limited] title guarantee

**6      Possession**

Subject but without prejudice to the provisions of this Agreement the Lease shall be granted with vacant possession of the Property upon completion

**[3714]**

**7      Title**

[Title shall commence with *(description of instrument)* dated *(date)* and made between *(parties)* [and the Tenant or the Tenant's Solicitors having been supplied with an epitome of the title prior to the date of this Agreement the Tenant shall be deemed to take the Lease with full knowledge of the title in all respects and shall not raise any requisitions or make any objection in relation to the title]
*or*
Title to the Property is registered at HM Land Registry with [absolute] title under title number *(number)* and title shall be deduced in accordance with the Land Registration Act 1925 Section 110 [save that copies of the entries on the register the filed plan and any documents referred to shall be office copies] [and the Tenant or the Tenant's Solicitors having been supplied with such copies prior to the date of this Agreement the Tenant shall be deemed to purchase with full knowledge of the title in all respects and shall not raise any requisitions or make any objection in relation to the title]]

**8      Encumbrances**

8.1     The Lease shall be granted subject to and (where appropriate) with the benefit of the matters contained or referred to in the [Documents *or* the property [proprietorship] and charges registers of title number *(number)*]

8.2     The Tenant or the Tenant's Solicitors having been supplied with copies of the [Documents *or* the property [proprietorship] and charges registers and the matters contained or referred to in the registers] prior to the date of this Agreement the Tenant shall be deemed to take with full notice and knowledge of the same and shall not raise any requisition or make any objection in relation to them

**9      Matters affecting the Property**

The Lease shall be granted subject to the following matters:

9.1     all local land charges whether registered or not before the date of this Agreement and all matters capable of registration as local land charges whether or not actually so registered

9.2     all notices served and orders demands proposals or requirements made by any local public or other competent authority whether before or after the date of this Agreement

9.3     all actual or proposed charges notices orders restrictions agreements conditions contraventions or other matters arising under the enactments relating to town and country planning and environmental law

9.4     all easements quasi-easements rights exceptions or other similar matters whether or not apparent on inspection or disclosed in any of the documents referred to in this Agreement

**[3715]**

**10      Disclaimer**[6]

10.1      The Tenant admits that:
          10.1.1      it enters into this Agreement solely as a result of its own inspection
                      and on the basis of the terms of this Agreement and not in reliance
                      upon any representation or warranty either written or oral or implied
                      made by or on behalf of [the Landlord or] the Developer (save for
                      any representation or warranty contained in written replies given by
                      the [Landlord's Solicitors or] the Developer's Solicitors to any
                      preliminary inquiries raised by the Tenant or the Tenant's Solicitors)
          10.1.2      this Agreement contains the entire agreement between the parties
10.2      The [Landlord or Developer] does not warrant that the Property may lawfully
          be used for any purpose authorised by the Lease

**11      Incorporation of conditions of sale**

The General Conditions shall apply to this Agreement in so far as they are applicable to
the grant of a lease by private treaty and are not varied by or inconsistent with the terms
of this Agreement [and shall be amended as follows: *(insert details of amendments required)*]

**12      Subsales and grants**[7]

The [Landlord or Developer] shall not be under any liability to grant the Lease (whether
pursuant to a direction by the Tenant or in any other manner) to anyone other than the
Tenant named in this Agreement and the Tenant shall itself take up occupation of the
Property and trade from it

**13      Merger on completion**[8]

The provisions of this Agreement shall not merge on grant of the Lease so far as they
remain to be performed

**14      VAT**[9]

14.1.1      The Tenant declares that it has no intention of using the Property or any part
            of it or of allowing it to be used whether by sub-letting or otherwise in such a
            way as to give rise to the disapplication of any election to waive exemption to
            tax made by the [Landlord or Developer]
14.1.2      The Tenant shall indemnify and keep indemnified the [Landlord or Developer]
            against all VAT which the [Landlord or Developer] has to repay to HM Customs
            and Excise including any under the capital goods scheme and against all VAT
            which is irrecoverable by the [Landlord or Developer] (together in each case
            with interest penalties and costs) due to the disapplication of any election to
            waive exemption to tax made by the [Landlord or Developer] arising in any way
            from the use of the Property or part or parts of it for an exempt purpose

**[15      Nature of this agreement**[10]

This Agreement is a deed and has been executed by the parties to it as a deed]

                                                                              **[3716]**


**C      DEFAULT**

**16      Events of Default**[11]

Each of the events specified in clauses 16.1–16.4 inclusive is an Event of Default:
16.1      the Tenant [or the Surety] becomes Insolvent

16.2    the Tenant [or the Surety] fails duly to perform or comply with any other obligation expressed to be assumed by it in this Agreement and

    16.2.1    (if in the opinion of the [Landlord *or* Developer] such default is capable of remedy) the Tenant [or the Surety] fails to remedy the default within [10] Working Days after the [Landlord *or* Developer] has given notice to the Tenant [or the Surety] specifying the default and the required remedy and

    16.2.2    such failure may in the reasonable opinion of the [Landlord *or* Developer] prejudice to a material extent the ability of the Tenant [or the Surety] to complete the Works

16.3    the Tenant [or the Surety] repudiates this Agreement or does or allows to be done or omitted any act or thing which the [Landlord *or* Developer] reasonably considers to evidence an intention to repudiate this Agreement

16.4    [the Tenant's Works (as defined in the [Third] Schedule) are not completed by *(insert date)*]

## 17    Consequences of Default

17.1    Where an Event of Default occurs the [Landlord *or* Developer] (without prejudice to any other available remedy) may serve notice of default on the Tenant whereupon:

    17.1.1    If completion of the Lease has not taken place the [Landlord *or* Developer] may by notice at any time rescind this Agreement

    [17.1.2    The Tenant shall [(if required by the [Landlord and/*or* [the] Developer)]] remove the Tenant's Works (as defined in the [Third] Schedule) and all goods and materials restore the Property in all respects to its former state and condition and indemnify the [Landlord and/*or* [the] Developer] [respectively] against all loss and damage howsoever arising]

    17.1.3    [Subject to the foregoing] if the Tenant shall have entered the Property for any permitted purpose the [Landlord *or* Developer] may re-enter upon the Property or any part of it in the name of the whole and the Property and any rights of the Tenant in relation to it will be forfeit and the [Landlord *or* Developer] shall not be liable to make any compensation or allowance to the Tenant

17.2    Any re-entry by the [Landlord *or* Developer] shall be without prejudice to the rights of either the [Landlord *or* Developer] [on the one hand] or the Tenant [on the other] concerning any antecedent breach on the part of the other. Subject thereto this Agreement shall determine absolutely

[3717]

## [D    SURETY

## 18    Surety

18.1    This Agreement has been entered into with the consent and at the request of the Surety

18.2    The Surety guarantees the due performance by the Tenant of all of the Tenant's obligations under this Agreement and will perform them or otherwise indemnify the Landlord in respect of any non-performance of such obligations including (for the avoidance of doubt) any obligation of the Tenant which is agreed or determined under paragraph 15.1 or 15.2 of the [Third] Schedule

18.3    The obligations of the Surety will not be affected by:

    18.3.1    any variation of this Agreement to which the Surety is not a party

    18.3.2    any other agreement entered into by the Tenant

| | |
|---|---|
| 18.3.3 | any time or indulgence given by the [Landlord and/*or* [the] Developer] |
| 18.3.4 | the Tenant becoming Insolvent |
| 18.3.5 | any other act deed or thing except an express release of the Surety or variation to the Surety's liability given in writing by the [Landlord and/*or* [the] Developer] |

18.4    If this Agreement shall in the hands of the Tenant become forfeit the [Landlord *or* Developer] may (but shall not be obliged to) by notice at any time require the Surety to undertake all the obligations of the Tenant under this Agreement and to take up the Lease as if it were the Tenant whereupon this Agreement shall bind the Surety accordingly]

[3718]

## E    MISCELLANEOUS

## 19    Communication

19.1    All Communications shall be in writing

19.2    A Communication from any party ('the Sender') to any other ('the Recipient') will be duly made if in writing and either delivered to the Recipient (including in a manner provided at clause 19.4) or sent within the United Kingdom by [first class prepaid or] registered or recorded delivery post addressed to the Recipient at his address as stated in this Agreement or as the Recipient may from time to time notify the Sender

19.3    A Communication sent by post will be deemed to have been made on the second Working Day next following the day of posting [and it will be sufficient proof of posting for first class prepaid post to show that a prepaid envelope containing the Communication was properly addressed and either delivered to or collected by the Post Office or placed in a Post Office letterbox]

19.4    In this clause 19 'writing' includes telex facsimile or other electronic means of communication (except e-mail) and 'delivered' includes transmission by such means in which event the Communication will be deemed to have been made when the Sender has finished its transmission without having any reasonable grounds for suspecting that the transmission has failed or was incomplete (except that if such transmission takes place outside normal business hours the Communication will be deemed to have been made when normal business hours next commence)

19.5    In this clause 19 'normal business hours' are [9.30 am to 5.30 pm] on Working Days

## 20    Waiver

No failure or delay by the[Landlord and/*or* [the] Developer] to exercise any right power or remedy under this Agreement will operate as a waiver of it in whole or in part nor will any partial exercise preclude any further exercise of the same or of some other right power or remedy

## 21    Headings

The clause and sub-clause and schedule headings do not affect the meaning of this Agreement

[3719]

FIRST SCHEDULE
The Property
*(describe the property)*

[SECOND SCHEDULE
The Documents
*(insert details)*]

[THIRD] SCHEDULE
Development Obligations

I      Definitions and Interpretation
II     Works
III    Tenant's Works and Obligations
IV     Disputes

Part I: Definitions and Interpretation

## 1      Definitions

In this Schedule the following words shall have the following meanings (unless the context otherwise requires):

### 1.1      'Access Date'[12]

The date (if any) prior to the Practical Completion Date upon which the [Architect *or* Employer's Agent] certifies that the Tenant may have access to the Property for the purpose of carrying out the Tenant's Works (but no such certificate shall be given unless the Works have reached a sufficiently advanced stage to enable the Tenant to commence and thereafter carry out the Tenant's Works without delaying completion of the Works)

### [1.2      'Architect'[13]

*(name and address)* or such other firm as may be appointed by the Developer]

### [1.3      'Building'[14]

The building of which the Property forms part [and forming part of the Works] [and the Estate]]

### 1.4      'Building Contract'

The contract or contracts made between the Developer and the Contractor (based upon the JCT [with contractor's design] [with or without quantities] form [1998] edition as amended) for the construction of the Works

[3720]

### [1.5      'Code'[15]

The Code of Measuring Practice of the Royal Institution of Chartered Surveyors and the Incorporated Society of Valuers and Auctioneers [Edition 4, 1993]

### 1.6      'Common Parts'

[The estate road and footpaths providing access to and egress from and fronting the Property and also associated Conduits and related facilities *or* As defined in the Lease]

### 1.7      'Contractor'

*(name and address)* or such other contractor as may be appointed by the Developer

### 1.8      'Conduits'

[As defined in the Lease *or (insert definintion)*]

### 1.9      'Consultants'

The [Employer's Agent] Architect Structural Engineer [Environmental Consultant] and Mechanical and Electrical Engineer *(add other consultants as appropriate and define them)* or (as the case may) be any person or firm appointed in substitution for any one or more of the foregoing

**[1.10     'Employer's Agent'**
*(name and address)* or such other firm as may be appointed by the Developer from time to time as employer's agent under the Building Contract]

**[1.11     'Environmental Consultant'**
*(name and address)* or such other firm as may be appointed by the Developer]

**[3721]**

**[1.12     'Estate'**
The Developer's Estate [as defined in the Lease] of which the Property forms part]

**[1.13     'Gross [External *or* Internal] Area'**[16]
The gross [external *or* internal] area of the Building as measured in accordance with the Code]

**[1.14     'Net Internal Area'**
The net internal area of the building as measured in accordance with the Code]

**1.15     'Mechanical and Electrical Engineer'**
*(name and address)* or such other firm as may be appointed by the Developer

**1.16     'Planning Permission'**
*(insert details)*

**1.17     'Practical Completion Date'**[17]
The date of practical completion as certified under the Building Contract and the expressions 'practical completion' and 'practically completed' shall be construed accordingly and without reference to:
1.17.1    any works of an unfinished nature which would normally be the subject of a snagging list
[1.17.2    any unfinished landscaping works the completion of which is to be postponed in whole or in part to the next planting season]
1.17.3    any defects liability period

**1.18     'Structural Engineer'**
*(name and address)* or such other firm as may be appointed by the Developer

**1.19     'Tenant's Works'**[18]
The fitting out works to the Property to be carried out by the Tenant pursuant and subject to paragraph 11 of this Schedule comprising the provision of interior fittings and equipment and the carrying out of other works to enable the Tenant to carry on and from the Property the use prescribed by the Lease

**1.20     'Works'**
The construction of [the Building and other facilities upon or in relation to] the Property [and the Estate] [(including Common Parts)] in accordance with the Documents and which are to be demised [or in relation to which rights are to be granted] by the Lease

**[3722]**

Part II: Works

**2          Execution of the Works**[19]

2.1          The Developer will as soon as practicable commence and diligently carry out the Works in accordance with the Planning Permission and all other relevant permissions and consents (which the Developer will use all reasonable endeavours to obtain as soon as possible) in a good and workmanlike manner and with good quality materials but for the avoidance of doubt the Developer is not obliged to comply with any fire or other regulations in so far as they concern the Tenant's Works or the Tenant's use of the [Building or the] Property

2.2     No alterations to the Documents [(so far as they relate to the Property [or any rights to be granted by the Lease])] shall be made without the prior approval of the Tenant (such approval not to be unreasonably withheld) but such approval shall not be required:

    2.2.1     for an alteration required for the purpose of obtaining any requisite permissions consents licences and approvals or complying with any requirements properly made by any competent authority

    2.2.2     where the alteration does not materially affect the layout size or appearance of the [Building *or* Property] [(or the exercise of any such rights above mentioned)]

    2.2.3     for the substitution of materials where those originally specified are not obtainable either at all or at a reasonable cost or within a reasonable time and where the substitute materials are of an equivalent (or better) quality

2.3     All items in the nature of the landlord's fixtures and fittings installed as part of the Works shall become landlord's fixtures and fittings and remain the property of the [Landlord *or* Developer]

2.4     The Developer will not use or permit or suffer to be used in the Works any materials which by their nature or application contravene any British standard or British code of practice or European Union equivalent current at the time of specification or use [and any of the following: *(insert details of deleterious materials)*]

## 3     Time for completion of the Works[20]

The Developer will use all reasonable endeavours to ensure that the Works are practically completed by *(insert date 12 months after signing)* [(and that grant of the Headlease is not delayed thereby)] unless prevented or delayed by any cause which under the terms of the Building Contract entitles the Contractor to an extension of time or any other cause or circumstance and in either case not within the reasonable control of the Developer in which case the Developer shall be entitled to an extension of time equal to the period of such delay

**[3723]**

## 4     Warranties

The Developer will procure that prior to the Date of Practical Completion there shall be delivered to the Tenant [(in escrow subject to completion of the Lease)] collateral agreements executed by the Contractor and by the Consultants and any sub-contractors having a substantial and significant design responsibility appointed by the Contractor for the purpose such collateral agreements to be in the form of each of the drafts annexed to this Agreement

## 5     Information

The Developer will keep the Tenant informed of progress of the Works and supply such other information in connection with the Works as the Tenant may reasonably require from time to time

**6      Inspection of Works**[21]

6.1     Subject to the Tenant giving the Developer or the [Architect *or* Employer's Agent] [5] Working Days' notice the Tenant or its duly authorised agent shall be allowed at all reasonable times in the company of the [Architect *or* Employer's Agent] to view the state and progress of the Works and to inspect the workmanship and the materials used (but not to test any of the materials) on the following conditions:

6.1.1       the person inspecting must report to the site office before making an inspection and act in accordance with the instructions of the Contractor's representatives

6.1.2       the person inspecting must comply with all relevant safety and security precautions and insurance requirements

6.1.3       every inspection is entirely at the risk of the person inspecting

6.1.4       there must be no communication with the Contractor about the Works

6.1.5       the progress of the Works must not be impeded

6.1.6       the Tenant shall not cause or suffer damage

6.2     If as a result of an inspection the Tenant wishes to make representations regarding the Works such representations shall be made exclusively to the Developer

[3724]

**7      Practical Completion**

7.1     The Developer will procure that the Tenant is given not less than [10] Working Days' notice in writing of the site meeting at which the [Architect *or* Employer's Agent] intends to inspect the Works with a view to issuing the certificate [or statement] of practical completion and will procure that the Tenant is afforded the opportunity of attending the inspection of the Works and that the [Architect *or* Employer's Agent] is informed of any representations made by or on behalf of the Tenant

7.2     In the event of the certificate [or statement] of practical completion being issued subject to a snagging list the Developer will procure that the works on the snagging list are carried out free of expense to the Tenant

7.3     The Developer will provide the Tenant with copies of the certificate [or statement] of practical completion and any snagging list

**8      Insurance**[22]

8.1     Until the Practical Completion Date the Developer will cause the Works [(or relevant part of them)] to be insured in accordance with the terms of the Building Contract

8.2     Thereafter the [Landlord *or* Developer] will insure the Works [(or relevant part of them)] or cause them to be kept insured against the Insured Risks as defined in and in like manner as under the Lease

8.3     The Developer will produce to the Tenant whenever reasonably required written evidence of the insurance cover mentioned at paragraph 8.1 and [so also the Landlord as to] such information concerning the insurance mentioned at paragraph 8.2 to which the Tenant would be entitled under the Lease

**[9      Measurement**[23]

9.1     The [Landlord and/*or* [the] Developer] and the Tenant shall procure that surveyors appointed by them shall measure the [Gross [External *or* Internal] *or*

Net Internal] Area of the Building within [5] Working Days of the Practical Completion Date and in the event of their failure to agree upon the [Gross [External *or* Internal] *or* Net Internal] Area within [10] Working Days after the Practical Completion Date the matter shall be referred to the decision of an independent expert pursuant to the provisions of paragraph 15

9.2 If the [Gross [External *or* Internal] *or* Net Internal] Area as agreed or determined is less than ... square metres or is more than ...... square metres then [(but not otherwise)] the Rent shall be the sum of the [Gross [External *or* Internal] *or* Net Internal] Area multiplied by £... instead of the sum specified in the form of the Lease

[9.3 The [Gross [External *or* Internal] *or* Net Internal] Area will be incorporated in clause *(number)* of the Lease]]

## 10 Defects

Any defects shrinkages or other faults in the Works [(or relevant part of them)] which shall appear within the defects liability period provided under the Building Contract and which shall be remediable thereunder shall be certified by the Tenant in a schedule of defects to be delivered by the Tenant to the Developer not later than [10] Working Days prior to the date of expiry of the defects liability period (time being of the essence at the discretion of the Developer) and the Developer shall take all reasonable steps to procure the making good of all such defects as are covered by the defects liability provisions of the Building Contract [(relative to the Property [and the respective rights to be granted by the Lease])] and the Tenant shall give reasonable access to the Contractor for this purpose

**[3725]**

Part III: Tenant's Works and Obligations

## 11 Tenant's Works[24]

11.1 As from the Access Date or (if none) the Practical Completion Date but subject to paragraph 11.2 the Tenant shall be afforded access to the Property (as licensee only and so that no tenancy shall be created thereby) for the purpose of carrying out the Tenant's Works

11.2 The Tenant shall

11.2.1 submit to [each of] the [Landlord and/*or* [the] Developer] for approval (such approval being subject to and in accordance with the relevant provisions of the Lease) [(including for approval in accordance with the terms of the Headlease)] within *(number)* months of the date of this Agreement plans or drawings in each case in [triplicate] of the Tenant's Works and shall not commence the Tenant's Works until

11.2.1.1 such approval has been obtained

11.2.1.2 the Tenant has executed and delivered to the [Landlord *or* Developer] such licence as shall or would be required under the Lease [(if the Lease has not been entered into the same to be expressed to be subject to the Lease when granted)]

11.2.2 obtain all requisite licences consents and permissions of the local planning and other authorities for the Tenant's Works and (subject to the foregoing) shall not commence the Tenant's Works until all such have been obtained and until copies have been provided to the Developer [and the Landlord]

11.2.3    subject as before carry out the Tenant's Works in a good and substantial manner with good quality materials in accordance with the said plans and the terms and conditions of all such licences consents and permissions in accordance with any such approval as may have been given and in accordance with paragraphs 11.2.1 and 11.2.2 and subject thereto to the reasonable satisfaction of the [Landlord and/or [the] Developer]

11.2.4    permit the [Landlord or Developer] and the [Architect or Employer's Agent] at all reasonable times to inspect the progress of the Tenant's Works and the quality of the materials and workmanship used therein

**[3726]**

11.3    The Tenant shall ensure that neither it nor its agents employees or contractors do anything to impede the progress of the Works or cause damage

11.4    As between the [Landlord or Developer] on the one hand and the Tenant on the other all materials goods plant machinery equipment and other items used in connection with the Tenant's Works shall be at the sole risk and responsibility of the Tenant and all agents employees and contractors engaged in the Tenant's Works shall be persons for whom the Tenant is responsible

11.5    The Tenant shall (without prejudice to any other liability arising under or pursuant to this Agreement or to any policy of insurance) be liable for and shall indemnify [each of] the [Landlord and/or [the] Developer] [respectively] against any expense liability loss claim or proceedings in respect of personal injury to or the death of any person whomsoever or injury or damage whatsoever to any property real or personal arising out of or in the course of or by reason of the carrying out of the Tenant's Works

## 12    Insurance of Tenant's Works

12.1    Until completion of the Tenant's Works the Tenant shall keep the Tenant's Works insured against the Insured Risks (as defined in the Lease) and on completion of the Lease shall advise the [Landlord and/or [the] Developer] in writing of the value of the Tenant's Works and within [10] Working Days of receipt of such written advice the [Landlord or Developer] shall insure or cause them (in so far as they are comprised within the Property and do not comprise tenant's fixtures for the purpose of the Lease) to be kept insured against the Insured Risks in accordance with the covenant on its behalf and subject to the conditions therein contained

12.2    The Tenant shall also during such period insure against public liability and such other risks as the Tenant is liable to indemnify the Landlord for under paragraph 11 in such amounts and upon such terms and with such insurance office as the [Landlord and/or [the] Developer] shall approve [(such approval not to be unreasonably withheld)]

12.3    The Tenant will produce to the [Landlord or Developer] whenever reasonably required written evidence of such insurance cover as mentioned in this paragraph 12

**[3727]**

## 13    Occupation

13.1    The Tenant shall use all reasonable endeavours to complete the Tenant's Works in accordance with the provisions of paragraph 11 of this Schedule within *(number)* weeks from the Access Date or (if none) the Practical Completion Date

13.2    As soon as the Tenant shall have completed the Tenant's Works in accordance with this Agreement the Tenant shall notwithstanding that the Lease may not then be completed take up occupation of and commence trading at and from the Property upon the terms and conditions of the Lease [(as if the same had been granted [paying to the [Landlord *or* Developer] from time to time a sum or sums equivalent to the rent and otherwise as reserved or becoming payable under the Lease until completion of the Lease)]] and with the benefit of but subject to the rights exceptions and reservations agreements and declarations and provisos therein contained and the [Landlord *or* Developer] shall have and be entitled to all remedies by distress action or otherwise for breach of any of the covenants or conditions on the part of the Tenant as if the Lease had actually been granted

## 14    Tenant's Obligations

The Tenant agrees to observe and perform the following stipulations:

14.1    Not to enter into occupation of the Property until the Access Date or (if none) the date of actual completion of the Lease

14.2    Pay the costs of such of the Consultants incurred in respect of the approval of the plans for the Tenant's Works and the inspection of the Tenant's Works [and all other costs of the [Landlord and/*or* [the] Developer] arising by virtue of the operation of paragraph 11 of this Schedule

**[3728]**

## Part IV: Disputes

## 15    Disputes

15.1    Any difference or dispute which may arise between the [Landlord *or* Developer] and the Tenant concerning the measurement of the Gross Internal Area shall be determined upon the application of either party by an independent chartered surveyor acting as an expert and not as an arbitrator such surveyor to be agreed upon by the parties and in default of agreement appointed by the President of the Royal Institution of Chartered Surveyors and whose fees shall be borne by the parties in equal shares provided that if such surveyor shall be unable or unwilling to act the before mentioned procedure shall be repeated as often as may be necessary

15.2    Whenever a person is to be appointed as an expert under this paragraph the following provisions shall have effect:

15.2.1    His decision shall be final and binding upon the parties

15.2.2    The person shall consider (inter alia) any written representations on behalf of either party to the dispute (if made promptly) but shall not be bound thereby

15.3    Any [other] dispute or difference arising between the [Landlord *or* Developer] on the one hand and the Tenant on the other as to any matter arising out of or in connection with the subject matter of this Schedule shall be referred to and determined by an independent person who has been professionally qualified in respect of the subject matter of the dispute or difference for not less than ten years and who is a specialist in relation to such subject matter such independent person to be agreed between the parties or failing such agreement to be nominated by the President or Vice-President or other duly authorised officer of the Royal Institution of Chartered Surveyors upon the application of any one of them and such reference shall (unless the parties otherwise agree) be a reference to arbitration in accordance with the Arbitration Act 1996 (and costs shall be in his award)

[15.4    Notwithstanding any of the foregoing the Surety shall not be a party to any dispute under this paragraph 15 but shall be bound by the results of any such dispute as it affects the Tenant]

## [[FOURTH] SCHEDULE
Contaminated Land[25]
*(insert appropriate provisions)]*

*(signatures of (or common seals or other execution by) the parties)[26]*
**[***(signatures of witnesses)***]**
**[3729]**

1    As to stamp duty see the Information Binder: Stamp Duties [1] (Lease; agreement for lease). Any stamp duty payable is payable on the agreement under the Finance Act 1999 s 112(3), Sch 13 para 14 (41 Halsbury's Statutes (4th Edn) STAMP DUTIES), and must be paid before the agreement may be used in civil proceedings. However, if entitlement to the lease is expressed as an option (not necessarily attractive to the landowner), liability to stamp duty is deferred to grant of the lease. As to agreements for lease between landowner and developer see Paragraph 322 [3604] et seq and for commentary on agreements for lease see vol 22(1) (1996 Reissue) LANDLORD AND TENANT (BUSINESS TENANCIES) Paragraph 101 [201] et seq.

      Because this Form includes an agreement for the grant of a lease, the agreement is capable of registration as an estate contract (either as a class C(iv) land charge under the Land Charges Act 1972 (37 Halsbury's Statutes (4th Edn) REAL PROPERTY) where the land is unregistered, or by way of notice (or caution) in the case of registered land).

      This precedent is set up to acknowledge the role of the developer quite separately from the landlord. If the developer himself is landlord, the precedent is designed to work by deleting all references to the landlord (once this is done the draftsman may then wish to redefine the developer as landlord).

      As to VAT see Paragraph 327 [3611] ante and see vol 38(1) (2000 Reissue) SALE OF LAND Paragraph 8 [16] et seq.

2    Use of a capital letter identifies a word as a definition. In this precedent some definitions are to be found in its schedules as well as in the main body of the agreement.

3    A form of lease is not here prescribed. Some definitions, such as 'estate' (in the third schedule), 'common parts' and 'conduits', may require re-definition.

4    As with the agreement for lease between landowner and developer (Form 82 [3651] ante), this is essentially an agreement for lease conditional upon the carrying out of development. A developer failing to perform a superior agreement may have it forfeit. By contrast, a developer failing to perform development obligations to his occupational tenant remains bound until the tenant treats the agreement as repudiated. For certainty, a tenant may therefore wish to qualify the developer's obligations (in the third schedule) by an express right of rescission in certain circumstances eg practical completion not achieved by a certain date. See also note 20 below.

      The main body of the agreement is otherwise essentially a conveyancing contract subject to the developer's obligations, but may need to be adapted if a superior lease is in contemplation, grant of which is also dependent on the developer carrying out works.

5    As to contaminated land generally see vol 38(1) (2000 Reissue) SALE OF LAND Paragraph 147 [341] et seq. For environmental and due diligence enquiries and definitions and interpretation for use with those enquiries see vol 38(1) (2000 Reissue) SALE OF LAND Forms 35 [1585] and 36 [1592]. For a schedule of environmental warranties and indemnities see vol 38(1) (2000 Reissue) SALE OF LAND Form 61 [2401]. For alternative shorter warranty clauses see Forms 144 [4587] and 145 [4588] post. Practitioners should consider what provisions are appropriate to be included in the fourth schedule to this Form having regard to the actual state of the site the subject of this agreement and draft appropriate provisions which may be based on the above mentioned Forms, ensuring that the definitions and wording used is compatible with those used in this Form.

6    A disclaimer clause will usually be found in a superior agreement as also in the lease and superior lease.

7    A landlord will always be concerned about the identity of a tenant under a rack-rented lease. The care taken over an alienation clause may be undone if the identity of the initial tenant is not confirmed by the enabling agreement.

8    Non-merger clauses are common to conveyancing contracts. A buyer of the investment will be keen to ensure that any outstanding obligations on the part of the tenant also remain enforceable. By contrast, as elsewhere provided in this agreement, the obligations of the developer are personal to the developer so that development obligations in favour of the tenant are not enforceable against the buyer of the investment: Landlord and Tenant (Covenants) Act 1995 s 3(6) (23 Halsbury's Statutes (4th Edn) LANDLORD AND TENANT).

9    Having regard to the Finance Act 1997 s 37 (48 Halsbury's Statutes (4th Edn) VALUE ADDED TAX), it is helpful if, depending on the user clause, the lease contains similar provisions. See also note 3 above.

10    It is not essential that an agreement for lease be executed.

11    The particular default clause is written only with tenant default in mind. Contrast Form 82 [3651] ante (agreement for lease between landowner and developer) where a disputes provision is also incorporated immediately after the default clause. There is no reason why a disputes clause should not appear in this agreement for lease also, but in the nature of the transaction, the greater need for a disputes clause under an agreement for occupational lease lies within the development provisions (see paragraph 15 of the third schedule of this Form).

      From a tenant's point of view, clauses 16 and 17 of this Form may be adapted for protection of the tenant's interests, particularly as to timing.

12      Reference to the architect or to the employer's agent distinguishes the type of building contract which may be used. If a design and build form, the employer's agent will usually issue a 'statement' of practical completion, rather than a certificate, but building contract amendments frequently reverse this terminology to a certificate.

**[3730]**

13      In the case of design and build, an architect is likely to be the appointee of the contractor rather than of the developer direct.

14      Terminology of this kind may require to be adapted depending on the circumstances eg if the developer is simply refurbishing, then the extent of the works may suggest a simpler regime. The entirety of the development provisions may require adaptation in any case to the particular development.

15      If the initial rent is to be fixed without reference to measurement then both this and other related provisions is this schedule may be deleted.

16      See paragraph 9 of the third schedule to this Form.

17      Practical completion is here made the trigger for completion of the lease. Where the development consists of more than one unit of occupation, the building contract may prescribe for sectional completion or rely upon the provisions for partial possession within its printed text (whether or not amended). Where partial possession is in contemplation, the developer as employer under the building contract must usually seek it, and modification of this precedent to accord is implied.

18      The provisions relating to tenant's works (as to which see paragraph 11 of the third schedule of this Form) need only be incorporated if it is perceived from the outset that the tenant may wish to carry out works. If not, the alterations clause (if any) in the lease may be operated when the lease is granted. Care should be taken to ensure that, if any tenant's works are in contemplation, the building contract makes adequate provision.

19      Unless the building is absolutely bespoke, general development provisions should suffice. Moreover, no question usually arises (and even then exceptionally) of the tenant being afforded step-in rights. Not least, this may be because the developer has commitments to other tenants and third parties.

20      Depending on the tenant's requirements, this clause may require substantial amendment to include a strict timescale which may also affect the tenant's works. The possibilities are too wide to suggest a general clause, but clearly a major consideration will be the grant of any related superior lease.

21      It is usually reasonable for the tenant to have some input to practical completion but not to the extent of controlling it. Apart from anything else, the building contract stands independently from the agreement, and in any case grant of a separate lease may be subject to separate criteria.

22      Particular care should be taken over insurance. The contractor's insurance will usually cease as at practical completion and it is usually considered sensible to bring the insurance provisions of the lease into force at that point.

23      The commercial terms should (if relevant) indicate the broad criteria for measurement, whether a maximum or minimum rent is to be imposed, whether the dimensions are also to be reflected in the lease for rent review purposes, whether the tenant may in the event rescind if certain parameters are breached, and so on. If measurement is not critical, of course, it is implicit that the initial rent may be fixed in any event, and the tenant will rely generally on the development obligations. Paragraph 9.3 of the third schedule is appropriate only if the form of the lease contains appropriate assumptions where these details may be inserted.

24      The tenant's works are discussed under note 18 above. This precedent assumes works of some substance, that these may be commenced prior to practical completion, and the possibility of consent being required from a superior lessor. It is important to ensure that adequate provision is made in the building contract to accommodate the implementation of tenant's works. Paragraph 12 et seq of the third schedule generally follow although, where tenant's works are not to be rentalised the value of insurance in context may be confined to the impact on the ongoing development.

     At paragraph 15 of the third schedule to this Form, depending on the extent of the works, an express disputes clause may be considered optional. So long as the lease is for a term expiring not earlier that twelve months following completion of the works, the agreement for lease is excluded as a construction contract by virtue of the Construction (England and Wales) Exclusion Order 1998, SI 1998/648 and so mandatory adjudication under the Housing Grants, Construction and Regeneration Act 1996 will not apply.

25      See note 5 above.

26      It is not usually necessary to have the contract executed as a deed unless the contract contains recitals which are intended to be binding or there are other special considerations (eg, there is a lack of valuable consideration or it is desired to extend the period set by the Limitation Act 1980 s 8 (24 Halsbury's Statutes (4th Edn) LIMITATION OF ACTIONS) for bringing claims).

     Where a contract is to be executed as a deed sealing is not necessary either in the case of an individual or in the case of a company, but all parties must sign either on the same document or each on one of two identical parts which are exchanged and the signatures of all individuals must be witnessed: see the Law of Property (Miscellaneous Provisions) Act 1989 s 1(3). As to the execution of a deed by an individual and by a corporation, see vol 12 (1994 Reissue) DEEDS, AGREEMENTS AND DECLARATIONS Paragraphs 16 [1525] and 28 [1554]–30 [1560] respectively.

     It is unnecessary for a contract by a corporate body to be under seal unless it would need to be a deed if made by private persons: see the Corporate Bodies' Contracts Act 1960 s 1 (11 Halsbury's Statutes (4th Edn) CONTRACT). A contract may be made by a company incorporated under the Companies Acts by writing under its common seal or on its behalf by any person acting under its authority, express or implied: Companies Act 1985 s 36 as substituted by the Companies Act 1989 s 130(1) (8 Halsbury's Statutes (4th Edn) COMPANIES).

**[3731]–[3750]**

# PART 8: INFRASTRUCTURE AND PLANNING OBLIGATIONS

## *Forms and Precedents*

### 84

**Planning agreement under the Town and Country Planning Act 1990
Section 106[1]**

This Agreement is made the ... day of ......BETWEEN:
(1)     *(name)* [company number *(number)*] [of *(address) or* whose registered office is at *(address)*] ('the Owner')
(2)     *(name)* [company number *(number)*] [of *(address) or* whose registered office is at *(address)*] ('the Mortgagee')
(3)     *(name)* [company number *(number)*] [of *(address) or* whose registered office is at *(address)*] ('the Applicant')
[(4)    *(name)* County Council of *(address)* ('the County Council')]
(5)     *(name)* District Council of *(address)* ('the Council')

## 1     Background

1.1     The Owner is [seised in fee simple in possession *or* is registered as proprietor under title number *(number)*] of the land at *(address)* shown for identification purposes only edged red on [the Plan *or* Plan No *(number)*] ('the Red Land')[2]
1.2     The Red Land is charged to the Mortgagee
1.3     The Council is the local planning authority [and the local housing authority]
[1.4    The County Council is [the local highway authority and/or the local education authority]]
1.5     The Applicant has by planning application number *(number)* applied to the Council for [outline] planning permission to develop the Red Land by *(describe intended development)*

                                                                                          **[3751]**

## 2     Interpretation

In this Agreement:
2.1     'the Act' means the Town and Country Planning Act 1990
2.2     'agreed' or 'approved' means agreed or approved in writing and given for the purpose of this Agreement
2.3     'the Application' means the planning application number *(number)* made by the Applicant to develop the [Application Site *or* Red Land] by *(describe intended development)*
2.4     'the Application Site' means the [Red Land *or* Blue Land]

2.5 'the Blue Land' means that part of the Red Land shown for the purposes of identification only edged blue on [the Plan *or* Plan No *(number)*]

2.6 'the Children's Play Area' means the children's play area [shown for identification purposes only edged *(colour)* on [the Plan *or* Plan No *(number)*] and] referred to in clause *(number)*

2.7 'the Community Facilities' means the facilities described in schedule [2]

2.8 'the Community Facilities Land' means the site of the Community Facilities [shown for identification purposes only edged *(colour)* on [the Plan *or* Plan No *(number)*] [having an area of *(number)* hectares] and] referred to in clause *(number)*

2.9 'Commuted Car Parking Payment' means the commuted car parking payment referred to in clause *(number)* to make good a deficiency in car parking provision arising from the Development

2.10 'the Development' means the development of the Application Site proposed in the Application or permitted by planning permission granted pursuant to the Application or carried out substantially in accordance with such planning permission

2.11 'Education Contribution' means the education contribution referred to in clause *(number)* to make good a deficiency in education provision arising from the Development

2.12 'the Green Land' means that part of the Red Land shown for the purposes of identification only edged green on [the Plan *or* Plan No *(number)*]

2.13 'the Highway Works' means the highway works referred to in clause *(number)*

**[3752]**

2.14 'Landscape Management Plan' means the landscape management plan referred to in clause *(number)*

2.15 'the Off-Site Infrastructure Works' means the off-site infrastructure works referred to in clause *(number)* to make good a deficiency in infrastructure provision arising from the Development

2.16 'the Public Open Space' means [that part of] the Green Land [shown for identification purposes hatched *(colour)* on [the Plan *or* Plan No *(number)*] [having an area of *(number)* hectares] and] referred to in clause *(number)*

2.17 'the Red Land' means the land shown for identification purposes edged red on [the Plan *or* Plan No *(number)*]

2.18 'Registered Social Landlord' means a registered social landlord within the meaning of the Housing Act 1996

2.19 'Social Housing Land' means that part of the Red Land shown for identification purposes only edged *(colour)* on [the Plan *or* Plan No *(number)*] [having an area of *(number)* hectares] and referred to in clause *(number)*

2.20 'Specified Date' means the date upon which an obligation arising under this Agreement is due to be performed

2.21 'the Transport Contribution' means the contribution referred to in clause *(number)*

2.22 'the Transport Facilities' means the transport facilities referred to in clause *(number)*

2.23 Words importing the masculine include the feminine and vice versa

2.24 Words importing the singular include the plural and vice versa

2.25 Words importing persons include companies and corporations and vice versa

2.26 Wherever there is more than one person named as a party and where more than one party undertakes an obligation all their obligations can be enforced against all of them jointly and against each individually

2.27 Any reference to a clause or schedule or plan is to one in to or attached to this Agreement

2.28    In the absence of contrary provision any reference to a statute includes any statutory modification or re-enactment of it and every statutory instrument direction or specification made or issued under the statute or deriving validity from it

2.29    References to any party to this Agreement shall include the successors in title to that party and to any deriving title through or under that party and in the case of the County Council and the Council the successors to their respective functions as [local highway authority and/*or* local education authority] and local planning authority [and local housing authority]

                                                                                                              **[3753]**

## 3      Enabling Provisions

This Agreement is made pursuant to Section 106 of the Act the Local Government Act 1972 Section 111 *(insert other powers)* and all other enabling powers and has been entered into by the Council pursuant to *(specify Committee)* Committee's resolution of *(date)* (Minute No *(number)*) and by the County Council pursuant to *(details)* resolution of *(date)* (Minute No *(number)*)

## 4      Commencement

This Agreement shall come into effect upon the date of [this Agreement *or* the grant of the planning permission granted pursuant to the Application] but the obligations in clause(s) *(number(s))* shall become effective only on the commencement of the Development in accordance with Section 56 of the Act[3]

## 5      Phasing

The Owner[4] [and the Applicant] agree[s] with the Council:

5.1     not to carry out or allow to be carried out any development on the Application Site before *(insert date or event)*

5.2     not to occupy or cause or allow to be occupied any of the dwellings forming part of the Development before *(insert date or event)*

                                                                                                              **[3754]**

## 6      Cessation/Modification/Revocation/Discontinuance of Development

The Owner agrees with the Council:

6.1     to cease to carry out the following development on the Red Land with effect from the date of this Agreement: *(specify prohibited development)*

6.2     not to implement nor cause or allow the implementation of planning permission *(insert reference number)*

6.3     not to claim nor to seek compensation in respect of the obligation arising under clauses[s] 6.1 [and 6.2] nor in respect of the exercise by the Council of its powers under Sections 97 99 and 102 of the Act in respect of the planning permission referred to in clause 6.2

6.4     to indemnify the Council from and against any claims or demands arising from the Council exercising its powers of modification revocation or discontinuance

## [7     Provision of Public Open Space

The Owner [and the Applicant] agree[s] with the Council:

7.1     to provide and lay out an area of open space having an area of *(number)* hectares [[within *or* comprising] the [Green] Land *or* substantially in the position shown edged *(colour)* on [the Plan *or* Plan No *(number)*]] in accordance with a specification approved by the Council and to the Council's satisfaction

7.2     to ensure that there is easy public access to the Public Open Space
7.3     to complete the works of provision and laying out in accordance with clause 7.1
        and to make the Public Open Space available for use by the public by no later
        than the [completion of the Development *or* first occupation of the *(insert
        number)* dwelling [forming part of the Development *or* on the Application Site]]
7.4     within 2 months of the completion of the works referred to in clause 7.3 to
        transfer the Public Open Space to the Council or to such body as it may direct
        substantially in the form of the transfer set out in schedule 1 although the Public
        Open Space may by agreement with the Council be handed over to the Council
        or its nominee for public use and for maintenance purposes in advance of the
        transfer[5]
7.5     upon the handover or transfer referred to in clause 7.4 (whichever in the earlier)
        to pay to the Council or its nominee the sum of £...]

                                                                                    **[3755]**

**[8      Provision of Children's Play Area**

The Owner [and the Applicant] agree[s] with the Council:
8.1     to provide layout and equip a children's play area substantially in the position
        shown edged *(colour)* on [the Plan *or* Plan No *(number)*] in accordance with a
        specification approved by the Council and to the Council's satisfaction
8.2     to ensure that there is easy public access to the Children's Play Area
8.3     to complete the works of provision laying out and equipment in accordance
        with clause 8.1 and to make the Children's Play Area available for use by the
        public by no later than [the completion of the Development *or* the first
        occupation of the *(insert number)* dwelling [forming part of the Development *or*
        on the Application Site]]
8.4     within 2 months of the completion of the works referred to in clause 8.3 to
        transfer the Children's Play Area to the Council or to such body as it may direct
        substantially in the form of the transfer set out in schedule 1 although the
        Children's Play Area may by agreement with the Council be handed over to the
        Council or its nominee for public use and for maintenance purposes in advance
        of the transfer[6]
8.5     upon the handover or transfer referred to in clause 8.4 (whichever is the earlier)
        to pay to the Council or its nominee the sum of £... by way of a commuted
        payment sum for future maintenance of the Children's Play Area[7]]

                                                                                    **[3756]**

**[9      Community Facilities**

The Owner [and the Applicant] agree[s] with the Council:
9.1     to provide [and lay out] an area of land of *(number)* hectares [[within *or*
        comprising the *(colour)* Land] *or* substantially in the position shown edged *(colour)*
        on [the Plan *or* Plan No *(number)*]] in accordance with a specification approved
        by the Council and to the Council's satisfaction for the purpose of
        accommodating the Community Facilities described in schedule [2]
9.2     to complete the works of provision and laying out in accordance with clause 9.1
        by no later than [*(date)* *or* the completion of the Development *or* the first
        occupation of the *(insert number)* dwelling [forming part of the Development *or*
        on the Application Site]]
9.3     within 2 months of the completion of the works referred to in clause 9.2 to
        transfer the Community Facilities Land to the Council or to such body as it may
        direct substantially in the form of the transfer set out in schedule [3][8]

[9.4     to pay to the Council [on the date of this Agreement *or* on *(date)*] the sum of
         £... in respect of a contribution towards the provision of the Community
         Facilities]][9]

**[3757]**

**[10    Social Housing** *(rural areas under 3000 population)*

The Owner [and the Applicant] agree[s] with the Council:

10.1     to provide [within the Red Land] the Social Housing Land [in such location or
         locations as may be approved by the Council] for the construction of *(number)*
         social housing units of such size tenure and type as shall be approved by the
         Council

10.2     to provide a vehicular access foul and surface water sewers and water gas
         electricity and telecommunication service systems for the Social Housing Land
         linking in each case to the estate roads sewers and service systems to be
         constructed and laid as part of the remainder of the Development and
         connected ultimately to highways and sewers maintainable at the public expense

10.3     to endeavour to agree with the Council on the identity of the Registered Social
         Landlord or other body to which the Social Housing Land is to be transferred
         within the period of *(specify)* from the date of this Agreement but if no
         agreement has been reached at the expiration of such period of *(specify)* the
         Council shall be entitled to nominate a Registered Social Landlord or other
         appropriate body for the purpose

10.4     to transfer the Social Housing Land to the Registered Social Landlord or other
         body agreed or determined in accordance with clause 10.3 at the purchase price
         as set out in clause 10.5 within one month of the Council giving its approval
         under clause 10.3[10]

[10.5    that the purchase price for the Social Housing Land shall be £...
         *or*
         that the purchase price for the Social Housing Land shall be calculated in
         accordance with the following formula: *(specify)*]

**[3758]**

10.6     not to occupy or cause or allow the occupation of more than *(number)* non-
         social housing units erected or to be erected on the Application Site before the
         transfer referred to in clause 10.4 shall have been completed

10.7     not to dispose of or cause or allow the disposal of any individual social housing
         unit built on the Social Housing Land other than:
         10.7.1    in respect of *(number)* units numbered *(numbers)* on [the Plan *or* Plan
                   No *(number)*] by way of shared ownership lease and
         10.7.2    in respect of *(number)* units numbered *(numbers)* on [the Plan *or* Plan
                   No *(number)*] by way of an assured tenancy agreement complying
                   with the guidance given by the Housing Corporation under the
                   Housing Act 1996 Section 36 or
         10.7.3    by way of the right to buy or the preserved right to buy under the
                   Housing Act 1985 or the right to acquire under the Housing Act
                   1996
         10.7.4    and to a person who satisfies the qualifications set out in clause 10.8

10.8     that the qualifications referred to in clause 10.7 are that the person:
         10.8.1    is an individual

10.8.2     is considered by the Registered Social Landlord in accordance with its rules to be in need of the accommodation provided by the dwelling

10.8.3     is not able easily to compete in the open market for housing accommodation in the district of *(specify name of Council)* and has a local connection within the meaning of clause 10.9

10.8.4     before taking up occupation of the social housing unit has never owned a freehold or a lease exceeding 3 years within the last 12 months (save that the condition shall not apply where the Council is satisfied that the circumstances of that person are such as to put him in need of housing) and

10.8.5     intends to occupy and subsequently occupies the social housing unit as his only or principal home

**[3759]**

10.9     for the purposes of clause 10.8 'local connection' means in relation to an individual:

10.9.1     such individual who:

10.9.1.1     immediately before taking up occupation of a social housing dwelling unit had his only or principal home in the [district of *(specify)* or parish of *(specify)*] for a continuous period of not less than 3 years or

10.9.1.2     has or a member of whose household has a parent adult child brother or sister whose only or principal home is and has been for a continuous period of not less than 3 years in the [district of *(specify)* or parish of *(specify)*] and he wishes to be near that relative or

10.9.1.3     is and has been permanently employed in the [district of *(specify)* or parish of *(specify)*] for a continuous period of not less than 3 years

10.9.2     where no person or insufficient persons have a connection with the parish of *(specify)* as described in clause 10.9.1 then the parish of *(specify)* shall be substituted for the parish of *(specify)* and then if no person or insufficient persons have a connection with the parish of *(specify)* then the parish of *(specify)* shall be substituted for the parish of *(specify)* and then if no person or insufficient persons have a connection with the parish of *(specify)* the district of *(specify)* shall be substituted for the parish of *(specify)*

10.10     upon transfer of the Social Housing Land to the Registered Social Landlord or other body agreed or determined in accordance with clause 10.3 to procure the execution by the Registered Social Landlord and delivery to the Council of a deed of nomination substantially in the form set out in schedule [4]

**[3760]**

10.11     to take all reasonable and prudent steps to avert the repossession of the Social Housing Land or any social housing unit erected on the Social Housing Land by any chargee or mortgagee or the exercise by any chargee or mortgagee of a power of sale and for these purposes in the event of default under the security or likely default to co-operate fully with the Council and the Housing Corporation to arrange a transfer of the Social Housing Land with sitting tenants to another Registered Social Landlord or (at the Council's option) to the Council and in particular to inform the Council immediately in the event of the Owner's receiving notification from such chargee or mortgagee of any breach or alleged breach by the Owner of any of its obligations under its security

10.12    that in the event of a default under any security referred to in clause 10.11 or in other circumstances warranting the intervention of the Housing Corporation (whether or not under the Housing Act 1996 Part 1 Chapter IV or Schedule 1 Part IV) clause 10.7 shall not prevent the transfer of the freehold of the Social Housing Land or any part of it to another Registered Social Landlord

10.13    that in the event the Housing Corporation exercises its right to require payment of social housing grant made in respect of the Social Housing Land in accordance with the Housing Act 1996 Section 27(2) the Owner shall pay to the Council on the date upon which the payment of social housing grant falls due in accordance with the Housing Corporation's direction the whole amount of any grant or loan made by the Council pursuant to the Housing Act 1996 Section 22 together with interest thereon in respect of the Social Housing Land

10.14    without prejudice to the provisions of clauses 10.1–10.13 to notify the Council immediately in the event of service of any notice under the Housing Act 1996 Sections 40 and 41 or any notice order or direction served made or given under the Housing Act 1996 Schedule 1 Part IV

**[3761]**

*or*

**10      Social Housing** *(General)*

The Owner [and the Applicant] agree[s] with the Council:

10.1     to provide within the Red Land the Social Housing Land in such location or locations as may be approved by the Council for the construction of *(number)* social housing units of such size and type as shall be approved by the Council

10.2     to provide a vehicular access foul and surface water sewers and water gas electricity and telecommunication service systems for the Social Housing Land linking in each case to the estate roads sewers and service systems to be constructed and laid as part of the remainder of the Development and connected ultimately to highways and sewers maintainable at the public expense

10.3     to endeavour to agree with the Council on the identity of the Registered Social Landlord or other body to which the Social Housing Land is to be transferred within the period of *(specify)* from the date of this Agreement but if no agreement has been reached at the expiration of such period of *(specify)* the Council shall be entitled to nominate a Registered Social Landlord or other appropriate body for the purpose

10.4     to transfer the Social Housing Land to the Registered Social Landlord or other body agreed or determined in accordance with clause 10.3 at the purchase price as set out in clause 10.5 within one month of the Council giving its approval under clause 10.3[11]

[10.5    that the purchase price for the Social Housing Land shall be £...
         *or*
         that the purchase price for the Social Housing Land shall be calculated in accordance with the following formula *(specify)*]

**[3762]**

10.6     not to occupy or cause or allow the occupation of more than *(number)* non-social housing units erected or to be erected on the Application Site before the transfer referred to in clause 10.4 shall have been completed

10.7     not to dispose of or cause or allow the disposal of any individual social housing unit built on the Social Housing Land other than:

10.7.1     in respect of *(number)* units numbered *(number)* on [the Plan *or* Plan No *(number)*] by way of shared ownership lease and

10.7.2     in respect of *(number)* units numbered *(number)* on [the Plan *or* Plan No *(number)*] by way of an assured tenancy agreement complying with the guidance given by the Housing Corporation under the Housing Act 1996 Section 36 or

10.7.3     by way of the right to buy or the preserved right to buy under the Housing Act 1985 and

10.7.4     to a person who satisfies the qualifications set out in clause 10.8

10.8     that the qualifications referred to in clause 10.7 are that the person:

10.8.1     is an individual

10.8.2     is considered by the Registered Social Landlord in accordance with its rules to be in need of the accommodation provided by the dwelling

10.8.3     is not able easily to compete in the open market for housing accommodation in the district of *(specify)*

10.8.4     before taking up occupation of the social housing unit has never owned a freehold or a lease exceeding 3 years within the last 12 months (save that the condition shall not apply where the Council is satisfied that the circumstances of that person are such as to put him in need of housing) and

10.8.5     intends to occupy and subsequently occupies the social housing unit as his only or principal home

**[3763]**

10.9     upon transfer of the Social Housing Land to the Registered Social Landlord or other body agreed or determined in accordance with clause 10.3 to procure the execution by the Registered Social Landlord and delivery to the Council of a deed of nomination substantially in the form set out in schedule [4]

10.10    to take all reasonable and prudent steps to avert the repossession of the Social Housing Land or any social housing unit erected on the Social Housing Land by any chargee or mortgagee or the exercise by any chargee or mortgagee of a power of sale and for these purposes in the event of default under the security or likely default to co-operate fully with the Council and the Housing Corporation to arrange a transfer of the Social Housing Land with sitting tenants to another Registered Social Landlord or (at the Council's option) to the Council and in particular shall inform the Council immediately in the event of the Owner's receiving notification from such chargee or mortgagee of any breach or alleged breach by the Owner of any of its obligations under its security

10.11    that in the event of a default under any security referred to in clause 10.10 or in other circumstances warranting the intervention of the Housing Corporation (whether or not under the Housing Act 1996 Part 1 Chapter IV or Schedule 1 Part IV) clause 10.7 shall not prevent the transfer of the freehold of the Social Housing Land or any part of it to another Registered Social Landlord

10.12    subject to and without prejudice to the powers and requirements of the Housing Corporation under the Housing Act 1996 that in the event of a default under any security referred to in clause 10.10 clause 10.7 shall not prevent the sale of the freehold of the Social Housing Land or of any social housing unit by the chargee or mortgagee in the exercise of its power of sale provided that the chargee or mortgagee shall have first followed the procedure set out in clause 10.13

**[3764]**

10.13    that the procedure referred to in clause 10.12 shall be as follows:

    10.13.1    the chargee or mortgagee shall give not less than 3 months' prior notice to the Council of its intention to exercise its power of sale to enable the Council to secure the transfer of the Social Housing Land to another Registered Social Landlord or to the Council

    10.13.2    the Council shall then have 3 months from the notice given pursuant to clause 10.13.1 within which to respond indicating that arrangements for the transfer of the Social Housing Land can be made in such a way as to safeguard the social housing character of the Social Housing Land and of any dwelling

    10.13.3    if within the 3 months the Council does not serve its response to the notice served under clause 10.13.1 then the chargee or mortgagee shall be entitled to exercise its power of sale free of the restrictions set out in clauses 10.7–10.9 inclusive

    10.13.4    if within 3 months of the date of receipt by it of the notice served under clause 10.13.1 the Council serves its response indicating that arrangements can be made in accordance with clause 10.13 then the chargee or mortgagee shall co-operate with such arrangements and use its best endeavours to secure such transfer

    10.13.5    the Council shall in formulating or promoting any arrangements referred to in clauses 10.13.2 and 10.13.4 give full consideration to protecting the interest of the chargee or mortgagee in respect of moneys outstanding under the charge or mortgage

    10.13.6    if the Council or any other person cannot within 12 months of the date of service of its response under clause 10.13.4 secure such transfer then provided that the chargee or mortgagee shall have complied with its obligations under clause 10.13.4 the chargee or mortgagee shall be entitled to exercise its power of sale free of the restrictions set out in clauses 10.7 and 10.8

    10.13.7    if the chargee or mortgagee does not wish to exercise its power of sale at any time after the giving of notice under clause 10.13.1 or the Council does not wish to continue with the exercise of its powers under clause 10.13.4 after the giving of its response under clause 10.13.2 that party shall give to the other not less than 7 days' written notice of its intention to discontinue

    10.13.8    in the event of the chargee or mortgagee exercising its power of sale the Owner shall pay to the Council no later than 14 days after the date of any such sale the whole amount of any grant or loan made by the Council in respect of the Social Housing Land pursuant to the Housing Act 1996 Section 22

**[3765]**

10.14    that in the event the Housing Corporation exercises its right to require payment of social housing grant made in respect of the Social Housing Land in accordance with the Housing Act 1996 Section 27(2) the Owner shall pay to the Council on the date upon which the payment of social housing grant falls due in accordance with the Housing Corporation's direction the whole amount of any grant or loan made by the Council pursuant to the Housing Act 1996 Section 22 together with interest thereon in respect of the Social Housing Land

10.15    without prejudice to the provisions of clauses 10.1–10.14 to notify the Council immediately in the event of service of any notice under the Housing Act 1996 Sections 40 and 41 of or any notice order or direction served made or given under the Housing Act 1996 Schedule 1 Part IV]

[11    **Highway Works**

The Owner [and the Applicant] agree[s] with the County Council and the Council:

11.1    to undertake and complete the Highway Works described in schedule [5] in accordance with the specification set out in schedule [5] and to the satisfaction of the County Council by no later than [*(insert event or date) or* the first occupation of the *(number)* dwelling built on the Application Site]

11.2    not to occupy or cause or allow to be occupied more than *(number)* dwellings built on the Application Site before the Highway Works have been completed in accordance with the specifications set out in schedule [5] and to the satisfaction of the County Council]

[3766]

[12    **Transport Contributions and Facilities**

The Owner [and the Applicant] agree[s] with the County Council and the Council:

[12.1    [on the date of this Agreement *or* on *(date or event)*] to pay to the Council the Transport Contribution of £... towards the provision of the Transport Facilities described in schedule [6][12]

        *or*

        to undertake and complete the Transport Facilities described in schedule [6] in accordance with the specification set out in schedule [6] and to the satisfaction of the [County Council *or* the Council] by no later than [*(date) or* the first occupation of the *(number)* dwelling built on the Application Site]]

12.2    not to occupy or cause or allow to be occupied more than *(number)* dwellings built on the Application Site before the Transport Facilities shall have been completed in accordance with the specification set out in schedule [6] and to the satisfaction of the Council]

[13    **Off-Site Infrastructure Works**

The Owner [and the Applicant] agree[s] with the Council:

13.1    to undertake and complete the Off-Site Infrastructure Works described in schedule [7] in accordance with the specification set out in schedule [7] by no later than [*(specify) or* the first occupation of the *(number)* dwelling built on the Application Site]

13.2    not to occupy or cause or allow to be occupied any more than *(number)* dwellings built on the Application Site before the Off-Site Infrastructure Works shall have been completed in accordance with the specification set out in schedule [7]]

[14    **Commuted Car Parking Payments**

The Owner [and the Applicant] agree[s] with the Council:

14.1    [on the date of this Agreement *or* on *(date)*] to pay to the Council the Commuted Car Parking Payment of £...[13]

14.2    not to occupy or cause or allow to be occupied any building forming part of the Development before the Commuted Car Parking Payment has been made]

[3767]

**[15      Landscape Management Plan**

The Owner [and the Applicant] agree[s] with the Council:

15.1      not to remove uproot destroy lop or damage any tree or shrub on the Application Site unless and until a landscape management plan providing for the retention of trees shrubs and other vegetation to be retained and the works planting management and maintenance works described in schedule [8] have been submitted to and approved by the Council

15.2      within *(number)* months of the date of this Agreement to submit to the Council for its approval the draft Landscape Management Plan

15.3      not to carry out any [development *or* works comprised within the Development] on the Application Site before the Landscape Management Plan has been approved by the Council

15.4      to implement the Landscape Management Plan approved by the Council]

**[16      Education Contribution**

The Owner [and the Applicant] agree with the County Council and the Council:

16.1      [on the date of this Agreement *or* on *(date or event)*] to pay to the [County Council *or* Council] the Education Contribution of £...[14]

16.2      not to occupy or cause or allow to be occupied any dwelling forming part of the Development before the Education Contribution shall have been made]

**17      Certificates**

The Owner and the Applicant agree with the County Council and the Council:

17.1      where this Agreement imposes a requirement for the making of a payment or the undertaking of an act or the cessation of an activity on a Specified Date the Owner and the Applicant shall give to the Council notice of the Specified Date not more than 7 days after such Specified Date

17.2      if the Owner and/or Applicant fail[s] to give the notice required under clause 17.1 the Council shall be entitled in its absolute discretion to determine the Specified Date and shall give notice to the Owner and Applicant of its determination

**[3768]**

**18      Index Linking**

The Owner and the Applicant agree with the County Council and the Council that any sums payable by the Owner and/or the Applicant under this Agreement shall be increased by the application of the formula $A = B \times C/D$ where:

18.1      A is the sum actually payable on the Specified Date

18.2      B is the original sum mentioned in this Agreement

18.3      C is the General Index of Retail Prices (All Items) for the month 2 months before the Specified Date

18.4      D is the General Index of Retail Prices (All Items) for the month 2 months before the date of this Agreement

18.5      C/D is equal to or greater than 1

**19      Interest**

The Owner and the Applicant agree with the County Council and the Council to pay interest on sums due to the County Council and the Council under this Agreement but not paid on the Specified Date from the Specified Date until actual payment. The rate of interest shall be 4% above the *(specify bank)* plc's base rate

**20      Costs**[15]

The Owner and the Applicant agree with the [County Council and the] Council:

20.1      to pay to the [County Council and the] Council [their *or* its] legal costs incurred in preparing and entering into this Agreement amounting to £… inclusive of VAT [and £… inclusive of VAT respectively]

20.2      to pay to the Council its legal costs incurred in connection with the transfers of land referred to in this Agreement [amounting to £… inclusive of VAT]

**[3769]**

**21      Mortgagee's Consent**[16]

The Mortgagee consents to the Owner entering into this Agreement and acknowledges that this Agreement binds the Red Land

**22      General**[17]

The parties agree that:

22.1      nothing in this Agreement constitutes or constitutes an obligation to grant planning permission

22.2      nothing in this Agreement grants planning permission or any other approval consent or permission required from the County Council or the Council in the exercise of any other statutory function

22.3      nothing in this Agreement fetters or restricts the exercise by the County Council and the Council of any of their powers

22.4      the obligations contained in clauses *(numbers)* are planning obligations for the purpose of Section 106 of the Act

22.5      this Agreement constitutes a deed

22.6      this Agreement is enforceable by the Council [and to the extent mentioned in clauses *(numbers)* by the County Council[18]]

22.7      this Agreement does not nor is intended to confer a benefit on a third party within the meaning of the Contracts (Rights of Third Parties) Act 1999

**[3770]**

[SCHEDULE 1[19]
(Transfer of public open space or children's play area)

*Use Land Registry form TP1 (for which see Form 114 [4181] post) and insert, in the panels specified below, the wording shown:*

**Panel 7  Transferee**

*(insert name of district council)*

**Panel 10  Consideration**

The Transferor has received from the Transferee for the Property the sum of one pound (£1)

**Panel 13  Additional Provisions**

**1      Definitions**

In this transfer:

1.1      'the Plan' means the plan annexed to this transfer [and if numbered plans are annexed any reference to a numbered plan is to the annexed plan so numbered]

1.2      'the Retained Land' means the land [and buildings] *(add description)* [outlined in green *or (as the case may be)*] on [the Plan *or* Plan No *(number)*] retained by the

Transferor [being that part of the land comprised in title number *(number)* as is not comprised in the Property *or* the land comprised in title number *(number)*]

[1.3    *(insert any others required)*]

## 2    Rights granted for the benefit of the Property

The Property is transferred together with the following rights: *(insert details of rights to be granted)*

## 3    Rights reserved for the benefit of other land

There are reserved out of the Property for the benefit of each and every part of the Retained Land the following rights: *(insert details of rights to be reserved)*

## [4    Restrictive covenant by the Transferee

The Transferee covenants with the Transferor for the benefit of the whole and every part of the Retained Land not to use the Property for any purpose other than as open space as defined in the Town and Country Planning Act 1990 Section 336]

## [5    Restrictive covenants by the Transferor

*(insert details)*]

## 6    Agreements and Declarations

It is agreed and declared as follows: *(insert details)*

## 7    Statements

The Transferee is acting pursuant to the Town and Country Planning Act 1990 Section 227]

**[3771]**

[SCHEDULE [2]
Community Facilities
*(insert details)*]

[SCHEDULE [3][20]
(Transfer of community facilities land)

*Use Land Registry Form TP1 (for which see Form 114 [4181] post) and insert, in the panels specified below, the wording shown:*

**Panel 7  Transferee**

*(insert name of district council)*

**Panel 10  Consideration**

The Transferor has received from the Transferee for the Property the sum of one pound (£1)

**Panel  13 Additional Provisions**

## 1    Definitions

In this transfer:

1.1     'the Plan' means the plan annexed to this transfer [and if numbered plans are annexed any reference to a numbered plan is to the annexed plan so numbered]

1.2     'the Retained Land' means the land [and buildings] *(add description)* [outlined in green *or (as the case may be)* on [the Plan *or* Plan No *(number)*]] retained by the Transferor [being that part of the land comprised in title number *(number)* as is not comprised in the Property *or* the land comprised in title number *(number)*]

[1.3     *(insert any others required)*]

**2     Rights granted for the benefit of the Property**

The Property is transferred together with the following rights: *(insert details of rights to be granted)*

**3     Rights reserved for the benefit of other land**

There are reserved out of the Property for the benefit of each and every part of the Retained Land the following rights: *(insert details of rights to be reserved)*

**[4     Restrictive covenant by the Transferee**

The Transferee covenants with the Transferor for the benefit of the whole and every part of the Retained Land not to use the Property for any purpose other than as open space as defined in the Town and Country Planning Act 1990 Section 336]

**[5     Restrictive covenants by the Transferor**

*(insert details)*]

**6     Agreements and Declarations**

It is agreed and declared as follows: *(insert details)*

**7     Statements**

The Transferee is acting pursuant to the Town and Country Planning Act 1990 Section 227]

**[3772]**

[SCHEDULE [4]

THIS DEED OF NOMINATION RIGHTS is made the … day of ……

BETWEEN:

(1)     *(name of Registered Social Landlord)* [company number *(number)*] whose registered address is at *(address)* ('the RSL') and

(2)     *(name)* District Council of *(address)* ('the Council')

**1     Definitions**

In this Deed:

1.1     'Initial Let' means the first tenancy or lease of such newly constructed and previously unoccupied Rented Unit or Shared Ownership Unit

1.2     'Local Connection' means in relation to an individual:

    1.2.1     such individual who:

        1.2.1.1     immediately before taking up occupation of a Rented Unit or Shared Ownership Unit had his only or principal home in the [district of *(specify)* or parish of *(specify)*] for a continuous period of not less than 3 years or

        1.2.1.2     has or a member of whose household has a parent adult child brother or sister whose only or principal home is and has been for a continuous period of not less than 3 years in the [district of *(specify)* or parish of *(specify)*] and he wishes to be near that relative or

        1.2.1.3     is and has been permanently employed in the [district of *(specify)* or parish of *(specify)*] for a continuous period of not less than 3 years

    1.2.2     where no person or insufficient persons have a connection with the parish of *(specify)* then the parish of *(specify)* shall be substituted for the parish of *(specify)* and then if no person or insufficient persons have a connection with the parish of *(specify)* then the parish of *(specify)* shall be substituted for the parish of *(specify)* and then if no person or insufficient persons have a connection with the parish of *(specify)* then the parish of *(specify)* shall be substituted for the parish of *(specify)* and then if no person or insufficient persons have a connection with the parish of *(specify)* the district of *(specify)* shall be substituted for the parish of *(specify)*

**[3773]**

1.3   Nomination List' means the list to be supplied by the Council pursuant to clauses 3.1.3 and 3.2.1 (as may be updated from time to time in accordance with clause 3.3.3)

1.4   'Nominee' means a person named in the Nomination List who satisfies the Local Connection and is specified by the Council as being suitable for the category of Rented Unit or Shared Ownership Unit in respect of which the RSL is in accordance with this Deed to select a person from the Nomination List to offer a Tenancy Agreement or Shared Ownership Lease

1.5   'Property' means the land at *(address)* shown edged red on the attached plan

1.6   'Rented Units' means *(number)* [houses *or* flats *or* maisonettes]

1.7   'Shared Ownership Units' means *(number)* [houses *or* flats *or* maisonettes]

1.8   'Shared Ownership Lease' means a lease substantially in the form annexed or agreed between the parties

1.9   'Subsequent Nominee' means a Nominee to be offered a Tenancy Agreement pursuant to clause 3.2.3

1.10   'Tenancy Agreement' means an assured tenancy agreement in a form prepared by the RSL and containing terms which accord with the form of tenancy agreement being used by the RSL from time to time for its general lettings

1.11   'Vacancy Notice' means a written notice given by the RSL to the Council (in a form to be agreed between the RSL and the Council within 5 weeks from the date of this Deed) the function of such notice being the notification to the Council by the RSL that the construction and fitting out of the Rented Unit or Shared Ownership Unit is completed

1.12   'Void' means a Rented Unit which is vacant otherwise than as a result of the tenant having:

    1.12.1   moved to other accommodation either by transfer or decant provided by the RSL

    1.12.2   moved to other accommodation under a reciprocal arrangement provided by another registered social landlord registered with the Housing Corporation under the Housing Act 1996

1.13   'Void Notice' means a written notice given by the RSL to the Council (in a form to be agreed between the RSL and the Council within 5 weeks from the date of this Deed) the function of such a notice being the notification to the Council of a Void

**[3774]**

## 2   Enabling Provisions

This Agreement is made pursuant to the Local Government Act 1972 Section 111 and all other enabling powers and the Local Government (Miscellaneous Provisions) Act 1982 Section 33

## 3   Procedure

The parties agree that the following nomination procedure shall apply to the nomination of persons in respect of the Rented Units or Shared Ownership Units

**3.1     Initial lets**

3.1.1     The RSL shall give the Council not less than 4 months' written notice of the date when the Initial Let units will be ready for occupation

3.1.2     The RSL shall serve Vacancy Notices in respect of the Rented Units or Shared Ownership Units not earlier than 2 months prior to such newly constructed and previously unoccupied Rented Units or Shared Ownership Units becoming available for occupation

3.1.3     The Council shall within 5 working days of receipt of a Vacancy Notice serve upon the RSL a list of the names of persons whom the Council considers have a Local Connection

3.1.4     The list to be served by the Council under clause 3.1.3 shall:

3.1.4.1     specify the appropriate category of Rented Unit or Shared Ownership Unit

3.1.4.2     indicate the priority for the housing of the persons named

**[3775]**

3.1.5     The RSL shall have the right to let the Initial Let in respect of the Rented Units or Shared Ownership Units to persons of its own choosing in the event of the Council's failure to serve the list of names referred to in clause 3.1.3 within the period of 5 working days of receipt of the Vacancy Notice

3.1.6     The RSL shall within 10 working days of the date of receipt of the list referred to in clause 3.1.3 select a Nominee from the Nomination List taking into account the priority for housing indicated by the Council and shall use its reasonable endeavours to arrange viewing of the relevant Rented Unit or Shared Ownership Unit and offer a Tenancy Agreement or Shared Ownership Lease to such selected Nominee

3.1.7     If the selected Nominee fails to enter into a Tenancy Agreement or Shared Ownership Lease within 3 working days of receipt of the RSL's offer of a Tenancy Agreement or Shared Ownership Lease such selected Nominee shall be deemed to have rejected the RSL's offer and the RSL shall select another Nominee whereupon the procedure set out in clause 3.1.6 and this clause shall be repeated

3.1.8     In the event of the second selected Nominee failing to accept the RSL's offer of a Tenancy Agreement or Shared Ownership Lease within the time prescribed by clause 3.1.7 then the RSL shall make an offer to a third Nominee and the procedure set out in clauses 3.1.6 or 3.1.7 shall apply but in the event of such third selected Nominee failing to accept the RSL's offer of a Tenancy Agreement or Shared Ownership Lease within the prescribed time limits the RSL shall not be bound to make any further offers of accommodation to Nominees in respect of such vacancy of the Rented Unit or Shared Ownership Unit but shall be entitled to let the Rented Unit or Shared Ownership Unit to a tenant of its own choosing

3.1.9     The RSL's obligations under clauses 3.1.3–3.1.8 shall cease when all of the Rented Units or Shared Ownership Units have been offered to Nominees in accordance with clauses 3.1.6–3.1.8

**[3776]**

**3.2     Voids**

3.2.1     Should a Rented Unit or Shared Ownership Unit become a Void after the Initial Let or the RSL has reasonable cause to believe it will become a Void then and in each case:

3.2.1.1     the RSL shall serve a Void Notice in respect of the relevant vacant Rented Unit or Shared Ownership Unit and

3.2.1.2    within 5 working days of receipt of the said notice the Council shall serve upon the RSL a list of the names of persons whom the Council considers to have a Local Connection and which shall contain the information referred to in clause 3.1.4

3.2.2    The RSL shall have the right to let the relevant vacant Rented Unit or Shared Ownership Unit to a person of its own choosing in the event of the Council's failure to serve the list referred to in clause 3.2.1.2 within 5 working days of receipt of the Void Notice

3.2.3    Upon receipt of the list referred to in clause 3.2.1.2 the RSL shall follow the procedure set out in clauses 3.1.6–3.1.8 mutatis mutandis

3.2.4    The RSL shall not be obliged to follow the procedure set out in clauses 3.2.1–3.2.3 if it would result in the Subsequent Nominees exceeding 75% of the Rented Units or Shared Ownership Units available after the Initial Let

**[3777]**

**3.3      Provision of information and alteration of lists**

3.3.1    The RSL shall give notification to the Council of the occurrence of the following events within 5 working days of their occurrence:

3.3.1.1    a Nominee failing to view a Rented Unit or Shared Ownership Unit within the time limit prescribed by this Deed

3.3.1.2    a Nominee failing to accept the offer of a Tenancy Agreement or Shared Ownership Lease within the time limit prescribed by this Agreement

3.3.1.3    a Nominee accepting an offer of a Tenancy Agreement or Shared Ownership Lease

3.3.1.4    a person accepting an offer of a tenancy from the RSL

3.3.1.5    the RSL rejecting a Nominee in accordance with clause 3.3.7

3.3.2    In the event of a notice being served pursuant to clause 3.3.1 then the name of such Nominee shall be removed from the Nomination List

3.3.3    Within 5 working days of the Council receiving notice served in accordance with clause 3.3.1 save for notice under clause 3.3.1.4 the Council shall serve upon the RSL the name and address of a Nominee to add to the Nomination List such notice to include the information set out in clause 3.1.4

3.3.4    If the Council shall within the period mentioned in clause 3.3.3 notify the RSL that the Council then has no suitable Nominee the Council shall advise the RSL of a suitable replacement Nominee as soon as reasonably practicable

3.3.5    The RSL shall have the right to let a Rented Unit or Shared Ownership Unit to a person of its choosing if the Council's failure to provide a Nominee creates a Void in respect of that Rented Unit or Shared Ownership Unit

3.3.6    On 1st January 1st April 1st July and 1st October in each year the RSL shall serve the Council with details of the letting activities of the Rented Units and Shared Ownership Units in a format to be agreed between the RSL and the Council

3.3.7    The RSL shall have the right to interview and make enquiries of each Nominee and by serving written notice upon the Council to that effect to reject any Nominee if in the opinion of the RSL the grant of an assured tenancy to such Nominee would be in contravention of the RSL's registered rules or its letting criteria

3.3.8    The Council shall immediately notify the RSL in writing if any Nominee is withdrawn from the Nomination List

3.3.9    When calculating percentages for the purposes of this Deed percentages in excess of 0.5 shall be rounded up and percentages equal to or less than 0.5 shall be rounded down

3.3.10    The Council and the RSL agree that the nomination rights contained in this Deed may be varied from time to time by agreement in writing by the parties

**[3778]**

**4    Notices**

Any notice required to be served hereunder shall be sufficiently served on the parties at the address indicated above or such other address notified by one party to the other and any notice shall be deemed to have been served 2 working days after posting

**5    Transfers to other Registered Social Landlords**

The RSL shall ensure that any registered social landlord to which the Property and Rented Units and Shared Ownership Units erected thereon are transferred otherwise than by direction of the Housing Corporation under its statutory powers shall enter into a similar agreement mutatis mutandis with the Council

**6    Disputes**

Where any matters fail to be agreed between the parties or any dispute or difference occurs the question shall be referred on the application of either party for the determination of a single expert to be agreed between the parties or in default of agreement to be nominated by or on behalf of the President for the time being of the Chartered Institute of Housing on the application of either party

**[3779]**

**7    Costs**

The RSL agrees with the Council to pay the legal costs which the Council incurs in preparing and entering into this deed

**8    Agreements and declarations**

The parties agree:

8.1    nothing in this Deed fetters or restricts the exercise by the Council of any of its powers

8.2    the obligations contained in this Deed are covenants for the purpose of the Local Government (Miscellaneous Provisions) Act 1982 Section 33

IN WITNESS etc]

[SCHEDULE [5]
Highway Works
*(insert details)*]

[SCHEDULE [6]
Transport Facilities
*(insert details)*]

[SCHEDULE [7]
Off-Site Infrastructure Works
*(insert details)*]

[SCHEDULE [8]
Landscape Management Plan
*(insert details)*]

*(signatures (and common seals) of the parties)*
*(signatures of witnesses)*
**[3780]**

1     This model Form is a planning obligation entered into between the local planning authority and all those with an interest in the land, under the Town and Country Planning Act 1990 s 106 as substituted by the Planning and Compensation Act 1991 s 12(1) (46 Halsbury's Statutes (4th Edn) TOWN AND COUNTRY PLANNING). As to planning obligations generally see vol 41 TOWN AND COUNTRY PLANNING Paragraph 13 [925]. This agreement contains a variety of obligations which are illustrative only; they and their related definitions should be omitted, amended, replaced and others added as appropriate.

2     Only those with a legal interest in the land can enter into a planning obligation: see the Town and Country Planning Act 1990 s 106(1), (3) as substituted. Any existing tenant should be joined as party if any of the obligations are to be binding on him.

3     The applicant should consider whether he should seek to provide that he can carry out preliminary works such as site clearance, site fencing and security, site investigations, archaeological investigations, laying of services and possibly even creating a temporary site access without this being treated as the commencement of development. For such a clause see vol 41 TOWN AND COUNTRY PLANNING Form 29 clause 2.4.2 [1186].

4     The parties should consider carefully whether it is appropriate for the owner to enter into each individual planning obligation in this agreement; on the assumption that the owner will sell the land to the applicant following the grant of planning permission, probably under a conditional contract or option, it may be appropriate for the applicant alone to enter into those obligations which involve payment of money or execution of works after completion of the sale. Covenanting parties are entitled to require that their liability ceases after they have parted with all interest in the land: see Town and Country Planning Act 1990 s 106(4) as substituted and for such a clause see vol 41 TOWN AND COUNTRY PLANNING Form 29.1 clause 3.3 [1188.3].

5     Planning obligations are often used to provide for the transfer of interests in land in connection with planning purposes. There is normally no objection in principle to the transfer of land for socially desirable purposes such as affordable housing or public open space. The precise mechanism is not wholly clear and there are conflicting authorities on the point: see *Wimpey Homes Holdings Ltd v Secretary of State for the Environment* [1993] 2 PLR, [1993] JPL 919 and *Jelson Ltd v Derby County Council* [1999] 39 EG 149, [2000] JPL 203. The position adopted here is that planning agreements may make provision for the transfer of land as has hitherto been regarded as the orthodox approach. Where land is to be transferred provision may be made for deduction of title; for such a clause see vol 41 TOWN AND COUNTRY PLANNING Form 29.1 clause 3.9 [1188.3]. It is usual, however, for title to be deduced before the agreement is entered into.

6     See note 5 above.

7     Where money is to be paid to the council to use in a specific way the applicant should consider trying to ring fence the money or perhaps have it held in trust for the specified purpose, with provision for it to be returned if the purpose for which the money is paid is not carried out within an agreed time. Such arrangements are sometimes unacceptable to councils but it is not an unreasonable request to make.

8     See note 5 above.

9     See note 7 above.

10    See note 5 above.

11    See note 5 above.

12    See note 7 above.

13    See note 7 above.

14    See note 7 above.

15    Where possible the amount of the costs should be agreed in advance and inserted in these clauses.

**[3781]**

16    A mortgagee may require the applicant or the owner or both to covenant in its favour to observe and perform the obligations and to indemnify the mortgagee.

17    Additional matters may include the following:
(a)    Town and Country Planning Act 1990 s 106(10) as substituted requires the council to be given a copy of the agreement; despite the fact that it is usually executed in duplicate and the council will hold the original it is prudent to obtain a receipt for it;
(b)    A provision for the council to give written confirmation when obligations have been fully performed;
(c)    A provision that any approval to be given by either council shall not be unreasonably withheld or delayed;
(d)    The applicant should consider whether he should seek to protect his position in the event of expiry of the permission without the development having commenced or the grant of subsequent permissions; for such clauses see vol 41 TOWN AND COUNTRY PLANNING Form 29.1 clauses 3.5 and 3.6 [1188.3].

18    The planning obligation must identify the authority by whom it is enforceable: see the Town and Country Planning Act 1990 s 106(9)(d) as substituted.

19     As to stamp duty see Information Binder: Stamp Duties [1] (Conveyance or transfer). As to Land
       Registry fees see Information Binder: Property [1]: (Fees in connection with property matters, Land
       Registry fees).
              Form TP1 (for which see Form 114 [4181] post) is the Land Registry form of transfer of part of
       freehold or leasehold land prescribed by the Land Registration Rules 1925, SR&O 1925/1093 r 98,
       Sch 1 as inserted by SI 1997/3037 and substituted by SI 1999/128. This Form should be used whenever
       part only of any registered title is transferred, even if the transfer also includes the whole of one or more
       other registered titles.
              The transferor's land or charge certificate must be placed on deposit (using Land Registry form
       DP1 as prescribed by SR&O 1925/1093 Sch 1 as inserted by SI 1997/3037 and substituted by SI 1999/
       128 (as to which see vol 25(1) (1999 Reissue) LAND REGISTRATION Form 3 [3076])) to meet the
       transferee's application to register the transfer. If the transferor's land is subject to any registered or noted
       charge, the consent of the chargee to the transfer should be obtained and lodged with the application
       to register the transfer.
              Form TP1 can also be used to transfer the land if it is unregistered. In that case panel 2 will be left
       blank and the property description in panel 4 will need to describe the land by reference to its being
       part of the land described in some suitable deed in the unregistered title (eg 'Land to the south side of
       Acacia Avenue being part of the land comprised in a conveyance dated *(date)* and made between *(parties)*')
       as well as by reference to the relevant plan referred to in the same panel. However, the application to
       register the land will then need to be on Form FR1 (as to which see vol 25(1) (1999 Reissue) LAND
       REGISTRATION Form 92 [3781]) accompanied by appropriate evidence of the transferor's title and
       Form DL (as to which see vol 25(1) (1999 Reissue) LAND REGISTRATION Form 93 [3786]) listing the
       documents lodged. Form TP1, suitably adapted, can also be used to transfer land that is a mixture of
       registered and unregistered land (although it will need to be lodged for registration under cover of two
       separate application forms: Form AP1 (as to which see vol 25(1) (1999 Reissue) LAND REGISTRATION
       Form 26 [3251]) dealing with the registered part and Forms FR1 and DL dealing with the unregistered
       part, and two fees will be payable.
              Reference should be made to Form 115 [4191] post for detailed footnotes on matters common
       to many forms of transfer, cross-references to the commentary in vol 35 (1997 Reissue) SALE OF LAND,
       for the location of alternative transfer clauses in that and other volumes and for footnotes relating to
       sales of part.
20     See note 19 above.

**[3782]–[3800]**

# 85

## Unilateral planning obligation under the Town and Country Planning Act 1990 Section 106[1]

This Unilateral Planning Obligation is dated *(date)* and is given by:

(1)     *(name)* [company number *(number)*] [of *(address) or* whose registered office is at
        *(address)*] ('the Owner')

(2)     *(name)* [company number *(number)*] [of *(address) or* whose registered office is at
        *(address)*] ('the Mortgagee')

(3)     *(name)* [company number *(number)*] [of *(address) or* whose registered office is at
        *(address)*] ('the Applicant')

## 1     Background

1.1     The Owner is [seised in fee simple in possession *or* is the registered proprietor
        under title number *(number)*] of the land at *(address)* shown for identification
        purposes only edged red on [the Plan *or* Plan No *(number)*] ('the Red Land')[2]

1.2     The Red Land is charged to the Mortgagee

1.3     *(name)* Council ('the Council') is the local planning authority [and the local
        housing authority]

1.4     *(name)* County Council ('the County Council') is the [local highway authority
        and/*or* the local education authority]

1.5       The Applicant has by planning application number *(number)* applied to the
          Council for [outline] planning permission to develop the Red Land by *(describe
          intended development)*
1.6       The Council has by a decision notice dated *(date)* refused the Application
1.7       The Applicant has appealed to the Secretary of State for the Environment
          Transport and the Regions against the Council's decision and is willing to give
          an undertaking to perform the obligations set out in this Unilateral Planning
          Obligation in the event of the appeal being allowed

                                                                                **[3801]**

## 2       Interpretation

In this Unilateral Planning Obligation:
2.1       'the Act' means the Town and Country Planning Act 1990
2.2       'agreed' or 'approved' means agreed or approved in writing and given for the
          purpose of this Unilateral Planning Obligation
2.3       'the Application' means the planning application numbered *(number)* made by
          the Applicant to develop the [Application Site *or* Red Land] by *(describe intended
          development)*
2.4       'the Application Site' means the [Red Land *or* Blue Land]
2.5       'the Blue Land' means that part of the Red Land shown for the purposes of
          identification only edged blue on [the Plan *or* Plan No *(number)*]
2.6       'the Children's Play Area' means the children's play area [shown for
          identification purposes only edged *(colour)* on [the Plan *or* Plan No *(number)*]
          and] referred to in clause *(number)*
2.7       'the Community Facilities' means *(insert details)*
2.8       'the Community Facilities Land' means the site of the Community Facilities
          [shown for identification purposes only edged *(colour)* on [the Plan *or* Plan No
          *(number)*] [having an area of *(number)* hectares] and] referred to in clause *(number)*
2.9       'Commuted Car Parking Payment' means the commuted car parking payment
          referred to in clause *(number)* to make good a deficiency in car parking provision
          arising from the Development
2.10      'the Development' means the development of the Application Site proposed in
          the Application or permitted by planning permission granted pursuant to the
          Application or carried out substantially in accordance with such planning
          permission
2.11      'Education Contribution' means the education contribution referred to in
          clause *(number)* to make good a deficiency in education provision arising from
          the Development
2.12      'the Green Land' means that part of the Red Land shown for the purposes of
          identification only edged green on [the Plan *or* Plan No *(number)*]
2.13      'the Highway Works' means the highway works referred to in clause *(number)*
2.14      'Landscape Management Plan' means the landscape management plan referred
          to in clause *(number)*
2.15      'the Off-Site Infrastructure Works' means the off-site infrastructure works
          referred to in clause *(number)* to make good a deficiency in infrastructure
          provision arising from the Development

                                                                                **[3802]**
2.16      'the Public Open Space' means [that part of] the Green Land [shown for
          identification purposes hatched *(colour)* on [the Plan *or* Plan No *(number)*]
          [having an area of *(number)* hectares] and] referred to in clause *(number)*
2.17      'the Red Land' means the land shown for identification purposes edged red on
          [the Plan *or* Plan No *(number)*]

| | |
|---|---|
| 2.18 | 'Registered Social Landlord' means a registered social landlord within the meaning of the Housing Act 1996 |
| 2.19 | 'Social Housing Land' means that part of the Red Land shown for identification purposes only edged *(colour)* on [the Plan *or* Plan No *(number)*] [having an area of *(number)* hectares] and referred to in clause *(number)* |
| 2.20 | 'Specified Date' means the date upon which an obligation arising under this Unilateral Planning Obligation is due to be performed |
| 2.21 | 'the Transport Contribution' means the contribution referred to in clause *(number)* |
| 2.22 | 'the Transport Facilities' means the transport facilities referred to in clause *(number)* |
| 2.23 | Words importing the masculine include the feminine and vice versa |
| 2.24 | Words importing the singular include the plural and vice versa |
| 2.25 | Words importing persons include companies and corporations and vice versa |
| 2.26 | Wherever there is more than one person named as a party and where more than one party undertakes an obligation all their obligations can be enforced against all of them jointly and against each individually |
| 2.27 | Any reference to a clause or schedule or plan is to one in to or attached to this Unilateral Planning Obligation |
| 2.28 | In the absence of contrary provision any reference to a statute includes any statutory modification or re-enactment of it and every statutory instrument direction specification made or issued under the statute or deriving validity from it |
| 2.29 | References to any party to this Unilateral Planning Obligation shall include the successors in title to that party and to any deriving title through or under that party and in the case of the County Council and the Council the successors to their respective functions as [local highway authority and/*or* local education authority] and local planning authority [and local housing authority] |

**[3803]**

**3 Enabling Provisions**

This Unilateral Planning Obligation is made pursuant to Section 106 of the Act the Local Government Act 1972 Section 111 *(insert other powers)* and all other enabling powers

**4 Commencement**

This Unilateral Planning Obligation shall come into effect upon the date of [this Unilateral Planning Obligation *or* the grant of the planning permission granted pursuant to the Application] but the obligations in clause(s) *(number(s))* shall become effective only on the commencement of the Development in accordance with Section 56 of the Act[3]

**5 Phasing**

The Owner[4] [and the Applicant] covenant[s] with the Council:

| | |
|---|---|
| 5.1 | not to carry out or allow to be carried out any development on the Application Site before *(insert date or event)* |
| 5.2 | not to occupy or cause or allow to be occupied any of the dwellings forming part of the Development before *(insert date or event)* |

**[3804]**

**6 Cessation/Modification/Revocation/Discontinuance of Development**

The Owner [and the Applicant] covenant[s]:

| | |
|---|---|
| 6.1 | to cease to carry out the following development on the Red Land with effect from the date of this Unilateral Planning Obligation: *(specify prohibited development)* |

6.2     not to implement nor cause or allow the implementation of planning permission *(insert reference number)*

6.3     not to claim nor to seek compensation in respect of the obligation arising under clauses[s] 6.1 [and 6.2] nor in respect of the exercise by the Council of its powers under Sections 97 99 and 102 of the Act in respect of the planning permission referred to in clause 6.2

6.4     to indemnify the Council from and against any claims or demands arising from the Council exercising its powers of modification revocation or discontinuance

## [7     Provision of Public Open Space

The Owner [and the Applicant] covenant[s]:

7.1     to provide and lay out an area of open space having an area of *(number)* hectares [[within *or* comprising] the [Green] Land *or* substantially in the position shown edged *(colour)* on [the Plan *or* Plan No *(number)*]] in accordance with a specification approved by the Council and to the Council's satisfaction

7.2     to ensure that there is easy public access to the Public Open Space

7.3     to complete the works of provision and laying out in accordance with clause 7.1 and to make the Public Open Space available for use by the public by no later than the [completion of the Development *or* first occupation of the *(insert number)* dwelling [forming part of the Development *or* on the Application Site]]

7.4     within 2 months of the completion of the works referred to in clause 7.3 to transfer the Public Open Space to the Council or to such body as it may direct substantially in the form of the transfer set out in schedule [1] although the Public Open Space may by agreement with the Council be handed over to the Council or its nominee for public use and for maintenance purposes in advance of the transfer[5]

7.5     upon the handover or transfer referred to in clause 7.4 (whichever in the earlier) to pay to the Council or its nominee the sum of £...]

                                                                              **[3805]**

## [8     Provision of Children's Play Area

The Owner [and the Applicant] covenant[s]:

8.1     to provide layout and equip a children's play area substantially in the position shown edged *(colour)* on [the Plan *or* Plan No *(number)*] in accordance with a specification approved by the Council and to the Council's satisfaction

8.2     to ensure that there is easy public access to the Children's Play Area

8.3     to complete the works of provision laying out and equipment in accordance with clause 8.1 and to make the Children's Play Area available for use by the public by no later than [the completion of the Development *or* the first occupation of the *(insert number)* dwelling [forming part of the Development *or* on the Application Site]]

8.4     within 2 months of the completion of the works referred to in clause 8.3 to transfer the Children's Play Area to the Council or to such body as it may direct substantially in the form of the transfer set out in schedule [1] although the Children's Play Area may by agreement with the Council be handed over to the Council or its nominee for public use and for maintenance purposes in advance of the transfer[6]

8.5     upon the handover or transfer referred to in clause 8.4 (whichever is the earlier) to pay to the Council or its nominee the sum of £... by way of a commuted payment sum for future maintenance of the Children's Play Area[7]]

                                                                              **[3806]**

**[9      Community Facilities**

The Owner [and the Applicant] covenant[s]:

9.1        to provide [and lay out] an area of land of *(number)* hectares [[within *or* comprising the *(colour)* Land] *or* substantially in the position shown edged *(colour)* on [the Plan *or* Plan No *(number)*]] in accordance with a specification approved by the Council and to the Council's satisfaction for the purpose of accommodating the Community Facilities described in schedule [2]

9.2        to complete the works of provision and laying out in accordance with clause 9.1 by no later than [*(date)* *or* the completion of the Development *or* the first occupation of the *(insert number)* dwelling [forming part of the Development *or* on the Application Site]]

9.3        within 2 months of the completion of the works referred to in clause 9.2 to transfer the Community Facilities Land to the Council or to such body as it may direct substantially in the form of the transfer set out in schedule [3][8]

[9.4        to pay to the Council [on the date of this Unilateral Planning Obligation *or* on *(date)*] the sum of £... in respect of a contribution towards the provision of the Community Facilities]][9]

**[3807]**

**[10      Social Housing** *(rural areas under 3000 population)*

The Owner [and the Applicant] covenant[s]:

10.1       to provide within the Red Land the Social Housing Land in such location or locations as may be approved by the Council for the construction of *(number)* social housing units of such size and type as shall be approved by the Council

10.2       to provide a vehicular access foul and surface water sewers and water gas electricity and telecommunication service systems for the Social Housing Land linking in each case to the estate roads sewers and service systems to be constructed and laid as part of the remainder of the Development and connected ultimately to highways and sewers maintainable at the public expense

10.3       to endeavour to agree with the Council on the identity of the Registered Social Landlord or other body to which the Social Housing Land is to be transferred within the period of *(specify)* from the date of this Agreement but if no agreement has been reached at the expiration of such period of *(specify)* the Council shall be entitled to nominate a Registered Social Landlord or other appropriate body for the purpose

10.4       to transfer the Social Housing Land to the Registered Social Landlord or other body agreed or determined in accordance with clause 10.3 at the purchase price as set out in clause 10.5 within one month of the Council giving its approval under clause 10.3[10]

[10.5       that the purchase price for the Social Housing Land shall be £...
            *or*
            that the purchase price for the Social Housing Land shall be calculated in accordance with the following formula: *(specify)*]

10.6       not to occupy or cause or allow the occupation of more than *(number)* non-social housing units erected or to be erected on the Application Site before the transfer referred to in clause 10.4 shall have been completed

10.7       not to dispose of or cause or allow the disposal of any individual social housing unit built on the Social Housing Land other than:

|  |  |  |
|---|---|---|
| 10.7.1 | in respect of *(number)* units numbered *(numbers)* on [the Plan *or* Plan No *(number)*] by way of shared ownership lease and |
| 10.7.2 | in respect of *(number)* units numbered *(numbers)* on [the Plan *or* Plan No *(number)*] by way of an assured tenancy agreement complying with the guidance given by the Housing Corporation under the Housing Act 1996 Section 36 or |
| 10.7.3 | by way of the right to buy or the preserved right to buy under the Housing Act 1985 or the right to acquire under the Housing Act 1996 and |
| 10.7.4 | to a person who satisfies the qualifications set out in clause 10.8 |

10.8     that the qualifications referred to in clause 10.7 are that the person:

10.8.1     is an individual

10.8.2     is considered by the Registered Social Landlord in accordance with its rules to be in need of the accommodation provided by the dwelling and

10.8.3     is not able easily to compete in the open market for housing accommodation in the district of *(specify name of Council)* and has a local connection within the meaning of clause 10.9

10.8.4     before taking up occupation of the social housing unit has never owned a freehold or a lease exceeding 3 years within the last 12 months (save that the condition shall not apply where the Council is satisfied that the circumstances of that person are such as to put him in need of housing) and

10.8.5     intends to occupy and subsequently occupies the social housing unit as his only or principal home

**[3808]**

10.9     for the purposes of clause 10.8 'local connection' means in relation to an individual:

10.9.1     such individual who:

10.9.1.1     immediately before taking up occupation of a social housing dwelling unit had his only or principal home in the [district of *(specify)* or parish of *(specify)*] for a continuous period of not less than 3 years or

10.9.1.2     has or a member of whose household has a parent adult child brother or sister whose only or principal home is and has been for a continuous period of not less than 3 years in the [district of *(specify)* or parish of *(specify)*] and he wishes to be near that relative or

10.9.1.3     is and has been permanently employed in the [district of *(specify)* or parish of *(specify)*] for a continuous period of not less than 3 years

10.9.2     where no person or insufficient persons have a connection with the parish of *(specify)* as described in clause 10.9.1 then the parish of *(specify)* shall be substituted for the parish of *(specify)* and then if no person or insufficient persons have a connection with the parish of *(specify)* then the parish of *(specify)* shall be substituted for the parish of *(specify)* and then if no person or insufficient persons have a connection with the parish of *(specify)* the district of *(specify)* shall be substituted for the parish of *(specify)*

10.10     upon transfer of the Social Housing Land to the Registered Social Landlord or other body agreed or determined in accordance with clause 10.3 to procure the execution by the Registered Social Landlord and delivery to the Council of a deed of nomination substantially in the form set out in schedule [4]

**[3809]**

10.11     to take all reasonable and prudent steps to avert the repossession of the Social Housing Land or any social housing unit erected on the Social Housing Land by any chargee or mortgagee or the exercise by any chargee or mortgagee of a power of sale and for these purposes in the event of default under the security or likely default to co-operate fully with the Council and the Housing Corporation to arrange a transfer of the Social Housing Land with sitting tenants to another Registered Social Landlord or (at the Council's option) to the Council and in particular to inform the Council immediately in the event of the Owner's receiving notification from such chargee or mortgagee of any breach or alleged breach by the Owner of any of its obligations under its security

10.12     that in the event of a default under any security referred to in clause 10.11 or in other circumstances warranting the intervention of the Housing Corporation (whether or not under the Housing Act 1996 Part 1 Chapter IV or Schedule 1 Part IV) clause 10.7 shall not prevent the transfer of the freehold of the Social Housing Land or any part to another Registered Social Landlord

10.13     that in the event the Housing Corporation exercises its right to require payment of social housing grant made in respect of the Social Housing Land in accordance with the Housing Act 1996 Section 27(2) the Owner shall pay to the Council on the date upon which the payment of social housing grant falls due in accordance with the Housing Corporation's direction the whole amount of any grant or loan made by the Council pursuant to the Housing Act 1996 Section 22 together with interest thereon in respect of the Social Housing Land

10.14     without prejudice to the provisions of clauses 10.1–10.13 to notify the Council immediately in the event of service of any notice under the Housing Act 1996 Sections 40 and 41 or any notice order or direction served made or given under the Housing Act 1996 Schedule 1 Part IV

**[3810]**

*or*

**10     Social Housing** *(General)*

The Owner [and the Applicant] covenant[s]:

10.1     to provide within the Red Land the Social Housing Land in such location or locations as may be approved by the Council for the construction of *(number)* social housing units of such size and type as shall be approved by the Council

10.2     to provide a vehicular access foul and surface water sewers and water gas electricity and telecommunication service systems for the Social Housing Land linking in each case to the estate roads sewers and service systems to be constructed and laid as part of the remainder of the Development and connected ultimately to highways and sewers maintainable at the public expense

10.3     to endeavour to agree with the Council on the identity of the Registered Social Landlord or other body to which the Social Housing Land is to be transferred within the period of *(specify)* from the date of this Unilateral Planning Obligation but if no agreement has been reached at the expiration of such period of *(specify)* the Council shall be entitled to nominate a Registered Social Landlord or other appropriate body for the purpose

10.4     to transfer the Social Housing Land to the Registered Social Landlord or other body agreed or determined in accordance with clause 10.3 at the purchase price as set out in clause 10.5 within one month of the Council giving its approval under clause 10.3[11]

[10.5     that the purchase price for the Social Housing Land shall be £...
*or*
that the purchase price for the Social Housing Land shall be calculated in accordance with the following formula: *(specify formula)*]

**[3811]**

10.6     not to occupy or cause or allow the occupation of more than *(number)* non-social housing units erected or to be erected on the Application Site before the transfer referred to in clause 10.4 shall have been completed

10.7     not to dispose of or cause or allow the disposal of any individual social housing unit built on the Social Housing Land other than:

     10.7.1     in respect of *(number)* units numbered *(number)* on [the Plan *or* Plan No *(number)*] by way of shared ownership lease and

     10.7.2     in respect of *(number)* units numbered *(number)* on [the Plan *or* Plan No *(number)*] by way of an assured tenancy agreement complying with the guidance given by the Housing Corporation under the Housing Act 1996 Section 36 or

     10.7.3     by way of the right to buy or the preserved right to buy under the Housing Act 1985 and

     10.7.4     to a person who satisfies the qualifications set out in clause 10.8

10.8     that the qualification referred to in clause 10.7 are that the person:

     10.8.1     is an individual

     10.8.2     is considered by the Registered Social Landlord in accordance with its rules to be in need of the accommodation provided by the dwelling

     10.8.3     is not able easily to compete in the open market for housing accommodation in the district of *(specify name of Council)*

     10.8.4     before taking up occupation of the social housing unit has never owned a freehold or a lease exceeding three years within the last 12 months (save that the condition shall not apply where the Council is satisfied that the circumstances of that person are such as to put him in need of housing) and

     10.8.5     intends to occupy and subsequently occupies the social housing unit as his only or principal home

**[3812]**

10.9     upon transfer of the Social Housing Land to the Registered Social Landlord or other body agreed or determined in accordance with clause 10.3 to procure the execution by the Registered Social Landlord and delivery to the Council of a deed of nomination substantially in the form set out in schedule [4]

10.10     to take all reasonable and prudent steps to avert the repossession of the Social Housing Land or any social housing unit erected on the Social Housing Land by any chargee or mortgagee or the exercise by any chargee or mortgagee of a power of sale and for these purposes in the event of default under the security or likely default to co-operate fully with the Council and the Housing Corporation to arrange a transfer of the Social Housing Land with sitting tenants to another Registered Social Landlord or (at the Council's option) to the Council and in particular shall inform the Council immediately in the event of the Owner's receiving notification from such chargee or mortgagee of any breach or alleged breach by the Owner of any of its obligations under its security

10.11     that in the event of a default under any security referred to in clause 10.10 or in other circumstances warranting the intervention of the Housing Corporation (whether or not under the Housing Act 1996 Part 1 Chapter IV or Schedule 1 Part IV) clause 10.7 shall not prevent the transfer of the freehold of the Social Housing Land or any part of it to another Registered Social Landlord

10.12     subject to and without prejudice to the powers and requirements of the Housing Corporation under the Housing Act 1996 that in the event of a default under any security referred to in clause 10.10 clause 10.7 shall not prevent the sale of the freehold of the Social Housing Land or of any social housing unit by the chargee or mortgagee in the exercise of its power of sale provided that the chargee or mortgagee shall have first followed the procedure set out in clause 10.13

**[3813]**

10.13     that the procedure referred to in clause 10.12 shall be as follows:

       10.13.1    the chargee or mortgagee shall give not less than 3 months' prior notice to the Council of its intention to exercise its power of sale to enable the Council to secure the transfer of the Social Housing Land to another Registered Social Landlord or to the Council

       10.13.2    the Council shall then have 3 months from the notice given pursuant to clause 10.13.1 within which to respond indicating that arrangements for the transfer of the Social Housing Land can be made in such a way as to safeguard the social housing character of the Social Housing Land and of any dwelling

       10.13.3    if within the 3 months the Council does not serve its response to the notice served under clause 10.13.1 then the chargee or mortgagee shall be entitled to exercise its power of sale free of the restrictions set out in clauses 10.7 to 10.9 inclusive

       10.13.4    if within 3 months of the date of receipt by it of the notice served under clause 10.13.1 the Council serves its response indicating that arrangements can be made in accordance with clause 10.13 then the chargee or mortgagee shall co-operate with such arrangements and use its best endeavours to secure such transfer

       10.13.5    the Council shall in formulating or promoting any arrangements referred to in clauses 10.13.2 and 10.13.4 give full consideration to protecting the interest of the chargee or mortgagee in respect of moneys outstanding under the charge or mortgage

       10.13.6    if the Council or any other person cannot within 12 months of the date of service of its response under clause 10.13.4 secure such transfer then provided that the chargee or mortgagee shall have complied with its obligations under clause 10.13.4 the chargee or mortgagee shall be entitled to exercise its power of sale free of the restrictions set out in clauses 10.7 and 10.8

       10.13.7    if the chargee or mortgagee does not wish to exercise its power of sale at any time after the giving of notice under clause 10.13.1 or the Council does not wish to continue with the exercise of its powers under clause 10.13.4 after the giving of its response under clause 10.13.2 that party shall give to the other not less than seven days' written notice of its intention to discontinue

       10.13.8    in the event of the chargee or mortgagee exercising its power of sale the Owner shall pay to the Council no later than 14 days after the date of any such sale the whole amount of any grant or loan made by the Council in respect of the Social Housing Land pursuant to the Housing Act 1996 Section 22

10.14    that in the event the Housing Corporation exercises its right to require payment of social housing grant made in respect of the Social Housing Land in accordance with the Housing Act 1996 Section 27(2) the Owner shall pay to the Council on the date upon which the payment of social housing grant falls due in accordance with the Housing Corporation's direction the whole amount of any grant or loan made by the Council pursuant to the Housing Act 1996 Section 22 together with interest thereon in respect of the Social Housing Land

10.15    without prejudice to the provisions of clauses 10.1–10.14 to notify the Council immediately in the event of service of any notice under the Housing Act 1996 Sections 40 and 41 of or any notice order or direction served made or given under the Housing Act 1996 Schedule 1 Part IV]

**[3814]**

## [11    Highway Works

The Owner [and the Applicant] covenant[s]:

11.1    to undertake and complete the Highway Works described in schedule [5] in accordance with the specification set out in schedule [5] and to the satisfaction of the County Council by no later than [*(insert event or date)* or the first occupation of the *(number)* dwelling built on the Application Site]

11.2    not to occupy or cause or allow to be occupied more than *(number)* dwellings built on the Application Site before the Highway Works shall have been completed in accordance with the specifications set out in schedule [5] and to the satisfaction of the County Council]

## [12    Transport Contributions and Facilities

The Owner [and the Applicant] covenant[s]:

[12.1    [on the date of this Agreement *or* on *(date or event)*] to pay to the Council the Transport Contribution of £… towards the provision of the Transport Facilities described in schedule [6][12]

*or*

to undertake and complete the Transport Facilities described in schedule [6] in accordance with the specification set out in schedule [6] and to the satisfaction of the [County Council *or* the Council] by no later than [*(date)* or the first occupation of the *(number)* dwelling built on the Application Site]]

12.2    not to occupy or cause or allow to be occupied more than *(number)* dwellings built on the Application Site before the Transport Facilities shall have been completed in accordance with the specification set out in schedule [6] and to the satisfaction of the Council]

**[3815]**

## [13    Off-Site Infrastructure Works

The Owner [and the Applicant] covenant[s]:

13.1    to undertake and complete the Off-Site Infrastructure Works described in schedule [7] in accordance with the specification set out in schedule [7] by no later than *(specify)* or the first occupation of the *(number)* dwelling built on the Application Site

13.2    not to occupy or cause or allow to be occupied any more than *(number)* dwellings built on the Application Site before the Off-Site Infrastructure Works shall have been completed in accordance with the specification set out in schedule [7]]

**[14     Commuted Car Parking Payments**

The Owner [and the Applicant] covenant[s]:

14.1     on the date of this Agreement *or* on *(date)* to pay to the Council the Commuted Car Parking Payment of £...[13]

14.2     not to occupy or cause or allow to be occupied any building forming part of the Development before the Commuted Car Parking Payment shall have been made]

**[15     Landscape Management Plan**

The Owner [and the Applicant] covenant[s]:

15.1     not to remove uproot destroy lop or damage any tree or shrub on the Application Site unless and until a landscape management plan providing for the retention of trees shrubs and other vegetation to be retained and the works planting management and maintenance works described in schedule [8] shall have been submitted to and approved by the Council

15.2     within *(number)* months of the date of this Agreement to submit to the Council for its approval the draft Landscape Management Plan

15.3     not to carry out any [development *or* works comprised within the Development] on the Application Site before the Landscape Management Plan has been approved by the Council

15.4     to implement the Landscape Management Plan approved by the Council]

**[3816]**

**[16     Education Contribution**

The Owner [and the Applicant] covenant[s]:

16.1     [on the date of this Agreement *or* on *(date or event)*] to pay to the [County Council *or* Council] the Education Contribution of £...[14]

16.2     not to occupy or cause or allow to be occupied any dwelling forming part of the Development before the Education Contribution shall have been made]

**17     Certificates**

The Owner and the Applicant covenant:

17.1     where this Unilateral Planning Obligation imposes a requirement for the making of a payment or the undertaking of an act or the cessation of an activity on a Specified Date the Owner and the Applicant shall give to the Council notice of the Specified Date not more than seven days after such Specified Date

17.2     if the Owner and/or Applicant fails to give the notice required under clause 17.1 the Council shall be entitled in its absolute discretion to determine the Specified Date and shall give notice to the Owner and Applicant of its determination

**18     Index Linking**

The Owner and the Applicant covenant that any sums payable by the Owner and/or the Applicant under this Unilateral Planning Obligation shall be increased by the application of the formula $A = B \times C/D$ where:

18.1     A is the sum actually payable on the Specified Date

18.2     B is the original sum mentioned in this Unilateral Planning Obligation

18.3     C is the General Index of Retail Prices (All items) for the month 2 months before the Specified Date

18.4     D is the General Index of Retail Prices (All items) for the month 2 months before the date of this Unilateral Planning Obligation

18.5     C/D is equal to or greater than 1

**[3817]**

**19     Interest**

The Owner and the Applicant covenant to pay interest on sums due to the County Council and the Council under this Unilateral Planning Obligation but not paid on the Specified Date from the Specified Date until actual payment. The rate of interest shall be 4% above the *(specify bank)* plc's base rate

**20     Costs**[15]

The Owner and the Applicant covenant:

20.1     to pay to the [County Council and the] Council [their *or* its] legal costs incurred in preparing and entering into this Unilateral Planning Obligation amounting to £... inclusive of VAT [and £... inclusive of VAT respectively]

20.2     to pay to the Council its legal costs incurred in connection with the transfers of land referred to in this Unilateral Planning Obligation [amounting to £... inclusive of VAT]

**21     Mortgagee's Consent**[16]

The Mortgagee consents to the Owner entering into this Unilateral Planning Obligation and acknowledges that this Unilateral Planning Obligation binds the Red Land

**22     General**[17]

The parties agree that:

22.1     nothing in this Unilateral Planning Obligation constitutes or constitutes an obligation to grant planning permission

22.2     nothing in this Unilateral Planning Obligation grants planning permission or any other approval consent or permission required from the County Council or the Council in the exercise of any other statutory function

22.3     nothing in this Unilateral Planning Obligation fetters or restricts the exercise by the County Council and the Council of any of their powers

22.4     the obligations contained in clauses *(number(s))* are planning obligations for the purpose of Section 106 of the Act

22.5     this Unilateral Planning Obligation constitutes a deed

22.6     this Unilateral Planning Obligation is enforceable by the Council [and to the extent mentioned in clauses *(numbers)* by the County Council[18]]

22.7     this Unilateral Planning Obligation does not nor is intended to confer a benefit on a third party within the meaning of the Contracts (Rights of Third Parties) Act 1999

**[3818]**

[SCHEDULE 1[19]

Transfer of Public Open Space or Children's Play Area

*Use Land Registry Form TP1 (for which see Form 114 [4181] post) and insert, in the panels specified below, the wording shown:*

**Panel 7     Transferee**

*(insert name of district council)*

**Panel 10     Consideration**

The Transferor has received from the Transferee for the Property the sum of one pound (£1)

## Panel 13  Additional Provisions

**1          Definitions**

In this transfer:

1.1      'the Plan' means the plan annexed to this transfer [and if numbered plans are annexed any reference to a numbered plan is to the annexed plan so numbered]

1.2      'the Retained Land' means the land [and buildings] *(add description)* [outlined in green *or (as the case may be)* on [the Plan *or* Plan No *(number)*]] retained by the Transferor [being that part of the land comprised in title number *(number)* as is not comprised in the Property *or* the land comprised in title number *(number)*]

[1.3      *(insert any others required)*]

**2          Rights granted for the benefit of the Property**

The Property is transferred together with the following rights: *(insert details of rights to be granted)*

**3          Rights reserved for the benefit of other land**

There are reserved out of the Property for the benefit of each and every part of the Retained Land the following rights: *(insert details of rights to be reserved)*

**[4          Restrictive covenants by the Transferor**

*(insert details)*]

**5          Agreements and Declarations**

It is agreed and declared as follows: *(insert details)*

**6          Statements**

The Transferee is acting pursuant to the Town and Country Planning Act 1990 Section 227]

**[3819]**

[SCHEDULE [2]
Community Facilities
*(insert details)*]

[SCHEDULE [3][20]
Transfer of Community Facilities Land

*Use Land Registry Form TP1 (for which see Form 114 [4181] ante) and insert, in the panels specified below, the wording shown:*

## Panel 7  Transferee

*(insert name of district council)*

## Panel 10  Consideration

The Transferor has received from the Transferee for the Property the sum of one pound (£1)

## Panel  13 Additional Provisions

**1          Definitions**

In this transfer:

1.1      'the Plan' means the plan annexed to this transfer [and if numbered plans are annexed any reference to a numbered plan is to the annexed plan so numbered]

1.2      'the Retained Land' means the land [and buildings] *(add description)* [outlined in green *or (as the case may be)* on [the Plan *or* Plan No *(number)*]] retained by the

Transferor [being that part of the land comprised in title number *(number)* as is not comprised in the Property *or* the land comprised in title number *(number)*]
1.3     *(insert any others required)*

**2      Rights granted for the benefit of the Property**
The Property is transferred together with the following rights: *(insert details of rights to be granted)*

**3      Rights reserved for the benefit of other land**
There are reserved out of the Property for the benefit of each and every part of the Retained Land the following rights: *(insert details of rights to be reserved)*

**[4     Restrictive covenants by the Transferor**
*(insert details)*]

**5      Agreements and Declarations**
It is agreed and declared as follows: *(insert details)*

**6      Statements**
The Transferee is acting pursuant to the Town and Country Planning Act 1990 Section 227]

**[3820]**

[SCHEDULE [4]

THIS DEED OF NOMINATION RIGHTS is made the … day of ……

BETWEEN:

(1)     *(name of Registered Social Landlord)* [company number *(number)*] whose registered address is at *(address)* ('the RSL') and
(2)     *(name)* District Council of *(address)* ('the Council')

**1      Definitions**

In this Deed:
1.1     'Initial Let' means the first tenancy or lease of such newly constructed and previously unoccupied Rented Unit or Shared Ownership Unit
1.2     'Local Connection' means in relation to an individual:
        1.2.1     such individual who:
                  1.2.1.1     immediately before taking up occupation of a Rented Unit or Shared Ownership Unit had his only or principal home in the [district of *(specify)* or parish of *(specify)*] for a continuous period of not less than 3 years or
                  1.2.1.2     has or a member of whose household has a parent adult child brother or sister whose only or principal home is and has been for a continuous period of not less than 3 years in the [district of *(specify)* or parish of *(specify)*] and he wishes to be near that relative or
                  1.2.1.3     is and has been permanently employed in the [district of *(specify)* or parish of *(specify)*] for a continuous period of not less than 3 years
        1.2.2     where no person or insufficient persons have a connection with the parish of *(specify)* then the parish of *(specify)* shall be substituted for the parish of *(specify)* and then if no person or insufficient persons have a connection with the parish of *(specify)* then the parish of *(specify)* shall

be substituted for the parish of *(specify)* and then if no person or insufficient persons have a connection with the parish of *(specify)* then the parish of *(specify)* shall be substituted for the parish of *(specify)* and then if no person or insufficient persons have a connection with the parish of *(specify)* the district of *(specify)* shall be substituted for the parish of *(specify)*

**[3821]**

1.3     'Nomination List' means the list to be supplied by the Council pursuant to clauses 3.1.3 and 3.2.1 (as may be updated from time to time in accordance with clause 3.3.3)

1.4     'Nominee' means a person named in the Nomination List who satisfies the Local Connection and is specified by the Council as being suitable for the category of Rented Unit or Shared Ownership Unit in respect of which the RSL is in accordance with this Deed to select a person from the Nomination List to offer a Tenancy Agreement or Shared Ownership Lease

1.5     'Property' means the land at *(address)* shown edged red on the attached plan

1.6     'Rented Units' means *(number)* [houses *or* flats *or* maisonettes]

1.7     'Shared Ownership Units' means *(number)* [houses *or* flats *or* maisonettes]

1.8     'Shared Ownership Lease' means a lease substantially in the form annexed or agreed between the parties

1.9     'Subsequent Nominee' means a Nominee to be offered a Tenancy Agreement pursuant to clause 3.2.3

1.10    'Tenancy Agreement' means an assured tenancy agreement in a form prepared by the RSL and containing terms which accord with the form of tenancy agreement being used by the RSL from time to time for its general lettings

1.11    'Vacancy Notice' means a written notice given by the RSL to the Council (in a form to be agreed between the RSL and the Council within 5 weeks from the date of this Deed) the function of such notice being the notification to the Council by the RSL that the construction and fitting out of the Rented Unit or Shared Ownership Unit is completed

1.12    'Void' means a Rented Unit which is vacant otherwise than as a result of the tenant having:

　　1.12.1  moved to other accommodation either by transfer or decant provided by the RSL

　　1.12.2  moved to other accommodation under a reciprocal arrangement provided by another registered social landlord registered with the Housing Corporation under the Housing Act 1996

1.13    'Void Notice' means a written notice given by the RSL to the Council (in a form to be agreed between the RSL and the Council within 5 weeks from the date of this Deed) the function of such a notice being the notification to the Council of a Void

**[3822]**

## 2     Enabling Provisions

This Agreement is made pursuant to the Local Government Act 1972 Section 111 and all other enabling powers and the Local Government (Miscellaneous Provisions) Act 1982 Section 33

## 3     Procedure

The parties agree that the following nomination procedure shall apply to the nomination of persons in respect of the Rented Units or Shared Ownership Units

**3.1      Initial lets**

3.1.1    The RSL shall give the Council not less than 4 months' written notice of the date when the Initial Let units will be ready for occupation

3.1.2    The RSL shall serve Vacancy Notices in respect of the Rented Units or Shared Ownership Units not earlier than 2 months prior to such newly constructed and previously unoccupied Rented Units or Shared Ownership Units becoming available for occupation

3.1.3    The Council shall within 5 working days of receipt of a Vacancy Notice serve upon the RSL a list of the names of persons whom the Council considers have a Local Connection

3.1.4    The list to be served by the Council under clause 3.1.3 shall:

   3.1.4.1    specify the appropriate category of Rented Unit or Shared Ownership Unit

   3.1.4.2    indicate the priority for the housing of the persons named

3.1.5    The RSL shall have the right to let the Initial Let in respect of the Rented Units or Shared Ownership Units to persons of its own choosing in the event of the Council's failure to serve the list of names referred to in clause 3.1.3 within the period of 5 working days of receipt of the Vacancy Notice

3.1.6    The RSL shall within 10 working days of the date of receipt of the list referred to in clause 3.1.3 select a Nominee from the Nomination List taking into account the priority for housing indicated by the Council and shall use its reasonable endeavours to arrange viewing of the relevant Rented Unit or Shared Ownership Unit and offer a Tenancy Agreement or Shared Ownership Lease to such selected Nominee

3.1.7    If the selected Nominee fails to enter into a Tenancy Agreement or Shared Ownership Lease within 3 working days of receipt of the RSL's offer of a Tenancy Agreement or Shared Ownership Lease such selected Nominee shall be deemed to have rejected the RSL's offer and the RSL shall select another Nominee whereupon the procedure set out in clause 3.1.6 and this clause shall be repeated

3.1.8    In the event of the second selected Nominee failing to accept the RSL's offer of a Tenancy Agreement or Shared Ownership Lease within the time prescribed by clause 3.1.7 then the RSL shall make an offer to a third Nominee and the procedure set out in clauses 3.1.6 or 3.1.7 shall apply but in the event of such third selected Nominee failing to accept the RSL's offer of a Tenancy Agreement or Shared Ownership Lease within the prescribed time limits the RSL shall not be bound to make any further offers of accommodation to Nominees in respect of such vacancy of the Rented Unit or Shared Ownership Unit but shall be entitled to let the Rented Unit or Shared Ownership Unit to a tenant of its own choosing

3.1.9    The RSL's obligations under clauses 3.1.3–3.1.8 shall cease when all of the Rented Units or Shared Ownership Units have been offered to Nominees in accordance with clauses 3.1.6–3.1.8

                                                                              **[3823]**

**3.2      Voids**

3.2.1    Should a Rented Unit or Shared Ownership Unit become a Void after the Initial Let or the RSL has reasonable cause to believe it will become a Void then and in each case:

   3.2.1.1    the RSL shall serve a Void Notice in respect of the relevant vacant Rented Unit or Shared Ownership Unit and

   3.2.1.2    within 5 working days of receipt of the said notice the Council shall serve upon the RSL a list of the names of persons whom the Council considers to have a Local Connection and which shall contain the information referred to in clause 3.1.4

3.2.2     The RSL shall have the right to let the relevant vacant Rented Unit or Shared Ownership Unit to a person of its own choosing in the event of the Council's failure to serve the list referred to in clause 3.2.1.2 within 5 working days of receipt of the Void Notice

3.2.3     Upon receipt of the list referred to in clause 3.2.1.2 the RSL shall follow the procedure mutatis mutandis set out in clauses 3.1.6–3.1.8

3.2.4     The RSL shall not be obliged to follow the procedure set out in clauses 3.2.1–3.2.3 if it would result in the Subsequent Nominees exceeding 75% of the Rented Units or Shared Ownership Units available after the Initial Let

**[3824]**

**3.3       Provision of information and alteration of lists**

3.3.1     The RSL shall give notification to the Council of the occurrence of the following events within 5 working days of their occurrence:

    3.3.1.1     a Nominee failing to view a Rented Unit or Shared Ownership Unit within the time limit prescribed by this Deed

    3.3.1.2     a Nominee failing to accept the offer of a Tenancy Agreement or Shared Ownership Lease within the time limit prescribed by this Agreement

    3.3.1.3     a Nominee accepting an offer of a Tenancy Agreement or Shared Ownership Lease

    3.3.1.4     a person accepting an offer of a tenancy from the RSL

    3.3.1.5     the RSL rejecting a Nominee in accordance with clause 3.3.7

3.3.2     In the event of a notice being served pursuant to clause 3.3.1 then the name of such Nominee shall be removed from the Nomination List

3.3.3     Within 5 working days of the Council receiving notice served in accordance with clause 3.3.1 above save for notice under clause 3.3.1.4 the Council shall serve upon the RSL the name and address of a Nominee to add to the Nomination List such notice to include the information set out in clause 3.1.4

3.3.4     If the Council shall within the period mentioned in clause 3.3.3 notify the RSL that the Council then has no suitable Nominee the Council shall advise the RSL of a suitable replacement Nominee as soon as reasonably practicable

3.3.5     The RSL shall have the right to let a Rented Unit or Shared Ownership Unit to a person of its choosing if the Council's failure to provide a Nominee creates a Void in respect of that Rented Unit or Shared Ownership Unit

3.3.6     On 1st January 1st April 1st July and 1st October in each year the RSL shall serve the Council with details of the letting activities of the Rented Units and Shared Ownership Units in a format to be agreed between the RSL and the Council

3.3.7     The RSL shall have the right to interview and make enquiries of each Nominee and by serving written notice upon the Council to that effect to reject any Nominee if in the opinion of the RSL the grant of an assured tenancy to such Nominee would be in contravention of the RSL's registered rules or its letting criteria

3.3.8     The Council shall immediately notify the RSL in writing if any Nominee is withdrawn from the Nomination List

3.3.9     When calculating percentages for the purposes of this Deed percentages in excess of 0.5 shall be rounded up and percentages equal to or less than 0.5 shall be rounded down

3.3.10    The Council and the RSL agree that the nomination rights contained in this Deed may be varied from time to time by agreement in writing by the parties

**[3825]**

**4      Notices**

Any notice required to be served hereunder shall be sufficiently served on the parties at the address indicated above or such other address notified by one party to the other and any notice shall be deemed to have been served 2 working days after posting

**5      Transfers to other Registered Social Landlords**

The RSL shall ensure that any registered social landlord to which the Property and Rented Units and Shared Ownership Units erected thereon are transferred otherwise than by direction of the Housing Corporation under its statutory powers shall enter into a similar agreement mutatis mutandis with the Council

**6      Disputes**

Where any matters fail to be agreed between the parties or any dispute or difference occurs the question shall be referred on the application of either party for the determination of a single expert to be agreed between the parties or in default of agreement to be nominated by or on behalf of the President for the time being of the Chartered Institute of Housing on the application of either party

**7      Costs**

The RSL agrees with the Council to pay the legal costs which the Council incurs in preparing and entering into this Deed

**8      Agreements and declarations**

The parties agree:

8.1      nothing in this Deed fetters or restricts the exercise by the Council of any of its powers

8.2      the obligations contained in this Deed are covenants for the purpose of the Local Government (Miscellaneous Provisions) Act 1982 Section 33

IN WITNESS etc]

[SCHEDULE [5]
Highway Works
*(insert details)*]

[SCHEDULE [6]
Transport Facilities
*(insert details)*]

[SCHEDULE [7]
Off-Site Infrastructure Works
*(insert details)*]

[SCHEDULE [8]
Landscape Management Plan
*(insert details)*]

*(signatures (and common seals) of the parties)*
*(signatures of witnesses)*
**[3826]**

1      This model Form is a unilateral planning obligation entered into by a potential developer of land under the Town and Country Planning Act 1990 s 106 as substituted by the Planning and Compensation Act 1991 s 12(1) (46 Halsbury's Statutes (4th Edn) TOWN AND COUNTRY PLANNING). As to planning obligations generally see vol 41 TOWN AND COUNTRY PLANNING Paragraph 13 [925]. This agreement contains a variety of obligations which are illustrative only; they and their related definitions should be omitted, amended, replaced and others added as appropriate.

2      Only those with a legal interest in the land can enter into a planning obligation: see the Town and Country Planning Act 1990 s 106(1), (3) as substituted. Any existing tenant should be joined as party if any of the obligations are to be binding on him.

3      The applicant should consider whether he should seek to provide that he can carry out preliminary works such as site clearance, site fencing and security, site investigations, archaeological investigations, laying of services and possibly even creating a temporary site access without this being treated as the commencement of development. For such a clause see vol 41 TOWN AND COUNTRY PLANNING Form 29 clause 2.4.2 [1186].

4      The parties should consider carefully whether it is appropriate for the owner to enter into each individual planning obligation in the agreement; on the assumption that the owner will sell the land to the applicant following the grant of planning permission, probably under a conditional contract or option, it may be appropriate for the applicant alone to enter into those obligations which involve payment of money or execution of works after completion of the sale. Covenanting parties are entitled to require that their liability ceases after they have parted with all interest in the land: see Town and Country Planning Act 1990 s 106(4) as substituted. For such a clause see vol 41 TOWN AND COUNTRY PLANNING Form 29.1 clause 3.3 [1188.3].

5      Planning obligations are often used to provide for the transfer of interests in land in connection with planning purposes. There is normally no objection in principle to the transfer of land for socially desirable purposes such as affordable housing or public open space. The precise mechanism is not wholly clear and there are conflicting authorities on the point: see *Wimpey Homes Holdings Ltd v Secretary of State for the Environment* [1993] 2 PLR, [1993] JPL 919 and *Jelson Ltd v Derby County Council* [1999] 39 EG 149, [2000] JPL 203. The position adopted here is that planning agreements may make provision for the transfer of land as has hitherto been regarded as the orthodox approach. Where land is to be transferred provision may be made for deduction of title; for such a clause see vol 41 TOWN AND COUNTRY PLANNING Form 29.1 clause 3.9 [1188.3]. It is usual, however, for title to be deduced before the agreement is entered into.

6      See note 5 above.

7      Where money is to be paid to the council to use in a specific way the applicant should consider trying to ring fence the money or perhaps have it held in trust for the specified purpose, with provision for it to be returned if the purpose for which the money is paid is not carried out within an agreed time. Such arrangements are sometimes unacceptable to councils but it is not an unreasonable request to make.

**[3827]**

8      See note 5 above.

9      See note 7 above.

10      See note 5 above.

11      See note 5 above.

12      See note 7 above.

13      See note 7 above.

14      See note 7 above.

15      Where possible the amount of the costs should be agreed in advance and inserted in these clauses.

16      A mortgagee may require the applicant or the owner or both to covenant in its favour to observe and perform the obligations and to indemnify the mortgagee.

17      Additional matters may include the following:

     (a)    Town and Country Planning Act 1990 s 106(10) as substituted requires the council to be given a copy of the agreement; despite the fact that it is usually executed in duplicate and the council will hold the original it is prudent to obtain a receipt for it;

     (b)    A provision for the council to give written confirmation when obligations have been fully performed;

     (c)    A provision that any approval to be given by either council shall not be unreasonably withheld or delayed;

     (d)    The applicant should consider whether he should seek to protect his position in the event of expiry of the permission without the development having commenced or the grant of subsequent permissions; for such clauses see vol 41 TOWN AND COUNTRY PLANNING Form 29.1 clauses 3.5 and 3.6 [1188.3].

18      The planning obligation must identify the authority by whom it is enforceable: see the Town and Country Planning Act 1990 s 106(9)(d) as substituted.

19      As to stamp duty see Information Binder: Stamp Duties [1] (Conveyance or transfer). As to Land Registry fees see Information Binder: Property [1] (Fees in connection with property matters, Land Registry fees).

Form TP1 (for which see Form 114 [4181] post) is the Land Registry form of transfer of part of freehold or leasehold land prescribed by the Land Registration Rules 1925, SR&O 1925/1093 r 98, Sch 1 as inserted by SI 1997/3037 and substituted by SI 1999/128. This Form should be used whenever part only of any registered title is transferred, even if the transfer also includes the whole of one or more other registered titles.

The transferor's land or charge certificate must be placed on deposit (using Land Registry form DP1 as prescribed by SR&O 1925/1093 Sch 1 as inserted by SI 1997/3037 and substituted by SI 1999/128 (as to which see vol 25(1) (1999 Reissue) LAND REGISTRATION Form 3 [3076])) to meet the transferee's application to register the transfer. If the transferor's land is subject to any registered or noted charge, the consent of the chargee to the transfer should be obtained and lodged with the application to register the transfer.

Form TP1 can also be used to transfer the land if it is unregistered. In that case panel 2 will be left blank and the property description in panel 4 will need to describe the land by reference to its being part of the land described in some suitable deed in the unregistered title (eg 'Land to the south side of Acacia Avenue being part of the land comprised in a conveyance dated *(date)* and made between *(parties)'*) as well as by reference to the relevant plan referred to in the same panel. However, the application to register the land will then need to be on Form FR1 (as to which see vol 25(1) (1999 Reissue) LAND REGISTRATION Form 92 [3781]) accompanied by appropriate evidence of the transferor's title and Form DL (as to which see vol 25(1) (1999 Reissue) LAND REGISTRATION Form 93 [3786]) listing the documents lodged. Form TP1, suitably adapted, can also be used to transfer land that is a mixture of registered and unregistered land (although it will need to be lodged for registration under cover of two separate application forms: Form AP1 (as to which see vol 25(1) (1999 Reissue) LAND REGISTRATION Form 26 [3251]) dealing with the registered part and Forms FR1 and DL dealing with the unregistered part, and two fees will be payable.

Reference should be made to Form 115 [4191] post for detailed footnotes on matters common to many forms of transfer, cross-references to the commentary in vol 35 (1997 Reissue) SALE OF LAND, for the location of alternative transfer clauses in that and other volumes and for footnotes relating to sales of part.

20    See note 19 above.

[3828]

# 86

## Agreement for construction and adoption of roads under the Highways Act 1980 Section 38 with guarantor joined[1]

THIS AGREEMENT is made the ...... day of .........

BETWEEN:

(1)    *(name)* ('the Council') [of *(address)*] [acting on behalf of *(name)* County Council of *(address)*][2]

(2)    *(name)* [company number *(number)*] [of *(address)* or whose registered office is at *(address)*] ('the Developer')

(3)    *(name)* [company number *(number)*] [of *(address)* or whose registered office is at *(address)*] ('the Surety')

NOW IT IS AGREED as follows:

### 1    Definitions and interpretation

In this Agreement:

1.1    'the Appropriate Officer' means [the Highway Engineer *or (as the case may be)*] of the Council

1.2    'the Coloured Land' means the parts of the Estate shown coloured [grey brown green and blue] on the Plan being the site of the Roads

1.3    'the Estate means the land situate at *(location of development)* and shown edged red on the Plan being [the whole *or* part of] the land comprised in title number *(number)*

1.4      'the Plan' means the plan attached to this Agreement [and if numbered plans are
         annexed any reference to a numbered plan is to the attached plan or plans so
         numbered]
1.5      'the Roads' means the road or roads to be constructed on the Coloured Land
1.6      'the Works' means the works specified in the schedule to this Agreement for the
         construction and making good of the Roads and the necessary surface water
         sewers and the provision of street lighting traffic signs and road markings
1.7      words importing one gender shall be construed as importing any other gender
1.8      words importing the singular shall be construed as importing the plural and vice
         versa
1.9      words importing persons shall be construed as importing a corporate body and/
         or a partnership and vice versa
1.10     where any party comprises more than one person the obligations and liabilities
         of that party under this Agreement shall be joint and several obligations and
         liabilities of those persons
1.11     the clause headings shall not form part of this Agreement and shall not be taken
         into account in its construction or interpretation

**[3829]**

## 2      Background

[2.1     The Council is the local highway authority for highways in *(name of county)*]
2.2      The Developer is registered as proprietor of the Estate with an absolute freehold
         title
2.3      The Developer proposes to develop the Estate as a building estate and intends
         to construct the Roads and it has requested that following completion of the
         Works the Roads are dedicated as highways and desires that the Roads shall on
         completion become highways maintainable at the public expense
[2.4     The *(name)* County Council has entered into arrangements under the Local
         Government Act 1972 Section 101[3] with the Council for the discharge of
         certain highway functions including the completion of agreements under the
         Highways Act 1980 Section 38[4]]
2.5      This Agreement is made in pursuance and under the authority of the Highways
         Act 1980 Section 38 and all other enabling powers

**[3830]**

## 3      Developer's covenants

The Developer for itself and its successors in the title covenants with the Council that:
3.1      **Easement for Highway Drainage:**  it will on demand and without cost to
         the Council grant to the Council an easement over or through any land (which
         does not form part of the highway to be adopted) through which any part of
         the surface water drainage system of the highway to be adopted under this
         Agreement passes and into which the system discharges and that any transfer of
         land the subject of such easement or which may become the subject of such
         easement shall be expressed to be subject to that easement
3.2      **Location of Roads:**  the position of any of the Roads constructed in
         pursuance of this Agreement shall unless otherwise agreed be in accordance
         with the Plan and in particular the carriageways footways verges and road
         drainage shall be constructed in the positions shown by [grey brown green and
         blue] colouring respectively on the Plan
3.3      **Works to be carried out by the Developer:** the Works shall be carried out
         by and at the expense of the Developer to the reasonable satisfaction of the
         Appropriate Officer in accordance with the schedule to this Agreement or as
         otherwise directed by the Appropriate Officer

3.4     **Inspection by Council:**  during the progress of the Works the Appropriate
        Officer and any other officer of the Council will be given free access to every
        part of the Estate for the purpose of inspecting the Works and all materials used
        or intended for use in them and that the Developer will give such notice as may
        be required to the Appropriate Officer regarding periodic inspection of the
        Works

3.5     **Time limit for completion:**  it will construct and complete the Works so that
        there shall be a direct connection to an existing public highway along the Roads
        completed in accordance with this Agreement from any building erected on the
        Estate within *(number)* months after that building shall have been occupied
        PROVIDED that the period of *(number)* months may be extended by the
        Council in cases where in the opinion of the Appropriate Officer undue
        damage might be caused to any street by the continuing building operations of
        the Developer PROVIDED that in any event the whole of the Roads and all
        works incidental to them shall be fully completed to the entire satisfaction of
        the Appropriate Officer in all respects within *(number)* years of the date of this
        Agreement

3.6     **Works in good order and repair:**  until the Roads have become highways
        maintainable at the public expense it will keep the whole of the Works in good
        order and repair and will reinstate and make good any defect or damage which
        may appear or arise and will upon the requirement of the Appropriate Officer
        make good and reconstruct any portion of the Works which the Appropriate
        Officer reasonably considers to be defective

3.7     **Indemnity:**  it will indemnify the Council against all actions claims charges
        demands proceedings costs expenses and liabilities arising directly or
        indirectly out of the failure by the Developer to perform or observe any of
        the covenants contained in this Agreement and in particular it will indemnify
        and keep indemnified the Council against all liabilities claims demands and
        expenses arising within a period of *(number)* years from the adoption of the
        Coloured Land under the Land Compensation Act 1973 Parts I and II and
        regulations made under it or the equivalent statutory provisions for the time
        being in force or arising from the construction adoption or lighting of the
        Roads

3.8     **Council's Costs:**  it will on or before the execution of this Agreement pay to
        the Council the sum of £... towards the cost of the supervision of the Works
        by the Council and its costs in connection with the completion of this
        Agreement

3.9     **Arrangements with other authorities:**  it will make arrangements with the
        appropriate authority or statutory undertaker for the future maintenance of
        lighting installations which do not come within the Highways Act 1980
        Section 270 or of any foul or surface water sewer laid in or under the Coloured
        Land and will indemnify the Council in respect of the cost of any works or
        measures considered necessary by any such authority or statutory undertaker in
        consequence of any such maintenance

                                                                              **[3831]**

## 4     Default

In default of the Developer executing or completing the Works or otherwise carrying
out its obligations under this Agreement the Council shall have the right (after 28 days
notice in writing to the Developer and the Surety of its intention to do so) to perform
these obligations and to charge the expenses of doing so to the Developer

## 5    Obligations of the Surety

Without prejudice to the right of the Council to exercise any of its rights and powers under the Highways Act 1980 or any other statutory provision the Surety shall in the event of non-observance or breach of any of the terms of the covenants of the Developer contained in this Agreement or if a receiving order in bankruptcy is made in respect of the Developer's estate or if the Developer is being wound up pay to the Council within 28 days of receiving notice in writing from the Appropriate Officer such sum of money as the Appropriate Officer may certify to be necessary to perform the obligations of the Developer under this Agreement PROVIDED that:

5.1      the obligation of the Surety under this Agreement shall not commence until the Developer begins to erect the first dwelling house on the Estate and

5.2      the sum payable by the Surety shall not exceed £...

                                                                                          **[3832]**

## 6    Council's covenants

The Council for itself and its successors in title covenants with the Developer and with the Surety that:

6.1      **Adoption of Highways and Surface Water Sewers:**  when:

      6.1.1      the Works have been completed in accordance with this Agreement to the reasonable satisfaction of the Appropriate Officer and

      6.1.2      have been maintained by the Developer for a period of **[12]** months from the date of the Appropriate Officer certifying such completion and

      6.1.3      all remedial works reasonably required by the Appropriate Officer have been completed and

      6.1.4      if all other covenants in this Agreement have been performed and observed

the Council shall take all necessary steps to secure that the Coloured Land together with any surface water sewers carrying highway drainage only which pass outside the Coloured Land shall become highways maintainable at the public expense PROVIDED that nothing in this Agreement shall impose on the Council any liability for the maintenance of any lighting installations which do not come within the Highways Act 1980 Section 270 or of any foul or surface water sewer laid in or under the Coloured Land (other than surface water sewers carrying highway drainage only) AND FURTHER PROVIDED THAT the Council may at its discretion before the Works as a whole shall have been completed take the necessary steps referred to above in respect of any part of the Works which have been completed and maintained as above

6.2      **Mitigation of Loss:**  it will use its best endeavours in consultation with the Surety to mitigate any loss or damage sustained by reason of any default by the Developer by taking such reasonable steps as the Council shall think fit

6.3      **Use of sums received from the Surety:**  the Council shall apply all sums received from the Surety solely to the completion of the Works and shall deduct such sums from any demands or charges which may be made by the Council on owners of properties abutting the Coloured Land in respect of any street works carried out under the Highways Act 1980 or any other statutory provision

6.4      **Refund to the Surety:**  if the sum paid by the Surety exceeds the final cost of the Works (including the Council's establishment and supervision charges) before the Coloured Land becomes a highway maintainable at the public expense such surplus money shall be refunded to the Surety

## 7 Arbitration

In the event of any dispute arising out of this Agreement the same shall be referred to a sole arbitrator to be agreed between the parties or failing agreement to be appointed by the President for the time being of the Institution of Civil Engineers in accordance with and subject to the Arbitration Act 1996

SCHEDULE
The Works
*(insert details)*

IN WITNESS etc

*(signatures (and common seals) of all parties)*
**[3833]**

1 No stamp duty. See Information Binder: Stamp Duties [1] (Agreement).
  As to section 38 agreements generally see Form 93 appendix 1 [3971] post. These agreements and bonds vary widely and this Form is an example only. It is usual for the agreement to be executed in duplicate, the surety receiving a certified copy.
2 If the County Council are acting in their capacity as local highway authority then the contents of the second set of square brackets can be deleted. Names of the two authorities are only necessary where another authority is acting as agent for the local highway authority under the Local Government Act 1972 s 101 as amended (25 Halsbury's Statutes (4th Edn) LOCAL GOVERNMENT).
3 Ie the Local Government Act 1972 s 101 as amended.
4 Ie the Highways Act 1980 s 38 as amended by the Local Government Act 1985 s 102, Sch 17 and by the New Roads and Street Works Act 1991 s 23 (20 Halsbury's Statutes (4th Edn) HIGHWAYS, STREETS AND BRIDGES). Clause 2 will need to contain either recital (1) or (4) depending on whether the highway authority is acting itself or another authority is acting as its agent.

**[3834]–[3850]**

# 87

**Agreement for the construction and adoption of roads and works on an existing highway under the Highways Act 1980 Sections 38 and 278 and the Local Government Act 1972 Section 111 adapted for use with an agreement under the Town and Country Planning Act 1990 Section 106 with mortgagee joined[1]**

THIS AGREEMENT is made the …… day of ………

BETWEEN:

(1) *(name)* of *(address)* ('the Council')
(2) *(name)* [company number *(number)*] [of *(address)* or whose registered office is at *(address)*] ('the Developer')
(3) *(name)* [company number *(number)*] [of *(address)* or whose registered office is at *(address)*] ('the Mortgagee')

**[3851]**

NOW IT IS AGREED as follows:

## 1 Definitions and interpretation

In this Agreement:
1.1 'the Appropriate Officer' means the highway engineer or other appropriate officer for the time being of the Council
[1.2 'the County Council' means the council for the county of *(name)*[2]]

1.3 'the Existing Roads' means the existing highways maintainable at public expense shown on the Plan and coloured [blue]

1.4 'the Final Certificate' means the certificate issued under clause 5.3 of this Agreement

1.5 'the First Specification' means the specification deposited with the Council in respect of the Section 38 Works and set out in the first schedule to this Agreement

1.6 'the Interim Certificate' means the certificate to be issued under clause 5.1 of this Agreement

1.7 'the Land' means the land situate at *(description of land)* shown [edged red] on the Plan being [the whole *or* part of] the land comprised in title number *(number)*

1.8 'the Maintenance Period' means the period of [12] months from the date of the Interim Certificate

1.9 'the Plan' means the plan annexed to this Agreement which has been approved by the Council [and if numbered plans are annexed any reference to a numbered plan is to the annexed plan or plans so numbered]

1.10 'the Planning Obligations' means the obligations set out in clauses 3.2 3.4 and 5.2

1.11 'the Roads' means the roads to be constructed on the Land by the Developer in connection with the Section 38 Works including all carriageways footways footpaths road islands and road verges shown on the Plan and coloured [brown] in the case of carriageways [grey] in the case of footways footpaths and road islands and [green] in the case of verges

1.13 'the Second Specification' means the specification in respect of the Section 111/278 Works and set out in the second schedule to this Agreement and includes any plan elevation or section of the Section 111/278 Works

1.14 'the Section 111/278 Works' means the improvements alterations and additions to the Existing Roads

1.15 'the Section 38 Works' means the construction of the Roads landscape features and the surface water drains and sewers shown by [blue] lines on the Plan

1.16 'the Street Lighting' means the street lighting facilities to be erected on the Land including the street lights the position of which is indicated on the Plan by [red circles] and all ancillary apparatus

1.17 words importing one gender shall be construed as importing any other gender

1.18 words importing the singular shall be construed as importing the plural and vice versa

1.19 words importing persons shall be construed as importing a corporate body and/or a partnership and vice versa

1.20 where any party comprises more than one person the obligations and liabilities of that party under this Agreement shall be joint and several obligations and liabilities of those persons

1.21 the clause headings shall not form part of this Agreement and shall not be taken into account in its construction or interpretation

[3852]

## 2 Background

2.1 The [County] Council is:

    2.1.1 the highway authority for the county of *(name)* [and the Council is the agent of the County Council for the purposes inter alia of the Highways Act 1980 Section 38 under an agreement dated *(date)* made between (1) the Council and (2) the County Council pursuant to the Local Government Act 1972 Section 101[3]] and

2.1.2       the Local Planning Authority (and for the purposes of Town and Country Planning Act 1990 Section 106[4]) by whom the Planning Obligations are enforceable

2.2     The Developer is registered as proprietor of the Land with an absolute freehold title under title number *(number)*

2.3     The Developer intends to carry out the Section 38 Works and the Section 111/ 278 Works on the Land in accordance with the Plan the First Specification and the Second Specification

2.4     The Developer desires that upon completion the Roads should become highways maintainable at the public expense

2.5     The Mortgagee is proprietor of the charge on the Land dated *(date)* registered on *(date)*

2.6     The Developer also wishes to carry out work on the Existing Roads

2.7     The Planning Obligations are planning obligations for the purposes of the Town and Country Planning Act 1990 Section 106

2.8     The covenants contained in clauses 3.2 3.4 and 5.2 are to bind the Developer as the owner of the site of the Roads and its successors in title to that land

2.9     This Agreement is entered into pursuant to the Highways Act 1980 Sections 38 and 278[5] the Local Government Act 1972 Section 111 and the Town and Country Planning Act 1990 Section 106

2.10    The Council has agreed with the Developer that subject to payment of the estimated cost of inspection of the Section 38 Works and their maintenance in a proper manner on the terms and conditions of this Agreement the Council will do and procure all acts and things necessary for the taking over and adoption of the Roads as highways maintainable at the public expense

**[3853]**

## 3     The Section 38 Works: construction of the Roads

### 3.1     Junctions

Where the Roads abut or join an existing highway the bellmouth joining the Roads to that highway shall be constructed at the expense of the Developer and to the satisfaction of the  Appropriate Officer

### 3.2     Construction of the Section 38 Works

3.2.1   The Developer shall at his own expense construct the Section 38 Works or cause the Section 38 Works to be constructed in accordance with the Plan and the First Specification in all respects to the satisfaction of the Appropriate Officer provided that any amendment to the Plan or the First Specification shall be previously approved in writing by the Council and the work comprised in the amendment shall not be commenced until notification in writing of approval has been received by the Developer

3.2.2   The Developer shall complete the Section 38 Works or any part of them:

    3.2.2.1     as soon as is practicable and in any case not later than *(number)* months after the completion of the buildings adjoining the Roads or

    3.2.2.2     in the case of any particular road or part of a road after the completion of so many of those buildings as would in the opinion of the Appropriate Officer reasonably justify the completion of the Section 38 Works or a portion of them or as the case may be

3.2.3   The Developer shall pay to the Council the cost of installation and erection of the Street Lighting by the Council and the Developer shall give to the Appropriate Officer and the Council's workmen free access for the purpose of installing erecting and afterwards maintaining the Street Lighting

### 3.3     Mortgagee's Consent
The Mortgagee hereby consents to the Developer entering into this Agreement and joins in the execution of this Agreement and acknowledges that this Agreement binds the Land

### 3.4     Restriction on occupation of houses
Prior to occupation of any house or other dwelling that fronts joins or abuts the Roads the Developer shall complete:
3.4.1     all road and other drainage contained within the Roads
3.4.2     all kerb foundations and those kerbs including lowering at vehicle crossings and pram ramps
3.4.3     carriageway sub-base road base and any supporting structures
3.4.4     carriageway base course surfacing where appropriate
3.4.5     demarcation of site lines and clearance of visibility splays
3.4.6     the columns for lighting erected in accordance with the specification
and make the carriageway to at least base course stage outside each house before that house shall be occupied

[3854]

### 4     The Section 111/278 Works: on the Existing Highway

### 4.1     Developer's Liability
The Developer shall carry out the Section 111/278 Works at its own expense but as agent for the Council in accordance with [the Plan and] the Second Specification and to the satisfaction of the Appropriate Officer within *(months)* of the date of this Agreement

### 4.2     Statutory Undertakers
The Developer shall pay all charges that may be levied on the Council or the Developer by any of the statutory undertakers in respect of the removal protection or alteration of any of their apparatus necessitated by the Section 111/278 Works

### 5     Provisions applying to both the Section 38 Works and the Section 111/278 Works

### 5.1     Interim Certificate
After the completion of the Section 38 Works and the Section 111/278 Works in accordance with this Agreement the Appropriate Officer shall issue to the Developer an Interim Certificate stating that those works have been carried out to his satisfaction and for the Maintenance Period the Developer shall execute all such works of repair reconstruction or rectification of any and all defects and imperfections and of any and all other faults of whatsoever nature that may be required of it in writing by the Appropriate Officer

### 5.2     Parties' obligations during the Maintenance Period
During the Maintenance Period:
5.2.1     the Developer shall at its own expense maintain the Section 38 Works and the Section 111/278 Works to enable safe use by vehicles and pedestrians to the satisfaction of the Appropriate Officer
5.2.2     the Council shall at its own expense undertake routine maintenance of and be responsible for payment for energy for all street lights and illuminated traffic signs

### 5.3     Final Certificate
If at the expiration of the Maintenance Period the Appropriate Officer is satisfied that the Section 38 Works and the Section 111/278 Works have been duly and properly

maintained and are not then subject to any defects and all other obligations under this Agreement have been performed he shall issue a certificate stating that the Section 38 Works are suitable for adoption and shall procure the adoption of the Roads by the [County] Council as highways maintainable at the public expense

**[3855]**

### 5.4      Issue of certificates for part

Notwithstanding the provisions of this Agreement the  Appropriate Officer may in his absolute discretion give an Interim Certificate and a Final Certificate in respect of such part or parts only of the Section 38 Works and the Section 111/278 Works as shall from time to time be constructed and maintained in accordance with this Agreement and clauses 5.1 and 5.3 shall apply accordingly to such part or parts of the Existing Roads or the Roads as shall from time to time be the subject of such certificates

### 5.5      Notice and access to be given to Surveyor

The Developer shall:

5.5.1      before commencing the Section 38 Works or the Section 111/278 Works give notice in writing to the Appropriate Officer of its intention to do so

5.5.2      during the progress of the Section 38 Works or the Section 111/278 Works and until the issue of the Final Certificate give to the Appropriate Officer and any person or persons duly authorised by him free access to any part of the Section 38 Works or the Section 111/278 Works

5.5.3      permit him or them to inspect the Section 38 Works or the Section 111/278 Works and all or any materials used or intended to be used in the Section 38 Works or the Section 111/278 Works

5.5.4      give effect to any requirements made or instructions given by the Appropriate Officer or any person duly authorised by him including the removal of specimens for analysis or other examination for securing that [the Section 38 Works shall conform to the Plan and First Specification and/or the Section 111/278 Works shall conform to the Plan and the Second Specification] and be executed to the satisfaction of the Appropriate Officer

### 5.6      No erection of overhead services

The Developer shall not at any time give consent to any service undertaking or supplier whether statutory or otherwise for the erection of overhead services in the Existing Roads or the Roads without the written consent of the Appropriate Officer being first obtained and the location and the disposition of underground services shall follow best practice

**[3856]**

### 5.7      Default provisions

If the Developer:

5.7.1      fails to perform or observe any of the conditions covenants agreements or obligations on the part of the Developer contained in this Agreement or described or referred to on the Plan or the First Specification or the Second Specification or

5.7.2      fails to proceed with the Section 38 Works and the Section 111/278 Works in respect of the Existing Roads or the Roads or any of them to the satisfaction of the Appropriate Officer (whose decision shall be conclusive) or

5.7.3      fails to complete the Section 38 Works and the Section 111/278 Works within the time limits set out in this Agreement or

5.7.4      being a company is wound up either voluntarily (except for the purpose of reconstruction or amalgamation) or compulsorily or being an individual becomes bankrupt or in either case enters into composition with its or his creditors or

5.7.5      suffers any distress or execution to be levied against its or his goods or

5.7.6    is the subject of the appointment of a receiver

the Council shall (after 28 days' notice in writing to the Developer of its intention so to do) have the right to exercise any powers whatsoever enabling it to carry out or cause to be carried out [the Section 38 Works or any part of them in respect of the Roads or any part of them and/*or* the Section 111/278 Works or any part of them in respect of the Existing Roads or any part of them] and to remedy any defect in them before their adoption as highways maintainable at the public expense and in addition shall have the right (without prejudice to any other rights claims and remedies of the Council arising out of matters listed in this clause or otherwise under this Agreement) by such written notice to determine this Agreement

**5.8    Notice of default in respect of part**

Where the Council serves a notice under clause 5.7 of this Agreement in respect of any of the Existing Roads or the Roads or part of them the service of the notice shall not in any way relieve the Developer from the performance and observance of the conditions covenants agreements or obligations on the part of the Developer contained in this Agreement in respect of the other Existing Roads or Roads or part of them included in this Agreement whether or not specified in the notice and so far as such other road or roads or parts of them are concerned the terms of this Agreement shall remain in full force and effect

**[3857]**

**5.9    Recovery of costs**

If the Council serves a notice under clause 5.7 of this Agreement and carries out the Section 38 Works and the Section 111/278 Works or any part of them or causes them to be carried out the Council shall be entitled to recover the cost of doing so from the Developer

**5.10    Limited action by Council**

5.10.1    If at any time after work has been done in or for the purpose of erecting any building adjoining the Roads or part of them and before the Developer has completed the Section 38 Works in respect of the Roads or parts of them the Council is of the opinion that the circumstances warrant action on its part but do not at that time warrant action under clause 5.7 the Council may by notice require the Developer to pay to the Council on demand such sum as the Council thinks fit not exceeding the estimated cost of completion of the parts of the Roads opposite the frontage of any such building and of any completed building (including any buildings built before the date of this Agreement) and of any parts intervening between any of those parts and between them and the nearest highway maintainable at the public expense PROVIDED that if the Council takes action under this clause such action shall not in any way prejudice the Council from taking further action under clause 5.7 of this Agreement should any further work subsequently be done in or for the purpose of erecting any building adjoining the Roads

5.10.2    The Highways Act 1980 Section 203(1) shall apply for the interpretation of this clause as it applies for the interpretation of the advance payments code of that Act[6]

**5.11    Indemnity**

The Developer on behalf of itself and its successors in title assigns undertakes and agrees with the Council that in the event of any claim for compensation damages charges costs or expenses arising in connection with or incidental to the carrying out of the Section 38 Works or the Section 111/278 Works (including claims relating to the infringement or destruction of any right easement or privilege and claims under Parts I and II of the Land Compensation Act 1973) or anything done or omitted to be done prior to the issue of the Final Certificate it will hold the Council harmless and safely indemnified from the claim

### 5.12    Dedication of land
Upon the issue of the Final Certificate or certificates as provided for in this Agreement the Developer shall give up and dedicate to the public the Land on which the Section 38 Works are constructed or such part of the Land as is covered by the Final Certificate to the intent that the Land shall become a public highway up to and including the boundary of the Land with other land as indicated on the Plan

[3858]

### 5.13    Developer may be called upon to transfer land[7]
If and when called upon by the Council to do so within 21 years from the date of this Agreement the Developer shall prove its title to the Land dedicated to the public and shall upon payment of 1p transfer with full title guarantee to the Council or its nominee the freehold estate in the Land

### 5.14    Bond
The Developer shall within [14] days of the execution of this Agreement and as a guarantee for the due performance of the terms and conditions contained in it procure a bond by *(surety)* whose registered office is at *(address)* in favour of the Council in the sum of £... and such bond will be terminated when a Final Certificate has been issued in respect of all the Section 38 Works and the Section 111/278 Works or at such earlier stage as to the whole bond or part of it as the Appropriate Officer may in his absolute discretion agree

### 5.15    Further bond
At any time after [12] months from the date of this Agreement the Developer shall if required by written notice served by the Council to do so procure a further bond by the *(surety)* in favour of the Council in such sum as the Appropriate Officer shall determine to guarantee further the terms and conditions contained in this Agreement which further bond shall be terminated in accordance with clause 5.15 PROVIDED that if within [14] days of service of any notice under this clause the Developer disputes the reasonableness of the sum specified the Developer shall give notice to that effect to the Council and the dispute or difference shall be referred to the determination of a single arbitrator to be agreed upon by the parties or failing agreement by a person nominated by the President of the Institution of Civil Engineers in the manner provided by the Arbitration Act 1996 or any statutory modification or re-enactment of it for the time being in force

### 5.16    Adoption not to include drains
It is agreed that the adoption of the Roads as highways maintainable at the public expense shall not include the adoption as part of such highways of the drains or sewers to be constructed by the Developer but subject to this exception the adoption shall include the surface water drains gullies and connections shown by blue lines on the Plan

[3859]

### 5.17    Service of notices
5.17.1    Any notice required to be given to the Developer under this Agreement shall be deemed to have been properly served if it is sent by the Council by pre-paid recorded delivery post to the Developer at the addresses given in this Agreement
5.17.2    Any notice required to be given by the Developer to the Council (which expression shall include any reference to the Appropriate Officer) shall be deemed to be properly served if sent by pre-paid recorded delivery post to the [Chief Executive] of the Council at the address given in this Agreement

**5.18    Arbitration**

In the event of any dispute arising out of the Section 38 Works or the Section 111/278 Works under this Agreement the same shall be referred to a sole arbitrator to be agreed between the parties or failing agreement to be appointed by the President for the time being of the Institution of Civil Engineers in accordance with and subject to the Arbitration Act 1996

FIRST SCHEDULE
Specification for the Section 38 Works
*(insert details)*

SECOND SCHEDULE
Specification for the Section 111/278 Works
*(insert details)*

The Section 278/111 Works shall be carried out in accordance with the 'Specification for Highway Works' (1991) published by the Department of Transport and any amendment or replacement thereof for the time being in force[8]

IN WITNESS etc

*(signatures (and common seals) of all parties)*
**[3860]**

1     No stamp duty. See Information Binder: Stamp Duties [1] (Agreement).
        As to these agreements generally see Form 93 appendix 1 [3971] post. These agreements and bonds vary widely and this Form is an example only. As to planning agreements generally see vol 41 TOWN AND COUNTRY PLANNING Paragraph 13 [925].

2     This definition is not necessary where the local highway authority is acting on its own behalf; clause 1.2 should be left in where agency arrangements are in place between the highway authority and 'the Council' under the Local Government Act 1972 s 101 (25 Halsbury's Statutes (4th Edn) LOCAL GOVERNMENT) for discharge of highway functions as recited in clause 2.1.1.

3     Ie the Local Government Act 1972 s 101 as amended.

4     Ie the Town and Country Planning Act 1990 s 106 as amended by the Planning and Compensation Act 1991 s 12 (46 Halsbury's Statutes (4th Edn) TOWN AND COUNTRY PLANNING).

5     Ie the Highways Act 1980 ss 38 (as amended by the Local Government Act 1985 s 102, Sch 17 and by the New Roads and Street Works Act 1991 s 23) and 278 (as substituted by the New Roads and Street Works Act 1991 s 23) (20 Halsbury's Statutes (4th Edn) HIGHWAYS, STREETS AND BRIDGES).

6     As to the advance payments code see the Highways Act 1980 s 219.

7     This clause contains an option which may be protected, where the land is registered, by a notice or caution and, where the land is unregistered, as a class C(iv) land charge. As to options generally see vol 38(1) (2000 Reissue) SALE OF LAND Paragraph 241 [611] et seq.

8     There may also be specifications issued by the local highway authority with regard to section 38 works, the provisions of which could be incorporated into the first schedule.

**[3861]**

# 88

**Application by owner to sewerage undertaker for agreement for adoption of sewers to be constructed[1]**

WATER INDUSTRY ACT 1991 SECTION 104(2)

To: *(sewerage undertaker)* of *(address)*

1     [I *or* We] *(name)* of *(address)* propose to construct [a sewer *or* sewers] on land situated at *(specify)* shown edged [green] on the attached plan which land is owned by [me *or* us] and is to be developed for use as *(give details)*

2         Acting under the Water Industry Act 1991 Section 104(2) **[I** *or* **we]** make application requesting you to make an agreement with **[me** *or* **us]** in accordance with the provisions contained in the Water Industry Act 1991 Section 104(1)

3         In support of this application **[I** *or* **we]** enclose the documents set out below[2] and agree to supply any further information which you may reasonably require[3]:

    3.1      Site plan number *(specify)*

    3.2      Drawing number *(specify)* showing the proposed route of the [sewer *or* sewers]: foul water and surface water sewers as the case may be are identified by [red] and [blue] lines respectively

    3.3      Drawing number *(specify)* showing details of all buildings connected to the [sewer *or* sewers]

    3.4      Sectional drawing number *(specify)* of [sewer *or* sewers]

    [3.5     *(list any other relevant documents enclosed)*]

Dated: *(date)*

*(signature of owner)*
**[3862]**

1   A sewerage undertaker may at the application of a person constructing or proposing to construct a sewer or a sewage disposal works agree that if the sewer or works is or are constructed in accordance with the terms of the agreement the undertaker will declare the sewer or works to be vested in the undertaker at some specified future date or on the happening of some future event: see the Water Industry Act 1991 s 104(1), (2) (49 Halsbury's Statutes (4th Edn) WATER). This Form is such an application.

    An applicant has a right of appeal to the Secretary of State for the Environment, Transport and the Regions where the sewage undertaker has:
(i)   refused the application
(ii)  offered to grant the application in terms to which the applicant objects or
(iii) has failed before the end of two months from the making of the application either to refuse the application or to give notice to the applicant of the terms on which it is prepared to grant the application (Water Industry Act 1991 s 105(2) as amended by the Competition and Service (Utilities) Act 1992 s 35(1), (7)).
2   An application must be accompanied and supplemented by all such information as the undertaker may reasonably require: see the Water Industry Act 1991 s 104(3).
3   Where an applicant fails to supply sufficient information the undertaker may be entitled to delay its response to the application: see further the Water Industry Act 1991 s 104(4).

**[3863]**

# 89

**Agreement for construction and adoption of sewers by sewerage undertaker under the Water Industry Act 1991 Section 104 with guarantor joined[1]**

THIS AGREEMENT is made the ...... day of .........

BETWEEN:

(1)    *(developer)* [company number *(number)*] [of *(address) or* whose registered office is at *(address)*] ('the Developer')

[(2)   *(surety)* [company number *(number)*] [of *(address) or* whose registered office is at *(address)*] ('the Surety')] and

(3)    *(sewerage undertaker)* company number *(number)* whose registered office is at *(address)* ('the Undertaker')

**[3864]**

IT IS AGREED as follows:

**1        Definitions and interpretation**

In this Agreement:

1.1        'the Act' means the Water Industry Act 1991

1.2        'the Defects Correction Period' means the period defined in clause 12

1.3        'the Drawings' means all plans drawings sections and other design or working documents as listed in the Schedule and attached to this agreement

1.4        'the Engineer' means such officer as may be designated by the Undertaker

1.5        'the Final Certificate' means the certificate defined in clause 16

1.6        'the Land' means land at *(specify)* shown edged [green] on the Plan

1.7        'the Plan' means the attached plan number *(specify)*

1.8        'the Provisional Certificate' means the certificate defined in clause 11

1.9        'the Sewers' includes not only the sewer pipes but also manholes ventilating shafts pumps and other accessories and pumping stations

1.10        'the Specification' means the guidance notes on design and construction of sewers and pumping stations as are issued from time to time by the Undertaker

1.11        'the Works' means the construction of the Sewers indicated by [red] lines as to foul sewers and [blue] lines as to surface water sewers on the Drawings and shall include any amended extra or substituted works permitted in accordance with clause 4

1.12        words importing one gender shall be construed as importing any other gender

1.13        words importing the singular shall be construed as importing the plural and vice versa

1.14        words importing persons shall be construed as importing a corporate body and/or a partnership and vice versa

1.15        where any party comprises more than one person the obligations and liabilities of that party under this agreement shall be joint and several obligations and liabilities of those persons

1.16        the clause headings shall not form part of this agreement and shall not be taken into account in its construction or interpretation

**[3865]**

**2        Background**

2.1        The Developer is registered as proprietor of the Land with an absolute freehold title under title number *(number)*

2.2        The Developer proposes to construct the Sewers in connection with the development of the Land and has agreed to carry out such construction on the terms set out in this Agreement

2.3        The Developer desires that upon completion the Sewers shall become public sewers vested in the Undertaker

[2.4        The Surety has agreed at the request of the Developer to be a party to this Agreement]

2.5        This Agreement is made pursuant to Section 104(1) of the Act

**3        Construction of Works**

The Developer shall construct the Works at its own expense and complete the Works in accordance with the Drawings and the Specification (as may be varied in accordance with clause 4) and any statutory provisions for the time being relating to new sewers and to the reasonable satisfaction of the Engineer in the positions and to the extent shown on the Drawings

**[3866]**

**4 Minor variations**

Without prejudice to clause 3 the Engineer may at the request of the Developer give permission (which permission shall not be unreasonably withheld) to the Developer to construct the Works or any part of them otherwise than in strict conformity with the Drawings and the Specification subject to the following:

4.1 the request by the Developer shall be made in writing (accompanied by such drawings as the Engineer may require) and the permission of the Engineer (if given) shall be in writing

4.2 the Developer shall not allow any variation from the Drawings and the Specification without such written permission having first been obtained

4.3 nothing contained in this clause shall permit or authorise any breach of the Specification

4.4 the granting of any permission by the Engineer under this clause shall not in any way prejudice any rights of the Undertaker against the Developer or the Surety in respect of any breach or non-observance of any part of this Agreement and the duties and obligations of the Surety shall apply in respect of the Works as varied as they apply to the Works as shown on the Drawings

4.5 the Developer shall pay on demand the Engineer's reasonable administrative costs incurred in connection with the granting of any permission given by virtue of this clause

**5 Notification of intended commencement**

The Developer shall:

5.1 give to the Engineer in writing *(specify)* months' notice of the date on which it proposes to commence the Works or any part of them and

5.2 shall at the same time submit to the Engineer for inspection such additional plans drawings and other design or working documents not previously submitted to him and which relate to the carrying out of the Works as the Engineer may require and

5.3 notwithstanding the notice previously given give the Engineer 48 hours' notice in writing of its intention to start the Works or any part of them

**[3867]**

**6 Period of construction**

The Developer shall:

6.1 construct and complete the Works within a period of *(specify)* years from the date of this Agreement (unless the Engineer shall in writing agree to an extension of that period) and in any event

6.2 ensure that before any building or property draining into any part of the Works is brought into occupation that part of the Works necessary to drain that building or property including all outfalls and all connections to existing public sewers shall be completed and in working order

**7 Easements**

The Developer shall at its own expense prior ro the commencement of the Works obtain:

7.1 easements from third parties having interests in land through which the Sewers are to pass for the Developer and the Undertaker its servants and agents to enter upon such land after the vesting of the Sewers in the Undertaker for the purpose of inspecting cleaning repairing maintaining reconstructing or renewing the same the form of such easements to be approved by the Undertaker

7.2    easements and consents in favour of the Developer and the Undertaker its
       servants and agents for the Works and the passage and running of soil and water
       through them

**[3868]**

## 8    Developer to obtain consents

It is expressly agreed that any consents to be obtained from any statutory or other body
or from any owner or occupier of other land or the owner or possessor of any other rights
(whether relating to land or not) shall be obtained with or without request by the
Undertaker and at the cost of and by and on the responsibility of the Developer

## 9    Building-over

Until such time as the Works shall have become vested in the Undertaker in accordance
with clause 16 the Developer shall ensure that:

9.1    no building or structure is erected over any part of the Works or on or over land
       within *(specify)* metres measured horizontally from the centre line of any Sewer
       without the written consent of the Undertaker
9.2    no pedestrian or vehicular access to the Works is obstructed and
9.3    in any transfer conveyance lease or other disposition of the Land or any part of
       it appropriate covenants are included in that respect binding upon the Land

but this clause shall not prohibit the erection of plot boundary walls or fences if they are
shown on the Drawings (or agreed in writing by the Engineer as a minor variation of the
Works) to lie across the Works or any part of them (manholes or ventilating shafts excepted)

## 10    Plans of Works as constructed

The Developer shall prior to the Works being vested in the Undertaker in accordance
with clause 16 supply to the Engineer 2 full sets of plans at a scale of *(specify)* and of
sections showing at the scales used for those sections which form part of the Drawings
the position level and type of construction of the Works as constructed

**[3869]**

## 11    Provisional Certificate

11.1    When the Developer is of opinion that the Works or any substantial part of them
        have been completed it shall serve a written notice upon the Engineer to that effect
11.2    After receiving such notice the Engineer shall satisfy himself as to whether or
        not the Works have been completed and if he is so satisfied shall issue a certificate
        on behalf of the Undertaker to that effect ('the Provisional Certificate') in
        respect of the whole or such substantial part as he considers appropriate
11.3    For the purposes of this clause the Works shall be deemed to be completed when:
        11.3.1    they shall have been substantially constructed in accordance with the
                  preceding clauses of this agreement and
        11.3.2    any premises intended to be served by those parts of the Works
                  which shall be sewers have been occupied and
        11.3.3    all necessary connections or other things have been made or done
                  whereby those premises may be effectually drained into an existing
                  public sewer

## 12    Defects Correction Period

12.1    If during the Defects Correction Period (being the period of 12 months after
        the date of the issue of the Provisional Certificate) or until the Works shall
        become vested in the Undertaker (whichever shall be the longer) any defect

damage or blockage shall appear arise or occur in the Works the Developer shall at its own expense and within 3 months after such defect damage or blockage has appeared arisen or occurred (or immediately if so required in writing by the Engineer) make the same good to the reasonable satisfaction of the Engineer and

12.2 Without prejudice to clause 12.1 the Developer shall during the period prior to the Works becoming vested in the Undertaker in accordance with clause 16 maintain the Works to the satisfaction of the Engineer

**[3870]**

## 13 Access to the Works

The Developer shall allow and arrange for the Engineer to have access to the Works and the Land at all reasonable times for the purposes of ensuring compliance with this agreement

## 14 Inspections

14.1 At any time before the Works shall have become vested in the Undertaker in accordance with clause 16 the Developer shall on being so requested in writing by the Engineer open for inspection any part of the Works which may have been covered up

14.2 Should the Developer fail to comply with any such request made under clause 14.1 (and without prejudice to all other rights accruing to the Undertaker on a breach of any part of this Agreement by the Developer) the Undertaker may itself open up the Works or any part of them

14.3 In the event of any part of the Works being found to be defective obstructed or otherwise failing to conform with the requirements of this Agreement the cost of such opening up rectification and reinstatement shall (subject to clause 14.4) be borne by the Developer

14.4 In any case other than those mentioned in clause 14.3 such cost shall be borne by the Undertaker except that in any case where the Engineer has not been given reasonable notice and facilities by the Developer in accordance with this Agreement to inspect any part of the Works and did not inspect them the cost of the opening reinstatement and rectification (if any) in relation to any part of the Works which shall have been opened up shall be borne by the Developer whether or not such opening up reveals any defect obstruction or other failure to comply with the requirements of this Agreement

**[3871]**

## 15 Undertaker's right to repair

If at any time before the Works shall have become vested in the Undertaker in accordance with clause 16 the Developer shall fail to construct complete make good and maintain the Works or any part of them in accordance with this Agreement:

15.1 the Undertaker shall be entitled at its discretion to construct complete make good and maintain such part of the Works as may be necessary in the opinion of the Engineer to drain effectually and properly all of those properties on the Land which have been occupied and may do so either by its own employees or by contract or in such other manner as it thinks fit after first giving reasonable notice in writing to the Developer and the Surety of its intention and

15.2 the Developer shall upon demand pay to the Undertaker the cost as certified by the Engineer of undertaking such part of the Works referred to in clause 15.1 including the cost of the preparation and service of notices and of administration

## 16    Final Certificate and vesting

16.1    The Undertaker shall (subject to the Developer complying with the terms of this agreement and in particular the terms of clause 16.2) by declaration vest those parts of the Works which shall be Sewers in the Undertaker

16.2    The Undertaker shall not be required to vest or to take over responsibility for the Works or any part of them until the following have occurred:

16.2.1    where any part of the land in which the Works are situated is outside the Land the Developer shall have produced to the Undertaker a good sufficient and marketable title to the land in which the Works are situated or evidence of sufficient rights in that land to enable the making of a valid and effectual declaration[2]

16.2.2    the Engineer shall have issued a certificate in writing ('the Final Certificate') (the Final Certificate not to be unreasonably withheld) certifying that:

16.2.2.1    the Works have been constructed and completed in accordance with the Drawings and the Specification to his reasonable satisfaction and have been maintained by the Developer during the Defects Correction Period and any defects arising or work required in connection with the Works during that period and prior to the date of the Final Certificate have been made good or carried out by the Developer to the reasonable satisfaction of the Engineer

16.2.2.2    no building or structure has been erected over any part of the Works or on or over land within *(specify)* metres measured horizontally from the centre line of any Sewer without the written consent of the Undertaker and no pedestrian or vehicular access to the Works has been obstructed

**[3872]**

16.2.2.3    where a Sewer (whether for foul sewage or surface water) is shown in the Drawings discharging to an existing public sewer that connection has been made (whether by the Developer or by or on behalf of the Undertaker) properly and in the manner shown in the Drawings

16.2.2.4    where a surface water Sewer is shown in the Drawings discharging to a watercourse that it does discharge properly to the watercourse in the manner shown in the Drawings and that all requisite consents have been obtained from the Undertaker

16.2.3    the Developer shall have made in full the payments required by clause 23

16.2.4    the Developer shall have complied with all requirements of the Undertaker in pursuance of clause 24

16.3    The Engineer shall not be obliged to issue a Final Certificate while any dispute exists between the Developer and any third party concerning the right of the Developer to construct the Works or any part of them in the position and the manner in which they have been constructed

16.4    To ensure that the Works shall so soon as practicable after the expiration of the Defects Correction Period receive the Final Certificate:

16.4.1    the Developer shall give notice *(specify)* months before the end of the Defects Correction Period

16.4.2      whether or not the Engineer shall have received a notice under clause 16.4.1 any inspection which the Engineer may require to make shall be made prior to the expiry of the Defects Correction Period and he shall within [14 days] after such inspection advise the Developer in writing of any defects arising or work required in connection with the Works and which he requires to be rectified or done before the issue of the Final Certificate

**[3873]**

## 17    No duty to Developer

Nothing in this Agreement shall imply any obligation on the part of the Engineer or the Undertaker to the Developer or to any other person to ensure that the Works or any part of them are properly constructed

## 18    Indemnity to Undertaker by Developer

The Developer shall indemnify the Undertaker against all claims costs losses or expenses which may be made against it in connection with the construction and completion of the Works and any defect in title

## 19    Termination

If the Developer shall:

19.1      fail to perform any of its obligations

19.2      [be adjudicated bankrupt or] shall go into liquidation voluntarily or otherwise or shall execute a deed of assignment for the benefit of or otherwise compound with its or his creditors (except for the purpose of reconstruction or amalgamation) the Undertaker may without prejudice to its other rights remedies and powers against the Developer for such breach by notice in writing to the Developer [and Surety] determine this agreement and upon such notice being served this Agreement shall immediately determine but without prejudice to the obligations of [the Surety to the Undertaker under clause 20 and of] the Developer to the Undertaker under this Agreement

**[3874]**

## [20    Obligation of Surety

20.1      If the Developer shall fail to perform any of its obligations under this agreement the Surety shall (subject to this clause) pay to the Undertaker any expenditure which the Undertaker may incur in accordance with this agreement by reason of the failure of the Developer to perform whether or not this agreement has been determined

20.2      The Surety shall in no circumstances be liable to pay a greater sum than £... for which sum the Surety binds itself and its successors and assigns to the Undertaker

20.3      The amount of any expenditure referred to in clause 20.1 shall be that certified by the Engineer whose certificate shall be final

20.4      The Surety shall be discharged or released from the covenant in clause 20.1 when those parts of the Works which shall be Sewers shall have become vested in the Undertaker [and those parts of the Works which shall not be Sewers but which the Undertaker requires to be conveyed or transferred together with the rights referred to in clause 24.1 shall have been effectually conveyed or transferred to the Undertaker] but it shall not be discharged or released from this covenant by any arrangement between the Developer and the Undertaker or by the execution of any amended extra or substituted works authorised by clause 4 or by any forbearance whether as to payment performance time or otherwise whether made with or without the assent of the Surety]

**21    Arbitration**

Any dispute or difference arising from the construction of the Works or application of this Agreement (clause 11.3 excepted) may be referred for determination to a person to be agreed between the parties (or failing such agreement to be appointed by or on behalf of the President for the time being of the Institution of Civil Engineers) on the application of any party in accordance with and subject to the provisions of the Arbitration Act 1996 the decision of the person so agreed or appointed to be final binding and conclusive

**[3875]**

**22    Notices**

Any notice to be served on or document to be supplied or submitted to the Undertaker shall be delivered or posted to *(address)* and any notices to be served on the Developer may be delivered or posted to [its last known address *or* its registered office] [and any notice to be served on the Surety may be delivered at or posted to its registered office]

**23    Fees and charges**

The Developer shall:

23.1    on the execution of this Agreement pay to the Undertaker the cost the Undertaker incurs in preparation and completion of this Agreement

23.2    on demand immediately after the Engineer carries out a first inspection of the Works or of any part of them pay the sum of £... in respect of the costs of the Undertaker for the inspection by the Engineer

[23.3    Upon the transfer of the land mentioned in clause 24.1 pay to the Undertaker the sum of £... in respect of the future cost to the Undertaker of maintaining and operating such part of the Works as comprise pumping stations and their pumps]

**24    Transfer of rights**

The Developer shall prior to the Works becoming vested in the Undertaker in accordance with clause 16:

[24.1    at the request of the Undertaker execute or secure the execution of a conveyance or transfer to the Undertaker (and at no cost to the Undertaker) vesting in the Undertaker the freehold estate free from incumbrances of the land forming the site and curtilage of those parts of the Works which are pumping stations and pumps together with all rights necessary to gain access with vehicles and shall pay the costs of the preparation and completion of the stamp duty upon and any Land Registry fees in respect of such conveyance or transfer][3]

24.2    at the request of the Undertaker secure (at no cost to the Undertaker) the transfer or grant to it of such of the rights referred to in clause 7 as the Undertaker may require so that such rights will be effectually vested in the Undertaker

**[3876]**

**25    Assignment**

The Developer shall not assign any interest or responsibility under this agreement without the express written consent of the Undertaker and upon such conditions and terms as the Undertaker may impose

**26    Other statutory functions**

Nothing in this Agreement shall in any way prejudice the exercise by the Undertaker of any of its statutory rights and powers arising otherwise than by virtue of this Agreement

IN WITNESS etc

## SCHEDULE
*(attach plans, drawings, sectional drawings and other working documents)*

*(signatures (or common seals) of the parties)*[4]
**[***(signatures of witnesses)***]**
**[3877]**

1     A sewerage undertaker (or a local authority acting in accordance with arrangements which it has entered into with the undertaker to carry out sewerage functions on the undertaker's behalf under the Water Industry Act 1991 s 97 as amended by the Government of Wales Act 1998 ss 129, 152, Sch 15 para 17, Sch 18 Pt IV and by the Statute Law (Repeals) Act 1998 (49 Halsbury's Statutes (4th Edn) WATER)) may agree with any person constructing or proposing to construct a sewer or sewage disposal works that if the sewer or works is or are constructed in accordance with the agreement, the undertaker will upon the completion of the work at some specified date or on the happening of some future event declare the sewer or works to be vested in the undertaker: Water Industry Act 1991 s 104(1). This provision applies also to drains but no declaration can be made until the drain becomes a sewer: Water Industry Act 1991 s 104(6). A sewerage undertaker must not enter into an agreement while the sewer, drain or sewage disposal works is situated in the area of another sewerage undertaker without the consent of that other undertaker unless the Secretary of State for the Environment, Transport and the Regions upon an application dispenses with the need for such consent: see the Water Industry Act 1991 s 104(7). The terms of the agreement will be settled by the sewerage undertaker (see Water Industry Act 1991 s 104(1)) but the terms can be challenged on appeal and may be modified at the discretion of the Secretary of State: see the Water Industry Act 1991 s 105(2), (4) as amended by the Competition and Service (Utilities) Act 1992 s 35(1), (7).

    An undertaker may not charge for the making of a declaration of vesting or in respect of any agreement to make such a declaration: Water Industry Act 1991 s 146(3). It is the duty of every sewerage undertaker to keep records of the location and other relevant particulars of every drain or sewer which is the subject of any such agreement to make a declaration which it has entered into: see the Water Industry Act 1991 s 199(1)(c).

2     With estate developments it is not unusual for part of a sewer forming part of the proposed sewerage system to be constructed by a developer to extend beyond the boundary of the developer's land. Unless the developer can satisfy the sewerage undertaker that he has obtained sufficient rights to lay the sewer in that other land (which will include the right to have the sewer adopted by the sewerage undertaker) then the undertaker should not make a declaration vesting the sewer. If such a sewer is vested in the undertaker and it is subsequently shown that the developer did not have sufficient rights, the owner of the sewer will be prevented from claiming compensation under the Water Industry Act 1991 Sch 12 para 4(1) by the provisions of the Water Industry Act 1991 Sch 12 para 4(5), which provides that no person may claim compensation on the ground that a sewerage undertaker has declared any sewer to be vested in the undertaker.

3     This clause should be deleted if there are no pumping stations.

4     As to the statutory requirements for valid execution of a deed see vol 12 (1994 Reissue) DEEDS AGREEMENTS AND DECLARATIONS.

**[3878]–[3890]**

## 90

**Bond supporting an agreement under the Highways Act 1980 Section 38 and/ or Section 278 (and Local Government Act 1972 Section 111) or the Water Industry Act 1991 Section 104**[1]

THIS BOND is made the ……. day of …… BETWEEN:

(1)     *(surety)* [company number *(number)*] [of *(address)* or whose registered office is at *(address)*] ('the Surety')

(2)     [*(authority)* of *(address)* ('the Council') or *(sewerage undertaker)* ('the Undertaker') company number *(number)* whose registered office is at *(address)* 'the Undertaker')][2] and

(3)     *(developer)* company number *(number)* whose registered office is at *(address)* ('the Developer')

## 1 Background

1.1 The Developer has entered into an agreement pursuant to [the Highways Act 1980 Section 38 [and Section 278 and the Local Government Act 1972 Section 111] *or* the Water Industry Act 1991 Section 104] with the [Council *or* Undertaker] dated *(date)* ('the Agreement') for [the making up of *or* works to existing *or* construction of] [roads *or* sewers] at *(location of development)* which are more particularly described in the Agreement
1.2 This Bond is supplemental to the Agreement
1.3 The Surety has agreed to guarantee the due performance of the Agreement in the following manner

**[3891]**

## 2 The Surety's Covenants

The Surety hereby covenants with the [Council *or* Undertaker] as follows:
2.1 The Surety will in all respects guarantee the due and proper performance of the Agreement and the due observance and punctual performance of all the obligations duties undertakings covenants and conditions by or on the part of the Developer and to be observed and performed by it which are set out in the Agreement (collectively 'the Obligations'), which guarantee shall extend to include any variation of or addition to the Agreement
2.2 If the Developer shall in any respect or for any reason fail or be unable to carry out observe or perform all or any of the Obligations (unless relieved of any of the Obligations by any condition of the Agreement or by the decision of a court or tribunal of competent jurisdiction) then the Surety will be liable for and shall indemnify the [Council *or* Undertaker] against all losses damages costs and expenses whatsoever which may be incurred by the [Council *or* Undertaker] by reason of or in consequence of any default or inability on the part of the Developer in performing any of the Obligations under the Agreement to the extent that such losses damages costs and expenses may be claimed by the [Council *or* Undertaker] against the Developer under the Agreement up to a maximum of £...

## 3 Avoidance of Obligation

The Surety shall not be discharged or released from this Bond by:
3.1 any agreement concession conduct forbearance or indulgence granted to the Developer under the Agreement or any alteration to the terms of the Agreement or
3.2 any other compromise or settlement of any dispute between the [Council *or* Undertaker] and the Developer (but so that the [Council *or* Undertaker] shall not pursue against the Surety a remedy contrary to the terms of any such compromise or settlement in so far as the Developer shall have complied with such terms)

**[3892]**

## 4 Duration of Bond

This Bond is a continuing guarantee and:
4.1 shall remain in operation until either:
    4.1.1 all the Obligations of the Developer under the Agreement shall have been satisfied or performed in full or
    4.1.2 the Surety has paid to the [Council *or* Undertaker] all the sums payable by the Developer to the [Council *or* Undertaker] under the terms of the Agreement [provided that the total sum payable by the Surety shall not exceed £...[3]]

4.2    is in addition to and not in substitution for any other security which the [Council *or* Undertaker] may at any time hold for the performance of such obligations and

4.3    may be enforced without first having recourse to any such security and without taking any other steps or proceedings against the Developer

## 5    Sums due from the Developer[4]

In so far as any sums are due by the Developer to the [Council *or* Undertaker] under the terms of the Agreement then the Surety shall not:

5.1    by paying any sum due in accordance with this Bond or by any other means or grounds claim or recover by the institution of proceedings or threat of proceedings or otherwise such sum from the Developer or

5.2    claim any set off or counterclaim against the Developer or

5.3    prove in competition with the [Council *or* Undertaker] in respect of any payment by the Surety in accordance with this Bond or

5.4    be entitled in competition with the [Council *or* Undertaker] to claim or have the benefit of any security which the [Council *or* Undertaker] holds or may hold for any money or liabilities due or incurred by the Developer to the [Council *or* Undertaker]

and in case the Surety receives any sums from the Developer in respect of any payment made by the Surety in accordance with this Bond the Surety shall hold such monies in trust for the [Council *or* Undertaker] so long as any sums are payable (contingently or otherwise) under this Bond

**[3893]**

## 6    Disclaimer of Agreement

The Surety's obligation and liability under this Bond shall continue notwithstanding any disclaimer of the Agreement by a liquidator or administrator appointed of the Developer and in the event of such a disclaimer the Agreement shall for the purposes of this Bond be deemed to continue

## 7    Surety's liability no greater than Developer's liability

This Bond shall not be construed as placing any greater liability upon the Surety than is upon the Developer under the terms of the Agreement

## 8    English law

This Bond shall be governed by and construed in accordance with English Law

IN WITNESS etc

*(signatures (or common seals) of the parties)*[5]
*(signatures of witnesses)*
**[3894]**

1    As to such agreements generally see Form 93 appendix 1 [3971] ante.
2    If the agreement is made under the Water Industry Act 1991 s 104 (49 Halsbury's Statutes (4th Edn) WATER) with the sewerage undertaker, the bond will be with the relevant undertaker instead of the relevant council.
3    Parties may wish to agree to retain only sub-clause 4.1.1 rather than providing for the two ways of ending the surety's obligation.
4    This clause is to protect the council or undertaker by ensuring that if the surety seeks to recover money paid by it from the developer, it will not do so in competition with the council or undertaker. Whether or not this clause is included is a matter for negotiation.
5    As to the statutory requirements for valid execution of a deed see vol 12 (1994 Reissue) DEEDS AGREEMENTS AND DECLARATIONS.

**[3895]**

# 91

**Transfer of part of registered freehold land being the site of an electricity sub-station¹**

*Use Land Registry Form TP1 (for which see Form 114 [4181] post) and insert, in the panels specified below, the wording shown:*

## Panel 3 Property

*(add after the description)*
[containing an area of *(number)* square metres or thereabouts]

## Panel 13  Additional Provisions

### 1      Definitions

In this transfer:
1.1     'the Authority' means *(name of local highway authority)* of *(address)*
1.2     'the Estate' means the land [edged brown] on the Plan being the land now and formerly comprised in title number *(number)*
1.3     'the Perpetuity Period' means the period of [21] [80] years commencing on the date of this transfer
1.4     'the Plan' means the plan annexed to this transfer [and if numbered plans are annexed any reference to a numbered plan is to the annexed plan so numbered]
[1.5    words importing one gender shall be construed as importing any other gender]
[1.6    words importing the singular shall be construed as importing the plural and vice versa]
[1.7    words importing persons shall be construed as importing a corporate body and/or a partnership and vice versa]
[1.8    where any party comprises more than one person the obligations and liabilities of that party under this transfer shall be joint and several obligations and liabilities of those persons]
[1.9    the panel and clause headings do not form part of this transfer and shall not be taken into account in its construction or interpretation]
[1.10   any reference to a clause is to one so numbered in this panel unless otherwise stated]
[1.11   any reference to a colour or letter is to one on the Plan]

                                                                    **[3896]**

### 2      Rights granted for the benefit of the Property

The Property is transferred together with:
2.1     the following rights:
          2.1.1    Full right and liberty for the Transferee and its successors in title and its or their tenants servants and licensees to enter the part of the Estate [coloured *or* edged [blue]]² for the purpose of erecting and maintaining an electricity sub-station on the Property the Transferee doing as little damage as possible to the Estate and making good any damage which may be caused
          2.1.2    Full right and liberty to go pass and repass at all times and for all purposes in connection with the sub-station over and along [the land coloured [brown] on the Plan] [and] the road and footpath abutting upon the Property [and any other roads and footpaths which are now

or may within the Perpetuity Period be constructed on the Estate]
and until constructed the intended site of such road[s] and
footpath[s]³

2.1.3 Full right and liberty to lay [underground] and maintain electric
cables and lines and conduits and pipes for containing the same
where necessary under and across:

[2.1.3.1 the strips of land *(number)* metres in width in the
approximate positions indicated by [broken red] lines
on the Plan]

[2.1.3.2 the land shown [coloured brown] on the Plan]

[2.1.3.3 any land forming part of the Estate [not being the site
of or intended to be the site of any building] in such
position as may be necessary for the purpose of affording
a supply of electricity to the properties erected or to be
erected on the Estate]

[2.1.3.4 the road abutting upon the Property [and any other
roads which are now or may within the Perpetuity
Period be constructed on the Estate and until
constructed the intended site of such road or roads]]

and to break up the surface of any land mentioned above so far as
may be necessary from time to time for the purpose of laying relaying
repairing and maintaining the electric cables and lines and conduits
or pipes doing as little damage as possible and restoring the surface as
soon as possible

2.2 the benefit of any rights reserved to the Transferor out of the transfer of any land
forming part of the Estate to lay and maintain electric cables lines pipes and
conduits under such land⁴

**[3897]**

## 3  Positive covenants by the Transferor

The Transferor covenants with the Transferee as follows:

3.1 The Transferor shall construct the carriageway and footpath upon which the
Property abuts to the specification of the Authority and shall maintain and keep
the same in good repair until taken over and adopted by the Authority as a
public highway and indemnify the Transferee from and against all costs charges
and expenses in respect of the carriageway and footpath

3.2 The Transferor shall not at any time after the date of this transfer construct or
permit to be constructed any building erection or structure of any kind
whatsoever over or within 1.5 metres on either side of the route of any electric
cables and lines and conduits or pipes laid or to be laid or placed by the
Transferee in pursuance of the rights granted by this transfer⁵

## 4  Agreements and Declarations

It is agreed and declared as follows:

4.1 The Transferee and the persons deriving title under it shall not by implication
prescription or otherwise become entitled to any right of light or air which
would restrict or interfere with the free use of the Estate for building or other
purposes

4.2 The Transferor reserves the right to modify waive or release all or any covenants
stipulations or restrictions relating to the Estate whether imposed or entered
into before at the same time as or after the date of this transfer

4.3     The Transferor shall not in any way be bound by the plotting or general scheme of development of any of the Estate as may be shown on any plans at any time prepared by it in regard to the Estate and may from time to time alter such plotting and scheme of development in such manner as it may deem fit

**[3898]**

1     As to stamp duty see Information Binder: Stamp Duties [1] (Conveyance or transfer). As to Land Registry fees see Information Binder: Property [1] (Fees in connection with property matters, Land Registry fees).

  Form TP1 is the Land Registry form of transfer of part of freehold or leasehold land prescribed by the Land Registration Rules 1925, SR&O 1925/1093 r 98, Sch 1 as inserted by SI 1997/3037 and amended by SI 1999/128. This Form should be used whenever part only of any registered title is transferred, even if the transfer also includes the whole of one or more other registered titles.

  The transferor's land or charge certificate must be placed on deposit (using Land Registry form DP1 as prescribed by SR&O 1925/1093 Sch 1 as inserted and amended (as to which see vol 25(1) (1999 Reissue) LAND REGISTRATION Form 3 [3076]) to meet the transferee's application to register the transfer. If the transferor's land is subject to any registered or noted charge, the consent of the chargee to the transfer should be obtained and lodged with the application to register the transfer.

  Reference should be made to Form 115 [4191] post for detailed footnotes on matters common to many forms of transfer, cross-references to the commentary in vol 35 (1997 Reissue) SALE OF LAND, for the location of alternative transfer clauses in that and other volumes and for footnotes relating to sales of part. The forms of rights and covenants are illustrative only; most electricity supply companies have their own standard forms of wording.

  The space required for an electricity sub-station is usually approximately the size of a garden shed and is generally enclosed by a brick wall or close-boarded fence. It is normal practice for the transfer to be drafted by the solicitors for the electricity company who usually have their own standard form. The consideration for the transfer is usually nominal.

2     Access should be restricted to such parts of the estate not already sold as is necessary for the purpose. Possibly access over the site of the estate road will be sufficient, in which case this paragraph can be simplified.

3     As to the adoption of roads generally see Form 93 appendix 1 [3971] post.

4     If the electricity company requires easements for laying cables etc over land which is not stipulated in this transfer, or which has already been transferred to an individual plot purchaser either a formal cable easement or an informal wayleave consent is required. For an example of the latter see vol 14 (1994 Reissue) ENERGY SUPPLY Form 13 [3310]. Electricity supply companies usually specify the forms of reservations that they require to be inserted in transfers of plots, although this would appear to be generally unnecessary as undertakers almost always have statutory rights which they can use.

5     This covenant may be drafted as a restrictive covenant if required. In any event the restriction must be carried forward into the relevant plot transfers either by imposing it as an additional restriction in favour of the transferor or by transferring subject to it and obtaining an indemnity covenant from the plot transferee.

**[3899]–[3950]**

# PART 9: RESIDENTIAL DEVELOPMENT

## *Forms and Precedents*

## (1): PRELIMINARY DOCUMENTS

### 92

**Form requesting instructions from the seller to set up a residential estate development[1]**

*(insert name of development)*

**A      PERSONNEL**

**1        Seller**
1.1      Full names:
1.2      Address:
1.3      Postcode:
1.4      Telephone number(s):
         1.4.1        office:
         1.4.2        mobile:
1.5      Fax number:
1.6      E-mail number:
1.7      DX number:

**[3951]**

**2        Developer (if not the Seller)**
2.1      Name:
2.2      Contact name:
2.3      Address:
2.4      Postcode:
2.5      Telephone number(s):
         2.5.1        office:
         2.5.2        mobile:
2.6      Fax number:
2.7      E-mail number:
2.8      DX number:
2.9      Relationship to the seller (if any)[2]:

**3        Site Office**
3.1      Name of site manager/foreman:
3.2      Telephone number(s):
         3.2.1        office:
         3.2.2        mobile:

3.3      Fax number:
3.4      E-mail number:

**4        Sales Office /Estate Agents**
4.1      Name of sales manager:
4.2      Address:
4.3      Postcode:
4.4      Telephone number(s):
       4.4.1        office:
       4.4.2        mobile:
4.5      Fax number:
4.6      E-mail number:
4.7      DX number:

**[3952]**

**5        Architect**
5.1      Name:
5.2      Contact name:
5.3      Address:
5.4      Postcode:
5.5      Telephone number(s):
       5.5.1        office:
       5.5.2        mobile:
5.6      Fax number:
5.7      E-mail number:
5.8      DX number:

**6        Bank**
6.1      Name:
6.2      Contact name:
6.3      Address:
6.4      Postcode:
6.5      Telephone number(s):
6.6      Fax number:
6.7      E-mail number:
6.8      DX number:

**[3953]**

**7        Mortgagees**
7.1      Name:
7.2      Contact name:
7.3      Address:
7.4      Postcode:
7.5      Telephone number(s):
7.6      Fax number:
7.7      E-mail number:
7.8      DX number:

**8        Mortgagees' Solicitors**
8.1      Name:
8.2      Contact name:
8.3      Address:
8.4      Postcode:

8.5     Telephone number(s):
8.6     Fax number:
8.7     E-mail number:
8.8     DX number:

**[3954]**

**B      DOCUMENTS**

9       Please supply the originals of the following documents *(delete any already held by the solicitor)*:
        9.1     the land certificate or charge certificate if outstanding (or details of lender from whom the charge certificate can be obtained)
        9.2     all title deeds
        9.3     all third party consents
        9.4     all restrictive covenant and defective title indemnity policies and the proposals forms for those policies

10      Please supply the originals or copies of the following:
        10.1    all planning permissions, the applications for those permissions, and all plans and drawings referred to
        10.2    all building regulation approvals
        10.3    all planning agreements
        10.4    certificate of registration as a member of the National House-Building Council[3]
        10.5    forms of agreement supplied by NHBC to be entered into with buyers[4]
        10.6    the latest draft of the proposed estate layout plan
        10.7    documents detailing the requirements of the providers of drainage, electricity, gas and telephone services
        10.8    documents detailing the requirements of the highway authority for the making up and adoption of the estate road
        10.9    all Advance Payment Code notices served and receipts for all payments made[5]
        10.10   any specification prepared for the buyers

**[3955]**

**C      DEVELOPMENT SCHEME**

11      Is the seller also the developer?
12      If not, what are the arrangements between the seller and the developer for the construction work[6]?
13      Has any construction work started on site?
14      If not, when is it expected or intended to start?
15      Will all the dwellings to be built be self-contained houses?
16      Are there any flats or maisonettes to be built?
17      What areas are to be provided for the general use of residents[7], eg:
        17.1    recreational areas
        17.2    children's play areas
        17.3    nature reserves
        17.4    landscaped areas and open space?

**D      INFRASTRUCTURE**

*(Where appropriate please mark the locations of services mentioned below on the draft estate layout plan or location plan)*

**18      Electricity**
18.1    Please supply the name and address of electricity supplier
18.2    What is the proposed route of the supply from the existing electricity main through the estate?
18.3    Will the supply be overhead or underground?
18.4    Is any substation site or cable easement required[8]? If so, where?
18.5    Who will deal with any supply agreement to be entered into?

[3956]

**19      Foul Drainage**
19.1    Where is the existing foul sewer into which the estate is to drain?
19.2    What evidence is there that it is a public sewer?
19.3    Has consent to connection been given?
19.4    What is the proposed route of the drainage system through and from the estate?
19.5    Are rights required from third parties to drain through their land? If so:
    19.5.1    where?
    19.5.2    how and by whom are the rights to be acquired[9]?
    19.5.3    what stage has been reached in acquiring those rights?
19.6    Will there be a sewer agreement for the construction and adoption of the foul sewer? If so:
    19.6.1    with whom?
    19.6.2    what stage has been reached in negotiating its terms?
    19.6.3    who will progress it?
    19.6.4    who will provide the bond or guarantee in support?

**20      Storm Water Drainage**
20.1    How is this to be dealt with?
20.2    Is it to be the subject of any agreement? If so:
    20.2.1    with whom?
    20.2.2    what stage has been reached in negotiating its terms?
    20.2.3    who will progress it?
    20.2.4    who will provide the bond or guarantee in support?
20.3    Are rights required from third parties to drain through their land? If so:
    20.3.1    where?
    20.3.2    how and by whom are the rights to be acquired?
    20.3.3    what stage has been reached in acquiring those rights?
20.4    Is any water to be discharged into a watercourse? If so:
    20.4.1    where?
    20.4.2    has consent to the discharge been obtained?

[3957]

**21      Water**
21.1    Please supply the name and address of water undertaker
21.2    Where is the existing water main from which the supply is to be taken?
21.3    What is the proposed route of the water main through the estate?
21.4    Are rights required from third parties to draw water through their land? If so:
    21.4.1    where?
    21.4.2    how and by whom are the rights to be acquired?
    21.4.3    what stage has been reached in acquiring those rights?
21.5    Is any agreement to be entered into with the water supplier?

**22      Gas**
22.1      Please supply the name and address of gas undertaker
22.2      Where is the existing gas main from which the supply is to be taken?
22.3      What is the proposed route of the gas main through the estate
22.4      Are rights required from third parties for a gas main to be laid through their land? If so:
  22.4.1      where?
  22.4.2      how and by whom will the rights be acquired[10]?
  22.4.3      what stage has been reached in acquiring those rights?
22.5      Is any agreement to be entered into with the gas supplier?

**23      Telephone**
23.1      Please supply the name and address of telephone undertaker
23.2      Where is the existing telephone supply from which the supply is to be taken?
23.3      What is the proposed route of the supply through the estate?
23.4      Will the supply be overhead or underground?
23.5      Who will deal with any service agreement to be entered into?

                            **[3958]**

**24      Services Generally**
24.1      Are there any other services to be provided to serve the estate?
24.2      Are any services to be provided (or the right reserved to provide services in the future) for the benefit of land or property:
  24.2.1      owned by the seller but not forming part of the estate?
  24.2.2      owned by third parties?
24.3      If so:
  24.3.1      what services?
  24.3.2      for what land are they to be provided?
  24.3.3      who will pay for their construction and future maintenance?

**25      Roads**
25.1      Please supply the name and address of the local highway authority
25.2      Has an Advanced Payments Code notice been served[11]?
25.3      Has the deposit been paid?
25.4      Is the road layout as shown on the draft estate layout plan approved by the local highway authority?
25.5      Is there to be an agreement with the local highway authority for the making up and adoption of the estate roads? If so:
  25.5.1      what stage has been reached in negotiating its terms?
  25.5.2      who will progress it?
  25.5.3      who will provide the bond or guarantee in support?
  25.5.4      will the agreement also deal with the storm water sewers under the estate road?
25.6      Are there any roads or footpaths not to be adopted as public highways? If so:
  25.6.1      which are they?
  25.6.2      what plots will they serve?
  25.6.3      who will subsequently own and maintain them?
25.7      Are there any roadside verges or service strips? If so, will they be adopted as part of the public highway?
25.8      Are there any detached car parking areas not exclusively for the use of one specified plot, eg visitor parking areas? If so:
  25.8.1      where?
  25.8.2      who will subsequently own and maintain them?

**E  SALE CONTRACTS**

26  Is the balance of the sale price to be paid only on completion of the dwelling ready for occupation, or by stage payments?

27  If there are to be stage payments, what are the stages for payment?

28  Are there to be any sales aids or inducements offered to buyers? If so, what[12]?

29  Is the sale price liable to be increased to take account of increases in building costs or inflation?

**[3959]**

1  This Form is intended as an aid to taking and recording instructions for preparation for development of a residential estate. It may be sent to the developer to complete although sometimes it may be better for the Form to be completed in conference with the estate layout plan to hand.

2  The relationship may be, eg, an associated company.

3  As to registration and structural guarantees given by the NHBC see Form 93 appendix 2 [3974] post.

4  The seller usually obtains the forms.

5  As to the Advance Payments Code under the Highways Act 1980 s 219 as amended (20 Halsbury's Statutes (4th Edn) HIGHWAYS, STREETS AND BRIDGES) see Form 93 appendix 2 [3974] post.

6  If the developer is not the seller the developer will require a licence to enter on the site to carry out the construction work.

7  As to the methods of dealing with unadopted amenity areas see Form 93 note 24 [3982] post.

8  For a form of transfer of an electricity substation site see Form 91 [3896] ante.

9  If the seller does not have the benefit of an easement to drain across land of a third party and cannot negotiate the right, it can requisition the right by serving a notice on the sewerage undertaker under the Water Industry Act 1991 ss 98–101 as amended (49 Halsbury's Statutes (4th Edn) WATER).

10  Usually the right will be acquired by the gas undertaker.

11  See note 5 above.

12  Selling aids or inducements which may be offered to the buyer include:

(a)  sale subject to satisfactory local searches;

(b)  sale conditional on mortgage offer;

(c)  mortgage interest subsidy;

(d)  redundancy protection scheme;

(e)  option for the buyer's existing house to be taken in part payment;

(f)  grant of a power of attorney for sub-sale by the developer of the buyer's existing house taken by the developer in part payment; and

(g)  sale conditional on sale of buyer's own property.

For Forms containing such provisions see Forms 104 [4129]–112 [4148] post.

**[3960]**

# 93

## Steps to be taken by the seller's solicitor in preparation for the sale of plots on a residential building estate[1]

### 1  Take instructions and some initial steps

On taking the seller's instructions to act:

1.1  obtain details of the estate development, roads, services and general layout[2]

1.2  obtain copies of all planning permissions, the applications for those permissions and all plans referred to, and all other consents

1.3  obtain copies of all restrictive covenant and defective title indemnity policies and the proposals for such insurance[3]

1.4  advise the seller of the necessity for registration of its title at HM Land Registry to be completed and for the estate layout plan and form of transfer to be approved by the Land Registry before draft contracts are sent out to the buyer's solicitors[4]

**[3961]**

**2      Site inspection**

Carry out a full inspection[5]

**3      Estate layout plan**

3.1      Brief the seller and his architect or surveyor on the Land Registry's requirements
         for the estate layout plan in order that it will be approved by the Land Registry[6],
         and on receipt of the plan apply to the appropriate Land Registry for approval
         of it

3.2      Advise the seller and his architect or surveyor of the difficulties and delays which
         will occur if the physical layout of the development departs from the approved
         layout plan and of the procedure to be followed when variations are necessary

3.3      Check that the number of dwelling units, garages and other buildings shown on
         the estate layout plan is the same as that authorised by the planning permission

3.4      Advise that before the draft contract is sent to the buyer's solicitors the site
         engineer or surveyor should check that the position of the buildings and fencing
         erected are in the positions shown on the estate layout plan so as to identify any
         discrepancies

                                                                              **[3962]**

**4      Infrastructure agreements**

**4.1     Electricity**

4.1.2    Liaise with the electricity supplier as to its requirements

4.1.3    Agree the form of any transfer of a site for an electricity substation and the grant
         of easements for cables and access[7]

4.1.4    Ascertain whether any cable or other rights are required to be reserved out of
         plot transfers in favour of the supply company and, if so, ensure that they are
         carried forward into the standard form of plot transfer[8]

**4.2     Estate roads**

4.2.1    Liaise with the local highway authority as to their requirements[9]

4.2.2    Agree the form of agreement with the highway authority for the construction,
         making up and adoption of the estate roads[10] and work on any existing public
         highways[11]

4.2.3    Obtain instructions on what contract provisions should be drafted to deal with
         the possibility that the highway agreement will not be complete by the date of
         exchange of plot contracts and for the refund to the seller of any advance
         payments made by it once the Section 38 agreement has been completed[12]

4.2.4    Agree the form of the bond, guarantee or other security in support of the
         highway agreement

4.2.5    If the development involves the alteration to a trunk road, agree the form of
         agreement with the Department of Transport[13]

                                                                              **[3963]**

**4.3     Gas**

4.3.1    Liaise with the gas supplier as to its requirements

4.3.2    Agree the form of any grant of easements for gas pipes and access[14]

4.3.3    Ascertain whether any rights are required to be reserved out of plot transfers in
         favour of the supply company and, if so, ensure that they are carried forward
         into the standard form of plot transfer

**4.4     Sewers**

4.4.1    Liaise with the sewerage undertaker and the local planning authority on their
         respective requirements for the foul and surface water drainage of the development[15]

4.4.2   Agree the terms of an agreement for the construction of foul and surface water sewers and for their adoption as publicly maintained sewers[16]

4.4.3   Agree the terms of any easements to be entered into where sewers will run across the land of a third party[17]

4.4.4   Ensure that any restrictions imposed by the sewer agreement for the protection of underground sewers and drains are carried forward into the standard form of plot transfer

4.4.5   Agree the form of the bond in support of the sewer agreement[18]

**[3964]**

**4.5   Telephone**
4.5.1   Liaise with the telephone supplier as to its requirements
4.5.2   Agree the form of any wayleave consents required

**4.6   Water**
4.6.1   Liaise with the water undertaker as to its requirements[19]

**5   Development programme**

5.1   Ascertain whether the development is to be carried out in a series of phases and, if so, check that the phases conform with the conditions imposed by the planning permission and any planning agreement or unilateral undertaking[20]

5.2   Check that the terms of the infrastructure agreements conform with the phasing programme

**[3965]**

**6   Method of plot disposals**

Ascertain the method of sale of each plot and in particular:

6.1   whether completion of the transfer is to take place only after the building is completed and fit for occupation or

6.2   whether the buyer is to pay stage payments during the course of construction and, if so:

6.2.1   at what stage is the land to be transferred to the buyer?

6.2.2   if the land is to be transferred before all stage payments have been paid, what security is to be given to the seller for the payments remaining to be paid[21]?

6.2.3   whether the seller is to retain ownership of the plot until completion of the building works, the works being carried out under a building licence[22]?

6.3   what selling aids or inducements are to be offered to the buyer, in particular[23]:

6.3.1   sale subject to satisfactory local searches

6.3.2   sale conditional on mortgage offer

6.3.3   mortgage interest subsidy

6.3.4   redundancy protection scheme

6.3.5   option for the buyer's existing house to be taken in part payment

6.3.6   grant of a power of attorney for sub-sale by the developer of the buyer's existing house taken by the developer in part payment

6.3.7   sale conditional on sale of the buyer's existing property

6.4   whether the purchase price is fixed or liable to increase in any circumstances

**[3966]**

**7   Unadopted amenity areas**

If there are to be any communal amenity areas such as play grounds, soft landscaping and parks, or facilities such as private sewage works:

7.1 who is to hold the legal ownership of the land and works?

7.2 who is to be entitled to use them and for what purposes?

7.3 how are they to be maintained, who will pay for them and how is payment to be recovered from plot owners[24]?

## 8 Construction

8.1 Obtain a copy of the specification to be supplied to each buyer[25]

8.2 Ascertain if the buyer is to be entitled to call on the seller to make additions to or omissions from the specification[26]

8.3 Ascertain whether the buyer is to be permitted to do any finishing works himself before completion of the purchase[27]

**[3967]**

## 9 NHBC and other construction guarantees[28]

9.1 Obtain particulars of the seller's registration as a member of the relevant insurance scheme and its registered number

9.2 Obtain from the seller the agreement for signature by each party for each plot and information documents to be supplied to the buyer

## 10 Draft documents

10.1 Prepare:

    10.1.1 the draft contract

    10.1.2 the draft transfer[29]

    10.1.3 the draft pre-contract information[30]

    10.1.4 the draft letter to accompany draft documents[31]

10.2 Obtain the developer's approval of all the drafts

**[3968]**

## 11 Mortgagee consents

Liase with the mortgagee's solicitors and agree with them:

11.1 the forms of release of plots from registered or noted charges[32]

11.2 the form of certificate of non-crystallisation of floating charges[33]

11.3 the form of consents to the grant of easements[34]

11.4 the procedure to be followed on each sale to procure delivery of the above documents to the seller's solicitors

## 12 Land Registry

12.1 Deposit the seller's land or charge certificate in the appropriate Land Registry if not already on deposit[35]

12.2 Make application to the appropriate Land Registry for approval of the form of draft transfer[36]

12.3 Make application for office copy entries of the seller's title and Form 102 in lieu of filed plan[37]

**[3969]**

## 13 Post office postal numbers

Send a copy of the estate layout plan to the local authority/head post office and request allocation of postal numbers to each dwelling and the postcode[38]

## 14    Local land charge search

Send a copy of the approved estate layout plan to the local land charges department of the local authority and request confirmation that it will accept applications for local searches without the submission of a plan provided that the application identifies each plot, garage plot, parking plot etc by the numbers specified on the approved layout plan

## 15    Plot sale record

15.1    Prepare a record table to record each plot sale, buyer, his solicitors, dates of instruction, exchange of contracts, completion; stage payments due and paid (if applicable) and other relevant information

15.2    Maintain a copy of the approved estate layout plan marking off each plot sold and its title number when allocated

**[3970]**

## 16    Financial matters

Establish:

16.1    appropriate procedures and documentation for recording payment of deposits, stage payments and balance purchase money, and payment to the seller or mortgagee

16.2    reporting procedures to the seller, sales manager, site manager, estate agents and others as required

16.3    procedure for release of the keys to the buyer on completion of the sale

### APPENDIX 1
### Roads And Sewers

## 1    General

The developer-buyer will be concerned to see that on completion of the development none of the land remains his responsibility. Occasionally, the roadways may be transferred to the private ownership of the adjoining residents, but more usually the developer arranges for the local authority to adopt the roads so that they are maintained at the public expense, and for the sewerage undertaker to adopt the sewers.

**[3971]**

## 2    Roads

The developer must apply for planning permission and approval under the Building Regulations[39] before starting work on the site. Within six weeks of the grant of approval under the Building Regulations the local authority serves on the developer a notice under the Highways Act 1980 Section 220[40]. The developer must then either deposit with the local authority a sum deemed by it to be sufficient to pay for construction of the roads to a standard suitable for adoption[41], or enter into an agreement with the local authority under the Highways Act 1980 Section 38[42].

An agreement under Section 38 may vary slightly from authority to authority, but the basic terms are constant. The developer must construct the road and/or footpaths to a standard laid down by the local authority within a specified time, and the authority agrees to take over and maintain the works once they have been completed, and have passed through a period of maintenance by the developer of up to a year[43].

Practice varies as to whether the agreement is, or is not, executed in duplicate. If only one copy is executed, the developer is provided with a certified copy.

## 3    Sewers

The adoption of sewers follows a procedure similar to that in respect of roads. The agreement is made under the Water Industry Act 1991 Section 104[44] usually supported by a bond. Although no longer common, a relevant authority[45] may carry out sewerage functions on behalf of a sewerage undertaker[46] and a single authority may enter into an agreement in respect of both the roads and the sewers.

**[3972]**

## 4    Bonds

Agreements for the adoption of services under the Highways Act 1980 Section 38[47] for roadways, and the Water Industry Act 1991 Section 104[48] for sewers, bind the developer as a company or an individual, but are of little comfort to a buyer of an individual plot unless they are supported by a bond deposited with the local authority or sewerage undertaker[49]. The bond, negotiated through an insurer or financial body, ensures that if the developer should fail to fulfil his obligations under the agreements, the local authority will do so and will recover the costs of the work out of the bond deposited with them.

It is becoming more common for bonds in support of agreements for the adoption of sewers to be waived in the case of substantial developers, or those whose financial status has been satisfactorily verified by the local authority.

## 5    Information required by the buyer of an individual plot

If a bond has been deposited with the local authority[50] the buyer of an individual plot should obtain written confirmation of that fact from the authority either direct or via the developer's solicitor or from his local search. If an agreement[51] and a bond have been executed, copies should be available for examination. The buyer's mortgagee will also be concerned to see that the bonds and the bondsmen are adequate and satisfactory.

If the agreements have not been concluded by the time contracts are exchanged, the buyer should seek to add a condition providing that an appropriate retention may be made from the purchase price pending execution of the relevant documents or adoption of the services by the local authority, whichever is sooner. The documentation ought to be available by completion[52].

**[3973]**

APPENDIX 2

Structural Guarantee Schemes For New Homes

(a)  General

## 1    Introduction

No new house will be readily saleable without confirmation that it has been built in accordance with the requirements of a recognised structural guarantee scheme such as 'Buildmark'[53] or 'Newbuild'[54]. A mortgagor will not usually make an offer on an unguaranteed property, and the public are generally aware of the importance of cover.

In addition to the various structural guarantee schemes, examples of which are outlined below[55], buyers of new properties are afforded a more wide-ranging statutory protection by the Defective Premises Act 1972[56], which places a duty on anyone taking on work in connection with the construction (or enlargement) of a dwelling house to ensure that the property is constructed in a workmanlike manner, using proper materials, and when completed, that it is fit for human habitation[57]. The disgruntled buyer is entitled to seek his remedy under the Act from not only the original builder, but also any architect, engineer or developer who was involved in the construction. The limitation period under the Act is, however, short, being six years from completion of construction[58].

**[3974]**

(b)  The National House Building Council Scheme

**2     Registration of a builder or developer**[59]

On 1st April 1988 the National House Building Council ('NHBC') introduced a procedure for registering homes under the trade mark 'Buildmark', which is the NHBC 10 year new home combined warranty protection scheme. The National Register maintained by the NHBC comprises two types of member:

2.1     'house-builders', who are entitled to build houses either direct for sale to the public or for developers;

2.2     'developers', who are not entitled to build houses themselves, but must employ a registered house builder as a main contractor.

Homes may also be sold by an unregistered developer within the scheme, if they have been registered by a registered house-builder and approval is given by the NHBC before construction begins. Housing associations or local authorities may choose this latter arrangement, in which case the NHBC must be informed of the intended method of disposal (eg renting or shared ownership) before building begins; alternatively, they may become registered developers. A housing association or local authority may be the first buyer (in the case of rented housing) or joint first buyer (in the case of shared ownership housing).

Annual certificates of registration on the National Register are issued and copies should be made available on request to prospective buyers.

**[3975]**

**3     NHBC agreement**

Developers who have registered with the NHBC will receive in respect of each house the following forms:

3.1     the Offer of Cover form (BM1);

3.2     the Acceptance form (BM2);

3.3     the 'Buildmark' booklet (BM3).

All the above documents should be sent to the buyer's solicitor on exchange of contracts for a sale. The protection for the buyer will come into effect upon completion of the Acceptance form (BM2).

Solicitors acting for a buyer of a new house should familiarise themselves with the procedures from the NHBC documentation supplied on exchange of contracts[60]. The NHBC will provide full details of the scheme to solicitors before exchange of contracts, on request.

**4     Buildmark cover**

Briefly, the 'Buildmark' cover afforded to the buyer comprises three parts:

4.1     Before completion: protection against loss arising from the builder's failure, through his insolvency or fraud, to complete the house in accordance with NHBC requirements;

4.2     The first two years after completion: protection in respect of defects which arise in the house as a result of the builder's failure to conform to NHBC standards for materials and workmanship.

4.3     The period from the beginning of the third year after completion until the end of the tenth year: protection in respect of major damage arising from structural defects or subsidence, resulting from a failure to comply with NHBC requirements, and (from 1 April 1999) the costs of clearing up contamination of the land on which the house is built.

**[3976]**

(c)  The Zurich Municipal Scheme

## 5    Zurich Municipal building guarantees

The insurer, Zurich Insurance Company, under its trading name Zurich Municipal, provides four types of structural building guarantee to cover buildings constructed or converted by a builder or developer:

5.1    'Newbuild', which covers new homes for sale;
5.2    'Rebuild', which covers newly converted homes for sale;
5.3    'Newstyle', which covers new homes for rent; and
5.4    'Restyle', which covers newly converted homes for rent.

A developer or builder must first register with Zurich Municipal[61] and may then notify Zurich Municipal of any development he wishes to have covered by the appropriate guarantee scheme. Notification should be made at least three weeks before commencement of the building works unless the ground on which the development is to be constructed is likely to be of abnormal risk[62]. Zurich Municipal's surveyor will carry out regular inspections during the construction and will, if necessary, set time limits for rectification of unsatisfactory work.

## 6    Documentation

Once notification of development has been received by Zurich Municipal, the policy documents and Initial Certificates will be issued to the developer and will eventually be distributed via the buyers' solicitors to the buyers and their mortgagees. The Initial Certificate, which should be kept with the policy document, gives details of the property and shows the effective dates of the first part of the Zurich Municipal guarantee.

For Newbuild and Rebuild guarantees, a Home Owner's Handbook and Buyer's Details form will be issued with the Initial Certificate. The form is to be completed by the buyer's solicitor and returned to Zurich Municipal in order that details may be included in the Final Certificate, issued on or before legal completion.

The Final Certificate will be issued upon both Zurich Municipal's surveyor and the Building Control Authority having satisfactorily completed all inspections. It is important that completion of the purchase by the buyer's solicitor should not take place until the Final Certificate has been issued[63].

**[3977]**

## 7    'Newbuild' cover

Briefly, the 'Newbuild' cover afforded to the buyer is as follows:

7.1    Before completion (ie during the Building Period[64]): protection against loss arising from the developer's failure, provided it is through his insolvency or fraud, to complete the property in accordance with Zurich Municipal's requirements;

7.2    The first two years after completion (ie the first two years of 'the Structural Insurance Period'[65]): protection in respect of Damage and Major Damage[66] (which includes ground movement) or Defects which arise in the house as a result of the developer's failure to rectify any damage or defect;

7.3    The period from the beginning of the third year after completion until the end of the tenth year (ie the remainder of the Structural Insurance Period): protection in respect of Major Damage[67] and any defects which are an imminent threat to physical health and safety;

7.4    There is provision to extend the Structural Insurance Period to 15 years[68].

**[3978]**

## APPENDIX 3
### Building Licences

**1    Building licences**[69]

Building licences are usually granted by a local authority wishing to develop land, although there is no reason why they should not also be used by a private developer.

Instead of selling land outright or subject to restrictions intended to ensure the fulfilment of housing needs in the area, the landowner grants a licence which permits the developer to enter and build on the land. It often also provides for the developer to sell the individual plots to a specified or general market. The contract for sale of such plots must provide for the landowner to join in the conveyance or transfer to convey or transfer the land to the buyer.

This arrangement does not require the developer to make any capital investment in the land, enabling it to concentrate all its available resources on the infrastructure and work in progress. However, the practitioner must ensure that the building licence fully protects the interests of the licensor who is allowing the builder onto his land. Some conditions of a licence may seem rather harsh, but it must be remembered that the licensor is committing his land to a speculative venture, and he must ensure that he has as much security and protection as possible.

If the developer is particularly concerned to avoid overstretching his resources he may require that the licence be split into phases, with a commitment to develop certain portions immediately and an option to develop others later.

**[3979]**

1    The steps listed in this checklist are in addition to the usual steps to be taken by the seller's solicitor on a residential conveyancing transaction, as to which see the checklist in vol 35 (1997 Reissue) SALE OF LAND Paragraphs 16 [22]–40 [59], although some of the steps in the latter checklist are superseded by the steps in this one. As to the completion requirements and procedure see vol 35 (1997 Reissue) SALE OF LAND Paragraphs 72 [107]–78 [114]. As to the use of the National Protocol (for which see vol 35 (1997 Reissue) SALE OF LAND Form 1 [1300]) see Paragraphs 1 [1]–14 [15] of that volume.

Although this checklist sets out the steps to set up a residential development for sale, the same steps need to be taken in respect of an industrial estate or business park, other than paragraph 9 relating to National Housebuilding and construction guarantees. On industrial and commercial estates the buyer may erect the buildings after completion of the purchase of a vacant plot.

In this checklist it is assumed that the seller is also the developer.

2    For a form requesting information from the seller to set up a development scheme see Form 92 [3951] ante.

3    The documents listed in paragraphs 1.2 and 1.3 of this checklist will be required, as copies will have to be supplied to the buyer.

4    In most cases the seller will have bought the land recently and the transfer or conveyance to the seller will have been compulsorily registrable. In those rare cases where the seller bought or acquired the land before compulsory registration of title applied, it should be advised to register its title voluntarily so as to speed the sale process. As to approval of the estate layout plan, see paragraph 3, and as to the approval of the draft transfer see paragraph 12, of this checklist.

5    If the seller's solicitor acted on the purchase of the land he should be fully acquainted with all physical features of the land at the time of purchase, but a site inspection in the company of seller and his architect or surveyor is advisable in order to observe changes since then and subsequent site works including access and infrastructure works, and to obtain any information necessary to complete the record of taking instructions. Throughout the course of the development the seller's solicitor should make periodic inspections to acquaint himself with the progress of the works and to make early discovery of any potential problems.

6    For general advice on the development of registered building estates see Land Registry Practice Leaflet No 7 (April 1999) *Developing Estates—Registration Services* and 5 supplements: 'Estate Boundary Approval'; 'Estate Plan Approval'; 'Approval of Draft Transfers and Leases'; 'Plot Sales—Transfers and Leases' and 'Detailed Plan Requirement and Surveying Specifications—Guidance for Surveyors'.

At the earliest possible stage in the development, the seller's solicitor should send two copies of the estate layout plan to the appropriate district land registry for approval. This will enable discrepancies between the registered title boundaries and the external boundaries of the development site to be identified and resolved before sales take place. The other advantages of obtaining approval of the estate layout plan are that: (1) negotiations for plot sales can proceed without the need to supply an office copy of the seller's filed plan, and (2) applications in Land Registry Form 109 (as to which see vol 25(1) (1999 Reissue) LAND REGISTRATION Form 9 [3141]) for certificates of inspection of the filed plan, and applications for official searches in Land Registry Form 94B (as to which see vol 25(1) (1999 Reissue) LAND REGISTRATION Form 17 [3187]), can describe the land being purchased merely by reference to the plot number(s) on the approved estate layout plan, so saving the cost and trouble of providing separate plans.

Any changes in the estate layout from that on the approved plan must be notified to the Land Registry at the earliest possible moment. The old approved layout plan should be returned to the Land Registry accompanied by a new estate layout plan in duplicate showing the proposed changes.

**[3980]**

7    For a form of transfer of part of the land in a title for an electricity substation and grant of easements for underground cables see Form 91 [3896] post. For a form of consent for a wayleave for overhead or underground cables see vol 14 (1994 Reissue) ENERGY SUPPLY Form 13 [3310].

8    Sometimes electricity supply companies require that the transfer of each plot reserves a right to place electric lines through the plot and/or to supply street lighting and apparatus affixed to buildings.

9    As to the construction, making up and adoption, dedication, stopping up or diversion of highways see vol 18 (1993 Reissue) HIGHWAYS generally and appendix 1 of this checklist. Estate roads are normally built under the Private Street Works Code, for which see the Highways Act 1980 ss 205–218 as amended (20 Halsbury's Statutes (4th Edn) HIGHWAYS, STREETS AND BRIDGES). As to the Advance Payments Code see vol 18 (1993 Reissue) HIGHWAYS Paragraph 50 [57].

10   For forms of agreement under the Highways Act 1980 s 38 as amended by the New Roads and Street Works Act 1991 s 22(1) and by the Local Government Act 1985 s 102, Sch 17 see Form 85 [3801] ante and vol 18 (1993 Reissue) HIGHWAYS Form 9 [127].

11   For a form of agreement which includes work on existing roads under the Highways Act 1980 s 278 and the Local Government Act 1972 s 111 (25 Halsbury's Statutes (4th Edn) LOCAL GOVERNMENT) see Form 87 [3851] ante.

12   If payment under the Advance Payment Code has been made the payment will be refunded on the agreement under the Highways Act s 38 being completed, but the repayment is made to the owner of the land for the time being: see vol 18 (1993 Reissue) HIGHWAYS Paragraph 52 [60]. Provision should be made in the plot sale contracts for any repayment made to the buyer to be repaid to the seller. For a form of such a clause see vol 36 (1997 Reissue) SALE OF LAND Form 297 [2432]. Where the section 38 agreement is not in existence at the date of exchange of the contract for sale, it is usual for a sum equal to the amount of the road charges specified in the advance payment notice in respect of the plot to be retained out of the purchase price and deposited in the joint names of the seller's and buyer's solicitors as security, the sum to be released to the seller when the agreement and bond are completed. For a form of such a clause see vol 36 (1997 Reissue) SALE OF LAND Form 296 [2431].

13   Such arrangements are made under the Highways Act 1980 s 278 as substituted by the New Roads and Street Works Act 1991 s 23, as to which see vol 18 (1993 Reissue) HIGHWAYS Paragraphs 16 [20] and 42 [48].

14   For a form of deed of grant of an easement for a gas main and for consent of an owner/occupier to lay gas pipes in land which is being developed see vol 14 (1994 Reissue) ENERGY SUPPLY Forms 29 [3902] and 32 [3920]).

15   As to the provision of public sewers see vol 14(2) (2000 Reissue) ENVIRONMENT Paragraph 372 [2801] et seq, and see appendix 1 of this checklist.

Under the Water Industry Act 1991 s 98(1) (49 Halsbury's Statutes (4th Edn) WATER) it is the duty of a sewerage undertaker to provide a public sewer to be used for the drainage for domestic purposes of premises in a particular locality in its area if: (a) the undertaker is so required by notice (a requisition) served by one or more of an owner or occupier of premises in the locality, a local authority whose area includes any part of the locality, the Commission for the New Towns, a development corporation for a new town or an urban development corporation; (b) the premises are ones on which there are or will be buildings; and (c) the financial conditions for compliance set out in the Water Industry Act 1991 s 99 are fulfilled. The duty is owed to all requisitioners and is enforceable by action: Water Industry Act 1991 s 98(3), (4) as amended by the Competition and Service (Utilities) Act 1992 s 56(6), Sch 1 para 26.

The Water Industry Act 1991 specifies only one type of financial condition to be imposed on a requisitioner: payment to the undertaker of an annual sum over 12 years on an annual deficit basis: see the Water Industry Act 1991 s 99(2). However, this does not appear to exclude the making of an up-front capital payment which could benefit both the undertaker and the local authority having regard to the controls on the raising and expenditure of capital moneys imposed by the Local Government and Housing Act 1989 (25 Halsbury's Statutes (4th Edn) LOCAL GOVERNMENT).

**[3981]**

16    Serious difficulties can be encountered if the drainage system is not to be connected to the public sewerage system because of the need to provide for the operation of a private sewage treatment works and the recovery of the cost of operation from house owners. A management company will have to be established to own and operate the system.

17    If the developer does not have the benefit of an easement to drain across the land of a third party to connect into a public sewer and is unable to negotiate terms for such an easement, it can requisition the right by serving notice on the sewerage undertaker.

18    The usual procedure is for the developer to enter into an agreement with the sewerage undertaker, or sometimes with the local authority as agent for the sewerage undertaker, under the Water Industry Act 1991 s 104, usually supported by a bond or guarantee. For the form of such an agreement see Form 87 [3851] ante.

19    As to the duty of a water undertaker to provide a water main for domestic purposes by requisition see vol 41 WATER Paragraph 20 [1523].

20    In large scale developments it is common for the development to be divided into phases and for planning conditions to be imposed to secure the orderly development of the site. Phasing conditions also may be imposed in an agreement or undertaking under the Town and Country Planning Act 1990 s 106 as substituted by the Planning and Compensation Act 1991 s 12(1) (46 Halsbury's Statutes (4th Edn) TOWN AND COUNTRY PLANNING).

21    Stage payments, whilst attractive to developers from a cash flow point of view, are not often found in mass produced housing developments because buyers cannot generally raise the stage payments without having completed the transfer of the land so that they can charge it by way of security, and developers are reluctant to transfer the land at the first stage of construction without themselves having a charge on it for future stage payments.

22    Building licences are usually granted by local authorities wishing to develop land, although they can also be granted by a private landowner if he wishes. For a form of building licence see Form 113 [4150] post.

23    For forms of, and commentary on, each selling aid see Form 104 [4129] et seq post.

24    Planning authorities often seek to impose, by way of condition or planning agreements under the Town and Country Planning Act 1990 s 106 as substituted (see note 20 above), requirements for recreational areas, nature reserves, gardens, parks and other facilities to be provided on developments (these sometimes also providing benefit to, or being available for use by, the public at large and not just the residents of the development), but without accepting the obligation to take over the land or facility and its future maintenance once the development is complete. This can cause considerable difficulty for the seller who will not wish to be left with ownership and maintenance liabilities after the development is completed. It is essential to address the problems of the future ownership and maintenance before accepting the obligation to provide the land or facility. Ideally there should be an agreement for the local authority to take over ownership and future maintenance on completion of the development, so relieving the developer of all future liability; this may involve the developer in making payment of a capital sum to the authority. For provisions in a planning agreement for a local authority to take over open space see Form 84 clause 7 [3755] ante. If the local authority refuse to take over the ownership and be responsible for the future maintenance and operation on completion of the development, then the developer should establish an estate management company to take over ownership, the cost of future maintenance being borne by all the plot owners who will pay by way of a service charge. For a form of deed of covenant where there is an estate management company which maintains communal land see Form 121 [4269] post. Some schemes reserve an estate rentcharge under the Rentcharges Act 1977 s 2 as amended by the Trusts of Land and Appointment of Trustees Act 1996 s 25(1), Sch 3, para 15(2) (37 Halsbury's Statutes (4th Edn) RENTCHARGES) coupled with an express right of re-entry, but the latter method is understood to be unacceptable to some lending institutions and its incorporation may cause difficulty in selling and resale.

**[3982]**

25    It is essential that there is a specification of the building works, including external works, fencing and landscaping, if dispute is to be avoided, although in mass produced housing it is not usual to provide a fully detailed architect's specification. A briefer form in layman's language perhaps running to a couple of pages is more common, the buyer sometimes being allowed to inspect a fuller specification at the site office. The contract should provide that the building works will conform with the specification, the planning permission and approved plans and the building regulation approval, and be built to the requirements of the relevant structural guarantee company, as to which see paragraph 9 of this checklist.

26    If variations are contemplated provision must be made in the contract for payment of or allowance for the added or omitted work.

27    Occasionally in developments at the lower price ranges, buyers are permitted to enter and complete fitting out works and do decorating and similar work before completion of the transfer. This is best avoided because of the problems which follow if the work is badly done which is likely to cause delay, or refusal by the buyer's lender to pay over the mortgage advance until remedial works have been done.

28    As to structural guarantees generally see appendix 2 of this checklist.

29      As to the matters to be considered on a transfer of part of the land in the seller's title see vol 35 (1997 Reissue) SALE OF LAND Paragraphs 494 [636]–516 [681] and for a table of such matters see vol 38(1) (2000 Reissue) SALE OF LAND Form 26 [1404]. For transfers of residential plots see Forms 114 [4181]–120 [4260] post.

30      The draft pre-contract information should give the same coverage of information (where appropriate) as would be requested by preliminary enquiries or given in the Seller's Property Information Form (for which see vol 35 (1997 Reissue) SALE OF LAND Form 3 [1323]), and in addition such other information on the scheme of development, the provision of access and services, title and procedural matters as will enable the buyer's solicitor to understand the papers and raise the minimum of enquiries. If the office copy entries of the seller's title are complex or contain irrelevant or superseded matter, notes of explanation should be provided. The fact that the estate layout plan and the form of transfer have been approved by the Land Registry should be stated, and evidence of that approval should be provided. For a specimen form of pre-contract information see Form 94 [4001] post.

31      For a list of documents to be sent to the buyer's solicitors with the draft contract see Form 95 [4007] post.

32      As to the procedure for discharge of plots from registered and noted charges see Land Registry Practice Leaflet No 25 (February 1998) *Discharge of Land from Registered Charges; Discharge of Land from Noted Charges; Deeds of Variation of Registered Charges*. The discharge, being of part of the land in the seller's title, should be made on Land Registry Form DS3 (for which see vol 25(1) (1999 Reissue) LAND REGISTRATION Form 47 [3371]) accompanied by a copy of the relevant part of the approved estate layout plan identifying the land discharged: Land Registration Rules 1925, SR&O 1925/1093 r 98(3)(c) as substituted by SI 1999/128. Form DS3 is not appropriate for the discharge of a plot from a noted charge; the person having the benefit of it must apply for cancellation of the entry, and deduce title to his interest if it has been assigned since the entry was made. See vol 25(1) (1999 Reissue) LAND REGISTRATION Paragraph 159 note 1 [2362].

33      As to certificates of non-crystallisation see vol 35 (1997 Reissue) Paragraph 34.7 [55]. For a form of certificate given by or on behalf of a seller see Form 129 [4352] post and vol 25(1) (1999 Reissue) LAND REGISTRATION Form 48 [3374], and for a form of certificate given by the chargee see Form 128 [4351] post. Evidence of non-crystallisation is not conclusive unless provided by the debenture holder, though the debenture holder is under no obligation to provide such evidence: see *Emmett on Title* (19th Edn) paragraph 10.86.

**[3983]**

34      There is no need to refer to the grant of easements in Land Registry Form DS3 if the transfer of the plot is in the approved form and the easements granted are in the standard wording in that form. If easements in a different form are granted, eg on the transfer of a site for an electricity substation, the Additional Provisions panel of Form DS3 must specifically refer to the easements granted so that the chargee consents to their grant.

35      As to the deposit of the land or charge certificate on a transfer of part see vol 25(1) (1999 Reissue) LAND REGISTRATION Paragraph 128 [2223] and vol 35 (1997 Reissue) SALE OF LAND Paragraph 30 [51]. Some lenders arrange with the Land Registry for their charge certificates generally to be retained on deposit, in which case the fact that the particular certificate is on deposit will normally be noted on the register.

36      The draft transfer together with a specimen of the plan referred to (which should conform with the approved estate layout plan) should be lodged for approval in the appropriate district land registry (as to which see note 6 above and the third supplement there referred to). This will avoid difficulties which may otherwise arise in connection with the proof of easements or generally in regard to the development. Where the form of transfer is approved, the letter of approval will contain an assurance that if easements are granted in the standard form these will be registered as appurtenant to the buyer's title. If the seller supplies to each buyer a copy of the Land Registry's letter, a buyer who relies upon this assurance is relieved of the duty of investigating in detail the seller's power to grant the easements which he purports to grant. This is particularly helpful where the transfer grants easements over the land of third parties, and also because the certificate of inspection of the filed plan in Land Registry Form 102 (for a form of which see vol 25(1) (1999 Reissue) LAND REGISTRATION Form 22 [3211]) does not show the extent of the land in the seller's title and accordingly does not enable the buyer's solicitor to satisfy himself that the seller has power to grant the easements which he contracts to grant.

37      It is recommended that application is made for office copy entries and certificates in Land Registry Form 102 in batches as the development proceeds and not as one bulk order at the start. In this way the later batches will include entries made in the register and on the filed plan as a result of earlier sale off.

38      The form of transfer of part, Land Registry Form TP1 (for which see Form 114 [4181] post), and the application for registration of each transfer in Land Registry Form AP1 (for which see vol 25(1) (1999 Reissue) LAND REGISTRATION Form 26 [3251]) require the full address and post code to be entered on the register to be given.

39      Ie the Building Regulations 1991, SI 1991/2768 as amended.

40      Ie the Highways Act 1980 s 220 as amended by the Local Government Act 1985 s 8, Sch 4 para 35 and by the Local Government (Wales) Act 1994 s 22(1), Sch 7 para 21.

41    Ie he must comply with the Advance Payments Code set out in the Highways Act 1980 s 219 as amended.

42    Highways Act 1980 s 219(4) as amended sets out exceptions to the Advance Payments Code, and sub-s (4)(d) provides that an agreement under the Highways Act 1980 s 38 as amended is a valid alternative.

43    For a form of agreement under the Highways Act 1980 s 38 as amended see Form 86 [3829] ante and vol 18 (1993 Reissue) HIGHWAYS Form 10 [133] and for a form of bond see Form 90 [3891] ante and vol 18 (1993 Reissue) HIGHWAYS Form 11 [145].

44    For a form of agreement under the Water Industry Act 1991 s 104 see Form 89 [3864] ante. For a form of bond see Form 90 [3891] ante.

45    See the Water Industry Act 1991 s 97(5) as amended by the Government of Wales Act 1998 ss 129, 152, Sch 15 para 17, Sch 18 Pt IV.

46    Water Industry Act 1991 s 97(1).

47    Ie the Highways Act 1980 s 38 as amended by the New Roads and Street Works Act 1991 s 22(1) and by the Local Government Act 1985 s 102, Sch 17. As to agreements under section 38 generally see appendix 1 paragraph 1 of this checklist.

48    As to agreements under the Water Industry Act 1991 s 104, see appendix 1 paragraph 3 of this checklist.

                                                                              **[3984]**

49    For a form of bond which can be adapted for roads or sewers see Form 90 [3891] ante and for highways bonds see also vol 18 (1993 Reissue) HIGHWAYS Form 11 [145].

50    Ie under the Advance Payments Code set out in the Highways Act 1980 ss 219, 220 as amended. See further vol 18 (1993 Reissue) HIGHWAYS Paragraph 48 [55] et seq.

51    Ie an agreement under the Highways Act 1980 s 38 as amended (see note 45 above) and/or an agreement under the Water Industry Act 1991 s 104. See appendix 1 paragraphs 2, 3 of this checklist.

52    For a form of such a clause see vol 36 (1997 Reissue) SALE OF LAND Form 296 [2431].

53    'Buildmark' is the registered trademark of the structural insurance scheme offered by the National House Building Council ('NHBC'). See appendix 2 paragraphs 2–4 of this checklist.

54    'Newbuild' is one of the registered trademarks of the structural insurance scheme offered by the Zurich Municipal. See appendix 2 paragraphs 5, 6 of this checklist.

55    See appendix 2 paragraph 2 et seq of this checklist.

56    Defective Premises Act 1972 s 1 (31 Halsbury's Statutes (4th Edn) NEGLIGENCE). Previously, properties built within the NHBC scheme were excluded from the protection of the Defective Premises Act 1972 s 1 by an agreement between the NHBC and the Secretary of State made under the Defective Premises Act 1972 s 2. However, following changes to the scheme made by the NHBC, the Defective Premises Act 1972 s 2 no longer operates to exclude from the Defective Premises Act 1972 s 1 properties within the NHBC 'Buildmark' Scheme. See appendix 2 paragraphs 2, 3 of this checklist.

57    See *Thompson v Clive Alexander and Partners and Associated Structural Design Ltd* (1992) 28 Con LR 49, 59 BLR 77.

58    Defective Premises Act 1972 s 1(5).

59    As a practitioner acting for a builder or developer it is wise to obtain a copy of the section dealing with legal requirements in *Registered House-Builder's Handbook* issued to all registered members. For the address of the NHBC see Information Binder: Addresses (Miscellaneous) [1].

60    See appendix 2 paragraph 2 of this checklist.

61    Before registration, an applicant will have his capabilities assessed by Zurich Municipal and must undertake to comply with all requirements of the scheme.

62    In cases of likely abnormal risk, notification, with a site investigation report and foundation details, should be made at least six weeks before commencement of the building works.

63    It is possible: (a) that the property might not have been completed in accordance with Zurich Municipal's requirements, or (b) that the Final Certificate might contain a restrictive endorsement.

64    The 'Building Period' is the period commencing on the effective date of the Initial Certificate (see appendix 2 paragraph 5 of this checklist) and, where no claims have been notified, ending on the date of the Final Certificate (see appendix 2 paragraph 5 of this checklist). Where a claim is notified the Building Period ends upon the notification of such a claim.

65    The 'Structural Insurance Period' is the period commencing on the effective date of the Final Certificate and ending 10 years later.

66    'Damage', 'Major Damage' and 'Defects' are defined in the Policy: 'Damage' is physical damage caused by a 'Defect' which, in turn, is a failure to comply with Zurich's Requirements. 'Major Damage' is: (a) damage including ground movement affecting the structural stability of the new home; or (b) damp penetration into the envelope of the new home; or (c) debonding of the internal plaster or external render; or (d) severe cracking.

67    See note 64 above.

68    Subject to the structural insurance period being free of claims, the buyer may pay an additional premium to extend the term for up to five additional years.
        Further information can be obtained from the Building Guarantee Dept, Zurich Municipal Insurance; for address see Information Binder: Addresses (Miscellaneous) [1].

69    For a form of building licence granted by a local authority see Form 113 [4150] post.

                                                                  **[3985]–[4000]**

# 94
### Pre-Contract Information[1]

*(insert name)* Estate

The following information is supplied on behalf of the seller. It is believed to be correct but the accuracy is not guaranteed and does not obviate the need to make appropriate searches, enquiries and inspections.

## 1    Boundaries

*(insert details of the ownership of the boundaries of the plot, and the maintenance of any the ownership of which is not known)* eg [The ownership and maintenance of boundaries of the individual plot is stated in the draft transfer and shown on the Estate layout plan attached to it]

**[4001]**

## 2    Access

2.1    The nearest existing publicly maintained highway is *(insert name and location by reference to the Estate layout plan)* and the Estate road will be connected to it as shown on the Estate layout plan

2.2    The Estate road and footpaths [are *or* are intended to be] the subject of an agreement under the Highways Act 1980 Section 38[2] [which is in the course of negotiation] with *(insert name of highway authority)* supported by a bond given by *(name of bondsman)* [and a copy of the agreement dated *(date)* and bond dated *(date)* is enclosed]

[2.3    [No payment has been made in respect of the plot under the Advance Payment Code[3] *or (insert details of any  payment made and of arrangements to be made for its refund to the seller)*]]

[2.4    *(if a retention is to be permitted until the highway agreement is entered into, insert details)*[4]]

## 3    Guarantees and similar documents

3.1    There are none at present in existence

3.2    The seller is registered with *(name of structural guarantee company)*[5] and will offer to enter into *(name of structural guarantee company)*'s agreement in respect of the building to be erected on the plot

3.3    The highway and sewer agreements mentioned above and below are supported by bonds copies of which are supplied

**[4002]**

## 4    Services

4.1    The dwelling house will be served by mains drainage, electricity, gas, telephone and water

[4.2    The routes of the foul and storm water sewers which are to be adopted are shown on the Estate layout plan]

4.3    Electricity, gas and water mains are provided [underground in the Estate road] by service undertakers and the dwelling houses will be directly connected to those mains

4.4    The nearest existing publicly maintained foul sewer is *(insert location by reference to the Estate layout plan)* and the foul [and storm water] sewers to serve the Estate will be connected to it as shown on the Estate layout plan

4.5     The foul [and storm water] sewers to serve the Estate [are *or* are intended to be] the subject of an agreement under the Water Industry Act 1991 Section 104[6] [which is in the course of negotiation] with *(insert name of authority or sewerage undertaker)* supported by a bond given by *(name of bondsman)* [and a copy of the agreement dated *(date)* and bond dated *(date)* is enclosed]

## 5     Planning

5.1     The previous use of the Estate was *(insert previous use)* and [outline] planning permission for residential development and the laying out of roads and sewers[7] was granted by *(name of local planning authority)* on *(date)* under reference number *(number)*

5.2     Notice of the decision on detailed plans for the development of the Estate was granted on *(date)* under reference number *(number)*

5.3     Building Regulation Approval[8] was granted on *(date)* under reference number *(number)*

5.4     Copies of the planning permission, notice of decision and approval are supplied

5.5     No building, engineering, mining or other operations have been carried out on the Estate except in pursuance of the above mentioned documents

                                                                                    **[4003]**

## 6     Disputes and notices

6.1     There are no [current] disputes concerning the Estate [and the seller is not aware of any past disputes concerning it *or (insert details)*]

6.2     No notices have been served by or on the seller [and so far as it is aware by or on its predecessors in title] except for those relating to planning and building regulation matters and infrastructure prior to or in the course of development of the Estate

## 7     Adverse rights

So far as the seller is aware the plot is not subject to any rights, easements, covenants or restrictions except as mentioned in the office copy entries of the seller's title, the draft contract and draft transfer and other documents supplied

## 8     Shared facilities

Details of shared facilities are set out or referred to in the draft transfer [and office copy entries of the seller's title]

## 9     Specification

[There is no specification but the buyer has been afforded the opportunity to inspect fully detailed approved drawings bearing construction and design notes and the construction will be in accordance with the planning permission and approved plans [and the requirements of *(name of structural guarantee company)*] *or* a full specification is supplied]

                                                                                    **[4004]**

## 10     Land Registration

10.1    The seller's land or charge certificate is on deposit at the *(name)* District Land Registry *(address)* [under deposit number *(number)*]

10.2    The Estate layout plan was approved by the Land Registry on *(date)* and official searches for the plot [and the [garage *or* parking] plot] may be made without supplying a plan provided that the plot number [and the plot number of the [garage *or* parking] plot] is stated on the application form

10.3    The form of transfer was approved by the Land Registry on *(date)* and a copy of
        the letter of approval is supplied

[10.4   *(insert any explanation of matters shown on the office copy entries)*]

## 11    Local searches

Local land charge searches and enquiries should be sent to *(insert name, address and DX
number of local authority)*. No plan need be supplied if the property is described as 'Plot
No *(number)* [and the plot number of the [garage *or* parking] plot] *(name of Estate and full
postal address)* development by *(name of developer)*'

**[4005]**

1       For a long form of preliminary enquiries suitable for residential property see vol 36 (1997 Reissue)
        SALE OF LAND Form 33 [1639]. This Form contains a specimen of the information which would have
        to be given in reply to relevant preliminary enquiries based on vol 36 (1997 Reissue) SALE OF LAND
        Form 33 [1639] if they were raised by the buyer following receipt of the draft contract.
2       Ie the Highways Act 1980 s 38 as amended by the Local Government Act 1985 s 102, Sch 17 and by
        the New Roads and Street Works Act 1991 s 22(1) (20 Halsbury's Statutes (4th Edn) HIGHWAYS
        STREETS AND BRIDGES) and see Form 93 appendix 1 [3971] ante.
3       As to the Advance Payments Code see vol 18 (1993 Reissue) HIGHWAYS Paragraph 50 [57] and see
        Form 93 appendix 1 paragraph 2 [3972] ante.
4       For such a clause see vol 36 (1997 Reissue) SALE OF LAND Form 296 [2431].
5       As to structural guarantee schemes see Form 93 appendix 2 [3974] ante.
6       Ie the Water Industry Act 1990 s 104 (49 Halsbury's Statutes (4th Edn) WATER) and see Form 93
        appendix 1 [3971] ante.
7       Planning permission for roads and sewers is sometimes granted in a separate permission; if so, the details
        should be set out.
8       Ie under the Building Act 1984 (35 Halsbury's Statutes (4th Edn) PUBLIC HEALTH AND
        ENVIRONMENTAL PROTECTION).

**[4006]**

# 95

**Checklist of documents to be sent with the initial contract for sale of a plot
on a residential estate**

1       Draft contract in duplicate
2       Office copy entries in the register and filed plan or Form 102[1]
3       Draft transfer in duplicate or triplicate[2]
4       Transfer plans[3]
5       Pre-contract information[4]
6       National House Building Council or other structural guarantee documentation[5]
7       Copies of all planning permissions and approvals under the Building Regulations[6]
8       Replies to standard requisitions on title
9       Copies of any agreements under the Highways Act 1980 Section 38[7] or the
        Water Industry Act 1991 Section 104[8] and supporting bonds where appropriate[9]
10      Copies of any other relevant documents eg an agreement under the Town and
        Country Planning Act 1990 Section 106[10]
11      Copy of specification (if any)
12      General information sheet[11]

**[4007]**

1          As to deduction of title generally see vol 35 (1997 Reissue) SALE OF LAND Paragraph 398 [509]
        et seq ante. As to Land Registry Form 102 certificates of inspection of the filed plan see vol 25(1) (1999
        Reissue) LAND REGISTRATION Paragraph 57 [1881].

2    An extra copy of the transfer is needed for registration purposes. It is usual for the builder's solicitors to provide the extra copies.

3    These are usually copies of or extracts from the estate plan. Enough plans should be supplied for one to be attached to each draft of the transfer and each engrossment and for use with any searches where plans are required.

4    For a specimen see Form 94 [4001] ante.

5    As to the National House Building Council scheme and its documentation generally see Form 93 appendix 2 [3974] ante.

6    Ie the Building Regulations 1991, SI 1991/2768 as amended.

7    Ie the Highways Act 1980 s 38 as amended by the Local Government Act 1985 s 102, Sch 17 and by the New Roads and Street Works Act 1991 s 22(1) (20 Halsbury's Statutes (4th Edn) HIGHWAYS, STREETS AND BRIDGES).

8    Ie the Water Industry Act 1991 s 104 (49 Halsbury's Statutes (4th Edn) WATER).

9    As to the adoption of roads and sewers generally see Form 93 appendix 2 [3974] ante.

10   Ie the Town and Country Planning Act 1990 s 106 as substituted by the Planning and Compensation Act 1991 s 12(1) (46 Halsbury's Statutes (4th Edn) TOWN AND COUNTRY PLANNING).

11   This should contain all information concerning the development likely to be of use to a buyer (if not included under pre-contract information) including instructions for submitting local land charges searches, mortgage arrangements available through the builder, use of retentions if the agreements for adoption of sewers and roads are not complete etc. It should be tailored to suit the individual requirements of each development.

**[4008]**

# (2):  AGREEMENTS FOR SALE

# 96

## Agreement for sale of part of a freehold property comprised in a single registered title being a building plot not on a building estate[1]

THIS AGREEMENT is made the ...... day of .........

BETWEEN:

(1)    *(seller)*[2] [company number *(number)*[3]] [of *(address)* *or* whose registered office is at *(address)*] ('the Seller') and

(2)    *(buyer)* [company number *(number)*] [of *(address)* *or* whose registered office is at *(address)*] ('the Buyer')

**[4009]**

**1      Definitions and interpretation[4]**

In this Agreement:

1.1     'the Buyer's Solicitors' means *(insert name and address of person or firm)*

1.2     'the Completion Date' means the ...... day of .........[5]

1.3     'the Contract Rate'[6] means *(insert interest rate or method of calculating the interest rate by reference eg to the base lending rate of a named bank)*

[1.4    'the Documents'[7] means the documents (if any) particulars of which are set out in the [second] schedule]

1.5     'the General Conditions'[8] means [the Standard Conditions of Sale (3rd Edn) *or* *(specify)*]

1.6     'the Plan' means the plan annexed to this Agreement [and if numbered plans are annexed any reference to a numbered plan is to the annexed plan so numbered]

1.7     'the Property'[9] means the property outlined in [red] on [the Plan *or* Plan No
        *(number)*] and described in the [first] schedule[10]
1.8     'the Purchase Price' means the sum of £…[11] [which is [inclusive *or* exclusive]
        of VAT at the standard rate as at the date of actual completion]
1.9     'the Retained Land' means the land [adjacent to the Property] *(add brief
        description)* which is outlined in [green] on [the Plan *or* Plan No *(number)*] (being
        that part of the land registered at HM Land Registry under title number
        *(number)* as is not comprised in the Property)
1.10    'the Seller's Solicitors' means *(insert name and address of person or firm)*
1.11    where the context so admits the expression[s] 'the Seller' [and 'the Buyer']
        include[s] the personal representatives of the Seller [and the Buyer] [and 'the
        Buyer' shall include any successors in title of the Buyer][12]
1.12    words importing one gender shall be construed as importing any other gender
1.13    words importing the singular shall be construed as importing the plural and vice
        versa
1.14    words importing persons shall be construed as importing a corporate body and/
        or a partnership and vice versa
1.15    where any party comprises more than one person the obligations and liabilities
        of that party under this Agreement shall be joint and several obligations and
        liabilities of those persons[13]
1.16    the clause headings do not form part of this Agreement and shall not be taken
        into account in its construction or interpretation
1.17    any reference to a clause or a paragraph or a schedule is to one in this Agreement
        so numbered
1.18    any reference to a colour or letter is to one on the Plan[s]

**[4010]**

## 2       Agreement for sale

The Seller shall sell and the Buyer shall buy the Property at the Purchase Price[14]

## [3      Rights and reservations

The Property is sold together with the rights contained in the [third] schedule and
subject to the reservations contained in the [fourth] schedule][15]

## 4       Deposit

The Buyer shall on or before the date of this Agreement pay a deposit of [10%] of the
Purchase Price to the Seller's Solicitors as [stakeholders *or* agents for the Seller][16] [by
means of cash or telegraphic or other direct transfer banker's draft or a building society
or bank guaranteed cheque or a cheque drawn on a solicitor's clients' account][17]

## 5       Completion

Completion of the sale and purchase and payment of the balance of the Purchase Price
shall take place on the Completion Date [at the offices of the Seller's Solicitors or where
they may direct][18]

## 6       Title guarantee

The Seller sells with [full *or* limited] title guarantee[19]

## 7       Possession

The Property is sold with vacant possession on completion[20]

**[4011]**

**8     Title**[21]

8.1     Title to the Property is registered at HM Land Registry with [absolute] title under title number *(number)* and title shall be deduced in accordance with the Land Registration Act 1925 Section 110[22] [save that copies of the entries on the register the filed plan and any documents referred to shall be office copies[23]] [and the Buyer or the Buyer's Solicitors having been supplied with such copies prior to the date of this Agreement the Buyer shall be deemed to purchase with full knowledge of the title in all respects and shall not raise any requisitions or make any objection in relation to the title]

[8.2     The Buyer shall not require the Seller to be registered as proprietor of the Property at HM Land Registry prior to the Completion Date and if such a requirement is made by the Buyer or any objection is raised with regard to the fact that the registration of the Seller as registered proprietor of the Property at HM Land Registry has not been completed on or before the Completion Date the Seller shall be entitled (but not obliged) to rescind this Agreement in the same manner and upon the same terms as if the Buyer had persisted in an objection to the title which the Seller was unable to deal with][24]

[9     **Incumbrances**[25] *(where the form of the assurance is not annexed)*

9.1     The Property is sold subject to and (where appropriate) with the benefit of the matters contained or referred to in the [Documents *or* the property [proprietorship][26] and charges[27] registers of title number *(number)* [save for the Seller's subsisting mortgage]]

9.2     The Buyer or the Buyer's Solicitors having been supplied with copies of the [Documents *or* the property [proprietorship] and charges registers and the matters contained or referred to in the registers] prior to the date of this Agreement the Buyer shall be deemed to purchase with full notice and knowledge of the same and shall not raise any requisition or make any objection in relation to them

9.3     The transfer of the Property shall contain a covenant by the Buyer that the Buyer will observe and perform the covenants and conditions [contained or referred to in the Documents *or* contained or referred to in the property [proprietorship] and charges registers of title number *(number)*] and will indemnify and keep the Seller and his successors in title fully and effectually indemnified against all actions proceedings damages costs claims and expenses which may be suffered or incurred by the Seller or his successors in title in respect of any future breach or non-observance or non-performance of those covenants and conditions[28]

9.4     The transfer shall be engrossed [in duplicate] by the Buyer's Solicitors and [the *or* both] engrossment[s] shall be executed by the Buyer before the Completion Date

[9.5     Immediately after completion the Buyer shall at his own expense procure the proper stamping of the duplicate transfer as a duplicate (including but not limited to the affixing of a particulars delivered stamp) and shall immediately after such stamping deliver the duly stamped duplicate to the Seller's Solicitors]

**[4012]**

*or*

**9     Incumbrances**[29] *(where the form of assurance is annexed)*[30]

9.1     The transfer to the Buyer shall be in the form of the annexed draft transfer

9.2     The Property is sold subject to and (where appropriate) with the benefit of the rights exceptions reservations covenants restrictions and other matters (if any) referred to in the annexed draft transfer and the property [proprietorship] and charges register of title number *(number)* [other than the charges referred to in the entries numbered *(numbers)* of the charges register of that title *or* other than the Seller's subsisting mortgage]

9.3      The Buyer or the Buyer's Solicitors having been supplied with copies of the documents referred to in clause 9.2 prior to the date of this Agreement shall be deemed to purchase with full notice and knowledge of them and shall not raise any requisition or make any objection in relation to them

9.4      The transfer shall be engrossed [in duplicate] by the Seller's Solicitors and [the *or* both] engrossment[s] shall be executed by the Buyer before the Completion Date

[9.5     Immediately after completion the Buyer shall at his own expense procure the proper stamping of the duplicate transfer as a duplicate (including but not limited to the affixing of a particulars delivered stamp) and shall immediately after such stamping deliver the duly stamped duplicate to the Seller's Solicitors]

9.6      On completion the Buyer shall in addition to the Purchase Price pay to the Seller's Solicitors the sum of £... and VAT for the Seller's Solicitors' costs of engrossment]

**[4013]**

## [10   New covenants[31]

10.1     The Buyer shall in the transfer enter into a covenant with the Seller to the intent that the burden of the covenant will run with and bind the Property and every part of it and that the benefit of the covenant will be annexed to and run with the Retained Land and every part of it to observe and perform the restrictions set out in the [fifth] schedule [but not so as to impose any personal liability on the Buyer or any successor in title of the Buyer after he has parted with all interest in the Property]

[10.2    The Buyer shall in the transfer enter into the covenants with the Seller in the form set out in the [sixth] schedule]

[10.3    The Seller shall in the transfer enter into the covenants with the Buyer in the form set out in the [seventh] schedule]]

## 11   Matters affecting the Property

The Property is sold subject to the following matters:

11.1     all local land charges whether registered or not before the date of this Agreement and all matters capable of registration as local land charges whether or not actually so registered[32]

11.2     all notices served and orders demands proposals or requirements made by any local public or other competent authority whether before or after the date of this Agreement

11.3     all actual or proposed charges notices orders restrictions agreements conditions contraventions or other matters arising under the enactments relating to town and country planning and environmental law

11.4     all easements quasi-easements rights exceptions or other similar matters whether or not apparent on inspection or disclosed in any of the documents referred to in this Agreement

**[4014]**

## [12   Shared facilities[33]

*(insert conditions concerning shared facilities if required; if necessary referring to a schedule)*]

## [13   Agreements and declarations[34]

The transfer to the Buyer shall contain declarations worded as follows:

'0.1     The Buyer and his successors in title shall not be entitled to any right of access of light and air or any other easement or right which would restrict or interfere with the free use of any Retained Land for building developing or any other purpose

0.2     The Buyer shall not be entitled to the continuance of nor shall he by virtue of this transfer or of the Law of Property Act 1925 Section 62[35] acquire any easement or right or privilege or advantage over or in respect of the Retained Land [or acquire any appurtenant right referred to in the property register of the title above mentioned] or be entitled to the benefit (which benefit is hereby exclusively reserved to the Seller) of or to enforce or to have enforced or to prevent the release or modification of any covenant agreement or condition entered into by any person with the Seller or his predecessors in title to the Retained Land save in so far as is specifically granted in this transfer[36]

0.3     No part of the soil of any road or lane [nor the bed foreshore or fundus of any estuary river or stream] abutting or adjoining the land hereby transferred is included in this transfer

0.4     No part of any hedge fence wall or gate separating the Property from the Retained Land is included in this transfer']

**14      Office copies**

The Buyer shall within 7 days of completion of the registration of the transfer supply the Seller with office copy entries of the register of the title to the Property[37]

**[4015]**

**15      Disclaimer[38]**

The Buyer admits that:

15.1    he has inspected the Property and purchases it with full knowledge of its actual state and condition and shall take the Property as it stands

15.2    he enters into this Agreement solely as a result of his own inspection and on the basis of the terms of this Agreement and not in reliance upon any representation or warranty either written or oral or implied made by or on behalf of the Seller (save for any representation or warranty contained in written replies given by the Seller's Solicitors to any preliminary inquiries raised by the Buyer or the Buyer's Solicitors)

15.3    this Agreement contains the entire agreement between the parties

**16      Incorporation of conditions of sale**

The General Conditions shall apply to this Agreement and are incorporated in it in so far as they are applicable to a sale by private treaty and are not varied by or inconsistent with the terms of this Agreement [and shall be amended as follows: *(insert details of amendments required)*][39]

**[17      Restriction on assignment[40]**

17.1    This Agreement is personal to the Buyer and shall not be capable of assignment

[17.2    The Seller shall not be required to transfer the Property [to anyone other than the Buyer named in this Agreement *or* at a price greater than the Purchase Price]]]

**18      Merger on completion[41]**

The provisions of this Agreement shall not merge on completion of the transfer of the Property so far as they remain to be performed

**19      Nature of this Agreement**

This Agreement [is *or* is not] a deed and [has *or* has not] been executed by the parties to it as a deed[42]

**[20     Contracts (Rights of Third Parties) Act 1999**

For the purposes of the Contracts (Rights of Third Parties) Act 1999 it is agreed that [with the exception only of *(specify clauses)*] nothing in this Agreement shall confer on any third party any right to enforce or any benefit of any term of this Agreement]

[AS *or* IN] WITNESS etc

**[4016]**

**[FIRST] SCHEDULE**
The Property
*(describe the property)*

**[SECOND SCHEDULE**
The Documents
*(insert details)*]

**[THIRD SCHEDULE**
The Rights Granted
*(insert details)*]

**[FOURTH SCHEDULE**
The Rights Reserved
*(insert details)*]

**[FIFTH SCHEDULE[43]**
The Restrictions

**1     Building site**

The Buyer must not use the Property for any purpose except as [permanent pasture for [mowing *or* grazing][44] *or*] a building site for the construction on it of one private dwelling house[45] and *(number)* private garage[s] and the laying out of gardens for such dwelling house PROVIDED ALWAYS that after such construction shall be completed this restriction shall cease to have effect

**2     Approval of plans**

The Buyer must not build or erect upon the Property any buildings [or] structures [or erections] other than one private dwelling house and *(number)* private garage[s] and boundary walls and fences as to the locations exterior design appearance finish and decoration [and foul drainage facilities] strictly in accordance with the drawings and specifications [approved by the Seller in writing (which approval [in relation to finish and decoration] will not be unreasonably withheld in respect of any of such matters as are approved by the local planning authority)] [attached and signed by the parties for the purpose of identification]

**[4017]**

**3     Alterations**

The Buyer must not:

3.1     make any deviation from the drawings and specification approved by the Seller affecting the location exterior design [and] appearance [finish and decoration] of all buildings and works as described therein

3.2     after completion of the buildings make any alterations or additions to the exterior of those buildings or of any other buildings subsequently erected on the Property [or to the walls hedges and fences on the Property]

3.3     erect any additional buildings walls hedges and fences on the Property except in all cases with the written approval of the Seller [which approval will not be unreasonably withheld and] whose fees and those of his professional advisors in connection with the consideration of any such application whether granted refused or withdrawn shall be paid by the Buyer

**4    Use**

The Buyer must not use the Property or any building for the time being on it for the purpose of any profession trade business or manufacture of any description nor use any dwelling house on it except as a private residence nor use any garage on it except as a private garage ancillary to the dwelling house

**5    Nuisance**[46]

The Buyer must not do or omit to be done any act or thing on or about the Property the doing or omission of which shall or may be or grow to be an annoyance nuisance damage danger or disturbance to the Seller or the owners or occupiers of any part of the Retained Land or adjoining or neighbouring property

**6    Parking**

The Buyer must not park boats caravans or trade vehicles (save in the course of delivery of goods or supply of services to the Property) on the Property

**7    Boundary support**

The Buyer must not deposit any soil or materials against or abutting upon any of the boundary walls hedges or fences dividing the Property from the Retained Land or use any such boundary features as a means of support

**[4018]**

**8    Levels**

The Buyer must not make any material alteration in the height or level of the surface of the Property as existing at the date of this transfer except so far as is essential to construct foundations and Service Installations

**9    Drainage**

The Buyer must not discharge water soil or effluent from the Property onto the Retained Land

**10    Trees**

The Buyer must not permit plants trees or shrubs which shall exceed *(number)* metres in height to remain on the part of the Property [hatched *or* tinted] *(colour)* on the Plan

**11    Laundry**

The Buyer must not hang out washing or laundry anywhere on the Property where it shall be visible from any part of the Retained Land

[SIXTH SCHEDULE
Buyer's covenants with the Seller][47]

[SEVENTH SCHEDULE
Seller's covenants with the Buyer][48]

*(signatures (or common seals) of the parties)*[49]
[*(signatures of witnesses)*]

**[4019]**

1     No stamp duty. See Information Binder: Stamp Duties [1] (Agreement).
      This Form is for use where the seller is selling part of his land (eg part of his garden) as a building
plot, the buyer to erect a house and garage on it in accordance with plans to be prepared by the buyer
but approved by the seller. For another form see vol 2(3) (1998 Reissue) ALLOTMENTS,
SMALLHOLDINGS AND GARDENS Form 131 [604].
      In the case of unregistered land the agreement is capable of being registered by the buyer against
the seller's name as an estate contract (see vol 25(1) (1999 Reissue) LAND CHARGES Paragraph 40.5
[75]) and additionally may be protected by way of caution against first registration (see vol 25(1) (1999
Reissue) LAND REGISTRATION Paragraph 204 [2661]). Registration should be effected against the
estate owner rather than the seller where the seller is a contracting buyer who has agreed to sub-sell or
a mortgagee exercising its power of sale.
      In the case of registered land, the agreement may be noted on the register as an estate contract if
the land certificate is placed on deposit or deemed to be on deposit, or it could be the subject of a
caution in other cases: see vol 25(1) (1999 Reissue) LAND REGISTRATION Paragraph 180 [2496].
Strictly, all contracts for the sale of land should be protected by registration as land charges irrespective
of whether the seller is in practice likely to resell, but the vast majority of such contracts are not so
registered unless eg completion is likely to be delayed. A buyer is not under a duty to register a contract:
*Wright v Dean* [1948] Ch 686, [1948] 2 All ER 415. However, it seems that in certain circumstances a
solicitor might be held to be negligent for failing to protect his client by registering his interest as buyer
under a contract: see eg *Midland Bank Trust Co Ltd v Hett, Stubbs & Kent (a firm)* [1979] 1 Ch 384, [1978]
3 All ER 571.
      As to the matters listed below see vol 35 (1997 Reissue) SALE OF LAND at the respective
references given:
(a)   identity of property: Paragraph 346 [453] et seq;
(b)   identity on sales of part: Paragraph 348 [455] et seq;
(c)   easements: Paragraph 485 [623] et seq;
(d)   matters to be considered on a transfer of part: Paragraph 494 [635] et seq;
(e)   restrictive covenants: Paragraph 517 [694] et seq;
(f)   positive covenants: Paragraph 527 [703] et seq;
(g)   parcels on a transfer of part: Paragraph 567 [753] et seq;
(h)   transfer of land in part of a registered title: Paragraph 590 [779];
(i)   plan on a transfer of unregistered land: Paragraph 623 [816] et seq; and
(j)   parcels and plans in a conveyance of unregistered land and HM Land Registry's colour code:
      Paragraph 652 [854] et seq.
For:
(a)   covenants (both restrictive and positive) and declarations see vol 13(1) (1996 Reissue)
      COVENANTS RELATING TO LAND generally;
(b)   easements and profits à prendre see vol 13(1) (1996 Reissue) EASEMENTS AND PROFITS À
      PRENDRE generally; and
(c)   covenants (both restrictive and positive), declarations, easements and profits à prendre relating to
      agricultural land, rural property and sporting matters, see vol 2(2) (1998 Reissue) AGRICULTURE
      Paragraph 113 [957] et seq.
      A plan must be used on a sale of part of a seller's property whether registered or unregistered and
the retained land must also be defined and identified on a plan. The plan must be of sufficient size and
scale to enable all salient features to be readily identified.
      It is good practice on sales of part for the draft assurance to be prepared by the seller's solicitors
and annexed to the contract and form part of the contract. This avoids the duplication involved in
setting out the covenants easements and declarations in full in the contract as well as the assurance.
      Where part only of a transferor's land is sold it is no longer necessary for the transferor to take a
duplicate transfer as evidence of the terms of the transfer and of the covenants, easements and
declarations which benefit the retained land. In many cases the need will be obviated by the fact that
details of the relevant matters will appear on the register of the transferee's title (which will be accessible
to the transferor due to the open register). The reserved rights will also be reflected as appurtenant
rights added onto the register of the transferor's title. Even with positive covenants, these will normally
be the subject of an entry on the transferee's title as a matter of Land Registry practice. It may be
desirable for the transferee to have a separate record of the positive covenants in case the 'chain of
covenants' in subsequent transfers of the transferee's title is broken (so that the entry on the positive
covenants on the register is cancelled). However, that need could be met by ensuring that the transfer
is executed first by the transferee (as would be prudent practice) and a certified copy of it, as executed
by both parties, is retained instead of a duplicate transfer.

2    The Standard Conditions of Sale (3rd Edn) (for which see vol 38(1) (2000 Reissue) SALE OF LAND Form 1 [1011]) use the terminology 'seller' and 'buyer' in place of the traditional 'vendor' and 'purchaser'. If this Form is to be used in conjunction with general conditions other than the Standard Conditions of Sale it is recommended that the expressions 'vendor' and 'purchaser' are used in place of 'seller' and 'buyer' in order to present a uniform approach to the definitions used in such other general conditions.

3    If any party is a company it is desirable to include the company registration number before the address of the registered office. This avoids any problems arising when a company has been wound up and a new company formed with the same name, or when the name of a company is changed, or if companies swap names, eg on a reconstruction of a group of companies. In addition the company registration number will be required by HM Land Registry under the provisions of the Land Registration Rules 1925, SR&O 1925/1093 r 259(1) as substituted by SI 1996/2973.

4    One view would add the words 'unless the context otherwise admits' or 'where the context admits' and this may be implied (see *Meux v Jacobs* (1875) LR 7 HL 481; *Law Society v United Services Bureau Ltd* [1934] 1 KB 343, DC). However, the better course is to use, whenever practicable, defined terms in such a way that there are no circumstances where the defined meanings do not apply.

        Clauses 1.12–14 are not strictly necessary as the Law of Property Act 1925 s 61 (37 Halsbury's Statutes (4th Edn) REAL PROPERTY) provides such definitions, but such definitions are usually inserted for the convenience of the parties.

        For additional definitions and interpretation clauses see vol 36 (1997 Reissue) SALE OF LAND Forms 191 [2231]–196 [2238].

5    If no date is specifically agreed for completion under a contract incorporating one of the sets of standard conditions the fall-back provisions of the relevant conditions will apply. See eg the Standard Conditions of Sale (3rd Edn) condition 6.1 (for which see vol 38(1) (2000 Reissue) SALE OF LAND Form 1 [1011]), the Law Society's Conditions of Sale (1984 Revision) condition 21(1) (for which see vol 38(1) (2000 Reissue) SALE OF LAND Form 3 [1131]) and the National Conditions of Sale (20th Edn) condition 5(1) (for which see vol 38(1) (2000 Reissue) SALE OF LAND Form 4 [1161]) (which latter two sets of conditions were replaced by the Standard Conditions of Sale as from March 1990: see vol 38(1) (2000 Reissue) SALE OF LAND Paragraph 290 [1001]).

6    Note that certain conditions in the Standard Conditions of Sale (3rd Edn) (see eg conditions 5.2.6, 7.3.2) provide for compensation payable at the 'contract rate' ie the Law Society's interest rate from time to time in force (for which see vol 38(1) (2000 Reissue) SALE OF LAND Form 1 condition 1.1.1(g) [1011]); there are also conditions (see eg conditions 2.2.3, 7.2(a), 7.5.2, 7.6.2) which provide for payment of 'accrued interest' (for which see vol 38(1) (2000 Reissue) SALE OF LAND Form 1 condition 1.1.1(a) [1011]).

7    Delete this definition and the schedule referred to if the draft assurance is annexed.

8    Other sets of standard conditions which might be referred to are the Statutory Form of Conditions of Sale 1925/779, which apply to contracts made by correspondence, and may, but only by express reference, be made to apply to any other cases (see the Law of Property Act 1925 s 46, the National Conditions of Sale (20th Edn) (for which see vol 38(1) (2000 Reissue) SALE OF LAND Form 4 [1161]), and the Law Society's General Conditions of Sale (1984 Revision) (for which see vol 38(1) (2000 Reissue) SALE OF LAND Form 3 [1131]). As to the replacement of the latter two sets of standard conditions by the Standard Conditions of Sale as from March 1990, see vol 38(1) (2000 Reissue) SALE OF LAND Paragraph 290 [1001] et seq. Neither set of conditions has been updated subsequently. A contract by correspondence can still be made in relation to a short lease, or the creation or operation of a resulting, implied or constructive trust: see the Law of Property (Miscellaneous Provisions) Act 1989 s 2 as amended by the Trusts of Land and Appointment of Trustees Act 1996 s 25(2), Sch 4 (37 Halsbury's Statutes (4th Edn) REAL PROPERTY).

**[4021]**

9    As to the identity of the property to be sold see vol 35 (1997 Reissue) SALE OF LAND Paragraph 346 et seq.

10    The size and scale of the plan should be sufficiently large to enable all salient features to be readily identified: see *Scarfe v Adams* [1981] 1 All ER 843, CA. If many plans are required it may be convenient to bind them in a separate bundle, suitably referred to in the contract. Each plan should be individually numbered if there is more than one. As to plans generally see vol 35 (1997 Reissue) SALE OF LAND Paragraph 623 [816].

11    As to circumstances in which VAT is payable see vol 35 (1997 Reissue) SALE OF LAND Paragraph 136 [173] et seq and Information Binder: Property [1] (VAT and Property).

        It should be noted that VAT forms part of the purchase price for the purposes of calculating stamp duty and land registration fees.

        If VAT is or may be chargeable in respect of any part of the purchase price, and the price is to be exclusive of the tax, a comprehensive clause dealing with all aspects of the tax should be included. For an example of such a clause see vol 38(1) (2000 Reissue) SALE OF LAND Form 57 clause 16.1–16.3

[2143]. The VAT provisions in that Form expand those in the Standard Conditions of Sale (3rd Edn) condition 1.4 (for which see vol 38(1) (2000 Reissue) SALE OF LAND Form 1 [1014]) and are inserted to act as a reminder to the parties of the importance of considering VAT aspects at an early stage.

    If the Value Added Tax Act 1994 s 89 (48 Halsbury's Statutes (4th Edn) VALUE ADDED TAX) is excluded or the purchase price is expressed to be inclusive of VAT any changes in the rate or incidence of VAT between contract and completion cannot be added to the price.

12    In the absence of any specific provision in the contract both seller and buyer are free to assign the benefit of the whole contract or a part of it (eg a charge of the benefit of the contract, or a sub-sale of part of the property). It may be thought desirable to limit these rights, whether because of the importance of the personality or standing of the buyer, or to avoid an immediate sub-sale of the whole or part of the property for tax or other reasons. For clauses preventing sub-sales by the buyer see clause 17 of this Form and the Law Society's Conditions of Sale (1984 Revision) condition 17(6) (for which see vol 38(1) (2000 Reissue) SALE OF LAND Form 3 [1131]). The Standard Conditions of Sale (3rd Edn) conditions 8.2.5 and 8.3.3 (for which see vol 38(1) (2000 Reissue) SALE OF LAND Form 1 [1011]), which prevent the buyer from transferring the benefit of the contract, apply only to leasehold property.

13    Where the Standard Conditions of Sale (3rd Edn) are incorporated this provision is rendered superfluous by condition 1.2 (for which see vol 38(1) (2000 Reissue) SALE OF LAND Form 1 [1011]). However, such words are commonly included for the convenience of the parties.

14    See note 11 above.

15    This clause and the third and fourth schedules are not required if the draft assurance is annexed.

16    As to the deposit generally see vol 35 (1997 Reissue) SALE OF LAND Paragraph 331 [432] et seq. For alternative clauses relating to the deposit see vol 36 (1997 Reissue) SALE OF LAND Forms 197 [2239]–204 [2246].

    As to the capacity in which the deposit is held see vol 35 (1997 Reissue) SALE OF LAND Paragraph 332 [433] et seq. As to the position when the deposit is held by an estate agent see vol 35 (1997 Reissue) SALE OF LAND Paragraph 334 [438].

    The Standard Conditions of Sale (3rd Edn) condition 2.2.2 (for which see vol 38(1) (2000 Reissue) SALE OF LAND Form 1 [1011]) provides that if the seller is buying another property in England and Wales for his residence he may use all or part of the deposit as a deposit in that transaction and his seller in turn may do the same, and condition 2.2.3 provides that any deposit or part of a deposit not so used is to be held by the seller's solicitor as stakeholder to be paid to the seller on completion with accrued interest (see note 6 above). If these provisions are unsuitable in the context of a particular transaction they should be amended accordingly. As to the position of a stakeholder generally see 9(1) Halsbury's Laws (4th Edn Reissue) CONTRACT para 1143. It should be remembered that VAT considerations may have a bearing on the capacity in which the deposit is to be held: see note 11 above.

17    The words in square brackets may be included if it is desired to expand the methods of payment (ie a banker's draft or cheque drawn on a solicitor's clearing bank account) permitted by the Standard Conditions of Sale (3rd Edn) condition 2.2.1 (for which see vol 38(1) (2000 Reissue) SALE OF LAND Form 1 [1011]) or where the contract incorporates the National Conditions of Sale (20th Edition) (for which see vol 38(1) (2000 Reissue) SALE OF LAND Form 4 [1161] (which latter set of conditions was replaced by the Standard Conditions of Sale as from March 1990: see vol 38(1) (2000 Reissue) SALE OF LAND Paragraph 290 [1001])) which do not cover the point.

**[4022]**

18    As to the completion date, delay and notice to complete generally see vol 35 (1997 Reissue) SALE OF LAND Paragraph 694 [902] et seq. For the provisions relating to payment of interest for late completion see the Standard Conditions of Sale (3rd Edn) condition 7.3 (for which see vol 38(1) (2000 Reissue) SALE OF LAND Form 1 [1011]), the Law Society's Conditions of Sale (1984 Revision) condition 22 (for which see vol 38(1) (2000 Reissue) SALE OF LAND Form 3 [1131]) and the National Conditions of Sale (20th Edn) condition 7 (for which see vol 38(1) (2000 Reissue) SALE OF LAND Form 4 [1161]). The differences between the three sets of conditions are great and should be carefully noted. As to the replacement of the latter two sets of standard conditions by the Standard Conditions of Sale as from March 1990, see vol 38(1) (2000 Reissue) SALE OF LAND Paragraph 290 [1001] et seq. Neither set of conditions has been updated subsequently.

    The inclusion of the words in brackets is not strictly necessary since the Standard Conditions of Sale (3rd Edn) condition 6.2 (for which see vol 38(1) (2000 Reissue) SALE OF LAND Form 1 [1011]) provides for completion to take place either at the seller's solicitor's office or at some other place which the seller reasonably specifies.

    Standard Conditions of Sale (3rd Edn) condition 6.1.2 (for which see vol 38(1) (2000 Reissue) SALE OF LAND Form 1 [1011]) states that if the money due on completion is received after 2.00 pm, completion is to be treated, for the purposes of apportionments and the provisions regarding late completion, as taking place on the next working day. Any amendments to this condition when incorporated should be included in clause 16.

19    As to implied covenants for title and the words importing them generally see vol 35 (1997 Reissue) SALE OF LAND Paragraph 472 [597] et seq.

Covenants for title are implied by the Law of Property (Miscellaneous Provisions) Act 1994 and (additionally in the case of registered land the Land Registration Rules 1925, SR&O 1925/1093 rr 76A–77A as substituted and amended by SI 1995/337) provided that key words are included in the assurance. Although under the Act and Rules no covenants are implied unless such key words are used, condition 4.5.2 of the Standard Conditions of Sale (for which see vol 38(1) (2000 Reissue) SALE OF LAND Form 1 [1011]) provide that if the contract for sale makes no provision as to title guarantee then subject to condition 4.5.3 the seller is to transfer the property with full title guarantee. Accordingly, in cases where it is inappropriate for any covenants for title to be given, a clause must be inserted expressly stating that no covenants for title will be given.

For a form varying the implied covenants for title see vol 36 (1997 Reissue) SALE OF LAND Form 190 [2226].

20    This clause, although regularly included in contracts, is strictly unnecessary since, in the absence of any indication to the contrary, it is an implied term that vacant possession will be given: see vol 35 (1997 Reissue) SALE OF LAND Paragraph 328 [429]. See also the Standard Conditions of Sale (3rd Edn) condition 4 (for which see vol 38(1) (2000 Reissue) SALE OF LAND Form 1 [1011]).

21    As to deduction of title to unregistered property see vol 35 (1997 Reissue) SALE OF LAND Paragraph 400 [515] and as to deduction of title to registered property see vol 35 (1997 Reissue) SALE OF LAND Paragraph 399 [510]. As to the seller's duty to disclose defects in the title see vol 35 (1997 Reissue) SALE OF LAND Paragraph 295 [391] et seq. It is clearly in the interests of the seller to disclose any defects of which he is aware before exchange of contracts; therefore it is now common for title to be deduced in its entirety before exchange and for restrictions to be placed on the right to raise requisitions.

As to the proving and investigation of title generally see vol 35 (1997 Reissue) SALE OF LAND Paragraph 398 [509] et seq.

22    Ie the Land Registration Act 1925 s 110 as amended by the Land Registration Act 1988 s 2, Schedule (37 Halsbury's Statutes (4th Edn) REAL PROPERTY).

23    The Standard Conditions of Sale (3rd Edn) condition 4.2.1 (for which see vol 38(1) (2000 Reissue) SALE OF LAND Form 1 [1011]) provides that the evidence of registered title is to be office copies of the items required to be furnished by the Land Registration Act 1925 s 110(2). However it is still advisable to include the words in square brackets because the Standard Conditions of Sale are incorporated only in so far as they are not varied by or inconsistent with the terms of the agreement, and it is arguable that the provisions of clause 8 without the words in square brackets form a complete provision replacing the equivalent provision in the Standard Conditions of Sale. As to the deduction of title using HM Land Registry's direct access system see vol 35 (1997 Reissue) SALE OF LAND Paragraph 399.3 [512].

The words in square brackets are required when the contract is made by reference to the National Conditions of Sale (20th Edn) (for which see vol 38(1) (2000 Reissue) Form 4 [1161] which do not include this provision (as to the replacement of these conditions see vol 38(1) (2000 Reissue) Paragraph 290 [1001]. As to the desirability of providing office copies see vol 35 (1997 Reissue) SALE OF LAND Paragraph 399.3 [512].

**[4023]**

24    It is not uncommon for contracts for the sale of property to provide for a contractual completion date prior to the date upon which the registration of the title of the seller at HM Land Registry as proprietor of the land to be sold is completed. In such cases, difficulties may arise as a result of the Land Registration Act 1925 s 110(5) which provides that where the seller is not himself registered as proprietor of the land or the charge giving a power of sale over the land, he shall, at the request of the buyer and at his own expense and notwithstanding any stipulation to the contrary, either procure the registration of himself as proprietor of the land or the charge as the case may be, or procure a disposition from the proprietor to the buyer. Clause 8.2 is intended to deter the buyer from insisting that the seller comply with the subsection by conferring upon the seller an option to withdraw from the proposed sale if the buyer does insist. If the buyer does so insist and the seller does not wish to withdraw from the sale, it is a moot point whether the buyer can rescind the contract if the registration of the seller as proprietor of the land is not completed on the contractual completion date or within a reasonable time after it: see *Re Stone and Saville's Contract* [1963] 1 All ER 353, [1963] 1 WLR 163, CA and contrast *Re Bryant and Barningham's Contract* (1890) 44 Ch D 218 with *Re Baker and Selmon's Contract* [1907] 1 Ch 238.

As to the limiting by contract of the time at which such a request may be made by the buyer see *Urban Manor Ltd v Sadiq* [1997] 1 WLR 1016, CA; *Country and Metropolitan Homes Surrey Ltd v Topclaim Ltd* [1996] Ch 307, [1997] 1 All ER 254.

For alternative clauses see Form 57 schedule 8 [2163] ante and vol 36 (1997 Reissue) SALE OF LAND Forms 174 [2188], 175 [2189] and 176 [2190].

It should be remembered in any case that the rule in *Bain v Fothergill* (1874) LR 7 HL 158 preventing a buyer from recovering damages for loss of bargain when a seller cannot make title in accordance with the terms of the contract has been abolished by the Law of Property (Miscellaneous Provisions) Act 1989 s 3 (37 Halsbury's Statutes (4th Edn) REAL PROPERTY). It is therefore preferable for the seller to ensure that he is registered as proprietor or will be so before the completion date.

25    As to the seller's duty to disclose incumbrances generally see vol 35 (1997 Reissue) SALE OF LAND
       Paragraph 295 [391]. Where registered land is concerned, the rights of any person in actual occupation
       of the land will be overriding interests to which any disposition of the land will be subject unless
       enquiry has been made of that person and the rights were not disclosed: see the Land Registration Act
       1925 s 70(1)(g). The same qualification does not apply in relation to other overriding interests listed in
       the Land Registration Act 1925 s 70(1) as amended.

26    The proprietorship register may need to be included if, eg, there is a restriction controlling dispositions
       of land which will remain on the register following sale.

27    Where certain charges, eg financial charges, are specifically excluded, a buyer may wish to ensure that
       any matters entered on the register before completion are also excluded. It might be argued that
       reference to exclusion of specific entries is to be interpreted as making the property subject to all other
       entries including new entries. It may be preferable to specify the entries to which the property is
       positively to be subject so that the position is clear.

28    This sub-clause should be omitted if there are no matters affecting the property in respect of which the
       seller will remain liable notwithstanding the completion of the conveyance or transfer of the property
       to the buyer. It may also be omitted in reliance upon the Standard Conditions of Sale (3rd Edn)
       condition 4.5.3 (for which see vol 38(1) (2000 Reissue) SALE OF LAND Form 1 [1011]) if incorporated.
       It should be omitted if the alternative sub-clauses 9.1 and 9.2 are used as the indemnity covenant will
       be set out in full in the draft transfer or conveyance.
            It may be preferred to set out the indemnity covenant the seller will require, rather than rely on
       standard conditions of sale, particularly if the contract is made by reference to the Law Society's
       Conditions of Sale (1984 Revision) (for which see vol 38(1) (2000 Reissue) SALE OF LAND Form 3
       [1131] which do not require the buyer to covenant to observe and perform the covenants and
       conditions. See also the Standard Conditions of Sale (3rd Edn) condition 4.5.3 (for which see vol 38(1)
       (2000 Reissue) SALE OF LAND Form 1 [1011]).

29    See note 25 above.

30    Whilst the annexation of a draft assurance is more usual on a sale of part of the seller's property it may
       be appropriate also on a sale of the whole of a property where there are numerous or complex
       incumbrances to be referred to in the assurance or covenants to be imposed.

31    This clause and the fifth, sixth and seventh schedules are not required if the draft assurance is annexed.

32    A buyer should bear in mind that certain financial charges in respect of costs incurred by a local
       authority are registrable as local land charges. If these relate to expenditure arising before the date of
       the contract the buyer may wish to ensure that they are borne by the seller.

33    This clause is not required if the draft assurance is annexed. For examples of what conditions might be
       inserted see, eg, vol 13(1) (1996 Reissue) COVENANTS RELATING TO LAND Forms 23 [1111] and 56
       [1219]).

34    This clause is not required if the draft assurance is annexed.

35    Ie the Law of Property Act 1925 s 62 (37 Halsbury's Statutes (4th Edn) REAL PROPERTY). As to the
       effect of such section see vol 35 (1997 Reissue) SALE OF LAND Paragraph 485 [623] et seq.

36    As to the reasons for this clause see vol 35 (1997 Reissue) SALE OF LAND Paragraph 490 [632] et seq.

37    This clause enables the seller to check that the buyer's title to the property has been correctly registered.

38    As an exclusion clause, this condition is subject to the test of reasonableness under the Unfair Contract
       Terms Act 1977 s 11 (11 Halsbury's Statutes (4th Edn) CONTRACT): see *Smith v Eric S Bush, Harris v
       Wyre Forest District Council* [1990] 1 AC 831, [1989] 2 All ER 514, HL. The seller cannot rely on a
       general disclaimer to avoid disclosing matters specifically known to him prior to sale: *Rignall
       Developments Ltd v Halil* [1988] 1 Ch 190, [1987] 3 All ER 170.

                                                                                                    **[4024]**

39    Consideration should be given to whether the conditions of sale incorporated require amendment in
       any way to suit the circumstances of the transaction or to ensure consistency with this agreement. As to
       possible modifications where the Standard Conditions of Sale (3rd Edn) are incorporated, see vol 38(1)
       (2000 Reissue) SALE OF LAND Form 12 [1245].

40    See note 12 above.

41    Where the Standard Conditions of Sale (3rd Edn) are being incorporated this clause can be omitted,
       although it is commonly included for the convenience of the parties: see the Standard Conditions of
       Sale (3rd Edn) condition 7.4 (for which see vol 38(1) (2000 Reissue) SALE OF LAND Form 1 [1011]).

42    It is essential to state on the face of a document that it is a deed if it is to be one: see the Law of Property
       (Miscellaneous Provisions) Act 1989 s 1(2)(a).

43    This schedule contains a specimen of stipulations, but there are many other forms which may be
       appropriate in particular cases. For alternative forms see vol 13(1) (1996 Reissue) COVENANTS
       RELATING TO LAND Forms 35 [1151]–55 [1198]. The stipulations set out in this Form cover the
       minimum range of stipulations likely to be required in most cases, although not necessarily in the
       wording shown; additional stipulations will be appropriate in some cases.

44    This stipulation prevents the land being used for some other temporary but unacceptable purpose until
       building work begins.

45    The phrase 'dwelling house' will prevent the buyer taking in paying guests: *Thorn v Madden* [1925] Ch 847. But it seems it would not restrict the buyer from erecting a garage ancillary to the dwelling house (see *Blake v Marriage* (1893) 9 TLR 569) and it is preferable to provide for this either by restricting any further construction work on the property or, as in this precedent, making it clear that an ancillary garage is permitted, although it may be prudent in that case to require the seller's approval of the plans (see vol 13(1) (1996 Reissue) COVENANTS AFFECTING LAND Form 50(1) [1188]).

46    In *Harrison v Good* (1871) LR 11 Eq 338 the word 'nuisance' was confined to a public nuisance but it seems this was too narrow an interpretation: *Tod-Heatly v Benham* (1889) 40 Ch D 80, CA. For the modern approach see *Hampstead and Suburban Properties Ltd v Diomedous* [1969] 1 Ch 248, [1968] 3 All ER 545 in which Megarry J said that the courts would regard the words 'nuisance' and 'annoyance' 'according to robust and common sense standards'. Certainly 'annoyance' has long been regarded as meaning an interference with the covenantee's enjoyment of his property: *Wood v Cooper* [1894] 3 Ch 671 (erection of trellis diminishing the light to the covenantee's property) and it seems preferable to include both words.

47    It is likely that a boundary wall or fence will have to be erected to separate the building site from the retained land. For covenants to erect and maintain boundaries see vol 13(1) (1996 Reissue) COVENANTS AFFECTING LAND Forms 70 [1276]–108 [1424]. The seller should consider whether it would be better for him to erect the boundary feature either before contract, or agree or covenant to erect it either before or after completion, either at his own cost or at the expense of the buyer. This will avoid the risk of the buyer failing to comply with his covenant to erect the boundary feature.

48    See note 47 above. If the seller is to erect the boundary feature a covenant to do so may be inserted here.

49    As to circumstances in which it may be desired to have the contract executed as a deed see vol 35 (1997 Reissue) SALE OF LAND Paragraph 21 note 3 [41].

      Where a contract is to be executed as a deed sealing is not necessary either in the case of an individual or in the case of a company, but all parties must sign either on the same document or each on one of two identical parts which are exchanged and the signatures of all individuals must be witnessed: see the Law of Property (Miscellaneous Provisions) Act 1989 s 1(3).

      It is unnecessary for a contract by a corporate body to be under seal unless it would need to be a deed if made by private persons: see the Corporate Bodies' Contracts Act 1960 s 1 (11 Halsbury's Statutes (4th Edn) CONTRACT). A contract may be made by a company incorporated under the Companies Acts by writing under its common seal or on its behalf by any person acting under its authority, express or implied: Companies Act 1985 s 36 as substituted by the Companies Act 1989 s 130(1) (8 Halsbury's Statutes (4th Edn) COMPANIES).

**[4025]**

# 97

### Agreement for sale of a plot on a freehold building estate, the buyer to erect the dwelling house to his own design, the design to be approved by the seller; form of transfer annexed[1]

THIS AGREEMENT is made the ...... day of .........

BETWEEN:

(1)    *(seller)* [company number *(number)*] [of *(address)* or whose registered office is at *(address)*] ('the Seller') and

(2)    *(buyer)* [company number *(number)*] [of *(address)* or whose registered office is at *(address)*] ('the Buyer')

**[4026]**

## 1    Definitions and interpretation

In this Agreement:

1.1    'the Buyer's Solicitors' means *(insert name and address of person or firm)*

1.2    'the Completion Date' means the ...... day of .........

1.3    'the Contract Rate' means *(insert interest rate or method of calculating the interest rate by reference eg to the base lending rate of a named bank)*

1.4    'the Estate' means the land now or formerly comprised in title number *(number)*

1.5    'the General Conditions' means [the Standard Conditions of Sale (3rd Edn) *or (specify)*]

1.6     'the Plan' means the plan annexed to the annexed draft transfer

1.7     'the Property' means the property outlined in [red] on the Plan and described in the schedule

1.8     'the Purchase Price' means the sum of £...[2] [which is [inclusive *or* exclusive] of VAT at the standard rate as at the date of actual completion]

1.9     'the Seller's Solicitors' means *(insert name and address of person or firm)*

1.10    where the context so admits the expression[s] 'the Seller' [and 'the Buyer'] include[s] the personal representatives of the Seller [and the Buyer] [and 'the Buyer' shall include any successors in title of the Buyer]

1.11    words importing one gender shall be construed as importing any other gender

1.12    words importing the singular shall be construed as importing the plural and vice versa

1.13    words importing persons shall be construed as importing a corporate body and/ or a partnership and vice versa

1.14    where any party comprises more than one person the obligations and liabilities of that party under this Agreement shall be joint and several obligations and liabilities of those persons

1.15    the clause headings do not form part of this Agreement and shall not be taken into account in its construction or interpretation

1.16    any reference to a clause or a paragraph or a schedule is to one in this Agreement so numbered

1.17    any reference to a colour or letter is to one on the Plan

1.18    words defined in the annexed draft transfer have the same meaning when used in this Agreement

## 2     Agreement for sale

The Seller shall sell and the Buyer shall buy the Property at the Purchase Price

## 3     Deposit

The Buyer shall on or before the date of this Agreement pay a deposit of [10%] of the Purchase Price to the Seller's Solicitors as [stakeholders *or* agents for the Seller] [by means of cash or telegraphic or other direct transfer banker's draft or a building society or bank guaranteed cheque or a cheque drawn on a solicitor's clients' account]

## 4     Completion

Completion of the sale and purchase and payment of the balance of the Purchase Price shall take place on the Completion Date [at the offices of the Seller's Solicitors or where they may direct]

[4027]

## 5     Title guarantee

The Seller sells with [full *or* limited] title guarantee

## 6     Possession

The Property is sold with vacant possession on completion

## 7     Title

Title to the Property is registered at HM Land Registry with [absolute] title under title number *(number)* and title shall be deduced in accordance with the Land Registration Act 1925 Section 110 [save that copies of the entries on the register the filed plan and any documents referred to shall be office copies and Land Registry Form 102 may be supplied in place of the filed plan³] [and the Buyer or the Buyer's Solicitors having been supplied with such copies prior to the date of this Agreement the Buyer shall be deemed to purchase with full knowledge of the title in all respects and shall not raise any requisitions or make any objection in relation to the title]

**8          Incumbrances**

8.1          The transfer to the Buyer shall be in the form of the annexed draft transfer

8.2          The Property is sold subject to and (where appropriate) with the benefit of the rights exceptions reservations covenants restrictions and other matters (if any) referred to in the annexed draft transfer and the property [proprietorship] and charges register of title number *(number)* [other than the charges referred to in the entries numbered *(numbers)* of the charges register of that title *or* other than charges to secure money] so far as the same relate to the Property (and no other rights and easements shall be implied)

8.3          The Buyer or the Buyer's Solicitors having been supplied with copies of the documents referred to in clause 8.2 prior to the date of this Agreement shall be deemed to purchase with full notice and knowledge of them and shall not raise any requisition or make any objection in relation to them

8.4          The transfer shall be engrossed [in duplicate] by the Seller's Solicitors and [the *or* both] engrossment[s] shall be executed by the Buyer before the Completion Date

[8.5          Immediately after completion the Buyer shall at his own expense procure the proper stamping of the duplicate transfer as a duplicate (including but not limited to the affixing of a particulars delivered stamp) and shall immediately after such stamping deliver the duly stamped duplicate to the Seller's Solicitors]

8.6          On completion the Buyer shall in addition to the Purchase Price pay to the Seller's Solicitors the sum of £... and VAT for the Seller's Solicitors' costs of engrossment and the supply of plans and draft documents

**[4028]**

**9          Matters affecting the Property**

The Property is sold subject to the following matters:

9.1          all local land charges whether registered or not before the date of this Agreement and all matters capable of registration as local land charges whether or not actually so registered

9.2          all notices served and orders demands proposals or requirements made by any local public or other competent authority whether before or after the date of this Agreement

9.3          all actual or proposed charges notices orders restrictions agreements conditions contraventions or other matters arising under the enactments relating to town and country planning and environmental law

9.4          all easements quasi-easements rights exceptions or other similar matters whether or not apparent on inspection or disclosed in any of the documents referred to in this Agreement

9.5          the easements and rights already granted or contracted to be granted to buyers of other parts of the Estate

**10          Seller's building works**

The Seller must at its own cost in a good and workmanlike manner carry out and complete the following works and acts so far as they afford access to and egress from the Property and services to and from it ('the Seller's Works'):

10.1     construct form make up drain and light the Estate Road[4] in the position shown
         on the Plan or in such other position as may be approved by the local planning
         highway and other competent authorities to the standard and specification and
         within the time required by the local highway authority for adoption as a public
         highway maintained at public expense and connect the same to the existing
         public highway called *(name)* and maintain the Estate Road in good repair and
         condition [and if necessary reinstate it] until it shall be adopted as a public
         highway maintained at public expense [and construct form make up and drain
         the Estate Road between the Property and the existing public highway to [base]
         course level by *(date)*][5] PROVIDED ALWAYS that the Seller shall not be liable
         to make good any damage caused to the Estate Road either by:

        10.1.1     improper or negligent use of the Estate Road by the Buyer or
                  persons working on or delivering materials to the Property or in
                  connection with any building operations on the Property or

        10.1.2     the opening up or reinstatement of the Estate Road in connection
                  with the installation of services to the Property

10.2     lay and construct foul sewers and storm water sewers under the Estate [and
         *(specify)*] in the approximate positions shown on the Plan or in such other
         positions as may be approved by the local planning and other competent
         authorities to the standard and specification required by those respective
         authorities for adoption as publicly maintained services and connect them to the
         public foul sewer and the public storm water sewer shown respectively on the
         Plan and maintain them in good repair and condition [and if necessary reinstate
         them] until they shall be adopted as publicly maintained services or become the
         responsibility of service undertakers PROVIDED ALWAYS that the Seller shall
         not be liable to make good any damage caused to the sewers by any cause
         mentioned in the proviso to sub-clause 10.1

10.3     lay and construct or use its reasonable endeavours to procure that *(name of water
         undertaker)* lays and constructs a water main in the approximate position shown
         on the Plan

10.4     lay or use its reasonable endeavours to procure that *(name of electricity supplier)* lays
         an underground electricity main under the [Estate Road *or* service strip shown
         on the Plan]

10.5     lay a duct for the accommodation of a main underground telephone cable under
         the [Estate Road *or* service strip] and use its reasonable endeavours to procure
         that *(name of telephone company)* lays a telephone cable in it

10.6     lay and construct or use its reasonable endeavours to procure that *(name of gas
         undertaker)* lays and constructs a gas main in the approximate position shown on
         the Plan

                                                                              **[4029]**

## 11     Delay in the Seller's Works[6]

The Seller shall not be responsible for any delay in executing the Seller's Works nor be
liable to the Buyer for any loss or inconvenience which may be due directly or indirectly
to:

11.1     strikes lockouts combinations and scarcity of labour

11.2     shortage of and delay in obtaining materials

11.3     hostilities and acts of the Queen's enemies

11.4     force majeure fire explosion flood lightning or bad weather

11.5     procedures required for obtaining all necessary permissions for or appertaining
         to the carrying out of the Seller's Works and all necessary services

11.6     compliance with all legislation statutory rules orders regulations or directions

11.7    accidents in the Seller's Works for which the Seller is not responsible
11.8    other causes beyond the control of the Seller
Where any such delay occurs the Seller shall be allowed a fair and reasonable extension
of the time mentioned in clause 10 for completion of the Seller's Works

## 12    Road and sewer agreements[7]

The Seller must use its reasonable endeavours to enter into an agreement with the local
highway authority under the Highways Act 1980 Section 38 relating to the construction
maintenance and adoption of the Estate Road and with the local water or public health
authority under the Water Industry Act 1991 Section 104 or other relevant legislation in
respect of the sewers referred to in sub-clause 10.2 and if required by the authorities to
provide to their satisfaction a bond or other security to secure the due performance by
the Seller of each of the agreements and after the agreement shall have been entered into
to perform and observe the terms of it

## 13    Buyer's obligations

The Buyer must:
13.1    make good forthwith all damage caused to the Estate Road the Service
        Apparatus and any other part of the Estate by any cause mentioned in the
        proviso to sub-clause 10.1
13.2    during the course of building operations on the Property keep the Property free
        of litter and refuse and reasonably tidy
13.3    not deposit or leave or permit or suffer to be deposited or left any soil building
        materials or other chattel or thing arising from or connected with the Buyer's
        operations upon any part of the Estate except the Property

**[4030]**

## 14    Contractor's sheds

Notwithstanding the provisions of clause [4] of panel 13 to the annexed draft transfer the
Buyer may place or permit to be placed on the Property one temporary building or
caravan for use (other than as living or sleeping accommodation) by workmen erecting
buildings on the Property conforming with the provisions of that clause

## 15    Estate layout

The Seller's estate layout plan represents the intention of the Seller as to the development
of the Estate of which the Property forms part but neither a slight variation in the actual
dimensions of the Property from the plan nor any variation in the development shall give
rise to any claim by the Buyer for compensation or otherwise[9]

## 16    Tree planting

There is reserved to the Seller a right of entry on the Property after completion of the
sale for itself its agents and workmen for the purpose of planting and maintaining trees
thereon in compliance with the conditions imposed (if any) by the grant of any planning
permission or consent

## 17    Disclaimer

The Buyer admits that:
17.1    he has inspected the Property and purchases it with full knowledge of its actual
        state and condition and shall take the Property as it stands

17.2    he enters into this Agreement solely as a result of his own inspection and on the basis of the terms of this Agreement and not in reliance upon any representation or warranty either written or oral or implied made by or on behalf of the Seller (save for any representation or warranty contained in written replies given by the Seller's Solicitors to any preliminary inquiries raised by the Buyer or the Buyer's Solicitors)

17.3    this Agreement contains the entire agreement between the parties

**[4031]**

## 18    Incorporation of conditions of sale

The General Conditions shall apply to this Agreement and are incorporated in it in so far as they are applicable to a sale by private treaty and are not varied by or inconsistent with the terms of this Agreement [and shall be amended as follows: *(insert details of amendments required)*]

## [19    Restriction on assignment

19.1    This Agreement is personal to the Buyer and shall not be capable of assignment

[19.2    The Seller shall not be required to transfer the Property [to anyone other than the Buyer named in this Agreement *or* at a price greater than the Purchase Price]]]

## 20    Merger on completion

The provisions of this Agreement shall not merge on completion of the transfer of the Property so far as they remain to be performed

## 21    Disputes

Any dispute or difference between the parties to this Agreement concerning the Seller's Works whether during the continuance of this Agreement or upon or after its determination shall be referred to arbitration in accordance with the Arbitration Act 1996 or any statutory modification or re-enactment thereof for the time being in force. The arbitrator shall be appointed either by agreement between the parties or in default of agreement within 14 days of one party giving notice to the other of its nomination be appointed by or on behalf of the President of the [Institute of Arbitrators] on the application of either party

## 22    Nature of this Agreement

This Agreement [is *or* is not] a deed and [has *or* has not] been executed by the parties to it as a deed

## [23    Contracts (Rights of Third Parties) Act 1999

For the purposes of the Contracts (Rights of Third Parties) Act 1999 it is agreed that [with the exception only of *(specify clauses)*] nothing in this Agreement shall confer on any third party any right to enforce or any benefit of any term of this Agreement]

[AS *or* IN] WITNESS etc

**[4032]**

THE SCHEDULE
The Property
*(describe the property)*

*(signatures (or common seals) of the parties)*
[*(signatures of witnesses)*]

1      No stamp duty. See Information Binder: Stamp Duties [1] Guide to stamp duties: Table of duties (Agreement).

          This Form is for use where a seller has laid out a residential estate and sells a single plot to a buyer who will then build a house and garage on it in accordance with plans to be prepared by him but approved by the seller. This Form differs from Form 96 [4009] ante in that the plot is on an estate and a standard form of transfer is annexed to the agreement. The transfer will be in the standard form for use on the estate for a form of which see Form 117 [4205] post. This Form of agreement may also be used where a seller sells a block of undeveloped plots on a residential estate to another builder or developer, the transfer in that case should be in Form 119 [4251] post as the rights and restrictions will differ in some respects from the standard form of transfer.

          Reference should be made to Form 96 [4009] ante for detailed footnotes on the terms common to most forms of contract for sale, for cross-references to the relevant part of the commentary in vol 35 (1997 Reissue) SALE OF LAND and for additional footnotes relating to sales of part.

          Consideration should be given to whether the Standard Conditions of Sale, or other general conditions used, require amendment in any way. For a table of amendments commonly made to the Standard Conditions of Sale (3rd Edn) see vol 38(1) (2000 Reissue) Form 12 [1245].

2      As to VAT see Form 96 note 11 [4022] ante.

3      As to Land Registry Form 102 certificates generally see vol 25(1) (1999 Reissue) LAND REGISTRATION Paragraph 57 [1881].

4      The estate road will be defined in the annexed draft transfer.

5      Where a seller sells a plot and contracts to build the house on it (as in Form 98 [4051] post), the buyer will be in a position to refuse to complete the purchase until the estate road is made up to at least base course level (or other state specified by a planning condition before any house may be occupied) so that there is a satisfactory road and pedestrian access to the property, and until all main services (as described in the specification) are connected so that the house is capable of occupation. For this reason, and because the buyer will be protected by a construction guarantee, probably from the National House Building Council, a buyer of a plot and house is usually willing to accept less precise obligations from the seller on these matters than appear in this Form. The agreement may also contain a right for the buyer to rescind the contract in the event of excessive delay.

          The buyer of a plot on which he is to build (as in this Form) may have to complete the purchase of the plot before the estate road and services to serve the plot are constructed, and in that case he needs specific agreements from the seller to construct the road and services by specified dates (without construction of which he may not be able to commence building) or occupy the finished building, and to enter into highway and sewer agreements. Even then he is at risk of the seller's default; ideally he should not contract to buy until the road and services are constructed up to the plot, although this may be impractical. For shorter forms of provision dealing only with roads and sewers see vol 13(1) (1996 Reissue) COVENANTS AFFECTING LAND Forms 62(1) [1229] and 62(2) [1230].

6      Anticipatory completion dates are most unwise from the seller's point of view because of the possibility of unforeseen delays. However for the reason given in note 5 above a compromise is necessary and the seller is protected by the provisions of clause 11.

7      It is preferable for the seller to have entered into these agreements before selling individual plots. Where that has not been done a retention of part of the purchase money may be required (for a clause dealing with which see vol 36 (1997 Reissue) SALE OF LAND Form 296 [2431]) and provision for refund to the seller of payments made under the Advance Payments Code (see vol 18 (1993 Reissue) HIGHWAYS Paragraph 50 [57] et seq) may also be appropriate (for a clause dealing with which see vol 36 (1997 Reissue) Form 297 [2434]).

8      Service installations will be defined in the annexed draft transfer.

9      As to variations to the Land Registry approved estate layout plan see Form 93 note 6 [3980] ante and Form 100 note 7 [4079] post.

**[4033]–[4050]**

# 98

### Agreement for sale of a plot on a freehold residential building estate, incorporating contract for the dwelling house to be built by the seller—long form; form of transfer annexed[1]

THIS AGREEMENT is made the ...... day of .........

BETWEEN:

(1)      *(seller)* [company number *(number)*] [of *(address) or* whose registered office is at *(address)*] ('the Seller') and

(2)      *(buyer)* [company number *(number)*] [of *(address) or* whose registered office is at *(address)*] ('the Buyer')

[4051]

## 1      Definitions and interpretation

In this Agreement:

1.1      'the Buyer's Solicitors' means *(insert name and address of person or firm)*

[1.2     'the Contract Price' means the Purchase Price plus the cost of any extras ordered by the Buyer]

1.3      'the Contract Rate' means *(insert interest rate or method of calculating the interest rate by reference eg to the base lending rate of a named bank)*

1.4      'the Dwelling House' means the dwelling house [and garage] erected or in the course of erection on the Land and described in the [first] schedule

1.5      'the General Conditions' means [the Standard Conditions of Sale (3rd Edn) *or (specify)*]

1.6      'the Land' means the plot of land described in the [first] schedule and in the draft transfer annexed to this Agreement

1.7      'the Period for Completion' means:
[within *(number)* days of the latest of the following [4] dates:

    1.7.1      the date of physical completion of the Dwelling House as notified to the Buyer's Solicitors or

    1.7.2      2 days after the date of posting of notification of the date of physical completion of the Dwelling House to the Buyer's Solicitors if that date is after the date of physical completion so notified or

    [1.7.3     the date upon which the Buyer receives a satisfactory offer of mortgage from his proposed lender whether it be a building society or not PROVIDED that if the lender is a building society the offer shall be deemed to have been received 2 days after it is known to have been posted but time shall not start to run until the instructions are sent out to the Buyer's Solicitors[2] or]

    1.7.4      the date of this Agreement

[4052]

*or*

not more than [14] days after the Buyer or the Buyer's Solicitors has been sent notice that the Dwelling House has been completed in accordance with this Agreement and is ready for occupation][3]

1.8      'the Plan' means the plan annexed to this Agreement [and if numbered plans are annexed any reference to a numbered plan is to the annexed plan so numbered]

1.9      'the Property' means the Land and the Dwelling House

1.10     'the Purchase Price' means the sum of £...[4] [which [includes *or* does not include] the cost of [construction of a garage] [installation of central heating]]

1.11     'the Seller's Solicitors' means *(insert name and address of person or firm)*

1.12     where the context so admits the expression[s] 'the Seller' [and 'the Buyer'] include[s] the personal representatives of the Seller [and the Buyer] [and 'the Buyer' shall include any successors in title of the Buyer]

1.13     words importing one gender shall be construed as importing any other gender

1.14     words importing the singular shall be construed as importing the plural and vice versa

1.15     words importing persons shall be construed as importing a corporate body and/or a partnership and vice versa

1.16    where any party comprises more than one person the obligations and liabilities of that party under this Agreement shall be joint and several obligations and liabilities of those persons

1.17    the clause headings do not form part of this Agreement and shall not be taken into account in its construction or interpretation

1.18    any reference to a clause or a paragraph or a schedule is to one in this Agreement so numbered

1.19    any reference to a colour or letter is to one on the Plan

1.20    words defined in the annexed draft transfer have the same meaning when used in this Agreement

[4053]

## 2    Agreement for sale

The Seller shall sell and the Buyer shall buy the Property at the Purchase Price

## 3    Deposit and completion

3.1    The Buyer shall pay [direct to the Seller *or* to the Seller's Solicitors as [stakeholders *or* agents for the Seller]] on the signing of this Agreement a deposit[5] of [5 *or* 10]% of the Purchase Price and the balance shall be paid and the purchase shall be completed at *(specify place of completion)* within the Period for Completion

3.2    If the balance of the Purchase Price has not been paid within the Period for Completion it shall bear interest at the Contract Rate as and from the first day following the expiry of the Period for Completion

3.3    If within the Period for Completion the Buyer has not notified the Seller in writing of any specific defects apparent in the Dwelling House the Buyer shall be deemed to have accepted the notification of completion of the Dwelling House as valid and be bound to complete PROVIDED that this shall not prejudice the right of the Buyer to require after completion the remedying of any defects in accordance with clause 10 of this Agreement

3.4    The Buyer shall not be entitled to delay completion by reason of minor defects or outstanding works of a minor nature which can reasonably be dealt with after completion (including in particular any landscaping erection of fences and final surfacing of driveways) and the Seller undertakes to complete such outstanding works (if any) as soon as practicable after completion

## 4    Title guarantee

The Seller sells with [full *or* limited] title guarantee

## 5    Possession

The Property is sold with vacant possession on completion

## 6    Title

Title to the Property is registered at HM Land Registry with [absolute] title under title number *(number)* and title shall be deduced in accordance with the Land Registration Act 1925 Section 110 [save that copies of the entries on the register the filed plan and any documents referred to shall be office copies and Land Registry Form 102 may be supplied in place of the Filed Plan[6]] [and the Buyer or the Buyer's Solicitors having been supplied with such copies prior to the date of this Agreement the Buyer shall be deemed to purchase with full knowledge of the title in all respects and shall not raise any requisitions or make any objection in relation to the title]

[4054]

**7       Transfer and encumbrances**

7.1        The transfer to the Buyer shall be in the form of the annexed draft transfer

7.2        The Property is sold subject to and (where appropriate) with the benefit of the
           rights exceptions reservations covenants restrictions and other matters (if any)
           referred to in the annexed draft transfer and the property [proprietorship] and
           charges register of title number *(number)* [other than the charges referred to in
           the entries numbered *(numbers)* of the charges register of that title *or* other than
           charges to secure money] (and no other rights and easements shall be implied)

7.3        The Buyer or the Buyer's Solicitors having been supplied with copies of the
           documents referred to in clause 7.2 prior to the date of this Agreement shall be
           deemed to purchase with full notice and knowledge of them and shall not raise
           any requisition or make any objection in relation to them

7.4        The transfer shall be engrossed [in duplicate] by the Seller's Solicitors and [the
           *or* both] engrossment[s] shall be executed by the Buyer before the date for
           completion

[7.5       Immediately after completion the Buyer shall at his own expense procure the
           proper stamping of the duplicate transfer as a duplicate (including but not
           limited to the affixing of a particulars delivered stamp) and shall immediately
           after such stamping deliver the duly stamped duplicate to the Seller's Solicitors]

7.6        On completion the Buyer shall in addition to the Purchase Price pay to the
           Seller's Solicitors the sum of £... and VAT for the Seller's Solicitors' costs of
           engrossment and the supply of plans and draft documents

**8       Matters affecting the Property**

The Property is sold subject to the following matters:

8.1        all local land charges whether registered or not before the date of this
           Agreement and all matters capable of registration as local land charges whether
           or not actually so registered

8.2        all notices served and orders demands proposals or requirements made by any
           local public or other competent authority whether before or after the date of
           this Agreement

8.3        all actual or proposed charges notices orders restrictions agreements conditions
           contraventions or other matters arising under the enactments relating to town
           and country planning and environmental law

8.4        all easements quasi-easements rights exceptions or other similar matters
           whether or not apparent on inspection or disclosed in any of the documents
           referred to in this Agreement

8.5        the easements and rights already granted or contracted to be granted to buyers
           of other parts of the Estate

                                                                                        **[4055]**

**9       Estate Plan**

The Seller's estate layout plan represents the intention of the Seller as to the development
of the Estate of which the Land forms part but neither any slight variation in the actual
dimensions of the Land from the plan nor any variation in the development shall give
rise to any claim by the Buyer for compensation or otherwise[7]

**10      Seller to construct the Dwelling House**

10.1       The Seller shall [on or before *(date)*[8] (but without any liability whatsoever to the
           Buyer should that completion date not be met)] construct or cause to be

constructed the Dwelling House together with all necessary works in a thorough and workmanlike manner and with materials of a suitable quality in accordance with:

10.1.1      the appropriate planning permission

10.1.2      the building regulations[9]

10.1.3      the prescribed mandatory requirements currently in force and laid down by the National House Building Council and

10.1.4      the plans and specifications prepared by or on behalf of the Seller which the Buyer has had the opportunity to inspect at the Seller's office or other suitable place and of which (whether he has inspected the same or not) he shall be deemed to have full knowledge

10.2      The Seller shall have the right to substitute materials as near as possible of the same quality and value in lieu of those contained or referred to in the plans and specifications if in its absolute discretion it deems it expedient so to do and to make reasonable modifications to the plans and specifications in such manner as may be necessary as a result of the use of such substituted materials or in accordance with the requirements of any competent authority but such substitution and modification shall not reduce the value of the Dwelling House nor substantially alter its accommodation

## 11      Alterations and extras

11.1      If the Buyer requires any alterations in the construction of the Dwelling House whether in the nature of extras or otherwise such requirements for alteration shall be notified in writing by the Buyer to the Seller

11.2      If such alterations are agreed to and executed by the Seller the Seller's costs shall be added to (or subtracted from as the case may be) the Purchase Price and any addition to the Purchase Price shall be paid for by the Buyer to the Seller's Solicitors no later than the completion date and if such addition is not paid within the Period for Completion it shall bear interest at the Contract Rate

[4056]

## [12      Price rises

The Contract Price is based on the prices of materials and labour subsisting at the date of this Agreement and if the rate of wages and other emoluments and expenses including the cost of National Insurance and third party insurance increases by reason of any alteration in the rules and decisions of the National Joint Council for the Building Industry or any other competent authority or if the market price of the fittings and materials used in the construction of the Dwelling House increases after the signing of this Agreement the amount of increase in such rates and other emoluments and expenses attributable to this Agreement and the increase in the cost of such fittings and materials shall be paid by the Buyer in addition to the price provided for in this Agreement and the same shall be paid to the Seller with the balance of purchase monies owing on completion of the Dwelling House [and the Buyer shall accept [a certificate from the Seller's estimating department *or (as the case may be)*] as to the amount of such increase and such certificate shall be conclusive and binding on the Buyer]][10]

## 13      Delays beyond the Seller's control

The erection and completion of the Dwelling House shall be carried out by the Seller as quickly as possible but in any of the cases specified below where delay is caused the Seller shall not be liable to the Buyer for any loss or inconvenience however occasioned:

13.1    strikes lockouts combinations and scarcity of labour
13.2    shortage of and delay in obtaining materials
13.3    hostilities and acts of the Queen's enemies
13.4    force majeure fire explosion flood lightning or bad weather
13.5    procedures required for obtaining all necessary permissions for or appertaining to the erection of the Dwelling House and all necessary services
13.6    compliance with all legislation statutory rules orders regulations or directions
13.7    accidents in the works for which the Seller is not responsible
13.8    other causes beyond the control of the Seller

[except that if from any cause outside the control of the Seller he is for a period of [6] months or more prevented from proceeding with work on the construction of the Dwelling House either party shall have the option to determine this Agreement upon giving to the other [14] days' notice in writing to that effect whereupon all monies paid by the Buyer to the Seller under the terms of this Agreement shall be repaid to the Buyer but without interest]

## 14    No possession prior to completion

Until payment of all money due under this Agreement by the Buyer to the Seller the Buyer will not without the prior written consent of the Seller take or attempt to take possession of the Dwelling House either personally or by agents

**[4057]**

## 15    Risk

The Dwelling House shall be at the sole risk of the Seller (notwithstanding any prior arrangement made by the Buyer or his mortgagees) in respect of damage or loss by fire storm explosion or lightning only and until the date for legal completion as described in clause 3 but if the Seller allows the Buyer at his request to store in the Dwelling House or upon the Land any of his possessions and such possessions are damaged or lost the Seller shall not be held liable for any such loss or damage in any manner whatsoever

## 16    National House Building Council

The Developer undertakes to make an irrevocable offer to provide the National House Building Council ('the NHBC') 'Buildmark' prior to the commencement of construction or to enter into any similar agreement or scheme which may be prescribed by the NHBC[11]

## 17    Tree planting

There is reserved to the Seller a right of entry on the Land after completion of the sale for itself its agents and workmen for the purpose of planting and maintaining trees thereon in compliance with the conditions imposed (if any) by the grant of any planning permission or consent

## 18    Disclaimer

The Buyer admits that:
18.1    he has inspected the Land and purchases it with full knowledge of its actual state and condition and shall take the Land as it stands
18.2    he enters into this Agreement solely as a result of his own inspection and on the basis of the terms of this Agreement and not in reliance upon any representation or warranty either written or oral or implied made by or on behalf of the Seller (save for any representation or warranty contained in written replies given by the Seller's Solicitors to any preliminary inquiries raised by the Buyer or the Buyer's Solicitors)
18.3    this Agreement contains the entire agreement between the parties

**[4058]**

**19      Incorporation of conditions of sale**

19.1      The General Conditions shall apply to this Agreement and are incorporated in
it in so far as they are applicable to a sale by private treaty and are not varied by
or inconsistent with the terms of this Agreement [and shall be amended as
follows: *(insert details of amendments required)*][12]

[19.2      The terms set out in Part[s] *(number(s))* of the second schedule are incorporated
in this Agreement[13]]

**[20      Restriction on assignment**

20.1      This Agreement is personal to the Buyer and shall not be capable of assignment

[20.2      The Seller shall not be required to transfer the Property [to anyone other than
the Buyer named in this Agreement *or* at a price greater than the Purchase
Price]]]

**21      Merger on completion**

The provisions of this Agreement shall not merge on completion of the transfer of the
Property so far as they remain to be performed

**22      Nature of this Agreement**

This Agreement [is *or* is not] a deed and [has *or* has not] been executed by the parties to
it as a deed

**23      Disputes**

Any dispute as to whether the home conforms to the mandatory requirements of the
NHBC shall be referred to the NHBC in accordance with its Resolution Scheme

**[24      Contracts (Rights of Third Parties) Act 1999**

For the purposes of the Contracts (Rights of Third Parties) Act 1999 it is agreed that
[with the exception only of *(specify clauses)*] nothing in this Agreement shall confer on
any third party any right to enforce or any benefit of any term of this Agreement]

[AS *or* IN] WITNESS etc

**[FIRST] SCHEDULE**
The Property

Name of development:
Town:
Plot no:
House type:
Postal address:

**[SECOND SCHEDULE**
*(insert appropriate special provisions from Forms 104 [4129]–112 [4148] post; each provision to
be inserted in a separate part)*

*(signatures (or common seals) of the parties)*
[*(signatures of witnesses)*]
**[4059]**

1    No stamp duty. See Information Binder: Stamp Duties [1] Guide to stamp duties: Table of duties (Agreement).

Reference should be made to Form 96 [4009] ante for detailed footnotes on the terms common to most forms of contract for sale, for cross-references to the relevant part of the commentary in vol 35 (1997 Reissue) SALE OF LAND, and for additional footnotes relating to sales of part.

2    This sub-clause is required if the agreement is conditional upon the issue of a mortgage offer to the buyer. For clauses making the agreement conditional, see Forms 106 [4131] and 107 [4136] post.

3    The second alternative is the easiest and most commonly used.

4    Unlike the arrangements in Form 97 [4026] ante the supply under this Form is of a freehold residential property and so a zero-rated supply for VAT purposes. Accordingly, no VAT is charged by the seller.

5    Buyers usually object to paying the deposit direct to the seller. If the deposit is paid to the seller's solicitors they will hold as stakeholders unless the agreement provides otherwise: see the Standard Conditions of Sale (3rd Edn) condition 2.2.3 (for which see vol 38(1) (2000 Reissue) SALE OF LAND Form 1 [1011].

6    As to Land Registry Form 102 certificates generally see vol 25(1) (1999 Reissue) LAND REGISTRATION Paragraph 57 [1881].

7    The practitioner needs to bear in mind that, if it is desired to reserve the right to make minor amendments to the approved estate plan, not only does the Land Registry need to be consulted about any amendment prior to its being made, but there may well be complications resulting from the existence of transfers that have already been effected on the estate and the existence of a defining plan in the transfer annexed to the current agreement. It is one thing to adjust a boundary between remaining unsold plots. It is quite another if any attempt is made to adjust the position of estate roads, pathways or common services, over which rights have been granted already, or are due to be granted under the form of transfer annexed to the agreement. In the latter case, the adjustments may well need to be agreed with the buyer and previous transferees, and embodied in suitable formal documents.

8    Anticipatory completion dates are most unwise from a builder's viewpoint in view of the possibility of unforeseen snags in the building work.

9    This may be an acceptance of an initial notice under the new building control system, but it would still be, technically, a building regulation consent, so that the old nomenclature is probably the best. For the current building regulations see the Building Regulations 1991, SI 1991/2768 as amended.

10   Price rise clauses are rare and operation of them in a normal housing development is very difficult. They are usually unacceptable to the buyer.

11   This wording may need to be changed from time to time in accordance with the requirements of the National House Building Council. As to the NHBC procedure generally see Form 93 appendix 2 [3974] ante.

12   Consideration should be given to whether the standard conditions of sale require amendment in any way. For a table of suggested amendments to the Standard Conditions of Sale (3rd Edn) see vol 38(1) (2000 Reissue) SALE OF LAND Form 12 [1245].

13   All special provisions in Forms 104 [3129]–112 [4148] post likely to be required in the development should be set out in the second schedule, each provision being headed with a part number.

**[4060]**

# 99

## Agreement for sale of a freehold plot or grant of a long lease of a plot on a residential building estate—incorporating contract for the dwelling house to be built by the seller—short form[1]

THIS AGREEMENT is made the ...... day of .........

BETWEEN:

(1)    *(seller)* [company number *(number)*] [of *(address)* or whose registered office is at *(address)*] ('the Seller') and

(2)    *(buyer)* [company number *(number)*] [of *(address)* or whose registered office is at *(address)*] ('the Buyer')

## 1      The Property

1.1    The Property is: *(insert development, plot number, type of dwelling and postal address if known)*

1.2 The tenure is: [Freehold *or* Leasehold for a term of *(number)* years from *(date)* at a ground rent of £... per year]

1.3 The title number is: *(specify)*

[4061]

## 2 Purchase Price

| | | |
|---|---|---|
| 2.1 | The Purchase Price is | £...[2] |
| 2.2 | The documentation fee is | £... |
| 2.3 | The total price is | £... |
| [2.4 | Less discount of | £...[3]] |
| 2.5 | Less deposit of | £... |
| 2.6 | Balance due on completion is | £... |

## 3 Contract Rate

The Contract Rate is: *(specify)*

## 4 Solicitors

4.1 the Seller's Solicitors' means: *(name and address)*

4.2 'the Buyer's Solicitors' means: *(name and address)*

## 5 Contract

[[The Seller shall sell with [full *or* limited] title guarantee and the Buyer shall purchase *or* The Seller shall grant with [full *or* limited] title guarantee] and the Buyer shall accept a lease of] the Property at the Purchase Price and upon the terms referred to above and in accordance with the conditions of sale set out in this Agreement

*or*

The Seller shall procure a transfer from *(name of freehold owner)* with [full *or* limited] title guarantee and the Buyer shall purchase the Property at the Purchase Price and upon the terms referred to above and in accordance with the conditions of sale set out in this Agreement and references to the Seller shall include references to the Seller acting as agent for *(name of freehold owner)* as freeholder][4]

[4062]

CONDITIONS OF SALE

## 1 Building works

1.1 The Seller shall erect and complete the Property in accordance with the terms of the relevant planning permission and the building regulation consent[5] and the current mandatory requirements of the National House Building Council and the Property shall be deemed to have been completed notwithstanding that any item of a minor or trivial nature may require to be corrected or completed by the Seller after completion of the sale

1.2 Plans and specifications of the Property are available for inspection by the Buyer at the site sales office or other suitable premises to be designated by the Seller and the Seller will use every endeavour to adhere to such plans and specifications and to the layout of the plot but reserves the right to make any reasonable variation to it not substantially affecting the value of the Property and such variation shall not annul the sale or entitle the Buyer to any damages and compensation

1.3 Where the plans provide for a garage space but do not provide for the erection of a garage the Seller shall provide sufficient space for the erection of a single garage but shall be under no obligation to carry out any works of any nature in respect of the garage space so as to prepare or render it fit for the erection of a garage

1.4      The cost of street sewer and other infrastructure works is included in the Purchase Price and no retention shall be made by the Buyer in relation to such matters under any circumstances whatsoever

## 2      Deposit

The deposit is paid to the Seller's Solicitors as [agents for the Seller *or* stakeholders][6]

## 3      Completion

The sale shall be completed and the balance due shall be paid at the office of the Seller's Solicitors within [14] days of the posting [by recorded delivery post] to the Buyer or his Solicitors of written notification of the completion of the Property fit for occupation[7]

## 4      Possession

The Property is sold with vacant possession on completion

**[4063]**

## 5      Assurance

The [transfer *or* lease] to the Buyer shall be in the model form annexed to this Agreement and the Buyer shall be deemed to have full knowledge of its contents and the Property [is sold *or* will be leased] together with the benefit of and subject to all matters contained in the [transfer *or* lease] [and the entries in the register of title number *(number)* [save for the Seller's subsisting mortgage]]

## 6      Title

Title to the Property is registered at HM Land Registry with [absolute] title under the title number specified in clause 1.3 of this Agreement and title shall be deduced in accordance with the Land Registration Act 1925 Section 110 [save that Land Registry Form 102 may be supplied in place of the Filed Plan]

## 7      Extras

Any extras or variations which the Seller may agree to supply or effect shall be paid for in addition to the Purchase Price and payment shall be made at such time as the Seller shall require[8]

## 8      Insurance

The Property will be at the Seller's risk until the release of the keys to the Buyer is authorised

## 9      National House Building Council

The Seller undertakes to make an irrevocable offer to provide the National House Building Council ('the NHBC') 'Buildmark' or to enter into any similar agreement or scheme prior to the commencement of construction which may be prescribed by the NHBC[9]

**[4064]**

## 10      General conditions

This Agreement incorporates [the Standard Conditions of Sale (3rd Edn) *or* *(specify)*] so far as they are not varied by or inconsistent with its express terms [and they shall be amended as follows: *(specify)*][10]

**11      Disputes**

Any dispute as to whether the home conforms to the mandatory requirements of the NHBC shall be referred to NHBC in accordance with its Resolution scheme[11]

**12      Agreement and declaration**

It is agreed and declared:

12.1    that the Seller shall not be liable for nor shall the Buyer be entitled to receive any compensation for any delay in the erection or completion of the Property or any other matter relating to it by reason of fire storm tempest snow accidents shortages of labour government control restrictions riots acts of war insurrection civil disturbance strikes lockouts or other causes outside the direct control of the Seller

12.2    that no representation either written or oral (except written answers to [standard] pre-contract enquiries [supplied with the estate documentation]) has been made to the Buyer prior to the date of this Agreement by the Seller or his servants or agents concerning the Property which has influenced or persuaded the Buyer to enter into this Agreement

**[13      Additional provisions**

The terms set out in Part[s] *(number(s))* of the schedule are incorporated in this Agreement]

**[4065]**

**14      Interpretation**

In this Agreement:

14.1    words importing one gender shall be construed as importing any other gender

14.2    words importing the singular shall be construed as importing the plural and vice versa

14.3    words importing persons shall be construed as importing a corporate body and/or a partnership and vice versa

14.4    where any party comprises more than one person the obligations and liabilities of that party under this Agreement shall be joint and several obligations and liabilities of those persons

14.5    the clause headings do not form part of this Agreement and shall not be taken into account in its construction or interpretation

14.6    any reference to a clause or a paragraph or a schedule is to one in this Agreement so numbered

**15      Nature of this Agreement**

This Agreement [is *or* is not] a deed and [has *or* has not] been executed by the parties to it as a deed

**[16      Contracts (Rights of Third Parties) Act 1999**

For the purposes of the Contracts (Rights of Third Parties) Act 1999 it is agreed that [with the exception only of *(specify clauses)*] nothing in this Agreement shall confer on any third party any right to enforce or any benefit of any term of this Agreement]

SCHEDULE

*(insert appropriate special provisions from Forms 104 [4129]–112 [4148] post, each provision to be in a separate part)*

*(signatures (or common seals) of both parties)*
*[(signatures of witnesses)]*
**[4066]**

1    No stamp duty. See Information Binder: Stamp Duties [1] (Agreement). This Form, which for convenience has all variable matters grouped at the beginning of the form, is designed to incorporate the additional provisions contained in Forms 104 [4129]–112 [4148] post if required.

2    Unlike the arrangements in Form 97 [4026] ante the supply under this Form is of a residential property and so a zero-rated supply for VAT purposes. Accordingly, no VAT is charged by the seller. As to VAT see Form 96 note 11 [4022] ante.

3    Discounts may play an important part in the price structuring of a new house.

4    The second alternative should be used where the developer is developing the site under a building licence as to which see Form 93 appendix 3 [3979] ante and Form 113 [4150] post. It is usual for the building licence to provide for the developer to enter into contracts without joining the owner who agrees in the licence that it will execute the necessary transfer or lease as the case may be.

5    This may be an acceptance of an initial notice under the new building control system, but it would still be, technically, a building regulation consent, so that the old nomenclature is probably the best. See the Building Regulations 1991, SI 1991/2768 as amended.

6    It is unusual for them to hold as stakeholders. See Form 98 note 5 [4060] ante.

7    If this contract is conditional on the buyer obtaining a mortgage offer, Forms 106 [4131] or 107 [4136] post will be incorporated in the schedule, and this clause will need to provide for the mortgage offer not having been received at the date of notification of completion of the property: see Form 98 clause 1.7.3 [4052] ante, which can be adapted to suit the circumstances.

8    Developers often prefer to have extras paid for direct to themselves, preferably upon an invoice rendered before legal completion, rather than have them dealt with by solicitors.

9    This wording may need to be changed from time to time in accordance with the requirements of the National House Building Council. As to the National House Building Council scheme generally see Form 93 appendix 2 [3974] ante. For alternative wording to this and other clauses where the guarantee is given by Zurich Municipal, see Form 103 [4121] post.

10    Consideration should be given to whether the standard conditions of sale require amendment in any way. For tables of suggested amendments see vol 38(1) (2000 Reissue) SALE OF LAND Form 12 [1245].

11    If required, additional wording concerning resolution of disputes about the construction of the contract itself may be added.

**[4067]**

# 100

### Agreement for sale of a plot on a freehold residential building estate, incorporating contract for the dwelling house to be built by the seller—long form with stage payments; form of transfer annexed[1]

THIS AGREEMENT is made the …… day of ………

BETWEEN:

(1)    *(seller)* [company number *(number)*] [of *(address)* or whose registered office is at *(address)*] ('the Seller') and

(2)    *(buyer)* [company number *(number)*] [of *(address)* or whose registered office is at *(address)*] ('the Buyer')

**[4068]**

**1     Definitions and interpretation**

In this Agreement:

1.1     'the Buyer's Solicitors' means *(insert name and address of person or firm)*

[1.2     'the Contract Price' means the Purchase Price plus the cost of any extras ordered by the Buyer]

1.3     'the Contract Rate' means *(insert interest rate or method of calculating the interest rate by reference eg to the base lending rate of a named bank)*

1.4     'the Dwelling House' means the dwelling house [and garage] erected or in the course of erection on the Land and described in the [first] schedule

1.5     'the General Conditions' means [the Standard Conditions of Sale (3rd Edn) *or (specify)*]

1.6     'the Land' means the plot of land described in the [first] schedule and in the draft transfer annexed to this Agreement

1.7     'the Period for Completion' means [within *(number)* days of the latest of the following [4] dates:

    1.7.1     the date of physical completion of the Dwelling House as notified to the Buyer's Solicitors or

    1.7.2     2 days after the date of posting of notification of the date of physical completion of the Dwelling House to the Buyer's Solicitors if that date is after the date of physical completion so notified or

    [1.7.3     the date upon which the Buyer receives a satisfactory offer of mortgage from his proposed lender whether it be a building society or not PROVIDED that if the lender is a building society the offer shall be deemed to have been received 2 days after it is known to have been posted but time shall not start to run until the instructions are sent out to the Buyer's Solicitors[2] or]

    1.7.4     the date of this Agreement
    *or*
    not more than [14] days after the Buyer or the Buyer's Solicitors has been sent notice that the Dwelling House has been completed in accordance with this Agreement and is ready for occupation][3]

1.8     'the Plan' means the plan annexed to this Agreement [and if numbered plans are annexed any reference to a numbered plan is to the annexed plan so numbered]

1.9     'the Property' means the Land and the Dwelling House

1.10     'the Purchase Price' means the sum of $£...$[4] [which [includes *or* does not include] the cost of [construction of a garage] [installation of central heating]]

1.11     'the Seller's Solicitors' means *(insert name and address of person or firm)*

1.12     where the context so admits the expression[s] 'the Seller' [and 'the Buyer'] include[s] the personal representatives of the Seller [and the Buyer] [and 'the Buyer' shall include any successors in title of the Buyer]

1.13     words importing one gender shall be construed as importing any other gender

1.14     words importing the singular shall be construed as importing the plural and vice versa

1.15     words importing persons shall be construed as importing a corporate body and/or a partnership and vice versa

1.16     where any party comprises more than one person the obligations and liabilities of that party under this Agreement shall be joint and several obligations and liabilities of those persons

1.17     the clause headings do not form part of this Agreement and shall not be taken into account in its construction or interpretation

1.18    any reference to a clause or a paragraph or a schedule is to one in this Agreement
        so numbered
1.19    any reference to a colour or letter is to one on the Plan
1.20    words defined in the annexed draft transfer have the same meaning when used
        in this Agreement

**[4069]**

## 2      Agreement for sale

The Seller shall sell and the Buyer shall buy the Property at the Purchase Price

## 3      Deposit

The Buyer shall on or before the date of this Agreement pay a deposit of [10%] of the
Purchase Price [direct to the Seller *or* to the Seller's Solicitors as [stakeholders *or* agents
for the Seller]][5]

## 4      Stage payments and Completion

4.1     The Purchase Price shall be paid at the following times or stages of construction
        and in the following amounts:

| Time or Stage | Amount £ |
|---|---|
| 4.1.1    [10]% deposit in accordance with clause 3 | ... |
| 4.1.2    *(stage)* | ... |
| 4.1.3    *(stage)* | ... |
| 4.1.4    *(stage)* | ... |
| 4.1.5    fully completed including external works | ... |
| **Total Purchase Price** | |

4.2     The Seller shall notify the Buyer's Solicitors in writing when each stage has been
        reached
4.3     If any stage payment (including the final stage payment) provided for in this
        clause shall not be paid within [14] days of such notification having been sent
        by the Seller the Buyer shall pay interest at the Contract Rate on the stage
        payment outstanding from the date of actual completion of that stage until the
        stage payment is received by the Seller
4.4     In the case of the final stage the Seller will endeavour to give to the Buyer's
        Solicitors as much notice as possible of the intended date of completion of the
        Dwelling House [but notwithstanding this the period of [14] days mentioned
        above shall run from the date of actual completion of the Dwelling House and
        the Seller shall be the sole arbiter of such date]
4.5     The final stage payment shall be paid and the Land transferred and the purchase
        shall be completed at *(specify place of completion)* within the Period for
        Completion

**[4070]**

## 5      Title guarantee

The Seller sells with [full *or* limited] title guarantee

## 6     Possession

The Property is sold with vacant possession on completion of the construction of the Dwelling House and the payment of all money due to the Seller under this Agreement [but the Buyer shall be entitled to reasonable access to the Land after the date of this Agreement at his own risk on prior appointment and only when accompanied by and complying with the safety instructions of a representative of the Seller for the purpose of inspecting the progress of the building works]

## 7     Title

Title to the Property is registered at HM Land Registry with [absolute] title under title number *(number)* and title shall be deduced in accordance with the Land Registration Act 1925 Section 110 [save that copies of the entries on the register the filed plan and any documents referred to shall be office copies and Land Registry Form 102 may be supplied in place of the Filed Plan[6] [and the Buyer or the Buyer's Solicitors having been supplied with such copies prior to the date of this Agreement the Buyer shall be deemed to purchase with full knowledge of the title in all respects and shall not raise any requisitions or make any objection in relation to the title]

**[4071]**

## 8     Transfer and incumbrances

8.1     The transfer to the Buyer shall be in the form of the annexed draft transfer

8.2     The Property is sold subject to and (where appropriate) with the benefit of the rights exceptions reservations covenants restrictions and other matters (if any) referred to in the annexed draft transfer and the property [proprietorship] and charges register of title number *(number)* [other than the charges referred to in the entries numbered *(numbers)* of the charges register of that title *or* other than charges to secure money] (and no other rights and easements shall be implied)

8.3     The Buyer or the Buyer's Solicitors having been supplied with copies of the documents referred to in clause 8.2 prior to the date of this Agreement shall be deemed to purchase with full notice and knowledge of them and shall not raise any requisition or make any objection in relation to them

8.4     The transfer shall be engrossed [in duplicate] by the Seller's Solicitors and [the *or* both] engrossment[s] shall be executed by the Buyer before the date for completion

[8.5     Immediately after completion the Buyer shall at his own expense procure the proper stamping of the duplicate transfer as a duplicate (including but not limited to the affixing of a particulars delivered stamp) and shall immediately after such stamping deliver the duly stamped duplicate to the Seller's Solicitors]

8.6     On completion the Buyer shall in addition to the Purchase Price pay to the Seller's Solicitors the sum of £... and VAT for the Seller's Solicitors' costs of engrossment and the supply of plans and draft documents

**[4072]**

## 9     Matters affecting the Property

The Property is sold subject to the following matters:

9.1     all local land charges whether registered or not before the date of this Agreement and all matters capable of registration as local land charges whether or not actually so registered

9.2     all notices served and orders demands proposals or requirements made by any local public or other competent authority whether before or after the date of this Agreement

9.3     all actual or proposed charges notices orders restrictions agreements conditions contraventions or other matters arising under the enactments relating to town and country planning and environmental law

9.4     all easements quasi-easements rights exceptions or other similar matters whether or not apparent on inspection or disclosed in any of the documents referred to in this Agreement

9.5     the easements and rights already granted or contracted to be granted to buyers of other parts of the Estate

## 10      Estate Plan

The Seller's estate layout plan represents the intention of the Seller as to the development of the Estate of which the Land forms part but neither any slight variation in the actual dimensions of the Land from the plan nor any variation in the development shall give rise to any claim by the Buyer for compensation or otherwise[7]

**[4073]**

## 11      Seller to construct the Dwelling House

11.1    The Seller shall [on or before *(date)*[8] (but without any liability whatsoever of the Seller should that completion date not be met)] construct or cause to be constructed the Dwelling House together with all necessary works in a thorough and workmanlike manner and with materials of a suitable quality in accordance with:

11.1.1      the appropriate planning permission

11.1.2      the building regulations[9]

11.1.3      the prescribed mandatory requirements currently in force and laid down by the National House Building Council and

11.1.4      the plans and specifications prepared by or on behalf of the Seller which the Buyer has had the opportunity to inspect at the Seller's office or other suitable place and of which (whether he has inspected the same or not) he shall be deemed to have full knowledge

11.2    The Seller shall have the right to substitute materials as near as possible of the same quality and value in lieu of those contained or referred to in the plans and specifications if in its absolute discretion it deems it expedient so to do and to make reasonable modifications to the plans and specifications in such manner as may be necessary as a result of the use of such substituted materials or in accordance with the requirements of any competent authority but such substitution and modification shall not reduce the value of the Dwelling House nor substantially alter its accommodation

## 12      Alterations and extras

12.1    If the Buyer requires any alterations in the construction of the Dwelling House whether in the nature of extras or otherwise such requirements for alteration shall be notified in writing by the Buyer to the Seller

12.2    If such alterations are agreed to and executed by the Seller the Seller's costs shall be added to (or subtracted from as the case may be) the Purchase Price and any addition to the Purchase Price shall be paid for by the Buyer to the Seller's Solicitors no later than the completion date and if such addition is not paid within the Period for Completion it shall bear interest at the Contract Rate

**[4074]**

**[13    Price rises**

The Contract Price is based on the prices of materials and labour subsisting at the date of this Agreement and if the rate of wages and other emoluments and expenses including the cost of National Insurance and third party insurance increases by reason of any alteration in the rules and decisions of the National Joint Council for the Building Industry or any other competent authority or if the market price of the fittings and materials used in the construction of the Dwelling House increases after the signing of this Agreement the amount of increase in such rates and other emoluments and expenses attributable to this Agreement and the increase in the cost of such fittings and materials shall be paid by the Buyer in addition to the price provided for in this Agreement and the same shall be paid to the Seller with the balance of purchase monies owing on completion of the Dwelling House [and the Buyer shall accept [a certificate from the Seller's estimating department *or (as the case may be)*] as to the amount of such increase and such certificate shall be conclusive and binding on the Buyer]][10]

**14    Delays beyond the Seller's control**

The erection and completion of the Dwelling House shall be carried out by the Seller as quickly as possible but in any of the cases specified below where delay is caused the Seller shall not be liable to the Buyer for any loss or inconvenience however occasioned:

14.1    strikes lockouts combinations and scarcity of labour
14.2    shortage of and delay in obtaining materials
14.3    hostilities and acts of the Queen's enemies
14.4    force majeure fire explosion flood lightning or bad weather
14.5    procedures required for obtaining all necessary permissions for or appertaining to the erection of the Dwelling House and all necessary services
14.6    compliance with all legislation statutory rules orders regulations or directions
14.7    accidents in the works for which the Seller is not responsible
14.8    other causes beyond the control of the Seller[11]

[except that if from any cause outside the control of the Seller he is for a period of [6] months or more prevented from proceeding with work on the construction of the Dwelling House either party shall have the option to determine this Agreement upon giving to the other [14] days' notice in writing to that effect whereupon all monies paid by the Buyer to the Seller under the terms of this Agreement shall be repaid to the Buyer but without interest]

**[4075]**

**15    No possession prior to completion**

Until payment of all money due under this Agreement by the Buyer to the Seller the Buyer agrees that he will not without the prior written consent of the Seller take or attempt to take possession of the Dwelling House either personally or by agents

**16    Risk**

The Dwelling House shall be at the sole risk of the Seller (notwithstanding any prior arrangement made by the Buyer or his mortgagees) in respect of damage or loss by fire storm explosion or lightning only and until the date for legal completion as described in clause 4 but if the Seller allows the Buyer at his request to store in the Dwelling House or upon the Land any of his possessions and such possessions are damaged or lost the Seller shall not be held liable for any such loss or damage in any manner whatsoever

## 17 National House Building Council

The Developer undertakes to make an irrevocable offer to provide the National House Building Council ('the NHBC') 'Buildmark' prior to the commencement of construction or to enter into any similar agreement or scheme which may be prescribed by the NHBC[12]

**[4076]**

## 18 Tree planting

There is reserved to the Seller a right of entry on the Land after completion of the sale for itself its agents and workmen for the purpose of planting and maintaining trees thereon in compliance with the conditions imposed (if any) by the grant of any planning permission or consent

## 19 Disclaimer

The Buyer admits that:

19.1 he has inspected the Land and purchases it with full knowledge of its actual state and condition and shall take the Land as it stands

19.2 he enters into this Agreement solely as a result of his own inspection and on the basis of the terms of this Agreement and not in reliance upon any representation or warranty either written or oral or implied made by or on behalf of the Seller (save for any representation or warranty contained in written replies given by the Seller's Solicitors to any preliminary inquiries raised by the Buyer or the Buyer's Solicitors)

19.3 this Agreement contains the entire agreement between the parties

## 20 Incorporation of conditions of sale and additional provisions

20.1 The General Conditions shall apply to this Agreement and are incorporated in it in so far as they are applicable to a sale by private treaty and are not varied by or inconsistent with the terms of this Agreement [and shall be amended as follows: *(insert details of amendments required)*][13]

[20.2 The terms set out in Part[s] *(number(s))* of the second schedule are incorporated in this Agreement[14]]

**[4077]**

## [21 Restriction on assignment

21.1 This Agreement is personal to the Buyer and shall not be capable of assignment

[21.2 The Seller shall not be required to transfer the Property [to anyone other than the Buyer named in this Agreement *or* at a price greater than the Contract Price]]]

## 22 Merger on completion

The provisions of this Agreement shall not merge on completion of the transfer of the Property so far as they remain to be performed

## 23 Disputes

Any dispute as to whether the home conforms to the mandatory requirements of the NHBC shall be referred to the NHBC in accordance with its Resolution Scheme

## 24 Nature of this Agreement

This Agreement [is *or* is not] a deed and [has *or* has not] been executed by the parties to it as a deed

**[25    Contracts (Rights of Third Parties) Act 1999**

For the purposes of the Contracts (Rights of Third Parties) Act 1999 it is agreed that [with the exception only of *(specify clauses)*] nothing in this Agreement shall confer on any third party any right to enforce or any benefit of any term of this Agreement]

[AS *or* IN] WITNESS etc

[FIRST] SCHEDULE
The Property

Name of development:
Town:
Plot no:
House type:
Postal address:

[SECOND SCHEDULE

*(insert appropriate special provisions from Forms 104 [4129]–112 [4148] post, each provision to be in a separate part)]*

*(signatures (or common seals) of the parties)*
[*(signatures of witnesses)*]
**[4078]**

1    No stamp duty. See Information Binder: Stamp Duties [1] (Agreement).
    Under this Form the buyer pays for the property in stage payments as the building work progresses. The buyer usually pays a deposit being a percentage of the total purchase price and the first stage payment may include the whole of the price of the land as well as the construction costs up to the first stage.
    If the buyer is able to pay the whole of the purchase price without raising any money on mortgage the transfer of the land can take place on completion of the construction work when the dwelling house is ready for occupation. If the buyer requires to mortgage the land in order to pay the stage payments then the land will have to be transferred, possibly as early as the date when the first stage payment is due, so that the land can be charged as security. The seller will then be left without ownership of the land as security for payment of the future stage payments. If the mortgage advance covers the whole of the balance to become due to the builder there may be little risk for the seller, but if the seller wishes he could require the buyer to execute a second legal charge or an equitable charge to secure the future payments.
    Reference should be made to Form 96 [4009] ante for detailed footnotes on the terms common to most forms of contract for sale, for cross-references to the relevant part of the commentary in vol 35 (1997 Reissue) SALE OF LAND and for additional footnotes relating to sales of part.
2    This sub-clause is required if the agreement is conditional upon the issue of a mortgage offer to the buyer. For clauses making the agreement conditional see Forms 106 [4131] and 107 [4136] post.
3    The second alternative is easier and more commonly used.
4    Unlike the arrangements in Form 97 [4026] ante, the supply under this Form is of a freehold residential property and so a zero-rated supply for VAT purposes. Accordingly, no VAT is charged by the seller.
5    Buyers usually object to paying the deposit direct to the seller. If the deposit is paid to the seller's solicitors they will hold as stakeholders unless the agreement provides otherwise: see the Standard Conditions of Sale (3rd Edn) condition 2.2.3 (for which see vol 38(1) (2000 Reissue) SALE OF LAND Form 1 [1011]).
6    As to Land Registry Form 102 certificates generally see vol 25(1) (1999 Reissue) LAND REGISTRATION Paragraph 57 [1881].
7    The practitioner needs to bear in mind that, if it is desired to reserve the right to make minor amendments to the approved estate plan, not only does the Land Registry need to be consulted about any amendment prior to its being made, but there may well be complications resulting from the existence of transfers that have already been effected on the estate and the existence of a defining plan in the transfer annexed to the current agreement. It is one thing to adjust a boundary between remaining unsold plots. It is quite another if any attempt is made to adjust the position of estate roads,

8 pathways or common services, over which rights have been granted already, or are due to be granted under the form of transfer annexed to the agreement. In the latter case, the adjustments may well need to be agreed with the buyer and previous transferees, and embodied in suitable formal documents.

8      Anticipatory completion dates are most unwise from a builder's viewpoint in view of the possibility of unforeseen snags in the building work.

9      See Form 98 note 9 [4060] ante. For the current building regulations see the Building Regulations 1991, SI 1991/2768 as amended.

10     Price rise clauses are rare and operation of them in a normal housing development is very difficult.

11     The seller should consider whether provision should be made to deal with any delay in payment of any stage payment; eg the seller being entitled to cease all building work and withdraw all labour and materials from the land and for the period for completion (if a specified date) to be extended proportionate to the time wasted by the buyer's default.

12     This wording may need to be changed from time to time in accordance with the requirements of the National House Building Council. As to the NHBC procedure generally see Form 93 appendix 2 [3974] ante.

13     Consideration should be given to whether the standard conditions of sale require amendment in any way. For tables of suggested amendments see vol 38(1) (2000 Reissue) SALE OF LAND Form 12 [1245].

14     All special provisions in Forms 104 [4129]–112 [4148] post likely to be required in the development should be set out in the second schedule, each provision being headed with a part number.

**[4079]**

# 101

## Agreement for sale of a plot on a freehold residential building estate—land only; for use in connection with a separate building agreement (for which see Form 102 [4085])—short form[1]

THIS AGREEMENT is made the ...... day of .........

BETWEEN

(1)     *(seller)* [company number *(number)*] [of *(address)* or whose registered office is at *(address)*] ('the Seller') and

(2)     *(buyer)* [company number *(number)*] [of *(address)* or whose registered office is at *(address)*] ('the Buyer')

**[4080]**

NOW IT IS AGREED as follows:

**1      Definitions and interpretation**

In this Agreement:

1.1     'the Building Agreement' means an agreement of even date with this Agreement made between the parties to this Agreement for erection of a dwelling house on the Plot

1.2     'the Buyer's Solicitors' means *(insert name and address of person or firm)*

1.3     'the Contract Rate' means *(insert interest rate or means of calculating the interest rate by reference eg to the base lending rate of a named bank)*

1.4     'the Deposit' means the sum of £... [which is [inclusive *or* exclusive] of VAT] being part of the Purchase Price

1.5     'the Estate Plan' means the Seller's estate plan

1.6     'the Plot' means *(description of plot)* described in the annexed draft transfer

1.7     'the Purchase Price' means the sum of £... [which is [inclusive *or* exclusive] of VAT at the standard rate as at the date of actual completion] [together with the certified value of the building works on the plot as at *(date)*][2]

1.8     'the Seller's Solicitors' means *(insert name and address of person or firm)*

1.9    where the context so admits the expression[s] 'the Seller' [and 'the Buyer'] include[s] the personal representatives of the Seller [and the Buyer] [and 'the Buyer' shall include any successors in title of the Buyer]

1.10    words importing one gender shall be construed as importing any other gender

1.11    words importing the singular shall be construed as importing the plural and vice versa

1.12    words importing persons shall be construed as importing a corporate body and/or a partnership and vice versa

1.13    where any party comprises more than one person the obligations and liabilities of that party under this Agreement shall be joint and several obligations and liabilities of those persons

1.14    the clause headings do not form part of this Agreement and shall not be taken into account in its construction or interpretation

[4081]

## 2    Agreement for sale

The Seller shall sell and the Buyer shall purchase the Plot at the Purchase Price

## 3    Deposit and completion

The deposit shall be paid to the Seller's Solicitors as [agents for the Seller *or* stakeholders] on the signing of this Agreement and the balance of the Purchase Price shall be paid and the purchase completed at the office of the Seller's Solicitors or such other place as they may direct [within 21 days of the Buyer's Solicitors being notified that [the *(specify which)* stage payment is due *or* the property is completed] under the Building Agreement *or* [28] days from the date of this Agreement][3]

## 4    Title Guarantee

The Seller sells with [full *or* limited] title guarantee

## 5    Title

The Seller is registered at HM Land Registry with title [absolute] under title number *(number)* and title shall be deduced in accordance with the Land Registration Act 1925 s 110[4] [save that copies of the entries on the register the filed plan and any documents referred to shall be office copies and Land Registry Form 102 may be supplied in place of the filed plan]

## 6    Transfer of the Plot

The transfer to the Buyer shall be in the form of the draft transfer annexed to this Agreement and the Plot is sold:

6.1    together with the benefit of and subject to the rights easements exceptions reservations agreements declarations covenants conditions stipulations and all other matters contained mentioned or referred to in the annexed draft transfer all of which shall be deemed to form part of this Agreement and

6.2    subject to all local land charges whether registered before or after the date of this Agreement and all other matters capable of registration as local land charges whether registered or not

## 7    Estate Plan[5]

The Estate Plan represents the intention of the Seller as to the development of the estate of which the Plot forms part but neither any slight variation in the actual dimensions of the Plot from the Estate Plan nor any variation in the development shall give rise to any claim by the Buyer for compensation or otherwise

**8 Incorporation of conditions of sale**

This Agreement incorporates the [Standard Conditions of Sale (3rd Edn) *or (specify)*] so far as they are applicable to a sale by private treaty and are not varied by or inconsistent with the express terms of this Agreement [and those conditions shall be amended as follows: *(insert amendments)*][6]

**9 Nature of this Agreement**

This Agreement [is *or* is not] a deed and [has *or* has not] been executed by the parties to it as a deed

**[10 Contracts (Rights of Third Parties) Act 1999**

For the purposes of the Contracts (Rights of Third Parties) Act 1999 it is agreed that [with the exception only of *(specify clauses)*] nothing in this Agreement shall confer on any third party any right to enforce or any benefit of any term of this Agreement]

*(signatures (or common seals) of both parties)*
[*(signatures of witnesses)*]
**[4082]**

1    No stamp duty. See Information Binder: Stamp Duties [1] (Agreement). For a form of building contract see Form 102 [4085] post.

      Reference should be made to Form 96 [4009] ante for detailed footnotes on the terms common to most forms of contract for sale and for cross references to the relevant part of the commentary in vol 35 (1997 Reissue) SALE OF LAND.

      This Form and Form 102 [4085] post are for use in an expenses paid scheme although they can also be used where that scheme is not operated. Under the expenses paid scheme the developer agrees to pay the expenses of the buyer incidental to the purchase, and attempts to mitigate his liability by requiring the buyer to enter into two separate contracts, one for the sale of the land and the other for erection of the building. These arrangements are outlined in Inland Revenue Statement of Practice SP 8/93.

      There are now two kinds of arrangement which may result in the desired effect of reducing the stamp duty payable, but this will depend on the precise facts in any particular case, and there will be no stamp duty saving where there is evidence of a sham or artificial transaction. Statement of Practice SP 8/93 reflects legal advice given to the Board of Inland Revenue following *Prudential Assurance Co Ltd v IRC* [1993] 1 WLR 211. However, the Statement does not necessarily bind the Board and the circumstances of any particular case may call for special consideration. It should be noted that, in the case of a residential estate, a builder would usually require a buyer to enter into the land contract and the building contract simultaneously, both for his protection and for administrative convenience, and that this would normally be the 'single transaction' situation referred to in (2) below. In this situation, it could be difficult to have contracts that are 'genuinely capable of independent completion' (see SP 8/93 para 2) and, if they are not, the stamp duty position would be as in (2)(a) below; if the contracts are genuinely independent (as in (2)(b) below), the stamp duty advantage would be lost if the transfer of the land is executed after all the building works have been completed.

      It is suggested that practitioners setting up an expenses paid scheme on behalf of a client builder apply initially to the Controller of Stamps for an adjudication of the particular scheme proposed.

(1)    **Two contracts and two separate transactions**
Where there is a contract for the purchase of land alone and, as a separate transaction, a second genuine contract for building works, ad valorem stamp duty on the transfer will be charged on the consideration payable for the purchase of the land only irrespective of whether any building work has commenced at the date of the transfer: Inland Revenue Statement of Practice SP 8/93 para 1.

**[4083]**

(2)    **Two contracts and a single transaction**
Where there is in reality only a single transaction between the parties, although there are two contracts, the stamp duty payable on the conveyance or transfer will depend on whether the contracts are genuinely independent of each other:

(a)    if the two contracts are inter-dependent, so that default on one contract means that the other is not enforceable, then the consideration chargeable to ad valorem stamp duty will be the total cost of the single transaction, including the total contract price for the buildings, whether or not the building works have been completed at the date of completion of the conveyance or transfer: *Statement of Practice* SP 8/93 para 2(i);

(b) if the two contracts are genuinely independent and separately enforceable, then the consideration chargeable to ad valorem stamp duty will be the total value of the land and any building works which have been completed at the date of execution of the conveyance or transfer: Statement of Practice SP 8/93 para 2(ii). See *Prudential Assurance Co Ltd v IRC* above, in which it was held that stamp duty was chargeable on the price paid for the transfer of the land and unfinished buildings, and not on the further sums payable under a development agreement for the completion of the buildings, even though the sale agreement and the development agreement comprised a single bargain. However, if the buildings have been completed at the date of the transfer of the land, then stamp duty will be chargeable on the total consideration for the land and buildings: see SP 8/93 para 2(ii).

2 As to VAT see Form 96 note 11 [4022] ante. The value of any building works on the plot at the date of the execution of the transfer, rather than the date of the agreement, may now be added to the value of the plot when assessing stamp duty payable: see note 1 above. Note that in Form 102 clause 1.1 [4085] post the certified value is deducted from the building price.

3 As to the current position with regard to saving stamp duty by using two contracts see note 1 above. The transfer of the plot would need to be executed before the building is completed: see note 1 above.

4 Ie the Land Registration Act 1925 s 110 as amended by the Land Registration Act 1988 s 2, Schedule (37 Halsbury's Statutes (4th Edn) REAL PROPERTY).

5 The practitioner needs to bear in mind that, if it is desired to reserve the right to make minor amendments to the approved estate plan, not only does the Land Registry need to be consulted about any amendment prior to its being made, but there may well be complications resulting from the existence of transfers that have already been effected on the estate and the existence of a defining plan in the transfer annexed to the current agreement. It is one thing to adjust a boundary between remaining unsold plots. It is quite another if any attempt is made to adjust the position of estate roads, pathways or common services, over which rights have been granted already, or are due to be granted under the form of transfer annexed to the agreement. In the latter case, the adjustments may well need to be agreed with the buyer and previous transferees, and embodied in suitable formal documents.

6 Consideration should be given to whether the standard conditions of sale require amendment in any way. For a table of suggested amendments see vol 38(1) (2000 Reissue) SALE OF LAND Form 12 [1244].

**[4084]**

# 102

## Building agreement for erection of a dwelling house on a plot on an estate with provision for stage payments—for use in conjunction with a separate plot sale contract (for which see Form 101)[1]

THIS [BUILDING][2] AGREEMENT is made the ...... day of .........

BETWEEN:

(1) *(builder)* [company number *(number)*] [of *(address) or* whose registered office is at *(address)*] ('the Builder') and

(2) *(buyer)* [company number *(number)*] [of *(address) or* whose registered office is at *(address)*] ('the Owner')

NOW IT IS AGREED as follows:

## 1 Definitions and interpretation

In this Agreement:

1.1 ['the Balance Owing' means the price of construction of the Dwelling House calculated in accordance with the [second] schedule [less the certified value of the building works on the Plot as at *(date)*][3]

*or*

'the Basic Price' means the sum of £... [less the certified value of the building works on the Plot as at *(date)*]][4]

1.2 'the Builder's Solicitors' means *(insert name and address of person or firm)*

1.3     'the Contract Rate' means *(insert interest rate or means of calculating the interest rate by reference eg to the base lending rate of a named bank)*

1.4     'the Dwelling House' means the dwelling house [and garage] to be erected on the Plot of the type specified in the [first] schedule

[1.5    'the Extras Price' means the cost of any extra work done in about or in respect of the Dwelling House at the request of the Owner and the cost of the materials used both to be as advised by the Builder]

1.6     'the Land Agreement' means an agreement dated *(date)* made between *(parties)* for the sale and purchase of the Plot

1.7     'the Owner's Solicitors' means *(insert name and address of person or firm)*

1.8     'the Plot' means the plot numbered *(number)* on the *(name)* estate at *(brief description)*

[1.9    'the Total Price' means the Basic Price plus the Extras Price]

1.10    where the context so admits the expression[s] 'the Builder' [and 'the Owner'] include[s] the personal representatives of the Builder and the Owner [and 'the Owner' shall include any successors in title of the Owner]

1.11    words importing one gender shall be construed as importing any other gender

1.12    words importing the singular shall be construed as importing the plural and vice versa

1.13    words importing persons shall be construed as importing a corporate body and/or a partnership and vice versa

1.14    where any party comprises more than one person the obligations and liabilities of that party under this Agreement shall be joint and several obligations and liabilities of those persons

1.15    the clause headings do not form part of this Agreement and shall not be taken into account in its construction or interpretation

**[4085]**

## 2     Construction of the Dwelling House

The Builder shall erect and complete on the Plot the Dwelling House for the Owner together with all necessary works in a thorough and workmanlike manner and with materials of a suitable quality in accordance with the drawings plans and specifications for the type of dwelling house selected by the Owner

## 3     Payment of the price

[3.1    [The Total Price *or* The Balance Owing][5] (together with any VAT chargeable thereon)[6] shall be paid by the Owner at the following stages and in the following amounts:

| No of Stage *(number)* | Stage of construction *(insert details)* | Amount payable £... |
|---|---|---|

3.2    The Builder shall notify the Owner's Solicitors in writing when each stage has been reached

3.3    If any stage payment (including the final stage) provided for in this clause shall not be paid within [14] days of such notification having been sent by the Builder the Owner shall pay interest at the Contract Rate on the stage payment or the amount outstanding from the date of actual completion of that stage until the stage payment is received by the Builder

3.4    In the case of the final stage [the Builder will endeavour to give to the Owner's Solicitors as much notice as possible of the intended date of completion but notwithstanding this] the period of [14] days mentioned above shall run from the actual date of completion and the Builder shall be the sole arbiter of such date

**[4086]**

*or*

3.1      [The Total Price *or* The Balance Owing] (together with any VAT chargeable thereon) shall be paid by the Owner within [14] days of the Builder notifying the Owner's Solicitors in writing that the Dwelling House is completed

3.2      If payment has not been made within the period of [14] days of such notification having been sent by the Builder the Owner shall pay interest at the Contract Rate on the total amount outstanding from the date that the Dwelling House was completed until the payment is received by the Builder

3.3      [The Builder will endeavour to give to the Owner's Solicitors as much notice as possible of the intended date of completion of the Dwelling House but notwithstanding this the *or* The] period of [14] days mentioned above shall run from the actual date of completion and the Builder will be the sole arbiter of such date]

[4087]

**[4     Price rises**

The price of construction of the Dwelling House is based on the prices of materials and labour subsisting at the date of this Agreement and if the rate of wages and other emoluments and expenses including the cost of National Insurance and third party insurance increases by reason of any alteration in the rules and decisions of the National Joint Council for the Building Industry or any other competent authority or if the market price of the fittings and materials used in the construction of the Dwelling House increases after the signing of this Agreement the amount of increase in such rates and other emoluments and expenses attributable to this Agreement and the increase in the cost of such fittings and materials shall be paid by the Owner in addition to the price provided for in this Agreement and the same shall be paid to the Builder with the balance of the [Total Price *or* Balance Owing] on completion of the Dwelling House [and the Owner shall accept [a certificate from the Builder's estimating department *or (as the case may be)*] as to the amount of such increase and such certificate shall be conclusive and binding on the Owner]]

**5     Delays beyond the Builder's control**

The erection and completion of the Dwelling House shall be carried out by the Builder as quickly as possible but in any of the cases specified below where delay is caused the Builder shall not be liable to the Owner for any loss or inconvenience however occasioned:

5.1      strikes lockouts combinations and scarcity of labour

5.2      shortage of and delay in obtaining materials

5.3      hostilities and acts of the Queen's enemies

5.4      force majeure fire explosion flood lightning or bad weather

5.5      procedures required for obtaining all necessary permissions for or appertaining to the erection of the Dwelling House and all necessary services

5.6      compliance with all legislation statutory rules orders regulations or directions

5.7      accidents in the works for which the Builder is not responsible

5.8      other causes beyond the control of the Builder[7]

except that if from any cause outside the control of the Builder he is for a period of [6] months or more prevented from proceeding with work on the construction of the Dwelling House either party shall have the option to determine this Agreement upon giving to the other [14] days' notice in writing to that effect [whereupon all monies paid by the Owner to the Builder under the terms of this Agreement shall be repaid to the Owner but without interest][8]

[4088]

## 6    Risk

The Dwelling House shall be at the sole risk of the Builder (notwithstanding any prior arrangement made by the Owner or his mortgagees) in respect of damage or loss by fire storm explosion or lightning only and until the date for payment of the final stage payment as described in clause 3 but if the Builder allows the Owner at his request to store in the Dwelling House or upon the Plot any of his possessions and such possessions are damaged or lost the Builder shall not be held liable for any such loss or damage in any manner whatsoever

## 7    National House Building Council[9]

The Builder undertakes to make an irrevocable offer to provide the National House Building Council ('the NHBC') 'Buildmark' prior to the commencement of construction or to enter into any similar agreement or scheme which may be prescribed by the NHBC

## [8    Time of the essence

In this Agreement where time limits are concerned time shall be of the essence of the agreement]

## [9    Exclusion of liability[10]

The Owner acknowledges that save as to such (if any) of the written statements of the Builder's Solicitors in answer to enquiries made or information supplied prior to the making of this Agreement as were not susceptible of independent verification by inspection and survey of the Plot [search and enquiry of the local or other public authority or inspection of the documents disclosed to the Owner] (and whether or not such inspections survey search and enquiry have been made) and have been relied on by the Owner he has not entered into this Agreement in reliance wholly or partly on any statement or representation made to him]

## 10    Disputes

Any dispute as to whether the home conforms to the mandatory requirements of the NHBC shall be referred to the NHBC in accordance with its Resolution Scheme

## 11    Nature of this Agreement

This Agreement [is *or* is not] a deed and [has *or* has not] been executed by the parties to it as a deed

## [12    Contracts (Rights of Third Parties) Act 1999

For the purposes of the Contracts (Rights of Third Parties) Act 1999 it is agreed that [with the exception only of *(specify clauses)*] nothing in this Agreement shall confer on any third party any right to enforce or any benefit of any term of this Agreement]

AS WITNESS etc

[4089]

### [FIRST] SCHEDULE
The House Type

Detached/terraced/semi–detached
House/chalet/bungalow/flat/maisonette
Type:

## [SECOND SCHEDULE
### The Balance Owing

Total construction cost of the Dwelling House     £.........
Cost of forms and plans     £.........
Total price     £.........
Less discount (if applicable)     £.........
Balance owing     £.........]

*(signatures (or common seals) of the parties)*
*[(signatures of witnesses)]*
**[4090]**

1    No stamp duty. See Information Binder: Stamp Duties [1] (Agreement). As to the use of separate land and building contracts generally see Form 101 note 1 [4083] ante. For a form of land contract see Form 101 [4080] ante.
2    Contracts of this type are commonly headed 'building agreement'.
3    See Form 101 notes 2, 3 [4084] ante.
4    The wording used depends on the method of definition of the price. The two methods given (ie (a) the balance owning; or (b) the basic price, the extras price and the total price) are examples only. The first alternative should be omitted if the basic price method is used.
5    The wording depends on which definition of the price is used. See note 4 above.
6    If the builder is a taxable person for VAT purposes, its construction services should be exclusive of VAT; the builder will charge the owner VAT.
7    The seller should consider whether provision should be made to deal with any delay in payment of any stage payment; eg the seller being entitled to cease all building work and withdraw all labour and materials from the land and for the period for completion (if a specified date) to be extended proportionate to the time wasted by the buyer's default.
8    The words in square brackets will not always be appropriate and the parties should consider what arrangements should apply. If by the time of rescission the plot has been transferred to the owner, it may not be equitable that the owner retains not only the plot for which he has paid, but also the value of the uncompleted building works and receives back all money paid by him for the construction of those works and delivery of materials.
9    As to the National House Building Council scheme generally see Form 93 appendix 2 [3974] ante.
10   This clause is more common in a contract for the sale of land, but there may have been enquiries or representation in relation to the building works.

**[4091]–[4120]**

# 103

**Agreement for the sale of a plot on a freehold residential building estate in consideration of the transfer of the buyer's existing freehold dwelling house and an additional payment by the buyer[1]**

THIS AGREEMENT is made the ...... day of .........

BETWEEN:

(1)      *(name)* [company number *(number)*] [of *(address) or* whose registered office is at *(address)*] ('the Developer') and

(2)      *(buyer)* [company number *(number)*] [of *(address) or* whose registered office is at *(address)*] ('the [First] Buyer')

[(3)     *(buyer)* [company number *(number)*] [of *(address) or* whose registered office is at *(address)*] ('the Second Buyer')][2]

**[4121]**

NOW IT IS AGREED as follows:

## 1     The First Property (to be taken by the Buyer)

The First Property is as follows:

1.1      Development:

1.2      Plot number:

1.3      Type of dwelling:

1.4      Postal address (if known):

1.5      Tenure: freehold/leasehold for a term of *(number)* years from *(date)* at a ground rent of £... per year

1.6      Title number: *(number)*

Subject to and with the benefit of all matters referred to in the draft [transfer *or* lease] annexed to this Agreement [and the entries in the register of title number *(number)* [save for the Developer's subsisting mortgage]]

## 2     The Second Property (to be taken by the Developer)

The Second Property is the following property of the [First] Buyer to be taken by the Developer:

2.1      Description and postal address: *(details)*

2.2      Tenure: freehold/leasehold for a term of *(number)* years from *(date)* at a ground rent of £... per year

2.3      [Title number *(number) or* comprised in a [conveyance *or (as the case may be)*] dated *(date)* made between *(parties)*]

Subject to and with the benefit of all matters referred to in the [entries in the register of title number *(number) or* the epitome of title] [save for the [First] Buyer's subsisting mortgage]

[4122]

## 3     The Additional Payment

[£... paid by the Buyer to the Developer *or* Nil] [plus *or* minus] the documentation fee of £...

## 4     Solicitors

4.1      The Developer's Solicitors are: *(name and address)*

4.2      The Buyer's Solicitors are : *(name and address)*

## 5     Contract

The Developer (being the owner of the First Property) will sell the First Property to the Buyer at the price of £... to be satisfied by the transfer by the [First] Buyer (being the owner of the Second Property) of the Second Property to the Developer and the Additional Payment and in accordance with the conditions of sale set out in this Agreement

## CONDITIONS OF SALE

### 1     Conditions applicable to the First Property

#### 1.1     Building works

1.1.1     The Developer shall erect and complete the First Property in accordance with the terms of the relevant planning permission and building regulation consent[3] and the current mandatory requirements of [the National House Building Council *or* Zurich Municipal] and the First Property shall be deemed to have been completed notwithstanding that any item of a minor or trivial nature may require attention the same to be corrected or completed by the Developer after completion of the [transfer *or* lease]

1.1.2     Plans and specifications of the First Property are available for inspection by the Buyer at the site sales office or other suitable premises to be designated by the Developer and the Developer will use every endeavour to adhere to such plans and specifications and to the layout of the plot but reserves the right to make any reasonable variation to it not substantially affecting the value of the Property and such variation shall not annul the sale or entitle the Buyer to any damages and compensation

1.1.3     Where the plans provide for a garage space but do not provide for the erection of a garage the Developer shall provide sufficient space for the erection of a single garage but shall be under no obligation to carry out any works of any nature in respect of the garage space so as to prepare or render it fit for the erection of a garage

**[4123]**

### 1.2     Assurance
The [transfer or lease] to the Buyer shall be in the form annexed to this Agreement and the Buyer shall be deemed to have full knowledge of its contents and the First Property is [transferred or leased] together with the benefit of and subject to all matters contained in the [transfer or lease]

### 1.3     Extras
Any extras or variations which the Developer may agree to supply or effect shall be paid for in addition to the Additional Payment shall be made at such time as the Developer shall require[4]

### 1.4     Insurance
The First Property will be at the Developer's risk until the release of the keys to the Buyer is authorised

### 1.5     [National House Building Council *or* Zurich Municipal]
The Developer undertakes to make an irrevocable offer to provide [the National House Building Council ('the NHBC') 'Buildmark' *or* Building Guarantee prescribed by Zurich Municipal ('Zurich')] or to enter into any similar agreement or scheme prior to the commencement of construction which may be prescribed by [the NHBC *or* Zurich] in relation to the First Property[5]

### 1.6     Disputes
Any dispute as to whether the home on the First Property conforms to the mandatory requirements of [the NHBC *or* Zurich] shall be referred to [the NHBC in accordance with its Resolution Scheme[6] *or* Zurich in accordance with its claims procedure]

**[4124]**

### 1.7     Agreement and declaration
It is agreed and declared:

1.7.1     that the Developer shall not be liable for nor shall the Buyer be entitled to receive any compensation for any delay in the erection or completion of the First Property or any other matter relating to it by reason of fire storm tempest snow accidents shortages of labour government control restrictions riots acts of war insurrection civil disturbance strikes lockouts or other causes outside the direct control of the Developer

1.7.2     that no representation either written or oral (except written answers to [standard] pre-contract enquiries [supplied with the estate documentation]) has been made to the Buyer prior to the date of this Agreement by the Developer or his servants or agents concerning the First Property which has influenced or persuaded the Buyer to enter into this Agreement

**2		Conditions applicable to the Second Property**
The Buyer shall permit the Developer and his agents:
2.1		to erect and maintain on the Second Property in positions to be determined by the Developer or his agents signboards and posters advertising the Second Property as being for sale
2.2		to show persons interested in purchasing the Second Property around the same at all reasonable times and
2.3		to arrange for valuers acting for building societies and other financial institutions to inspect the Second Property during normal working hours

**[3		Additional terms**

The terms set out in [Parts *(insert relevant numbers)* of] the schedule are incorporated in this Agreement]

**[4125]**

**4		Conditions applicable to both properties**

**4.1		Title Guarantee**
The Developer and Buyer shall transfer their respective properties with [full *or* limited] title guarantee

**4.2		Completion**
The [sale and purchase *or* grant of the lease] of the First Property and the transfer of the Second Property shall be completed and the Additional Payment shall be paid at the offices of the Developer's Solicitors within [14] days of written notification being posted [by recorded delivery post *or (as the case may be)*] to the Buyer or his solicitors to the effect that the First Property is complete and fit for occupation[7]

**4.3		Possession**
The First Property and the Second Property are to be transferred with vacant possession on completion

**4.4		Title**
The Developer and the Buyer shall respectively deduce a good and marketable title in respect of the First Property and the Second Property in accordance with the Land Registration Act 1925 Section 110

**4.5		Agreement and declaration**
The Developer and the Buyer enter into this Agreement as a result of their own personal inspection of the respective properties and not as a result of any express or implied written or oral representation or warranty made or alleged to have been made by or on behalf of them

**4.6		General conditions**
This Agreement incorporates the [Standard Conditions of Sale (3rd Edn) *or (specify)*] so far as they are not varied by nor inconsistent with its express terms

**[4126]**

## 5     Interpretation

5.1     where the context so admits the expression[s] 'the Developer' [and 'the Buyer'] include[s] the personal representatives of the Developer [and the Buyer] [and 'the Buyer' shall include any successors in title of the Buyer]

[5.2     'the Buyer' means the First Buyer and the Second Buyer]

5.3     words importing one gender shall be construed as importing any other gender

5.4     words importing the singular shall be construed as importing the plural and vice versa

5.5     words importing persons shall be construed as importing a corporate body and/ or a partnership and vice versa

5.6     where any party comprises more than one person the obligations and liabilities of that party under this Agreement shall be joint and several obligations and liabilities of those persons

5.7     the clause headings do not form part of this Agreement and shall not be taken into account in its construction or interpretation

5.8     any reference to a clause or a paragraph or a schedule is to one in this Agreement so numbered

## 6     Nature of this agreement

This Agreement [is *or* is not] a deed and [has *or* has not] been executed by the parties to it as a deed

## [7     Contracts (Rights of Third Parties) Act 1999

For the purposes of the Contracts (Rights of Third Parties) Act 1999 it is agreed that [with the exception only of *(specify clauses)*] nothing in this Agreement shall confer on any third party any right to enforce or any benefit of any term of this Agreement]

### THE SCHEDULE
### Part [1]
*(insert appropriate special provisions from Forms 104 [4129]–112 [4148] post, each provision to be in a separate part)*

*(signatures (or common seals) of the parties)*
*[(signatures of witnesses)]*
**[4127]**

---

1     As to stamp duty see Information Binder: Stamp Duties [1] (Conveyance or transfer on sale) and see vol 35 (1997 Reissue) SALE OF LAND Paragraph 774 [1032] et seq. This Form is designed to incorporate selling aids contained in Forms 104 [4129]–112 [4148] post as agreed.

Reference should be made to Form 96 [4009] ante for detailed footnotes on the terms common to most forms of contract for sale and for cross-references to the relevant part of the commentary in vol 35 (1997 Reissue) SALE OF LAND. As to exchanges generally see vol 35 (1997 Reissue) SALE OF LAND Paragraph 760 [1014] et seq. The wording of the contract is critical to whether the transaction constitutes a single-sale of the more expensive property (on which one amount of ad valorem stamp duty is payable) or an exchange of two properties where two charges to stamp duty will arise. The practitioner should pay careful attention to the Inland Revenue's Press Release dated 18 April 1994. See also Form 110 note 1 [4145] post.

For a form containing fuller provisions on title, incumbrances, matters affecting the properties etc, see vol 36 (1997 Reissue) SALE OF LAND Form 112 [1876].

2     The buyers should be divided into first and second buyers if their existing property is in the name of only one of them. The transfer of the new home to the buyer should include the direction of the party who is the owner of the second property that the new house is to be transferred to the buyers jointly in the appropriate shares. As between the buyers, there is a voluntary disposition of the appropriate share of the new house.

3      Ie consent under the Building Regulations 1991, SI 1991/2768 as amended.

4      Developers often prefer to have extras paid for direct to themselves, preferably upon an invoice rendered
       before legal completion, rather than have them dealt with by solicitors.

5      This wording may need to be changed from time to time in accordance with the requirements of the
       National House Building Council or Zurich Municipal. As to the National House Building Council
       and Zurich Municipal's schemes generally see Form 93 appendix 2 [3974] ante.

6      If required, additional wording concerning resolution of disputes about the construction of the contract
       itself may be added.

7      If this contract is conditional on the buyer obtaining a mortgage offer Forms 106 [4131] or 107 [4136]
       post will be incorporated in the schedule, and this clause will need to provide for the mortgage offer
       not having been received at the date of notification of completion of the first property; see Form 98
       clause 1.7.3 [4052] ante which can be adapted to suit the circumstances.

                                                                                              **[4128]**


# (3): CLAUSES FOR INSERTION IN AGREEMENTS FOR THE SALE OF RESIDENTIAL PLOTS


## 104

### Clause stating that the agreement is conditional on satisfactory results of a local land charges search already submitted

0.1    If the Buyer's Solicitors have submitted to the appropriate authority a local land
       charges search and additional enquiries on Form [Con 29 (1991)] prior to the
       date of this Agreement this Agreement is exchanged upon the basis that if the
       certificate of such search or replies to such enquiries reveal any matter which
       materially adversely affects the value or the beneficial occupation of the
       Property as a private dwelling house[1] the Buyer may rescind this Agreement by
       serving notice in writing on the Seller's Solicitors within [7] days of receipt by
       the Buyer's Solicitors of the certificate and replies and this Agreement shall be
       deemed to have been rescinded [7] days after such notice is served unless within
       that period the Seller undertakes in writing to secure the removal of such matter

0.2    In this clause where the time limits are concerned time shall be of the essence
       of the contract and in any event the Buyer's Solicitors shall notify the Seller's
       Solicitors immediately they receive the certificate and replies

1      The precise meaning of this phrase has not been litigated, which perhaps indicates that is has been found
       to be clear in practice, or that developers do not insert this condition in a contract unless certain that it
       will not be invoked.

                                                                                              **[4129]**


## 105

### Clause stating that the agreement is conditional on a satisfactory local land charges search—search deemed satisfactory in certain events[1]

0.1    This Agreement is exchanged upon the basis that if the Buyer's Solicitors'
       local land charges search certificate or replies to additional enquiries on Form

[Con 29 (1991)] reveal any matter which materially adversely affects the value or the beneficial occupation of the Property as a private dwelling house the Buyer may rescind this Agreement by serving notice in writing on the Seller's Solicitors within [7] days of receipt by the Buyer's Solicitors of the certificate and replies and this Agreement shall be deemed to have been rescinded *(number)* days after such notice is served unless within that period the Seller undertakes in writing to secure the removal of such matter

0.2     If within [6] weeks of *(date)* being the date on which the Seller's Solicitors posted a draft of this Agreement and the accompanying documentation to the Buyer's Solicitors the Buyer's Solicitors have not advised the Seller's Solicitors in writing that they have received an unsatisfactory certificate and/or unsatisfactory replies or that they have not then received any form of certificate and/or replies the Seller shall be entitled to assume that a satisfactory local land charges search certificate and replies have been received by the Buyer's Solicitors and this Agreement shall become unconditional so far as the local land charges search and replies to additional enquiries are concerned

0.3     In this clause where time limits are concerned time shall be of the essence of the contract

1     This Form differs from Form 104 [4129] ante in not requiring the search to have been submitted to the appropriate authority before the date of the agreement and in providing for the result to be deemed satisfactory in the events mentioned in clause 0.2. This Form is rarely used.

[4130]

# 106

### Clause stating that the agreement is conditional on mortgage offer being obtained by the buyer—provision for the seller to lend any shortfall[1]

0.1     This Agreement is conditional upon an offer of advance (including a second mortgage offer) of not less than £...[2] ('the Offer') [on terms acceptable to the Buyer *or* repayable over [25] years on the normal terms of *(name)* Building Society][3] being made available to the Buyer on or before *(date)* or such later date as shall be agreed by the Seller in writing ('the Offer Date')

[4131]

0.2     If the Offer is not made available to the Buyer on or before the Offer Date this Agreement shall be deemed to be rescinded and the Buyer shall be entitled to the return of all deposit monies paid by him to the Seller (other than the reservation deposit) [PROVIDED that:
        [0.2.1     if an offer of advance is received for an amount less than that stated above and the shortfall represents *(insert percentage)*% or less of the Purchase Price the Seller may elect within *(number)* [weeks] of the Offer Date to provide the shortfall out of his own funds PROVIDED that the amount of the shortfall together with the amount of the advance offered shall not exceed *(specify percentage)*% of the Purchase Price and
        0.2.2     if the Seller so elects the condition specified above shall be deemed to be satisfied and the Buyer shall enter into a [second] legal charge in the form annexed to this Agreement (which has already been

shown to the Buyer as the Buyer acknowledges) to provide for repayment to the Seller of the shortfall together with interest at the current recommended rate of *(name of building society or bank)* at the date of this Agreement by equal monthly instalments over a maximum period of *(number)* months [and provided that the Buyer pays the monthly instalments under the second legal charge within 14 days of the due dates the Seller will waive all payment of interest thereon][4]

**[4132]**

*or*

0.2.1    if the Buyer is a First Time Buyer and an offer of advance is received for an amount less than that stated above and the shortfall represents 10% or less of the Purchase Price the Seller may elect within *(number)* [weeks] of the Offer Date to provide the shortfall out of his own funds PROVIDED that the amount of the shortfall together with the amount of the advance offered shall not exceed *(specify percentage)*% of the Purchase Price and

0.2.2    if the Seller so elects the condition specified above shall be deemed to be satisfied and the Buyer shall enter into a [second] legal charge in the form annexed to this Agreement (which has already been shown to the Buyer as the Buyer acknowledges) to provide for repayment to the Seller of the shortfall together with [simple] interest on it at *(specify rate)*% on the fifth anniversary of the completion of this Agreement or upon sale of the Property whichever shall be the sooner and

0.2.3    a 'First Time Buyer' means a Buyer who has not previously owned a dwelling house or in the case of 2 or more joint buyers none of whom has previously owned a dwelling house

0.2.4    the Buyer and if more than one each of them warrants to the Seller that he is a First Time Buyer]][5]

**[4133]**

0.3    The Buyer agrees that he will do all things and acts necessary either to assist the Seller in obtaining an offer of mortgage for him or to obtain such an offer himself whether such acts or things be concerned with completing the application forms paying survey fees answering correspondence or any other matter appertaining to the obtaining of such an offer and the Buyer agrees that once the mortgage application has been lodged he will not withdraw it and will accept a suitable offer of mortgage when available and that should he either withdraw the application or fail to accept an offer in circumstances in which the Seller can establish that had the Buyer not withdrawn or failed as aforesaid [an Offer would have been made to the Buyer *or* the preconditions to an election under sub-clause 0.2.1 would have existed and the Seller would have so elected][6] then this Agreement shall as regards the provisions of this condition be deemed to have become unconditional

**[4134]**

---

1    A contract which is conditional on the buyer receiving a satisfactory mortgage offer may provide that, failing a satisfactory offer, a mortgage facility shall be available from the seller by way of deferred payment loan or otherwise. A deferred payment loan is simply a loan from the seller secured by a second charge on the property. A special condition in the contract contains an agreement for the loan and provides for a form of charge. For a form of condition more favourable to the buyer which can be adapted see vol 36 (1997 Reissue) SALE OF LAND Form 181 [2200]. No precedent for such a scheme is given because of the many variations currently in use.

2      The amount inserted should be the net offer expected after deducting any guarantee premium etc.
3      Without one of these alternative wordings the buyer may be forced to accept a prejudicial offer.
4      The words in square brackets should be included where an interest free loan is being used as a selling aid.
5      The second alternative (sub-clauses 0.2.1–0.2.4) should be used where the loan is to be a deferred
       payment loan.
6      If the seller will not make up any shortfall the first alternative should be used.

**[4135]**

## 107

### Clause stating that the agreement is conditional on a mortgage offer being obtained by the seller or the buyer[1]

This Agreement is conditional upon either:

0.1        the Seller obtaining through his own connections an offer of mortgage ('Offer
           of Mortgage') in terms [reasonably] satisfactory to the Buyer from a building
           society to be nominated by the Seller and:

    0.1.1      the amount of the loan required is [the amount so stated in the
               Reservation Form or £...]

    0.1.2      the Seller anticipates that the Offer of Mortgage will be issued by the
               date of expiry of the (number) weeks' reservation period as set out in
               the reservation form signed by the Buyer copies of which are held by
               both the Seller and the Buyer ('the Reservation Form') but if the
               Offer of Mortgage is delayed beyond that date for any reason the
               validity of this Agreement shall not be affected

    0.1.3      this Agreement shall be deemed to have become unconditional in so
               far as the Offer of Mortgage is concerned [2] days after the building
               society is known to have posted the Offer of Mortgage to the Buyer
               PROVIDED that if the instructions to the Buyer's Solicitors are
               issued separately by the building society this Agreement shall become
               unconditional when the Buyer receives the offer and not when the
               Buyer's Solicitor receives the instructions

    0.1.4      if for any reason the Seller is unable to obtain an Offer of Mortgage
               for the Buyer he shall notify the Buyer in writing by recorded
               delivery post and this Agreement shall be deemed to have been
               rescinded following the expiry of the [seventh] day after the date of
               posting of the notice of rescission ('the Last Day') PROVIDED that
               the Buyer has not elected by notice in writing sent by recorded
               delivery post to reach the Seller before last post on the Last Day to
               arrange for his own mortgage in which case sub-clause [0.2] shall
               immediately come into effect save that the period within which the
               Buyer shall obtain his mortgage offer shall be calculated from the Last
               Day instead of the date upon which the Buyer signed the
               Reservation Form and shall be limited to [6] weeks from the Last
               Day

**[4136]**

           or

0.2        the Buyer obtaining an offer of mortgage in terms [reasonably] satisfactory to
           the Buyer for the amount so stated in the Reservation Form from a building
           society or other lending institution agency or individual within (number) weeks
           of the date on which the Reservation Form is signed by the Buyer and:

    0.2.1      the Seller and Buyer may agree in writing for an extension of the
               period[2] in which the Offer of Mortgage is to be made

0.2.2    this Agreement shall be deemed to have become unconditional in so far as the Offer of Mortgage is concerned [2] days after the building society is known to have posted its offer of mortgage to the Buyer PROVIDED that if the instructions to the Buyer's Solicitors are issued separately by the building society this Agreement shall become unconditional when the Buyer receives the offer and not when the Buyer's Solicitor receives the instructions

0.2.3    if by the last day of *(number)* of weeks from the date of signature of the Reservation Form by the Buyer or any extension of that period agreed between the Seller and the Buyer ('the Expiry Date') the Buyer has not obtained an offer of mortgage [reasonably satisfactory to the Buyer] and he wishes to rescind this Agreement he shall notify the Seller in writing by recorded delivery post within [14] days of the Expiry Date that an offer of mortgage has not been received and that he is rescinding this Agreement for that reason and

0.2.4    should the Buyer not so notify the Seller within that period of [14] days immediately following the Expiry Date the Seller shall be entitled to assume that the Buyer is proceeding with his purchase and thereupon this Agreement shall become unconditional in so far as the Offer of Mortgage is concerned

0.2.5    for the purposes of this clause the first day of the [14] day period within which notice of rescission may be given shall be the day immediately following the Expiry Date and the notice may be posted at any time up to midnight on the [14th] day

0.2.6    the Seller may rescind this Agreement at any time following the Expiry Date by sending to the Buyer or the Buyer's Solicitors by recorded delivery post notice of rescission and this Agreement shall accordingly be deemed to have been rescinded as from the date of such posting

PROVIDED that the Seller may elect on receiving notice from the Buyer that the Buyer is unable to obtain a [reasonably] satisfactory offer of mortgage to attempt to obtain one for the Buyer through his own connections and in the case of such election the provisions of sub-clause [0.1] shall come into effect save that if the Seller has not procured for the Buyer a [reasonably] satisfactory offer of mortgage within [6] weeks of the Seller giving to the Buyer written notice of election the Buyer shall be entitled to give notice of rescission in writing to the Seller by recorded delivery post and this Agreement shall be rescinded as from the date of posting such notice

**[4137]**

0.3    In the event of this Agreement being rescinded under the terms of sub-clauses [0.1] or [0.2]:

0.3.1    the Seller shall return to the Buyer £... of the £... reservation fee the balance of £... being retained by the Seller as an administration fee

0.3.2    in respect of any further deposit paid by the Buyer to the Seller the whole amount shall be returned to the Buyer PROVIDED that if the Buyer has requested any extras and either the materials for them have been ordered by the Seller and cancellation of the order is impossible or the materials have been ordered and delivered (whether or not any work has taken place) the cost incurred by the Seller in satisfying the order so placed by the Buyer shall be deducted from the further deposit returned to the Buyer and shall be forfeited to the Seller and

0.3.3       it is a condition of this clause that in the case of any such orders for extras the Seller shall notify the Buyer in writing within [14] days of the order being placed that this forfeiture clause operates

0.4      In respect of both sub-clauses [0.1] and [0.2] the Buyer agrees:

0.4.1       that he will do all things and acts necessary either to assist the Seller in obtaining an offer of mortgage for him or to obtain such an offer himself whether such acts or things be concerned with completing the application forms paying survey fees answering correspondence or any other matter appertaining to the obtaining of the offer

0.4.2       that once the mortgage application has been lodged he will not withdraw the application or fail to accept the offer

0.4.3       this Agreement shall become unconditional as far as the Offer of Mortgage is concerned if the Seller shows that had the Buyer complied with this sub-clause a mortgage offer would have been made available to him

**[4138]**

1    Under this Form the contract is conditional on a mortgage offer of the required amount being obtained either by the seller for the buyer, or by the buyer for himself. Form 106 [4131] ante should be used if the parties wish to make provision for a mortgage offer of less than the required sum being made and the seller requires the option to make up the shortfall out of his own funds.

2    Any extension of time should be in a form complying with the Law of Property (Miscellaneous Provisions) Act 1989 (37 Halsbury's Statutes (4th Edn) REAL PROPERTY) because it will be a variation of the terms of the agreement. For a form of variation contract see vol 36 (1997 Reissue) SALE OF LAND Form 156 [2141].

**[4139]**

# 108

### Mortgage interest subsidy clause[1]

0.1      For a period of [one year] from completion of this Agreement or until the Buyer legally completes the resale of the Property if that should occur earlier the Seller will pay [monthly] to the Buyer the difference between the actual monthly repayment which the Buyer is making to his mortgagee and the monthly repayment he would have made had the mortgage interest rate been *(insert percentage)*%

0.2      The Buyer shall notify the Seller of any variation in his mortgage interest rate within [7] days of receiving notice of the same himself from his mortgagee

**[4140]**

1    The mortgage interest subsidy scheme is an effective marketing device in times of high interest rates.

The subsidy is usually an amount equal to the difference over a specified period between the mortgage instalments actually payable by the buyer and the instalments which would be payable if the interest rate were lower. Some schemes use the rate of interest on a particular date, others use an artificial figure. The subsidy may be made payable as a lump sum on completion or from time to time.

During a period of frequent changes in interest rates, the seller may wish to withdraw and reintroduce the scheme from time to time, and therefore from the seller's point of view it is probably desirable for his solicitor to record the buyer's cover by way of letter rather than as a term in the contract. From the buyer's point of view a binding contract is preferable, whether it takes the form of a separate contract or is a term of the main contract. The consideration need be only nominal eg 10p. Sellers usually prefer a more informed approach, confirming the scheme.

The difficulties of creating binding arrangements by way of separate letters arising out of the Law of Property (Miscellaneous Provisions) Act 1989 s 2 as amended by the Trusts of Land and Appointment of Trustees Act 1996 s 25(2), Sch 4 (37 Halsbury's Statutes (4th Edn) REAL PROPERTY) are well publicised and it is probably better now to ensure that all terms of the transaction are contained in the contract: see vol 35 (1997 Reissue) SALE OF LAND Paragraph 200 [257].

**[4141]**

# 109

## Redundancy protection scheme clause[1]

Upon the Buyer completing this Agreement he shall be eligible (subject to acceptance by the insurers underwriting the Seller's redundancy protection scheme) to participate in the scheme and the Seller warrants that it will thereupon enter the Buyer in the scheme

1    A redundancy protection scheme offers the buyer the security of knowing that, if he should be made redundant, either his mortgage instalments will be paid for a stated period (usually one or two years) or the property will be bought back from him at a price representing the market value. There are many permutations of this scheme, but the basic protection is an attractive incentive.

It is debatable whether a record of a buyer's participation in the scheme should be by special condition in the contract, confirmatory letter from the seller, or otherwise. Most sellers who offer this scheme do so by insuring the risk of having to make payments under it, and the insurer issues the explanatory paperwork itself. Any condition in the agreement in this case should address itself solely to the participation of the buyer in the scheme otherwise the condition becomes unnecessarily complicated and lengthy.

The difficulties of creating binding arrangements by way of separate letters arising out of the Law of Property (Miscellaneous Provisions) Act 1989 s 2 as amended by the Trusts of Land and Appointment of Trustees Act 1996 s 25(2), Sch 4 (37 Halsbury's Statutes (4th Edn) REAL PROPERTY) are well publicised and it is probably better now to ensure that all terms of the transaction are contained in the contract: see vol 35 (1997 Reissue) SALE OF LAND Paragraph 200 [257].

**[4142]**

# 110

## Put option for the buyer to require the seller to take the buyer's existing house in part payment[1]

In consideration of the Buyer's agreement to purchase the Property the Seller grants to the Buyer an option ('the Option') to require the Seller to take the Buyer's Existing property described in schedule *(insert number of schedule)* below ('the Buyer's Existing Property') by way of part payment for the Property at the agreed value set out below PROVIDED that:

**[4143]**

0.1    the Option may be exercised by notice in writing at any time up to and including the [third] day after the posting of written notification of completion of the Property under condition *(insert condition number)* of this Agreement

0.2    in the event of there being more than one Buyer under this Agreement the Option may only be exercised by the Buyer in whom the Buyer's Existing Property is vested (the 'Owner Buyer') and upon the exercise of the Option the parties shall be bound as if the Agreement had always been one whereby the Seller would take and the Owner Buyer would transfer the Buyer's Existing Property in part payment for the purchase price of the Property and the balance of the Purchase Price would be paid by all Buyers jointly and severally

0.3      for the avoidance of doubt the General Conditions referred to in condition *(insert number of incorporating condition)* shall apply to the sale of the Buyer's Existing Property as well as to the sale of the Property mutatis mutandis

SCHEDULE [*(number)*]

The Buyer's Existing Property

**1      Tenure**

[Freehold *or* leasehold for a term of *(number)* years from *(date)* at a ground rent of £...
per year]

**2      Description**

*(insert description and title number (if any))*

**3      Agreed value**

£...

[4144]

1      The part-exchange scheme is one of the most effective selling aids operated by developers. The scheme enables the buyer to require the seller to take his existing property in part payment for a new property, and make an equality payment of the difference in the value of the two properties. It is an alternative to Form 103 [4121] ante.

     The buyer avoids having to sell his existing property before committing himself to a new property and avoids selling agents' fees, but there is no longer any stamp duty saving. A part exchange is disadvantageous if the agreed sale price is less than might have been achieved on the open market. However, some developers who operate such a scheme do additionally agree to credit the buyer with any profit eventually made on the sale of the original property.

     The buyer cannot enter into a contract for sale of his property to a third party while the option remains in force.

     Where one property is sold and another is given in part payment of the sale price, stamp duty is charged on the total consideration for the sale: Finance Act 1999 s 112(3), Sch 13 (41 Halsbury's Statutes (4th Edn) STAMP DUTIES).

     A transfer of a new house in consideration of the transfer of the buyer's present house, plus payment of equality money (in the agreement for sale (for a form of which see Form 103 [4121] ante) called the 'additional payment'), is stamped as if it were a conveyance on sale for the total value of the buyer's present house plus the additional payment: Finance Act 1994 s 241(1) as amended by the Finance Act 1999 s 112(4), Sch 14 para 30 (42–44 Halsbury's Statutes (4th Edn) TAXATION). The value of the buyer's present house (if this is not stated in the transfer) is taken to be its market value immediately before the transfer to the seller is executed: Finance Act 1994 s 241(1) (as amended), (2). See vol 38(1) (2000 Reissue) SALE OF LAND Paragraph 30 [81] et seq, the Information Binder: Stamp Duties [1] (Guide to Stamp Duties: Paragraph 23 [42]) and see vol 35 (1997 Reissue) SALE OF LAND Paragraph 774.2 [1032]. The transfer of the buyer's present house to the seller in consideration of the transfer of the new house is not a regarded as a separate sale for stamp duty purposes and is liable only to the fixed duty of £5.00: see the Inland Revenue Press Release dated 18 April 1994, which is printed in [1994] LS Gaz 4 May, 32. For a form of contract for exchange of properties see vol 36 (1997 Reissue) SALE OF LAND Form 112 [1876].

     As to the effect of the Law of Property (Miscellaneous Provisions) Act 1989 s 2 as amended by the Trusts of Land and Appointment of Trustees Act 1996 s 25(2), Sch 4 (37 Halsbury's Statutes (4th Edn) REAL PROPERTY) in relation to the grant and the exercise of options see *Spiro v Glencrown Properties Ltd* [1991] Ch 537, [1991] 1 All ER 600 and vol 38(1) (2000 Reissue) SALE OF LAND Form 40 note 6 [1665].

     An option agreement is chargeable to stamp duty on any consideration as a conveyance on sale: *George Wimpey & Co Ltd v IRC* [1975] 2 All ER 45, [1975] 1 WLR 995, CA. See Information Binder: Stamp Duties (Conveyance or transfer).

     This Form is drafted on the assumption that the developer's property being sold to the buyer is more valuable than the buyer's existing property.

     Occasionally the parties may wish to have the option of a part-exchange, but not be bound initially. In such circumstances, they should agree a valuation of the prospective exchange property and enter into a contract comprising the usual provisions and the option conditions, (having due regard for the matters referred to in the first paragraph of this note). There must be an agreed time limit within which the option must be exercised, together with a description and agreed valuation of the buyer's existing property. It is crucial to the effective operation of this scheme that the addition to the standard form of agreement for sale states that, upon exercise of the option, the parties will be bound as if the agreement had always been one whereby the owner buyer's existing property would be taken in part payment of the purchase price. When the option has been exercised, the transaction proceeds in the same way, including stamping, as if such a transaction had been fixed from the beginning.

**[4145]**

# 111

## Power of attorney to enable a developer to transfer the buyer's existing property taken in part payment to a sub-buyer[1]

0.1     The whole money consideration for the Property due to the Seller under this Agreement is to be paid by the Buyer immediately upon exchange of this Agreement (and receipt of that sum is acknowledged)

0.2     The Seller intends to effect a sub-sale of the Buyer's Existing Property and accordingly:
      0.2.1          completion of the transfer of the Buyer's Existing Property to the Seller shall not take place until such time as the Seller may direct when the Buyer's Existing Property will be transferred into the name of such person or persons as the Seller may direct
      0.2.2          the Buyer shall immediately upon the exchange of this Agreement apply or concur in an application for the registration of [a notice in respect of this Agreement against the title of the Buyer to the Buyer's Existing Property pursuant to the Land Registration Act 1925 Section 49 *or* a class C(iv) Land Charge pursuant to the Land Charges Act 1972 Section 2]
      [0.2.3          in the event that the consideration received by the Seller on a sub-sale of the Buyer's Existing Property is greater than the purchase price for the Property under this Agreement the Seller shall pay to the Buyer the difference between such sums after deduction of all costs and expenses incurred by the Seller in respect of such sub-sale][2]

0.3     The Buyer irrevocably appoints the Seller or any person nominated by the Seller the attorney of the Buyer for and in the name and on behalf of the Buyer and as the Buyer's act and deed or otherwise to take all steps necessary to procure that the Buyer's Existing Property be transferred to the Seller or to such person or persons as the Seller may direct [and that the title to the Buyer's Existing Property be registered at HM Land Registry in the name of such transferee]

**[4146]**

1     A clause appointing the buyer as attorney for the seller for the purpose of executing a transfer of the property may be included in the agreement for sale if the buyer intends to resell immediately, so that no transfer to the buyer himself need be taken. These clauses, which are often used where a company purchases a property belonging to its employee to facilitate relocation, are also often used in residential estate conveyancing, particularly in connection with part-exchange schemes. This clause is designed for use in conjunction with Form 110 [4143] ante to effect a transfer of the buyer's existing property by the developer on resale. The seller (developer) saves land registry fees and, to a lesser extent, stamp duty. Where several such transactions are being carried out at once, administrative time is also saved.

Features of the arrangement where, in connection with residential estate development, the developer is taking the buyer's existing property in part exchange are:

(1)  the buyer pays the whole of the balance of the purchase price over and above the value of the buyer's existing property on exchange of contracts;

(2)  the contract contains a power of attorney appointing the developer or his nominee as the attorney of the buyer to transfer the buyer's existing property;

(3)  the title deeds of the buyer's existing property are given to the developer on exchange; and

(4)  because the contract contains a power of attorney under the Powers of Attorney Act 1971 s 1(1) (1 Halsbury's Statutes (4th Edn) AGENCY) the contract requires execution as a deed.

The practitioner will need to consider the effect of the Trustee Delegation Act 1999 where there is more than one joint buyer.

The developer, as the attorney of the buyer, transfers the buyer's existing property to a sub-buyer, and the transfer rather than the contract attracts ad valorem stamp duty. The developer must protect his interest under the contract by registration, either by a notice on the register under the Land Registration Act 1925 s 49 as amended (37 Halsbury's Statutes (4th Edn) REAL PROPERTY) or a class C(iv) land charge under the Land Charges Act 1972 s 2(4)(iv) (37 Halsbury's Statutes (4th Edn) REAL PROPERTY) and a caution against first registration under the Land Registration Act 1925 s 53.

2    This clause should be omitted if the profit is not to be passed on.

[4147]

# 112

## Clause stating that the agreement is conditional on the sale of the buyer's own property

0.1     This Agreement is conditional upon the Buyer entering into a contract for the sale of the Buyer's own [freehold or leasehold] property known as *(specify)* registered at HM Land Registry under Title Number *(number)* ('the Buyer's Property')

0.2     If the Buyer has not by the expiration of [14] days from the date of this Agreement or such later date as shall be agreed by the Seller in writing[1] exchanged an unconditional contract for the sale of the Buyer's Property to a third party [at a sale price of not less than £...] or if the Seller shall at any time within such period reasonably form the view (from information provided to it by the Buyer and the Buyer's [Solicitors or agents]) that the condition in clause [0.1] is unlikely to be satisfied within such period then either party may at any time thereafter prior to the exchange of contracts for the sale of the Buyer's Property by written notice to the other or their solicitors rescind this Agreement whereupon the Seller shall be entitled to retain for its own benefit the reservation deposit paid to the Seller by the Buyer and following such rescission all the provisions of this Agreement shall become null and void and any further deposit paid under this Agreement (other than the reservation deposit) shall be reimbursed to the Buyer

0.3     In the event that the Buyer exchanges contracts for the sale of the Buyer's Property prior to the rescission of this Agreement this Agreement shall become unconditional

[4148]

0.4     The Buyer agrees that he will:

0.4.1     instruct [*(name of estate agents)* or estate agents approved by the Seller in writing such approval not to be unreasonably withheld] ('the Agents') to advertise and market the Buyer's Property for sale and instruct them to erect and maintain upon the Buyer's Property a signboard or poster advertising the Buyer's Property for sale and

0.4.2    use his [best *or* reasonable] endeavours to procure a sale of the Buyer's Property at or above the above-mentioned sale price as soon as reasonably practicable and

0.4.3    permit prospective buyers their surveyors and valuers and the surveyors and valuers acting for the prospective buyer's intended mortgagees to inspect the Buyer's Property at all reasonable times and

0.4.4    do all acts and things reasonably necessary to enable a prospective purchaser to purchase the Buyer's Property

0.5    The Buyer will forthwith authorise the Agents and the Buyer's Solicitors to provide to the Seller such information as the Seller may from time to time request regarding the sale of the Buyer's Property in order to enable the Seller to monitor the progress with regard to it and undertakes immediately to notify the Seller's Solicitors of exchange of contracts for the sale of the Buyer's Property

---

1    Any extension of time should be in a form complying with the Law of Property (Miscellaneous Provisions) Act 1994 (37 Halsbury's Statutes (4th Edn) REAL PROPERTY) because it will be a variation of the terms of the agreement. For a form of variation contract see vol 36 (1997 Reissue) SALE OF LAND Form 156 [2141].

**[4149]**

# (4): BUILDING LICENCES

# 113

### Building licence granted by a local authority[1]

THIS AGREEMENT is made the ...... day of .........

BETWEEN:

(1)    *(name of local authority granting the licence)* of *(address)* ('the Council') and
(2)    *(name of developer)* [company number *(number)*] [of *(address)* or whose registered office is at *(address)*] ('the Developer')

**[4150]**

NOW IT IS AGREED as follows:

## 1    Definitions and interpretation

In this Agreement:

1.1    'the Accounting Day' means the *(date)* [and *(date)*] in each year and the [28th] day following the sale of the last Dwelling forming part of the Development

1.2    'the Additional Payment' means a payment calculated in accordance with clause 4 due from the Developer to the Council

1.3    'the Approved Plans' means the layout plans elevations sections landscaping schemes and other drawings and specifications describing the Developer's proposals for the development of the Site approved in writing by the Council [listed in schedule 4] together with any variation of them which may be agreed in writing by the Council

1.4    'the Completion Date' means *(date)* or such other date as the Council shall agree to in writing for the completion of the Development by the Developer under the provisions of this Agreement

1.5    the 'Council's Surveyor' means *(name of officer)* of the Council for the time being or such other officer of the Council as the Council may appoint from time to time

1.6    'the Development' means the works described in the Approved Plans including any preparation of the Site by the demolition of any existing buildings and other such preparatory works

1.7    'the Development Programme' means the timetable (if any) for the completion of the various stages of the Development and in particular any roads footpaths and cycleways which may be needed to serve other developments adjoining or neighbouring the Site [approved of or specified in writing by the Council *or* set out in schedule 5] with such variations as may be approved in writing by the Council

1.8    'Dwelling' means a dwelling of any type including a flat or maisonette and shall include any garage outbuildings car parking area and garden land and any other land or structure appurtenant to it

1.9    'the Index' means *(specify index to be used)*

1.10   'the Site' means *(describe the land)*

1.11   'the Site Highways' means the roads footways footpaths and cycleways with the verges street-lighting landscaped areas and other things appurtenant which it is intended shall become highways maintainable at the public expense and which form part of the Development

1.12   words importing one gender shall be construed as importing any other gender

1.13   words importing persons shall be construed as importing a corporate body and/or a partnership and vice versa

1.14   words importing persons shall be construed as importing a corporate body and/or a partnership and vice versa

1.15   where any party comprises more than one person the obligations and liabilities of that party under this Agreement shall be joint and several obligations and liabilities of those persons

1.16   the clause headings do not form part of this Agreement and shall not be taken into account in its construction or interpretation

**[4151]**

## 2    Powers and authority

This Agreement is entered into by the Council pursuant to [the Local Authorities (Land) Act 1963 Section 2 *or* the Town and Country Planning Act 1990 Section 235] the Local Government Act 1972 Section 111 and all other enabling powers and the resolution of its *(name)* Committee dated *(date)* (minute No *(number)*)

## 3    Conditional agreement

3.1    This Agreement is conditional upon the Developer:

3.1.1    obtaining planning permission for the Development and approval under the Building Regulations[2] in respect of the Development in accordance with the Approved Plans with if need be such reasonable modifications of the Approved Plans as the planning or local authority may require and the Council approve in writing

3.1.2    entering into an agreement with the highway authority pursuant to the Highways Act 1980 Section 38[3] in respect of the construction and adoption of the Site Highways and other agreements with the sewerage undertaker for the adoption of all main foul and surface water sewers and with the Council for the adoption of the landscaped areas (not part of the Site Highways) children's play areas and recreation areas forming part of the Development

3.1.3    negotiating and obtaining on reasonable terms and at its own expense the supply of water gas electricity and other necessary services to the Site sufficient to serve the Development

3.2    The Developer shall use its [best *or* reasonable] endeavours[4] to obtain the satisfaction and fulfilment of the conditions referred to in clause 3.1 and shall provide any bonds and pay any capital sums as are in all the circumstances reasonable and obtain any necessary consents of third parties within the period of [3] months from the date of this Agreement (or such extended period as the Council may agree to in writing) but in the event of the conditions not being satisfied and fulfilled within that period or extended period this Agreement may be rescinded by either party giving notice to the other in writing to that effect

3.3    In the event of this Agreement being rescinded pursuant to the provisions of clause 3.2 neither party shall have any claim against the other and the licence fee paid by the Developer under the provisions of this Agreement to the Council shall be refunded [without interest *or* together with interest at the rate of *(insert rate)*]

[4152]

## 4    Financial arrangements

The Council and the Developer agree the following financial arrangements:

4.1    The deposit to be paid by the Developer to the Council shall be £... to be set off against the final payments due to the Council from the Developer under the provisions of this Agreement

4.2    Within [14 days] of the completion of the sale of a Dwelling forming part of the Development the Developer shall pay to the Council a proportion of the sale price of that Dwelling calculated in accordance with schedule 1

4.3    The numbers of the plots on which each type of Dwelling is to be erected in accordance with the Approved Plans are set out in schedule 2

4.4    On each Accounting Day the Developer shall supply to the Council a list of the Dwellings and their type sold by it since the commencement of this Agreement or the last Accounting Day (as the case may be) together with the actual sale price for each Dwelling and where the sale price of any Dwelling exceeds the basic price as set out in column 2 of schedule 1 the Developer shall within [14 days] of the receipt of a demand from the Council pay a further sum in respect of that Dwelling calculated as set out in clause 4.5 below

4.5    The Additional Payment shall be [60%] of the increase of the sale price over the basic price after taking into consideration the increase in house building costs since *(specify base date)* such increase in building costs to be calculated on the difference between the basic price and the share of it due to the Council as set out in schedule 1 by reference to the Index and the point on the Index relative to the calculation of the basic price shall be taken as *(specify)* and all movements of the Index above this value shall be taken into account in calculating any additional payment due to the Council under this clause

4.6    For additional guidance only a formula for calculating the increased share of the sale price due to the Council under the provisions of clause 4.4 is set out in schedule 3

4.7    On each Accounting Day the figure of the Index to be taken into consideration shall be the latest then available (published or not) but on no account is such latest figure to be more than 6 months prior to the Accounting Day

4.8      In the event of the latest Index figure available on an Accounting Day being calculated for a period ending more than 6 months prior to that Accounting Day the payment due to the Council under clauses 4.4 and 4.5 shall be postponed until a date [14 days] after more up-to-date figures become available or where the delay before such figures become available appears in the opinion of the Council likely to be extensive the sum due to the Council shall be determined by agreement between the parties or failing agreement as set out below

4.9      It is agreed that:

4.9.1      in the event of any change in the base date in the base used to compile the Index the figure taken to be shown in the Index after such change shall be the figure which would have been shown in the Index if the reference base at present in use had been retained

4.9.2      in the event of it becoming impossible by reason of any change in the methods used to compile the Index or for any other reason to calculate by reference to it or if any dispute or question shall arise between the parties with respect to the amount of increase the amount of increase shall be determined as provided in clause 9.13 of this Agreement and the expert shall have full power to determine what would have been the increase in the Index had it continued on the present basis

4.9.3      the minimum sum to be received by the Council on the sale of each Dwelling is set out in column 3 of schedule 1 for the relevant Dwelling type as a proportion of the basic price for that type and the minimum sum in total to be received by the Council under this Agreement shall be £...

[4153]

## 5     Licence

Subject to the provisions of clause 3 of this Agreement the Council grants to the Developer immediate licence and authority for the purpose of the carrying out of this Agreement but for no other purpose whatsoever:

5.1      **Entry onto Site:** to enter upon the Site with all necessary plant machinery equipment and materials for carrying out the development of the Site in accordance with the Approved Plans

5.2      **Right of passage:** to pass and repass with or without vehicles (in common with all other persons having the like right) at all times and for all purposes in connection with the Development over and along the private roads serving the Site

5.3      **Connections to services:** to make (in so far as the Council can give such authority) such connections as may be necessary with the sewers drains pipes wires and cables now laid or during the period of [5] years from the date of this Agreement to be laid in the roads adjoining or neighbouring the Site so as to enable the Dwellings and Site Highways to be erected upon the Site to be served but for no other purpose

5.4      **Adjoining land:** to enter upon the Council's land adjoining the Site so far only as may be necessary to enable the Developer to construct in accordance with the Approved Plans any road footway footpath or cycleway necessary to connect the Site Highways to [the roads footways footpaths and cycleways provided by the Council as part of its development of *(specify)* of which the Site is part or *(as the case may be)*]

[4154]

**6     Obligations of the Developer**

The Developer undertakes and agrees with the Council:

6.1     **Entry:** to enter upon the Site as licensee only for the purpose of carrying out the Development and the Developer acknowledges that as between itself and the Council the Council is entitled to possession of the Site subject to the rights of the Developer under this Agreement

6.2     **Further agreements:** as soon as possible after entering upon the Site to produce to the Council the agreements referred to in clause 3.1.2 for inspection together with copies for retention by the Council

6.3     **Method of working:** to carry out the Development at its exclusive expense and in accordance with the Approved Plans in a good and workmanlike manner to the reasonable satisfaction of the Council diligently continuously and with all practicable speed (and in any event in accordance with the Development Programme) so that the Development shall be completed by the Completion Date

6.4     **Materials:** in carrying out the Development to use sound materials and to take down and remove any work or materials which shall not be in accordance with statute or building regulations or the Approved Plans or which shall not otherwise have been carried out in accordance with this Agreement within [14] days of service by the Council of notice to do so

6.5     **Outgoings:** from the date of entry upon the Site and during the continuance of this Agreement to pay all rates taxes claims assessments and other outgoings (if any) now or after the date of this Agreement chargeable against an owner or occupier of the Site or any part or parts of it remaining unsold during the period of this Agreement

6.6     **No assignment:** not to assign or part with its licence or interest under this Agreement or any part of it [except to a [bank] as security for a loan to enable the Development to be carried out][5]

**[4155]**

6.7     **Avoidance of damage:** during the development of the Site to take all reasonable care to avoid damage to adjoining or neighbouring roads and footpaths including their verges and any landscaped areas associated with them and not to bring upon or allow any person to bring upon those roads and footpaths any carts or vehicles without having previously removed from the wheels any mud clay or other material adhering to them and likely to cause a nuisance or damage to other persons using the roads and footpaths and on demand to repay to the Council the reasonable cost incurred by it (as certified by the Council's Surveyor) in making good any damage to or cleansing of the roads and footpaths caused or made necessary by any failure on the part of the Developer to obey the requirements of this Agreement

6.8     **Protection of trees etc:** not to cut down any trees or hedgerows at present growing upon the Site without the written consent of the Council and to take all reasonable steps to preserve such trees and hedgerows during the Development

6.9     **Avoidance of nuisance etc:** not knowingly to do or permit or suffer to be done upon the Site or any part of it during the Development anything which may be or become a nuisance or annoyance or cause damage to the Council or the tenants or occupiers of neighbouring premises except so far as may be reasonable and necessary in the development of the Site as envisaged by this Agreement

6.10     **Safeguards for the environment:** not to permit any deleterious objectionable dangerous poisonous or explosive matter or substance or controlled waste to be discharged into the atmosphere ditches watercourses culverts drains or sewers on or near the Site and to take all reasonable measures for ensuring that any emissions or effluent so discharged shall not be corrosive or otherwise harmful to the atmosphere ditches watercourses culverts drains or sewers or cause obstruction or deposit in them

6.11 **No excavations:** not to excavate for sale or dispose of any minerals earth clay gravel chalk or sand from the Site or permit or suffer any of those materials to be removed except so far as is approved by the Council's Surveyor or necessary for the Development

**[4156]**

6.12 **User:** not to use or permit or suffer to be used the Site or any part of it for any purposes other than that of performing this Agreement without the previous written consent of the Council

6.13 **Protection of highways etc:** to keep the Site Highways main sewers play recreation and landscaped areas forming part of the Development in good repair and in a clean and tidy condition to the reasonable satisfaction of the Council's Surveyor until the same shall be adopted by the appropriate authority undertaker or other body or some other arrangement is made to the reasonable satisfaction of the Council for the future repair maintenance and use of them until adoption

6.14 **Staff:** to observe and be responsible for ensuring that its employees and sub-contractors and suppliers observe the reasonable directions from time to time given by the Council's Surveyor for gaining access to the Site

6.15 **Advertising etc:** not to erect or build or permit to be erected or built on the Site any temporary structures or advertising signs save such as may be authorised in writing by the Council's Surveyor

6.16 **Tidiness:** until the completion of the Development to keep and maintain the Site (or the parts of it for the time being remaining unsold) in a neat and tidy condition and to prevent so far as may be reasonably practicable any matters or things which may be unnecessarily unsightly or offensive visually or otherwise and to maintain all completed but unsold Dwellings in repair and good marketable condition

6.17 **Street naming:** not to name any of the Site Highways or give any name to the Development as a whole or any part of it without the prior written approval of the Council to the name or names

6.18 **Storage of materials:** not to deposit on the Site or make up or manufacture on it any building or other materials or goods except those required for the Development and as soon as the Development is completed to remove immediately from the Site all surplus building and other materials and rubbish

6.19 **Compliance with statutes etc:** in carrying out the Development to do all acts and things required by and to perform the building work in conformity in all respects with the provisions of all statutes applicable and any orders or regulations made under them and the byelaws or regulations of any statutory undertakers public utilities and other such bodies including in particular planning permission and to pay all proper fees charges fines penalties and other payments whatsoever which during the progress of the Development may become payable or be demanded by such undertakers utilities or other such bodies in respect of the Development or anything done under the licence and authority granted by this Agreement

**[4157]**

6.20 **Indemnity—materials etc:** to indemnify and keep indemnified the Council from and against all claims demands and liabilities however arising in respect of the materials and workmanship used by the Developer in the Development or any part of it

6.21    **Indemnity—works etc:**  to indemnify the Council (notwithstanding any
        supervision or approval of the Council or any person acting on behalf of the
        Council) against any liability loss claim or proceeding in respect of any injury
        or damage whatsoever to any person or to any property real or personal in so
        far as such injury or damage arises out of or in the course of or by reason of the
        negligent execution of the Development and to insure against any such liability
        in an insurance office approved by the Council (such approval not to be
        unreasonably withheld) and in a sum to be approved by the Council and to pay
        all premiums in respect of such insurance

6.22    **Insurances:**  at all times during the Development to insure the Development
        or such parts of it as have not been sold in a sum sufficient to cover the cost of
        reinstating the same completely in the event of total destruction together with
        professional fees and other expenses incidental to the reinstatement against loss
        or damage by fire and any other risk usually insured against in respect of a
        development of this nature and to pay all premiums and other monies necessary
        for this purpose and to produce to the Council's Surveyor on demand the
        policies of insurance maintained under the provisions contained in this
        Agreement and all receipts as evidence of payment of the current premiums and
        if so requested to have recorded on the policy or policies the Council's interest
        in it or them as the owner of the Site

6.23    **Registrations with NHBC:**  that it is registered with the National House
        Building Council ('the NHBC') and that every Dwelling built by it on the site
        will also be so registered and built in accordance with the requirements as to
        standards of workmanship and materials of the NHBC and that it will offer to
        every buyer of a Dwelling erected pursuant to this Agreement the benefit of the
        NHBC 'Buildmark' combined warranty and protection scheme or any similar
        agreement or scheme which may from time to time be prescribed by the
        NHBC[6]

                                                                                            **[4158]**

**7        Obligations of the Council**

The Council undertakes and agrees with the Developer:

7.1     **Execution of documents etc:**  to join in a [transfer *or* [shared ownership]
        lease] (which shall so far as practicable be in [a standard form *or* the form
        attached as appendix 1]) to a nominee of the Developer previously approved of
        by the Council of the [freehold *or* leasehold] interest in any Dwelling
        constructed by the Developer on the Site the [transfer *or* [shared ownership]
        lease] including the plan incorporated by it to be in a form previously agreed
        by the Council and to contain the grants reservations restrictions and
        stipulations reasonably specified by the Council for the proper enjoyment of
        that Dwelling and the protection and the enjoyment of the Council's other land
        both within the Site and adjoining and neighbouring it

7.2     **Sales:**  that the Council will consent to sales of Dwellings on the Site to
        nominees of the Developer who intend to use the Dwellings as their principal
        place of residence *(insert any conditions eg as to occupancy and local connection)*[7]

7.3     **Deduction of title:**  to supply the Developer with evidence of its title to the
        land sufficient to enable the Developer to deduce title to the buyers of the
        Dwellings constructed by the Developer on the Site and such information as the
        Developer may need to reply to the usual enquiries raised on behalf of buyers
        of Dwellings

7.4     **Further agreements:**  that it will if required by the appropriate authority or
        undertaker enter into any of the agreements referred to in clause 3.1.2 in its

capacity as estate owner for the purpose of dedicating or agreeing to dedicate any road as a highway and for the adoption of sewers that the relevant authority or undertaker may reasonably require PROVIDED that the Developer shall indemnify the Council from and against all proceedings costs charges claims and demands whatsoever arising by reason of the Council having entered into any covenant with the relevant authority or undertaker

**[4159]**

8 **Further obligations of the Developer**

The Developer further undertakes and agrees with the Council:

8.1 **Execution of documents:** to comply with any reasonable procedures the Council may from time to time specify relating to the sealing of the [transfers *or* [shared ownership] leases] to the buyers of the Dwellings constructed on the Site and completion of the sales

8.2 **Licence fee:** to pay to the Council on the signing of this Agreement by way of licence fee the sum specified as a deposit in clause 4 on account of the money due to the Council under the provisions of this Agreement

8.3 **Payment of sale proceeds:** following completion of every sale of a Dwelling constructed on the Site in accordance with the provisions of this Agreement (which completions it will handle as agent for the Council) to forward to the Council the proper proportion of the proceeds of sale due to the Council as landowner calculated in accordance with the provisions of clause 4 and in the manner specified in this Agreement

8.4 **Information:** to supply such details and produce such documents as the Council may reasonably request to verify the selling prices of the Dwellings

8.5 **No disposal:** not to dispose of or attempt to dispose of any part of the Site other than in accordance with the provisions of this Agreement

**[4160]**

9 **Agreement and declaration**

It is agreed and declared that:

9.1 **Sale negotiations:** the Developer shall be solely responsible at its own expense for negotiating the sale of the Dwellings to be built by it on the Site

9.2 **Inspections:** the Council its Surveyor and other authorised persons may enter upon the Site to view the state and progress of the Development and to inspect and test the materials and workmanship and for any other reasonable purpose including the exercise of the rights given to the Council by this Agreement upon default of the Developer and may enter upon the Site (other than any Dwelling the sale of which has been legally completed) and any building for the time being unsold for the purpose of protecting repairing and maintaining the same and for the removal of any works which are in contravention of this Agreement and the cost of any works carried out by the Council under this clause shall be recoverable from the Developer

9.3 **Default and termination:** if the Developer:

9.3.1 fails to commence or proceed with the Development with proper diligence

9.3.2 fails to complete the Development and any Dwellings being part of it fit for immediate use and occupation by the Completion Date

9.3.3 fails to observe and perform in material respects the other stipulations and conditions on its part contained in this Agreement

9.3.4    fails to remedy the breach of any of the stipulations and conditions on its part contained in this Agreement within [2 months] after receipt of written notice requiring it to remedy the breach or within such reasonable time in excess of [2 months] as may be specified by the Council's Surveyor

9.3.5    enters into liquidation whether compulsory or voluntary (except for the purpose of reconstruction amalgamation or other similar purpose not involving a realisation of assets) or

9.3.6    suffer its goods to be taken in execution

the Council may terminate this Agreement and eject the Developer from the Site (save for those Dwellings in respect of which there exists a binding contract for sale within the provisions of this Agreement) and the Development works and erections and fixtures (except the Developer's plant and equipment) on the Site with power to hold and dispose of them but if this Agreement is terminated under this provision the Council shall pay to the Developer the value to the Council of any works executed by the Developer on that part of the Site then unsold and not contracted for sale in so far as they add to the value of the Site after the deduction of any money then due from the Developer to the Council and the value to the Council of those works shall be the amount they add to the value of the Site or the part of it then under consideration after also taking into consideration any element of depreciation in the value of the Site caused by such works or any part of them

**[4161]**

9.4    **Consequences of termination:**   in the event of termination of this Agreement before completion of the Development the Developer shall assign or cause to be assigned to the Council the copyright in the Approved Plans or other plans forming part of this Agreement and the design of the Development in so far as may be necessary to enable the Development to be completed

9.5    **Survival of Agreement:**  notwithstanding the completion of any transfer of a Dwelling this Agreement shall remain in full force and effect in regard to anything remaining to be done performed or observed on the part of the Developer

9.6    **Antiquities:**  any relic article or thing whatsoever of antiquity rarity or value which may be found or discovered by the Developer in or upon the Site or any buildings on it shall belong to the Council and be delivered up by the Developer to the Council and immediately any such relic article or thing is found or discovered the Developer shall give notice to the Council and afford all reasonable facilities to the Council to remove the same and the Council shall grant to the Developer such an extension of the time for the completion of the Development as is reasonable following the Developer's compliance with these provisions

9.7    **No liability for plans:**  the Council shall not be under any liability whatsoever in respect of any defect in the design of the Development by reason of having approved the Approved Plans or otherwise

9.8    **Disclaimer for information:**  any information given to the Developer by the Council in this Agreement or otherwise as to the position of sewers wires cables pipes or other conduits within or over the Site or any information given as to levels or soil conditions is to the best of the Council's knowledge correct but is given on the understanding that the Council and its servants and agents shall not be liable for any inaccuracies and the Developer is expected to carry out its own surveys and site investigations

**[4162]**

9.9    **Notices:** any notice under the terms of this Agreement or by statute required to be served by the parties to this Agreement shall be sufficiently served by the Council by being left or sent by post to the Developer at its [registered office *or (as appropriate)*] for the time being and by the Developer by being left or sent by post to the Council's Chief Executive at its principal office

9.10   **No fetters:** nothing contained or implied in this Agreement shall prejudice or affect the rights powers duties and obligations of the Council in the exercise of its functions as a local authority and the rights powers duties and obligations of the Council under all statutes byelaws orders and regulations may be as fully and effectually exercised in relation to the Site and the Development as if the Council were not the owner of the Site and this Agreement had not been executed by it

9.11   **Delay and extension of time:** if the Developer is delayed in completing or proceeding with the Development solely by reason of any outbreak of war or civil insurrection or by fire tempest frost or other severe weather or by other unavoidable cause or accident or by any strike or lock-out in the building trade or any kindred trade or by unreasonable delay of the Council in complying with its obligations under this Agreement or by any other authority or body needing to give approval to the proposed development or provide essential services or by reason of an extension variation or alteration made to the Development (which has been approved by the Council) the Council shall allow such further time for the completion of the Development as is in all the circumstances reasonable and shall notify the Developer in writing of the extended time

9.12   **Arbitration:** in the event of any dispute or difference arising between the parties as to the construction of this Agreement or as to the rights duties or obligations of the parties or as to any other matter in any way arising out of or in connection with the subject matter of this Agreement (except for the matters covered by clause 9.13) the dispute shall be referred to the arbitration or decision of an independent arbitrator to be appointed by the President for the time being of the Law Society (this Agreement being deemed to be a submission to arbitration within the meaning of the Arbitration Act 1996 or any statutory modification or re-enactment of it for the time being in force) and it is agreed and declared that the decision of the arbitrator shall be final and binding

9.13   **Dispute resolution:** in so far as the provisions of this Agreement require any calculation or valuation to be made and agreed by the parties the calculation or valuation shall failing agreement be referred to an expert to be agreed upon by the parties or failing agreement appointed as provided in clause 9.12 and his determination shall be conclusive and binding

9.14   **Costs of awards:** any costs payable by reason of the provisions of clauses 9.12 and 9.13 shall be borne initially in equal proportions by the parties and then as may be adjusted by the award pursuant to its provisions

**[4163]**

IN WITNESS etc

SCHEDULE 1

| **Dwelling type** | **Agreed basic sale price** | **Share of sale price due to the Council** |
|---|---|---|
| *(specify)* | *(specify)* | *(specify)* |

## SCHEDULE 2

**Dwelling type**
*(specify)*

**Plots on which each dwelling type is to be constructed**
*(specify)*

## SCHEDULE 3
Formula for calculating increased share of sale price

The formula referred to in clause 4.6 above is:

$$A - \frac{(B \times I)}{100} \times 60\,\%$$

Where:
A = the difference between the actual sale price and the agreed basic price for the Dwelling as set out in schedule 1
B = the agreed basic price less the share due to the Council as set out in schedule 1 and
I = the difference between the Index applicable on the relevant Accounting Day and the base index relevant at the time of the calculation of the basic prices set out in this Agreement

## SCHEDULE 4
Approved Plans

## SCHEDULE 5
Development Programme

*(signatures (or common seals) of the parties)*
[*(signatures of witnesses)*]
**[4164]**

1   No stamp duty. See Information Binder: Stamp Duties [1] (Licence). This Form is based on a form previously supplied by Neville Smallman Esq, formerly Chief Legal Officer, Peterborough Development Corporation.
    As to building licences generally see Form 93 appendix 3 [3979] ante.
2   Ie the Building Regulations 1991, SI 1991/2768 as amended.
3   Ie the Highways Act 1980 s 38 as amended by the New Roads and Street Works Act 1991 s 22(1) and by the Local Government Act 1985 s 102, Sch 17 (20 Halsbury's Statutes (4th Edn) HIGHWAYS, STREETS AND BRIDGES). As to agreements for the adoption of roads and sewers generally see Form 93 appendix 1 [3971] ante.
4   As to the distinction between 'all reasonable', 'reasonable' and 'best' endeavours, see *UBH (Mechanical Services) Ltd v Standard Life Assurance Co* (1986) Times, 13 November. The use of expressions such as 'best endeavours' or 'all reasonable endeavours' can give rise to problems. The former expression has (in the context of trying to obtain the landlord's consent to assign a lease) been held to mean 'something less than efforts which go beyond the bounds of reason but are considerably more than casual and intermittent activities': see *Pips (Leisure Productions) Ltd v Walton* (1982) 43 P & CR 415 at 420, per Megarry V-C. This would seem to entail the developer doing what a reasonable person would do in the circumstances. 'All reasonable endeavours' is probably seen generally as a lesser obligation than 'best endeavours', but in the light of the above definition it is not clear how much less. It may be preferable for the developer to omit both expressions, though the council may wish to see some definition of the degree of obligation on the developer.
5   It is possible that this clause will prevent the developer's interest being charged as security to a bank if the words in square brackets are not included.
6   As to the National House Building Council insurance scheme and alternative clauses generally see Form 93 appendix 2 [3974] ante.
7   For a clause more restrictive of the persons to whom the developer may sell which could be adapted see Form 84 clause 10 [3758] ante.

**[4165]–[4180]**

# (5): TRANSFERS

## 114

### Transfer of part of registered title(s)—Land Registry Form TP1[1]

**Transfer of part
of registered title(s)**

**HM Land Registry**

*(if you need more room than is provided for in a panel, use continuation sheet CS and staple to this form)*

---

**1. Stamp Duty**

*Place "X" in the box that applies and complete the box in the appropriate certificate.*

☐ It is certified that this instrument falls within category ☐ in the Schedule to the Stamp Duty (Exempt Instruments) Regulations 1987

☐ It is certified that the transaction effected does not form part of a larger transaction or of a series of transactions in respect of which the amount or value or the aggregate amount or value of the consideration exceeds the sum of

£

---

**2.** Title number(s) out of which the Property is transferred *(leave blank if not yet registered)*

---

**3.** Other title number(s) against which matters contained in this transfer are to be registered *(if any)*

---

**4.** Property **transferred** *(Insert address, including postcode, or other description of the property transferred. Any physical exclusions, e.g. mines and minerals, should be defined. Any attached plan must be signed by the transferor and by or on behalf of the transferee.)*

The Property is defined: *(place "X" in the box that applies and complete the statement)*

☐ on the attached plan and shown *(state reference e.g. "edged red")*

☐ on the Transferor's filed plan and shown *(state reference e.g. "edged and numbered 1 in blue")*

---

**5.** Date

---

**6.** Transferor *(give full names and Company's Registered Number if any)*

---

**7.** Transferee **for entry on the register** *(Give full names and Company's Registered Number if any; for Scottish Co. Reg. Nos., use an SC prefix. For foreign companies give territory in which incorporated.)*

*Unless otherwise arranged with Land Registry headquarters, a certified copy of the transferee's constitution (in English or Welsh) will be required if it is a body corporate but is not a company registered in England and Wales or Scotland under the Companies Acts.*

---

**8.** Transferee's intended **address(es) for service in the U.K.** *(including postcode)* **for entry on the register**

---

**9. The Transferor transfers the Property to the Transferee.**

---

**10.** Consideration *(Place "X" in the box that applies. State clearly the currency unit if other than sterling. If none of the boxes applies, insert an appropriate memorandum in the additional provisions panel.)*

☐  The Transferor has received from the Transferee for the Property the sum of *(in words and figures)*

☐  *(insert other receipt as appropriate)*

☐  The transfer is not for money or anything which has a monetary value

---

**11.** The Transferor transfers with *(place "X" in the box which applies and add any modifications)*

☐  full title guarantee          ☐  limited title guarantee

---

**12.** Declaration of trust *Where there is more than one transferee, place "X" in the appropriate box.*

☐  The Transferees are to hold the Property on trust for themselves as joint tenants.

☐  The Transferees are to hold the Property on trust for themselves as tenants in common in equal shares.

☐  The Transferees are to hold the Property *(complete as necessary)*

---

**13.** Additional Provisions
  *1. Use this panel for:*
  - *definitions of terms not defined above*
  - *rights granted or reserved*
  - *restrictive covenants*
  - *other covenants*
  - *agreements and declarations*
  - *other agreed provisions*
  - *required or permitted statements, certificates or applications.*
  *2. The prescribed subheadings may be added to, amended, repositioned or omitted.*

Definitions




Rights granted for the benefit of the Property

Rights reserved for the benefit of other land *(the land having the benefit should be defined, if necessary by reference to a plan)*

Restrictive covenants by the Transferee *(include words of covenant)*

Restrictive covenants by the Transferor *(include words of covenant)*

14. *The Transferors and all other necessary parties (including the proprietors of all the titles listed in panel 3) should execute this transfer as a deed using the space below and sign the plan. Forms of execution are given in Schedule 3 to the Land Registration Rules 1925. If the transfer contains transferees' covenants or declarations or contains an application by them (e.g. for a restriction), it must also be executed by the Transferees.*

1    Form TP1 is the transfer of part of the land in a registered title prescribed by the Land Registration Rules
     1925, SR&O 1925/1093 r 98, Sch 1 as inserted by SI 1999/128 and is Crown Copyright. This Form
     should be used whenever part only of any registered title is transferred, even if the transfer also includes
     the whole of one or more other registered titles. This Form must be prepared in accordance with the
     requirements of SR&O 1925/1093 rr 308, 308A as respectively substituted and inserted by SI 1997/
     3037 and amended by SI 1999/128 and by SI 1999/2097, as to which see Form 115 note 1 [4195] post.
     Reference should be made to Form 115 [4191] post for:
     (a)    detailed footnotes on matters common to many forms of transfer;
     (b)    cross references to the commentary in vol 35 (1997 Reissue) SALE OF LAND and for the location
            of alternative transfer clauses in this and other volumes.
     Panel 3:  Particulars should be inserted of any other title numbers of land affected by matters contained
     in the transfer; eg land over which rights are to be granted.
     Panel 4:  The second box and wording in panel 4 may be completed where the land to be transferred is
     sufficiently defined by a reference on the transferor's title plan but the Form assumes (as will normally be
     the case) that one or more plans will be annexed to the transfer to show not only the land transferred but
     also the extent of the retained land, as defined, and the land affected by any easements such as rights of way.

**[4185]–[4190]**

# 115

**Transfer of part of registered freehold land granting and reserving easements imposing new positive and restrictive covenants and declarations: transferor's retained land registered under the same or another title, or unregistered**[1]

*Use Land Registry Form TP1 (for which see Form 114 [4181] ante) and insert, in the panels specified below, the wording shown:*

### Panel 3   Title number[2]

*(insert number)*

### Panel 6   Transferor[3]

*(insert full names and company number (if any))*

### Panel 8   Transferee's address for service[4]

*(insert full postal address including postcode for entry on the register)*

### Panel 10   Consideration[5]

*(place 'X' in the box which applies. State clearly the currency unit if other than sterling. If none of the boxes applies insert an appropriate memorandum in the additional provisions panel)*

### Panel 11   Title Guarantee[6]

*(place 'X' in the box which applies and add any modifications)*

### Panel 12   Declaration of Trust[7]

*(where there is more than one transferee, place 'X' in the appropriate box)*

**[4191]**

### Panel 13 Additional Provisions
### 1       Definitions and interpretation[8]

In this transfer:
[1.1    'the Perpetuity Period' means the period of [21] [80] years commencing on the
        date of this transfer]

1.2     'the Plan' means the plan annexed to this transfer[9] [and if numbered plans are annexed any reference to a numbered plan is to the annexed plan so numbered]

1.3     'the Retained Land' means the land [and buildings] *(add description)* [outlined in green *or (as the case may be)* [on Plan *(number)*]] retained by the Transferor [being that part of the land comprised in title number *(number)* as is not comprised in the Property *or* the land comprised in title number *(number) or* the land comprised in a conveyance dated *(date)* made between *(parties)*]

[1.4    'Services' means water soil effluent [including without limitation farm effluent] gas fuel oil electricity telephone [telephonic signals television visual audio fax electronic mail data information communications] and other services]

[1.5    'Service Apparatus' means sewers drains channels pipes watercourses gutters wires cables ducts flues conduits laser optic fibres electronic data or impulse communication transmission or reception systems and other conducting media [septic tanks holding tanks and sewage treatment works] and associated equipment]

[1.6    words importing one gender shall be construed as importing any other gender]

[1.7    words importing the singular shall be construed as importing the plural and vice versa]

[1.8    words importing persons shall be construed as importing a corporate body and/or a partnership and vice versa][10]

[1.9    where any party comprises more than one person the obligations and liabilities of that party under this transfer shall be joint and several obligations and liabilities of those persons][11]

[1.10   the panel and clause headings do not form part of this transfer and shall not be taken into account in its construction or interpretation]

[1.11   any reference to a clause is to one so numbered in this panel unless otherwise stated]

[1.12   any reference to a colour or letter is to one on the Plan]

                                                                                      **[4192]**

## 2      Rights granted for the benefit of the Property[12]

2.1     The Property is transferred together with the following rights [but subject to the observance and performance of the [covenants *or* conditions] contained in clause 2.2]: *(insert details of rights to be granted)*

[2.2    *(insert details of covenants or conditions)*]

## 3      Rights reserved for the benefit of other land[13]

3.1     There are reserved out of the Property for the benefit of each and every part of the Retained Land the following rights [but subject to the observance and performance of the [covenants *or* conditions] contained in clause 3.2]: *(insert details of rights to be reserved)*

[3.2    *(insert details of covenants or conditions)*]

## 4      Restrictive covenants by the Transferee[14]

4.1     The Transferee covenants with the Transferor to observe and perform the Restrictions specified below and it is agreed and declared that:

        4.1.1    the benefit of this covenant and the Restrictions is to be attached to and enure for each and every part of the Retained Land [that remains unsold by the Transferor or has been sold by the Transferor [or by any person claiming through the Transferor otherwise than by a transfer on sale] with the express benefit of this covenant and the Restrictions]

        4.1.2    the burden of this covenant and the Restrictions is intended to bind and binds each and every part of the Property into whomsoever's hands it may come [but not so as to render the Transferee personally liable for any breach of this covenant or a Restriction arising after the Transferee has parted with all interest in the Property or the part of the Property on which such breach is committed]

4.1.3     a Restriction not to do any act or thing includes an obligation not to permit or suffer that act or thing to be done by another person

4.2     The Restrictions mentioned in clause 4.1 are the following: *(insert details)*

**[4193]**

## 5     Restrictive covenants by the Transferor[15]

5.1     The Transferor covenants with the Transferee to observe and perform the Restrictions specified below and it is agreed and declared that:

5.1.1     the benefit of this covenant and the Restrictions is to be attached to and enure for each and every part of the Property [that remains unsold by the Transferee or has been sold by the Transferee [or by any person claiming through the Transferee otherwise than by a transfer on sale] with the express benefit of this covenant and the Restrictions]

5.1.2     the burden of this covenant and the Restrictions is intended to bind and binds each and every part of the Retained Land into whomsoever's hands it may come [but not so as to render the Transferor personally liable for any breach of this covenant or a Restriction arising after the Transferor has parted with all interest in the Retained Land or the part of the Retained Land on which such breach is committed]

5.1.3     a Restriction not to do any act or thing includes an obligation not to permit or suffer that act or thing to be done by another person

5.2     The Restrictions mentioned in clause 5.1 are the following: *(insert details)*

## 6     Positive covenants by the Transferee[16]

6.1     The Transferee covenants with the Transferor that the Transferee will observe and perform the covenants and conditions contained or referred to in the [property [proprietorship][17] and charges registers of title number *(number)*[18] and/or *(insert details)*] [so far as they relate to the Property] and will indemnify and keep the Transferor and his successors in title fully and effectually indemnified against all actions proceedings damages costs claims and expenses which may be suffered or incurred by the Transferor or his successors in title in respect of any future breach or non-observance or non-performance of those covenants and conditions

6.2     The Transferee covenants with the Transferor as follows: *(insert details)*[19]

## 7     Positive covenants by the Transferor[20]

The Transferor covenants with the Transferee as follows: *(insert details)*

## 8     Agreements and Declarations[21]

It is agreed and declared as follows: *(insert details)*

## 9     Statements[22]

## 10     Applications[23]

**[4194]**

1        As to stamp duty see Information Binder: Stamp Duties [1] (Conveyance or transfer). As to Land
Registry fees see Information Binder: Property [1]: Fees in connection with property matters, Land
Registry fees.
        Form TP1 (for which see Form 114 [4181] ante) is the Land Registry form of transfer of part of
freehold or leasehold land prescribed by the Land Registration Rules 1925, SR&O 1925/1093 r 98,
Sch 1 as inserted by SI 1999/128. This Form should be used whenever part only of any registered title
is transferred, even if the transfer also includes the whole of one or more other registered titles.
        The transferor's land or charge certificate if not already on deposit must be placed on deposit using
Land Registry Form DP1 as prescribed by SR&O 1925/1093 Sch 1 as inserted by SI 1997/3037 and
substituted by SI 1999/128 (as to which see vol 25(1) (1999 Reissue) LAND REGISTRATION Form 3
[3076]) to meet the transferee's application to register the transfer. If the transferor's land is subject to
any registered charge, that charge will require to be released by use of Land Registry Form DS3 (for
which see vol 25(1) (1999 Reissue) LAND REGISTRATION Form 47 [3371]). If the charge is a noted
charge, the consent of the chargee to the transfer should be obtained and lodged with the application
to register the transfer.
        As to the matters listed below see vol 35 (1997 Reissue) SALE OF LAND at the respective
references given:
(a)      as to sales of part generally: Paragraph 348 [455] et seq;
(b)      identity on sales of part: Paragraph 349 [456] et seq and 591 [780] et seq;
(c)      easements: Paragraph 485 [623] et seq;
(d)      matters to be considered on a transfer of part: Paragraph 494 [636] et seq;
(e)      restrictive covenants: Paragraph 517 [682] et seq;
(f)      positive covenants: Paragraph 527 [703] et seq;
(g)      parcels on a transfer of part: Paragraph 591 [780] et seq;
(h)      transfer of land in part of a registered title: Paragraph 590 [779] et seq;
For forms of:
(i)      covenants (both restrictive and positive) and declarations: see vol 13(1) (1996 Reissue)
         COVENANTS RELATING TO LAND generally;
(ii)     easements and profits à prendre: see vol 13(1) (1996 Reissue) EASEMENTS AND PROFITS À
         PRENDRE generally; and
(iii)    covenants (both restrictive and positive), declarations, easements and profits à prendre relating to
         agricultural land, rural property and sporting matters: see vol 2(2) (1998 Reissue)
         AGRICULTURE.
        Where part only of a transferor's land is sold it is no longer necessary for the transferor to take a
duplicate transfer as evidence of the terms of the transfer and of the covenants, easements and
declarations which benefit the retained land. In many cases the need will be obviated by the fact that
details of the relevant matters will appear on the register of the transferee's title (which will be accessible
to the transferor due to the open register). The reserved rights will also be reflected in appurtenant
rights added on to the register of the transferor's title. Even with positive covenants, these will normally
be the subject of an entry on the transferee's title as a matter of Land Registry practice. It may be
desirable for the transferee to have a separate record of the positive covenants, in case the 'chain of
covenants' in subsequent transfers of the transferee's title is broken. (so that the entry on the positive
covenants on the register is cancelled). However that need could be met by ensuring that the transfer
is executed first by the transferee (as would be prudent practice) and a certified copy of it, as executed
by both parties, is retained instead of a duplicate transfer.

                                                                                              **[4195]**

        For the prescribed forms of execution of transfers see SR&O 1925/1093 Sch 3 as inserted by
SI 1997/3037, as to which see vol 37 (1998 Reissue) SALE OF LAND Form 4 [59]. As to the statutory
requirements for the valid execution of a deed see vol 12 (1994 Reissue) DEEDS, AGREEMENTS AND
DECLARATIONS.
        As to the method of reproduction of Land Registry prescribed forms see SR&O 1925/1093
rr 308, 308A as substituted by SI 1997/3037 r 47 and amended by SI 1999/128 and by SI 1999/2097:
        '308.—(1) Subject to rule 308A, any application or instrument in one of the Schedule
        1 forms must:
        (a) be printed in black on durable white A4 size paper;
        (b) be reproduced as set out in the Schedule, that is to say as to its wording, layout, ruling,
        font and point size, and
        (c) contain all the information required in an easily legible form.
                (2) Where on a Schedule 1 form (other than Form DL) any panel is insufficient in
        size to contain the required insertions, and the method of production of the form does
        not allow the depth of the panel to be increased, the information to be inserted in the
        panel shall be continued on a continuation sheet in form CS.
                (3) When completing a Schedule 1 form containing an additional provisions panel,

any statement, certificate or application required or permitted by these rules to be included in the form for which the form does not otherwise provide and any additional provisions desired by the parties shall be inserted in that panel or on a continuation thereof.

(4) Where the form consists of more than one sheet of paper, or refers to an attached plan or a continuation sheet, all the sheets including any plan shall be securely fastened together.'

'Electronically produced forms

**308A.** Where the method of production of a Schedule 1 form permits—

(a) the depth of a panel may be increased or reduced to fit the material to be comprised in it, and a panel may be divided at a page break;

(b) instructions in italics may be omitted;

(c) inapplicable certificates and statements may be omitted;

(d) the plural may be used instead of the singular and the singular instead of the plural;

(e) panels which would contain only the panel number and the panel heading, if any, may be omitted, but such omission shall not affect the numbering of subsequent panels.'

(f) "x" boxes may be omitted where all inapplicable statements and certificates have been omitted;

(g) the sub-headings in an additional provisions panel may be added to, amended, repositioned or omitted;

(h) 'Seller' may be substituted for 'Transferor' and 'Buyer' for 'Transferee' in a transfer on sale;

(i) the vertical lines which define the left and right boundaries of any panel may be omitted.'

Paragraphs (f), (g) and (h) are inserted by the Land Registration Rules 1999, SI 1999/128 r 2(1) Sch 1 para 22. Paragraph (i) is insertd by the Land Registration (No 2) Rules 1999, SI 1999/2097 r 2(1), Sch 1 para 13.

'Form of documents to be filed

**308B.** All documents (other than Schedule 1 forms, maps or plans) to be filed in the Registry shall be printed, typewritten, lithographed or written on durable paper, A4 size, and shall allow a sufficient margin, in order that they may be conveniently bound.'

**[4196]**

For further advice on completion of Land Registry Form TP1 see Form 114 [4181] ante and see vol 25(1) (1999 Reissue) LAND REGISTRATION Form 28(2) [3273].

As to registered land generally see vol 25(1) (1999 Reissue) LAND REGISTRATION. For commentary on transfers of registered land generally see vol 35 (1997 Reissue) SALE OF LAND Paragraphs 544 [727] et seq and as to the following specific matters at the respective references given:

(a)  Administrative Area 549 [732];

(b)  consideration 558 [741] and receipt 559 [742];

(c)  address of transferee 561 [744];

(d)  implied covenants for title 562 [748] et seq and 472 [597]–484 [622];

(e)  parcels 567 [753] et seq and H M Land Registry's colour code 656 [858];

(f)  certificate of value 577 [763];

(g)  execution as a deed 579 [765];

(h)  references to trusts 581 [767] et seq;

(i)  transfers of unregistered land 621 [813] et seq.

Land Registry Form CS (for which see vol 25(1) (1999 Reissue) LAND REGISTRATION Form 29 [3277]) is only for use with Land Registry forms completed using printed versions supplied by law stationers. On electronically produced forms the depth of a panel should be increased or reduced depending on the amount of material to be comprised in it as shown in panel 13.

2    Particulars should be inserted of any other title numbers of land affected by matters contained in the transfer; eg land over which rights are to be granted.

3    Where the transferor is not the registered proprietor words identifying his capacity should be added, eg: 'as [executor *or* administrator] of *(name of deceased proprietor)*' or 'as trustee in bankruptcy of *(name of registered proprietor)*'. There is no legal requirement to include words of capacity and the inclusion does not obviate the need to produce appropriate evidence of the transferor's capacity (eg office copy probate or bankruptcy order), but it can be useful to the registrar and the parties. Where the capacity is closely connected with statements in panel 13 of this Form and would be confusing if separated from those statements, the capacity may be given in that panel instead.

4    See vol 35 (1997 Reissue) SALE OF LAND Paragraph 561 [744] et seq.

5    The box 'This transfer is not for money or anything which has a monetary value' should be ticked where the transferee gives an indemnity covenant but no other consideration of any kind passes (eg on a gift). The Land Registry do not seek to attribute any particular value to indemnity covenants for fee purposes.

6      The panel should be completed in accordance with the contract terms. Where the contract provides
       for a modification of the title guarantee, such modification should be set out in this panel. The Standard
       Conditions of Sale (3rd Edn) (for which see vol 38(1) (2000 Reissue) SALE OF LAND Form 1 [1011])
       provide that if the contract for sale makes no provision as to title guarantee then subject to condition
       4.5.3 the seller is to transfer the property with full title guarantee. Where the contract contains an
       express term that no covenants for title are given, panel 11 of this Form should be deleted on printed
       forms supplied by law stationers and omitted completely on electronically produced forms. Where a
       panel is omitted, the subsequent panel should be reproduced with their existing numbering and should
       not be renumbered. For forms of variation of the implied covenants for title see vol 36 (1997 Reissue)
       SALE OF LAND Form 190 [2226].

                                                                                                          **[4197]**

7      In beneficial joint ownership cases there is no need to insert a statement that the transferee can or
       cannot give a valid receipt for capital money arising on a disposition of the property. A reference in
       the transfer to the buyers holding on trust for themselves as joint tenants, provided that the transfer
       is executed by the buyers, informs the Registrar that the usual joint proprietor restriction need not
       be entered on the register. Conversely, if the transfer refers to the buyers holding on trust for
       themselves as tenants in common or for others as trustees under an express trust, it will be clear to
       the Registrar that the restriction should be entered. The Registrar is obliged to enter a restriction
       unless it is shown to his satisfaction that the joint proprietors are entitled for their own benefit, or can
       give a valid receipt for capital money, or that one of them is a trust corporation: Land Registration
       Act 1925 s 58(3) (37 Halsbury's Statutes REAL PROPERTY). As to co-owners see vol 35 (1997
       Reissue) SALE OF LAND Paragraph 573 [759] and as to the protection of beneficial interests of joint
       proprietors and of beneficiaries under a trust of land see vol 35 (1997 Reissue) SALE OF LAND
       Paragraph 983 [1287] et seq.

8      One view would add 'unless the context otherwise requires' or 'where the context so admits' and in
       fact this may be implied (see *Meux v Jacobs* (1875) LR 7 HL 481 at 493; *Law Society v United Services
       Bureau* [1934] 1 KB 343, DC) but the better course is to use defined terms in such a way that there are
       no circumstances where the defined meaning does not apply. Additional definitions should be inserted
       in alphabetical order.

9      The second box and wording in panel 4 may be completed where the land to be transferred is
       sufficiently defined by a reference on the transferor's title plan but this Form assumes (as will normally
       be the case) that one or more plans will be annexed to the transfer to show not only the land transferred
       but also the extent of the retained land, as defined, and the land affected by any easements such as rights
       of way.
              The size and scale of the plan should be sufficiently large to enable all salient features to be readily
       identified: see *Scarfe v Adams* [1981] 1 All ER 843, CA. If many plans are required it may be convenient
       to bind them together in a separate bundle, suitably referred to in the transfer. Each plan should be
       individually numbered if there is more than one. As to the Land Registry's colour code see vol 35 (1997
       Reissue) SALE OF LAND Paragraph 656 [858]. Where a plan has a legend with texturing, hatching or
       words of identification or notation an additional definition clause can be added: '[the Car Park, the
       Public Open Space *or (as the case may be)*] mean respectively those parts of the [Property *or* Estate] which
       are shown on the Plan and defined by reference to the legend endorsed on it'.

10     The clauses concerning gender, singular including the plural and persons including corporations can be,
       and in most simple transfers are, omitted in reliance on the Law of Property Act 1925 s 61 (37 Halsbury's
       Statutes (4th Edn) REAL PROPERTY) but they are sometimes inserted for the convenience of the
       parties.

11     This clause may be inserted where there are a number of covenanting clauses. If there is only one such
       clause an alternative is to insert the joint and several liability wording in that clause. If the interpretation
       clause is used it will require amendment if the transferors are trustees and their liability is to be limited.

12     For forms of clauses see vol 37 (1998 Reissue) SALE OF LAND Forms 254 [3265]–255 [3266] and vol 13(1)
       (1996 Reissue) EASEMENTS AND PROFITS À PRENDRE Form 13 [5601] et seq.

13     For forms of clauses see vol 37 (1998 Reissue) SALE OF LAND Forms 252 [3262]–254 [3265] and vol 13(1)
       (1996 Reissue) EASEMENTS AND PROFITS À PRENDRE Form 13 [5601] et seq.

14     For other forms of imposing covenants and for forms of restrictions see vol 13(1) (1996 Reissue)
       COVENANTS RELATING TO LAND generally. This Form is based on vol 13(1) (1996 Reissue)
       COVENANTS RELATING TO LAND Form 10(4) [1084].

15     See note 14 ante.

16     The transferee or grantee takes subject to the incumbrances and other entries appearing on the
       register and, unless the contrary is expressed on the register, to any overriding interests affecting the
       estate or land transferred or created. Such matters as appear on the register and overriding interests
       should not be mentioned in the transfer. See vol 25(1) (1999 Reissue) LAND REGISTRATION
       Paragraph 121 [2165]. The clause is based on the indemnity covenant in the basic agreement for sale
       in vol 36 (1997 Reissue) SALE OF LAND Form 102 clause 8.3 [1813]. For other forms of indemnity

covenant see vol 13(1) (1996 Reissue) COVENANTS RELATING TO LAND Forms 437 [2391]–443 [2397]. For indemnity covenants in respect of a selling landlord's liability see vol 13(1) (1996 Reissue) COVENANTS RELATING TO LAND Form 444 [2398]–446 [2401].

17    This register may need to be included if, for example, there is a restriction controlling dispositions of land which will remain on the register following completion of the transfer.

18    If the property comprises land in a number of titles and the covenants and conditions in respect of which an indemnity is required are contained in only some of those titles, the title numbers should be inserted.

19    For forms of clauses see vol 13(1) (1996 Reissue) COVENANTS RELATING TO LAND Form 1 [1001] et seq.

20    See note 19 above.

21    For forms of declaration see vol 37 (1997 Reissue) SALE OF LAND Forms 246 [3253]–247 [3255], vol 13(1) (1996 Reissue) COVENANTS RELATING TO LAND Form 5(1) [1051] inter alia, vol 13(1) (1996 Reissue) EASEMENTS AND PROFITS À PRENDRE Form 108 [5855] inter alia and vol 36 (1997 Reissue) SALE OF LAND Form 105 clause 13 [1833]. The Registrar normally arranges for a note of declarations to be entered in the property register of the title of the land transferred without any specific application being made.

22    Insert details of: (a) the statutory powers or instrument conferring authority to buy or sell or required by SR&O 1925/1093 as amended; (b) the capacity of the transferor if he is not the registered proprietor or estate owner or the capacity of the transferee respectively if the information cannot conveniently be inserted in panels 6 or 7 of this Form (as appropriate); (c) statements required by statute (eg in relation to charities required by SR&O 1925/1093 rr 61, 62, 122 and 128 as substituted by SI 1996/2975); (d) in the case of unregistered land, confirmation that personal representatives have not given or made any previous assent or conveyance; (e) statements of account, as to the nature of the transaction or consideration, as to merger, (or as the case may be). Information usually given by way of recital in unregistered conveyancing should not be inserted: see vol 35 (1997 Reissue) SALE OF LAND Paragraph 552 [735] et seq.

23    For forms of restriction see vol 25(1) (1999 Reissue) LAND REGISTRATION Forms 80(1) [3599]–80(43)–[3641].

**[4198]**

# 116

## Transfer of part of registered freehold land being a building plot not on a building estate[1]

*Use Land Registry Form TP1 (for which see Form 114 [4181] ante) and insert, in the panels specified below, the wording shown:*

**Panel 13    Additional Provisions**

**1      Definitions**

In this transfer:

1.1    'the Perpetuity Period' means the period of [21] [80] years commencing on the date of this transfer

1.2    'the Plan' means the plan annexed to this transfer [and if numbered plans are annexed any reference to a numbered plan is to the annexed plan so numbered]

1.3    'the Retained Land' means the land [and buildings] *(add description)* [outlined in green *or (as the case may be)* [on Plan *(number)*]] retained by the Transferor being that part of the land comprised in title number *(number)* as is not comprised in the Property

1.4    'Services' means water soil effluent gas fuel oil electricity telephone [telephonic signals television visual audio fax electronic mail data information communications] and other services

1.5    'Service Apparatus' means sewers drains channels pipes watercourses gutters wires cables ducts flues conduits laser optic fibres electronic data or impulse communication transmission or reception systems and other conducting media [septic tanks holding tanks] and associated equipment

[1.6        words importing one gender shall be construed as importing any other gender]

[1.7        words importing the singular shall be construed as importing the plural and vice versa]

[1.8        words importing persons shall be construed as importing a corporate body and/ or a partnership and vice versa]

[1.9        where any party comprises more than one person the obligations and liabilities of that party under this transfer shall be joint and several obligations and liabilities of those persons]

[1.10       the panel and clause headings do not form part of this transfer and shall not be taken into account in its construction or interpretation]

[1.11       any reference to a clause is to one so numbered in this panel unless otherwise stated]

[1.12       any reference to a colour or letter is to one on the Plan]

[4199]

**2        Rights granted for the benefit of the Property**

2.1        The Property is transferred together with the following rights [but subject to the observance and performance of the [covenants *or* conditions] contained in clause 2.2]: *(insert details of rights to be granted)*

[2.2        *(insert details of covenants or conditions)*]

**3        Rights reserved for the benefit of other land**

3.1        There are reserved out of the Property for the benefit of each and every part of the Retained Land the following rights [but subject to the observance and performance of the [covenants *or* conditions] contained in clause 3.2]: *(insert details of rights to be reserved)*

[3.2        *(insert details of covenants or conditions)*]

**4        Restrictive covenants by the Transferee**

4.1        The Transferee covenants with the Transferor to observe and perform the Restrictions specified below and it is agreed and declared that:

   4.1.1        the benefit of this covenant and the Restrictions is to be attached to and enure for each and every part of the Retained Land [that remains unsold by the Transferor or has been sold by the Transferor [or by any person claiming through the Transferor otherwise than by a transfer on sale] with the express benefit of this covenant and the Restrictions]

   4.1.2        the burden of this covenant and the Restrictions is intended to bind and binds each and every part of the Property into whomsoever's hands it may come [but not so as to render the Transferee personally liable for any breach of this covenant or a Restriction arising after the Transferee has parted with all interest in the Property or the part of the Property on which such breach is committed]

   4.1.3        a Restriction not to do any act or thing includes an obligation not to permit or suffer that act or thing to be done by another person

[4200]

4.2        The Restrictions mentioned in clause 4.1 are the following:

   4.2.1        **Building site:** The Transferee must not use the Property for any purpose except as [permanent pasture for [mowing *or* grazing] *or (as the case may be)*] [or] a building site for the construction on it of one private dwelling house and *(insert number)* private garage[s] and the laying out of gardens for such dwelling house PROVIDED ALWAYS that after such construction shall be completed this restriction shall cease to have effect

4.2.2    **Approval of plans:** The Transferee must not build or erect upon the Property any buildings [or] structures [or erections] other than one private dwelling house and *(insert number)* private garage[s] and boundary walls and fences as to the locations exterior design appearance finish and decoration [and foul drainage facilities] strictly in accordance with the drawings and specifications [approved by the Transferor in writing (which approval [in relation to finish and decoration] will not be unreasonably withheld [in respect of any of such matters as are approved by the local planning authority)]] [attached and signed by the parties for the purpose of identification]

**[4201]**

4.2.3    **Alterations:** The Transferee must not:

4.2.3.1    make any deviation from the drawings and specification approved by the Transferor affecting the location exterior design [and] appearance [finish and decoration] of all buildings and works as described therein

4.2.3.2    after completion of the buildings make any alterations or additions to the exterior of those buildings or of any other buildings subsequently erected on the Property [or to the walls hedges and fences on the Property]

4.2.3.3    erect any additional buildings walls hedges and fences on the Property

except in all cases with the written approval of the Transferor [which approval will not be unreasonably withheld and] whose fees and those of its professional advisors in connection with the consideration of any such application whether granted refused or withdrawn shall be paid by the Transferee

4.2.4    **Use:** The Transferee must not use the Property or any building for the time being on it for the purpose of any profession trade business or manufacture of any description nor use any dwelling house on it except as a [single] private dwelling house nor use any garage on it except as a private garage ancillary to the dwelling house

4.2.5    **Nuisance:** The Transferee must not do or omit to be done any act or thing on or about the Property the doing or omission of which shall or may be or grow to be an annoyance nuisance damage danger or disturbance to the Transferor or the owners or occupiers of any part of the Retained Land or adjoining or neighbouring property

4.2.6    **Parking:** The Transferee must not park boats caravans or trade vehicles (save trade vehicles in the course of delivery of goods or supply of services to the Property) on the Property

4.2.7    **Boundary support:** The Transferee must not deposit any soil or materials against or abutting upon any of the boundary walls hedges or fences dividing the Property from the Retained Land or use any such boundary features as a means of support

4.2.8    **Levels:** The Transferee must not make any material alteration in the height or level of the surface of the Property as existing at the date of this transfer except so far as is essential to construct foundations and Service Apparatus

4.2.9    **Drainage:** The Transferee must not discharge water soil or effluent from the Property onto the Retained Land

4.2.10    **Trees:**  The Transferee must not permit plants trees or shrubs which shall exceed *(number)* metres in height to remain on the part of the Property [hatched *or* tinted] *(colour)* on the Plan

4.2.11    **Laundry:**  The Transferee must not hang out washing or laundry anywhere on the Property where it shall be visible from any part of the Retained Land

**[4202]**

## 5    Restrictive covenants by the Transferor

5.1    The Transferor covenants with the Transferee to observe and perform the Restrictions specified below and it is agreed and declared that:

5.1.1    the benefit of this covenant and the Restrictions is to be attached to and enure for each and every part of the Property [that remains unsold by the Transferee or has been sold by the Transferee [or by any person claiming through the Transferee otherwise than by a transfer on sale] with the express benefit of this covenant and the Restrictions]

5.1.2    the burden of this covenant and the Restrictions is intended to bind and binds each and every part of the Retained Land into whomsoever's hands it may come [but not so as to render the Transferor personally liable for any breach of this covenant or a Restriction arising after the Transferor has parted with all interest in the Retained Land or the part of the Retained Land on which such breach is committed]

5.1.3    a Restriction not to do any act or thing includes an obligation not to permit or suffer that act or thing to be done by another person

5.2    The Restrictions mentioned in clause 5.1 are the following: *(insert details)*

## 6    Positive covenants by the Transferee

6.1    The Transferee covenants with the Transferor that the Transferee will observe and perform the covenants and conditions contained or referred to in the [property [proprietorship] and charges registers of title number *(number) and/or (insert details)*] [so far as they relate to the Property] and will indemnify and keep the Transferor and his successors in title fully and effectually indemnified against all actions proceedings damages costs claims and expenses which may be suffered or incurred by the Transferor or his successors in title in respect of any future breach or non-observance or non-performance of those covenants and conditions

6.2    The Transferee covenants with the Transferor as follows: *(insert details)*

## 7    Positive covenants by the Transferor

The Transferor covenants with the Transferee as follows: *(insert details)*

## 8    Agreements and Declarations

It is agreed and declared as follows: *(insert details)*

**[4203]**

---

1    As to stamp duty see Information Binder: Stamp Duties [1] (Conveyance or transfer). As to Land Registry fees see Information Binder: Property [1]: Fees in connection with property matters, Land Registry fees.

Form TP1 (for which see Form 114 [4181] ante) is the Land Registry form of transfer of part of freehold or leasehold land prescribed by the Land Registration Rules 1925, SR&O 1925/1093 r 98, Sch 1 as inserted by SI 1999/128. This Form should be used whenever part only of any registered title is transferred, even if the transfer also includes the whole of one or more other registered titles.

The transferor's land or charge certificate if not already on deposit must be placed on deposit using Land Registry Form DP1 as prescribed by SR&O 1925/1093 Sch 1 as inserted by SI 1997/3037 and substituted by SI 1999/128 (as to which, see vol 25(1) (1999 Reissue) LAND REGISTRATION Form 3 [3076]) to meet the transferee's application to register the transfer. If the transferor's land is subject to any registered charge, that charge will require to be released by use of Land Registry Form DS3 (for which see vol 25(1) (1999 Reissue) LAND REGISTRATION Form 47 [3371]). If the charge is a noted charge, the consent of the chargee to the transfer should be obtained and lodged with the application to register the transfer.

Reference should be made to Form 115 [4191] ante for detailed footnotes on matters common to many forms of transfer and for cross references to the commentary in vol 35 (1997 Reissue) SALE OF LAND, for the location of alternative transfer clauses in that and other volumes and for additional footnotes relating to the sale of part of a property.

**[4204]**

# 117

## Transfer of part of registered freehold land being a plot on a building estate with a dwelling house and garage on it not comprised in a building scheme[1]

*Use Land Registry Form TP1 (for which see Form 114 [4181] ante) and insert, in the panels specified below, the wording shown:*

### Panel 4   Property

Plot number *(number)* [and garage plot number *(number)*] on the approved estate layout plan lodged at HM Land Registry known as *(description)* [including the walls hedges and fences marked on the Plan with a 'T' mark inside the red edging and the buildings erected on [it *or* them]]

**[4205]**

### Panel 13   Additional Provisions

### 1        Definitions

In this transfer:

1.1        'the Estate' means the land [edged brown] on the Plan now and formerly comprised in title number *(number)* known as the *(name)* Estate at *(address)*

1.2        ['the Estate Road'] ['the Private Road'] ['the Drive'] ['the Car Park'] [and *(specify)*] mean respectively those parts of the Estate which are shown on the Plan and defined by reference to the legend endorsed on it

1.3        'the Perpetuity Period' means the period of [21] [80] years commencing on the date of this transfer

1.4        'the Plan' means the plan annexed to this transfer [and if numbered plans are annexed any reference to a numbered plan is to the annexed plan so numbered]

1.5        'the Projections' means eaves gutters spouts downpipes chimney cappings foundations supporting pillars and stanchions and any similar structures

1.6        'Services' means water soil effluent gas fuel oil electricity telephone telephonic signals television and other services

1.7        'Service Apparatus' means sewers drains channels pipes watercourses gutters wires cables ducts flues conduits and other conducting media [septic tanks holding tanks and sewage treatment works] and associated equipment

[1.8        words importing one gender shall be construed as importing any other gender]

[1.9        words importing the singular shall be construed as importing the plural and vice versa]

[1.10      words importing persons shall be construed as importing a corporate body and/ or a partnership and vice versa]

[1.11    where any party comprises more than one person the obligations and liabilities of that party under this transfer shall be joint and several obligations and liabilities of those persons]

[1.12    the panel and clause headings do not form part of this transfer and shall not be taken into account in its construction or interpretation]

[1.13    any reference to a clause is to one so numbered in this panel unless otherwise stated]

[1.14    any reference to a colour or letter is to one on the Plan]

                                                                      **[4206]**

## 2      Rights granted for the benefit of the Property

The Property is transferred together with the following rights in common with the Transferor and all other persons who have or may in future have the like rights:

2.1      The right at all times hereafter for the purpose of access to and egress from the Property to pass and repass on foot and with or without vehicles over the carriageway of the Estate Road and on foot only over the footways and footpaths on the Estate

2.2      The right so far as the same serve the Property of taking passage and running (as appropriate) of Services through the Service Apparatus which are now or may within the Perpetuity Period be laid in on over or under the Estate SUBJECT to the Transferee paying a fair proportion of the cost of cleaning maintaining repairing and whenever necessary renewing the same

2.3      The right to maintain enjoy and use over on or under the adjoining land comprised in the Estate the Projections incidental to the user of the buildings on the Property which overhang stand on or protrude beneath the adjoining land comprised in the Estate

2.4      The right to enter after the giving of reasonable notice and at all reasonable times (or in the case of emergency at any time without notice) upon the adjoining land comprised in the Estate [other than any land covered by a building] so far as may be necessary for the purposes of inspecting cleaning maintaining repairing and renewing the buildings walls hedges fences and other boundary structures on the Property the Service Apparatus and the Projections causing as little damage as possible and making good to the reasonable satisfaction of the registered proprietors from time to time of the adjoining land any damage caused

[2.5     The right to pass and repass on foot and with or without motor vehicles over that part of the [Private Road *or* Drive] which is not hereby transferred for the purpose of gaining access to and egress from the Property SUBJECT to the payment to the owner of that part of *(specify)*% of the cost of cleaning maintaining repairing and whenever necessary renewing that part of the [Private Road *or* Drive]][2]

[2.6     The right to park one private motor car belonging to or used by the owner or occupier for the time being of the Property or his visitors on the Car Park for reasonable periods only when space is available the Car Park being available to all those entitled to use it and the Transferee on a first come first served basis SUBJECT to the payment to the owner of it of *(specify)*% of the cost of cleaning maintaining repairing and whenever necessary renewing the Car Park]

                                                                      **[4207]**

## 3      Rights reserved for the benefit of other land

There are reserved out of the Property for the benefit of each and every part of the remainder of the Estate the following rights:

3.1      The right (in common with all others entitled thereto and so far as the same serve other parts of the Estate) to take pass and run (as appropriate) Services through the Service Apparatus now or at any time within the Perpetuity Period laid in on over or under the Property

3.2     The right to maintain enjoy and use over on or under the Property the Projections incidental to the user of the buildings on the adjoining land comprised in the Estate which overhang stand on or protrude beneath the Property

3.3     The right at any time within the Perpetuity Period to enter upon the Property [other than any land covered by a building] and:

    3.3.1     to lay place or erect in on over or under it and thereafter at all times to use any Service Apparatus for the supply and passage of Services to or from any other part of the Estate and likewise to alter enlarge or duplicate Service Apparatus

    3.3.2     to construct lay place or erect in on over or under it and thereafter at all times to maintain enjoy and use the Projections incidental to the user of the buildings to be constructed on the adjoining land comprised in the Estate overhanging standing on or protruding beneath the Property

3.4     The right to enter after the giving of reasonable notice and at all reasonable times (or in the case of emergency at any time without notice) upon the Property so far as may be necessary for the purposes of constructing laying altering inspecting cleaning maintaining repairing renewing and demolishing the buildings walls hedges fences and other boundary structures upon the adjoining land comprised in the Estate and Service Apparatus and the Projections and for the purpose of complying with any covenant agreement or condition entered into by the Transferor with the Transferee or any other person causing as little damage as possible and making good to the reasonable satisfaction of the Transferee any damage caused

[3.5     The right (in common with the Transferee and all others entitled thereto) to pass and repass on foot and with or without vehicles over that part of the [Private Road *or* Drive] which is hereby transferred for the purpose of obtaining access to and egress from other parts of the Estate SUBJECT to the person exercising such right paying to the Transferee *(specify)*% of the cost of maintaining repairing and whenever necessary renewing that part of the [Private Road *or* Drive]][3]

[3.6     The right (in common with the Transferee and all other entitled thereto) for the owners and occupiers of Plot No *(number)* on the Plan to pass and repass on foot and with or without motor vehicles over that part of the [Private Road *or* Drive] which is hereby transferred for the purpose of gaining access to and egress from Plot No *(number)* on the Plan SUBJECT to the owner of Plot No *(number)* paying to the Transferee *(specify)*% of the cost of maintaining and repairing and whenever necessary renewing that part of the [Private Road *or* Drive]][4]

**[4208]**

## 4     Restrictive covenants by the Transferee

4.1     The Transferee covenants with the Transferor to observe and perform the Restrictions specified below and it is agreed and declared that:

    4.1.1     the benefit of this covenant and the Restrictions is to be attached to and enure for each and every part of the Estate [that remains unsold by the Transferor or has been sold by the Transferor [or by any person claiming through the Transferor otherwise than by a transfer on sale] with the express benefit of this covenant and the Restrictions][5]

4.1.2      the burden of this covenant and the Restrictions is intended to bind and binds each and every part of the Property into whomsoever's hands it may come [but not so as to render the Transferee personally liable for any breach of this covenant or a Restriction arising after the Transferee has parted with all interest in the Property or the part of the Property on which such breach is committed]

4.1.3      a Restriction not to do any act or thing includes an obligation not to permit or suffer that act or thing to be done by another person

4.2      The Restrictions mentioned in clause 4.1 are the following:

4.2.1      The Transferee must not without the previous written consent of the Transferor use the Property for the purpose of any profession trade business or manufacture of any description nor for any purpose other than as a single private dwelling house and ancillary private garage

4.2.2      The Transferee must not do or omit to be done any act or thing on or about the Property the doing or omission of which shall or may be or grow to be an annoyance nuisance damage danger or disturbance to the Transferor or the owners or occupiers of any part of the Estate

4.2.3      The Transferee must not make any alterations to the exterior of the buildings now or subsequently erected on the Property or to the walls hedges and fences on the Property nor erect any additional buildings [walls hedges and fences] on the Property except with the written approval of the Transferor whose fees and those of its professional advisers in connection with the consideration of any such application whether granted refused or withdrawn shall be paid by the Transferee

4.2.4      The Transferee must not plant any tree or shrub or erect any wall hedge or fence or other structure forward of the front line of the dwelling house and garage on the Property nor do anything to interfere with or destroy the open plan layout of the Estate

4.2.5      The Transferee must not park motor vehicles on or obstruct in any other manner any part of the [Estate Road *or* Private Road *or* Drive]

4.2.6      The Transferee must not park boats caravans or trade vehicles (except trade vehicles in the course of delivering goods to or supplying services to the Property) on the Property or on any other part of the Estate

[4.2.7      The Transferee must not transfer the smaller plot hereby transferred separately from the larger plot and vice versa or permit or suffer the garage on the smaller plot to be used or occupied except by the occupier for the time being of the dwelling house on the larger plot hereby transferred]

[4209]

## 5      Positive covenants by the Transferee

5.1      The Transferee covenants with the Transferor that the Transferee will observe and perform the covenants and conditions contained or referred to in the [property [proprietorship] and charges registers of title number *(number) and/or (insert details)*] [so far as they relate to the Property] and will indemnify and keep the Transferor and his successors in title fully and effectually indemnified against all actions proceedings damages costs claims and expenses which may be suffered or incurred by the Transferor or his successors in title in respect of any future breach or non-observance or non-performance of those covenants and conditions

5.2         The Transferee covenants with the Transferor as follows:

      5.2.1        Unless express provision is elsewhere contained in this Transfer or the same are maintained at public expense the Transferee must pay a fair proportion of the expense of cleaning maintaining repairing and renewing the Service Apparatus and any entrance drive path or access way or other land or thing used by the Transferee jointly with others

      5.2.2        The Transferee must maintain and keep in good repair the walls hedges and fences hereby transferred

      5.2.3        The Transferee must replace to the satisfaction of the local planning authority any tree or shrub originally planted by the Transferor on the Property which dies or is cut down

      [5.2.4       The Transferee must maintain repair and whenever necessary properly renew the part of the [Private Road *or* Drive] which is hereby transferred]

      5.2.5        The Transferee must forthwith on demand pay to the owner or other person entitled thereto all money payable by the Transferee as a condition of the exercise of any easement granted to the Transferee by this transfer

      5.2.6        The Transferee must observe and perform all conditions contained in any planning permission affecting the Property

                                                                                        **[4210]**

## 6          Agreements and Declarations

It is agreed and declared as follows:

6.1         The Transferee and his successors in title shall not be entitled to any right of access of light or air or other easement or right which would restrict or interfere with the free use of any land comprised in the Estate or any adjoining or neighbouring land of the Transferor for building or any other purpose

6.2         The Transferor shall be at liberty to modify waive or release all or any covenants stipulations or restrictions relating to the Property the Estate or any adjoining or neighbouring land now or in the future belonging to the Transferor whether imposed or entered into before at the same time as or after the date of this transfer AND to sell or dispose of any part of the Estate free from any restriction or stipulation AND the Transferor shall not in any way be bound by the plotting or general scheme of development of the Estate

6.3         Unless the contrary appears on the Plan by 'T' marks the walls hedges and fences separating the Property from the adjoining plots and the buildings on them are party walls and fences and the rights and liabilities in respect of them shall be in accordance with the Law of Property Act 1925 Section 38(1)

6.4         If there shall be any dispute between the owners of any part of the Estate who are entitled to use and liable to pay for cleaning maintaining repairing or renewing any part of the Estate including Service Apparatus or any one or more of such owners as to the necessity for cleaning repair maintenance or renewal of any such part of thing their nature execution or cost or as to the proportions in which the owners are liable to pay or contribute to such cost the same shall be referred to the decision of a chartered surveyor appointed by agreement between all the owners or in default of agreement within 14 days of one owner giving notice to all of the others of his nomination appointed by or on behalf of the President of the [Royal Institution of Chartered Surveyors] on the application of any of the owners and the surveyor shall act as an expert and not as an arbitrator and his decision shall be final and binding on all such owners and the costs of his appointment and decision shall be as he may award

                                                                                        **[4211]**

1        As to stamp duty see Information Binder: Stamp Duties [1] (Conveyance or transfer). As to Land
         Registry fees see Information Binder: Property [1]: Fees in connection with property matters, Land
         Registry fees.
                 Form TP1 (for which see Form 114 [4181] ante) is the Land Registry form of transfer of part of
         freehold or leasehold land prescribed by the Land Registration Rules 1925, SR&O 1925/1093 r 98,
         Sch 1 as inserted by SI 1999/128. This Form should be used whenever part only of any registered title
         is transferred, even if the transfer also includes the whole of one or more other registered titles.
                 The transferor's land or charge certificate if not already on deposit must be placed on deposit using
         Land Registry Form DP1 as prescribed by SR&O 1925/1093 Sch 1 as inserted by SI 1997/3037 and
         substituted by SI 1999/128 (as to which, see vol 25(1) (1999 Reissue) LAND REGISTRATION Form 3
         [3076]) to meet the transferee's application to register the transfer. If the transferor's land is subject to
         any registered charge, that charge will require to be released by use of Land Registry Form DS3 (for
         which see vol 25(1) (1999 Reissue) LAND REGISTRATION Form 47 [3371]). If the charge is a noted
         charge, the consent of the chargee to the transfer should be obtained and lodged with the application
         to register the transfer.
                 Reference should be made to Form 115 [4191] ante for detailed footnotes on matters common
         to many forms of transfer, for cross references to the commentary in vol 35 (1997 Reissue) SALE OF
         LAND, for the location of alternative transfer clauses in that and other volumes and for additional
         footnotes relating to the sale of part of a property.
                 The forms of rights, exceptions, covenants, restrictions, agreements and declarations are
         illustrative only and should be altered or replaced as the circumstances may require.
                 This Form, unlike Form 118 [4213] post, does not expressly create a building scheme so that the
         restrictions are mutually enforceable as between individual plot owners. As to the necessary elements
         to constitute a building scheme see *Elliston v Reacher* [1908] 2 Ch 374. See also 16 Halsbury's Laws
         (4th Edn Reissue) EQUITY para 797 et seq. Because of the possibility that such covenants may be
         enforceable by other plot owners who are not parties to the transfer even if a building scheme is not
         expressly created (*Re Ecclesiastical Commrs for England's Conveyance* [1936] Ch 430) an express
         declaration negativing such a scheme may be inserted if desired, although practitioners may feel that
         clause 4.1.1 is sufficient indication if the words in brackets remain in this clause. See note 5 below.
2        This right is for use where there is a private road or drive giving access to two or a few more plots which
         is not to be adopted as a public highway maintained at public expense. The freehold ownership of that road
         or drive will be divided up between the owners of the adjacent plots and part transferred to each owner as
         part of his plot but he will require rights over the other parts of that private road or drive and vice versa.
3        This is the reservation corresponding to the right granted in clause 2.5 of this Form.
4        This clause may be used where access is to be reserved for just one specific plot, eg the private drive
         serves only two plots. Clause 3.5 is appropriate where the right is to be reserved for the benefit of all
         of the plots on the estate.
5        The benefit of the restriction on plots sold is expressed not to pass to buyers of later plots sold, nor will
         the buyers of later plots sold acquire the benefit of the restrictions imposed on the transfer of plots sold
         earlier unless expressly granted. If the benefit is to pass all the words in square brackets should be deleted.

**[4212]**

# 118

**Transfer of part of registered freehold land being a plot on a building estate
comprised in a building scheme**[1]

*Use Land Registry Form TP1 (for which see Form 114 [4181] ante) and insert, in the panels
specified below, the wording shown:*

**Panel 4  Property**

Plot number *(number)* [and garage plot number *(number)*] on the approved estate layout
plan lodged at HM Land Registry known as *(description)* [including the walls hedges and
fences marked on the Plan with a 'T' mark inside the red edging and the buildings
erected on [it *or* them]] subject to and with the benefit of the restrictive covenants
referred to below in accordance with the building scheme affecting or intended to affect
the Estate as constituted by this and transfers of other parts of the Estate

**[4213]**

## Panel 13  Additional Provisions

### 1      Definitions

In this transfer:

1.1      'the Estate' means the land [edged brown] on the Plan now and formerly comprised in title number *(number)* known as *(name)* Estate at *(address)*

1.2      'the Perpetuity Period' means the period of [21] [80] years commencing on the date of this transfer

1.3      'the Plan' means the plan annexed to this transfer[2] [and if numbered plans are annexed any reference to a numbered plan is to the annexed plan so numbered]

[1.4      words importing one gender shall be construed as importing any other gender]

[1.5      words importing the singular shall be construed as importing the plural and vice versa]

[1.6      words importing persons shall be construed as importing a corporate body and/or a partnership and vice versa]

[1.7      where any party comprises more than one person the obligations and liabilities of that party under this transfer shall be joint and several obligations and liabilities of those persons]

[1.8      the panel and clause headings do not form part of this transfer and shall not be taken into account in its construction or interpretation]

[1.9      any reference to a clause is to one so numbered in this panel unless otherwise stated]

[1.10    any reference to a colour or letter is to one on the Plan]

[4214]

### 2      Rights granted for the benefit of the Property

The Property is transferred together with the following rights for the Transferee in common with the Transferor and all other persons who have or may in future have the like right:

2.1      at all times and for all usual and reasonable purposes to pass and repass with or without motor and other vehicles from and to the Property over and along all roads and footways now constructed or at any time during the Perpetuity Period to be constructed on the Estate and intended to be declared by the appropriate local authority as repairable at the public expense[3] PROVIDED that such right shall be restricted to a right to pass and repass on foot only over such parts of the roads and footways as are not intended for vehicular use

[2.2      at all times and for all usual and reasonable purposes connected with the use of the Property as a private dwelling to pass and repass with or without motor and other vehicles over and along the accessway shown coloured [yellow] on the Plan (being other portions of private common garage accessways) and to use any oil grease and petrol traps (if any) constructed in the accessways the Transferee contributing a due proportion of the expense of keeping and maintaining the accessway and oil grease and petrol traps (if any) in good repair]

[2.3      at all times but on foot only to pass and repass over and along the footpath shown coloured [brown] on the Plan the Transferee contributing a due proportion of the expense of keeping and maintaining the footpath in good repair]

2.4      to take water electricity gas and other appropriate services and to the passage of water and soil through the pipes cables sewers and drains and other conducting media respectively now laid or at any time during the Perpetuity Period to be laid in under or through any land (other than the Property) included in the Estate and the pipes cables sewers and drains and other conducting media shall unless and until they are adopted by the appropriate authorities or undertakers be maintained and repaired at the joint and equal expense of the owners for the time being of the Property and of any other land entitled to use them

2.5        if a garage is now or shall at any time within 80 years of the date of this transfer be erected on any adjoining land included in the Estate against the boundary of the Property for the Transferee to break into and build on to the wall of that garage for the sole purpose of erecting a garage on the Property contiguous to that garage making good at his own expense any damage to that garage to the reasonable satisfaction of its owner TOGETHER with a right of support for the walls and eaves of the garage erected on the Property

2.6        to enter on the land (other than the Property) included in the Estate for the purpose of:

2.6.1        laying maintaining replacing and inspecting any pipes cables sewers and drains and other conducting media used by the Property

2.6.2        renewing repairing and inspecting the facing walls of any house garage or other structure which may be built on the boundary line of the Property

the Transferee making good all damage which may be done in the exercise of such powers as specified in this sub-clause at his own cost and without unnecessary delay

[2.7        *(continue with rights to use other communal areas)*]⁴

PROVIDED that none of the rights granted by this schedule shall apply to or be exercised over any land transferred to or vested in any service undertaker

**[4215]**

## 3        Rights reserved for the benefit of other land

There are reserved out of the Property for the benefit of each and every part of the remainder of the Estate the following rights for the Transferor the owner or owners for the time being of the remainder of the Estate and of the adjoining and neighbouring land now or formerly owned by the Transferor and of any part or parts of that land intended to be benefitted and all other persons having the like right or similar rights:

[3.1        at all times and for all usual and reasonable purposes to pass and repass with or without motor and other vehicles over and along the accessway now transferred shown coloured [purple] on the Plan to and from the adjoining and neighbouring land served by that accessway together with the right to use any oil grease and petrol traps constructed in that accessway the person or persons exercising such rights contributing a due proportion of the expense of keeping and maintaining that accessway and oil grease and petrol traps (if any) in good repair]

[3.2        at all times when the same shall be available to use the parking space or spaces shown coloured [black] on the Plan for parking vehicles for reasonable periods only the parking space or spaces being available to all those for whom the benefit of this clause is intended and the Transferee together on a first come first served basis]

[3.3        at all times but on foot only to go and return over and along the footpath shown coloured [blue] [and the grassed area shown coloured [orange]] on the Plan to and from the adjoining and neighbouring land served by the footpath [and the grassed area] such persons mentioned above contributing a due proportion of the expense of keeping and maintaining the footpath [and the grassed area] in good repair]

3.4        to take water electricity gas and other appropriate services and to pass water and soil through the pipes cables sewers and drains and other conducting media respectively now laid or at any time during the Perpetuity Period to be laid in under or through the Property and the pipes cables sewers and drains and other conducting media shall unless and until they are adopted by the appropriate authorities or undertakers be maintained and repaired at the joint and equal expense of the owners for the time being of the Property and of the other land entitled to use them

3.5 if a garage is now or shall at any time within the Perpetuity Period be erected on the Property against the boundary of any adjoining land included in the Estate to break into and build on to the wall of that garage for the sole purpose of erecting an adjoining garage contiguous to the garage on the Property the person exercising such right making good at his own expense any damage to the garage on the Property to the reasonable satisfaction of the Transferee TOGETHER with a right of support for the walls and eaves of the adjoining garage

3.6 to enter on the Property for the following purposes:

3.6.1 to lay maintain and replace inspect and connect to such pipes cables sewers and drains and other conducting media

3.6.2 to renew repair and inspect the facing walls of any house garage or other structure built upon any adjoining land and upon the boundary line of the Property

3.6.3 (such rights also to be reserved to the appropriate local authority) to plant on the Property trees and/or shrubs in accordance with the requirements of the local authority and afterwards as occasion may require to stake cultivate or replace such trees and/or shrubs[5]

all damage which may be done in the exercise of such powers as are specified in this sub-clause being made good without unnecessary delay at the cost of the Transferor or other person so entering

**[4216]**

## 4    Restrictive covenants by the Transferee

4.1 The Transferee so as to bind the Property [but not so as to render him personally liable after having parted with all interest in the Property] covenants separately with each of the Transferor and every other person who is now the owner of any land forming part of the Estate (subject to the right of the Transferor to vary and release covenants set out below) for the benefit of the whole and every part of[6] the Estate to observe and perform the Restrictions set out below[7]

4.2 The Restrictions mentioned in clause 4.1 are the following:

4.2.1 The Transferee shall not erect on the Property in front of the prescribed building line any fence or wall [other than a brick wall not exceeding (*height*) with gatepiers not exceeding (*height*)] such wall to be erected in a proper and workmanlike manner and to be constructed of facing bricks PROVIDED that no such wall or fence shall be erected if prohibited by planning conditions relating to the Property

4.2.2 The Transferee shall not use the Property or any buildings on the Property for the carrying on of any trade or business whatsoever and shall use the same as a single private dwelling house only

4.2.3 The Transferee shall not mutilate or remove the trees and/or shrubs which may be planted within the boundary of the Property

[4.2.4 (*insert any other restrictions as required*)]

4.3 In this clause an obligation not to do any act or thing includes an obligation not to permit or suffer that act or thing to be done by another person

**[4217]**

**5          Covenants by the Transferor**

5.1          The Transferor so as to bind the part of the Estate retained by the Transferor [but not so as to render himself personally liable after having parted with all interest in the Estate] covenants with the Transferee for the benefit of the whole and every part of the Property in the terms to which all the land in the Estate is to be subject to observe and perform the obligations set out below

5.2          The obligations mentioned in clause 5.1 are the following:

   5.2.1          The Transferor shall at his own expense well and sufficiently form metal and kerb the new roads and footways on the Estate and shall complete all sewers (both foul and storm water) on the Estate and shall maintain and repair the roads footpaths and sewers so far as they are not under this transfer to be maintained by any other person until such time as they are adopted as highways and sewers maintainable at the public expense and shall indemnify the Transferee from and against all costs charges claims and demands for sewering levelling paving metalling flagging channelling and making good the new roads and footways and for constructing the sewers

   [5.2.2          The Transferor shall so long as any part of the land comprised in the Estate remains vested in the Transferor pay to (*name of management company*) such part of any costs and expenses incurred by (*name of management company*) in providing procuring and performing in respect of the Estate the services set out in the schedule to a deed of covenant made between (*name of management company*) (1) and the Transferee (2) and bearing the same date as this transfer as if the Transferor had entered into a deed of covenant in like terms with (*name of management company*) in respect of the land remaining vested in the Transferor]

   [5.2.3          (*insert any other covenants as required*)]

[4218]

**6          Positive covenants by the Transferee**

6.1          The Transferee covenants with the Transferor that the Transferee will observe and perform the covenants and conditions contained or referred to in the [property [proprietorship] and charges registers of title number (*number*) and/or (*insert details*)] [so far as they relate to the Property] and will indemnify and keep the Transferor and his successors in title fully and effectually indemnified against all actions proceedings damages costs claims and expenses which may be suffered or incurred by the Transferor or his successors in title in respect of any future breach or non-observance or non-performance of those covenants and conditions

6.2          The Transferee covenants with the Transferor as follows:

   6.2.1          The Transferee shall at all times in the future maintain the fences on the sides of the Property where marked 'T' within the boundaries on the Plan

   6.2.2          The Transferee shall perform and observe all conditions contained in any planning permission affecting the Property

   [6.2.3          (*continue with other positive covenants as required*)]

[4219]

**7          Agreements and Declarations**

It is agreed and declared as follows:

7.1          All the restrictive covenants imposed on different transferees by this and other transfers of land on the Estate pursuant to the building scheme referred to above are intended to be mutually enforceable between such transferees and their respective successors in title regardless of the date or dates of the transfers to them

7.2     The Transferor expressly reserves the right:

   7.2.1      to make from time to time any alteration in:

      7.2.1.1      the mode of laying out the Estate

      7.2.1.2      the number and area of the plots

      7.2.1.3      the class of building or

      7.2.1.4      the special and general conditions of sale and

   7.2.2      to withdraw release vary or abandon in favour of the owner or owners from time to time of any part of the Estate (including the Property) any of the special conditions or any covenants restrictions stipulations and conditions entered into or to be entered into

in such manner as the Transferor shall think fit[8]

7.3     the Transferee shall not by virtue of this transfer acquire or be entitled to any easement or right of light or air which would prejudice the free use or enjoyment of any adjoining or neighbouring land of the Transferor for building or other purposes and any enjoyment of light or air had by the Transferee from or over any adjoining or neighbouring land of the Transferor shall be deemed to be had by consent of the Transferor

7.4     any wall erected or to be erected which shall separate the buildings erected or to be erected on the Property from any buildings erected or to be erected on the Estate shall after erection be deemed to be a party wall and shall be maintained and repaired accordingly

7.5     all eaves gutters down spouts cisterns passages drains sewers pipes wires and cables and all other matters and things now used or intended to be used and enjoyed in common by the owners and occupiers for the time being of the Property and of any other land comprised in the Estate shall continue to be so used and enjoyed and shall be repaired and maintained at the fair and proportionate expense of those persons entitled to the use and enjoyment of them

## 8      Applications

[8.1     The Transferor and the Transferee apply to the Registrar to enter a restriction on the title to the Property that except under an order of the Registrar no transfer lease or disposition by the proprietor [or in exercise of the power of sale in any registered charge][9] of the land is to be registered without the consent in writing of (*name of management company*)][10]

8.2     The Transferee and the Transferor apply to the Registrar to make all necessary entries on the register of their respective titles so as to give effect to this deed and the building scheme declared in it[11]

**[4220]**

1      As to stamp duty see Information Binder: Stamp Duties [1] (Conveyance or transfer). As to Land Registry fees see Information Binder: Property [1]: Fees in connection with property matters, Land Registry fees.
       Form TP1 (for which see Form 114 [4181] ante) is the Land Registry form of transfer of part of freehold or leasehold land prescribed by the Land Registration Rules 1925, SR&O 1925/1093 r 98, Sch 1 as inserted by SI 1999/128. This Form should be used whenever part only of any registered title is transferred, even if the transfer also includes the whole of one or more other registered titles.
       The transferor's land or charge certificate if not already on deposit must be placed on deposit using Land Registry Form DP1 as prescribed by SR&O 1925/1093 Sch 1 as inserted by SI 1997/3037 and

substituted by SI 1999/128 (as to which, see vol 25(1) (1999 Reissue) LAND REGISTRATION Form 3 [3076]) to meet the transferee's application to register the transfer. If the transferor's land is subject to any registered charge, that charge will require to be released by use of Land Registry Form DS3 (for which see vol 25(1) (1999 Reissue) LAND REGISTRATION Form 47 [3371]). If the charge is a noted charge, the consent of the chargee to the transfer should be obtained and lodged with the application to register the transfer.

    Reference should be made to Form 115 [4191] ante for detailed footnotes on matters common to many forms of transfer, for cross references to the commentary in vol 35 (1997 Reissue) SALE OF LAND, for the location of alternative transfer clauses in that and other volumes and for additional footnotes relating to the sale of part of a property.

    The forms of rights, exceptions, covenants, restrictions, agreements and declarations are illustrative only and should be altered or replaced as the circumstances may require.

    This Form is intended to enable restrictive covenants contained in this and other transfers of plots on the same estate, in identical terms, to be mutually enforceable as between individual plot holders notwithstanding that the original seller has disposed of all the land. As to the necessary elements required to constitute a building scheme see *Elliston v Reacher* [1908] 2 Ch 374. See also 16 Halsbury's Laws (4th Edn Reissue) EQUITY para 797 et seq.

2     The extent of the land intended to be subject to the building scheme must be identifiable on the Ordnance Map so that the extent affected can be noted on the seller's title.

3     As to agreements with the local authority for adoption of roads under the Highways Act 1980 s 38 as amended by the New Roads and Street Works Act 1991 s 22(1) and by the Local Government Act 1985 s 102, Sch 17 (20 Halsbury's Statutes (4th Edn) HIGHWAYS, STREETS AND BRIDGES) see Form 93 appendix 1 [3971] ante and see vol 18 (1993 Reissue) HIGHWAYS Paragraph 13 [16] and for examples of such agreements see Form 86 [3829] ante and vol 18 (1993 Reissue) HIGHWAYS Forms 19 [178] and 20 [181].

4     Where there are communal amenity areas such as landscaped areas, gardens, tennis courts and other recreational facilities these are likely to be transferred to and maintained by a management company, the members of which will be the residents of the estate. The communal areas should be defined in clause 1 of panel 13 of this Form and rights granted to use them. The buyer will enter into a deed of covenant with the management company, for a form of which see Form 121 [4269] post, under which the company will undertake to maintain the areas and the buyer to pay a service charge. A restriction should be entered on the Land Register to prevent a transfer of the plot without the transferee having entered into the deed of covenant.

**[4221]**

5     This important reservation permits the local authority to carry out any duties it may have under an open space agreement.

6     Use of these words ensures that the covenants are capable of being enforced by the successor in title to any part of the land which the covenant in fact benefits, even where there is no express assignment of the benefit. See vol 35 (1997 Reissue) SALE OF LAND Paragraph 517 [682] et seq.

7     As to entry of restrictive covenants on the register generally see vol 25(1) (1999 Reissue) LAND REGISTRATION Paragraph 133 [2263]. For alternative forms of covenanting clauses see vol 13(1) (1996 Reissue) COVENANTS AFFECTING LAND Forms 6(1)[1054]–6(4)[1057]. Such covenants may be enforceable by the owners of other parts of the estate who are not parties to the transfer even if a building scheme such as that contemplated by this Form is not created: *Re Ecclesiastical Commrs for England's Conveyance* [1936] Ch 430.

8     The inclusion of this clause may be considered prejudicial to the setting up of a valid building scheme, but it is contended that its inclusion in fact has little effect either for or against the existence of a building scheme: *Re Wembley Park Estate Co Ltd's Transfer, London Sephardi Trust v Baker* [1968] Ch 491, [1968] 1 All ER 457. As to the possibility of their being a restriction on the seller's powers to effect a 'radical' variation of the covenants see *Whitehouse v Hugh* [1906] 2 Ch 283, CA. If the Land Registry has approved an estate layout plan, the Registry must be informed immediately of the details of any alteration to the layout of the estate affecting the extent of plots yet to be disposed of, and a revised plan must be submitted for approval before further transfers are made, otherwise considerable difficulties can arise with later official searches and registration of transfers relating to revised plots.

9     For additional security, the deed creating the covenants should require the covenantor to extract a covenant from any chargee to the effect that the chargee will, in turn, require any transferee under a transfer in exercise of the power of sale to covenant direct with the covenantee, or his successors, that he will observe the original positive covenants. If this is not done, then the registration of a charge, and a subsequent exercise of the power of sale can have the effect of breaking the chain of covenants. The alternatives in square brackets cover this case.

10    This restriction will be required only if there is to be a management company responsible for maintenance of common parts of the estate. For a form of deed of covenant for use where common parts of an estate are to be looked after by a management company see Form 121 [4269] post.

11      In general such an application is unnecessary but, in the case of a building scheme the specific
        application may well be helpful to the Land Registry.
              A practitioner acting for a developer of a registered title who intends to dispose of properties under
        a building scheme must have the draft form of transfer approved by the Land Registry well in advance
        of the plot disposal, as to which see Form 93 note 36 [3984] ante.
              There are no provisions under the Land Registration Act 1925 (37 Halsbury's Statutes (4th Edn)
        REAL PROPERTY) or the rules made under it, that require the Registrar to enter notice of the existence
        of a building scheme on the register. In practice, however, provided the scheme has been properly
        instituted, entries may be made on the register referring to the building scheme and its extent: see
        further vol 25(1) (1999 Reissue) LAND REGISTRATION Paragraph 134 [2266] and Form 112 [3928].

                                                                                            **[4222]–[4250]**

# 119

## Transfer of part of registered freehold land being a block of undeveloped plots on a building estate[1]

*Use Land Registry Form TP1 (for which see Form 114 [4181] ante) and insert, in the panels specified below, the wording shown:*

### Panel 4  Property

The block of land comprising Plots numbers *(numbers)* [and garage plots numbers *(numbers)*] on the approved estate layout plan lodged at HM Land Registry known as *(description)* [including the walls hedges and fences marked on the Plan with a 'T' mark inside the red edging]

                                                                                            **[4251]**

### Panel 13  Additional Provisions

### 1      Definitions

In this transfer:

1.1      'the Estate' means the land [edged yellow] on the Plan now and formerly comprised in title number *(number)* known as *(name)* Estate at *(address)*

1.2      'the Estate Road' means the carriageways and footways [constructed *or* to be constructed] on the part of the Estate [tinted brown] on the Plan

1.3      'the Perpetuity Period' means the period of [21] [80] years commencing on the date of this transfer

1.4      'the Plan' means the plan annexed to this transfer [and if numbered plans are annexed any reference to a numbered plan is to the annexed plan so numbered]

1.5      'Services' means water soil effluent gas fuel oil electricity telephone telephonic signals television and other services

1.6      'Service Apparatus' means sewers drains channels pipes watercourses gutters wires cables ducts flues conduits and other conducting media and associated equipment

[1.7      words importing one gender shall be construed as importing any other gender]

[1.8      words importing the singular shall be construed as importing the plural and vice versa]

[1.9      words importing persons shall be construed as importing a corporate body and/ or a partnership and vice versa]

[1.10      where any party comprises more than one person the obligations and liabilities of that party under this transfer shall be joint and several obligations and liabilities of those persons]

[1.11     the panel and clause headings do not form part of this transfer and shall not be taken into account in its construction or interpretation]

[1.12     any reference to a clause is to one so numbered in this panel unless otherwise stated]

[1.13     any reference to a colour or letter is to one on the Plan]

**[4252]**

## 2        Rights granted for the benefit of the Property

The Property is transferred together with the following rights in common with the Transferor and all others who have or may in future have the like rights:

2.1       The right at all times hereafter for the purpose of access to and egress from the Property to pass and repass on foot and with or without vehicles over the carriageway and on foot only over the footways of the Estate Road and the site of them

2.2       The right so far as the same serve the Property of taking passage and running (as appropriate) of Services through the Service Apparatus which are now or may within the Perpetuity Period be laid in on over or under the Estate SUBJECT to the Transferee paying a fair proportion of the cost of cleaning maintaining repairing and whenever necessary renewing the same

2.3       The right at any time before *(specify)*[2] to enter upon the Estate Road and the site of it so far as is necessary to lay under it and at all times thereafter to use any Service Apparatus for the taking passage and running of Services from the respective mains under it to the Property and with the consent of the relevant service undertakers or suppliers to make connections to those mains and to excavate the surface of the Estate Road and site of it for such purposes SUBJECT to the Transferee causing as little damage and inconvenience as possible and reinstating the surface of the Estate Road to the standard prior to excavation and making good all damage caused forthwith and keeping the Estate Road open for traffic at all times

2.4       The right to enter after the giving of reasonable notice and at all reasonable times (or in the case of emergency at any time without notice) upon the adjoining land comprised in the Estate (other than any land covered or intended to be covered by a building) so far as may be necessary for the purposes of [constructing laying] inspecting cleaning maintaining repairing and renewing the [buildings] walls hedges fences and other boundary structures on the Property and the Service Apparatus causing as little damage as possible and making good to the reasonable satisfaction of the registered proprietors from time to time of the adjoining land any damage caused

**[4253]**

## 3        Rights reserved for the benefit of other land

There are reserved out of the Property for the benefit of each and every part of the remainder of the Estate the following rights:

3.1       The right (in common with all others entitled and so far as the same serve other parts of the Estate) to take pass and run (as appropriate) Services through the Service Apparatus now or at any time within the Perpetuity Period laid in on over or under the Property

3.2       The right at any time within the Perpetuity Period to enter upon the Property [other than land covered by a building] and to lay place or erect in on over or under it and thereafter at all times to use any Service Apparatus for the supply and passage of Services to or from any other part of the Estate and likewise to alter enlarge or duplicate Service Apparatus

3.3      · The right to enter after the giving of reasonable notice and at all reasonable times (or in the case of emergency at any time without notice) upon the Property so far as may be necessary for the purposes of constructing laying altering inspecting cleaning maintaining repairing renewing and demolishing the buildings walls hedges fences and other boundary structures upon the adjoining land comprised in the Estate and the Service Apparatus and for the purpose of complying with any covenant agreement or condition entered into by or binding on the Transferor with the Transferee or any other person causing as little damage as possible and making good to the reasonable satisfaction of the Transferee any damage caused

[4254]

**4        Restrictive covenants by the Transferee**

4.1      The Transferee covenants with the Transferor to observe and perform the Restrictions specified below and it is agreed and declared that:

4.1.1      the benefit of this covenant and the Restrictions is to be attached to and enure for each and every part of the Estate [that remains unsold by the Transferor or has been sold by the Transferor [or by any person claiming through the Transferor otherwise than by a transfer on sale] with the express benefit of this covenant and the Restrictions][3]

4.1.2      the burden of this covenant and the Restrictions is intended to bind and binds each and every part of the Property into whomsoever's hands it may come [but not so as to render the Transferee personally liable for any breach of this covenant or a Restriction arising after the Transferee has parted with all interest in the Property or the part of the Property on which such breach is committed]

4.1.3      a Restriction not to do any act or thing includes an obligation not to permit or suffer that act or thing to be done by another person

4.2      The Restrictions mentioned in clause 4.1 are the following:

4.2.1      The Transferee must not use the Property for any purpose except as a building site for the construction thereon of *(number)* private dwelling houses and *(number)* ancillary private garages and the laying out of gardens for each such dwelling house PROVIDED ALWAYS that after such construction shall be completed this restriction shall cease to have effect

4.2.2      The Transferee must not build or erect upon the Property any buildings or structures except *(number)* private dwelling houses and *(number)* ancillary private garages and boundary walls and fences as to the locations exterior design appearance finish and decoration strictly in accordance with the drawings [numbers *(specify)* and the design and construction notes thereon and the specification therefor respectively signed by or on behalf of the Transferor and Transferee for the purposes of identification] [already approved by the local planning authority on *(date)* under reference number *(number)* and the design and construction notes thereon] [to be approved by the Transferor in writing such approval not to be unreasonably withheld]

[4255]

4.2.3      The Transferee must not:

4.2.3.1      make any deviation from the above mentioned drawings [design and construction notes and specification] affecting the locations exterior design appearance finish and decoration of all buildings [boundary walls and fences] and works as described therein

4.2.3.2    after completion of the buildings boundary walls and fences make any alterations to the exterior of those buildings or of any other buildings later erected on the Property [or to the walls hedges and fences on the Property]

4.2.3.3    erect any additional buildings [walls hedges and fences] on the Property

except in all cases with the written approval of the Transferor whose fees and those of its professional advisors in connection with the consideration of any such application whether granted refused or withdrawn shall be paid by the Transferee

4.2.4    Except for the erection of the buildings the Transferee must not without the previous written consent of the Transferor use the Property or any building for the time being on it for the purpose of any profession trade business or manufacture of any description nor use any dwelling house on it except as a single private residence nor use any garage on it except as an ancillary private garage

4.2.5    The Transferee must not do or omit to be done any act or thing on or about the Property the doing or omission of which shall or may be or grow to be an annoyance nuisance damage or danger or disturbance to the Transferor or the owners or occupiers of any adjoining or neighbouring property

4.2.6    The Transferee must not plant any tree or shrub or erect any wall hedge or fence or other structure forward of the front line of the dwelling house and garage on the Property nor do anything to interfere with or destroy the open plan layout of the Estate

4.2.7    The Transferee must not park motor vehicles on or obstruct in any other manner any part of the Estate Road

4.2.8    The Transferee must not park boats caravans or trade vehicles (except trade vehicles in the course of construction work delivering goods to or supplying services to the Property) on the Property or on any other part of the Estate

4.2.9    The Transferee must not erect any building or structure over any part of any sewer or drain (which expression shall include manholes ventilating shafts pumps and the access areas thereto belonging) or on or over any land within 3 metres measured horizontally from the centre line of any sewer or drain without the written consent of *(name of sewerage undertaker)* nor obstruct access to them on foot and with any necessary vehicles plant or equipment

**[4256]**

## 5    Positive covenants by the Transferee

5.1    The Transferee covenants with the Transferor that the Transferee will observe and perform the covenants and conditions contained or referred to in the [property [proprietorship] and charges registers of title number *(number)* and/or *(insert details)*] [so far as they relate to the Property] and will indemnify and keep the Transferor and his successors in title fully and effectually indemnified against all actions proceedings damages costs claims and expenses which may be suffered or incurred by the Transferor or his successors in title in respect of any future breach or non-observance or non-performance of those covenants and conditions

5.2      The Transferee covenants with the Transferor as follows:

5.2.1      Unless express provision is elsewhere contained in this Transfer or the same are maintained at public expense the Transferee must pay a fair proportion of the expense of cleaning maintaining repairing and renewing the Service Apparatus and any land or thing used by the Transferee jointly with others

5.2.2      The Transferee must maintain and keep in good repair the walls fences and hedges hereby transferred

5.2.3      The Transferee must replace to the satisfaction of the local planning authority any tree or shrub originally planted by the Transferor on the Property which dies or is cut down

5.2.4      The Transferee must within one month of the date of this Transfer or before building operations excavation or site works are commenced on the Property whichever is the earlier erect and at all times thereafter maintain fences between the points marked *(specify)* and *(specify)* on the Plan constructed of *(insert specification)*

5.2.5      The Transferee must clean maintain repair and whenever necessary properly renew the parts of the foul and storm water sewers and drains serving the Estate which are under the Property unless or until they are adopted as public sewers maintained at public expense

**[4257]**

## 6    Agreements and Declarations

It is agreed and declared as follows:

6.1      The Transferee and his successors in title shall not be entitled to any right of access of light or air or other easement or right which would restrict or interfere with the free use of any land comprised in the Estate or any adjoining or neighbouring land of the Transferor for building or any other purpose

6.2      The Transferor shall be at liberty to modify waive or release all or any covenants stipulations or restrictions relating to the Property the Estate or any adjoining or neighbouring land now or in the future belonging to the Transferor whether imposed or entered into before at the same time as or after the date of this transfer AND to sell or dispose of any part of the Estate free from any restriction or stipulation AND the Transferor shall not in any way be bound by the plotting or general scheme of development of the Estate

6.3      Unless the contrary appears on the Plan by 'T' marks the walls hedges and fences separating the Property from the adjoining plots and the buildings on them are party walls and fences and the rights and liabilities in respect of them shall be in accordance with the Law of Property Act 1925 Section 38(1)

6.4      If there shall be any dispute between the owners of any part of the Estate who are entitled to use and liable to pay for cleaning maintaining repairing or renewing any part of the Estate including Service Apparatus or any one or more of such owners as to the necessity for cleaning repair maintenance or renewal of any such part or thing their nature execution or cost or as to the proportions in which the owners are liable to pay or contribute to such cost the same shall be referred to the decision of a chartered surveyor appointed by agreement between all the owners or in default of agreement within 14 days of one owner giving notice to all the others of his nomination appointed by or on behalf of the President of the [Royal Institution of Chartered Surveyors] on the application of any of the owners. The surveyor shall act as an expert and not as an arbitrator and his decision shall be final and binding on all such owners and the costs of his appointment and decision shall be as he may award

**[4258]**

1    As to stamp duty see Information Binder: Stamp Duties [1] (Conveyance or transfer). As to Land
     Registry fees see Information Binder: Property [1]: Fees in connection with property matters, Land
     Registry fees.
         Form TP1 (for which see Form 114 [4181] ante) is the Land Registry form of transfer of part of
     freehold or leasehold land prescribed by the Land Registration Rules 1925, SR&O 1925/1093 r 98,
     Sch 1 as inserted by SI 1999/128. This Form should be used whenever part only of any registered title
     is transferred, even if the transfer also includes the whole of one or more other registered titles.
         The transferor's land or charge certificate if not already on deposit must be placed on deposit
     (using Land Registry Form DP1 as prescribed by SR&O 1925/1093 Sch 1 as inserted by SI 1997/3037
     and substituted by SI 1999/128 (as to which, see vol 25(1) (1999 Reissue) LAND REGISTRATION
     Form 3 [3076]) to meet the transferee's application to register the transfer. If the transferor's land is
     subject to any registered charge, that charge will require to be released by use of Land Registry Form
     DS3 (for which see vol 25(1) (1999 Reissue) LAND REGISTRATION Form 47 [3371]). If the charge is
     a noted charge, the consent of the chargee to the transfer should be obtained and lodged with the
     application to register the transfer.
         Reference should be made to Form 115 [4191] ante for detailed footnotes on matters common
     to many forms of transfer, for cross references to the commentary in vol 35 (1997 Reissue) SALE OF
     LAND, for the location of alternative transfer clauses in that and other volumes and for additional
     footnotes relating to the sale of part of a property.
         The forms of rights, exceptions, covenants, restrictions, agreements and declarations are
     illustrative only and should be amended or replaced as the circumstances require. When the contract
     includes provision for the seller to provide infrastructure works (as in Form 97 [4026] ante) these
     obligations may be carried forward if desired into this Form. This Form, unlike Form 118 [4213] ante,
     does not expressly create a building scheme so that the restrictions are mutually enforceable as between
     individual plot owners. As to the necessary elements to constitute a building scheme see *Elliston v
     Reacher* [1908] 2 Ch 374. See also 16 Halsbury's Laws (4th Edn Reissue) EQUITY para 797 et seq.
     Because of the possibility that such covenants may be enforceable by other plot owners who are not
     parties to the transfer even if a building scheme is not expressly created (*Re Ecclesiastical Commrs for
     England's Conveyance* [1936] Ch 430) an express declaration negativing such a scheme may be inserted
     if desired, although practitioners may feel that clause 4.1.1 is sufficient indication if the words in brackets
     remain in this clause.
2    The date to be inserted should be well before the date for completion of the estate road as specified in
     the agreement under the Highways Act 1980 s 38 as amended by the New Roads and Street Works Act
     1991 s 22(1) and by the Local Government Act 1985 s 102, Sch 17 (20 Halsbury's Statutes (4th Edn)
     HIGHWAYS, STREETS AND BRIDGES), for a specimen of which see Form 86 [3829] ante.
3    The benefit of the restriction on plots sold is expressed not to pass to buyers of later plots sold, nor will
     the buyers of later plots sold acquire the benefit of the restrictions imposed on the transfer of plots sold
     earlier unless expressly granted. If the benefit is to pass all the words in square brackets should be deleted.

                                                                                              **[4259]**


# 120

## Transfer of part of registered freehold land being a plot on a building estate with a completed dwelling house built on it under a building licence, local authority transferring[1]

*Use Land Registry Form TP1 (for which see Form 114 [4181] ante) and insert, in the panels specified below, the wording shown:*


### Panel 4  Property

Plot number *(number)* [and garage plot number *(number)*] on the approved estate layout
plan lodged at HM Land Registry known as *(description)* [including:
[3.1    the walls hedges and fences marked on the Plan with a 'T' mark inside the red
        edging and the buildings erected on [it *or* them]]
[3.2    the Private Garage Accessway (if any) and]
3.3    the Private Footpath (if any)]

                                                                                              **[4260]**

## Panel 6   Transferor

*(the local authority registered proprietor)*

## Panel 10   Consideration

The Contractor has received from the Transferee for the Property the sum of *(in words and figures)* paid to him at the request and direction of the Transferor

## Panel 13   Additional Provisions

### 1      Definitions

In this transfer:

1.1      'the Adjoining Land' means any land of the Transferor adjoining or adjacent to or neighbouring the Estate now owned by the Transferor or any part of such land

1.2      'the Contractor' means *(builder)* [company number *(number)*] [of *(address)* or whose registered office is at *(address)*]

1.3      'the Estate' means the land [edged yellow] on the Plan being [all *or* part of] the land now and formerly comprised in title number *(number)*

1.4      'the Perpetuity Period' means the period of [21] [80] years commencing on the date of this transfer

1.5      'the Plan' means the plan annexed to this transfer [and if numbered plans are annexed any reference to a numbered plan is to the annexed plan so numbered]

1.6      'the Private Footpath' means the private footpath (if any) tinted [blue] on the Plan

1.7      'the Private Garage Accessway' means the private garage accessway and forecourt (if any) tinted [brown] on the Plan

1.8      'Services' means water soil effluent gas fuel oil electricity telephone telephonic signals television and other services

1.9      'Service Apparatus' means sewers drains channels pipes watercourses gutters wires cables ducts flues conduits and other conducting media and associated equipment

[1.10    words importing one gender shall be construed as importing any other gender]

[1.11    words importing the singular shall be construed as importing the plural and vice versa]

[1.12    words importing persons shall be construed as importing a corporate body and/or a partnership and vice versa]

[1.13    where any party comprises more than one person the obligations and liabilities of that party under this transfer shall be joint and several obligations and liabilities of those persons]

[1.14    the panel and clause headings do not form part of this transfer and shall not be taken into account in its construction or interpretation]

[1.15    any reference to a clause is to one so numbered in this panel unless otherwise stated]

[1.16    any reference to a colour or letter is to one on the Plan]

**[4261]**

### 2      Rights granted for the benefit of the Property

The Property is transferred together with the following rights in common with all other persons now or similarly entitled in the future:

2.1      A right of way at all times and for all usual and reasonable purposes connected with the enjoyment of the Property over the roads and footpaths on the Estate and the Adjoining Land [which are intended to become highways maintainable at the public expense]

2.2    The right of passage of water soil gas electricity and telephone communications through the Service Apparatus serving the Property which are now or may during the Perpetuity Period be situated on in over or under the Estate and the Adjoining Land

2.3    The right for the eaves gutters and foundations of any building erected on the Property to protrude into or over any other part of the Estate

[2.4    Subject to the Transferee's compliance with the appropriate provisions as to maintenance and repair and payments by way of contribution to maintenance and repair a right of way at all times for all usual and reasonable purposes connected with the enjoyment of the Property over the Private Garage Accessway and the Private Footpath]²

2.5    The right to enter upon the Estate or the Adjoining Land on giving reasonable notice to the occupier of the land entered (or in case of emergency without notice) for the purpose of inspecting maintaining repairing and renewing:

2.5.1    anything necessary for the proper enjoyment of the easements granted by this transfer

2.5.2    any building including boundary walls and fences forming part of the Property

the Transferee doing as little damage as possible to the land entered and making good without undue delay to the reasonable satisfaction of the owner and the occupier of the land entered any damage caused or occasioned by or during the exercise of such rights

[4262]

### 3    Rights reserved for the benefit of other land

There are reserved out of the Property for the benefit of the whole and every part of the Estate and the Adjoining Land to the Transferor the Contractor the owners and occupiers for the time being of the Estate and the Adjoining Land and all other persons now or in the future similarly entitled the following rights and so far as the rights have already been created at the date of this transfer the Property is transferred subject to them:

3.1    The right of passage of water soil gas electricity and telephone communications from and to the Estate and the Adjoining Land through the Service Apparatus which are now or may during the Perpetuity Period be situated on in over or under the Property

3.2    The right for the eaves gutters and foundations of any building including boundary walls and fences erected or to be erected on the Estate or the Adjoining Land to protrude into or over the Property

[3.3    A right of way for the Transferor and the owners and occupiers for the time being of other properties served by them for all usual and reasonable purposes connected with the enjoyment of properties served by them over and along the Private Garage Accessway and Private Footpath (if any) included in the Property subject always to the payment of the appropriate contributions in respect of the maintenance and repair of the Private Garage Accessway and Private Footpath]³

3.4    The right to enter upon the Property for the purpose of inspecting maintaining repairing or renewing:

3.4.1    anything necessary for the proper enjoyment of the rights reserved by this transfer

3.4.2    any buildings including boundary walls and fences forming part of the Estate or the Adjoining Land on giving reasonable notice to the Transferee (or in cases of emergency without notice) and doing as little damage as possible to the Property and making good without undue delay to the reasonable satisfaction of the Transferee any damage caused or occasioned by or during the exercise of such rights

[4263]

**4       Restrictive covenants by the Transferee**

4.1      The Transferee covenants with the Transferor and all other persons claiming under it as transferee of any part of the Estate to observe and perform the Restrictions specified below and it is agreed and declared that:

4.1.1      the benefit of this covenant and the Restrictions is to be attached to and enure for each and every part of the Estate[4]

4.1.2      the burden of this covenant and the Restrictions is intended to bind and binds each and every part of the Property into whomsoever's hands it may come [but not so as to render the Transferee personally liable for any breach of this covenant or a Restriction arising after the Transferee has parted with all interest in the Property or the part of the Property on which such breach is committed]

4.1.3      a Restriction not to do any act or thing includes an obligation not to permit or suffer that act or thing to be done by another person

4.2      The Restrictions mentioned in clause 4.1 are the following[5]:

4.2.1      Not to carry on any trade business or manufacture upon or on the Property nor to use the Property for any purpose other than as a private dwelling house garage and parking space

4.2.2      Not at any time to do or cause to be done in or upon the Property anything which may be or become a nuisance annoyance danger or detriment to the Estate or any part of the Estate or to the Adjoining Land or to the owners or occupiers of the Estate or the Adjoining Land

4.2.3      Not to keep on the Property poultry pigs pigeons or noisy offensive or dangerous birds or animals

4.2.4      Not to erect or place or allow to remain upon the Property any hut shed caravan house on wheels or other chattel intended or adapted for use as a dwelling house or sleeping apartment or boat with or without trailer unless screened from view from the Estate roads and any other roads nearby and from the other dwellings forming part of the Estate and not to place any advertisement or hoarding on the Property (save for a 'For Sale' or 'To Let' notice of reasonable size) nor to use any boundary wall or fence or part of a building on the Property for the display of advertisements (save as mentioned above)

[4264]

4.2.5      Not to park or place or allow to remain upon the Property any lorry or trailer or similar vehicle other than a motor car or light motor van which could reasonably be parked inside the garage forming part of the Property or in cases where there is no such garage inside a garage of a size usual for the type of dwelling erected on the Property

4.2.6      Not to erect on the external parts of any building on the Property a reception or transmission aerial for radio or television or otherwise

4.2.7      Not to erect on any part of the Property for a period of 10 years from the date of this transfer any building or structure of any kind and not to carry out additions or structural alterations to the buildings now

on the Property without the Transferor's prior written approval [any
application for such approval to be accompanied by a fee to the
Transferor of £... plus VAT [(which shall not be returnable whether
or not the application is ultimately granted)]]

4.2.8     Not to obstruct the accessways footpaths and roads including the
          Private Garage Accessway and the Private Footpath [over which
          rights of way are granted by this transfer *or* which form part of the
          Property]

4.2.9     Not to fell any trees shrubs groups of trees shrubs or hedges planted
          on the Property at the date of this transfer nor remove or alter the
          position or height of any boundary fences or walls or screen walls or
          fences erected on the Property without the prior written approval of
          the Transferor or the planning authority

4.2.10    Not to erect any new building or structure of any kind over or within
          3 feet of any private drain or sewer in over or under the Property nor
          to cover or otherwise obstruct any access or inspection chamber for
          such drain or sewer or the means of access to it

[4.2.11   Not to exercise the rights referred to in clause 2.4 during such time
          as any proper demand for reimbursement of the cost of maintaining
          repairing and renewing the whole of the Private Garage Accessway
          and the Private Footpath remains unsatisfied and has remained
          unsatisfied for more than 21 days]

                                                                         [4265]

## 5        Positive covenants by the Transferee

5.1       The Transferee covenants with the Transferor that the Transferee will observe and
          perform the covenants and conditions contained or referred to in the [property
          [proprietorship] and charges registers of title number *(number) and/or (insert
          details)*] [so far as they relate to the Property] and will indemnify and keep the
          Transferor and its successors in title fully and effectually indemnified against all
          actions proceedings damages costs claims and expenses which may be suffered or
          incurred by the Transferor or its successors in title in respect of any future breach
          or non-observance or non-performance of those covenants and conditions

5.2       The Transferee covenants with the Transferor as follows:

          5.2.1    To pay a fair proportion of the expense of repairing maintaining and
                   cleansing all party walls Service Apparatus Private Garage Accessways
                   Private Footpaths (except any roads footpaths or Service Apparatus
                   intended to become maintained at the public expense or by the
                   appropriate service undertaker) and other facilities used or to be used
                   in common by the occupiers of the Property and the occupiers of
                   other plots forming part of the Estate

          5.2.2    From the date of this transfer forever to maintain and renew the fence
                   on the side(s) of the Property marked 'T' within the red edging on
                   the Plan

          5.2.3    To keep the verge (if any) shown coloured [pink] on the Plan in
                   good order and in a clean and tidy condition with the grass properly
                   cut [until such time as the same may be adopted by the appropriate
                   local authority]

          5.2.4    To keep the garden or garden land forming part of the Property
                   properly planted and in a good state of cultivation and order and in
                   a clean condition and free from weeds

[5.2.5    To maintain repair and where necessary renew the surface of those parts of any Private Garage Accessway and any parking space included in the Property]

[4266]

## 6    Agreements and Declarations

It is agreed and declared as follows:

6.1      the Transferee shall not by virtue of this transfer:

6.1.1      acquire any right or easement of light or air or otherwise except as set out in clause 2 which would restrict or in any way interfere with the free use and enjoyment of the Estate or the Adjoining Land for building or for other purposes

6.1.2      be entitled to the benefit (if any) of restrictions which the Transferor might have imposed or may in future impose on any owner or lessee of the Adjoining Land

6.1.3      acquire any right title or interest in the soil of any road or footpath intended to become publicly maintainable and not included in the Property

6.2      the walls of the dwelling and/or garage constructed on the Property separating it from any other dwelling and/or garage on the Estate shall be deemed to be party walls and shall be repaired and maintained as such

6.3      it is the intention of the Transferor and the Transferee and the Transferee buys upon the express understanding that each transferee of a plot on the Estate is to have the benefit of the restrictions conditions and stipulations binding on all other plots forming part of the Estate regardless of the date or dates of the transfers to him and them

6.4      the Transferor shall have power while any of the plots within the Estate are unsold:

6.4.1      to alter the layout of the Estate and vary the plots on the unsold parts of the Estate and

6.4.2      to vary or waive any of the restrictions conditions and stipulations affecting any plot on the Estate but not so far as to effect any radical alterations to the general building scheme effected by this and transfers of other parts of the Estate[6]

6.5      nothing contained in this transfer shall subject any part of the Adjoining Land to any scheme of development or operate to impose any control on development of it by the Transferor

## 7    Contractor's covenant

The Contractor covenants with the Transferee and his successors in title to construct the roads footpaths street lighting and sewers of the Estate intended to be publicly maintained at his expense and to the satisfaction of the highway authority or other proper authority and to indemnify the Transferee against all charges which may be levied in respect of the cost of the construction and to maintain such roads footpaths street lighting and sewers until such time as they are taken over and become maintainable at the public expense[7]

## 8    Statement

The Transferor is acting pursuant to the [Local Government Act 1972 Section 123 *or* Town and Country Planning Act 1990 Section 233]

[4267]

1     As to stamp duty see Information Binder: Stamp Duties [1] (Conveyance or transfer). As to Land
      Registry fees see Information Binder: Property [1]: Fees in connection with property matters, Land
      Registry fees.
            Form TP1 is the Land Registry form of transfer of part of freehold or leasehold land prescribed
      by the Land Registration Rules 1925, SR&O 1925/1093 r 98, Sch 1 as inserted by SI 1999/128. This
      Form should be used whenever part only of any registered title is transferred, even if the transfer also
      includes the whole of one or more other registered titles.
            The transferor's land or charge certificate must be placed on deposit (using Land Registry Form
      DP1 as prescribed by SR&O 1925/1093 Sch 1 as inserted by SI 1997/3037 and substituted by SI 1999/
      128 (as to which, see vol 25(1) (1999 Reissue) LAND REGISTRATION Form 3 [3076]) to meet the
      transferee's application to register the transfer. If the transferor's land is subject to any registered charge,
      that charge will require to be released by use of Land Registry Form DS3 (for which see vol 25(1)
      (1999 Reissue) LAND REGISTRATION Form 47 [3371]). If the charge is a noted charge, the consent
      of the chargee to the transfer should be obtained and lodged with the application to register the
      transfer.
            Reference should be made to Form 115 [4191] ante for detailed footnotes on matters common
      to many forms of transfer, for cross references to the commentary in vol 35 (1997 Reissue) SALE OF
      LAND, for the location of alternative transfer clauses in that and other volumes and for additional
      footnotes relating to the sale of part of a property.
            The extent of the property transferred and the forms of rights, exceptions, covenants, restrictions
      and agreements and declarations are illustrative only and should be altered or replaced as the
      circumstances may require.
            As to development of estates under a building licence generally see Form 93 appendix 3 [3979]
      ante. As to restrictions on the power of a local authority to dispose of land see vol 35 (1997 Reissue)
      SALE OF LAND Paragraph 256 [336].

2     Omit this clause if the private garage accessway and the private footpath are transferred by this transfer
      and insert clause 3.3 instead.

3     Only insert this clause if the private accessway and the private footpath are transferred by this transfer.

4     Use of these words ensures that the covenants are capable of being enforced by the successor in title to
      any part of the land which the covenant in fact benefits, even where there is no express assignment of
      the benefit. See vol 35 (1997 Reissue) SALE OF LAND Paragraph 517 [682] et seq.

5     As to entry of restrictive covenants on the register generally see vol 25(1) (1999 Reissue) LAND
      REGISTRATION Paragraph 133 [2263]. For alternative forms of covenanting clauses see vol 13(1) (1996
      Reissue) COVENANTS AFFECTING LAND Forms 6(1) [1054]–6(4) [1057]. Such covenants may be
      enforceable by the owners of other parts of the estate who are not parties to the transfer even if a
      building scheme such as that contemplated by this Form is not created: *Re Ecclesiastical Commrs for
      England's Conveyance* [1936] Ch 430.

6     The inclusion of this clause may be considered prejudicial to the setting up of a valid building
      scheme, but it is contended that its inclusion in fact has little effect either for or against the existence
      of a building scheme: *Re Wembley Park Estate Co Ltd's Transfer, London Sephardi Trust v Baker* [1968]
      Ch 491, [1968] 1 All ER 457. As to the possibility of there being a restriction on the seller's powers
      to effect a 'radical' variation of the covenants see *Whitehouse v Hugh* [1906] 2 Ch 283, CA. If the
      Land Registry has approved an estate layout plan, the Registry must be informed immediately of the
      details of any alteration to the layout of the estate affecting the extent of plots yet to be disposed of,
      and a revised plan must be submitted for approval before further transfers are made, otherwise
      considerable difficulties can arise with later official searches and registration of transfers relating to
      revised plots.

7     As to agreements for adoption of roads under the Highways Act 1980 s 38 as amended by the New
      Roads and Street Works Act 1991 s 22(1) and by the Local Government Act 1985 s 102, Sch 17
      (20 Halsbury's Statutes (4th Edn) HIGHWAYS, STREETS AND BRIDGES) generally see Form 93
      appendix 1 [3971] ante.

                                                                                           **[4268]**

# (6): MANAGEMENT DOCUMENTS

## 121

### Deed of covenant by a buyer with a management company responsible for maintenance of common parts of an estate[1]

THIS DEED OF COVENANT is made the ...... day of .........

BETWEEN:

(1)      *(management company)* company number *(number)* whose registered office is at *(address)* ('the Company') and

(2)      *(buyer)* of *(address)* ('the Transferee')

NOW IT IS AGREED as follows:

## 1      Definitions

In this deed:

1.1      'the Communal Land' means the land shown coloured [blue] on the Plan

1.2      'the Plan' means the plan annexed to the Transfer

1.3      'the Property' means *(description of the property)*

1.4      'the Scheduled Services' means the services set out in the schedule to this deed

1.5      'the Transfer' means a transfer [bearing the same date as this deed *or* dated *(date)*] and made between *(developer)* and [the Transferee *or* *(initial purchaser)*][2]

1.6      'the Transferee' includes where the context so admits the successors in title of the Transferee and where the Transferee is more than one person all covenants and agreements on the part of the Transferee contained in this deed shall be deemed to have been made jointly and severally by all such persons constituting the Transferee

**[4269]**

## 2      Recitals

2.1      The Transferee has agreed to purchase the Property together with the easements and other rights in respect of the Communal Land set out in clause 2 of panel 13 to the Transfer

2.2      [The Transferee has agreed to enter into this deed in the manner appearing below *or* The Transfer provides that the Transferee and his successors in title shall enter into a deed of covenant in the manner set out in the Transfer and the parties to this deed have agreed to enter into this deed accordingly]

## 3      Registration as a member of the Company

The Transferee applies to be registered as a member of the Company and the Company undertakes to register the Transferee as a member of the Company[3]

## 4      Company's covenants

The Company covenants with the Transferee that it will:

4.1      provide procure and perform in relation to the Communal Land the Scheduled Services

4.2      enter into a deed of covenant in the terms of this deed with any intended
         transferee of the Property in the terms of this deed and give any consent
         required to HM Land Registry to allow registration of any proposed dealing
         with the Property[4] provided that the Transferee has observed and performed the
         covenants on his part contained in this deed and fulfilled the obligations on his
         part contained in the articles of association of the Company

                                                                                  **[4270]**

5        **Transferee's covenants**

The Transferee covenants with the Company that he will:

5.1      pay to the Company a *(fraction)*[5] part of the costs and expenses incurred by the
         Company in providing securing and performing the Scheduled Services
         including the costs of and incidental to the administration and conduct of the
         Company's affairs

5.2      in any contract for the sale of the Property include a condition that the
         intending buyer shall upon completion of the contract apply to become
         registered as a member of the Company

5.3      include in any contract for the sale of the Property a condition precedent to
         performance of the contract that the intending buyer shall enter into a deed of
         covenant with the Company in the terms of this deed and that the intending
         buyer shall bear all costs of and incidental to the preparation and execution of
         the deed including any stamp duty payable on it

IN WITNESS etc

SCHEDULE[6]
The Scheduled Services

1        The provision and maintenance of all boundary walls fences roads footpaths
         drives sewers and other services passing in under upon and over the Communal
         Land

2        The mowing and upkeep of all grassed areas and the upkeep of garden areas
         when considered expedient

3        The provision of lighting including the cost of replacement of equipment and
         supply of electricity where the same is not the responsibility of any local
         authority or other authority

4        The provision of all such other services and matters which the Company may
         from time to time consider necessary

5        The employment of all such agents managers contractors or other persons as
         shall in the opinion of the Company be necessary

6        The payment of all rates insurance premiums and other charges of a like nature
         which may be charged upon or incurred in relation to the Communal Land

                                              *(signatures (or common seals) of the parties)*[7]
                                                      [*(signatures of witnesses)*]
                                                                                  **[4271]**

1        No stamp duty. See Information Binder: Stamp Duties [1] (Covenant).
              This Form is intended for use where a transfer provides for maintenance of external common areas
         by establishing a management company. The members of the management company, who are assumed
         to be the residents of the area concerned, sub-contract to a commercial company the maintenance
         duties as set out in the schedule (see eg paragraph 5 of the schedule to this Form). Usually, the
         subscribers of the management company are officers of the development company who resign when

the owners of all the plots have become members of the company. The freehold of the communal areas is transferred to the management company whilst the company is still under the control of the subscribers. It is important to remind the parties that the management company must not be allowed to become moribund and dissolved by being struck off the register of companies. This can cause considerable difficulties in the future if allowed to happen.

    Every incoming buyer must execute a deed in this form or a suitable similar form. As to building schemes generally see 16 Halsbury's Laws (4th Edn Reissue) EQUITY para 797 et seq.

2    The first alternative in each set of square brackets should be used when the deed of covenant is entered into by the initial buyer of the plot and the second alternative when the covenants are entered into by a subsequent buyer.

3    The management company envisaged here is intended to be one limited by guarantee rather than shares. If a company limited by shares is required, this provision must be supplemented by a transfer of the shares signed by the existing shareholder.

4    For the wording of the restriction entered on the register see Form 118 panel 13 clause 8.1 [4220] ante.

5    The proportion of the costs to be borne may relate directly to the number of dwelling houses concerned, but may also be affected by other factors. The figures are usually decided by the developer. The percentages attributable to all the properties when fully developed must, of course, total 100% so that all costs are fully covered. Where a development is phased and there is doubt as to whether all phases will be completed, it is better to arrange for each phase to be covered by a separate deed of covenant. If changes in the estate layout during the course of a development result in a change in the overall number of units, the proportions to be borne by units as yet unsold must be adjusted so that the aggregate payments total 100%.

6    The schedule contains examples of services frequently included in such deeds. It should be adapted to suit particular circumstances.

7    As to the statutory requirements for the valid execution of deeds see vol 12 (1994 Reissue) DEEDS, AGREEMENTS AND DECLARATIONS.

**[4272]**

# 122

## Consent to dealing by a management company in whose favour there is a restriction on the register[1]

### HM LAND REGISTRY LAND REGISTRATION ACTS 1925 to 1986

| | |
|---|---|
| Administrative Area | *(insert details)* |
| Title Number | *(title number)* |
| Property | *(describe property)* |
| DATE | *(date)* |

*(Management company)* [company number *(number)*] whose registered office is at *(address)* consents to the registration of a transfer dated *(date)* made between *(parties)* in respect of *(description of property transferred)* being [part of] the land comprised in the title above referred to provided that the restriction remains entered on the register of the title above referred to[2]

Dated:

        *(signatures on behalf of (or common seal) of the management company)*[3]

1    For the wording of a restriction preventing dealings without the consent of a management company see Form 118 panel 13 clause 8.1 [4220] ante.

2    This proviso makes it clear to the Land Registry that the restriction is not of a kind which may be cancelled following a transfer of the land.

3    For forms of execution see vol 37 (1998 Reissue) SALE OF LAND Form 4 [59]. As to the statutory requirements for the valid execution of deeds see vol 12 (1994 Reissue) DEEDS, AGREEMENTS AND DECLARATIONS.

**[4273]**

# 123

**Agreement between owners entitled to use common facilities and services as to proportions in which they are liable for maintenance[1]**

THIS AGREEMENT is made the ... day of ......BETWEEN the owners of properties on the *(name and address of building estate)* ('the Estate') whose names and signatures are set out in the schedule below

WHEREBY IT IS AGREED as follows:

1 In this Agreement words defined in transfers of plots on the Estate have the same meaning in this Agreement

2 This Agreement is entered into to define the proportions in which the owners of properties on the Estate are liable to bear the cost of inspecting cleaning maintaining repairing and renewing the Service Apparatus and land or things used by the owners of plots on the Estate jointly with other owners in accordance with clause *(insert number of clause requiring payment of a fair proportion of the expenses: eg Form 117 panel 13 clause 5.2.1 [4210] ante)* of the plot transfers

3 Each signatory to this Agreement is mutually bound to every other present or future signatory from the date upon which he signs this Agreement

4 Each signatory shall cease to be liable to contribute to any expenses incurred after the date upon which the transferee from him of his property signs this Agreement

[4274]

5 The signatories to this Agreement agree that the proportions are as set out below[2]

5.1 The proportions applicable to the [Entrance Drive] are as follows: *(insert each plot number and its proportion)*

5.2 The proportions applicable to the [Estate Road] are as follows: *(insert each plot number and its proportion)*

5.3 The proportions applicable to the [Private Road] are as follows: *(insert each plot number and its proportion)*

5.4 The proportions applicable to the [Car Park] are as follows: *(insert each plot number and its proportion)*

5.5 The proportions applicable to the [Footpath] are as follows: *(insert each plot number and its proportion)*

5.6 The proportions applicable to the private foul drainage system by reference to the inspection chamber numbers ('Numbers') shown on the annexed plan are as follows:

5.6.1 The septic tank and pumping system: Plots 1–10 inclusive in equal shares

5.6.2 Between Numbers 1 and 2: Plots 1–10 inclusive in equal shares

5.6.3 Between Numbers 2 and 3: Plots *(insert plot numbers and proportions applicable to each plot)*

5.6.4 Between Numbers 3 and 4: Plots *(insert plot numbers and proportions applicable to each plot)*

Where the proportions change at any Number the cost shall be divided as to one half in the proportions applicable to the incoming drain and as to one half in the proportions applicable to the outgoing drain

6    The proportions have been fixed on the assumption that [every dwelling house on each plot is occupied as a single private residence *or* Plots 1–8 inclusive are dwelling houses each occupied as a single private residence Plot 9 is a block of 5 two-bedroom flats and Plot 10 a retirement home with 7 patients' rooms *or (as the case may be)*]

7    If the circumstances of occupation and use of the plots or any of them change from the assumptions set out in clause 6 above any signatory to this Agreement may at any time afterwards give notice in writing to all the other signatories terminating this Agreement and on service of such notice the provisions of the plot transfers shall apply as to the proportions payable after termination and the resolution of any disputes[3]

8    This Agreement may be signed in any number of counterparts or duplicates each of which shall be an original but such counterparts or duplicates shall together constitute one and the same agreement[4]

## THE SCHEDULE

| **Plot number** | **Owner** | **Owner' signature** | **Date of signature** |
|---|---|---|---|

*(insert details in the order in which plots are sold)*

**[4275]**

1    This agreement is for use where the repairing liability in respect of shared service apparatus and facilities is shared and where the plot transfers provide that the transferees are to pay a fair proportion of the expenses according to user (as in Form 117 panel 13 clause 5.2.1 [4210] ante). This Form must be adapted to the particular circumstances of the development and is only applicable to those service apparatus and facilities which are not to be adopted and publicly maintained. This Form is only likely to be satisfactory with a small number of plots; larger developments are likely to be better served by vesting the shared service apparatus and facilities in an estate management company with the transfer reserving an estate rentcharge; for a form of which see vol 37 (1998 Reissue) SALE OF LAND Form 142 [1776].

2    The matters to be the subject of agreement will depend on the particular development. Those set out in the following clauses are illustrative only and should be omitted, altered or added to as the circumstances require.

3    The dispute arrangements are those set out in the plot transfers (eg Form 117 panel 13 clause 6.4 [4211] ante). This agreement only deals with the proportions in which plot owners are to contribute; any dispute as to the necessity for work or its nature, execution or cost, remains governed by the transfer dispute clause.

4    Ideally all plot owners should all sign each agreement form so that each plot owner holds an original or duplicate signed by all plot owners. That may prove impractical if there are more than a very few plots in which case arrangements could be made for a solicitor, or the plot owner who acts as the manager in dealing with the repairs, to hold all the signed originals and to supply certified true copies to each plot owner.

**[4276]–[4290]**

# (7):  COUNTRY HOUSE FREEHOLD DIVISION SCHEME

## 124

**Agreement for sale on a freehold basis of a dwelling house comprising a part of a country mansion house, with garages and/or other land, incorporating a contract for the seller to carry out works of conversion[1]**

THIS AGREEMENT is made the ...... day of ......... BETWEEN:
(1)      *(seller)* [company number *(number)*] [of *(address) or* whose registered office is at *(address)*] ('the Seller') and
(2)      *(buyer)* of *(address)* ('the Buyer')

[4291]

**1        Definitions and interpretation**

In this Agreement:
1.1      'the Architect' means *(insert name and address of person or firm)*
1.2      'the Buyer's Solicitors' means *(insert name and address of person or firm)*
1.3      'the Certificate' means the Certificate of Practical Completion referred to in clause 11.4
1.4      'the Completion Date' means [the ...... day of ...... *or* 10 working days after the date on which the Buyer has been given notice of the issue of the Certificate and a copy of the Certificate]
1.5      'the Contract Price' means the Purchase Price plus the cost of any extras ordered by the Buyer
1.6      'the Contract Rate' means *(insert interest rate or method of calculating the interest rate by reference eg to the base lending rate of a named bank)*
1.7      'the Dwelling House' means the dwelling house [and garages] erected or in the course of conversion on the Land and described in the schedule and in the draft transfer annexed to this Agreement
1.8      'the General Conditions' means [the Standard Conditions of Sale (3rd Edn) *or (specify)*]
1.9      'the Land' means the plot[s] of land described in the schedule and in the draft transfer annexed to this Agreement
1.10     'the Management Company' means *(name)* company number *(number)* whose registered office is at *(address)*
[1.11    'the Plan' means the plan annexed to this Agreement [and if numbered plans are annexed any reference to a numbered plan is to the annexed plan so numbered]]
1.12     'the Property' means the Land and the Dwelling House
1.13     'the Purchase Price' means the sum of £......
1.14     'the Seller's Solicitors' means *(insert name and address of person or firm)*
1.15     'the Works' means the works of construction alteration and conversion to create the Dwelling House as more fully described in the Architect's drawings numbers *(numbers)* and specification annexed to this Agreement
1.16     where the context so admits the expression[s] 'the Seller' [and 'the Buyer'] include[s] the personal representatives of the Seller and the Buyer [and 'the Buyer' shall include any successors in title of the Buyer]

1.17    words importing one gender shall be construed as importing any other gender

1.18    words importing the singular shall be construed as importing the plural and vice versa

1.19    words importing persons shall be construed as importing a corporate body and/or a partnership and vice versa

1.20    where any party comprises more than one person the obligations and liabilities of that party under this Agreement shall be joint and several obligations and liabilities of those persons

1.21    the clause headings do not form part of this Agreement and shall not be taken into account in its construction or interpretation

1.22    any reference to a clause or a paragraph or a schedule is to one in this Agreement so numbered

1.23    any reference to a colour or letter is to one on the Plan

1.24    words defined in the annexed draft transfer have the same meaning when used in this Agreement

**[4292]**

## 2    Agreement for sale

The Seller shall sell and the Buyer shall buy the Property at the Purchase Price

## 3    Deposit

The Buyer shall on or before the date of this Agreement pay a deposit of [10%] of the Purchase Price to the Seller's Solicitors as [stakeholders *or* agents for the Seller] [by means of cash or telegraphic or other direct transfer banker's draft or a building society cheque or a cheque drawn on a solicitor's client account]

## 4    Completion

4.1    Completion of the sale and purchase and payment of the balance of the Purchase Price shall take place on the Completion Date [at the offices of the Seller's Solicitors or where they may reasonably direct]

4.2    If the Buyer has not notified the Seller in writing within [5] working days of the receipt by him of the Certificate of any specific defects apparent in the Dwelling House the Buyer shall be deemed to have accepted the Certificate as valid and be bound to complete PROVIDED that this shall not prejudice the right of the Buyer to require after completion the remedying of any defects in accordance with clause 11 of this Agreement

4.3    The Buyer shall not be entitled to delay completion by reason of minor defects or outstanding works of a minor nature which can reasonably be dealt with after completion (including in particular any landscaping erection of fences and final surfacing of driveways) and the Seller undertakes to complete such outstanding works (if any) as soon as practicable after completion

## 5    Title guarantee

The Seller sells with [full *or* limited] title guarantee

## 6    Possession

The Property is sold with vacant possession on completion

## 7    Title

Title to the Property is registered at HM Land Registry with [absolute] title under title number *(number)* and title shall be deduced in accordance with the Land Registration Act

1925 Section 110 [save that copies of the entries on the register the filed plan and any documents referred to shall be office copies and Land Registry Form 102 may be supplied in place of the filed plan²] [and the Buyer or the Buyer's Solicitors having been supplied with such copies prior to the date of this Agreement the Buyer shall be deemed to purchase with full knowledge of the title in all respects and shall not raise any requisitions or make any objection in relation to the title]

**[4293]**

## 8　　　Transfer and incumbrances

8.1　　　The transfer to the Buyer ('the Transfer') shall be in the form of the annexed draft transfer

8.2　　　The Property is sold subject to and (where appropriate) with the benefit of the rights exceptions reservations covenants restrictions and other matters (if any) referred to in the annexed draft transfer and the property [proprietorship] and charges register of title number *(number)* [other than the charges referred to in the entries numbered *(numbers)* of the charges register of that title *or* other than charges to secure money]

8.3　　　The Buyer (the Buyer's Solicitors having been supplied with copies of the documents referred to in clause 8.2 prior to the date of this Agreement) shall be deemed to purchase with full notice and knowledge of them and shall not raise any requisition or make any objection in relation to them

8.4　　　The transfer shall be engrossed [in duplicate] by the Seller's Solicitors and [the *or* both] engrossment[s] shall be executed by the Buyer before the Completion Date

[8.5　　　Immediately after completion the Buyer shall at his own expense procure the proper stamping of the duplicate transfer as a duplicate (including but not limited to the affixing of a particulars delivered stamp) and shall immediately after such stamping deliver the duly stamped duplicate to the Seller's Solicitors]

8.6　　　On completion the Buyer shall in addition to the Purchase Price pay to the Seller's Solicitors the sum of £...... and VAT for the Seller's Solicitors' costs of engrossment and the supply of plans and draft documents

**[4294]**

## 9　　　Matters affecting the Property

The Property is sold subject to the following matters:

9.1　　　all local land charges whether registered or not before the date of this Agreement and all matters capable of registration as local land charges whether or not actually so registered

9.2　　　all notices served and orders demands proposals or requirements made by any local public or other competent authority whether before or after the date of this Agreement

9.3　　　all actual or proposed charges notices orders restrictions agreements conditions contraventions or other matters arising under the enactments relating to town and country planning and environmental law

9.4　　　all easements quasi-easements rights exceptions or other similar matters whether or not apparent on inspection or disclosed in any of the documents referred to in this Agreement

9.5　　　the easements and rights already granted or contracted to be granted to buyers of other parts of the Estate

## 10    Estate Plan

The Seller's plan of the division and use of the mansion its outbuildings and grounds represents the intention of the Seller as to the development of the Estate of which the Land forms part but neither any slight variation in the actual dimensions of the Land from those plans nor any variation in the development shall give rise to any claim by the Buyer for compensation or otherwise[3]

**[4295]**

## 11    Seller to construct

11.1    The Seller shall on or before *(date)*[4] (but without any liability whatsoever to the Seller should that completion date not be met) carry out and complete the Works in a thorough and workmanlike manner and with materials of suitable quality in accordance with the appropriate planning permissions listed building consents the building regulations[5] and the annexed drawings and specification and to the satisfaction of the Architect

11.2    The Buyer acknowledges that he has had the opportunity to inspect the documents mentioned in clause 11.1 (whether he has inspected the same or not) and he shall be deemed to have full knowledge of them

11.3    The Seller shall have the right to substitute materials as near as possible of the same quality and value in lieu of those contained or referred to in the drawings and specification if in its absolute discretion it deems it expedient so to do and to make reasonable modifications to the drawings and specification in such manner as may be necessary as a result of the use of such substituted materials or in accordance with the requirements of any competent authority but such substitution and modification shall not reduce the value of the Dwelling House nor substantially alter its accommodation

11.4    The Architect shall give to the Buyer not less than [10] working days notice of his intention to issue a certificate of practical completion ('the Certificate'). Any architect or surveyor acting for the Buyer may make representations in writing to the Architect on matters to be considered by him before he issues the Certificate and the Architect shall have due regard to any such representations and this process may be repeated as often as necessary

11.5    When the Works have been completed to the satisfaction of the Architect he shall issue the Certificate

11.6    The Certificate may be issued notwithstanding that works of a minor nature have not been completed and the Seller undertakes to complete such works as soon as practical after completion

11.7    Within [3] working days of receipt of the Certificate by the Seller it shall give notice in writing to the Buyer of the issue of the Certificate and serve a copy of the Certificate on the Buyer and General Condition 1.3 shall apply as to service and receipt

11.8    The Property is sold in its existing state but subject to the carrying out of the Works and any warranty as to its state and condition is expressly excluded

**[4296]**

## 12    Alterations and extras

12.1    If the Buyer requires any alterations additions [or omissions] in the Works whether in the nature of extras or otherwise he shall notify the Seller as soon as practical

12.2    If the Seller agrees to and executes the alterations additions [or omissions] the cost [including profit] to the Seller of executing such alterations shall be added to (or subtracted from as the case may be) the Purchase Price

12.3     Any addition to the Purchase Price shall be paid for by the Buyer to the Seller's
         Solicitors no later than the Completion Date and if such addition not be paid
         by that date it shall bear interest at the Contract Rate

## 13     Delays beyond the Seller's control

The Works shall be carried out by the Seller as quickly as possible but in any of the cases
specified below where delay is caused the Seller shall not be liable to the Buyer for any
loss or inconvenience however occasioned:
13.1     strikes lockouts combinations and scarcity of labour
13.2     shortage of and delay in obtaining materials
13.3     hostilities and acts of the Queen's enemies
13.4     force majeure fire explosion flood lightning or bad weather
13.5     procedures required for obtaining all necessary permissions for or appertaining
         to the Works and all necessary services
13.6     compliance with all legislation statutory rules orders regulations or directions
13.7     accidents in the Works for which the Seller is not responsible
13.8     other causes beyond the control of the Seller
[except that if from any cause outside the control of the Seller he is for a period of [6]
months or more prevented from proceeding with Works either party shall have the
option to determine this Agreement upon giving to the other [14] days' notice in
writing to that effect whereupon all monies paid by the Buyer to the Seller under the
terms of this Agreement shall be repaid to the Buyer but without interest]

**[4297]**

## 14     No possession prior to completion; access for inspection

14.1     Until payment of all money due under this Agreement by the Buyer to the
         Seller the Buyer will not without the prior written consent of the Seller take or
         attempt to take possession of the Dwelling House either personally or by agents
14.2     The Buyer and his professional advisors may by prior appointment with the
         Seller enter upon the Property and the parts of the Estate affording access to it
         to inspect the progress of the Works subject to the following conditions:
         14.2.1     the persons entering do so at their own risk
         14.2.2     they shall comply with all safety directions and requirements of the
                    Seller and its site manager
         14.2.3     they shall not impede the progress of the Works
         14.2.4     they shall not give instructions to any workmen on the site

## 15     Risk

The Dwelling House shall be at the sole risk of the Seller (notwithstanding any prior
arrangement made by the Buyer or his mortgagees) in respect of damage or loss by fire
storm explosion or lightning only until the Completion Date but if the Seller allows the
Buyer at his request to store in the Dwelling House or upon the Land any of his
possessions and such possessions are damaged or lost the Seller shall not be held liable for
any such loss or damage in any manner whatsoever

## 16     Management Company[6]

16.1     The Seller shall procure that the Management Company executes the Transfer
         before the Completion Date
16.2     The Buyer shall on completion apply to become a member of the Management
         Company and shall covenant with the Management Company in the terms set
         out in the Transfer

**[4298]**

## 17    Tree planting

There is reserved to the Seller a right of entry on the part of the Land edged *(colour)* for itself its agents and workmen for the purpose of planting and maintaining trees thereon in compliance with the conditions imposed (if any) by the grant of any planning permission or consent

## 18    Disclaimer

The Buyer admits that:

18.1    he has inspected the Land and purchases it with full knowledge of its actual state and condition and shall take the Land as it stands

18.2    he enters into this Agreement solely as a result of his own inspection and on the basis of the terms of this Agreement and not in reliance upon any representation or warranty either written or oral or implied made by or on behalf of the Seller (save for any representation or warranty contained in written replies given by the Seller's Solicitors to any preliminary enquiries raised by the Buyer or the Buyer's Solicitors)

18.3    this Agreement contains the entire agreement between the parties

## 19    Incorporation of conditions of sale

The General Conditions shall apply to this Agreement and are incorporated in it in so far as they are applicable to a sale by private treaty and are not varied by or inconsistent with the terms of this Agreement [and shall be amended as follows[7]:

19.1    General Conditions 5.1.1 and 5.1.2 shall not apply

19.2    The following condition shall be added in place of General Conditions 5.1.1 and 5.1.2:

'If [on or before the Completion Date *or* before the issue of the Certificate] [the Property suffers substantial damage rendering it unfit for occupation as a residence *and/or* the [mansion house *or* outbuildings] of which the Dwelling House forms part suffers substantial damage whether or not rendering the Dwelling House unfit for occupation as a residence] the following provisions shall apply:

5.1.1    Within [4] working days of the event causing the damage the Seller shall give notice in writing to the Buyer of the event stating whether in the Seller's opinion the damaged or destroyed part can or cannot be reinstated and made good [[before *or* within [14] working days after] the Completion Date *or* within [3] months after the date of damage or destruction]

5.1.2    If the Seller's notice shall state that in his opinion the damaged or destroyed part cannot be reinstated and made good within the time specified in Condition 5.1.1 either party may rescind this Agreement by notice in writing to the other and General Condition 7.2 shall apply'

19.3    *(insert details of any other amendments required)*][8]

**[4299]**

## [20    Restriction on assignment

20.1    This Agreement is personal to the Buyer and shall not be capable of assignment

[20.2    The Seller shall not be required to transfer the Property [to anyone other than the Buyer named in this Agreement *or* at a price greater than the Purchase Price]]]

## 21    Merger on completion

The provisions of this Agreement shall not merge on completion of the transfer of the Property so far as they remain to be performed

## 22    Nature of this Agreement

This Agreement [is *or* is not] a deed and [has *or* has not] been executed by the parties to it as a deed

## [23    Insolvency

If either party:

23.1    enters into voluntary liquidation (other than for the purpose of reconstruction or amalgamation not involving a realisation of assets) or has a winding-up order made against it by the court or has a receiver appointed over all or any part of its assets or an administration order is made pursuant to the Insolvency Act 1986 or

23.2    becomes insolvent or enters into any composition with its or his creditors or enters into a voluntary arrangement (within the meaning of the Insolvency Act 1986 Sections 1 or 253) or distress sequestration or execution is levied on its or his goods

then and in any such case the other party may rescind this Agreement by notice to the party suffering the relevant event referred to in clause 23.1 Condition 7.2 of the General Conditions shall apply save that in this instance the Seller shall not be obliged to pay any interest which has accrued on the deposit]

## 24    Arbitration

If any question difference or dispute shall at any time arise between the parties to this Agreement as to the execution of the Works the dispute shall be referred to the arbitration and final decision of a person to be agreed upon between the parties or failing such agreement within [14] days after either party has given to the other a written request to concur in such appointment a person to be appointed on the written request of either party by or on behalf of the President for the time being of the Royal Institute of British Architects

## [25    Contracts (Rights of Third Parties) Act 1999

For the purposes of the Contracts (Rights of Third Parties) Act 1999 it is agreed that [with the exception only of *(specify clauses)*] nothing in this Agreement shall confer on any third party any right to enforce or any benefit of any term of this Agreement]

[AS *or* IN] WITNESS etc

**[4300]**

THE SCHEDULE
The Property

(1)    the freehold land together with the part of the structure of the [[stables *or* coachhouses] of the] mansion house situate and known as *(insert name and address)* which part comprises a separate dwelling house to be called Number *(number) (name of mansion)*

(2)    the freehold land together with the garage[s] on it situate near to the mansion house known as Garage[s] number[s] *(number(s))*

(3)    the freehold land comprising part of the gardens and grounds of the mansion house

All of which are more fully described in the annexed form of transfer and shown on the plans attached to it [and for the purpose of identification only and not by way of limitation or enlargement shown edged in *(colour)* and numbered [1A 1B and 1C] on the Plan]

*(signatures (or common seals) of the parties)*
[*(signatures of witnesses)*]
**[4301]**

1    No stamp duty. See Information Binder: Stamp Duties [1].
        Reference should be made to Form 115 [4191] ante for detailed footnotes on the terms common to most forms of contract for sale, for cross-references to the relevant part of the commentary in vol 35 (1997 Reissue) SALE OF LAND and for additional footnotes relating to sales of part.
        This form is an alternative to the usual leasehold flat scheme and is only suitable for use where the architectural design and construction of the mansion or outbuildings is capable of vertical division to create what is, in effect, a run of terraced dwelling houses. Each house will comprise a part of the mansion, stables or coachhouses, such as a complete wing, and will comprise the freehold of the land on which it stands, the cellars (if any) and all the accommodation directly above it, the roof over it and airspace above it. The house will have its own exclusive direct entrance and there will be no common parts within the mansion. Sometimes each dwelling will also have its own freehold garages and piece of garden. The remainder of the grounds of the mansion, park, drives, and possibly a freehold column of accommodation comprising the principal rooms of the mansion which are unsuitable for division into smaller units, and the service apparatus which serves more that one dwelling house, will be owned by a management company of which the buyer will become a member; the buyer will have rights to use those common parts which will be maintained by the management company out of a service charge.

2    As to Land Registry Form 102 certificates generally see vol 25(1) (1999 Reissue) LAND REGISTRATION Paragraph 57 [1881]. It will generally be more useful to the buyer's solicitors to see the filed plan.

3    The practitioner needs to bear in mind that, if it is desired to reserve the right to make minor amendments to the approved estate plan, not only does the Land Registry need to be consulted about any amendment prior to its being made, but there may well be complications resulting from the existence of transfers that have already been effected on the estate and the existence of a defining plan in the transfer annexed to the current agreement. It is one thing to adjust a boundary between remaining unsold plots. It is quite another if any attempt is made to adjust the position of estate roads, pathways or common services, over which rights have been granted already, or are due to be granted under the form of transfer annexed to the agreement. In the latter case, the adjustments may well need to be agreed with the buyer and previous transferees, and embodied in suitable formal documents.

4    Anticipatory completion dates are most unwise from a builder's viewpoint in view of the possibility of unforeseen snags in the building work.

5    This may be an acceptance of an initial notice under the new building control system, but it would still be, technically, a building regulation consent, so that the old nomenclature is probably the best. For the current building regulations see the Building Regulations 1991, SI 1991/2768 as amended.

6    The management company may be either a private company limited by shares (for which see vol 9 (1994 Reissue) COMPANIES Paragraph 136 [605]) or one limited by guarantee without a share capital (as to which see vol 9 (1994 Reissue) COMPANIES Paragraph 146 [618]). For forms of memorandum of association of companies limited by shares which may be adapted see vol 9 (1994 Reissue) COMPANIES Form 130 [688] and vol 23 LANDLORD AND TENANT Forms 734 [2757] and 748 [2876].
        The management company is required to execute the transfer to grant the rights over the common parts to the buyer and to covenant with the buyer to provide the maintenance services in relation to them. Alternatively, the management company may be joined in the agreement for sale as a party to it and enter into direct agreements with the buyer in relation to these matters.

7    Consideration should be given to whether the standard conditions of sale require amendment in any way. For a table of suggested amendments see vol 38(1) (2000 Reissue) SALE OF LAND Form 12 [1245].

8    The possibility of damage or destruction should be carefully considered. If other parts of the mansion are substantially destroyed but not the buyer's dwelling house, the buyer might not wish to proceed with the purchase if the result is to leave him owning the one undamaged wing of what is otherwise a ruin which might not be rebuilt, or which at the very least would be subject to major demolition and construction works over a long period.

**[4302]**

# 125

**Transfer of part of registered freehold land, being parts of the grounds of a country mansion house which is being converted into a number of freehold dwelling houses, to a management company to hold and administer for the benefit of the dwelling house owners[1]**

*Use Land Registry Form TP1 (for which see Form 115 [4191] ante) and insert, in the panels specified below, the wording shown:*

## Panel 4  Property

The land forming part of the gardens park woodlands lakes and landscaped areas of the mansion house situate and known as *(insert name and address)*
[including the walls hedges and fences marked on Plan *(number)* with a 'T' mark inside the red edging]

The Property is defined *(place 'X' in the first box and complete the statement as follows)*
on the attached plan *(number)* (being the approved estate layout plan lodged at HM Land Registry) and edged [green]

**[4303]**

## Panel 13  Additional Provisions

**1        Definitions**

In this transfer:

1.1       'the Company'[2] means the Transferee and its successors in title to the Common Parts

1.2       'the Common Parts'[3] means the land edged [green] on Plan *(number)* being the Property and being the parts of the Estate to be owned by the Company and the facilities on them for the use in common by the owners and occupiers of Dwelling Houses on the Estate and visitors to the Estate or any of them including but not limited to the communal gardens park woodlands lakes landscaped areas and the Drives the Car Park paths and tracks on such lands

1.3       'the Drives' 'the Car Park' [and *(specify)*] mean respectively those parts of the Estate which are shown on Plan *(number)* and defined by reference to the legend endorsed on it and include all cattle grids speed ramps gates gate piers signs lighting drainage facilities and ancillary works

1.4       'Dwelling House' means any parcel of land being part of the Estate together with the part of the structure of the [stables or coachhouses of the] mansion house situate and known as *(insert name and address)* which comprises or will comprise a separate dwelling house

1.5       'the Estate' means the land [edged brown] on Plan *(number)* now comprised in title number *(number)* comprising the mansion [outbuildings] gardens and the Common Parts collectively known as the *(name)* Estate at *(address)*

1.6       'the Perpetuity Period' means the period of [21] [80] years commencing on the date of this transfer

1.7       'Plan' followed by a number means the annexed plan so numbered

1.8       'the Projections' means eaves gutters spouts downpipes chimney cappings foundations supporting pillars architraves pediments ornaments and stanchions shutes cellar lights and gratings and any similar structures

1.9       'the Service Charge' has the meaning given in clause 6

1.10      'Services' means water soil effluent gas fuel oil electricity telephone telephonic signals television and other services

1.11      'Service Apparatus' means sewers drains channels pipes watercourses gutters wires cables ducts flues conduits and other conducting media [septic tanks holding tanks and sewage treatment works] and associated equipment

[1.12     words importing one gender shall be construed as importing any other gender]

[1.13     words importing the singular shall be construed as importing the plural and vice versa]

[1.14     words importing persons shall be construed as importing a corporate body and/or a partnership and vice versa]

[1.15     where any party comprises more than one person the obligations and liabilities of that party under this transfer shall be joint and several obligations and liabilities of those persons]

[1.16     the panel and clause headings do not form part of this transfer and shall not be taken into account in its construction or interpretation]

[1.17     any reference to a clause is to one so numbered in this panel unless otherwise stated]

[1.18     any reference to a colour or letter is to one on the Plan]

[4304]

## 2          Rights granted by the Transferor for the benefit of the Property[4]

The Property is transferred together with the following rights in common with the Transferor and all other persons who have or may in future have the like rights:

### 2.1          Services
The right so far as the same serve the Property of taking passage and running (as appropriate) of Services through the Service Apparatus which are now or may within the Perpetuity Period be laid in on over or under the Estate SUBJECT to the Transferee paying a fair proportion of the cost of cleaning maintaining repairing and whenever necessary renewing the same

### 2.2          Projections
The right to maintain enjoy and use over on or under the adjoining land comprised in the Estate the Projections incidental to the user of the buildings on the Property which overhang stand on or protrude beneath the adjoining land comprised in the Estate

### 2.3          Access
The right to enter after the giving of reasonable notice and at all reasonable times (or in the case of emergency at any time without notice) upon the adjoining land comprised in the Estate [other than any land covered by a building] so far as may be necessary for the purposes of inspecting cleaning maintaining repairing and renewing the buildings walls hedges fences and other boundary structures on the Property the Service Apparatus and the Projections causing as little damage as possible and making good to the reasonable satisfaction of the registered proprietors from time to time of the adjoining land any damage caused

### 2.4          Support and protection
The right of support and protection for the benefit of the Property that is now enjoyed from all other parts of the Estate

[2.5      (insert any other rights)]

[4305]

**3      Rights reserved for the benefit of other land**

There are reserved out of the Property for the benefit of each and every part of the remainder of the Estate [subject to the observance and performance of such reasonable regulations to be made by the Company relating to the use of the Common Parts] the following rights[5]:

**3.1      Rights of way**

The right at all times hereafter for the purpose of access to and egress from the remainder of the Estate to pass and repass on foot and with or without vehicles [horses and dogs] over the Drives and on foot only over the paths [on the Common Parts *or* coloured *(colour)* and *(colour)* respectively on Plan *(number)*]

**3.2      Parking**

The right to park motor vehicles and building and construction plant equipment and materials on the Car Park for reasonable periods only when space is available the Car Park being available to all those entitled to use it and the Transferor and his successors in title on a first come first served basis[6]

**3.3      Services**

The right (in common with the Transferee and all others entitled thereto and so far as the same serve other parts of the Estate) to take pass and run (as appropriate) Services through the Service Apparatus now or at any time within the Perpetuity Period laid in on over or under the Property

**3.4      Projections**

The right to maintain enjoy and use over on or under the Property the Projections incidental to the user of the buildings on the adjoining land comprised in the Estate which overhang stand on or protrude beneath the Property

**[3.5      Future service apparatus**

The right at any time within the Perpetuity Period to enter upon the Property and:

3.5.1      to lay place or erect in on over or under it and thereafter at all times to use any Service Apparatus for the supply and passage of Services to or from any other part of the Estate and likewise to alter enlarge or duplicate Service Apparatus

3.5.2      to construct lay place or erect in on over or under the Property and thereafter at all times to maintain enjoy and use the Projections incidental to the user of the buildings to be constructed on the adjoining land comprised in the Estate overhanging standing on or protruding beneath the Property]

**[4306]**

**3.6      Access**

The right to enter after the giving of reasonable notice and at all reasonable times (or in the case of emergency at any time without notice) upon the Property so far as may be necessary for the purposes of constructing laying altering inspecting cleaning maintaining repairing renewing and demolishing the buildings walls hedges fences and other boundary structures upon the adjoining land comprised in the Estate and Service Apparatus and the Projections and for the purpose of complying with any covenant agreement or condition entered into by the Transferor with the Transferee or any other person causing as little damage as possible and making good to the reasonable satisfaction of the Transferee any damage caused

**3.7    Support and protection**

The right of support and protection for the benefit of the remainder of the Estate that is now enjoyed from the Property

**3.8    Recreation**

The right to use the gardens park woodlands [lakes] and landscaped areas and facilities on the Property for recreation subject to complying with such reasonable regulations as may from time to time be made by the Company

**[3.9    *(insert any other rights)*]**

**4       Restrictive covenants by the Transferee**

4.1     The Transferee covenants with the Transferor to observe and perform the Restrictions specified below and it is agreed and declared that:

    4.1.1     the benefit of this covenant and the Restrictions is to be attached to and enure for each and every part of the remainder of the Estate

    4.1.2     the burden of this covenant and the Restrictions is intended to bind and binds each and every part of the Property into whomsoever's hands it may come [but not so as to render the Transferee personally liable for any breach of this covenant or a Restriction arising after the Transferee has parted with all interest in the Property or the part of the Property on which such breach is committed]

    4.1.3     a Restriction not to do any act or thing includes an obligation not to permit or suffer that act or thing to be done by another person

4.2     The Restrictions mentioned in clause 4.1 are the following:

    4.2.1     The Transferee must not use the Property or any part of it for any purpose except the provision of amenities to and leisure and recreation uses by the owners and occupiers of any part of the Estate

    4.2.2     The Transferee must not transfer or grant a lease of the Property or any part of it except to a person who has first executed a deed[7] expressed to be made in favour of the owners of every property on the remainder of the Estate by which that person covenants in the terms set out in clause 5.2 and this clause 4.2.2

**[4307]**

**5       Positive covenants by the Transferee**

**5.1    Indemnity**

The Transferee covenants with the Transferor that the Transferee will observe and perform the covenants and conditions contained or referred to in the [property [proprietorship] and charges registers of title number *(number)* and/or *(insert details)*] [so far as they relate to the Property] and will indemnify and keep the Transferor and his successors in title fully and effectually indemnified against all actions proceedings damages costs claims and expenses which may be suffered or incurred by the Transferor or his successors in title in respect of any future breach or non-observance or non-performance of those covenants and conditions

**5.2    With the Transferor and his successors in title**

The Transferee covenants with the Transferor and his successors in title as owners of the remainder of the Estate that it will on request join in any transfer of any part of the remainder of the Estate or enter into a separate deed with the owner of each part of it and covenant with the transferee or owner of each such part in the following terms:

**'[0.1]     Covenants and provisions affecting the Company's obligations**

**[0.1.1]    Covenants by the Company[8]**

The Company covenants with the Transferee and his successors in title that subject to the payment by the Transferee of the Service Charge and to the provisions of clause [0.1.2] the Company will [so far as practical use it best endeavours] to:

0.1.1.1     *Drives and car park maintenance*:  maintain the Drives and the Car Park in the same state of repair as they [shall be in upon the issue of the certificate of practical completion by the architect in charge of the conversion and construction work on the Estate *or* are in at the date of this transfer namely *(describe present state of surfacing)*] and rebuild resurface and renew the same whenever and wherever necessary

0.1.1.2     *Drive verges maintenance*:  mow and maintain the grass verges of the Drives

**[4308]**

0.1.1.3     *Paths and tracks maintenance*:  mow and keep open and tidy the [principal] paths and tracks within the Common Parts[9] [shown coloured *(colour)* on Plan *(number)*]

0.1.1.4     *Boundary features maintenance*:  maintain in proper repair and where necessary stockproof the walls hedges fences and gates within or bounding the Common Parts except in so far as they are the responsibility of the Transferee or adjoining owners

0.1.1.5     *Grounds maintenance*:  maintain cultivate mow and care for and so far as practical keep in a clean and tidy condition the gardens park lakes woodlands and grounds of the Common Parts

0.1.1.6     *Service Apparatus*:   maintain repair and whenever necessary renew or replace all Service Apparatus in on over or under the Estate the use of which is common to more than one property within the Estate and is not the responsibility of service undertakers or suppliers

0.1.1.7     *Ornamental features*:  maintain and repair all statuary and architectural and ornamental features on the Common Parts unless this is impossible or can only be done at a cost that is unreasonable in all the circumstances

0.1.1.8     *Enforcement of covenants*:  if so required by the Transferee take all reasonable steps to enforce the observance and performance by the owners of other properties within the Estate of the covenants and conditions to be observed and binding on them [subject to the Transferee indemnifying the Company against all costs of such enforcement and providing such security or deposit of money in respect of costs and expenses as the Company may reasonably require]

0.1.1.9     *Third party covenants*:  observe and perform all covenants and obligations in favour of third parties affecting the Common Parts

**[4309]**

**[0.1.2]    Provisions affecting the Company's obligations**

0.1.2.1    *Relief from liability to perform*: The Company is not to be liable to the Transferee for any failure or interruption in any of the Maintenance Services *(as defined in clause [0.2.1.6] for which see clause 6.1 [4312] post)* or the temporary closure of access to or over any part of the Common Parts caused by necessary repair replacement cultivation or maintenance or damage to them or destruction of them or anything beyond the Company's control [provided and to the extent that the failure or interruption could not [reasonably] have been prevented or shortened by the exercise of proper care attention diligence and skill by the Company or those undertaking the Maintenance Services on its behalf and provided that the Company uses and continues to use [its best *or* reasonable] endeavours to restore the Maintenance Services or reopen the part of the Common Parts in question and] Provided that the Company shall not close off all pedestrian and vehicular access to the Property at the same time

0.1.2.2    *Acts of servants*: The Company is not to be liable to the Transferee for any act omission or negligence of any person undertaking any of the Maintenance Services on its behalf [provided that this clause is not to be construed as relieving the Company from liability for breach by it of any covenants on its part contained in this transfer]

0.1.2.3    *Variation of the Maintenance Services*: The Company may withhold add to or change the Maintenance Services or any of them from time to time [if at its absolute discretion it considers it desirable to do so (or as required) provided that the variation complies with the principles of good estate management and is reasonable in all the circumstances]

**[[0.1.3]**    *(insert any specific covenants for the benefit of the property only)*]

**5.3    For the benefit of specific property**

The Transferee covenants with the Transferor and its successors in title as owners of *(insert details of specific property to be benefited or protected)* as follows: *(insert details)*
                                                                                          **[4310]**

**6    Transferor's covenants**

6.1    The Transferor covenants with the Company that any transfer of any part of the remainder of the Estate which includes a building which is or is intended to be used as a dwelling house will contain a covenant by the transferee with the Transferor and as a separate covenant with the Company to pay a service charge to the Company in accordance with clause [0.2] set out below ('the Service Charge'):

'**[0.2]**      **Service Charge provisions**[10]
**[0.2.1]**    **Definitions**

In this clause:

0.2.1.1      'The Additional Items' means the fees costs and outgoings set out in clause [0.2.7]

0.2.1.2      'The Annual Expenditure' means:

　　　　　　　0.2.1.2.1      the costs expenses and outgoings [reasonably and properly] incurred by the Company during a financial year in or incidental to providing all or any of the Maintenance Services and

　　　　　　　0.2.1.2.2      the expense [reasonably and properly] incurred by the Company during a financial year in relation to the Additional Items

and any VAT payable on such costs expenses and outgoings to the extent that it cannot be recovered by the Company. The Annual Expenditure excludes any expenditure in respect of any part of the Estate for which the Transferee or any other transferee is wholly responsible and excludes any expenditure that the Company recovers or that is met under any insurance policy maintained by it or that it recovers in whole or in part from any person other than the Transferee or any other transferee of any part of the Estate

**[4311]**

0.2.1.3      References to 'a computing date' are references to [31st December *or (as the case may be)*] in every year or any other date that the Company from time to time nominates and references to 'computing dates' are to be construed accordingly

0.2.1.4      References to a 'financial year' are references to the period commencing on [1st January *or (as the case may be)*] and ending on the first computing date and subsequently to the period between 2 consecutive computing dates excluding the first computing date but including the second computing date

0.2.1.5      'the Initial Provisional Service Charge' means £...... a year [plus any VAT payable thereon]

0.2.1.6      'The Maintenance Services' mean the obligations of the Company set out in clauses [0.1.1.1]–[0.1.1.9] inclusive *(for which see clause 5.2 [4308] ante)*

0.2.1.7      'the Manager' means the agent acting for the Company in relation to the Maintenance Services and collection of the Service Charge

0.2.1.8      'the Service Charge' means the Service Charge Percentage of the Annual Expenditure [plus any VAT payable thereon]

0.2.1.9      'the Service Charge Percentage' means ...% [subject to the provisions for variation contained in clause [0.2.6]]

**[4312]**

**[0.2.2]   Preparation of accounts**

As soon as convenient after each computing date the Company must prepare an account showing the Annual Expenditure for the financial year ending on that computing date and containing a fair summary of the expenditure referred to in it and when that account is certified by chartered accountants it is to be conclusive evidence of all matters of fact referred to in it for the purposes of this transfer [except in the case of manifest error]

**[0.2.3]   Initial Provisional Service Charge**

For the period from the date of this transfer to the computing date next following the date of this transfer the Transferee must pay the Initial Provisional Service Charge. The first payment being a proportionate sum in respect of the period commencing on the date of this transfer and ending on the next computing date must be made on the date of this transfer. The subsequent payments must be made in advance on [1st January *or (as the case may be)*] in each year

**[0.2.4]   Interim payments**

For the next and each subsequent financial year the Transferee must pay on [1st January *or (as the case may be)*] a provisional sum [equal to the Service Charge payable for the previous financial year—or the Service Charge that would have been payable had that financial year been a period of 12 months calculated by establishing a monthly figure for that financial year by apportionment and multiplying it by 12] increased by [*(state percentage, eg 10%) or (as required)*] calculated on [an estimate *or* a reasonable and proper estimate] by the Manager acting as an expert and not as an arbitrator of what the Annual Expenditure is likely to be for that financial year

**[0.2.5]   Adjustments**

If the Service Charge for any financial year exceeds the provisional sum for that financial year the excess must be paid to the Company on demand. If the Service Charge for any financial year is less than the provisional sum for that financial year the overpayment must be credited to the Transferee against the next annual payment of the Service Charge

**[4313]**

**[0.2.6]   Variation of the Service Charge Percentage**

If at any time the total property that enjoys or is capable of enjoying the benefit of any of the Maintenance Services or the Additional Items is permanently increased or decreased [or if some other event occurs as a result of which the Service Charge Percentage is no longer appropriate to the Property] then with effect from the computing date following that event the Service Charge Percentage may be varied by agreement between the Company and the Transferee or in default of agreement within *(state period, eg 3 months)* of the first proposal for variation made by the Company in such a manner as the Manager acting as an expert and not as an arbitrator determines to be fair and reasonable in the light of the event in question

**[0.2.7]**     **The Additional Items**

0.2.7.1    *Fees*: The [proper] fees and disbursements of:

       0.2.7.1.1     any surveyor accountant and other person employed or retained by the Company for or in connection with any surveying or accounting functions relating to or the management of the Common Parts

       0.2.7.1.2     the Manager for or in connection with:

             0.2.7.1.2.1     management of the Common Parts

             0.2.7.1.2.2     collection of the sums due to the Company from the transferees of the Estate

             0.2.7.1.2.3     performance of the Maintenance Services [and any other duties in and about the Common Parts or any part of them relating without prejudice to the generality of the foregoing to the general management administration security maintenance protection and cleanliness of the Common Parts]

       0.2.7.1.3     any person providing caretaking or security arrangements and Maintenance Services to the Estate and

       0.2.7.1.4     any other person employed or retained by the Company to perform any of the Maintenance Services or in connection with them or to perform any of the functions or duties referred to in this clause

**[4314]**

0.2.7.2    *Staff*: The cost of seeking and employing such staff as the Company in its absolute discretion thinks necessary to perform the Maintenance Services and the other functions and duties referred to in clause [0.2.7.1] and all other incidental expenditure in relation to employing the staff including but without prejudice to the generality of the foregoing:

       0.2.7.2.1     insurance pension and welfare contributions

       0.2.7.2.2     transport facilities and benefits in kind

       0.2.7.2.3     the provision of uniforms and working clothing

       0.2.7.2.4     the provision of vehicles tools appliances and other equipment for the proper performance of their duties and a store for housing them

0.2.7.3    *Contracts for Maintenance Services:* The cost of entering into any contracts to carry out all or any of the Maintenance Services and other functions and duties that the Company in its absolute discretion considers desirable or necessary

0.2.7.4    *Outgoings:* All rates taxes assessments duties charges impositions and outgoings that are at any time charged assessed or imposed on the Common Parts and on any residential accommodation for caretakers groundsmen and other staff employed in connection with the Common Parts

0.2.7.5    *Cost of fuel*: The cost of the supply of electricity gas oil or other fuel for the provision of the Maintenance Services and for all purposes in connection with the Common Parts

0.2.7.6     *Road and Service Apparatus charges*:   The amount the Company is called on to pay as a contribution towards the expense of making repairing maintaining rebuilding and cleaning any ways roads paths or structures Service Apparatus or anything that may belong to or be used for the Common Parts or any part of them exclusively or in common with other neighbouring or adjoining premises

0.2.7.7     *Cost of regulations*:  The costs charges and expenses of preparing any regulations made by the Company relating to the Common Parts or the use of them and supplying copies of them to the transferees

**[4315]**

0.2.7.8     *Cost of meeting statutory requirements*:   The cost of taking any [reasonable] steps the Company considers desirable or expedient to comply with make representations against or otherwise contest the incidence of the provisions of any statute byelaw or notice concerning town planning public health highways streets drainage or other matters relating to or alleged to relate to the Common Parts or any part of them for which no transferee is directly and exclusively liable

0.2.7.9     *Costs of borrowing money*:  Any interest and fees in respect of money borrowed to finance the provision of the Maintenance Services or the Additional Items

0.2.7.10    *Professional advice*:  The cost of obtaining any professional advice and services including the prosecution of legal proceedings in relation to the Maintenance Services the Service Charges the Common Parts and the enforcement of covenants in favour of and rights enjoyed by the Company

0.2.7.11    *Reserve funds for anticipated expenditure*:  Subject as provided in clause [0.2.7.12] and if requested by the Company reasonable provision— to be determined by the Manager acting as an expert not an arbitrator—towards the anticipated expenditure in respect of:
            0.2.7.11.1    periodically recurring items whether or not recurring at regular or irregular intervals and
            0.2.7.11.2    such of the Company's obligations set out in clause [0.1.1] *(for which see clause 5.2 [4308] ante)* as relate to the renewal or replacement of the items referred to there

**[4316]**

0.2.7.12    *Conditions applying to the fund*
            0.2.7.12.1    *The replacement fund*:   The reasonable provision in relation to items referred to in clause [0.2.7.11.2] is to be calculated on the basis of such life expectancy of those items referred as the Manager acting as an expert not an arbitrator [reasonably] determines and on the assumption that each year the Transferee will pay a rateable proportion towards the anticipated cost of renewal or replacement of them to the intent that a fund will be accumulated sufficient to cover the cost of renewal or replacement by the end of the anticipated life of each such item
            0.2.7.12.2    *No obligation to establish any fund*:  Nothing in this clause obliges the Company to establish or maintain any fund to cover the cost of replacement or renewal of any item

0.2.7.12.3  *Expenditure to be met out of funds in order*: Where either a specific fund has been established in connection with a recurring item referred to in clause [0.2.7.11.1] or the Company's obligations set out in clause [0.1.1] to renew or replace any item referred to there or part of a general fund has been allocated by the Company to that recurring item or the renewal or replacement concerned then any expenditure by the Company in respect of that recurring item or the renewal or replacement concerned must be met first out of the specific fund or out of the general fund to the extent of the credit allocated for it by the Company

0.2.7.12.4  *Accounts to indicate existence of the sinking fund*: The account referred to in clause [0.2.2] must indicate whether or not the Company has established and is maintaining any fund pursuant to this clause and must provide full details of any such fund

**[4317]**

0.2.7.12.5  *Separate account for the fund*: All sums received by the Company pursuant to this clause ('the Fund') must be credited to an account separate from the Company's own money. The Fund must be held by the Company during the Perpetuity Period on trust for the persons who from time to time are the owners of the dwelling houses on the Estate to apply the Fund and any interest accruing for the purposes set out in this clause. At the end of the Perpetuity Period any of the Fund unexpended must [either] be paid to the persons who are then the owners of the dwelling houses on the Estate in the same proportion the Service Charge payable by each owner respectively bears to the total of all the Service Charges paid by the owners of the dwelling houses [or for the benefit of any new trust then established in relation to the Maintenance Services to be provided to the Common Parts]'

6.2     Until completion of the first sale of each of the dwelling houses on the Estate the Transferor will pay to the Company the payments which would be due to the Company in respect of each such dwelling house [and observe and perform such obligations as the transferee of such dwelling house would be liable to observe and perform] if the sale had been completed

**[4318]**

## 7     Agreements and declarations

It is agreed and declared as follows:

7.1     The Transferee and its successors in title shall not be entitled to any right of access of light or air or other easement or right which would restrict or interfere with the free use of any land comprised in the Estate or any adjoining or neighbouring land of the Transferor for building or any other purpose

7.2     The Transferor shall be at liberty to modify waive or release all or any covenants stipulations or restrictions relating to the Property or the Estate (other than the service charge provision referred to in clause 6 of this transfer) whether imposed or entered into before at the same time as or after the date of this transfer AND to sell or dispose of any part of the Estate free from any restriction or stipulation (other than the service charge provision referred to in clause 6 of this transfer) or subject to other covenants as may be appropriate to the transferred property AND the Transferor shall not in any way be bound by the plotting or general scheme of development of the Estate

7.3 Unless the contrary appears on the Plans by 'T' marks the walls hedges and fences separating the Property from the adjoining land and the buildings on it are party walls and fences and the rights and liabilities in respect of them shall be in accordance with the Law of Property Act 1925 Section 38(1)

## 8 Application

The parties apply to the Registrar for entry of a restriction in the proprietorship register of the title to the Property in the following terms:

'Except under an order of the Registrar no disposition or dealing by the proprietor is to be registered unless there is furnished to the Registrar a certificate from the solicitors acting for *(disponee)* that a deed complying in all respects with the provisions of clause [4.2.2] of a deed dated *(date)* made between *(parties)* [referred to in the charges register of this title] has been delivered to the registered proprietor of every dwelling house on the *(name)* Estate[11]

## 9 Statement

The Transferor is converting the mansion house [and outbuildings] on the land comprised in title number *(number)* into separate dwelling houses and has incorporated the Transferee as the management company to own the Property described in panel 4 and to hold maintain and manage it for the benefit of the owners of the dwelling houses who are to be granted rights to use the Property subject to payment of a service charge

**[4319]**

1    As to stamp duty see Information Binder: Stamp Duties [1] (Conveyance or transfer). As to Land Registry fees see Information Binder: Property [1]: Fees in connection with property matters, Land Registry fees.

Form TP1 is the Land Registry form of transfer of part of freehold or leasehold land prescribed by the Land Registration Rules 1925, SR&O 1925/1093 r 98, Sch 1 as inserted by SI 1999/128. This Form should be used whenever part only of any registered title is transferred, even if the transfer also includes the whole of one or more other registered titles.

The transferor's land or charge certificate must be placed on deposit (using Land Registry Form DP1 as prescribed by SR&O 1925/1093 Sch 1 as inserted by SI 1997/3037 and substituted by SI 1999/128 (as to which see vol 25(1) (1999 Reissue) LAND REGISTRATION Form 3 [3076]) to meet the transferee's application to register the transfer. If the transferor's land is subject to any registered charge, that charge will require to be released by use of Land Registry Form DS3 (for which see vol 25(1) (1999 Reissue) LAND REGISTRATION Form 47 [3371]). If the charge is a noted charge, the consent of the chargee to the transfer should be obtained and lodged with the application to register the transfer.

Reference should be made to Form 115 [4191] ante for detailed footnotes on matters common to many forms of transfer, for cross references to the commentary in vol 35 (1997 Reissue) SALE OF LAND, for the location of alternative transfer clauses in that and other volumes and for additional footnotes relating to sale of part of a property.

The forms of rights, exceptions, covenants, restrictions, agreements and declarations in this Form are illustrative only and should be altered or replaced as the circumstances may require. Reference may be made to the clauses used in flat letting schemes and to vol 13(1) (1996 Reissue) COVENANTS RELATING TO LAND; EASEMENTS AND PROFITS À PRENDRE for alternative and additional clauses.

This form is for use in conjunction with Forms 124 [4291] ante (agreement) and 126 [4322] post (transfer). For an outline of the scheme see Form 124 [4291] ante. This transfer of the common parts should be completed and the transfer registered before the transfer of any dwelling house (for which see Form 126 [4322] post) is completed.

2    This definition is inserted because clauses 5.2 and 6.1 contain copies of provisions which appear in the transfers of dwelling houses and those provisions use the words 'Company' and 'Common Parts'.

3    See note 2 above.

4    It is unlikely that most of these rights will be required; no right of way is granted to the transferee because all the drives and paths will themselves be part of the common parts and land transferred.

**[4320]**

5    These reservations, apart from clause 3.5 which is additional, are the same as those to be granted by the company to the dwelling house owners by clause 3 of the transfer of dwelling houses (for which see Form 126 [4322] post). The rights granted by this clause are required by the transferor until such time as all the dwelling houses have been sold and to give the transferor the power to grant such rights to buyers of dwelling houses in the unlikely event that the company defaults in making such grant itself.

Clause 10.4 of the dwelling house transfer (for which see Form 126 [4322] post) excludes the buyer from getting the benefit of the rights reserved by this clause because the exercise of these rights is not conditional on payment of the service charge and observance and performance of the covenants in favour of the company in clause 6.2 of the dwelling house transfer. The buyer will be granted these rights by the company conditional on payment of the service charge and compliance with the covenants in the company's favour.

6    The parking rights reserved are wider than that in the dwelling house transfer (for which see Form 126 panel 13 clause 3.2 [4326] post) because the transferor may need to park trade and construction vehicles and deposit equipment plant and materials on the car park in connection with unfinished building work. As the car park is not the best area for this activity and is likely to interfere with the reasonable use of it by buyers, consideration should be given to reserving such rights over a separate less intrusive area such as a yard or other screened area. If that is done the clause can then follow clause 3.2 of the dwelling house transfer but without any limit on the number of vehicles which can park.

7    For a form of deed of covenant adapted for use in this case see Form 127 [4347] post.

8    This is a copy of the company's covenant to be inserted in the dwelling house transfer (for which see Form 126 panel 13 clause 7 [4333] post). The numbering of the clause will need to be altered according to the numbering of the deed into which it is to be inserted. It has been given the number '0.1' to differentiate it from the clause set out in panel 13 clause 6.1 of this Form ('service charge provisions'), which has been given the number '0.2'. The numbering is not meant to imply that the two clauses are sub-clauses, nor that they follow on from one another.

9    Ie the land transferred by this transfer.

10   This is a copy of the service charge clause to be inserted in the dwelling house transfer: see Form 126 panel 13 clause 9 [4335] and notes 17 [4343]–36 [4345] post. Some practitioners may wish the transferor also to covenant to impose in the dwelling house transfer the covenants in clauses 6.2.1–6.2.8 and 6.2.10 of panel 13 of that transfer, but that has not been done in this Form because those covenants are more for the other dwelling house owners' benefit than the company's benefit. Those covenants are expressed also to be made with the company to enable the company principally to enforce those covenants for the benefit of dwelling house owners.

The numbering of the clause will need to be altered according to the numbering of the deed into which it is to be inserted. It has been given the number '0.2' to differentiate it from the clause set out in panel 13 clause 5.2 of this Form ('covenants and provisions affecting the company's obligations'), which has been given the number '0.1'. The numbering is not meant to imply that the two clauses are sub-clauses, nor that they follow on from one another.

11   Early forms of such restrictions required the deed to be lodged with the land registry and in effect for the registry to check whether the deed complied with the terms of the covenant. This was not desirable and most modern forms of the restriction seek to leave control of the form of the deed with the seller or his solicitor, who then furnishes a certificate to the subsequent buyer that the obligations under the covenant have been complied with, and this certificate is lodged with the application for registration.

This Form does not include the additional covenant and restriction in relation to a charge inserted in the dwelling house transfer (for which see Form 126 panel 13 clause 5.2.12 [4330] and note 10 [4343] post) because the chance of the common parts being charged is remote.

**[4321]**

# 126

## Transfer of part of registered freehold land being a dwelling house comprising part of a country mansion house, with garages and/or other land, not comprised in a building scheme, management company joined as party[1]

*Use Land Registry Form TP1 (for which see Form 114 [4181] ante) and insert, in the panels specified below, the wording shown:*

### Panel 3  Title Number

*(insert title numbers of the estate and of the common parts)*

### Panel 4  Property

First the land together with the part of the structure of the [[stables *or* coachhouses] of the] mansion house situate and known as *(insert name and address)* which part comprises a separate dwelling house to be called Number *(number) (name of mansion)*
Secondly the land together with the garage[s] on it situate near to the mansion house known as Garage[s] *(number(s))*
Thirdly the land comprising the part of the gardens of the mansion house which is to be the private garden of the Dwelling House
[including the walls hedges and fences marked on Plan *(number)* with a 'T' mark inside the red edging]'

The Property is defined *(place 'X' in the first box and complete the statement as follows:)* on the attached plan *(number)* (being the approved estate layout plan lodged at HM Land Registry):
As to the land first described: edged and numbered [1A] in red
As to the land secondly described: edged and numbered [1B] in red
As to the land thirdly described: edged and numbered [1C] in red

[4322]

### Panel 13 Additional Provisions

#### 1      Definitions

In this transfer:
1.1      'the Company' means *(name and company registration number)* whose registered office is at *(address)* and its successors in title to the Common Parts
1.2      'the Common Parts' means the land edged [green] on Plan *(number)* being the land comprised in title number *(number)*[2] and being the parts of the Estate owned by the Company and the facilities on them for the use in common by the owners and occupiers of dwelling houses on the Estate and visitors to the Estate or any of them including but not limited to the communal gardens park woodlands [lakes] landscaped areas and the Drives Car Park paths and tracks on such land
1.3      'the Drives' 'the Car Park' [and *(specify)*] mean respectively those parts of the Estate which are shown on Plan *(number)* and defined by reference to the legend endorsed on it and include all cattle grids speed ramps gates gate piers signs lighting drainage facilities and ancillary works
1.4      'the Dwelling House' means the part of the Property first described in panel 4
1.5      'the Estate' means the land [edged brown] on Plan *(number)* now and formerly comprised in title number *(number)* comprising the mansion outbuildings gardens and the Common Parts collectively known as the *(name)* Estate at *(address)*
1.6      'the Garage' means the part of the Property secondly described in panel 4

1.7     'the Private Garden' means the part of the Property thirdly described in panel 4
1.8     'the Maintenance Services' has the meaning given in clause 9.1.6
1.9     'the Perpetuity Period' means the period of [21] [80] years commencing on the date of this transfer

[4323]

1.10    'Plan' followed by a number means the annexed plan so numbered
1.11    'the Projections' means eaves gutters spouts downpipes chimney cappings foundations supporting pillars architraves pediments ornaments and stanchions shutes cellar lights and gratings and any similar structures
1.12    'the Property' means the whole of the property described in panel 4
1.13    'the Service Charge' has the meaning given in clause 9.1.8
1.14    'Services' means water soil effluent gas fuel oil electricity telephone telephonic signals television and other services
1.15    'Service Apparatus' means sewers drains channels pipes watercourses gutters wires cables ducts flues conduits and other conducting media [septic tanks holding tanks and sewage treatment works] and associated equipment
[1.16   words importing one gender shall be construed as importing any other gender]
[1.17   words importing the singular shall be construed as importing the plural and vice versa]
[1.18   words importing persons shall be construed as importing a corporate body and/ or a partnership and vice versa]
[1.19   where any party comprises more than one person the obligations and liabilities of that party under this transfer shall be joint and several obligations and liabilities of those persons]
[1.20   the panel and clause headings do not form part of this transfer and shall not be taken into account in its construction or interpretation]
[1.21   any reference to a clause is to one so numbered in this panel unless otherwise stated]
[1.22   any reference to a colour or letter is to one on the Plan]

[4324]

## 2      Rights granted by the Transferor for the benefit of the Property

The Property is transferred together with the following rights in common with the Transferor and all other persons who have or may in future have the like rights:

### 2.1      Services

The right so far as the same serve the Property of taking passage and running (as appropriate) of Services through the Service Apparatus which are now or may within the Perpetuity Period be laid in on over or under all parts of the Estate except the Common Parts[3] SUBJECT to the Transferee paying a fair proportion of the cost of cleaning maintaining repairing and whenever necessary renewing the same

### 2.2      Projections

The right to maintain enjoy and use over on or under the adjoining land comprised in the Estate the Projections incidental to the user of the buildings on the Property which overhang stand on or protrude beneath the adjoining land comprised in the Estate

### 2.3      Access

The right to enter after the giving of reasonable notice and at all reasonable times (or in the case of emergency at any time without notice) upon the adjoining land comprised in the Estate except the Common Parts[4] so far as may be necessary for the purposes of inspecting cleaning maintaining repairing and renewing the buildings walls hedges fences and other boundary structures on the Property the Service Apparatus and the Projections causing as little damage as possible and making good to the reasonable satisfaction of the registered proprietors from time to time of the adjoining land any damage caused

**2.4 Support and protection**
The right of support and protection for the benefit of the Property that is now enjoyed from all other parts of the Estate except the Common Parts[5]

**[2.5** *(insert any other rights)]*

[4325]

**3 Rights granted by the Company for the benefit of the Property**

In consideration of the covenants by the Transferee contained in clause 6.2 the Company with [full *or* limited] title guarantee grants to the Transferee as appurtenant to the Property the following rights in common with the Company and all other persons who have or may in future have the like rights but subject to the observance and performance of the covenants and conditions contained in clauses 6.2 and 9:

**3.1 Rights of way**
The right at all times hereafter for the purpose of access to and egress from the Property to pass and repass on foot and with or without vehicles [horses and dogs] over the Drives and on foot only over the paths [on the Common Parts *or* coloured *(colour)* and *(colour)* respectively on Plan *(number)*]

**3.2 Parking**
The right to park *(number)* private motor car[s] belonging to or used by the owner or occupier for the time being of the Property or his visitors on the Car Park for reasonable periods only when space is available the Car Park being available to all those entitled to use it and the Transferee on a first come first served basis

**3.3 Services**
The right so far as the same serve the Property of taking passage and running (as appropriate) of Services through the Service Apparatus which are now or may within the Perpetuity Period be laid in on over or under the Common Parts

**3.4 Access**
The right to enter after the giving of reasonable notice and at all reasonable times (or in the case of emergency at any time without notice) upon the adjoining land comprised in the Common Parts so far as may be necessary for the purposes of inspecting cleaning maintaining repairing and renewing the buildings walls hedges fences and other boundary structures on the Property the Service Apparatus and the Projections causing as little damage as possible and making good to the reasonable satisfaction of the registered proprietors from time to time of the Common Parts any damage caused

**3.5 Support and protection**
The right of support and protection for the benefit of the Property that is now enjoyed from the Common Parts

**3.6 Recreation**
The right to use the gardens park woodland [lakes] and landscaped areas and facilities of the Common Parts for recreation subject to complying with such reasonable regulations as may from time to time be made by the Company

**[3.7**      *(insert any other rights)*]

**3.8      Covenants**

The benefit of the following covenants contained in a transfer dated *(date)* of *(number of dwelling house subject to the covenants)* in the following terms: *(insert copy of covenanting clause and restrictions etc)*

[4326]

**4      Rights reserved for the benefit of other land**

There are reserved out of the Property for the benefit of each and every part of the remainder of the Estate[6] the following rights:

**4.1      Services**

The right (in common with all others entitled thereto and so far as the same serve other parts of the Estate) to take pass and run (as appropriate) Services through the Service Apparatus now or at any time within the Perpetuity Period laid in on over or under the Property

**4.2      Projections**

The right to maintain enjoy and use over on or under the Property the Projections incidental to the user of the buildings on the adjoining land comprised in the Estate which overhang stand on or protrude beneath the Property

**[4.3      Future service apparatus**

The right at any time within the Perpetuity Period to enter upon the Property and:

4.3.1          to lay place or erect in on over or under it and thereafter at all times to use any Service Apparatus for the supply and passage of Services to or from any other part of the Estate and likewise to alter enlarge or duplicate Service Apparatus

4.3.2          to construct lay place or erect in on over or under the Property and thereafter at all times to maintain enjoy and use the Projections incidental to the user of the buildings to be constructed on the adjoining land comprised in the Estate overhanging standing on or protruding beneath the Property]

**4.4      Access**

The right to enter after the giving of reasonable notice and at all reasonable times (or in the case of emergency at any time without notice) upon the Property so far as may be necessary for the purposes of [constructing] laying altering inspecting cleaning maintaining repairing renewing and demolishing the buildings walls hedges fences and other boundary structures upon the adjoining land comprised in the Estate and Service Apparatus and the Projections and for the purpose of complying with any covenant agreement or condition entered into by the Transferor with the Transferee or any other person causing as little damage as possible and making good to the reasonable satisfaction of the Transferee any damage caused

**4.5      Support and protection**

The right of support and protection for the benefit of the remainder of the Estate that is now enjoyed from the Property

**[4.6      *(insert any other rights)*]**

[4327]

## 5     Restrictive covenants by the Transferee with the Transferor and the Company

5.1     The Transferee covenants with the Transferor and separately with the Company to observe and perform the Restrictions specified below and it is agreed and declared that:

    5.1.1     the benefit of this covenant and the Restrictions is to be attached to and enure for each and every part of the Estate [that remains unsold by the Transferor or has been sold by the Transferor [or by any person claiming through the Transferor otherwise than by a transfer on sale] with the express benefit of this covenant and the Restrictions][7]

    5.1.2     the burden of this covenant and the Restrictions is intended to bind and binds each and every part of the Property into whomsoever's hands it may come [but not so as to render the Transferee personally liable for any breach of this covenant or a Restriction arising after the Transferee has parted with all interest in the Property or the part of the Property on which such breach is committed]

    5.1.3     a Restriction not to do any act or thing includes an obligation not to permit or suffer that act or thing to be done by another person

5.2     The Restrictions mentioned in clause 5.1 are the following[8]:

    5.2.1     *No trade or business*:  The Transferee must not use the Property or any part of it for the purpose of any profession trade business [holiday lettings] or manufacture of any description nor for any public spectacle or entertainment

    5.2.2     *Single private dwelling*:  The Transferee must not use the Dwelling House for any purpose other than as a single private dwelling house in the occupation of one family only nor use the Garage except as a domestic garage and the Private Garden as a leisure garden both ancillary to occupation of the Dwelling House

    5.2.3     *Nuisance*:  The Transferee must not do or omit to be done any act or thing on or about the Property the doing or omission of which shall or may be or grow to be an annoyance nuisance damage danger or disturbance to the Transferor or the owners or occupiers of any part of the Estate

**[4328]**

    5.2.4     *Alterations and additions*:  The Transferee must not make any alterations to the exterior of the buildings now or subsequently erected on the Property or to the walls hedges fences statuary and architectural and ornamental features on the Property nor erect any additional buildings [walls hedges fences and statuary or architectural and ornamental features] on the Property except with the written approval of the Transferor [or if it shall so direct with the written approval of the Company] whose fees and those of its professional advisers in connection with the consideration of any such application whether granted refused or withdrawn shall be paid by the Transferee

    5.2.5     *Exterior decoration*:  The Transferee must not paint decorate or treat the external woodwork and ironwork of the Property in any colour except *(specify)* nor the external stone or brickwork [plaster or rendering] in any manner [whatsoever *or* in any colour except *(specify)*]

    5.2.6     *Exterior chattels shrubs etc*:  The Transferee must not plant or place any tree or shrub seats or chattels anywhere on the Property except in the Private Garden

**[4329]**

5.2.7    *Trees*:  The Transferee must not fell lop or cut any trees on the Property without the written consent of the Company but this restriction does not prohibit the pruning and trimming of shrubs and hedges in the normal course of good horticultural practice

5.2.8    *Parking*:  The Transferee must not park motor vehicles anywhere on the Estate except in or on the Garage or its forecourt or the Car Park if space is available nor obstruct in any manner any part of the Drives or footpaths

5.2.9    *Boats caravans and trade vehicles*:  The Transferee must not park boats caravans or trade vehicles (except trade vehicles in the course of delivering goods to or supplying services to the Property which may park on the Garage forecourt [or Car Park if space is available] so long only as is reasonably necessary) on the Property or on any other part of the Estate

5.2.10   *Animals*:  The Transferee must not keep animals birds or reptiles on the Property except a maximum of [2] dogs and [2] domestic cats provided that such dogs or cats do not wander unaccompanied over other parts of the Estate or cause annoyance or inconvenience to other occupiers of the Estate

5.2.11   *Severance*:  The Transferee must not transfer charge mortgage or grant a lease or tenancy or part with possession of part only of the Property as distinct from the entirety of the Property

5.2.12   *Alienation*:  The Transferee must not transfer or grant a lease of the Property except to a person who has first applied to become a member of the Company and executed a deed[9] expressed to be made in favour of the Company by which that person covenants in the terms set out in clause 6.2 and this clause 5.2.12 [and will not charge the whole or any part of the Property except to a person who:

5.2.12.1    covenants with the Company that no transfer will be made or lease or tenancy granted under the power of sale or of leasing arising by virtue of the charge except to a person who has executed a deed in the terms referred to above and

5.2.12.2    applies to the Registrar for entry of a restriction in the proprietorship register of the charge in the following terms:

'Except under an order of the Registrar no transfer under a power of sale or grant of a lease under the power of leasing by the proprietor of this charge is to be registered unless there is furnished to the Registrar a certificate from the solicitors acting for proprietor of this charge that a deed complying in all respects with the provisions of clause [5.2.12] of a deed dated *(date)* made between *(parties)* [referred to in the charges register of this title] has been delivered to *(name of the company)*'][10]

**6        Positive covenants by the Transferee**

**6.1        Indemnity**

The Transferee covenants with the Transferor that the Transferee will observe and perform the covenants and conditions contained or referred to in the [property [proprietorship] and charges registers of title number *(number)* and/or *(insert details)*] [so far as they relate to the Property] and will indemnify and keep the Transferor and his successors in title fully and effectually indemnified against all actions proceedings damages costs claims and expenses which may be suffered or incurred by the Transferor or his successors in title in respect of any future breach or non-observance or non-performance of those covenants and conditions

**6.2        Covenants with the Transferor and the Company**

The Transferee covenants with the Transferor and as a separate covenant with the Company as follows:

6.2.1        *Joint facilities*:  Unless express provision is elsewhere contained in this Transfer or the same are to be maintained by the Company the Transferee must pay a fair proportion of the expense of cleaning maintaining repairing and renewing the Service Apparatus and any entrance drive path or access way or other land or thing used by the Transferee jointly with others

6.2.2        *Repairs*:  The Transferee must maintain and keep in good and substantial repair the whole of the buildings and the Service Apparatus on or exclusively serving the Property and the walls hedges fences statuary and architectural and ornamental features on it so as to afford shelter and protection to the remainder of the buildings on the Estate using materials labour and workmanship of the quality and standard appropriate to the maintenance and preservation of a building of architectural and historic importance

6.2.3        *Decoration*:  The Transferee must paint decorate or treat all the external woodwork and ironwork of the Property in *(year)* and at least once in every [4] years thereafter or more frequently if necessary with *(specify)* and the external stone or brickwork [plaster or rendering] in *(year)* and at least once in every [10] years thereafter or more frequently if necessary with *(specify)* using materials labour and workmanship of the quality and standard appropriate to the decoration maintenance and preservation of a building of architectural and historic importance

**[4331]**

6.2.4        *Company membership*:  The Transferee must forthwith apply to become a member of the Company and must remain a member so long as he is the registered proprietor of the Property

6.2.5        *Regulations*: The Transferee must observe and perform all regulations made by the Company relating to the use and enjoyment of the Common Parts

6.2.6        *To grant easements for Services*: The Transferee must on the request of the Transferor or the Company grant to statutory undertakers or suppliers by deed easements over any part of the Property [not covered by a building] as may reasonably be necessary to enable mains Service Apparatus to be laid to serve the Estate or any part of it

6.2.7        *Insurance*: The Transferee must insure and keep insured all buildings on the Property in the full cost of rebuilding and reinstatement including VAT professional fees shoring up debris removal site clearance and incidental expenses with the insurers or underwriters from time to time nominated by the Company and against the risks and generally on the terms of the nominated insurer's comprehensive residential policy of insurance for all buildings on the Estate[11]

6.2.8    *Rebuilding and reinstatement*: In the event of damage or destruction to the Property or any part of it the Transferee must use his best endeavours to obtain all requisite permissions required to enable him to rebuild and reinstate the Property or damaged part and on receipt of such permissions as soon as reasonably practical lay out all insurance money received in rebuilding and reinstating the Property and make up any deficiency out of his own money

6.2.9    *Service Charge*: The Transferee must pay the Service Charge to the Company in accordance with the provisions of clause 9

6.2.10    *Deed of covenant*: The Transferee must pay all costs and expenses incurred by the Company incidental to the preparation and execution of the deed to be entered into pursuant to clause 5.2.12 on the occasion of any distribution of the Property by the Transferee including any stamp duty payable on that deed

## 6.3    For the benefit of specific property

The Transferee covenants with the Transferor and his successors in title as owners of *(insert details of specific property to be benefited or protected)* as follows: *(insert details)*

[4332]

## 7    Covenants by the Company

### 7.1    Company's Obligations

The Company covenants with the Transferee and his successors in title that subject to the payment by the Transferee of the Service Charge and to the provisions of clause 7.2 the Company will [so far as practical use it best endeavours to]:

7.1.1    *Drive and Car Park maintenance*: maintain the Drives and the Car Park in the same state of repair as they [shall be in upon the issue of the certificate of practical completion by the architect in charge of the conversion and construction work on the Estate *or* are in at the date of this transfer namely *(describe present state of surfacing)*] and rebuild resurface and renew the same whenever and wherever necessary

7.1.2    *Drive verges maintenance*: mow and maintain the grass verges of the Drives

7.1.3    *Paths and tracks maintenance*: mow and keep open and tidy the [principal] paths and tracks within the Common Parts [shown coloured *(colour)* on Plan *(number)*]

7.1.4    *Boundary features maintenance*: maintain in proper repair and where necessary stockproof the walls hedges fences and gates within or bounding the Common Parts except in so far as they are the responsibility of the Transferee or adjoining owners

7.1.5    *Grounds maintenance*: maintain cultivate mow and care for and so far as practical keep in a clean and tidy condition the gardens park [lakes] woodlands and grounds of the Common Parts

7.1.6    *Service Apparatus*: maintain repair and whenever necessary renew or replace all Service Apparatus in on over or under the Estate[12] the use

of which is common to more than one property within the Estate
and is not the responsibility of service undertakers or suppliers

7.1.7     *Ornamental features*:  maintain and repair all statuary and architectural
and ornamental features on the Common Parts unless this is
impossible or can only be done at a cost that is unreasonable in all the
circumstances

**[4333]**

7.1.8     *Enforcement of covenants*:  if so required by the Transferee take all
reasonable steps to enforce the observance and performance by the
owners of other properties within the Estate of the covenants and
conditions to be observed and binding on them [subject to the
Transferee indemnifying the Company against all costs of such
enforcement and providing such security or deposit of money in
respect of costs and expenses as the Company may reasonably require][13]

7.1.9     *Third Party covenants*: observe and perform all covenants and
obligations in favour of third parties affecting the Common Parts

**7.2     Provisions affecting the Company's obligations**

7.2.1     *Relief from liability to perform*[14]:  The Company is not to be liable to
the Transferee for any failure or interruption in any of the
Maintenance Services or the temporary closure of access to or over
any part of the Common Parts caused by necessary repair
replacement cultivation or maintenance or damage to them or
destruction of them or anything beyond the Company's control
[provided and to the extent that the failure or interruption could not
[reasonably] have been prevented or shortened by the exercise of
proper care attention diligence and skill by the Company or those
undertaking the Maintenance Services on its behalf and provided
that the Company uses and continues to use [its best *or* reasonable]
endeavours to restore the Maintenance Services or reopen the part
of the Common Parts in question and] Provided that the Company
shall not close off all pedestrian and vehicular access to the Property
at the same time

7.2.2     *Acts of servants*[15]:  The Company is not to be liable to the Transferee
for any act omission or negligence of any person undertaking any of
the Maintenance Services on its behalf [provided that this clause is
not to be construed as relieving the Company from liability for
breach by it of any covenants on its part contained in this transfer]

7.2.3     *Variation of the Maintenance Services*:  The Company may withhold add
to or change the Maintenance Services or any of them from time to
time [if at its absolute discretion it considers it desirable to do so *or*
provided that the variation complies with the principles of good
estate management and is reasonable in all the circumstances][16]

**[7.3     *(insert any specific covenants for the benefit of the Property only)*]**

**8     Transferor's covenants**

Until completion of the first sale of each of the dwelling houses on the Estate the
Transferor will pay to the Company the payments which would be due to the Company
in respect of each such dwelling house [and observe and perform such obligations as the
transferee of such dwelling house would be liable to observe and perform] if the sale had
been completed

**[4334]**

**9        Service Charge Provisions**

**9.1      Definitions**

In this clause:

9.1.1        'The Additional Items' means the fees costs and outgoings set out in clause 9.7

9.1.2        'The Annual Expenditure' means:

9.1.2.1        the costs expenses and outgoings [reasonably and properly] incurred by the Company during a financial year in or incidental to providing all or any of the Maintenance Services and

9.1.2.2        the expense [reasonably and properly] incurred by the Company during a financial year in relation to the Additional Items

and any VAT payable on such costs expenses and outgoings to the extent that it cannot be recovered by the Company. The Annual Expenditure excludes any expenditure in respect of any part of the Estate for which the Transferee or any other transferee is wholly responsible and excludes any expenditure that the Company recovers or that is met under any insurance policy maintained by it or that it recovers in whole or in part from any person other than the Transferee or any other transferee of any part of the Estate

9.1.3        References to 'a computing date' are references to [31st December or *(as the case may be)*] in every year or any other date that the Company from time to time nominates and references to 'computing dates' are to be construed accordingly

9.1.4        References to a 'financial year' are references to the period commencing on [1st January *or (as the case may be)*] and ending on the first computing date and subsequently to the period between 2 consecutive computing dates excluding the first computing date but including the second computing date

9.1.5        'the Initial Provisional Service Charge' means £...... a year [plus any VAT payable thereon]

9.1.6        'The Maintenance Services' mean the obligations of the Company set out in clauses 7.1.1–7.1.9 inclusive

9.1.7        'the Manager' means the agent acting for the Company in relation to the Maintenance Services and collection of the Service Charge

9.1.8        'the Service Charge' means the Service Charge Percentage of the Annual Expenditure [plus any VAT payable thereon]

9.1.9        'the Service Charge Percentage' means ...% [subject to the provisions for variation contained in clause 9.6]

**9.2      Preparation of accounts**

As soon as convenient[17] after each computing date the Company must prepare an account showing the Annual Expenditure for the financial year ending on that computing date and containing a fair summary of the expenditure referred to in it and when that account is certified by chartered accountants it is to be conclusive evidence of all matters of fact referred to in it for the purposes of this transfer [except in the case of manifest error]

**9.3      Initial Provisional Service Charge**

For the period from the date of this transfer to the computing date next following the date of this transfer the Transferee must pay the Initial Provisional Service Charge. The first payment being a proportionate sum in respect of the period commencing on the date of this transfer and ending on the next computing date must be made on the date of this transfer. The subsequent payments must be made in advance on [1st January *or (as the case may be)*] in each year

[4335]

### 9.4      Interim payments

For the next and each subsequent financial year the Transferee must pay on [1st January *or (as the case may be)*] a provisional sum [equal to the Service Charge payable for the previous financial year—or the Service Charge that would have been payable had that financial year been a period of 12 months calculated by establishing a monthly figure for that financial year by apportionment and multiplying it by 12] increased by [*(state percentage, eg 10%) or (as required)*] calculated on [an estimate *or* a reasonable and proper estimate] by the Manager acting as an expert and not as an arbitrator of what the Annual Expenditure is likely to be for that financial year]

### 9.5      Adjustments

If the Service Charge for any financial year exceeds the provisional sum for that financial year the excess must be paid to the Company on demand. If the Service Charge for any financial year is less than the provisional sum for that financial year the overpayment must be credited to the Transferee against the next annual payment of the Service Charge[18]

### [9.6      Variation of the Service Charge Percentage[19]

If at any time the total property that enjoys or is capable of enjoying the benefit of any of the Maintenance Services or the Additional Items is permanently increased or decreased [or if some other event occurs as a result of which the Service Charge Percentage is no longer appropriate to the Property][20] then with effect from the computing date following that event the Service Charge Percentage may be varied by agreement between the Company and the Transferee or in default of agreement within *(state period, eg 3 months)* of the first proposal for variation made by the Company in such a manner as the Manager acting as an expert and not as an arbitrator determines to be fair and reasonable in the light of the event in question]

### 9.7      The Additional Items
### 9.7.1      Fees

The [proper] fees and disbursements of:

9.7.1.1      any surveyor accountant and other person employed or retained by the Company for or in connection with any surveying or accounting functions relating to or the management of the Common Parts

9.7.1.2      the Manager for or in connection with:

9.7.1.2.1      management of the Common Parts[21]

9.7.1.2.2      collection of the sums due to the Company from the transferees of the Estate[22]

9.7.1.2.3      performance of the Maintenance Services[23] [and any other duties in and about the Common Parts or any part of it relating without prejudice to the generality of the foregoing to the general management administration security maintenance protection and cleanliness of the Common Parts][24]

9.7.1.3      any person providing caretaking or security arrangements and Maintenance Services to the Estate and

9.7.1.4      any other person employed or retained by the Company to perform any of the Maintenance Services or in connection with them or to perform any of the functions or duties referred to in this clause

[4336]

**9.7.2    Staff[25]**

The cost of seeking and employing such staff as the Company in its absolute discretion thinks necessary to perform the Maintenance Services and the other functions and duties referred to in clause 9.7.1 and all other incidental expenditure in relation to employing the staff including but without prejudice to the generality of the foregoing:

9.7.2.1    insurance pension and welfare contributions

9.7.2.2    transport facilities and benefits in kind

9.7.2.3    the provision of uniforms and working clothing

9.7.2.4    the provision of vehicles tools appliances and other equipment for the proper performance of their duties and a store for housing them

**9.7.3    Contracts for Maintenance Services**

The cost of entering into any contracts to carry out all or any of the Maintenance Services and other functions and duties that the Company in its absolute discretion considers desirable or necessary

**9.7.4    Outgoings**

All rates taxes assessments duties charges impositions and outgoings that are at any time charged assessed or imposed on the Common Parts and on any residential accommodation for caretakers groundsmen and other staff employed in connection with the Common Parts

[4337]

**9.7.5    Cost of fuel**

The cost of the supply of electricity gas oil or other fuel for the provision of the Maintenance Services and for all purposes in connection with the Common Parts

**9.7.6    Road and Service Apparatus charges**

The amount the Company is called on to pay as a contribution towards the expense of making repairing maintaining rebuilding and cleaning any ways roads paths or structures Service Apparatus or anything that may belong to or be used for the Common Parts or any part of them exclusively or in common with other neighbouring or adjoining premises

**9.7.7    Cost of regulations**

The costs charges and expenses of preparing any regulations made by the Company relating to the Common Parts or the use of them and supplying copies of them to the transferees

**9.7.8    Cost of meeting statutory requirements**

The cost of taking any [reasonable] steps the Company considers desirable or expedient to comply with make representations against or otherwise contest the incidence of the provisions of any statute byelaw or notice concerning town planning public health highways streets drainage or other matters relating to or alleged to relate to the Common Parts or any part of them for which no transferee is directly and exclusively liable

**9.7.9    Costs of borrowing money**

Any interest and fees in respect of money borrowed to finance the provision of the Maintenance Services or the Additional Items[26]

[4338]

**9.7.10   Professional advice**

The cost of obtaining any professional advice and services including the prosecution of legal proceedings in relation to the Maintenance Services the

Service Charges the Common Parts and the enforcement of covenants in favour of and rights enjoyed by the Company

**9.7.11   Reserve funds for anticipated expenditure**[27]
Subject as provided in clause 9.7.12 and if requested by the Company[28] reasonable provision—to be determined by the Manager acting as an expert not an arbitrator—towards the anticipated expenditure in respect of:

9.7.11.1   periodically recurring items whether or not recurring at regular or irregular intervals and

9.7.11.2   such of the Company's obligations set out in clause 7.1 as relate to the renewal or replacement of the items referred to there[29]

**9.7.12   Conditions applying to the fund**

9.7.12.1   *The replacement fund*:  The reasonable provision in relation to items referred to in clause 9.7.11.2 is to be calculated on the basis of such life expectancy of those items referred to as the Manager acting as an expert not an arbitrator [reasonably] determines and on the assumption that each year the Transferee will pay a rateable proportion towards the anticipated cost of renewal or replacement of them to the intent that a fund will be accumulated sufficient to cover the cost of renewal or replacement by the end of the anticipated life of each such item

9.7.12.2   *No obligation to establish any fund*:  Nothing in this clause obliges the Company to establish or maintain any fund to cover the cost of replacement or renewal of any item

9.7.12.3   *Expenditure to be met out of funds in order*:  Where either a specific fund has been established in connection with a recurring item referred to in clause 9.7.11.1 or the Company's obligations set out in clause 7.1 to renew or replace any item referred to there or part of a general fund has been allocated by the Company to that recurring item or the renewal or replacement concerned then any expenditure by the Company in respect of that recurring item or the renewal or replacement concerned must be met first out of the specific fund or out of the general fund to the extent of the credit allocated for it by the Company[30]

9.7.12.4   *Accounts to indicate existence of the sinking fund*:  The account referred to in clause 9.2 must indicate whether or not the Company has established and is maintaining any fund pursuant to this clause and must provide full details of any such fund

9.7.12.5   *Separate account for the fund*:  All sums received by the Company pursuant to this clause ('the Fund') must be credited to an account separate from the Company's own money. The Fund must be held by the Company during the Perpetuity Period[31] on trust[32] for the persons who from time to time[33] are the owners of the dwelling houses on the Estate[34] to apply the Fund and any interest[35] accruing for the purposes set out in this clause. At the end of the Perpetuity Period any of the Fund unexpended must [either] be paid to the persons who are then the owners of the dwelling houses on the Estate in the same proportion the Service Charge payable by each owner respectively bears to the total of all the Service Charges paid by the owners of the dwelling houses [or for the benefit of any new trust then established in relation to the Maintenance Services to be provided to the Common Parts][36]

**10      Agreements and declarations**

It is agreed and declared as follows:

10.1    The Transferee and his successors in title shall not be entitled to any right of access of light or air or other easement or right which would restrict or interfere with the free use of any land comprised in the Estate or any adjoining or neighbouring land of the Transferor for building or any other purpose

10.2    The Transferor shall be at liberty to modify waive or release all or any covenants stipulations or restrictions relating to the Property the Estate or any adjoining or neighbouring land now or in the future belonging to the Transferor whether imposed or entered into before at the same time as or after the date of this transfer AND to sell or dispose of any part of the Estate free from any restriction or stipulation or subject to other covenants as may be appropriate to the transferred property AND the Transferor shall not in any way be bound by the plotting or general scheme of development of the Estate

10.3    Unless the contrary appears on the Plans by 'T' marks the walls hedges and fences separating the Property from the adjoining land and the buildings on it are party walls and fences and the rights and liabilities in respect of them shall be in accordance with the Law of Property Act 1925 Section 38(1)

10.4    This transfer does not include the benefit so far as appurtenant to the Property of the rights reserved to the Transferor out of the transfer of the Common Parts dated *(date)* referred to in entry *(number)* of the [property *or* charges] register of title number *(transferor's title number)* so far as such rights are the same or substantially similar to those granted by the Company in clause 3[37]

10.5    If at any time or times not less that [75%] of the owners of the dwelling houses on the Estate who are members of the Company resolve to construct additional recreational facilities with associated buildings on the Common Parts ('the Works')[38] and the Company agrees to such construction:

   10.5.1    the Transferee shall not object to or impede or delay the construction of the Works or oppose the grant of any requisite permission licence or consent from any public authority

   10.5.2    the Transferee shall not be liable to contribute to the cost of construction of the facility or its insurance maintenance and operation ('Operational Costs')

                                                            **[4340]**

   10.5.3    the Transferee may give notice in writing to the Company before construction commences that he is willing to contribute to the cost of construction and Operational Costs and he shall thereafter be liable to pay his contributions

   10.5.4    only those who have contributed to the construction of the Works and contribute to the Operational Costs shall be entitled to use the Works and no part of such costs shall be borne by the Company

   10.5.5    the Company may consent to the Works on such terms as it sees fit including imposing on the parties entitled to use the Works a licence fee to be credited to the Service Charge account to compensate those owners who do not elect to contribute to the Operational Costs of the Works for the loss of use of the area occupied by the Works

   10.5.6    All costs fees and expenses incurred by the Company and those of its professional advisors in connection with the consideration of any such application whether granted refused or withdrawn and in connection with the construction and operation of the facility shall be borne by the applicants and those entitled to use the facility and no part of such costs fees and expenses shall form part of the Service Charge

10.5.7     Subsequent owners of the Property shall be entitled to use the Works on such terms as to contribution to the Operational Costs as the Company shall from time to time determine

## 11     Application

The parties apply to the Registrar for entry of a restriction in the proprietorship register of the title to the Property in the following terms:

'Except under an order of the Registrar no disposition or dealing [including a disposition or dealing in exercise of the power of sale or power of leasing in any registered charge] is to be registered unless there is furnished to the Registrar a certificate from [*(name of the Company) or* the solicitors acting for *(name of the Company)*]* that a deed complying in all respects with the provisions of clause [5.2.12] of a deed dated *(date)* made between *(parties)* [referred to in the charges register of this title] has been delivered to *(name of the Company)*'[39]

**[4341]**

1     As to stamp duty see Information Binder: Stamp Duties [1] (Conveyance or transfer). As to Land Registry fees see Information Binder: Property [1]: Fees in connection with property matters, Land Registry fees.

Form TP1 is the Land Registry form of transfer of part of freehold or leasehold land prescribed by the Land Registration Rules 1925, SR&O 1925/1093 r 98, Sch 1 as inserted by SI 1999/128. This Form should be used whenever part only of any registered title is transferred, even if the transfer also includes the whole of one or more other registered titles.

The transferor's land or charge certificate must be placed on deposit (using Land Registry Form DP1 as prescribed by SR&O 1925/1093 Sch 1 as inserted by SI 1997/3037 and substituted by SI 1999/128 (as to which see vol 25(1) (1999 Reissue) LAND REGISTRATION Form 3 [3076]) to meet the transferee's application to register the transfer. If the transferor's land is subject to any registered charge, that charge will require to be released by use of Land Registry Form DS3 (for which see vol 25(1) (1999 Reissue) LAND REGISTRATION Form 47 [3371]). If the charge is a noted charge the consent of the chargee to the transfer should be obtained and lodged with the application to register the transfer.

Reference should be made to Form 115 [4191] ante for detailed footnotes on matters common to many forms of transfer, for cross references to the commentary in vol 35 (1997 Reissue) SALE OF LAND, for the location of alternative transfer clauses in that and other volumes and for additional footnotes relating to sale of part of a property.

The forms of rights, exceptions, covenants, restrictions, agreements and declarations in this Form are illustrative only and should be altered or replaced as the circumstances may require. Reference may be made to the clauses used in flat letting schemes and to vol 13(1) (1996 Reissue) COVENANTS RELATING TO LAND; EASEMENTS AND PROFITS À PRENDRE for alternative and additional clauses.

This form is for use in conjunction with Forms 124 [4291] and 125 [4303] ante. For an outline of the scheme see Form 124 [4291] ante. The transfer of the common parts should be completed and the transfer registered before the transfer of any dwelling house is completed.

2     The title number of the common parts should be inserted in panel 3 in addition to the title number of the estate.

3     The rights in this clause are not over the common parts; rights over the common parts are conditional on payment of the service charge and are granted by the company in panel 13 clause 3. Although the transferor has the right to grant such rights over the common parts by virtue of the reservation of those rights to him in the transfer of the common parts, the transferee is not granted the benefit of those reservations so far as they benefit the property as he would then be able to exercise those rights without paying the service charge: see clause 9 for a declaration excluding the passing of such reserved rights which would otherwise pass automatically without express mention.

4     See note 3 above.

5     See note 3 above.

6     The reservations can only operate for the benefit of the land comprised in the transferor's title and should exclude the common parts. The common parts are unlikely to require rights over the property transferred but so far as necessary such rights should be granted to the management company in the transfer to it of the common parts.

**[4342]**

7    The benefit of the restriction on plots sold is expressed not to pass to buyers of later plots sold nor will the buyers of later plots sold acquire the benefit of the restrictions imposed on the transfer of plots sold earlier unless expressly granted. This Form, unlike Form 118 [4213] ante, does not expressly create a building scheme so that the restrictions are mutually enforceable as between individual plot owners. As to the necessary elements to constitute a building scheme see *Elliston v Reacher* [1908] 2 Ch 374. See also 16 Halsbury's Laws (4th Edn Reissue) EQUITY para 797 et seq. Because of the possibility that such covenants may be enforceable by other plot owners who are not parties to the transfer even if a building scheme is not expressly created (*Re Ecclesiastical Commrs for England's Conveyance* [1936] Ch 430) an express declaration negativing such a scheme may be inserted if desired, although practitioners may feel that clause 5.1 is sufficient indication. There may be advantages in expressly creating a building scheme in view of the close relationship of the dwelling houses to each other and the comfort which each owner would derive from being able to enforce covenants direct rather than rely on the management company doing so. In that case this Form should be adapted to follow the relevant parts of Form 118 [4213] ante and in particular panel 13 clauses 4.1 [4217] and 7.1 and 7.2 [4220] of that Form.

8    For other restrictions which may be appropriate see vol 13(1) (1996 Reissue) COVENANTS RELATING TO LAND Forms 126 [1483]–143(12) [1604]. Consideration should be given to such additional matters as refuse storage, hanging out of washing, and satellite dishes and external television aerials.

9    For a form of deed of covenant adapted for use in this case see Form 127 [4347] post.

10    A restriction in the proprietorship register may not be cancelled on the exercise of a power of sale by a registered chargee, but nevertheless there is doubt whether the transferee would be bound by the covenants. It may be deemed prudent, therefore, particularly in the case of a charge executed prior to or contemporaneously with the application for the registration, to ensure that any registered chargee applies for a restriction to be registered against the charge, so as to put the matter beyond doubt. The chargee or his solicitors must sign the application for this restriction. It may be incorporated within the text of a transfer or deed of covenant, or application may be made by letter accompanying the application for registration of the charge.

11    Unlike in a flat letting scheme the transferee is responsible for insurance of his property. This Form provides for all the dwellings and other buildings to be insured by the same insurer to avoid the inevitable problems which will arise if a number of different insurers are involved in the event of major damage affecting a number of dwellings in the mansion or outbuildings. Whilst the adjoining owners and the management company have no insurable interest in the transferee's property they will want the comfort of knowing that if the transferee's property is damaged it will be rebuilt and that it is adequately insured. Careful consideration of all the insurance aspects is essential including the possibility of major destruction which may leave a few dwelling houses undamaged but surrounded by or attached to a ruin and which it may be impractical or unlawful to rebuild. It is likely to be impossible to provide for all contingencies and this clause and clause 6.2.8 contain the bare minimum of provision. For other and more detailed insurance clauses which may be adapted see vol 22(3) (1997 Reissue) LANDLORD AND TENANT (BUSINESS TENANCIES). Consideration should be given to imposing the obligations of insurance, external repairs and external decoration on the management company, to be paid for out of the service charge.

12    There may be common service apparatus within the mansion or outbuildings.

13    See note 7 above as to the possibility of creating a building scheme which would allow direct action by one dwelling owner against another.

14    This clause is likely to be viewed as an exclusion clause: see vol 22(1) (1996 Reissue) LANDLORD AND TENANT (BUSINESS TENANCIES) Paragraph 338 notes 5 and 6 [592].

15    See note 14 above.

16    As to 'sweeping-up' provisions see vol 22(1) (1996 Reissue) LANDLORD AND TENANT (BUSINESS TENANCIES) Paragraph 350 [609].

17    Time is not of the essence in relation to the preparation of the service charge account where a lease provides for the account to be prepared within a specified period: see *West Central Investments Ltd v Borovik* (1977) 241 Estates Gazette 609 and vol 22(1) (1996 Reissue) LANDLORD AND TENANT (BUSINESS TENANCIES) Paragraph 355 [621].

**[4343]**

18    The Transferee may wish to have large overpayments refunded immediately, or at least on being credited with interest. Where repayments are made and VAT is normally charged, a VAT credit note will need to be issued.

19    As to the need for this provision, see vol 22(1) (1996 Reissue) LANDLORD AND TENANT (BUSINESS TENANCIES) Paragraph 353.1 [613]. An alternative is to have a completely independent expert such as an outside chartered surveyor to make the determination.

20    This wording gives greater flexibility to the company, permitting a change in the percentage in circumstances other than an increase or decrease in the number of dwelling houses.

21    If such items are to be recovered, there must be express references in the transfer: see *Cleve House Properties v Schildof* [1980] CLY 1641.

22    See note 21 above.

23    The company is likely to perform the maintenance services either by means of third parties whose fees it pays, being reimbursed by the transferees, or by its own staff. In the latter case the company would wish to be able to include the cost of employing the staff as part of the service charge.

24    These words serve to widen the maintenance services further, and the transferee should resist them.

25    As to employment of staff see vol 22(1) (1996 Reissue) LANDLORD AND TENANT (BUSINESS TENANCIES) Paragraph 346 [603].

26    See *Boldmark Ltd v Cohen* (1985) 19 HLR 136, [1986] 1 EGLR 47, CA.

27    As to sinking funds see vol 22(1) (1996 Reissue) LANDLORD AND TENANT (BUSINESS TENANCIES) Paragraph 364 [632].

28    In view of the taxation implications (for which see vol 22(1) (1996 Reissue) LANDLORD AND TENANT (BUSINESS TENANCIES) Paragraph 365.6 [635]) the landlord will not wish to be compelled to operate a sinking fund.

29    The fund is divided into two categories: the equalisation fund and the replacement fund for plant and machinery. As to this division see vol 22(1) (1996 Reissue) LANDLORD AND TENANT (BUSINESS TENANCIES) Paragraphs 363 [631] and 364 [632].

30    As to the need to ensure that the sinking fund is tapped as necessary see vol 22(1) (1996 Reissue) LANDLORD AND TENANT (BUSINESS TENANCIES) Paragraph 365.2 [633].

31    The life of a trust has to be limited to a perpetuity period and the express choice of 80 years would seem to be the most practical. As to the rule against perpetuities see vol 22(1) (1996 Reissue) LANDLORD AND TENANT (BUSINESS TENANCIES) Paragraph 153 [290].

32    As to the need to keep the sinking fund separate from the company's own money see vol 22(1) (1996 Reissue) LANDLORD AND TENANT (BUSINESS TENANCIES) Paragraph 365.1 [633].

33    There is perhaps the technical argument that making future dwelling house owners beneficiaries would prevent the transferor from changing the form of the transfer with regard to future sales. See also *Leahy v A-G for New South Wales* [1959] AC 457, [1959] 2 All ER 300, PC.

**[4344]**

34    A trust expressed for a purpose that is not charitable is invalid if there are no beneficiaries: see *Re Denley's Trust Deed, Holman v HH Martyn & Co Ltd* [1969] 1 Ch 373, [1968] 3 All ER 65 in which Goff J held that such a trust was not invalid where it was directly or indirectly for the benefit of individuals. It is suggested that any doubt be avoided by expressly dealing with the question of beneficiaries in such a way that it would also remove any uncertainty as to who would be entitled to enforce the trust.

35    In the case of a lease, a landlord, who is holding the fund on trust, may invest it only as permitted by the Trustee Investments Act 1961 (48 Halsbury's Statutes (4th Edn) TRUSTS AND SETTLEMENTS). A landlord who accepts the principle of a trust may seek to widen the provision by means of a variation on the type of investments clause found in wills or settlements. The tenant could well resist on the grounds that interest earned, or rather the difference between that earned on 'safe' and 'speculative' investments, is unlikely to be very material; what is far more important is that the fund should be available when the redecoration or replacement is undertaken.

36    Provision should be made for the disposal of any surplus funds at the end of the period, although there could be difficulties with this format. Inclusion of the alternative provisions in square brackets may help.

       Consideration should also be given to any circumstances in which the dwelling house owner should be entitled to a refund of his sinking fund contributions before the end of the 80-year period.

37    See note 3 above.

38    Occasionally some owners wish to provide some additional leisure facility (eg a tennis court), but others, such as the elderly, do not want it. This clause is designed to allow it to be built at the expense only of those who are to use it. However, such provisions can be divisive and should only be inserted if there is a real possibility of some additional facility being required.

       Provision should be made to allow subsequent owners of dwelling houses, whose predecessors have not contributed to its construction, to have the right to use it or appropriate terms.

39    Early forms of such restrictions required the deed to be lodged with the land registry and in effect for the registry to check whether the deed complied with the terms of the covenant. This was not desirable and most modern forms of the restriction seek to leave control of the form of the deed with the seller or his solicitor, who then furnishes a certificate to the subsequent buyer that the obligations under the covenant have been complied with, and this certificate is lodged with the application for registration.

**[4345]–[4346]**

# 127

### Deed of covenant by a second or subsequent buyer with a management company responsible for maintenance of parts of the grounds of a country mansion which has been converted into a number of freehold dwelling[1]

THIS DEED OF COVENANT is made the ...... day of ......... BETWEEN

(1)     *(management company)* [company number *(number)*] whose registered office is at *(address)* ('the Company') and

(2)     *(buyer)* of *(address)* ('the Transferee')

NOW THIS DEED WITNESSES as follows:

[4347]

## 1       Definitions and interpretation

In this deed:

1.1     'the 'Common Parts' has the meaning given in clause [1.2] of the Transfer[2]

1.2     'the Property' means *(address of the dwelling house)* registered at HM Land Registry under title number *(number)*

1.3     'the Service Charge' has the meaning given in clause [1.13] of the Transfer

1.4     'the Transfer' means a transfer of the Property dated *(date)* and made between *(seller)* and *(first buyer)* referred to in entry number *(number)* of the [property or charges] register of title number *(number)*

1.5     'the Transferee' includes where the context so admits the successors in title of the Transferee and where the Transferee is more than one person all covenants and agreements on the part of the Transferee contained in this deed shall be deemed to have been made jointly and severally by all such persons constituting the Transferee

1.6     any reference to a clause in the Transfer is to a clause in panel 13 of the Transfer

## 2       Recitals

2.1     This deed is supplemental to the Transfer and is executed pursuant to clause [5.2.12] of the Transfer

2.2     The Transferee has agreed to purchase the Property together with the rights in respect of the Common Parts granted by the Company by clause [3] of the Transfer

## 3       Registration as a member of the Company

The Transferee applies to be registered as a member of the Company and the Company undertakes to register the Transferee as a member of the Company[3]

[4348]

## 4       Company's covenants

The Company covenants with the Transferee that it will:

4.1     subject to payment by the Transferee to the Company of the Service Charge in accordance with the provisions of clause [9] of the Transfer and to the provisions of clause [7.2] of the Transfer [so far as practical use its best endeavours to] observe and perform the obligations of the Company set out in clause [7] of the Transfer as if such obligations were repeated here in full

4.2      enter into a deed of covenant in the terms of this deed with any transferee or
         intended transferee of the Property and give any certificate required to HM
         Land Registry to allow registration of any proposed dealing with the Property
         provided that the Transferee has observed and performed the covenants on his
         part contained in this deed and fulfilled the obligations on his part contained in
         the articles of association of the Company
4.3      give to HM Land Registry a certificate in accordance with clause [11] of the
         Transfer to allow registration of the transfer of the Property to the Transferee[4]

## 5      Transferee's covenants

The Transferee covenants with the Company that he will:

5.1      pay to the Company the Service Charge in accordance with the provisions of
         clause [9] of the Transfer
5.2      in any contract for the sale of the Property include a condition that the
         intending buyer shall upon completion of the contract apply to become
         registered as a member of the Company
5.3      include in any contract for the sale of the Property a condition precedent to
         performance of the contract that the intending buyer shall enter into a deed of
         covenant with the Company in the terms of this deed and that the intending
         buyer shall bear all costs of and incidental to the preparation and execution of
         the deed including any stamp duty payable on it

IN WITNESS etc

*(signatures (or common seals) of the parties)*[5]
**[***(signatures of witnesses)***]**
**[4349]**

---

1     No stamp duty. See Information Binder: Stamp Duties [1] (Covenant).
          This Form is intended for use on the second or subsequent purchase of a freehold dwelling house
      which is part of a country mansion house which is subject to the scheme set up in Forms 124 [4291]–
      126 [4322] ante. Every incoming buyer of a dwelling house must execute a deed in this Form or a
      suitable similar form.
2     See Form 126 [4322] ante.
3     The management company envisaged here is intended to be one limited by guarantee rather than
      shares. If a company limited by shares is required, this provision must be supplemented by a transfer of
      the shares signed by the existing shareholder.
4     For the wording of the restriction entered on the register see Form 126 panel 13 clause 11 [4341] ante.
5     As to the statutory requirements for the valid execution of deeds see vol 12 (1994 Reissue) DEEDS,
      AGREEMENTS AND DECLARATIONS.

**[4350]**

# (8): RELEASES FROM SECURITY

## 128

### Letter of non-crystallisation issued by a chargee[1]

*(Letterhead of the chargee)*

To all whom it may concern

*(date)*

Re: *(address of property)*

We refer to the floating charge created by a mortgage debenture dated *(date)* in our favour and confirm that we are not aware of the happening of any event and have taken no action whereby the floating charge created by the debenture has crystallised.

We also consent to the sale of the above property free from the floating charge created by the debenture.

Yours faithfully,

*(signature of or on behalf of the chargee)*

---

1    Evidence of non-crystallisation is not conclusive unless provided by the debenture holder, though a debenture holder is under no obligation to provide such evidence: see *Emmet on Title* (19th Edn) Paragraph 10.86. A letter of non-crystallisation should also be sought from the company concerned. For an example of such a letter see Form 129 [4352] post. Letters of non-crystallisation should be lodged with the application for registration of the dealing where the relevant floating charge has been noted on the register of title. The Registrar will then be satisfied that the entry can be cancelled following the transfer and need not be carried forward to any new title.

**[4351]**

## 129

### Letter of non-crystallisation issued by the chargor[1]

*(Letterhead of the company)*

To all whom it may concern

*(date)*

Charge dated *(date)* to *(chargee)*
*(address of property)*

I certify on behalf of the above-named company that the floating charge above referred to has not crystallised and I further certify that I do not know of any reason why it should have done so.

Yours faithfully,

*(signature of authorised signatory on behalf of the company)*

---

1    A letter of non-crystallisation should also be obtained from the chargee: see Form 128 [4351] ante.

**[4352]**

## 130

### Release of plot from noted debenture

HM LAND REGISTRY LAND REGISTRATION ACTS 1925 to 1986

| | |
|---|---|
| Administrative area | *(insert details)* |
| Title Number | *(title number)* |
| Property | *(describe property)* |
| Date | *(date)* |

We, *(name of debenture holder)*, being entitled to the benefit of the equitable charge created by the debenture dated *(date)* referred to in Entry number *(number)* of the Charges Register of the title above referred to:

1        release the land shown and edged with red on the accompanying plan signed for and on our behalf being Plot Number *(number)* [and Garage Plot number *(number)*] and being part of the land comprised in the title above mentioned from all claims and demands under the debenture and

2        consent to the registration of the transfer dated *(date)* of [that *or* those] plots by *(transferor)* to *(name of transferee)*

*(signature of authorised signatory on behalf of the company)*
**[4353]–[4370]**

# PART 10: PROFESSIONALS: APPOINTMENT AND COLLATERAL WARRANTIES

## *Forms and Precedents*

### 131
#### Appointment of a professional[1]

THIS AGREEMENT is made the ... day of ......

BETWEEN:

(1)      *(name)* [company number *(number)*][2] [of *(address) or* whose registered office is at *(address)*] ('the Client') which expression includes his successors in title and assigns)

(2)      *(name)* [company number *(number)*] [of *(address) or* whose registered office is at *(address)*] ('the Consultant')

[4371]

NOW IT IS AGREED as follows:

**1       Definitions and interpretation**

In this Agreement:

1.1      'Adjudicator' means the person appointed pursuant to clause 16 and schedule 7[3]

1.2      'Building Contract' means the building contract in respect of the Project in the form agreed or to be agreed between the Client and the Building Contractor

1.3      'Building Contractor' means the contractor employed or to be employed by the Client under the Building Contract

1.4      'design' includes all drawings design details specifications and bills of quantities (including specification of articles or substances) in relation to any part of the Project

1.5      'Designer' means any person who prepares a design or arranges for any person under his or her control to prepare a design

1.6      'Fees' means the fees specified in or calculated on the basis set out in schedule 1

1.7      'Group Company'[4] means a company within the group of companies of which the Client is from time to time a member

1.8      'Health and Safety File'[5] means the file or other record in permanent form containing adequate information about any aspect of the Project or any structure or materials therein (including articles and substances) which might affect the health and safety (or it is reasonably foreseeable will be necessary to ensure the health and safety) of any person at work who is carrying out or will carry out any work on the Site at any time or of any person who may be affected by the work of such a person at work

1.9     'Health and Safety Plan'[6] means the health and safety plan prepared in accordance with the provisions of the Construction (Design and Management) Regulations 1994

1.10    'Insurer' means any person providing decennial or project insurance and the members of any technical inspection team he may appoint[7]

**[4372]**

1.11    'Joint Venture Partner' means any person who may enter into a joint venture at any time with the Client in respect of the Site and/or the Project

1.12    'Key Personnel' means the persons specified in schedule 2

1.13    'Lender' means any person who may provide or agree to provide loan facilities or other finance in respect of the acquisition of the Site or the carrying out of the Project or the acquisition of the Project (complete or incomplete) or secured on any of the foregoing for any purpose and his successors in title or assignees

1.14    'Materials' means all designs drawings models design details brochures reports notes of meetings computer-aided design materials documents papers calculations specifications software computerised information data plans drawings photographs and any other materials prepared by or on behalf of the Consultant for the purposes of the Project

1.15    'Other Consultants' means the other consultants involved in the Project identified in schedule 3 or such other consultants as the Client may from time to time engage in connection with the Project

1.16    'Programme' means the Client's programme for the carrying out of the Project as amended from time to time

1.17    'Prohibited Materials' means the materials referred to in clause 3.2.9

1.18    'Project' means the development described in schedule 4 and references to the Project include part or parts thereof and/or any building erected or to be erected thereon

1.19    'Project Brief' means the statement of the Client's requirements and objectives for the Project details of which have been supplied to the Consultant as may be amended or supplemented from time to time

1.20    'Purchaser' means any purchaser or prospective purchaser of the Site or the Project and his successors in title or assignees

1.21    'Services' means the services described in schedule 5 and any additional services requested by the Client and agreed to be undertaken by the Consultant in respect of the Project

1.22    'Site' means the land upon which the Project will be carried out and references to the Site include part or parts of it

1.23    'Site Staff' means staff appointed in accordance with clause 6

1.24    'Statutory Requirements' means all relevant acts of parliament regulations instruments or orders made thereunder all regulations and bye-laws of any relevant local and statutory authority and any modification extension or re-enactment of them from time to time

1.25    'Sub-contractor' means any sub-contractor supplier or sub-consultant (of any tier) involved with the Project

1.26    'Tenant' means any tenant or prospective tenant (whether on a pre-let basis or following completion of the Project) of the Site or the Project and his successors in title or assignees

1.27    'Warranty' means one or other of the form of warranties set out in schedule 6 and 'Warranties' means [both *or* all] of them

1.28    Clause headings are for convenience only and shall not affect the construction of this Agreement and all references to clauses sub-clauses or schedules are to clauses and sub-clauses of and schedules to this Agreement

1.29    Words denoting the singular number include the plural and vice versa
1.30    References to persons include references to bodies corporate and unincorporate

**[4373]**

**2       Background**

2.1     The Client intends to proceed with the Project at the Site. The Project is
        intended to be used as *(insert description)*
2.2     The Client wishes to engage the Consultant to act in the capacity of *(specify)* on
        the terms and subject to the provisions of this Agreement
[2.3    The Project is not designed for occupation by the Client. It is to be let and/or
        sold in its entirety or in parts⁸]
2.4     The Client wishes to appoint the Other Consultants to provide services for the
        Client
2.5     The Client requires the Consultant to provide warranties in the form of the
        Warranty

**3       Appointment**

3.1     The Client appoints the Consultant to provide the Services and the Consultant
        accepts such appointment which shall be deemed to take effect from the date of
        the commencement of the provision of the Services
3.2     The Consultant covenants with the Client that in the provision of the Services
        and in the execution of all matters which lie within the scope of his professional
        skill judgment and responsibilities which he has undertaken and will undertake
        in relation to the Project he:

   3.2.1    has exercised and will continue to exercise all the reasonable skill care
            and diligence expected of a properly qualified and competent *(insert
            discipline)* carrying out the Services and experienced in projects of a
            similar size scope complexity and purpose as the Project
   3.2.2    acknowledges that the Client shall be deemed to have relied
            exclusively upon his professional skill judgment and responsibilities
            in respect of his duties under this Agreement
   3.2.3    has performed and will continue to perform his duties so that to the
            extent to which the design of the Project has been carried out by or
            on his behalf such design complies with the requirements of the
            Project Brief the Building Contract and all relevant Statutory
            Requirements and to the best of the Consultant's knowledge and
            belief the completed Project or such part of the Project as has been
            constructed in accordance with his design criteria complies and will
            continue to comply in all respects with the Project Brief the Building
            Contract and all relevant Statutory Requirements

**[4374]**

   3.2.4    has performed and will continue to perform his duties in
            conjunction with the Client the Designers the Other Consultants
            the Building Contractor and any Sub-contractors and their
            respective officers employees agents and representatives
   3.2.5    has co-ordinated and will continue to co-ordinate both the design
            for which he is responsible and the design of any part of the Project
            undertaken by any of the Other Consultants with the overall design
            of the Project
   3.2.6    has performed and will continue to perform his duties so as to
            comply with the Programme

| | |
|---|---|
| 3.2.7 | has the competence to perform the Services and to conduct his undertaking without contravening any prohibition imposed on him by or under any relevant acts and regulations and will at all relevant times employ an adequate number of competent and suitably qualified and experienced personnel in the performance of the Services |
| 3.2.8 | has allocated and will continue to allocate adequate resources to enable him to undertake the Services |
| 3.2.9 | has not specified and will not specify any goods materials products or substances for use in the Project which are not in accordance with the relevant British and European Standards and Codes of Practice or which are generally known or suspected within the construction or engineering industries at the time of use to be deleterious to health and safety or to the durability of the Project in the particular circumstances in which they are used ('Prohibited Materials') and if he becomes aware that any Prohibited Material has been or is about to be used he will immediately alert the Client[9] |

**[4375]**

| | |
|---|---|
| 3.2.10 | has exercised and will continue to exercise all reasonable skill care and diligence to see so far as is consistent with his duties under this Agreement that no Prohibited Materials have been specified for use in the Project by any of the Other Consultants |
| 3.2.11 | shall if requested by the Client issue to the Client and to any person as the Client may require a certificate stating that no Prohibited Materials have been specified for use by the Consultant in the Project |
| 3.2.12 | has used and will continue to use his reasonable endeavours to procure that in the provision of the Services full compliance is made with all relevant Statutory Requirements relating to site safety and in the event that the Consultant becomes aware of any working or other practice which may give rise to any injury to a person during the course of the carrying out of the Project he shall forthwith give written details thereof to the Client |
| 3.2.13 | has used and will continue to use his best endeavours to give effect to the requirements of the Insurer and any member of the Insurer's technical inspection team[10] |

**[4376]**

## 4    Other consultants and the designers

| | |
|---|---|
| 4.1 | The Client intends to employ the Other Consultants and such other consultants as he deems necessary in connection with the design and carrying out of the Project |
| 4.2 | The Consultant shall liaise and co-operate as necessary with the Building Contractor the Designers the Insurer the Sub-contractors and the Other Consultants and provide each with and co-ordinate any required information using reasonable endeavours to ensure that the Project is designed carried out and completed in accordance with the Project Brief and he shall produce all relevant information or advice required of him punctually so as not to cause any delay in the Programme |
| 4.3 | The Consultant will take such steps as it is reasonable for him to take to ensure co-operation between himself the Designers and the Other Consultants so far as is necessary to enable him the Designers and the Other Consultants to ensure that any design prepared includes among the design considerations adequate regard to the need to: |

4.3.1    avoid foreseeable risks to the health and safety of any person at work carrying out any construction work or cleaning work at any time or of any person who may be affected by the work of such a person at such work and

4.3.2    combat at source risks to the health and safety of any person at work carrying out any construction work or cleaning work at any time or of any person who may be affected by the work of such a person at such work and

4.3.3    give priority to measures which will protect all persons at work who may carry out any construction work or cleaning work at any time and all persons who may be affected by the work of such persons at such work over measures which only protect each person carrying out such work[11]

**[4377]**

## 5    Key Personnel

5.1    The Consultant shall ensure that the Key Personnel shall be employed on the Project on a full-time basis

5.2    Any Key Personnel who shall die be incapacitated suffer serious illness or cease to work for the Consultant shall be replaced by another who shall previously have been approved by the Client in writing

5.3    The Consultant shall ensure that at least one of the Key Personnel is present at all meetings at which the Consultant's attendance is required

## 6    Site Staff

6.1    The Consultant shall recommend the appointment of Site Staff to the Client if in his opinion such appointment is necessary to allow him to provide the Services

6.2    The Consultant shall confirm in writing to the Client the Site Staff to be appointed their disciplines the expected duration of their employment the party to appoint them and the party to pay for such appointment

6.3    Any such Site Staff shall be under the direction and control of the Consultant

**[4378]**

## 7    Remuneration

7.1    The remuneration of the Consultant for the Services shall be the Fees which the Client will pay to the Consultant in accordance with schedule 1 as long as the Consultant provides the Client with VAT invoices in proper form

7.2    If for any reason and at any time the design or carrying out of the Project is postponed or delayed the Client's liability for payment of the Fees shall be deferred by an interval equal to the length of such postponement or delay and the Consultant shall be entitled to a proportion of the Fees commensurate with the Services undertaken by him up to the date of the postponement or delay calculated on a quantum meruit basis

7.3    If the Client fails to make payment of any amounts payable under this Agreement by the date [14] days after the date on which any amount payable under this Agreement becomes due for payment (referred to in this clause as 'the Final Date for Payment') the Consultant may give notice in writing to the Client of his intention to suspend performance of his obligations under this Agreement[12]

7.4     The notice referred to in sub-clause 7.3 shall specify the ground or grounds on which the Consultant intends to suspend performance of his obligations under this Agreement[13]

7.5     If within [7] days of receipt of a notice under sub-clause 7.3 the Client has not made payment in full of the amount due and specified in the said notice the Consultant may suspend performance of his obligations under this Agreement[14]

7.6     The Consultant's right to suspend performance of his obligations under this Agreement ceases when the Client makes payment in full of the amounts payable under this Agreement specified in the notice served under sub-clause 7.3[15]. The Consultant shall thereupon proceed regularly and diligently with performance of his obligations under this Agreement and he shall not be entitled to any payment or damages whatsoever in addition to the Fees by virtue of exercising his right to suspend performance

7.7     Where the Client proposes to withhold payment after the Final Date for Payment of a sum due or to become due to the Consultant under this Agreement he shall serve a notice of intention to withhold payment on the Consultant in writing not later than [7] days before the Final Date for Payment[16] stating the amount proposed to be withheld and the ground for withholding payment or if there is more than one ground each ground and the amount attributable to it

**[4379]**

## 8     Assignment

8.1     This Agreement is personal to the Consultant and he shall not assign charge or transfer any right or obligation under this Agreement to any other person

8.2     The Consultant may recommend to the Client that he be permitted to appoint specialists to design a certain part of the Project in which case and if the recommendation is accepted by the Client in writing the Consultant shall be responsible to the Client for their design of any such part as if the design were his and shall co-ordinate and integrate their design of such part within the overall design of the Project

8.3     The Client shall be freely entitled to assign charge novate or otherwise transfer the benefit of all or any of the Consultant's obligations under this Agreement and/or any benefit arising under or out of this Agreement to any person and in this connection and upon the Client's written request the Consultant shall enter into a deed of novation with any such person in the form set out in schedule 8 with all necessary changes

8.4     The Consultant hereby irrevocably appoints the Client to be his attorney for the purpose of executing and completing any assignment charge novation or transfer required to satisfy the provisions of sub-clause 8.3 which is not executed and completed within [7] days of any request by the Client. The Consultant agrees to ratify any action taken by the Client by virtue of this power of attorney

8.5     Immediately upon notice of any such assignment charge novation or transfer being given to the Consultant he shall become and be fully bound to such person as if that person had originally been a party to this Agreement and had been named herein as the Client

**[4380]**

## 9     Insurance[17]

9.1     Without prejudice to his obligations under this Agreement the Consultant warrants that he has and that he will maintain insurance cover in respect of all claims under this Agreement:

9.1.1       for negligence with a limit of indemnity of not less than £... and an excess of not more than £... for each and every event unlimited in number (or in the case of claims for pollution or contamination with not less than such limit of indemnity in the aggregate for any and all claims notified in the year of insurance) and

9.1.2       for public liability in the sum of not less than £... for each and every occurrence unlimited in number

and in each case for a period of 12 years from the date of practical completion of the Project and under a policy issued by a reputable insurance company or underwriters carrying on business in the United Kingdom

9.2     On request the Consultant shall produce for inspection by the Client or any person authorised by the Client documentary evidence that the insurance required under sub-clause 9.1 is being maintained

9.3     If the Consultant fails to comply with this clause 9 he shall repay to the Client on demand any money the Client reasonably spends to effect insurance against any risk or amount with respect to which such default has occurred

9.4     The Consultant has prior to the date of this Agreement notified his insurers of the terms of this Agreement and will disclose the same to any new insurers before changing insurers

**[4381]**

## 10     Determination

10.1     The Client may at any time by notice in writing of not less than *(specify)* given to the Consultant determine his appointment under this Agreement and the Consultant shall if required to do so by the Client hand over copies of the Materials (in the format referred to in sub-clause 13.6) to the Client without further payment therefor other than the Fees accrued due

10.2     If at any time the Client decides to postpone or suspend the Project the Client may thereupon by reasonable notice in writing to the Consultant require him to suspend performance of the Services

10.3     If the Client shall not have required the Consultant to resume performance of the Services following any postponement or suspension within a period of *(specify)* from the notice given under sub-clause 10.2 then for the purposes of this Agreement the Project shall be considered to have been abandoned and the Consultant's appointment under this Agreement determined

10.4     The Consultant shall upon receipt of any notice or requirement in accordance with sub-clauses 10.1 and 10.2 proceed in an orderly manner but with all reasonable speed and economy to take such steps as are necessary to bring the Services to an end or postpone or suspend the same and he shall if required to do so by the Client hand over copies of the Materials (in the format referred to in sub-clause 13.6) to the Client without further payment

10.5     Any determination postponement or suspension of the Consultant's appointment hereunder shall not prejudice or affect the accrued rights claims or liabilities of either party under this Agreement or otherwise

## 11     Payment following determination postponement or suspension by the Client

11.1     Upon determination postponement or suspension pursuant to clause 10 the Client shall pay to the Consultant a proportion of the Fees calculated on a quantum meruit basis less any amounts payable to the Client by the Consultant under this Agreement

11.2    Except as stated in clause 11.1 no further payments shall be made to the Consultant

11.3    In the event of the Client giving written notice to the Consultant requiring him to resume the carrying out of the Services which may have been postponed or suspended pursuant to sub-clause 10.2 any payment made to the Consultant pursuant to sub-clause 11.1 shall rank as a payment on account of the Fees payable to the Consultant

**[4382]**

## 12    Default

If the Consultant shall commit a material breach of this Agreement which is capable of remedy and fails to remedy such breach within [7] days of being given written notice specifying the breach and requiring it to be remedied the Client shall be entitled to terminate the Consultant's appointment under this Agreement forthwith but without prejudice to any rights the Client may have against the Consultant in respect of any non-performance failure or neglect of the Consultant and the Consultant shall if required so to do by the Client hand over copies of the Materials (in the format referred to in sub-clause 13.6) to the Client for use in connection with the Project without further payment

## 13    Copyright

13.1    The Consultant grants the Client an irrevocable royalty-free non-exclusive licence to use and reproduce the Materials for any purpose relating to the Project whether completed or uncompleted including (without limitation) the construction completion reconstruction modification extension repair reinstatement refurbishment redevelopment maintenance use letting promotion and advertisement of the Project

13.2    The licence carries the right to grant sub-licences and is transferable without the prior consent of the Consultant

13.3    The Consultant will not be liable for the use of any of the Materials by the beneficiary of the licence or sub-licence for any purpose other than that for which they were prepared

13.4    The Consultant agrees on request at any time to give the Client or any person authorised by the Client access to the Materials and to provide copies of them at the Client's expense

13.5    The Consultant will after completion of the Project provide the Client free of charge with 3 comprehensive sets of the Materials and drawings showing the Project 'as built' the main lines of drainage the services installations maintenance and operation manuals and all guarantees provided by suppliers of materials and/or components together with any additional comprehensive sets as the Client may require and for which the Client will pay the Consultant his reasonable copying charges

13.6    All such Materials and drawings showing the Project 'as built' the main lines of drainage the services installations maintenance and operation manuals and all guarantees provided by suppliers of materials and/or components shall if required by the Client be provided on magnetic and/or optical media or in other computer readable format compatible with the Client's information technology systems and shall be free from any virus and shall be Year 2000 compliant

13.7    If the Consultant shall be prevented by insolvency or other incapacity from performing his obligations under this Agreement the Client may make free use of the Materials notwithstanding any lien on them against unpaid Fees

13.8     All royalties or other sums payable in respect of the supply and use of any patented articles processes or inventions required in connection with the performance of the Services shall be paid by the Consultant and the Consultant shall indemnify the Client from and against all claims proceedings damages costs and expenses suffered or incurred by the Client by reason of the Consultant infringing or being held to infringe any intellectual property rights in the performance of the Services

**[4383]**

## 14     Warranties

14.1     [Contemporaneously with the exchange of the Building Contract the Consultant shall execute and hand to the Building Contractor a warranty in favour of the Building Contractor in the form of the warranty set out in schedule 6(A)[18] and/*or* the Consultant shall when requested by the Client execute and hand to the Client the Warranty in favour of any or all of the Purchaser the Tenant the Lender the Group Company the Insurer and the Joint Venture Partner as and when required by the Client in the form of the warranty set out in schedule 6(B)]

14.2     The Consultant irrevocably appoints the Client to be his attorney for the purposes of executing and completing [the Building Contractor's Warranty and] the Warranty required to satisfy the provisions of sub–clause 14.1 which is not executed and completed within [7] days of any request by the Client. The Consultant agrees to ratify and confirm any action taken by the Client by virtue of this power of attorney

## 15     Variations, omissions, alterations, modifications, confidentiality and approvals relating to the Project

15.1     The Consultant shall not without the written consent of the Client agree any variation omission alteration or modification relating to the Project and shall not (save as may be necessary for his proper performance under this Agreement) disclose to any third party or make use of any information of any kind whatsoever in relation to the Project

15.2     The Consultant shall inform the Client upon it becoming apparent that there is any incompatibility between the Project Brief the Building Contract the Programme the Health and Safety Plan and the requirements of the Insurer or any need to vary any part of them

15.3     The obligations of the Consultant under this Agreement shall not be lessened or affected by any power or duty of the Client or any of the Other Consultants to grant or withhold approval of or object to any matter in connection with the Project or to inspect the Project or the grant or failure to grant such approval or the making or failure to make such objection or any such inspection of or failure to inspect the Project

**[4384]**

## 16     Disputes[19]

16.1     If any dispute or difference as to the construction of this Agreement or any matter or thing of whatsoever nature arising under it or in connection with it shall arise between the Client and the Consultant it shall be determined in the courts of England and Wales or by adjudication and not in arbitration

16.2     If any dispute or difference arises under this Agreement either party may refer it to adjudication in accordance with the provisions of this clause and subject thereto final determination of disputes or differences arising herein shall be determined in accordance with this clause 16

16.3    Where either party requires a dispute or difference to be referred to adjudication the matter shall be dealt with in accordance with the provisions set out in schedule 7

## 17    Communications

17.1    All notices or other communications under or in respect of this Agreement to either party shall be deemed to be duly given or made when delivered (in the case of personal delivery or letter) or when despatched (in the case of facsimile) to the party addressed to him at the address appearing below (or at such address as the party may after the date of this Agreement specify for this purpose to the other):
17.1.1    In the case of the Client:
17.1.1.1    Address:
17.1.1.2    Facsimile number:
17.1.2    In the case of the Consultant:
17.1.2.1    Address:
17.1.2.2    Facsimile number:

17.2    A written notice includes a notice by facsimile. A notice or other communication received on a non-working day or after business hours in the place of receipt shall be deemed to be given or made on the next following working day in that place

**[4385]**

## [18    Third party rights[20]

A person who is not a party to this Agreement has no rights under the Contracts (Rights of Third Parties) Act 1999 to enforce any terms of this Agreement]

## [19    Novation

The Client and Consultant agree that the Client may novate this Agreement to the Building Contractor in accordance with the terms of the Deed of Novation set out in schedule 8 and the Consultant shall within 10 working days of the Client's written request so to do execute the Deed of Novation and deliver it to the Client[21]]

## 20    Nature of this Agreement

This Agreement [is *or* is not] a deed and [has *or* has not] been executed by the parties to it as a deed

IN WITNESS etc[22]

*(signatures (or common seals) of the parties)*
*(signatures of witnesses)*
**[4386]**

SCHEDULE 1
The Fees

## 1    Calculation of fees

The Fees for the Services are the sum of *(insert figure or basis upon which the Fees are to be paid)*. This sum shall be deemed to include reimbursement for all expenses and disbursements incurred by the Consultant including (without limitation) expenses and disbursements in connection with attendance at meetings site visits and the provision of drawings and specifications

**2      VAT**

VAT properly chargeable will be paid to the Consultant in addition to the sum set out in paragraph 1 of this schedule

**3      Payment of the fees**

3.1     The Fees shall be paid by the following instalments: *(specify)*
3.2     Not later than [5] days after the date on which any instalment of Fees becomes due from the Client to the Consultant the Client shall give notice to the Consultant specifying the amount (if any) of the payment made or proposed to be made and the basis on which that amount is calculated[23]

**[4387]**

**4      Fees for additional services**

4.1     Unless otherwise agreed between the parties the Fees for additional services (if any) shall be calculated according to the following hourly rates for:

| Type of Consultant | Hourly Rate |
| --- | --- |
|  | £ |
| Partners/Directors | *(specify)* |
| Project Consultants | *(specify)* |
| Assistant Consultants | *(specify)* |
| Other Staff | *(specify)* |

4.2     These above rates include all fringe benefits mark-ups overheads and profits and reimbursement for the matters referred to in paragraph 1 of this schedule
4.3     Fees for additional services (if any) shall be invoiced on the last day of each relevant month in arrears
4.4     The Consultant will be paid not later than [28] days after each instalment date referred to in paragraph 3.1 and/or each invoice date where the parties agree that the Consultant should undertake any additional services in respect of the Project[24]

SCHEDULE 2
The Key Personnel
*(insert details)*

SCHEDULE 3
The Other Consultants
*(insert details)*

SCHEDULE 4
The Project
*(insert details)*

SCHEDULE 5
The Services[25]
Introduction

**1      Commentary**

The Services are divided into work stages based upon the RIBA Plan of Work. Subject to the need for the Consultant to obtain the Client's approval to move on from one stage to another this division shall not limit or affect the Consultant's general obligation to provide the Services as and when may be necessary or appropriate for the proper and timely completion of the Project.

**[4388]**

## PART 1: BASIC SERVICES

**2      Consultancy Services**

Provide the services of a consultant [architect *or* [structural *or* civil *or* mechanical *or* electrical *or* plumbing *or* lift] engineer *or* quantity surveyor *or* planning supervisor *or* contract administrator *or* Employer's Agent[26] *or* (specify)] in relation to all elements of the Project

**3      Generally**

*(Note: the Services listed in this paragraph 3 are to be provided at each Stage of the Project)*

3.1      Obtain details of the Client's requirements budget and timetable and give the Client general advice on how to proceed

3.2      Advise on the need for and the scope of other consultants' services and the conditions of their appointment

3.3      Arrange for and assist in the selection of other consultants

3.4      Assist and provide information to the Client and other consultants in the carrying out their services

3.5      Assist others employed by the Client to provide any specialist services

3.6      Attend such meetings or procure that one of the Key Personnel attend such meetings as reasonably required by the Client

3.7      Assist and provide information to the Client and the Other Consultants to enable the preparation of estimates cash flow forecasts and cost monitoring reports for construction and development costs

3.8      Provide assistance in the preparation and monitoring of the Programme

3.9      Prepare and regularly revise a plan of work and programme for the execution of the Services incorporating where necessary the services of the Other Consultants

3.10    Review and update the Project Brief and the Programme

3.11    Provide assistance in the preparation reviewing and updating of the Project Brief and the Programme

3.12    Provide information to discuss proposals with and incorporate input of the Other Consultants

3.13    Prepare presentation drawings brochures models or technical information for use of the Client

**[4389]**

3.14    Assist the Client with negotiations with third parties

3.15    The Client may enter into agreements with third parties with regard to the Project such as funding agreements building agreements and agreements for lease and sale ('the Third Party Agreements'). Subject to the Consultant receiving copies of any other such Third Party Agreements or copies of such parts of the same as are relevant the Consultant shall:

3.15.1      be responsible for the issue of certificates as to the state of completion or readiness of the Project for completion or the start of a Tenant's fitting-out works or as to similar matters as required under the Third Party Agreements and

3.15.2      comply with procedures laid down in the Third Party Agreements for the draw down of funding and for changes in design specifications or materials and for the inspection of the Project prior to the issue of any certificates or statements of practical completion or of making good defects under the Building Contract and for similar matters and

3.15.3     carry out the Services in such a manner so that no act omission or default of the Consultant shall cause the Client to be in breach of any of the Third Party Agreements

3.16     In the undertaking of the Services the Consultant shall liaise and co-operate throughout as necessary with the Other Consultants the Designers and the Building Contractor so as to ensure that anything provided by the Consultant is up-to-date produced punctually and can be integrated and co-ordinated into the Project and is compatible with the information technology systems of the Other Consultants

**[4390]**

*(The following additional paragraphs should be included where the Consultant is a Planning Supervisor:)*

[3.17     Provide and carry out all of the planning supervisor's duties services and functions as set out in and as contemplated by the Construction (Design and Management) Regulations 1994 ('the 1994 Regulations')[27] together with the following Services whether or not the primary responsibility for providing them rests with the planning supervisor under the 1994 Regulations and whether or not the Services are required by the 1994 Regulations

3.18     Advise the Client of his duties under the provisions of the 1994 Regulations and of any practical guidance issued from time to time by the Health and Safety Commission with respect to the requirements of the 1994 Regulations

3.19     Before tenders are invited for the carrying out of the Project prepare the pre-tender Health and Safety Plan for later development by the principal contractor to be appointed under the provisions of the 1994 Regulations. Thereafter up-date and re-issue the pre-tender Health and Safety Plan to include post-tender design development

3.20     Monitor the completion of the Health and Safety Plan by the principal contractor

3.21     Advise the Client upon the need for further advice and/or reports relating to the carrying out of the Project and compliance with the 1994 Regulations in the light of any known or suspected contamination or pollution likely to affect the Project or the impact which the Project might have upon any adjoining or neighbouring property or third parties

3.22     Prepare the Health and Safety File and pass the completed file together with two certified copies to the Client as soon as practicable following practical completion of the Project

3.23     Assess tenders and advise the Client on the adequacy of resources for the work to be carried out in compliance with the 1994 Regulations

3.24     Advise the Client on the appointment of other competent persons as required by the 1994 Regulations

3.25     Advise the Client of his duties under the 1994 Regulations and monitor compliance by the Client with those duties

**[4391]**

3.26     Give notice of the Project to the Health and Safety Executive immediately following the Consultant's appointment in accordance with Regulation 7(3) of the 1994 Regulations and immediately following the appointment of the principal contractor and in any event before the start of construction work in accordance with Regulation 7(4) of the 1994 Regulations

3.27     Check that the Building Contractor keeps an up-to-date Health and Safety Plan reflecting design development

3.28     Provide the Client with a regular statement regarding health and safety issues and administration throughout the design and construction of the Project

3.29    Monitor health and safety implications of any proposed changes to production information and design input and any variation to the works referred to in the Building Contract

3.30    Ensure that the Health and Safety File is updated at the issue of the notice of completion of making good defects under the Building Contract in respect of each structure comprised in the Project

3.31    Following the receipt of tenders review the considerations given by them to health and safety issues relating to the 1994 Regulations and advise the Client as to the adequacy of such considerations

3.32    Carry out regular health and safety audits

3.33    Make such visits to the Site as the Consultant shall consider necessary to satisfy himself as to the compliance by the principal contractor with the requirements and procedures of the Health and Safety Plan and immediately advise the principal contractor and the Client of any shortcomings requiring action]

                                                                                    **[4392]**

**4        Stages A and B—Inception and feasibility**

4.1    Advise the Client on the investigations required to obtain information about the Site local infrastructure and any other matters which may affect the Project

4.2    Visit the Site and carry out an initial appraisal

4.3    Assist the Client in the preparation of the employer's requirements

4.4    Advise the Client on methods of procuring construction

4.5    Advise on the need for the services of other consultants specialist contractors sub-contractors and suppliers to [design and/*or* carry out the construction of any part of] the Project

4.6    Advise on the need to obtain planning permission approvals under Building Acts[28] and/or Building Regulations[29] and all other relevant statutory requirements

4.7    [Prepare proposals and make *or* Assist with preparing proposals and making] applications for outline planning permission

4.8    Carry out such studies as may be necessary to determine the feasibility of the Client's requirements

4.9    Review with the Client alternative design and construction approaches and cost implications

4.10    Develop the Client's requirements

4.11    Prepare and submit an outline feasibility estimate

4.12    Submit the design for the Client's comment

4.13    Review and sign the Project Brief

4.14    Provide a written statement to the Client confirming:
          4.14.1    that the design is in accordance with the Project Brief
          4.14.2    that the design is fully co-ordinated
          4.14.3    progress against the [plan of work and the] Programme
          4.14.4    a timetable for the completion of the Services for the Project

4.15    Provide a written statement to the Client on the progress of design consents cost management and Programme

4.16    Seek the Client's instructions to proceed with the next Stage

                                                                                    **[4393]**

**5        Stage C—Outline proposals**
*(The Services in this Stage are to be provided in addition to those described in Stages A and B)*
5.1    Analyse and where necessary revise the Client's requirements
5.2    Prepare outline proposals comprising general arrangement plans and sketches including inter alia initial studies of:

|       |       |                                                                  |
|-------|-------|------------------------------------------------------------------|
|       | 5.2.1 | main space and circulation locations and arrangements            |
|       | 5.2.2 | type of foundations and structure                                |
|       | 5.2.3 | regulations and views of statutory authorities adjoining owners etc |
|       | 5.2.4 | services loadings                                                |
|       | 5.2.5 | major services supply and distribution requirements              |
|       | 5.2.6 | possible services solutions and ramifications                    |

all as defined in the RIBA Plan of Work

5.3    Prepare a budget estimate of construction cost

5.4    Propose and operate a procedure for cost planning and management of construction [and development] costs

5.5    Submit the design for the Client's comment

5.6    Review and sign the Project Brief and general arrangement drawings

5.7    Provide a written statement to the Client confirming:

    5.7.1    that the design is in accordance with the Project Brief

    5.7.2    that the design is fully co-ordinated

    5.7.3    progress against the plan of work and Programme

    5.7.4    a timetable for the completion of the Services for the Project

5.8    Provide a written statement to the Client on the progress of design consents cost management and the Programme

5.9    Seek the Client's instructions to proceed to the next Stage

[4394]

## 6    Stage D—Scheme design

*(The Services in this Stage are to be provided in addition to those described in Stages A–C)*

6.1    Develop the scheme design from approved outline proposals to the extent to obtain unconditional planning permission including inter alia:

    6.1.1    general arrangement sectional and elevational drawings

    6.1.2    spatial arrangements

    6.1.3    sketch details and schematics

    6.1.4    types of external materials and appearance

    6.1.5    outline specification

    6.1.6    forms of construction

    6.1.7    approximate sizes of major plant rooms equipment ducts etc

    6.1.8    routing and locations of major services engineering elements

    6.1.9    calculations to define full scheme

    6.1.10   slab thicknesses floor loadings and column/section sizes

    6.1.11   analysis of environmental and functional requirements

    6.1.12   schedules of power heating and cooling loads

    6.1.13   thermal performance and insulation standards

    6.1.14   selection of energy sources

all as defined in the RIBA Plan of Work

6.2    Prepare a detailed cost plan and provide regular cost checks

6.3    Prepare a preliminary timetable for [construction and/*or* the completion of the Project]

6.4    [Prepare *or* Assist in preparing] [an application *or* multiple applications] and any necessary resubmissions for full planning permission

6.5    Make revisions to scheme design to deal with the requirements of the statutory authorities and third parties

6.6    Submit the design for the Client's comment

6.7    Review and sign the Project Brief

6.8    Provide a written statement to the Client confirming:

    6.8.1    that the design is in accordance with the Project Brief

    6.8.2    that the design is fully co-ordinated

| | |
|---|---|
| 6.8.3 | progress against the plan of work and the Programme |
| 6.8.4 | a timetable for the completion of the Services for the Project |
| 6.9 | Seek the Client's instructions to proceed to the next stage |

**[4395]**

**7          Stage E—Detail design**

*(The Services in this Stage are to be provided in addition to those described in Stages A–D)*

7.1     Develop the detail design from approved scheme design including [but without limiting the generality of this service]:

| | |
|---|---|
| 7.1.1 | detailed design drawings |
| 7.1.2 | details of user studies |
| 7.1.3 | complete calculations |
| 7.1.4 | complete selection of materials |
| 7.1.5 | confirm loadings |
| 7.1.6 | detailed specifications |
| 7.1.7 | such calculations and details as may be required for submission to statutory authorities or other third party consents |
| 7.1.8 | general arrangement reinforcement drawings |

all as defined in the RIBA Plan of Work

7.2     Revise the cost plan and provide regular cost checks

7.3     Prepare applications for approvals and notices under Building Acts and/or Building Regulations and all other relevant statutory requirements

7.4     Agree the form of Building Contract and explain to the Client his obligations under it

7.5     [Prepare information for *or* Apply for] all necessary approvals notices and the like required to comply with the Statutory Requirements

7.6     Advise on the need and method for pre-ordering of materials to comply with the Client's requirements and timetable

7.7     [Assist in the co-ordination of *or* Co-ordinate] the design prepared by the Consultant and the Other Consultants

7.8     [Assist with *or* Carry out] a value engineering exercise and report to the Client

7.9     Submit the design for the Client's comment

7.10    Review and sign the Project Brief

7.11    Provide a written statement to the Client confirming:

| | |
|---|---|
| 7.11.1 | that the design is in accordance with the Project Brief |
| 7.11.2 | that the design is fully co-ordinated |
| 7.11.3 | progress against the plan of work and the Programme |
| 7.11.4 | a timetable for the completion of the Services for the Project |

7.12    Seek the Client's instructions to proceed to the next stage

**[4396]**

**8          Stages F and G—Production information**

*(The Services in this Stage are to be provided in addition to those described in Stages A–E)*

8.1     Develop the production information from approved detailed design including [but without limiting the generality of this service]:

| | |
|---|---|
| 8.1.1 | production and builder's work drawings |
| 8.1.2 | complete material and workmanship specifications |
| 8.1.3 | complete final specification notes on drawings |
| 8.1.4 | detailed reinforcement drawings and bending schedules |

all as defined in the RIBA Plan of Work or in the Project Brief

8.2     Prepare tender documentation comprising [employer's requirements *or* bills of quantities]

8.3     Advise on the selection of Building Contractors and Sub-contractors

8.4     Provide information for the preparation of [bills of quantities *or* schedules of works *or* schedules of rates *or* employer's requirements *or* contract sum analysis] for tendering purposes

8.5     Submit the design for the Client's comment

8.6     Review and sign the Project Brief

8.7     Provide a written statement to the Client confirming:

8.7.1     that the design is in accordance with the Project Brief

8.7.2     that the design is fully co-ordinated

8.7.3     progress against the plan of work and the Programme

8.7.4     a timetable for the completion of the Services for the Project

8.8     Seek the Client's instructions to proceed to the next Stage

[4397]

**9         Stage H—Tender action**

*(The Services in this Stage are to be provided in addition to those described in Stages A–G)*

9.1     Provide assistance in the preparation of the terms and conditions of the Building Contract and any related agreements

9.2     Advise on and obtain the Client's approval to a list of tenderers for the Building Contract

9.3     [Invite tenders *or* Select a Building Contractor by *(describe method of selection)*]

9.4     Examine the Building Contractors' proposals submitted by the tenderers for compliance with the employer's requirements

9.5     Appraise and report on tenders

9.6     [Assist other consultants in negotiating *or* Negotiate] with a tenderer

9.7     Advise the Client on the appointment of a Building Contractor

9.8     Revise the pre-contract detailed design production information [and employer's requirements] to reflect the adjusted tender sum

9.9     Provide a written statement to the Client on the tender sums the Building Contractor's proposals programme and contract sum

9.10    Seek the Client's instructions to proceed to the next Stage

**10        Stage J—Project planning**

*(The Services in this Stage are to be provided in addition to those described in Stages A–H)*

10.1    Advise the Client on the appointment of the Building Contractor the form of the Building Contract and all ancillary documentation such as bonds guarantees and warranties and on the responsibilities of the parties under these documents

10.2    Prepare the Building Contract and all ancillary documentation such as bonds guarantees and warranties and arrange for its execution as a deed in each case

10.3    Provide [the employer's requirements *or* other] such documentation as required by the Building Contract

10.4    Seek the Client's instructions to proceed to the next Stage

[4398]

**11        Stage K—Operations on Site**

*(The Services in this Stage are to be provided in addition to those described in Stages A–J)*

11.1    Provide all necessary *(insert discipline)* information to enable all necessary instructions to be given to the Building Contractor

11.2    Administer the terms of the Building Contract

11.3    Act as the [Employer's Agent *or* contract administrator] for the purposes of the Building Contract

11.4    Liaise with the Client and the Other Consultants and assemble the necessary information to be given to the Building Contractor as and when appropriate

11.5    [Attend *or* Conduct] meetings with the Building Contractor to review progress

11.6      Advise the Client of items of inadequate quality or otherwise of items of non-compliance with the Building Contract

11.7      Assist in the preparation of any instructions and information required by the Contractor under the terms of the Building Contract

11.8      Generally inspect materials delivered to the Site

11.9      As appropriate instruct on sample taking and carrying out tests of materials components techniques and workmanship and examine the conduct and results of such tests whether on or off-site

11.10    As appropriate instruct on the opening up of completed work to determine that it is generally in accordance with the Building Contract

11.11    As appropriate visit the sites of the extraction and fabrication and assembly of materials and components to inspect such materials and workmanship before delivery to the Site

11.12    At intervals appropriate to the stage of construction visit the Site to inspect the progress and quality of the Project to determine that they are being executed generally in accordance with the Building Contract

11.13    Comment on the as-built drawings and information prepared by the Building Contractor or others

11.14    Prepare valuations of work carried out and completed

**[4399]**

11.15    Review the Building Contractor's applications for payment

11.16    Agree the cost of any variations with the Building Contractor

11.17    Arrange for the measurement of work and if necessary adjust or agree the value of any variations and fluctuations in accordance with the terms of the Building Contract

11.18    Inspect and check the Building Contractor's final account advising on it and agreeing the totals with the Building Contractor

11.19    Comment on the maintenance and operational manuals prepared by the Building Contractor or others [and incorporate information prepared by others in maintenance manuals]

11.20    Produce a monthly written report to the Client covering:
       11.20.1    Quality and compliance with the Project Brief
       11.20.2    Progress of the Project and design completion
       11.20.3    Change management procedures and cost and time implications of all variations issued and under consideration
       11.20.4    Cash flow analysis
       11.20.5    Health and safety

11.21    Supply the Building Contractor with any documentation required to be supplied to him by the Client under the Building Contract

11.22    Take delivery of any documentation due from the Building Contractor to the Client under the Building Contract and pass the same to the Client and if appropriate copies to the Other Consultants

**[4400]**

11.23    Subject to getting instructions from the Client act for the Client for the purposes of receiving or issuing (in due time) any applications consents instructions notices requests opinions accounts decisions certificates or statements under the Building Contract and exercise the Client's powers under the Building Contract

11.24    Co-ordinate the Other Consultants after the Building Contract has been let

11.25    In connection with all site meetings which take place both prior to and after the letting of the Building Contract keep a full and proper record of the meetings and circulate copies to the Client and all others who were or who should have been present at the meetings

11.26 Advise the Client on all insurance matters arising in relation to the construction of the Project

11.27 Keep full and proper records of amounts authorised to be paid to the Building Contractor and of all information and documents sent or received by the Consultant and in any way relating to the construction of the Project

11.28 At every stage of design work and in the Consultant's inspections of the work in respect of the Project in progress monitor the need for the completed Project to meet any target gross internal areas referred to in the Third Party Agreements and report to the Client accordingly

11.29 Monitor the Building Contractor's applications and notices in relation to the Statutory Requirements to determine that the Building Contractor has complied with them

11.30 Seek confirmation that the requirements of any statutory bodies which have any jurisdiction in relation to the Project have been complied with

11.31 Seek the Client's instructions to proceed to the next Stage

[4401]

## 12 Stage L—Completion

*(The Services in this Stage are to be provided in addition to those described in Stages A–K)*

12.1 Administer the terms of the Building Contract relating to the completion of the Project

12.2 Inspect the Project and provide a written statement to the Client that it complies with the Project Brief and that a [Certificate *or* Notice] of Practical Completion can be given

12.3 Inspect the Project and provide a written statement to the Client that it complies with the Project Brief and that a [Certificate *or* Notice] of Making Good Defects can be given

12.4 Obtain record drawings and other information from the Building Contractor and collate and pass them on to the Client

12.5 See that the Building Contractor compiles maintenance and operational manuals incorporating information and record drawings prepared by his consultants specialist contractors sub-contractors and suppliers

12.6 Negotiate and agree the final account with the Building Contractor

12.7 Assist in the settling of any dispute or difference relating to the Project between the Client and the Building Contractor

[4402]

## PART 2: OTHER SERVICES[30]

*(The Services in Part 2 are to be provided in addition to those contained in Part 1)*

### 13 Administration and management services

13.1 Prepare the Project Brief

13.2 Prepare a manual as a guide to the administration and procurement of the Project ('the Project Manual')

13.3 Advise the Client on the need for Site Staff

13.4 Prepare co-ordinated detailed programmes for the Project incorporating construction activities and the plan of works and programmes prepared by the Consultant and the Other Consultants for their Services

13.5 Direct and control the activities of Site Staff

13.6 Administer the terms of the Building Contract

13.7 Conduct meetings with the Building Contractor to review progress

13.8 [Advise on *or* Prepare a programme] [and arrange for] the maintenance of the completed Project

13.9       Monitor the progress of the Project against the Building Contractor's programme and report to the Client

13.10      [Assist with the co-ordination of *or* Organise and co-ordinate] the issue of all as-built drawings warranties and completion certificates to the Client

                                                                                    **[4403]**

**14         Design services**

14.1       Carry out and advise on interior design

14.2       [Design and/*or* advise on] the selection of furniture and fittings

14.3       Advise on prepare information for and inspect the installation of works of special quality [*eg shopfittings or (specify)*]

14.4       Develop a building system or components for mass production

14.5       Carry out and advise on town planning and urban design

14.6       Carry out the civil engineering design of [the Project *or* highway works outside the boundary of the Site comprising *(insert details)*]

14.7       Carry out the landscape design of [the Project *or* works outside the boundary of the Site comprising *(insert details)*]

14.8       Carry out and advise on graphic and signage design

14.9       Carry out acoustical design

14.10      Advise on the use of energy in new buildings

14.11      Carry out the design of fire protection [*(insert any other specialist services)*] installations

14.12      Carry out the traffic management design of [the Project *or* highway works outside the boundary of the Site comprising *(insert details)*]

14.13      Advise and provide specialist cladding and glazed material design

14.14      Carry out the design of [all] underground [services *or* drainage] installations beneath the Site [up to and including the first [manhole *or* termination point *or (specify)*] *or* to a point *(specify)* beyond the Site perimeter] [and provide assistance and information to enable the design of the remaining underground services]

14.15      Carry out the design of the waterproofing of the entire Project and below ground construction

14.16      Audit the co-ordination of the design prepared by the Consultant and the Other Consultants

14.17      Provide information and assistance to the Insurer and its technical inspection team and make revisions to the design to deal with their requirements

14.18      Advise on a design audit process and agree with the Client the selection terms and appointment of consultants to undertake the audits and co-ordinate their reports and any necessary actions arising from them

14.19      [Assist *or* Consult with submit details and negotiate] as necessary for the purposes of obtaining a Building Research Establishment Environmental Assessment Method certificate

                                                                                    **[4404]**

**15         Negotiations with third parties**

15.1       Consult with provide information and where necessary [assist the Client in obtaining *or* obtain] consents from all necessary statutory authorities

15.2       Provide information in connection with [make applications for and conduct negotiations for] local authority government and other grants

15.3       Consult with provide information and where necessary [assist the Client in obtaining *or* obtain] consents from all relevant heritage bodies and non-statutory bodies

15.4       Consult with provide information and where necessary [assist the Client in obtaining *or* obtain] consents from all relevant advisory bodies

15.5     Advise provide information and negotiate on rights including easements and responsibilities of relevant owners and lessees

15.6     Consult with provide information and where necessary [assist the Client in obtaining *or* obtain] consents from relevant adjoining owners and lessees

15.7     Consult with provide information and where necessary [assist the Client in obtaining *or* obtain] consents from adjoining owners in connection with party wall matters

15.8     Consult with provide information and where necessary [assist the Client in obtaining *or* obtain] consents in connection with [existing *or* future] Tenants

15.9     Submit plans for the Project for approval by Purchasers Tenants Lenders Joint Venture Partners or others

15.10    Conduct negotiations for approvals waivers or relaxations by all relevant statutory authorities

15.11    Negotiate with Purchasers Tenants Lenders Joint Venture Partners or others

**[4405]**

**16       Surveys and investigations**

16.1     Advise on the suitability and selection of alternative [sites *or* buildings]

16.2     [Arrange for *or* Make *or* Advise on the need for] measured surveys take levels and prepare plans of [the Site *or* existing buildings] [and adjoining property]

16.3     [Arrange for *or* Make] investigations of soil conditions of the Site

16.4     Prepare a desk top study and preliminary land quality statement of the Site

16.5     Prepare a land quality statement for the Site [and review and update at each stage of the Project] [and procure updates from other parties]

16.6     Advise on the environmental impact of the Project and prepare an Environmental Impact Assessment for the Site [and review and update at each stage of the Project] [and procure updates from other parties]

16.7     Inspect advise and report on the following in respect of existing buildings on the Site:

    16.7.1     existing building systems and forms of construction
    16.7.2     use of energy
    16.7.3     schedule of conditions
    16.7.4     schedule of dilapidations
    16.7.5     means of escape
    16.7.6     building failures
    16.7.7     floor loadings
    16.7.8     sound insulation
    16.7.9     services installations particularly: *(specify: eg fire protection fire alarms security systems)*

16.8     Inspect and prepare a report and schedule of condition of adjoining properties

16.9     [Arrange for *or* Make] acoustic surveys on the Site [and adjoining property]

16.10    [Arrange for *or* Make] structural surveys and report on the structural elements of the buildings on the Site [and adjoining properties]

**[4406]–[4407]**

**17       Development services**

17.1     Prepare special perspective and other illustrations

17.2     Prepare special presentation drawings brochures models or technical information for use of the Client

17.3     Make photographic record services

17.4     Act as [witness as to fact *or* expert witness *or* arbitrator *or* adjudicator *or* *(specify)*]

17.5     Prepare a layout for the development of alternative sites

17.6     Prepare a layout for a greater area than that which is to be developed immediately comprising *(specify)*

17.7     [Prepare *or* Check] calculations of floor and site areas from coloured plans prepared by others delineating the measured areas

17.8     Prepare coloured plans delineating floor and site areas for measurement

17.9     Carry out special constructional research for the Project including design of prototypes mock-ups or models

17.10    Monitor testing of prototypes mock-ups or models

**18       Cost management services**

18.1     Prepare life cycle analyses of the proposed or existing buildings to determine their likely cost in use

18.2     Prepare estimates for the replacement and reinstatement of buildings and plant

18.3     Prepare submit and negotiate claims following damage by fire and other causes

**[4408]**

**[PART 3:  ADDITIONAL SERVICES**[31]**]**

*(The Services in Part 3 may be required by the Client in addition to those contained in Parts 1 and 2, in which case the parties will negotiate a fee for them and the Client will issue a separate instruction)*

**19       Administration and management services**
*(insert details)*

**20       Design services**
*(insert details)*

**21       Negotiations with third parties**
*(insert details)*

**22       Surveys and investigations**
*(insert details)*

**23       Development services**
*(insert details)*

**24       Cost management services**
*(insert details)]*

**[4409]**

SCHEDULE 6
THE WARRANTIES
(A):  Warranty in favour of the Building Contractor[32]

THIS DEED is made the ... day of ......

BETWEEN:

(1)      *(name)* [company number *(number)*][33] [of *(address) or* whose registered office is at *(address)*] ('the Consultant') which expression includes his successors in title and assigns)

(2)      *(name)* [company number *(number)*] [of *(address) or* whose registered office is at *(address)*] ('the Building Contractor')

NOW IT IS AGREED AS FOLLOWS:

**1          Background**

1.1          The Consultant was appointed by *(name)* [company number *(number)*] [of *(address)* or whose registered office is at *(address)*] ('the Building Owner') to act for the Building Owner in the capacity of *(specify)* in connection with the development ('the Development') brief details of which are set out in the first schedule upon the terms and conditions contained in an agreement dated *(date)* ('the Deed of Appointment') a copy of which is annexed[34]

1.2          The Building Owner is the owner of the Development and by a Building Contract [dated *(insert date if the contract has been let)*] ('the Building Contract') the Building Owner [has employed or will employ] the Building Contractor to construct the Development

1.3          At the request of the Building Owner the Consultant has agreed to enter into this Deed in favour of the Building Contractor

[4410]

**2          Interpretation**

In this Deed unless the context otherwise requires:

2.1          clause headings are inserted for convenience only and shall not affect the construction of this Deed and any references to a clause or schedule is to a clause of and schedule to this Deed

2.2          words denoting the singular number include the plural and vice versa

2.3          references to persons include references to bodies corporate and unincorporate

**3          Exercise of skill care and diligence**

The Consultant warrants and undertakes to the Building Contractor that in respect of all matters which lie within the scope of his professional responsibilities in relation to the Development:

3.1          he has exercised and will continue to exercise all reasonable skill care and diligence to be expected of a properly qualified and competent consultant experienced in carrying out work of a similar size scope complexity and purpose as the Development in the provision of his duties under the Deed of Appointment

3.2          he shall owe a duty of care to the Building Contractor in respect of such matters and the Building Contractor shall be deemed to have relied exclusively upon the Consultant's professional skill and judgment in respect of such matters

3.3          he has performed and shall continue properly and diligently to perform all of his duties and obligations under the Deed of Appointment

**4          Copyright and licence to use the Materials**

4.1          The Consultant grants to the Building Contractor an irrevocable royalty-free non-exclusive licence to use and reproduce the Materials as defined in the Deed of Appointment (whether in existence or to be prepared in the future) for any purposes connected with the Development

4.2          The licence carries the right to grant sub-licences and is transferable without the prior consent of the Consultant

4.3          The Consultant will not be liable for the use of any of the Materials by the beneficiary of the licence or sub-licence for any purpose other than that for which they were prepared by or on behalf of the Consultant

## 5      Prohibited materials

The Consultant further warrants to the Contractor that:

5.1      he has not specified and will not specify any goods materials products or substances for use in the Development which are not in accordance with the relevant British and European Standards and Codes of Practice or which are generally known or suspected within the construction or engineering industries at the time of use to be deleterious to health and safety or to the durability of the Development in the particular circumstances in which they are used ('Prohibited Materials')[35]

5.2      without prejudice to the generality of the foregoing he has exercised and will continue to exercise all reasonable skill care and diligence to see so far as is consistent with his duties under the Deed of Appointment that no Prohibited Material has been specified for use in the Development by any of the Other Consultants as defined in the Deed of Appointment

**[4411]**

## 6      Variation of deed of appointment

The Consultant undertakes to the Building Contractor not to vary or depart from the terms of the Deed of Appointment without the prior written consent of the Building Contractor and agree that any variation or departure made without such consent shall not be binding on the Beneficiary or affect or prejudice the Beneficiary's rights under this Deed or under the Deed of Appointment or in any other way

## 7      Indemnity insurance[36]

7.1      The Consultant warrants that he has and that he will maintain insurance cover in respect of all claims for negligence with a limit of indemnity of not less than £... and an excess of not more than £... for each and every event unlimited in number (or in the case of claims for pollution or contamination with not less than such limit of indemnity in the aggregate for any and all claims notified in the year of insurance) for a period of 12 years from the date of practical completion of the Project and under a policy or policies issued by a reputable insurance company carrying on business in the United Kingdom

7.2      On request the Consultant shall produce for inspection by the Building Contractor documentary evidence that the insurance required under sub-clause 7.1 is being maintained

7.3      If the Consultant fails to comply with this clause 7 he shall repay to the Building Contractor on demand any money the Building Contractor reasonably spends to effect insurance against any risk or amount with respect to which such default has occurred

7.4      The Consultant has prior to the date of this Deed notified his insurers of the terms of this Deed and will disclose the terms to any new insurers before changing insurers

**[4412]**

## 8      Concurrent liabilities

The obligations of the Consultant under or pursuant to this Deed shall be in addition to and without prejudice to any other present or future liability of the Consultant to the Building Contractor including any liability in negligence

**9      Continuing effect**

Notwithstanding the completion of the Development or any part of it this Deed shall
continue to have effect

**10     Limitation period**

The liability of the Consultant under this Deed shall cease 12 years after the date of
practical completion of the Development save so far as concerns any matter in respect of
which proceedings (whether by way of action adjudication or otherwise) shall have been
commenced before the expiry of the period of 12 years

**11     Disputes**[37]

11.1    If any dispute or difference as to the construction of this Deed or any matter or
        thing of whatsoever nature arising under it or in connection with it shall arise
        between the Consultant and the Building Contractor it shall be determined in
        the Courts of England and Wales or by adjudication and not in arbitration

11.2    If any dispute or difference arises under this Deed either party may refer it to
        adjudication in accordance with the provisions of this clause and subject thereto
        final determination of disputes or differences arising shall be determined in
        accordance with this clause 11

11.3    Where either party requires a dispute or difference to be referred to adjudication
        the matter shall be dealt with in accordance with the provisions set out in the
        second schedule to this Deed

                                                                              **[4413]**

**[12    Third party rights**[38]

A person who is not a party to this Deed has no rights under the Contracts (Rights of
Third Parties) Act 1999 to enforce any terms of this Deed]

**13     Notices**

13.1    All notices or other communications under or in respect of this Deed to either
        party shall be deemed to be duly given or made when delivered (in the case of
        personal delivery or letter) or when despatched (in the case of facsimile) to the
        party addressed to him at the address appearing below (or at such address as the
        party may after the date of this Deed specify for this purpose to the other):
        13.1.1    In the case of the Consultant:
                  13.1.1.1    Address:
                  13.1.1.2    Facsimile number:
        13.1.2    In the case of the Building Contractor:
                  13.1.2.1    Address:
                  13.1.2.2    Facsimile number:

13.2    A written notice includes a notice by facsimile. A notice or other
        communication received on a non-working day or after business hours in the
        place of receipt shall be deemed to be given or made on the next following
        working day in that place

                                                                              **[4414]**

IN WITNESS etc[39]

First Schedule
The Development
*(insert details)*

Second Schedule
Adjudication Provisions

1     The adjudicator to decide the dispute or difference shall be either an individual agreed by the parties or on the application of either party an individual to be nominated as the adjudicator (the individual so agreed or nominated is in this schedule called 'the Adjudicator') by the President or Vice-President of *(insert details of an appropriate professional body)* ('the Nominator')

2     If the Adjudicator dies or becomes ill or is unavailable for some other cause and is thus unable to adjudicate on a dispute or difference referred to him the parties may either agree upon a person to replace the Adjudicator or either party may apply to the Nominator for the nomination of an adjudicator to adjudicate the dispute or difference

3     When a party requires a dispute or difference to be referred to adjudication then that party shall give notice to the other party of its intention to refer the dispute or difference briefly identified in the notice to adjudication. Within 7 days from the date of such notice the party giving the notice of intention shall refer the dispute or difference to the Adjudicator for his decision ('the Referral') and shall include with that Referral particulars of the dispute or difference together with a summary of the contentions on which it relies a statement of the relief or remedy which is sought and any material it wishes the Adjudicator to consider. The Referral and its accompanying documentation shall be copied simultaneously to the other party

4     The Adjudicator shall immediately upon receipt of the Referral and its accompanying documentation confirm that receipt to the parties

**[4415]**

5     The party not making the Referral may by the same means stated in paragraph 3 of this Schedule send to the Adjudicator within [7] days from the date of receipt of the Referral or confirmation from the Adjudicator whichever is later with a copy to the other party a written statement of the contentions on which it relies and any material it wishes the Adjudicator to consider

6     The Adjudicator shall within 28 days of his receipt of the Referral and its accompanying documentation under paragraph 3 of this Schedule and acting as an Adjudicator for the purposes of the Housing Grants, Construction and Regeneration Act 1996 Section 108 and not as an expert or an arbitrator reach his decision and forthwith send that decision in writing to the parties. Provided that:

6.1     the party who has made the referral may consent to allowing the Adjudicator to extend the period of 28 days by up to 14 days and

6.2     if after the referral has been made and the parties agree they may jointly notify the Adjudicator that he be allowed a longer period than 28 days within which to reach his decision

7     The Adjudicator shall [not] be obliged to give reasons for his decision

8     In reaching his decision the Adjudicator shall act impartially set his own procedure and at his absolute discretion may take the initiative in ascertaining the facts and the law as he considers necessary in respect of the referral which may include the following:

8.1     using his own knowledge and/or experience

8.2     opening up reviewing and revising any certificate direction statement opinion decision requirement or notice issued given or made as if no such certificate direction opinion decision requirement or notice had been given or made

8.3     requiring further information from the parties than that contained in the notice of Referral and its accompanying documentation or in any written statement provided by the parties including the results of any tests that have been made or of any opening up

8.4     requiring the parties to carry out tests or additional tests or to open up work or further open up work

8.5     visiting the Site

8.6     obtaining such information as he considers necessary from any employee or representative of the parties provided that before obtaining information from an employee of a party he has given prior notice to that party

8.7     obtaining from others such information and advice as he considers necessary on technical and on legal matters subject to giving prior notice to the parties together with a statement or estimate of the cost involved

**[4416]**

9       The Adjudicator in his decision shall state how payment of his fee and reasonable expenses is to be apportioned as between the parties. In default of such statement the parties shall bear the cost of the Adjudicator's fee and reasonable expenses in equal proportions

10      The parties shall be jointly and severally liable to the Adjudicator for his fee and for all expenses reasonably incurred by the Adjudicator pursuant to the Adjudication

11      The decision of the Adjudicator shall be binding on the parties until the dispute or difference is finally determined by legal proceedings or by an agreement in writing between the parties made after the decision of the Adjudicator has been given

12      The Adjudicator shall not be liable for anything done or omitted in the discharge or purported discharge of his functions as Adjudicator unless the act or omission is in bad faith and this protection from liability shall similarly extend to any employee or agent of the Adjudicator

*(signatures (or common seals) of the parties)*
*(signatures of witnesses)*
**[4417]**

(B):  Warranty in favour of Purchasers Lenders Group Companies the Insurer and Joint Venture Partners[40]

THIS DEED is made the ...... day of .........

BETWEEN:

(1)     *(name)* [company number *(number)*[41]] [of *(address)* or whose registered office is at *(address)*] ('the Consultant')

(2)     *(name)* [company number *(number)*] [of *(address)* or whose registered office is at *(address)*] ('the Beneficiary') which expression shall include its successors in title and assigns

## 1      Background

1.1      The Consultant was appointed by *(name of developer)* [company number *(number)*] [of *(address)* or whose registered office is at *(address)*] ('the Building Owner') to act for the Building Owner in the capacity of *(insert discipline)* in connection with the development brief details of which are set out in the first schedule below ('the Development') upon the terms and conditions contained in an Agreement dated *(date)* ('the Deed of Appointment') a copy of which is annexed[42]

1.2      [The Beneficiary has [acquired or taken an interest in or taken a lease of] [part of] the Development [more particularly known as *(specify)*][43]

or

The Beneficiary has agreed to provide loan facilities or other finance in respect of the [carrying out of the Development or acquisition of the Development when complete][44]

or

The Beneficiary is a company within the group of companies of which the Building Owner is a member[45]

or

The Beneficiary has entered into a joint venture with the Building Owner in respect of *(specify)*][46]

1.3      The Consultant has agreed to enter into this Deed in favour of the Beneficiary and its successors in title and assigns

**[4418]**

## 2      Interpretation

In this Deed unless the context otherwise requires:

2.1      clause headings are inserted for convenience only and shall not affect the construction of this Deed and any references to a clause or schedule is to a clause of and schedule to this Deed

2.2      words denoting the singular number include the plural and vice versa

2.3      references to persons include references to bodies corporate and unincorporate

## 3      Exercise of skill care and diligence

The Consultant warrants and undertakes to the Beneficiary that in respect of all matters which lie within the scope of his professional responsibilities in relation to the Development:

3.1      he has exercised and will continue to exercise all the reasonable skill care and diligence to be expected of a properly qualified and competent consultant experienced in carrying out work of a similar size scope complexity and purpose as the Development in the provision of his duties under the Deed of Appointment

3.2      he shall owe a duty of care to the Beneficiary in respect of such matters and the Beneficiary shall be deemed to have relied exclusively upon the Consultant's professional skill and judgment in respect of such matters

3.3      he has performed and shall continue properly and diligently to perform all of his duties and obligations under the Deed of Appointment

## 4      Copyright and licence to use the Materials

4.1      The Consultant grants to the Beneficiary an irrevocable royalty free non-exclusive licence to use and reproduce all of the Materials as defined in the Deed of Appointment (whether in existence or to be prepared in the future) and any works designs or inventions of the Consultant incorporated or referred to in them for any purposes connected with the Development

4.2     The licence carries the right for the Beneficiary to grant sub-licences and is transferable without the prior consent of the Consultant

4.3     The Consultant will not be liable for the use of any of the Materials by the beneficiary of the licence or sub-licence for any purpose other than that for which they were prepared by or on behalf of the Consultant

**[4419]**

## 5      Prohibited Materials

The Consultant further warrants to the Beneficiary that:

5.1     he has not specified and will not specify any goods materials products or substances for use in the Development which are not in accordance with the relevant British and European Standards and Codes of Practice or which are generally known or suspected within the construction or engineering industries at the time of use to be deleterious to health and safety or to the durability of the Development in the particular circumstances in which they are used ('Prohibited Materials')[47]

5.2     without prejudice to the generality of the foregoing he has exercised and will continue to exercise all reasonable skill care and diligence to see so far as is consistent with his duties under the Deed of Appointment that no Prohibited Materials have been specified for use in the Development by any other consultant involved with the Development

## 6      Variation of Deed of Appointment

The Consultant undertakes to the Beneficiary not to vary or depart from the terms of the Deed of Appointment without the prior written consent of the Beneficiary and agrees that any variation or departure without such consent shall not be binding on the Beneficiary or affect or prejudice the Beneficiary's rights under this Deed or under the Deed of Appointment or in any other way

## 7      Indemnity insurance[48]

7.1     The Consultant warrants to the Beneficiary that he has and that he will maintain insurance cover in respect of all claims for negligence with a limit of indemnity of not less that £... and an excess of not more than £... for each and every event unlimited in number (or in the case of claims for pollution or contamination with not less than such limit of indemnity in the aggregate for any and all claims notified in the year of insurance) for a period of 12 years from the date of practical completion of the Development and under a policy or policies issued by a reputable insurance company carrying on business in the United Kingdom

7.2     On request the Consultant shall produce for inspection by the Beneficiary documentary evidence that the insurance required under this clause 7 is being maintained

7.3     If the Consultant fails to comply with this clause 7 he shall repay to the Beneficiary on demand any money the Beneficiary reasonably spends to effect insurance against any risk or amount with respect to which such default has occurred

7.4     The Consultant has prior to the date of this Deed notified his insurers of the terms of this Deed and will disclose the terms to any new insurers before changing insurers

**[4420]**

## 8       Indemnity

[Save that the Sub-contractor shall owe the Beneficiary no greater duty than it owes to the Contractor under the Sub-contract the *or* The] Sub-contractor further undertakes to indemnify the Beneficiary from and against the consequences of any breach by the Sub-contractor of any of the warranties covenants and undertakings contained in this Deed

## 9       Concurrent liabilities

The obligations of the Consultant under or pursuant to this Deed shall be in addition to and without prejudice to any other present or future liability of the Consultant to the Beneficiary including any liability in negligence provided always that the Consultant shall owe no greater liability to the Beneficiary under the terms of this Deed than he owes to the Building Owner under the Deed of Appointment

## 10      Continuing effect

Notwithstanding the completion of the Development or any part of it this Deed shall continue to have effect

## 11      Limitation period

The liability of the Consultant under this Deed shall cease 12 years after the date of practical completion of the Development save so far as concerns any matter in respect of which proceedings (whether by way of action adjudication or otherwise) shall have been commenced before the expiry of the period of 12 years

**[4421]**

## 12      Assignment

The Beneficiary and its successors in title shall be entitled to assign by way of absolute legal assignment and/or charge the benefit of this Deed and/or any of the present or future rights interests and benefits of the Beneficiary to any third party at any time during the period of 12 years from the date of practical completion of the Development [on *(number)* occasions only without the consent of the Consultant and thereafter only with the consent of the Consultant such consent not to be unreasonably withheld or delayed][49]

## 13      Further warranty deeds

The Consultant covenants that if required by the Beneficiary he will enter into further deeds of warranty with all and each of such persons who shall acquire or agree to acquire an interest in the whole or any part of the Development. Each such deed of warranty shall be in the same form as this Deed mutatis mutandis save for this clause

## 14      Disputes[50]

14.1    If any dispute or difference as to the construction of this Deed or any matter or thing of whatsoever nature arising under it or in connection with it shall arise it shall be determined in the Courts of England and Wales or by adjudication and not in arbitration

14.2    If any dispute or difference arises under this Deed either party may refer it to adjudication in accordance with the provisions of this clause and subject thereto final determination of disputes or differences arising herein shall be determined in accordance with this clause 14

14.3    Where either party requires a dispute or difference to be referred to adjudication the matter shall be dealt with in accordance with the provisions set out in second schedule to this Deed

**[4422]**

**[15    Third party rights**[51]

A person who is not a party to this Deed has no rights under the Contracts (Rights of Third Parties) Act 1999 to enforce any terms of this Deed]

**16    Law and jurisdiction**

This Deed shall be governed by and construed in accordance with English Law and the parties submit to the [non-exclusive] jurisdiction of the English courts

**17    Notices**

17.1    All notices or other communications under or in respect of this Deed to either party shall be deemed to be duly given or made when delivered (in the case of personal delivery or letter) or when despatched (in the case of facsimile) to the party addressed to it at the address appearing below (or at such address as the party may after the date of this Agreement specify for this purpose to the other):

   17.1.1    In the case of the Consultant:
       17.1.1.1    Address: *(address)*
       17.1.1.2    Facsimile number: *(number)*

   17.1.2    In the case of the Beneficiary:
       17.1.2.1    Address: *(address)*
       17.1.2.2    Facsimile number: *(number)*

17.2    A written notice includes a notice by facsimile. A notice or other communication received on a non-working day or after business hours in the place of receipt shall be deemed to be given or made on the next following working day in that place

**[18    Determination** *(for insertion only where the beneficiary is a lender)*

The Consultant covenants and agrees with the Lender that he will not exercise or seek to exercise any right he may now or at any time hereafter have under the Deed of Appointment or serve notice to determine his appointment under the Deed of Appointment or discontinue the performance of any of his obligations or duties thereunder without first giving to the Lender not less than 28 days' prior written notice of the Consultant's intention specifying the ground or grounds for the purported determination of his appointment and notwithstanding any provision of the Deed of Appointment (unless the Consultant's appointment is determined by the Building Owner) the Consultant's appointment under the Deed of Appointment shall not otherwise determine]

**[4423]**

IN WITNESS etc

First Schedule
The Development
*(insert description and address of the site of it)*

Second Schedule
Adjudication Provisions

1    The adjudicator to decide the dispute or difference shall be either an individual agreed by the parties or on the application of either party an individual to be nominated as the adjudicator (the individual so agreed or nominated is in this schedule called 'the Adjudicator') by the President or Vice-President of *(insert details of an appropriate professional body)* ('the Nominator')

2    If the Adjudicator dies or becomes ill or is unavailable for some other cause and is thus unable to adjudicate on a dispute or difference referred to him the parties may either agree upon a person to replace the adjudicator or either party may apply to the Nominator for the nomination of an adjudicator to adjudicate the dispute or difference

3    When a party requires a dispute or difference to be referred to adjudication then that party shall give notice to the other party of its intention to refer the dispute or difference briefly identified in the notice to adjudication. Within 7 days from the date of such notice the party giving the notice of intention shall refer the dispute or difference to the Adjudicator for his decision ('the Referral') and shall include with that Referral particulars of the dispute or difference together with a summary of the contentions on which it relies a statement of the relief or remedy which is sought and any material it wishes the Adjudicator to consider. The Referral and its accompanying documentation shall be copied simultaneously to the other party

4    The Adjudicator shall immediately upon receipt of the Referral and its accompanying documentation confirm  that receipt to the parties

**[4424]**

5    The party not making the Referral may by the same means stated in paragraph 3 of this Schedule send to the Adjudicator within [7] days from the date of receipt of the Referral or confirmation from the Adjudicator whichever is later with a copy to the other party a written statement of the contentions on which it relies and any material it wishes the Adjudicator to consider

6    The Adjudicator shall within 28 days of his receipt of the Referral and its accompanying documentation under paragraph 3 of this Schedule and acting as an Adjudicator for the purposes of the Housing Grants, Construction and Regeneration Act 1996 Section 108 and not as an expert or an arbitrator reach his decision and forthwith send that decision in writing to the parties. Provided that:

6.1      the party who has made the referral may consent to allowing the Adjudicator to extend the period of 28 days by up to 14 days and

6.2      if after the referral has been made and the parties agree they may jointly notify the Adjudicator that he be allowed a longer period than 28 days within which to reach his decision

7    The Adjudicator shall [not] be obliged to give reasons for his decision

8    In reaching his decision the Adjudicator shall act impartially set his own procedure and at his absolute discretion may take the initiative in ascertaining the facts and the law as he considers necessary in respect of the referral which may include the following:

8.1     using his own knowledge and/or experience

8.2     opening up reviewing and revising any certificate direction statement opinion decision requirement or notice issued given or made as if no such certificate direction opinion decision requirement or notice had been given or made

8.3     requiring further information from the parties than that contained in the notice of Referral and its accompanying documentation or in any written statement provided by the parties including the results of any tests that have been made or of any opening up

8.4     requiring the parties to carry out tests or additional tests or to open up work or further open up work

8.5     visiting the Site

8.6     obtaining such information as he considers necessary from any employee or representative of the parties provided that before obtaining information from an employee of a party he has given prior notice to that party

8.7     obtaining from others such information and advice as he considers necessary on technical and on legal matters subject to giving prior notice to the parties together with a statement or estimate of the cost involved

**[4425]**

9     The Adjudicator in his decision shall state how payment of his fee and reasonable expenses is to be apportioned as between the parties. In default of such statement the parties shall bear the cost of the Adjudicator's fee and reasonable expenses in equal proportions

10     The parties shall be jointly and severally liable to the Adjudicator for his fee and for all expenses reasonably incurred by the Adjudicator pursuant to the Adjudication

11     The decision of the Adjudicator shall be binding on the parties until the dispute or difference is finally determined by legal proceedings or by an agreement in writing between the parties made after the decision of the Adjudicator has been given

12     The Adjudicator shall not be liable for anything done or omitted in the discharge or purported discharge of his functions as Adjudicator unless the act or omission is in bad faith and this protection from liability shall similarly extend to any employee or agent of the Adjudicator

*(signatures (or common seals) of the parties)*
*(signatures of witnesses)*
**[4426]**

### SCHEDULE 7
### ADJUDICATION PROVISIONS[52]

1     The adjudicator to decide the dispute or difference shall be either an individual agreed by the parties or on the application of either party an individual to be nominated as the adjudicator (the individual so agreed or nominated is in this schedule called 'the Adjudicator') by the President or Vice-President of *(insert details of an appropriate professional body)* ('the Nominator')

2     If the Adjudicator dies or becomes ill or is unavailable for some other cause and is thus unable to adjudicate on a dispute or difference referred to him the parties

may either agree upon a person to replace the adjudicator or either party may apply to the Nominator for the nomination of an adjudicator to adjudicate the dispute or difference

3    When a party requires a dispute or difference to be referred to adjudication then that party shall give notice to the other party of its intention to refer the dispute or difference briefly identified in the notice to adjudication. Within 7 days from the date of such notice the party giving the notice of intention shall refer the dispute or difference to the Adjudicator for his decision ('the Referral') and shall include with that Referral particulars of the dispute or difference together with a summary of the contentions on which it relies a statement of the relief or remedy which is sought and any material it wishes the Adjudicator to consider. The Referral and its accompanying documentation shall be copied simultaneously to the other party

4    The Adjudicator shall immediately upon receipt of the Referral and its accompanying documentation confirm  that receipt to the parties

5    The party not making the Referral may by the same means stated in paragraph 3 of this Schedule send to the Adjudicator within [7] days from the date of receipt of the Referral or confirmation from the Adjudicator whichever is later with a copy to the other party a written statement of the contentions on which it relies and any material it wishes the Adjudicator to consider

6    The Adjudicator shall within 28 days of his receipt of the Referral and its accompanying documentation under paragraph 3 of this Schedule and acting as an Adjudicator for the purposes of the Housing Grants, Construction and Regeneration Act 1996 Section 108 and not as an expert or an arbitrator reach his decision and forthwith send that decision in writing to the parties. Provided that:

6.1    the party who has made the referral may consent to allowing the Adjudicator to extend the period of 28 days by up to 14 days and

6.2    if after the referral has been made and the parties agree they may jointly notify the Adjudicator that he be allowed a longer period than 28 days within which to reach his decision

7    The Adjudicator shall [not] be obliged to give reasons for his decision

**[4427]**

8    In reaching his decision the Adjudicator shall act impartially set his own procedure and at his absolute discretion may take the initiative in ascertaining the facts and the law as he considers necessary in respect of the referral which may include the following:

8.1    using his own knowledge and/or experience

8.2    opening up reviewing and revising any certificate direction statement opinion decision requirement or notice issued given or made as if no such certificate direction opinion decision requirement or notice had been given or made

8.3    requiring further information from the parties than that contained in the notice of Referral and its accompanying documentation or in any written statement provided by the parties including the results of any tests that have been made or of any opening up

8.4    requiring the parties to carry out tests or additional tests or to open up work or further open up work

8.5    visiting the Site

8.6     obtaining such information as he considers necessary from any employee or representative of the parties provided that before obtaining information from an employee of a party he has given prior notice to that party

8.7     obtaining from others such information and advice as he considers necessary on technical and on legal matters subject to giving prior notice to the parties together with a statement or estimate of the cost involved

9     The Adjudicator in his decision shall state how payment of his fee and reasonable expenses is to be apportioned as between the parties. In default of such statement the parties shall bear the cost of the Adjudicator's fee and reasonable expenses in equal proportions

10     The parties shall be jointly and severally liable to the Adjudicator for his fee and for all expenses reasonably incurred by the Adjudicator pursuant to the Adjudication

11     The decision of the Adjudicator shall be binding on the parties until the dispute or difference is finally determined by legal proceedings or by an agreement in writing between the parties made after the decision of the Adjudicator has been given

12     The Adjudicator shall not be liable for anything done or omitted in the discharge or purported discharge of his functions as Adjudicator unless the act or omission is in bad faith and this protection from liability shall similarly extend to any employee or agent of the Adjudicator

**[4428]**

## SCHEDULE 8
## DEED OF NOVATION[53]

THIS DEED is dated the ... day of ......

BETWEEN:

(1)     *(name)* [company number *(number)*[54]] [of *(address)* or whose registered office is at *(address)*] ('the Consultant')

(2)     *(name)* [company number *(number)*] [of *(address)* or whose registered office is at *(address)*] ('the 'Client')

(3)     *(name)* [company number *(number)*] [of *(address)* or whose registered office is at *(address)*] ('the Building Contractor')

## 1   Definitions

1.1     'the Agreement' means an agreement dated *(date)* and made between the Client and the Consultant a copy of which is annexed

1.2     'the Building Contract' means the building contract in respect of the Works dated *(date)* and made between the Client and the Building Contractor

1.3     'the Further Consultants' means the further consultants appointed by the Client in respect of the Project being *(insert details)*

1.4     'the Other Consultants' means the other consultants appointed by the Client in respect of the Project whose appointment is also subject to a novation agreement being *(insert details)*

1.5     'the Project' means *(insert description)*

1.6     'Works' means the works to be carried out by the Building Contractor pursuant to the Building Contract

**2          Background**

2.1       By the Agreement the Client appointed the Consultant to act as *(insert discipline)* to provide services more particularly specified in the Agreement. The Client similarly appointed the Further Consultants and the Other Consultants

2.2       By the Building Contract the Client has appointed the Building Contractor to carry out the Works

2.3       It is a term of the Building Contract that the Building Contractor accepts full responsibility for the design services already supplied by the Consultant to the Client

2.4       It is also a condition of the Building Contract that the Building Contractor and the Consultant enter into this Deed for the purpose of the novation of the benefit and burden of the Agreement to the Building Contractor

2.5       This Deed is supplemental to the Agreement

**[4429]**

**3          Release by Client**

The Client releases and discharges the Consultant from further performance of the Consultant's obligations under the Agreement and from all claims and demands whatsoever arising out of or in respect of the Agreement whether arising prior to on or subsequent to the date of this Deed but without prejudice to the provisions of clause 5 or to the provisions of the collateral warranty to be provided to the Client by the Consultant pursuant to the Agreement

**4          Release by Consultant**

The Consultant releases and discharges the Client from further performance of the Client's obligations under the Agreement and from all claims and demands whatsoever arising out of or in respect of the Agreement whether arising prior to on or subsequent to the date of this Deed

**5          Acceptance of liability by the Building Contractor**

The Building Contractor accepts the responsibilities and the liabilities of the Client under the Agreement and agrees to perform all the duties and to discharge all the obligations of the Client under it and to be bound by all its terms and conditions in every way as if it were named in the Agreement as a party to it from the start in place of the Client. Without limiting the generality of the foregoing the Building Contractor acknowledges and agrees that he will receive and accept responsibility for negotiating and settling all claims and demands whatsoever against the Client arising out of or in respect of the Agreement whether arising prior to on or subsequent to the date of this Deed

**6          Acceptance of liability by the Consultant**

6.1       The Consultant agrees to perform all his duties and to discharge all his obligations under the Agreement and to be bound by all its terms and conditions in favour of the Building Contractor in every way as if the Building Contractor were named in the Agreement as a party to it from the start in place of the Client

6.2       Without limiting the generality of the foregoing the Consultant acknowledges and agrees that the Building Contractor shall have the right to enforce the Agreement and pursue all claims and demands (future or existing) by the Client whatsoever arising out of or in respect of the Agreement whether arising prior to on or subsequent to the date of this Deed

6.3 Nothing in this Deed shall operate to extend or increase the liability of the Consultant beyond that which would have existed but for this Deed and without limiting the generality of the foregoing it is expressly agreed that nothing in this Deed shall operate to enable any claims to be brought against the Consultant which but for this Deed would be statute barred if made by the Client

**[4430]**

## 7 Acknowledgement of payment

The Consultant acknowledges that up to the date of this Deed he has been paid the sum of £... exclusive of VAT by the Client

## 8 Further deeds of novation

The Client and the Building Contractor hereby covenant with the Consultant that each of them will contemporaneously with this Deed execute and complete with the Other Consultants deeds of novation of the appointment of the Other Consultants in substantially similar form as this Deed

## 9 The Agreement in force

The terms and conditions of this Deed represent the entire agreement between the parties relating to the novation of the Agreement and except as specifically amended by this Deed all the terms and conditions of the Agreement remain in full force and effect

## 10 No discharge of Consultant's liability

Nothing in this Deed shall operate to discharge the Consultant from any liability in respect of duties performed prior to the execution of this Deed

## [11 Third Party Rights[55]

A person who is not a party to this Deed has no rights under the Contracts (Rights of Third Parties) Act 1999 to enforce any terms of this Deed]

IN WITNESS etc[56]

*(signatures (or common seal) of the parties)*
*(signatures of witnesses)*
**[4431]**

1 This is a form of appointment which can be adapted for the appointment of various professionals involved in a development. See also the RIBA standard forms of agreement for the appointment of an architect in vol 12 (1994 Reissue) CONTRACTS FOR SERVICES Form 12 [1179].

2 If any party is a company it is desirable to include the company registration number before the address of the registered office. This avoids any problems arising when a company has been wound up and a new company formed with the same name, or when the name of a company is changed, or if companies swap names eg on a reconstruction of a group of companies.

3 See the Housing Grants, Construction and Regeneration Act 1996 s 108 (11 Halsbury's Statutes (4th Edn) CONTRACT).

4 See vol 38(1) (2000 Reissue) SALE OF LAND Paragraph 226.5 [554].

5 A health and safety file is required if the Construction (Design and Management) Regulations 1994, SI 1994/3140 apply. See vol 38(1) (2000 Reissue) SALE OF LAND Paragraph 121 [250].

6 A health and safety plan is required if the Construction (Design and Management) Regulations 1994, SI 1994/3140 apply. See vol 38(1) (2000 Reissue) SALE OF LAND Paragraph 120 [249].

7 See vol 38(1) (2000 Reissue) SALE OF LAND Paragraph 231 [576] et seq.

8    If the project is not designed for occupation by the client, this recital will put the consultant on notice that third parties may have rights. See *St Martins Property Corporation Ltd v Sir Robert McAlpine & Sons Ltd* (1992) 57 BLR 57, CA and *Linden Gardens Trust Ltd v Lenesta Sludge Disposals Ltd* [1994] 1 AC 85, [1993] 3 All ER 417, HL.

9    Alternatively, if the prohibited materials are listed in the building contract, an identical list should be included in the consultant's appointment.

10   See vol 38(1) (2000 Reissue) SALE OF LAND Paragraph 231 [576] et seq.

11   Clause 2.3 summarises relevant provisions of the Construction (Design and Management) Regulations 1994, SI 1994/3140. See vol 38(1) (2000 Reissue) SALE OF LAND Paragraph 119 [242] et seq.

12   See the Housing Grants, Construction and Regeneration Act 1996 s 112(1).

13   See the Housing Grants, Construction and Regeneration Act 1996 s 112(2).

14   See the Housing Grants, Construction and Regeneration Act 1996 s 112(2).

15   See the Housing Grants, Construction and Regeneration Act 1996 s 112(3).

16   See the Housing Grants, Construction and Regeneration Act 1996 s 111.

17   Insurance can be a topic which involves protracted negotiations. Clients should take professional advice as to the amount of cover required for both professional indemnity and public liability insurance. Much will depend upon the size of the project and the degree of involvement of the consultant in the project. A client would wish to see professional indemnity cover for each and every event unlimited in number. Present market conditions suggest that pollution or contamination claims are only insurable on an aggregate basis. Consultants may seek to include a provision whereby insurance cover will be kept on foot only as long as it is available at 'commercially reasonable rates'. Clients find this to be too subjective a test to be acceptable in the current market conditions.

18   If a design and build building contract is used (for example, the JCT Standard Form of Building Contract, With Contractor's Design, 1998 Edition) and the building contractor is to be fully responsible for both the design and the construction of the project, the consultants who have played a major role in its design will be required to provide warranties in favour of the building contractor if their appointments are not novated to the building contractor. If it is not a design and build contract, the opening words of the clause should be deleted.

**[4432]**

19   The disputes procedure is compliant with the Housing Grants, Construction and Regeneration Act 1996.

20   See the Contracts (Rights of Third Parties) Act 1999 (11 Halsbury's Statutes (4th Edn) CONTRACT); and see vol 38(1) (2000 Reissue) SALE OF LAND Paragraph 230 [574].

21   See vol 38(1) (2000 Reissue) SALE OF LAND Paragraph 224 [547]. If the appointment is not to be novated to the building contractor, delete this clause.

22   Usually this documentation is executed as a deed so that consideration is unnecessary and any action for breach of contract is subject to a 12-year limitation period instead of the normal 6-year limit. See vol 5 (1994 Reissue) BUILDING AND ENGINEERING CONTRACTS Paragraph 140 [483]. It must be executed as a deed if it contains any power of attorney: eg clauses 8.4 and 14.2 of this Form.

23   See the Housing Grants, Construction and Regeneration Act 1996 s 110(2).

24   See the Housing Grants, Construction and Regeneration Act 1996 s 110(1).

25   The schedule of services is intended to provide a list of services commonly provided by the principal consultants involved in a construction project. The list is not intended to be exhaustive and consideration should be given to the nature and complexity of the project and the experience of each consultant.
     The services are in three parts:
     (a)   Part 1: Basic Services: the services to be provided by the Consultant
     (b)   Part 2: Other Services: the services to be provided by the Consultant in addition to the Basic Services. Some or all of these services may be the subject of a separate fee quotation
     (c)   Part 3: Additional Services: the services not selected from Part 2 or any other additional service which may be required to be provided by the Consultant at some time during the course of the project. These services will be the subject of an additional fee and instruction.

26   Under the JCT Standard Form of Building Contract, With Contractor's Design, 1998 Edition the 'contract administrator' is called the Employer's Agent.

27   As to the Construction (Design and Management) Regulations 1994, SI 1994/3140 see vol 38(1) (2000 Reissue) SALE OF LAND Paragraph 119 [242] et seq.

28   Ie the Building Act 1984 (35 Halsbury's Statutes (4th Edn) PUBLIC HEALTH AND ENVIRONMENTAL PROTECTION).

29   Ie the Building Regulations 1991, SI 1991/2768 as amended.

**[4433]**

30   The Services in Part 2 are to be provided in addition to those contained in Part 1. Those items not selected can be transferred to Part 3 as appropriate.

31   The Services in Part 3 may be required in addition to those contained in Parts 1 and 2, for which a separate fee will be negotiated and a separate instruction issued.

32     See clause 14.1 of this Form. if a design and build building contract is used (for example, the JCT Standard Form of Building Contract, With Contractor's Design, 1998 Edition) the building contractor is to be fully responsible for both the design and the construction of the project. The consultants who have played a major role in the design of the project will be required to provide warranties in favour of the building contractor if their appointments are not novated to the building contractor.

33     See note 2 above.

34     It is essential for the building contractor to have seen and to be happy with the terms of the consultant's appointment. It is preferable for a copy to be annexed to the warranty.

35     Alternatively, if the prohibited materials are listed in the consultant's appointment, an identical list should be included in the warranty.

36     Insurance can be a topic which involves protracted negotiations. Building contractors should take professional advice as to the amount of cover required for both professional indemnity and public liability insurance. Much will depend upon the size of the project and the degree of involvement of the consultant in the project. Building contractors would wish to see professional indemnity cover for each and every event unlimited in number. Present market conditions suggest that pollution or contamination claims are only insurable on an aggregate basis. Consultants may seek to include a provision whereby insurance cover will be kept on foot only as long as it is available at 'commercially reasonable rates'. Building contractors find this to be too subjective a test to be acceptable in the current market conditions.

37     The disputes procedure is compliant with the Housing Grants, Construction and Regeneration Act 1996.

38     See the Contracts (Rights of Third Parties) Act 1999, and see vol 38(1) (2000 Reissue) SALE OF LAND Paragraph 230 [574].

39     Usually this documentation is executed as a deed so that consideration is unnecessary and any action for breach of contract is subject to a 12-year limitation period instead of the normal 6-year limit. See vol 5 (1994 Reissue) BUILDING AND ENGINEERING CONTRACTS Paragraph 140 [483]. It must be executed as a deed if it contains any power of attorney.

40     No stamp duty. As to collateral warranties generally see vol 38(1) (2000 Reissue) SALE OF LAND Paragraph 225 [548] et seq. This Form is the same as Form 137 [4551] post, except:

          (a)   in this Form the consultant is a single individual rather than plural, or a corporate body; and

          (b)   in sub-clauses 13.2 and 13.3 of this Form the dispute procedure is adjudication in accordance with the provisions of the second schedule to this warranty deed.

41     If any party is a company it is desirable to include the company registration number before the address of the registered office. This avoids any problems arising when a company has been wound up and a new company formed with the same name, or when the name of a company is changed, or if companies swap names eg on a reconstruction of a group of companies.

42     The deed of appointment must be annexed, as reference is made to its terms in various clauses of this Form.

43     Identify the transaction which has taken place which allows the beneficiary to obtain the warranty.

**[4434]**

44     Identify the transaction which has taken place which allows the beneficiary to obtain the warranty.

45     Identify the transaction which has taken place which allows the beneficiary to obtain the warranty.

46     Identify the transaction which has taken place which allows the beneficiary to obtain the warranty.

47     Alternatively, if the prohibited materials are listed in the consultant's appointment, an identical list should be included in the warranty. See Form 134 note 7 [4494] post as to the risks of inserting a list.

48     Indemnity insurance is often a topic which can involve protracted negotiations. Warrantors often seek to include a provision whereby insurance cover is available at 'commercially reasonable rates'. Beneficiaries find this to be too subjective a test to be acceptable.

        Insurers often cap liability for claims relating to contamination or pollution.

        The required limit of indemnity and the amount of any excess are figures upon which the beneficiary should take professional advice. A commercial decision should then be taken in the light of the extent of cover that is in place.

        The clause requires cover for each and every claim. Some warrantors seek to include a provision whereby the amount of the insurance cover is capped for any one year. Beneficiaries tend to reject this proposal.

        A warrantor's liability under the provisions of the warranty should be contrasted with the amount of insurance cover that exists. Strictly, any shortfall would be a liability that remains with the warrantor.

49     Unless the parties agree otherwise, the benefits can be assigned freely without consent of the warrantor. If the number of assignments is to be limited, care should be taken in choosing the number. Two or three assignments appear to be acceptable in the market but particular circumstances may require a greater number. Practitioners should appreciate the difference between the availability of a warranty itself and the ability to assign its benefits to third parties. If a development is to be multi-let a developer will wish to ensure that professionals will be providing warranties to first purchasers and tenants. See clause 14.1 [4384] of this Form.

50    Some commentators have suggested that this type of warranty could be regarded as a 'construction contract' for the purposes of the Housing Grants, Construction and Regeneration Act 1996 Pt II (11 Halsbury's Statutes (4th Edn) CONTRACT) which came into effect on 1 May 1998. The Act allows the parties to refer disputes to adjudication (Housing Grants, Construction and Regeneration Act 1996 s 108). If a contract does not comply with any one of the requirements of the Act, a statutory scheme will apply (Housing Grants, Construction and Regeneration Act 1996 s 108(5)) and this provides the procedures for the appointment of an adjudicator. Parties drafting or negotiating construction contracts will therefore have four choices:

(a)    leave the contract silent and allow the statutory scheme to apply;

(b)    incorporate one of the sets of rules which have been published by, for example, the Technology and Construction Solicitors' Association ('TeCSA'), (formerly the Official Referees Solicitors' Association), the Centre for Dispute Resolution ('CEDR') or the Institution of Civil Engineers ('ICE'). Form 137 [4551] post incorporates TeCSA's Adjudication Rules;

(c)    incorporate the statutory scheme with amendments;

(d)    draft their own provisions which meet the requirements of the Act. This Form contains its own provisions, but practitioners should be aware that there are others.

51    See the Contracts (Rights of Third Parties) Act 1999 and see vol 38(1) (2000 Reissue) SALE OF LAND Paragraph 230 574 et seq.

52    This schedule contains the adjudication provisions relating to disputes under the deed of appointment.

53    This is a form of novation whereby the building contractor is substituted for the client as the consultant's employer. In circumstances where, for example, the client disposes of its interest in the project prior to its completion the buyer may wish to retain the services of the consultant. Clause 8.3 of the appointment of the consultant allow this to happen. In this case the deed of novation can be adapted. Clauses 2.2–2.4 would have to recite the background to the assignment and references to the building contractor would be changed to the new client.

54    If any party is a company it is desirable to include the company registration number before the address of the registered office. This avoids any problems arising when a company has been wound up and a new company formed with the same name, or when the name of a company is changed, or if companies swap names eg on a reconstruction of a group of companies.

55    See the Contracts (Rights of Third Parties) Act 1999, and see vol 38(1) (2000 Reissue) SALE OF LAND Paragraph 224 [547] et seq.

56    Usually this documentation is executed as a deed so that consideration is unnecessary and any action for breach of contract is subject to a 12-year limitation period instead of the normal 6-year limit. See vol 5 (1994 Reissue) BUILDING AND ENGINEERING CONTRACTS Paragraph 140 [483]. It must be executed as a deed if it contains any power of attorney.

**[4435]–[4450]**

# 132

### Terms and conditions for appointment of environmental expert[1]

THIS DEED OF APPOINTMENT is made the ...... day of .........

BETWEEN:

(1)    *(name)* [company number *(number)*] [of *(address) or* whose registered office is at *(address)*] ('the Client') and

(2)    *(Assignee)* [company number *(number)*] [of *(address) or* whose registered office is at *(address)*] ('the Consultant')

## 1    Background

1.1    The Consultant is engaged in business offering consultancy services in relation to environmental matters and has considerable skill knowledge and experience in that field.

1.2    In reliance upon that skill knowledge and experience the Client wishes to engage the Consultant to provide services in relation to environmental matters and the Consultant agrees to accept the engagement on the following terms

**[4451]**

## 2       Definitions and interpretation

2.1      In this Agreement:

    2.1.1      'Affiliate' means any company partnership or other entity which directly or indirectly controls is controlled by or is under common control of either the Client or the Consultant

    2.1.2      'Agreement' means this instrument and any and all schedules to this Agreement as the same may be amended modified or supplemented from time to time in accordance with these provisions

    2.1.3      'the Board' means the Board of Directors from time to time of the Client

    2.1.4      'the Commencement Date means *(date)*

    2.1.5      'Confidential Information' means all unpatented designs drawings data specifications manufacturing processes testing procedures and all other technical business and similar information relating to the Project or relating to the business of the Consultant or its operation including all readable or computer or other machine readable data logic logic diagrams flow charts orthographic representations coding sheets coding source or object codes listings test data test routines diagnostic programs or other material relating to or comprising software which is part of the Project

    2.1.6      'control' means the legal power to direct or cause the direction of the general management and policies of the party in question

    2.1.7      'Documents' means all records reports documents papers and other materials whatsoever originated by or on behalf of the Consultant pursuant to this Agreement

    2.1.8      'the Project' means the job specification set out in schedule 1

    2.1.9      'the Services' means the services more particularly set out in schedule 2 and

    2.1.10    'the Site(s)' means the property and places more particularly set out in schedule 3

2.2      In this Deed unless the context otherwise requires:

    2.2.1      the headings in this Agreement are inserted only for convenience and shall not affect its construction

    2.2.2      where appropriate words denoting a singular number only shall include the plural and vice versa

    2.2.3      reference to any statute or statutory provision includes a reference to the statute or statutory provisions as from time to time amended extended or re-enacted

## 3     Duration

The Consultant shall commence the provision of the Services on the Commencement Date and shall continue to provide the Services until termination of this Agreement as provided in clause 6

**[4452]**

## 4     Positive obligations of the Consultant

4.1      *Services:* The Consultant shall provide the Services at the Site provided that it may provide the Services at such other place or places as may be necessary for the due performance of them

4.2       *Records:*  The Consultant shall keep detailed records of all acts and things done by it in relation to the provision of the Services and at the Client's request shall make them available for inspection and/or provide copies to the Client

4.3       *Duties:*  The Consultant shall at all times during the period of this Agreement:
          4.3.1       faithfully and diligently perform those duties and exercise such powers consistent with them which are from time to time necessary in connection with the provision of the Services
          4.3.2       obey all lawful and reasonable directions of the Client

4.4       *Confidentiality:*
          4.4.1       The Consultant agrees to treat as secret and confidential and make no disclosure of and to ensure that its personnel shall treat as secret and confidential and make no disclosure of the Confidential Information the Documents and all other matters arising or coming to its or their attention in connection with the provision of the Services and not at any time for any reason whatsoever to disclose them or permit them to be disclosed to any third party except as permitted in this Appointment to enable the Consultant to carry out its duties and obligations
          4.4.2       The Consultant shall procure that its personnel and all others of its employees having access to any of the Confidential Information the Documents or such matters shall be subject to the same obligations as the Consultant and shall enter into a suitable secrecy agreement in a form approved by the Client or in so far as this is not reasonably practicable the Consultant shall take all reasonable steps to ensure that its employees are made aware of and perform such obligations
          4.4.3       The Consultant agrees to treat as secret and confidential and not at any time for any reason to disclose or permit to be disclosed to any person or persons or otherwise make use of or permit to be made use of any information relating to the Client's technology technical processes business affairs or finances or any such information relating to any Affiliate suppliers or customers of the Client where knowledge or details of the information was received during the period of this Agreement
          4.4.4       The obligations of the parties under this clause 4.4 shall survive the expiry or the termination of this Agreement for whatever reason

                                                                                    **[4453]**

4.5       *Liability:*
          4.5.1       The Client will be relying upon the Consultant's skill expertise and experience and also upon the accuracy of all representations or statements made and the advice given by the Consultant in connection with the provision of the Services and the accuracy of any Confidential Information or Documents conceived originated made or developed by the Consultant in connection with the provision of the Services and the Consultant agrees to indemnify the Client against all loss damage costs legal costs and professional and other expenses of any nature whatsoever incurred or suffered by the Client or by a third party whether direct or consequential including but without limitation any economic loss or other loss of turnover profits business or goodwill as a result of such reliance
          4.5.2       The Consultant accepts:
                      4.5.2.1       liability for death or personal injury howsoever resulting from the Consultant's negligence or that of its employees or sub-contractors and

4.5.2.2      liability for damage to property howsoever resulting from the Consultant's negligence or that of its employees or sub-contractors where such negligence has arisen or arises in connection with the provision of the Services or in connection with any other activities undertaken by the Consultant pursuant to or for any purpose related to this Agreement

4.5.3      The Consultant hereby agrees to indemnify the Client against all and any liability loss damage costs and expense of whatsoever nature incurred or suffered by the Client or by any third party whether arising from any disputes contractual or tortious or other claims or proceedings which seek to recover loss and/or damage incurred by reason of any such death personal injury or damage to property

4.5.4      The Consultant's personnel shall at all times be deemed to be the Consultant's employees whether such personnel are at the Site or anywhere else

**[4454]**

4.5.5      The Consultant's liability under clauses 4.5.1 4.5.2 and 4.5.3 above shall be limited to the sum of £...

4.5.6      The Consultant expressly acknowledges that the provisions of this clause 4.5 satisfy the requirements of reasonableness specified in the Unfair Contract Terms Act 1977 and that it shall be estopped from claiming the contrary at any future date in the event of any dispute with the Client concerning the Consultant's liability under this Appointment

4.5.7      The Consultant undertakes and agrees to take out and maintain for the whole period of the Project adequate insurance cover with an insurance office of repute to cover the liability accepted by it in this clause 4.5 and agrees to produce at the Client's request a copy of the insurance policy or policies and relevant renewal receipts for inspection by the Client

4.5.8      The provisions of this clause 4.5 shall survive the termination of this Agreement for any reason

4.6      *Third parties:* If the Consultant shall consider it necessary to use the services of a third party whether for information or for the supply of goods or services including without limitation manufacture of models prototypes mock-ups art work drawings printing photography testing and the like the Consultant shall except in matters of a minor and obvious nature obtain the prior consent of the Client before using such services

4.7      *Indemnity:* The Consultant shall indemnify the Client against all liability loss damage and expense of whatsoever nature incurred or suffered by the Client or any third party as a result of the breach of any warranty in clause 4

**[4455]**

## 5      Payment

5.1      In consideration of the provision of the Services the Client shall pay to the Consultant the fees as set out in Schedule 4

5.2      All payments to the Consultant shall be made against the Consultant's invoices which shall be presented at the end of each calendar month during the term of this Agreement in respect of the provision of the Services provided in each such month. All payments shall be made by the Client within [30] days following receipt by the Client of the Consultant's invoice. All payments shall be made by the Client by a cheque or bank transfer to the account of the Consultant at a bank to be nominated in writing by the Consultant

5.3 Payment by the Client shall be without prejudice to any claims or rights which the Client may have made against the Consultant and shall not constitute any admission by the Client as to the performance by the Consultant of its obligations under this Appointment. Prior to making any such payment the Client shall be entitled to make deductions or deferments in respect of any disputes or claims whatsoever with or against the Consultant

## [6 Obligations of the Client

Throughout the period of this Agreement the Client shall in so far as possible afford the Consultant such access to the Site and the Client's information records and other material relevant to the Project as the Consultant may require to provide the Services provided always that the Client shall be obliged to afford such access only during its normal business hours. Further the Client shall:

6.1 advise the Consultant of the rules and regulations which are then in force for the conduct of personnel at the Site. The Consultant shall ensure that its personnel comply with any such rules and regulations

6.2 make available such working space and facilities at the Site as the Consultant may reasonably require. Such working space and facilities shall be comparable to but not better than those given by the Client to its own personnel of similar status

6.3 make available appropriate personnel to liaise with the Consultant

6.4 secure and otherwise keep safe all and any property of the Consultant]

**[4456]**

## 7 Termination

7.1 This Agreement shall terminate automatically on completion of the Project by the Consultant to the satisfaction of the Client by the service of a written notice to that effect from the Client but such termination shall be without prejudice to any provision intended to operate thereafter

7.2 Upon any breach by the Consultant of any of its duties and obligations under this Agreement in relation to the provision of the Services the Client shall have the rights specified in clauses 7.2.1 and 7.2.2:

    7.2.1 The Client shall have the right to seek an order for specific performance together with a mandatory injunction against the Consultant in addition to bringing a claim in damages

        7.2.1.1 The Consultant expressly acknowledges that the Client is relying upon the Consultant to perform all the Consultant's duties and obligations in connection with the provision of the Services and that upon any breach by the Consultant of any such duties and obligations the Client may not wish to exercise its right to terminate this Agreement pursuant to clause 7.2.2 and thereafter to engage the services of another consultant to complete the provision of the Services seeking to recover the cost thereof as damages from the Consultant since any such other consultant will not have the familiarity with the Client's business affairs necessary to enable such other consultant to provide the Services pursuant to the terms of this Agreement

7.2.1.2    By reason of the foregoing the Consultant hereby agrees that in circumstances where it is in breach of its duties and obligations in connection with the provision of the Services and the Client elects to affirm this Agreement and claim for damages the claim for damages will be an inadequate remedy for the Client and subject always to the discretion of the court the Client shall be entitled to an interlocutory order for specific performance together with a mandatory injunction (if the circumstances are appropriate to the grant of such an injunction) either or both in terms compelling the Consultant and its personnel thereafter to provide the Services pursuant to this Agreement

7.2.1.3    The Consultant further agrees that such relief shall not affect the Client's right to seek to recover any loss and damage suffered by it in respect of the Consultant's prior breach of its duties and obligations in connection with the provision of the Services

7.2.2    The Client shall have the right to terminate this Agreement forthwith by notice in writing to the Consultant and to engage another consultant to complete the provision of the Services. Following any such termination of this Agreement the Consultant shall indemnify the Client against all loss damage cost including management and similar costs expenses including professional fees and expenses and all other expenditure or loss of opportunity or revenue whatsoever incurred or suffered by the Client as a result of the Consultant's breach. This indemnity shall survive the termination of this Agreement

**[4457]**

7.3    In addition to and notwithstanding the Client's rights of termination pursuant to clause 7.2 either party may terminate this Agreement forthwith by notice in writing to the other if the other:

7.3.1    commits a breach of this Agreement which in the case of a breach capable of remedy shall not have been remedied within 30 days of the receipt by the other of a notice from the innocent party identifying the breach and requiring its remedy

7.3.2    is unable to pay its debts or enters into compulsory or voluntary liquidation (other than for the purpose of effecting a reconstruction or amalgamation in such manner that the company resulting from such reconstruction or amalgamation if a different legal entity shall agree to be bound by and assume the obligations of the relevant party under this Agreement) or compounds with or convenes a meeting of its creditors or proposes a voluntary arrangement with its creditors or has a receiver or manager or administrative receiver or administrator appointed or ceases for any reason to carry on business or takes or suffers any similar action which in the opinion of the party giving notice means that the other may be unable to pay its debts

7.4    The Client shall have the right to terminate this Agreement forthwith by written notice to the Consultant if the Consultant shall have been prevented by any cause from providing the Services for an aggregate period of [20] working days in any period of [12] calendar months

**[4458]**

7.5 Upon termination of this Agreement:

    7.5.1 for whatever reason the Consultant shall deliver up to the Client all of the Confidential Information and the Documents and any copies of them in the possession power custody or control of the Consultant at the time and shall execute all such deeds and documents as the Client's legal advisers may require to transfer and assign to the Client the property and intellectual property in such Confidential Information and the Documents and the Consultant shall not at any time afterwards utilise or exploit the Confidential Information or the Documents in any way whatsoever

    7.5.2 for whatever reason the Client shall have the right to utilise and exploit the Confidential Information and the Documents in any way whatsoever without restriction

    7.5.3 by the Consultant pursuant to clause 7.3 the Client shall remain liable to pay to the Consultant all sums which have accrued due and owing to the Consultant under this Appointment

7.6 Termination of this Agreement for whatever reason shall not affect the accrued rights of the parties arising in any way out of this Agreement as at the date of termination and in particular but without limitation the right to recover damages against the other and all provisions which are expressed to survive this Agreement shall remain in force and effect

**[4459]**

## 8 Assignment

8.1 Subject to the provisions of clause 8.2 below neither party shall assign transfer sub-contract or in any other manner make over to any third party the benefit and/or burden of this Agreement without the prior written consent of the other

8.2 The Client shall be entitled without the prior written consent of the Consultant to assign transfer or in any manner make over the benefit and/or burden of this Agreement to an Affiliate or to any 50/50 joint venture company where it is the beneficial owner of 50% of the issued share capital thereof or to any company or partnership with which it may merge or to any company or partnership to which it may transfer its assets and undertaking provided that such Affiliate or other company or partnership undertakes and agrees in writing to assume observe and perform the rights and power and/or duties and obligations of the Client under the provisions of this Agreement being assigned transferred or otherwise made over

8.3 This Agreement shall be binding upon the successors and assigns of the parties hereto and the name of a party appearing herein shall be deemed to include the names of its successors and assigns provided always that nothing shall permit any assignment by either party except as expressly provided

## 9 Governing law and jurisdiction

9.1 The validity construction and performance of this Agreement shall be governed by English Law

9.2 All disputes claims or proceedings between the parties relating to the validity construction or performance of this Agreement shall be subject to the non-exclusive jurisdiction of the High Court of Justice in England to which the parties hereto irrevocably submit. Each of the parties irrevocably consents to the award or grant of any relief in any such proceedings before the High Court of

Justice in England. Either party shall have the right to take proceedings in any other jurisdiction for the purposes of enforcing a judgment or order obtained from the High Court of Justice in England

**[4460]**

## 10 Force majeure

10.1 Neither party shall be in breach of this Agreement if there is any total or partial failure of performance by it of its duties and obligations under this Agreement occasioned by any act of God fire act of government or state war civil commotion insurrection embargo prevention from or hindrance in obtaining any raw materials energy or other supplies and any other reason beyond the control of either party

10.2 If either party is unable to perform its duties and obligations under this Agreement as a direct result of the effect of one of those reasons that party shall give written notice to the other of the inability setting out full details of the reason in question

10.3 The operation of this Agreement shall be suspended during the period (and only during the period) in which the reason continues

10.4 Forthwith upon the reason ceasing to exist the party relying upon it shall give written notice to the other of this fact

10.5 If the reason continues for a period of more than [90] days and substantially affects the commercial intention of this Agreement the party not claiming relief under this clause 10 shall have the right to terminate this Agreement upon giving 30 days written notice of such termination to the other party

## 11 Illegality

If any provision or term of this Agreement or any part of it shall become or be declared illegal invalid or unenforceable for any reason whatsoever including but without limitation by reason of the provisions of any legislation or other provisions having the force of law or by reason of any decision of any court or other body or authority having jurisdiction over the parties or this Agreement including the EC Commission and the European Court of Justice such terms or provisions shall be divisible from this Agreement and shall deemed to be deleted from this Agreement in the jurisdiction in question provided always that if any such deletion substantially affects or alters the commercial basis of this Agreement the parties shall negotiate in good faith to amend and modify the provisions and terms of this Agreement as may be necessary or desirable in the circumstances

**[4461]**

## 12 Amendment

12.1 This Agreement shall not be amended modified varied or supplemented except in writing signed by a duly authorised representative of each of the parties

12.2 No failure or delay on the part of either party hereto to exercise any right or remedy under this Agreement shall be construed or operated as a waiver thereof nor shall any single or partial exercise of any right or remedy as the case may be. The rights and remedies provided in this Agreement are cumulative and are not exclusive of any rights or remedies provided by law

12.3 The text of any press release or other communication to be published by or in the media concerning the subject matter of this Agreement shall require the approval of each party

12.4    Each of the parties hereto shall be responsible for its respective legal and other costs incurred in relation to the preparation of this Agreement

**[4462]**

## 13    Notices

13.1    Any notice or other document to be given under this Agreement shall be in writing and shall be deemed to have been duly given if left or sent by:
    13.1.1    first class post or express or air mail or other fast postal service or
    13.1.2    registered post or
    13.1.3    telex facsimile or other electronic media to a party at the address or relevant telecommunications number for such party or such other address as the party may from time to time designate by written notice to the other(s)

13.2    All such notices and documents shall be in the English language. Any notice or other document shall be deemed to have been received by the addressee two working days following the date of dispatch of the notice or other document by post or where the notice or other document is sent by hand or is given by telex facsimile or other electronic media simultaneously with the delivery or transmission. To prove the giving of a notice or other document it shall be sufficient to show that it was dispatched

SCHEDULE 1
Job Specification

SCHEDULE 2
The Services

SCHEDULE 3
The Site(s)

SCHEDULE 4
The Fees

**[4463]**

---

1    Terms of appointment could be set out in a letter, or, as here, in a more formal contract. The clauses contained in this agreement have been drafted on the basis of other, well-established precedents for similar consultancy agreements, adapted for use in the environmental field, but practitioners may take the view that many of the clauses are more complex than need be for a relatively simple survey of a target site by a surveyor.
    Most firms of consultants or experts have standard terms and conditions which are substantially briefer, and usually much more restrictive of the client's rights, than this model, and those standard terms may well be adequate, once the main restrictions have been dealt with.

**[4464]–[4480]**

# 133

## Deed of assignment of a professional's appointment[1]

THIS DEED OF ASSIGNMENT is made the ...... day of .........

BETWEEN:

(1)    *(Assignor)* [company number *(number)*[2]] [of *(address)* or whose registered office is at *(address)*] ('the Assignor') and

(2)    *(Assignee)* [company number *(number)*] [of *(address)* or whose registered office is at *(address)*] ('the Assignee')

## 1      Background

1.1      The Assignor appointed *(name and address of professional)* to act on its behalf in the capacity of *(insert discipline)* in connection with a development brief details of which are set out in the schedule below ('the Development') upon the terms and conditions contained in an Agreement dated *(date)* ('the Deed of Appointment') a copy of which is annexed[3]

1.2      [The Assignee] has by an agreement made between *(parties)* agreed to [purchase *or* take a lease of *or* provide funds for] [the whole *or* part] of the Development [more particularly known as *(description)*]

1.3      The Assignor has the benefit of the Deed of Appointment and has agreed to assign the benefit of its interest in it to the Assignee

**[4481]**

## 2      Assignment

The Assignor with limited title guarantee assigns to the Assignee absolutely the whole of the rights title and benefit which the Assignor may now have or become entitled to under the Deed of Appointment

## 3      Assignee's covenants

The Assignee covenants with the Assignor from the date of this Deed to observe and perform the Assignor's obligations in the Deed of Appointment[4]

## [4      Third party rights

A person who is not a party to this Deed has no rights under the Contracts (Rights of Third Parties) Act 1999 to enforce any terms of this Deed[5]]

IN WITNESS etc[6]

THE SCHEDULE
The Development
*(insert details)*

*(signatures (and common seals) of the parties)*
*(signatures of witnesses)*
**[4482]**

1      No stamp duty. As to assignment of rights generally see vol 38(1) (2000 Reissue) SALE OF LAND Paragraph 222 [543].

2      If any party is a company it is desirable to include the company registration number before the address of the registered office. This avoids any problems arising when a company has been wound up and a new company formed with the same name, or when the name of a company is changed, or if companies swap names eg on a reconstruction of a group of companies.

3      It is essential for the assignee to have seen and to be happy with the terms of the consultant's appointment. It is preferable for a copy to be annexed to the assignment.

4      It is assumed the Assignee will observe and perform the Assignee's obligations in the Deed of Appointment. If not, the clause should be amended.

5      See vol 38(1) (2000 Re issue) SALE OF LAND Paragraph 230 [574] et seq.

6      Usually this documentation is executed as a deed so that consideration is unnecessary and any action for breach of contract is subject to a 12-year limitation period instead of the normal 6-year limit. See vol 5 (1994 Reissue) BUILDING AND ENGINEERING CONTRACTS Paragraph 140 [483].

**[4483]**

# 134

## Deed of warranty by a contractor in favour of third party beneficiaries[1]

THIS DEED is made the ...... day of .........

BETWEEN

(1)       *(name)* [company number *(number)*[2]] [of *(address)* *or* whose registered office is at *(address)*] ('the Contractor') and

(2)       *(name)* [company number *(number)*] [of *(address)* *or* whose registered office is at *(address)*] ('the Beneficiary') and

(3)       *(name)* [company number *(number)*] [of *(address)* *or* whose registered office is at *(address)*] ('the Developer')

## 1       Background

1.1       By the Building Contract the Developer has employed the Contractor to carry out the Development

1.2       [The Beneficiary has [acquired *or* taken and interest in *or* taken a lease of] [part of] the [Development *or* Premises] [more particularly known as *(insert details)*][3]
          *or*
          The Beneficiary has agreed to provide loan facilities or other finance in respect of [the carrying out of the Development *or* the acquisition of the [Development *or* Premises] when complete][4]
          *or*
          The Beneficiary is a company within the group of companies of which the Building Owner is a member[5]
          *or*
          The Beneficiary has entered into a joint venture with the Building Owner in respect of *(specify)*][6]

1.3       The Contractor has agreed to enter into this Deed for the benefit of the Beneficiary and its successors in title and assigns

                                                                          **[4484]**

## 2       Definitions and interpretation

2.1       In this Deed:

          2.1.1       'the Building Contract' means the building contract made or to be made for the carrying out of the Development brief details of which are set out in schedule 1 and includes any documents or arrangements which are supplemental or ancillary to it by way of variation or otherwise

          2.1.2       'the Contract Works' means the works performed or to be performed by the Contractor under the Building Contract

          2.1.3       'the Development' means the development of the Premises brief details of which are out in schedule 2

          2.1.4       'Prohibited Materials' means the materials referred to in clause 7[7]

          2.1.5       'Notice of Completion of Making Good Defects' means the notice to that effect under the terms of the Building Contract

          2.1.6       'Practical Completion' means the date of practical completion of the Development under the terms of the Building Contract

          2.1.7       'the Premises' means the premises described in Schedule 3

2.2      In this Deed unless the context otherwise requires:

       2.2.1      clause headings are inserted for convenience only and shall not affect the construction of this Deed and any references to clauses or schedules are to clauses of and schedules to this Deed

       2.2.2      words denoting the singular number include the plural and vice versa

       2.2.3      references to persons include references to bodies corporate and unincorporate

**[4485]**

## 3     Exercise of skill care and diligence

3.1      The Contractor warrants and undertakes to the Beneficiary that it has exercised and will continue to exercise all the reasonable skill care and diligence which may reasonably be expected of a contractor acting within the scope of the Contractor's appointment under the provisions of the Building Contract including without prejudice to the generality of the foregoing the design of the Contract Works and the selection of goods and materials for the Contract Works

3.2      The Contractor further warrants and undertakes to the Beneficiary that:

       3.2.1      the Contract Works will at Practical Completion satisfy all performance specifications and other requirements contained or referred to in the Building Contract and

       3.2.2      the Contract Works and all materials and goods comprised in them will correspond as to description quality and condition with the requirements of the Building Contract and will be of sound manufacture and workmanship

## [4     Obligations prior to determination of the Building Contract[8]

4.1      The Contractor warrants and undertakes to the Beneficiary that it will not exercise or seek to exercise any right of determination of its employment under the Building Contract or to discontinue the performance of any of its obligations in relation to the Development by reason of breach on the part of the Developer without giving to the Beneficiary not less than 28 days' notice of its intention to do so and specifying the grounds for the proposed determination or discontinuance

4.2      Compliance by the Contractor with the provisions of clause 4.1 shall not be treated as a waiver of any breach on the part of the Developer giving rise to the right of determination nor otherwise prevent the Contractor from exercising its rights after the expiration of the notice unless the right of determination shall have ceased under the provisions of clause 5]

**[4486]**

## [5     Obligations of the Contractor to the Beneficiary

5.1      The right of the Contractor to determine its employment under the Building Contract shall cease within the period of 28 days referred to in clause 4.1 if the Beneficiary shall give notice to the Contractor:

       5.1.1      requiring it to continue its obligations under the Building Contract in relation to the Development

       5.1.2      acknowledging that the Beneficiary is assuming all the obligations of the Developer under the Building Contract and

       5.1.3      undertaking unconditionally to the Contractor to discharge all payments which may subsequently become due to the Contractor under the terms of the Building Contract and shall pay to the Contractor all sums which have become due and payable to it under the Building Contract but which were then unpaid

5.2      Upon compliance by the Beneficiary with the requirements of clause 5.1 the Building Contract shall continue in full force and effect as if the right of determination on the part of the Contractor had not arisen and in all respects as if the Building Contract had been made between the Contractor and the Beneficiary

5.3      The Contractor acting in accordance with the provisions of this clause 5 shall not by so doing incur any liability to the Developer]

## 6     Copyright and licence to use documents

6.1      The Contractor grants and agrees to grant to the Beneficiary an irrevocable royalty-free non-exclusive licence to use and reproduce all designs drawings models plans specifications design details photographs brochures reports notes of meetings details schedules levels setting-out dimensions documents papers calculations software computerised information data and any other materials and work prepared by or on behalf of the Contractor in connection with the Development (whether in existence or to be made) and all amendments and additions to them and any works designs or inventions of the Contractor incorporated or referred to in them for any purpose whatsoever relating to the Development ('the Documents') including (without limitation) the construction completion reconstruction modification extension repair reinstatement refurbishment development maintenance use letting promotion and advertisement of the Development. Such licence carries the right for the Beneficiary to grant sub-licences and to be transferable without the prior consent of the Contractor provided that the Contractor shall have no liability to the beneficiary of the licence or sub-licence arising from the use of the Documents other than that for which they were prepared by or on behalf of the Contractor

6.2      The Contractor agrees on request at any time to give the Beneficiary or any persons authorised by the Beneficiary access to the Documents and at the Beneficiary's expense to provide copies of them

6.3      All royalties or other sums payable in respect of the supply and use of any patented articles processes or inventions required in connection with the Building Contract shall be paid by the Contractor and the Contractor shall indemnify the Beneficiary from and against all claims proceedings damages costs and expenses suffered or incurred by the Beneficiary by reason of the Contractor infringing or being held to infringe any intellectual property rights in the course of or in connection with the Building Contract

**[4487]**

## 7     Prohibited Materials[9]

The Contractor further warrants to the Beneficiary that it:

7.1      has not used any of the following in the Development: *(insert list of prohibited materials to correspond with the terms of the Building Contract)*

7.2      has exercised and will continue to exercise all reasonable skill care and diligence to see so far as is consistent with its duties under this Deed that none of the matters referred to in clause 7.1 has been specified for use in the Development and that none are used in the Development

**[8      Year 2000 compliance**[10]

8.1      In this clause unless the context otherwise requires the following expressions
         have the following meanings:

    8.1.1      'Equipment' means all computer hardware (including Firmware) and
         associated documentation to be supplied by the Contractor or its
         sub-contractors for inclusion in the Development

    8.1.2      'Firmware' means the microcode which is an integral part of and
         required by a specific item of the Equipment

    8.1.3      'Software' means the software to be provided by the Contractor or
         its sub-contractors under the Building Contract including but not
         limited to operating systems compilers utilities and other
         programmes including developed programmes and the application
         software identified in the Building Contract

    8.1.4      'System' means the Equipment and Software

         For the purposes of this clause the twentieth century shall be deemed to have
         ended and the twenty-first century shall be deemed to have begun on 1st
         January 2000 at 00.00 hours in the time zone local to the System

         **[4488]**

8.2      The Contractor represents and warrants to the Beneficiary that the System has
         Year 2000 conformity as defined in the British Standards Institution Definition
         of Year 2000 Conformity Requirements[11] and that the System has 'general
         integrity' and 'date integrity' as specified in rules 1 and 2 of such Definition.
         Without prejudice to the generality of the foregoing:

    8.2.1      no error or interruption in the operation of the System will result
         directly or indirectly from the passage from the twentieth century to
         the twenty-first century or from the extra day occurring in any leap
         year in the twentieth or twenty-first century or from the occurrence
         of any other date

    8.2.2      no reduction or alteration in the functionality of the System will
         result directly or indirectly from the passage from the twentieth
         century to the twenty-first century or from the extra day occurring
         in any leap year in the twentieth or twenty-first century or from the
         occurrence of any other date

    8.2.3      the System will not process any data which includes a date which
         does not specify the century

    8.2.4      all date-related output and results produced by the System shall
         include an indication of the century

    8.2.5      the System will produce accurate results in the calculations and other
         data processing which span the twentieth century to the twenty-first
         century

    8.2.6      inter-faces and reporting facilities comprised by the System will
         support four-digit year processing]

         **[4489]**

**9      Variation of the building licence**

The Contractor undertakes to the Beneficiary not to vary or depart from the terms and
conditions of the Building Contract without the prior written consent of the Beneficiary
and agrees that any variation or departure made without such consent shall not be
binding on the Beneficiary or affect or prejudice the Beneficiary's rights under this Deed
or under the Building Contract or in any other way

## 10      Insurance[12]

10.1      The Contractor warrants to the Beneficiary that it has at all relevant times maintained and (so long as such insurance is available in the market) will continue to maintain for a period of 12 years from the date of issue of the Notice of Completion of Making Good Defects [both] [professional indemnity and/or product liability] insurance[s] with [a] reputable insurance [company or companies] with [a] limit[s] of [indemnity and/or liability] of not less than £... [and £... respectively] and an excess of not more than £... in respect of each and every claim to cover any claims made against the Contractor in relation to the Development

10.2      As and when reasonably required by the Beneficiary the Contractor shall produce for inspection satisfactory documentary evidence that the insurance[s] referred to in clause 10.1 [is or are] being properly maintained and confirm that payment has been made in respect of the last preceding premium[s] due under [it or them]

10.3      If the contractor fails to comply with this clause 10 it shall repay to the Beneficiary on demand any money the Beneficiary reasonably spends to effect insurance against any risk or amount with respect to which such default has occurred

10.4      The Contractor has prior to the date of this Deed notified its insurers of the terms of this Deed and will disclose the terms to any new insurers before changing insurers

**[4490]**

## 11      Indemnity

[Save that the Contractor shall owe the Beneficiary no greater duty than it owes to the Developer under the Building Contract] the Contractor further undertakes to indemnify the Beneficiary from and against the consequences of any breach by the Contractor of any of the warranties covenants and undertakings contained in this Deed

## 12      Concurrent liabilities

The rights and benefits conferred upon the Beneficiary by this Deed are in addition to any other rights and remedies it may have against the Contractor including without prejudice to the generality of the foregoing any remedies in negligence

## 13      Continuing effect

Notwithstanding the completion of the Development or any part of it this deed shall continue to have effect

## 14      Limitation period

The liability of the Contractor under this Deed shall cease 12 years after the date of issue of the Notice of Completion of Making Good Defects save so far as concerns any matter in respect of which proceedings (whether by way of action adjudication or otherwise) shall have been commenced before the expiry of the period of 12 years

**[4491]**

## 15      Assignment

The benefit of all or any of the Contractor's obligations under this Deed and/or any benefit arising under or out of this Deed may be assigned without the consent of the

Contractor [on *(number)* occasions only and thereafter with the Contractor's consent which consent may not be unreasonably withheld or delayed][13]

## 16    Further warranty deeds

The Contractor covenants that if required by the Beneficiary it will enter into further deeds of warranty with all and each of such persons who shall acquire or agree to acquire an interest in or who shall provide or agree to provide loan facilities or other finance (secured or unsecured) in respect of the whole or any part of the [Development *or* Premises]. Each such deed of warranty shall be in the same form mutatis mutandis as this Deed save for this clause

## 17    Disputes[14]

17.1    If any dispute or difference as to the construction of this Deed or any matter or thing of whatsoever nature arising hereunder or in connection therewith shall arise it shall be determined in the courts of England and Wales or by adjudication and not in arbitration

17.2    The parties' right to refer a dispute arising under this Deed to adjudication shall be in accordance with this clause 17

17.3    The Technology and Construction Solicitors' Association's Adjudication Rules shall apply if a dispute or difference is required to be referred to adjudication. Therefore it is agreed that the provisions of Part I of the Schedule to the Scheme for Construction Contracts (England and Wales) Regulations 1998[15] shall not apply

**[4492]**

## [18    Third party rights[16]

A person who is not a party to this Deed has no rights under the Contracts (Rights of Third Parties) Act 1999 to enforce any terms of this Deed]

## 19    Law and jurisdiction

This Deed shall be governed by and construed in accordance with English Law and the parties submit to the [non-exclusive] jurisdiction of the English courts

## 20    Notices

20.1    All notices or other communications under or in respect of this Deed to any party shall be deemed to be duly given or made when delivered (in the case of personal delivery or letter) or when despatched (in the case of facsimile) to the party addressed to it at the address appearing below (or at such address as the party may after the date of this Deed specify for this purpose to the other):

20.1.1    In the case of the Contractor:
    20.1.1.1    Address: *(address)*
    20.1.1.2    Facsimile No: *(number)*

20.1.2    In the case of the Beneficiary:
    20.1.2.1    Address: *(address)*
    20.1.2.2    Facsimile No: *(number)*

20.1.3    In the case of the Developer:
    20.1.3.1    Address: *(address)*
    20.1.3.2    Facsimile No: *(number)*

20.2    A written notice includes a notice by facsimile. A notice or other communication received on a non-working day or after business hours in the place of receipt shall be deemed to be given or made on the next following working day in that place

IN WITNESS etc[17]

## SCHEDULE 1
### The Building Contract
The Building Contract made between the Developer of the one part and the Contractor of the other part dated *(date)*

## SCHEDULE 2
### The Development
*(insert description)*

## SCHEDULE 3
### The Premises
*(insert description)*

*(signatures (and common seals) of the parties)*
*(signatures of witnesses)*
**[4493]**

1    No stamp duty. As to collateral warranties generally see vol 38(1) (2000 Reissue) SALE OF LAND Paragraph 225 [548] et seq.

2    If any party is a company it is desirable to include the company registration number before the address of the registered office. This avoids any problems arising when a company has been wound up and a new company formed with the same name, or when the name of a company is changed, or if companies swap names eg on a reconstruction of a group of companies.

3    Identify the transaction which has taken place which allows the beneficiary to obtain the warranty.

4    Identify the transaction which has taken place which allows the beneficiary to obtain the warranty.

5    Identify the transaction which has taken place which allows the beneficiary to obtain the warranty.

6    Identify the transaction which has taken place which allows the beneficiary to obtain the warranty.

7    Reference to a list of 'deleterious materials' is to be avoided. Manufacturers of materials that commonly appear in such lists may have a right of action. There is nothing objectionable for an employer to require any particular material to be excluded from a project as long as he does not describe the material as being deleterious when it may not be so if used in particular circumstances. This clause provides for a list for practitioners who wish to insert one. For alternative wording not listing materials see Form 137 clause 5.1 [4553] post.

8    Clauses 4 and 5 provide the beneficiary with 'step-in' rights and should be deleted if such rights are not required.

9    See note 7 above. For a generic definition of non-stipulated materials see Prec 7/7 clause 3.1 post.

10    In the event, the major problems anticipated with the passing of 1 January 2000 did not materialise. However, clients and end-users will be concerned to ensure that computer equipment is able to cope with the fact that the year 2000 is a leap year and any other 'troublesome' dates which may occur in the future. See clauses 8.2.1 and 8.2.2. With the passage of time this clause will become redundant, but clients should obtain specialist advice before deleting it altogether.

11    Published by the British Standard Institution, reference DISC PD 2000-1.

**[4494]**

12    Insurance is often a topic which can involve protracted negotiations. As the contractor may be responsible for the design of a significant element of the development and the installation of materials and goods, both professional indemnity insurance and product liability insurance should be considered. Warrantors often seek to include a provision whereby insurance cover is available at 'commercially reasonable rates'. Beneficiaries find this to be too subjective a test to be acceptable.

Insurers often cap liability for claims relating to contamination or pollution.

The required limit of indemnity and the amount of any excess are figures upon which the beneficiary should take professional advice. A commercial decision should then be taken in the light of the extent of cover that is in place.

The clause requires cover for each and every claim. Some warrantors seek to include a provision whereby the amount of the insurance cover is capped for any one year. Beneficiaries tend to reject this proposal.

A warrantor's liability under the provisions of the warranty should be contrasted with the amount of insurance cover that exists. Strictly, any shortfall would be a liability that remains with the warrantor.

13   Unless the parties agree otherwise, the benefits can be assigned freely without consent of the warrantor. If the number of assignments is to be limited, care should be taken in choosing the number. Two or three assignments appear to be acceptable in the market but particular circumstances may require a greater number.

14   Some commentators have suggested that this type of warranty could be regarded as a 'construction contract' for the purposes of the Housing Grants, Construction and Regeneration Act 1996 Pt II (11 Halsbury's Statutes (4th Edn) CONTRACT) which came into effect on 1st May 1998. The Act allows the parties to refer disputes to adjudication (Housing Grants, Construction and Regeneration Act 1996 s 108). If a contract does not comply with any one of the requirements of the Act, a statutory scheme will apply (Housing Grants, Construction and Regeneration Act 1996 s 108(5)) and this provides the procedures for the appointment of an adjudicator. Parties drafting or negotiating construction contracts will therefore have four choices:

(a)   leave the contract silent and allow the statutory scheme to apply;

(b)   incorporate one of the sets of rules which have been published by, for example, the Technology and Construction Solicitors' Association ('TeCSA') (formerly the Official Referees Solicitors' Association), the Centre for Dispute Resolution ('CEDR') or the Institution of Civil Engineers ('ICE'). This Form incorporates TeCSA's Adjudication Rules, but practitioners should be aware that there are others;

(c)   incorporate the statutory scheme with amendments;

(d)   draft their own provisions which meet the requirements of the Act. For an example, see Form 131 clause 16 [4385] and schedule 7 [4427] ante.

15   Ie the Scheme for Construction Contracts (England and Wales) Regulations 1998, SI 1998/649.

16   See vol 38(1) (2000 Reissue) SALE OF LAND Paragraph 230 [574] et seq.

17   Usually this documentation is executed as a deed so that consideration is unnecessary and any action for breach of contract is subject to a 12-year limitation period instead of the normal 6-year limit. See vol 5 (1994 Reissue) BUILDING AND ENGINEERING CONTRACTS Paragraph 140 [483].

**[4495]–[4510]**

# 135

### Deed of warranty by a sub-contractor in favour of the employer[1]

THIS DEED is made the ...... day of .........

BETWEEN

(1)   *(name)* [company number *(number)*[2]] [of *(address) or* whose registered office is at *(address)*] ('the Sub-contractor')

(2)   *(name)* [company number *(number)*] [of *(address) or* whose registered office is at *(address)*] ('the Employer')

## 1      Background

1.1   By the Building Contract the Employer has employed or will employ the Contractor to carry out the Development

1.2   By the Sub-contract the Contractor has engaged or will engage the Sub-contractor to carry out the Sub-contract Works

1.3   The engagement of the Sub-contractor has been approved by the Employer under the terms of the Building Contract

1.4   The Sub-contractor has agreed to enter into this Deed for the benefit of the Employer and its successors in title and assigns

**[4511]**

## 2          Definitions and interpretation

2.1       In this Deed:

2.1.1       'the Building Contract' means the building contract made or to be made between the Employer and the Contractor for the carrying out of the Development and includes any documents or arrangements which are supplemental or ancillary to it by way of variation or otherwise

2.1.2       'the Contractor' means *(name)* [company number *(number)*] [of *(address) or* whose registered office is at *(address)*]

2.1.3       'the Development' means the construction of *(description of development)*

2.1.4       'Prohibited Materials' means the materials referred to in clause 7[3]

2.1.5       'Practical Completion' means the date of practical completion of the Development under the terms of the Building Contract

2.1.6       'the Premises' means the premises described in schedule 2

2.1.7       'the Sub-contract' means the sub-contract for the carrying out of the *(description)* works in relation to the Development brief details of which are set out in schedule 1 and a copy of which is annexed[4]

2.1.8       'the Sub-contract Works' means works performed or to be performed by the Sub-contractor under the Sub-contract

2.2       In this Deed unless the context otherwise requires:

2.2.1       clause headings are inserted for convenience only and shall not affect the construction of this Deed and any references to a clause or schedule is to a clause of and schedule to this Deed

2.2.2       words denoting the singular number include the plural and vice versa

2.2.3       references to persons include references to bodies corporate and unincorporate

                                                                                          **[4512]**

## 3          Exercise of skill care and diligence

3.1       The Sub-contractor warrants and undertakes to the Employer that it has exercised and will continue to exercise all the reasonable skill care and diligence which may reasonably be expected of a sub-contractor in relation to the Development acting within the scope of the Sub-contractor's appointment under the provisions of the Sub-contract including without prejudice to the generality of the foregoing the design of the Sub-contract Works and the selection of goods and materials for the Sub-contract Works

3.2       The Sub-contractor further warrants and undertakes to the Employer that:

3.2.1       the Sub-contract Works will at Practical Completion satisfy all performance specifications and other requirements contained or referred to in the Building Contract and the Sub-contract and

3.2.2       the Sub-contract Works and all materials and goods comprised in them will correspond as to description quality and condition with the requirements of the Building Contract and Sub-contract and will be of sound manufacture and workmanship

                                                                                          **[4513]**

## [4          Novation[5]

4.1       In the event that the Building Contract or the employment of the Contractor thereunder is determined for any reason whatsoever including but without prejudice to the generality of the foregoing the insolvency or winding-up of the

Contractor (voluntary or otherwise) the Sub-contractor shall without allowing any break or intermission to occur in the performance of its duties:

4.1.1      continue to observe and carry out its obligations under the Sub-contract and this Deed

4.1.2      if so required by notice in writing from the Employer treat the Employer as employer under the Sub-contract to the exclusion of the Contractor whereupon all rights and obligations of the employer under the Sub-contract shall thereafter be exercisable and performed by the Employer

4.1.3      accept and enter into any deeds or other documents as are reasonably required to put into legal effect any further novation of the Sub-contract reasonably required by the Employer subject to an undertaking by any person taking such a novation to pay all sums due and payable to the Sub-contractor under the Sub-contract and

4.1.4      if the Sub-contractor fails to execute any such Deeds or other documents within 14 days of a request the Employer may execute them on behalf of the Sub-contractor and for such purpose the Sub-contractor irrevocably appoints the Employer as the Sub-contractor's attorney for the purpose of executing such deeds or other documents

4.2      Subject to clause 5 the Employer shall from the date of such determination until any further novation of the Sub-contract be responsible for the payment of all sums properly payable to the Sub-contractor under the Sub-contract whether accruing due before or after such determination but subject to the same right to deduct retentions as would have applied to the Contractor under the Sub-contract

4.3      The Sub-contractor shall have no claim whatsoever against the Employer in respect of any damage loss or expense howsoever arising out of or in connection with any determination of the Building Contract or the Sub-contract]

**[5      Notice of novation**

Notwithstanding anything contained in this Deed and notwithstanding any payments which may be made by the Employer to the Sub-contractor the Employer shall not be under any obligation to the Sub-contractor unless the Employer shall have given written notice to the Sub-contractor pursuant to clause 4.1.2]

**[4514]**

**6      Copyright and licence to use documents**

6.1      The Sub-contractor grants and agrees to grant to the Employer an irrevocable royalty-free non-exclusive licence to use and reproduce all designs drawings models plans specifications design details photographs brochures reports notes of meetings details schedules levels setting-out dimensions documents papers calculations software computerised information data and any other materials and work prepared by or on behalf of the Sub-contractor in connection with the Sub-contract Works (whether in existence or to be made) and all amendments and additions to them and any works designs or inventions of the Sub-contractor incorporated or referred to in them for all purposes relating to the Sub-contract Works ('the Documents') including (without limitation) the construction completion reconstruction modification extension repair reinstatement refurbishment development maintenance use letting promotion and advertisement of the Development. Such licence carries the right for the

Beneficiary to grant sub-licences and to be transferable without the prior consent of the Sub-contractor provided that the Sub-contractor shall have no liability to the beneficiary of the licence or sub-licence arising from the use of the Documents other than that for which they were prepared by or on behalf of the Sub-contractor

6.2     The Sub-contractor agrees:

6.2.1     on request at any time to give the Employer or any persons authorised by the Employer access to the Documents and at the Employer's expense to provide copies of them and

6.2.2     at the Sub-contractor's expense to provide the Employer with a set of all the Documents on practical completion of the Sub-Contract

6.3     All royalties or other sums payable in respect of the supply and use of any patented articles processes or inventions required in connection with the Sub-contract Works shall be paid by the Sub-contractor and the Sub-contractor shall indemnify the Employer from and against all claims proceedings damages costs and expenses suffered or incurred by the Employer by reason of the Sub-contractor infringing or being held to infringe any intellectual property rights in the course of or in connection with the Sub-contract Works

**[4515]**

**7     Prohibited Materials[6]**

The Sub-contractor further warrants to the Employer that it:

7.1     has not used and will not use any of the following in the Development: *(insert appropriate list of prohibited materials to correspond with that in the Building Contract)*

7.2     has exercised and will continue to exercise all reasonable skill care and diligence to see so far as is consistent with its duties under the Sub-contract that none of the materials referred to in clause 7.1 have been specified for use in the Development and that none are used in the Development

**[8     Year 2000 compliance[7]**

8.1     In this clause unless the context otherwise requires the following expressions have the following meanings:

8.1.1     'Equipment' means all computer hardware (including Firmware) and associated documentation to be supplied by the Sub-contractor for inclusion in the Development

8.1.2     'Firmware' means the microcode which is an integral part of and required by a specific item of the Equipment

8.1.3     'Software' means the software to be provided by the Sub-contractor under the Sub-contract including but not limited to operating systems compilers utilities and other programmes including developed programmes and the application software identified in the Sub-contract

8.1.4     'System' means the Equipment and the Software

8.2     The Sub-contractor represents and warrants to the Employer that the System has Year 2000 conformity as defined in the British Standards Institution Definition of Year 2000 Conformity Requirements[8] and that the System has 'general integrity' and 'date integrity' as specified in rules 1 and 2 of such Definition. Without prejudice to the generality of the foregoing:

8.2.1    no error or interruption in the operation of the System will result directly or indirectly for the passage from the twentieth century to the twenty-first century or from the occurrence of any other date

8.2.2    no reduction or alteration in the functionality of the System will result directly or indirectly from the passage from the twentieth to the twenty-first century or from the extra day occurring in any leap year in the twentieth or twenty-first century or from the occurrence of any other date

8.2.3    the System will not process any data which includes a date which does not specify the century

8.2.4    all date-related output and results produced by the System shall include an indication of the century

8.2.5    the System will produce accurate results in the calculations and other data processing which span the twentieth century to the twenty-first century

8.2.6    inter-faces and reporting facilities comprised by the System will support four-digit year processing]

**[4516]**

## 9    Variation of the Sub-contract

The Sub-contractor undertakes to the Employer not to vary or depart from the terms and conditions of the Sub-contract without the prior written consent of the Employer and agrees that any variation or departure made without such consent shall not be binding on the Employer or affect or prejudice the Employer's rights under this Deed or under the Sub-contract or in any other way

## 10    Insurance[9]

10.1    The Sub-contractor warrants to the Employer that he has at all relevant times maintained and (so long as such insurance is available in the market) will continue to maintain throughout the duration of the Building Contract and for a period of 12 years from the date of Practical Completion [both] [professional indemnity and/or product liability] insurance[s] with [a] reputable insurance [company or companies] with [a] limit[s] of [indemnity and/or liability] of not less than £... [and £... respectively] and an excess of not more than £... in respect of each and every claim to cover any claims made under this Deed against the Sub-contractor in relation to the Development

10.2    As and when reasonably required by the Beneficiary the Contractor shall produce for inspection satisfactory documentary evidence that the insurance[s] referred to in clause 10.1 [is or are] being properly maintained and confirm that payment has been made in respect of the last preceding premium[s] due under [it or them]

10.3    If the Sub-contractor fails to comply with this clause 10 he shall repay to the Employer on demand any money the Employer reasonably spends to effect insurance against any risk or amount with respect to which such default has occurred

10.4    The Sub-contractor has prior to the date of this Deed notified its insurers of the terms of this Deed and will disclose the terms to any new insurers before changing insurers

**[4517]**

## 11    Indemnity

[Save that the Sub-contractor shall owe the Employer no greater duty than it owes to the Contractor under the Sub-contract] the Sub-contractor further undertakes to indemnify the Employer from and against the consequences of any breach by the Sub-contractor of any of the warranties covenants and undertakings contained in this Deed

## 12    Concurrent liabilities

The rights and benefits conferred upon the Employer by this Deed are in addition to any other rights and remedies it may have against the Sub-contractor including without prejudice to the generality of the foregoing any remedies in negligence

## 13    Continuing effect

Notwithstanding the completion of the Development or any part of it this deed shall continue to have effect

## 14    Limitation Period[10]

The liability of the Sub-contractor under this Deed shall cease 12 years after the date of Practical Completion save so far as concerns any matter in respect of which proceedings (whether by way of action adjudication or otherwise) shall have been commenced before the expiry of the period of 12 years

## 15    Assignment

The benefit of all or any of the Sub-contractor's obligations under this Deed and/or any benefit arising under or out of this Deed may be assigned without the consent of the Sub-contractor [on *(number)* occasions only and thereafter with the Sub-contractor's consent which consent may not be unreasonably withheld or delayed][11]

**[4518]**

## 16    Further warranty deeds

The Sub-contractor covenants that if required by the Employer it will enter into further deeds of warranty with all and each of such persons who shall acquire or agree to acquire an interest in the whole or any part of the [Development *or* Premises]. Each such deed of warranty shall be in the same form mutatis mutandis as this Deed save for this clause

## 17    Disputes[12]

17.1    If any dispute or difference as to the construction of this Deed or any matter or thing of whatsoever nature arising hereunder or in connection therewith shall arise it shall be determined in the Courts of England and Wales and not in arbitration

17.2    The parties' right to refer a dispute arising under this Deed to adjudication shall be in accordance with this clause 16

17.3    The Technology and Construction Solicitors' Association's Adjudication Rules shall apply if a dispute or difference is required to be referred to adjudication. Therefore it is agreed that the provisions of Part I of the Schedule to the Scheme for Construction Contracts (England and Wales) Regulations 1998[13] shall not apply

**[18    Third party rights**[14]

A person who is not a party to this Deed has no rights under the Contracts (Rights of Third Parties) Act 1999 to enforce any terms of this Deed**]**

**[4519]**

## 19    Law and jurisdiction

This Deed shall be governed by and construed in accordance with English Law and the parties submit to the [non-exclusive] jurisdiction of the English courts

## 20    Notices

20.1    All notices or other communications under or in respect of this Deed to either party shall be deemed to be duly given or made when delivered (in the case of personal delivery or letter) or when despatched (in the case of facsimile) to the party addressed to it at the address appearing below (or at such address as the party may after the date of this Deed specify for this purpose to the other):
20.1.1    In the case of the Sub-contractor:
20.1.1.1    Address: *(address)*
20.1.1.2    Facsimile No: *(number)*
20.1.2    In the case of the Employer:
20.1.2.1    Address: *(address)*
20.1.2.2    Facsimile No: *(number)*

20.2    A written notice includes a notice by facsimile. A notice or other communication received on a non-working day or after business hours in the place of receipt shall be deemed to be given or made on the next following working day in that place

IN WITNESS etc[15]

SCHEDULE 1
Particulars of the Sub-contract
*(insert details)*

SCHEDULE 2
The Premises
*(insert description)*

*(signatures (and common seals) of the parties)*
*(signatures of witnesses)*
**[4520]**

1    No stamp duty. As to collateral warranties generally see vol 38(1) (2000 Reissue) SALE OF LAND Paragraph 225 [548] et seq.
2    If any party is a company it is desirable to include the company registration number before the address of the registered office. This avoids any problems arising when a company has been wound up and a new company formed with the same name or when the name of a company is changed or if companies swap names eg on a reconstruction of a group of companies.
3    Reference to a list of 'deleterious materials' is to be avoided. Manufacturers of materials that commonly appear in such lists may have a right of action. There is nothing objectionable for an employer to require any particular material to be excluded from a project as long as he does not describe the material as being deleterious when it may not be so if used in particular circumstances. This clause provides for a list for practitioners who wish to insert one. For alternative wording not listing materials see Form 137 clause 5.1 [4553] post.

| | |
|---|---|
| 4 | The sub-contract must be annexed as reference is made to its terms in various clauses of this Form. |
| 5 | Clauses 4 and 5 provide the beneficiary with 'step-in' rights and should be deleted if such rights are not required. |
| 6 | See note 3 above. For a generic definition of prohibited materials see Form 137 clause 5.1 [4553] ante. |
| 7 | In the event, the major problems anticipated with the passing of 1 January 2000 did not materialise. However, clients and end-users will be concerned to ensure that computer equipment is able to cope with the fact that the year 2000 is a leap year and any other 'troublesome' dates which may occur in the future. See clauses 8.2.1 and 8.2.2. With the passage of time this clause will become redundant, but clients should obtain specialist advice before deleting it altogether. |
| 8 | Published by the British Standard Institution, reference DISC PD 2000-1. |
| 9 | Insurance is often a topic which can involve protracted negotiations. If the sub-contractor is responsible for the design of any significant element of the development, professional indemnity insurance should be considered. If he is to install materials and goods, product liability insurance may be necessary. Warrantors often seek to include a provision whereby insurance cover is available at 'commercially reasonable rates'. Beneficiaries find this to be too subjective a test to be acceptable. |

Insurers often cap liability for claims relating to contamination or pollution.

The required limit of indemnity and the amount of any excess are figures upon which the beneficiary should take professional advice. A commercial decision should then be taken in the light of the extent of cover that is in place.

The clause requires cover for each and every claim. Some warrantors seek to include a provision whereby the amount of the insurance cover is capped for any one year. Beneficiaries tend to reject this proposal.

A warrantor's liability under the provisions of the warranty should be contrasted with the amount of insurance cover that exists. Strictly, any shortfall would be a liability that remains with the warrantor.

This form requires the sub-contractor to keep insurance on foot for 12 years from practical completion of the project as opposed to a period that runs from the making good of its defects (cf Form 134 clause 10.1 [4490] ante). A sub-contractor's work may be completed early on in the undertaking of the development and it might be considered unreasonable for cover to be maintained for an extended period by virtue of a problem which was not of his making.

| | |
|---|---|
| 10 | The limitation period is 12 years following practical completion for the reason given in note 9 above. |
| 11 | Unless the parties agree otherwise, the benefits can be assigned freely without consent of the warrantor. If the number of assignments is to be limited, care should be taken in choosing the number. Two or three assignments appear to be acceptable in the market but particular circumstances may require a greater number. |
| 12 | Some commentators have suggested that this type of warranty could be regarded as a 'construction contract' for the purposes of the Housing Grants, Construction and Regeneration Act 1996 Pt II (11 Halsbury's Statutes (4th Edn) CONTRACT) which came into effect on 1st May 1998. The Act allows the parties to refer disputes to adjudication (Housing Grants, Construction and Regeneration Act 1996 s 108). If a contract does not comply with any one of the requirements of the Act, a statutory scheme will apply (Housing Grants, Construction and Regeneration Act 1996 s 108(5)) and this provides the procedures for the appointment of an adjudicator. Parties drafting or negotiating construction contracts will therefore have four choices: |

(a)    leave the contract silent and allow the statutory scheme to apply;

(b)    incorporate one of the sets of rules which have been published by, for example, the Technology and Construction Solicitors' Association ('TeCSA') (formerly the Official Referees Solicitors' Association), the Centre for Dispute Resolution ('CEDR') or the Institution of Civil Engineers ('ICE'). This Form incorporates TeCSA's Adjudication Rules, but practitioners should be aware that there are others;

(c)    incorporate the statutory scheme with amendments;

(d)    draft their own provisions which meet the requirements of the Act. For an example, see Form 131 clause 16 [4385] and schedule 7 [4427] ante.

| | |
|---|---|
| 13 | Ie the Scheme for Construction Contracts (England and Wales) Regulations 1998, SI 1998/649. |
| 14 | See vol 38(1) (2000 Reissue) SALE OF LAND Paragraph 230 [574] et seq. |
| 15 | Usually this documentation is executed as a deed so that consideration is unnecessary and any action for breach of contract is subject to a 12-year limitation period instead of the normal 6-year limit. See vol 5 (1994 Reissue) BUILDING AND ENGINEERING CONTRACTS Paragraph 140 [483]. |

**[4521]**

# 136

## Deed of warranty by a sub-contractor in favour of third party beneficiaries[1]

THIS DEED is made the ...... day of .........

BETWEEN

(1)     *(name)* [company number *(number)*[2]] [of *(address) or* whose registered office is at *(address)*] ('the Sub-contractor')

(2)     *(name)* [company number *(number)*] [of *(address) or* whose registered office is at *(address)*] ('the Beneficiary')

## 1      Background

1.1     By the Building Contract the Employer has employed or will employ the Contractor to carry out the Development

1.2     By the Sub-contract the Contractor has engaged or will engage the Sub-contractor to carry out the Sub-contract Works

1.3     The engagement of the Sub-contractor has been approved by the Employer under the terms of the Building Contract

1.4     [The Beneficiary has [acquired *or* taken an interest in *or* taken a lease of] [part of] the [Development *or* Premises] [more particularly known as *(insert details)*][3]
         *or*
         The Beneficiary has agreed to provide loan facilities or other finance in respect of the [carrying out of the Development *or* acquisition of the [Development *or* Premises] when complete][4]
         *or*
         The Beneficiary is a company within the group of companies of which the Building Owner is a member[5]
         *or*
         The Beneficiary has entered into a joint venture with the Building Owner in respect of *(specify)*][6]

1.5     The Sub-contractor has agreed to enter into this Deed for the benefit of the Beneficiary and its successors in title and assigns

                                                                                    **[4522]**

## 2      Definitions and interpretation

2.1     In this Deed:

         2.1.1     'the Building Contract' means the building contract made or to be made between the Employer and the Contractor for the carrying out of the Development and includes any documents or arrangements which are supplemental or ancillary to it by way of variation or otherwise

         2.1.2     'the Contractor' means *(name)* [company number *(number)*] [of *(address) or* whose registered office is at *(address)*]

         2.1.3     'the Development' means *(description)*

         2.1.4     'the Employer' means *(name)* [company number *(number)*] [of *(address) or* whose registered office is at *(address)*]

         2.1.5     'Prohibited Materials' means the materials so defined in clause 5[7]

         2.1.6     'Practical Completion' means the date of practical completion of the Development under the terms of the Building Contract

2.1.7    'the Premises' means the premises described in Schedule 2

2.1.8    'the Sub-contract' means the sub-contract for the carrying out of the *(details)* works in relation to the Development brief details of which are set out in Schedule 1 and a copy of which is annexed[8]

2.1.9    'the Sub-contract Works' means works performed or to be performed by the Sub-contractor under the Sub-contract

2.2    In this Deed unless the context otherwise requires:

2.2.1    clause headings are inserted for convenience only and shall not affect the construction of this Deed and any references to a clause or schedule is to a clause of and schedule to this Deed

2.2.2    words denoting the singular number include the plural and vice versa

2.2.3    references to persons include references to bodies corporate and unincorporate

**[4523]**

**3    Exercise of skill and care**

3.1    The Sub-contractor warrants and undertakes to the Beneficiary that it has exercised and will continue to exercise all the reasonable skill care and diligence which may reasonably be expected of a sub-contractor acting within the scope of the Sub-contractor's appointment under the provisions of the Sub-contract including without prejudice to the generality of the foregoing the design of the Sub-contract Works and the selection of goods and materials for the Sub-contract Works

3.2    The Sub-contractor further warrants and undertakes to the Beneficiary that:

3.2.1    the Sub-contract Works will at Practical Completion satisfy all performance specifications and other requirements contained or referred to in the Building Contract and the Sub-contract and

3.2.2    the Sub-contract Works and all materials and goods comprised in them will correspond as to description quality and condition with the requirements of the Building Contract and the Sub-contract and will be of sound manufacture and workmanship

**4    Copyright and licence to use documents**

4.1    The Sub-contractor grants and agrees to grant to the Beneficiary an irrevocable royalty-free non-exclusive licence to use and reproduce all designs drawings models plans specifications design details photographs brochures reports notes of meetings details schedules levels setting out dimensions documents papers calculations software computerised information data and any other materials and work prepared by or on behalf of the Sub-contractor in connection with the Sub-contract Works (whether in existence or to be made) and all amendments and additions to them and any works designs or inventions of the Sub-contractor incorporated or referred to in them for any purpose whatsoever relating to the Sub-contract Works ('the Documents') including (without limitation) the construction completion reconstruction modification extension repair reinstatement refurbishment development maintenance use letting promotion and advertisement of the Development such licence carries the right for the Beneficiary to grant sub-licences and to be transferable without the prior consent of the Sub-contractor provided that the Sub-contractor shall have no liability to the beneficiary of the licence or sub-licence arising from the use of the Documents other than that for which they were prepared by or on behalf of the Sub-contractor

4.2      The Sub-contractor agrees on request at any time to give the Beneficiary or any persons authorised by the Beneficiary access to the Documents and at the Beneficiary's expense to provide copies of them

4.3      All royalties or other sums payable in respect of the supply and use of any patented articles processes or inventions required in connection with the Sub-contract Works shall be paid by the Sub-contractor and the Sub-contractor shall indemnify the Beneficiary from and against all claims proceedings damages costs and expenses suffered or incurred by the Beneficiary by reason of the Sub-contractor infringing or being held to infringe any intellectual property rights in the course of or in connection with the Sub-contract Works

**[4524]**

## 5      Prohibited materials[9]

The Sub-contractor further warrants to the Beneficiary that it:

5.1      has not used and will not use any of the following in the Development: *(insert list of prohibited materials to correspond with that in the Building Contract)*

5.2      has exercised and will continue to exercise all reasonable skill care and diligence to see so far as is consistent with its duties under the Sub-contract that none of the materials referred to in clause 5.1 has been specified for use in the Development and that none are used in the Development

## [6      Year 2000 compliance[10]

6.1      In this clause unless the context otherwise requires the following expression have the following meanings:

  6.1.1      'Equipment' means all computer hardware (including Firmware) and associated documentation to be supplied by the Sub-contractor for inclusion in the Development

  6.1.2      'Firmware' means the microcode which is an integral part of and required by a specific item of the Equipment

  6.1.3      'Software' means the software to be provided by the Sub-contractor under the Sub-contract including but not limited to operating systems compilers utilities and other programmes including developed programmes and the application software identified in the Sub-contract

  6.1.4      'System' means the Equipment and the Software

For the purposes of this clause the twentieth century shall be deemed to have ended and the twenty-first century to have begun on 1st January 2000 at 00.00 hours in the time zone local to the System

**[4525**

6.2      The Sub-contractor represents and warrants to the Beneficiary that the System has Year 2000 conformity as defined in the British Standards Institution Definition of Year 2000 Conformity Requirements[11] and that the System has 'general integrity' and 'date integrity' as specified in rules 1 and 2 of such Definition. Without prejudice to the generality of the foregoing:

  6.2.1      no error or interruption in the operation of the System will result directly or indirectly from the passage from the twentieth century to the twenty-first century or from the extra day occurring in any leap year in the twentieth or twenty-first century or from the occurrence of any other date

6.2.2    no reduction or alteration in the functionality of the System will result directly or indirectly from the passage from the twentieth century to the twenty-first century or from the occurrence of any other date

6.2.3    the System will not process any data which includes a date which does not specify the century

6.2.4    all date-related output and results produced by the System will include an indication of the century

6.2.5    the System will produce accurate results in the calculations and other data processing which span the twentieth century to the twenty-first century

6.2.6    inter-faces and reporting facilities comprised by the System will support four-digit year processing]

[4526]

## 7    Variation of the Sub-contract

The Sub-contractor undertakes to the Beneficiary not to vary or depart from the terms and conditions of the Sub-contract without the prior written consent of the Beneficiary and agrees that any variation or departure made without such consent shall not be binding on the Beneficiary or affect or prejudice the Beneficiary's rights under this Deed or under the Sub-contract or in any other way

## 8    Insurance[12]

8.1    The Sub-contractor warrants to the Beneficiary that it has at all relevant times maintained and (so long as such insurance is available in the market) will continue to maintain throughout the duration of the Sub-contract and for a period of 12 years from the date of Practical Completion [both] [professional indemnity and/or product liability] insurance[s] with a reputable insurance [company or companies] with [a] limit[s] of [indemnity and/or liability] of not less than £... [and £... respectively] and an excess of not more than £... in respect of each and every claim to cover any claims made against the Sub-contractor in relation to the Development

8.2    As and when reasonably required by the Beneficiary the Sub-contractor shall produce for inspection satisfactory documentary evidence that the insurance[s] referred to in clause 8.1 [is or are] being properly maintained and confirm that payment has been made in respect of the last preceding premium[s] due under [it or them]

8.3    If the Sub-contractor fails to comply with this clause 8 he shall repay to the Beneficiary on demand any money the Beneficiary reasonably spends to effect insurance against any risk or amount with respect to which such default has occurred

8.4    The Sub-contractor has prior to the date of this Deed notified its insurers of the terms of this Deed and will disclose the terms to any new insurers before changing insurers

[4527]

## 9    Indemnity

[Save that the Sub-contractor shall owe the Beneficiary no greater duty than it owes to the Contractor under the Sub-contract the or The] Sub-contractor further undertakes to indemnify the Beneficiary from and against the consequences of any breach by the Sub-contractor of any of the warranties covenants and undertakings contained in this Deed

### 10    Concurrent liabilities

The rights and benefits conferred upon the Beneficiary by this Deed are in addition to any other rights and remedies it may have against the Sub-contractor including without prejudice to the generality of the foregoing any remedies in negligence

### 11    Continuing effect

Notwithstanding the completion of the Development or any part thereof this Deed shall continue to have effect

### 12    Limitation Period[13]

The liability of the Sub-contractor under this Deed shall cease 12 years after the date of Practical Completion save so far as concerns any matter in respect of which proceedings (whether by way of action adjudication or otherwise) shall have been commenced before the expiry of the period of 12 years

### 13    Assignment

The benefit of all or any of the Sub-contractor's obligations under this Deed and/or any benefit arising under or out of this Deed may be assigned without the consent of the Sub-contractor [on *(number)* occasions only and thereafter with the Sub-contractor's consent which consent may not be unreasonably withheld or delayed][14]

**[4528]**

### 14    Further warranty deeds

The Sub-contractor covenants that if required by the Beneficiary it will enter into further deeds of warranty with all and each of such persons who shall acquire or agree to acquire an interest in the whole or any part of the [Development *or* Premises]. Each such deed or warranty shall be in the same form mutatis mutandis as this Deed save for this clause

### 15    Disputes[15]

15.1    If any dispute or difference as to the construction of this Deed or any matter or thing of whatsoever nature arising hereunder or in connection therewith shall arise it shall be determined in the Courts of England and Wales or by adjudication and not in arbitration

15.2    The parties' right to refer a dispute arising under this Deed to adjudication shall be in accordance with this clause 15

15.3    The Technology and Construction Solicitors' Association's Adjudication Rules shall apply if a dispute or difference is required to be referred to adjudication. Therefore it is agreed that the provisions of Part I of the Schedule to the Scheme for Construction Contracts (England and Wales) Regulations 1998[16] shall not apply

### [16    Third party rights[17]

A person who is not a party to this Deed has no rights under the Contracts (Rights of Third Parties) Act 1999 to enforce any terms of this Deed]

### 17    Law and jurisdiction

This Deed shall be governed by and construed in accordance with English Law and the parties submit to the [non-exclusive] jurisdiction of the English courts

**[4529]**

## 18     Notices

18.1     All notices or other communications under or in respect of this Deed to either party shall be deemed to be duly given or made when delivered (in the case of personal delivery or letter) or when despatched (in the case of facsimile) to the party addressed to it at the address appearing below (or at such address as the party may after the date of this Deed specify for this purpose to the other):

18.1.1     In the case of the Sub-contractor:

18.1.1.1     Address: *(address)*

18.1.1.2     Facsimile No: *(number)*

18.1.2     In the case of the Beneficiary:

18.1.2.1     Address: *(address)*

18.1.2.2     Facsimile No: *(number)*

18.2     A written notice includes a notice by facsimile. A notice or other communication received on a non-working day or after business hours in the place of receipt shall be deemed to be given or made on the next following working day in that place

IN WITNESS etc[18]

SCHEDULE 1
Particulars of the Sub-contract
*(insert details)*

SCHEDULE 2
The Premises
*(insert description)*

*(signatures (and common seals) of the parties)*
*(signatures of witnesses)*
**[4530]**

1     No stamp duty. As to collateral warranties generally, see vol 38(1) (2000 Reissue) SALE OF LAND Paragraph 225 [548] et seq.
2     If any party is a company it is desirable to include the company registration number before the address of the registered office. This avoids any problems arising when a company has been wound up and a new company formed with the same name, or when the name of a company is changed, or if companies swap names eg on a reconstruction of a group of companies.
3     Identify the transaction which has taken place which allows the beneficiary to obtain the warranty.
4     Identify the transaction which has taken place which allows the beneficiary to obtain the warranty.
5     Identify the transaction which has taken place which allows the beneficiary to obtain the warranty.
6     Identify the transaction which has taken place which allows the beneficiary to obtain the warranty.
7     Reference to a list of 'deleterious materials' is to be avoided. Manufacturers of materials that commonly appear in such lists may have a right of action. There is nothing objectionable for an employer to require any particular material to be excluded from a project as long as he does not describe the material as being deleterious when it may not be so if used in particular circumstances. This clause provides for a list for practitioners who wish to insert one. For alternative wording not listing materials see Form 137 clause 5.1 [4553] post.
8     The sub-contract must be annexed as reference is made to its terms in various clauses of this Form.
9     See note 7 above. For a generic definition of prohibited materials see Form 137 clause 5.1 [4553] ante.
10     In the event, the major problems anticipated with the passing of 1 January 2000 did not materialise. However, clients and end-users will be concerned to ensure that computer equipment is able to cope with the fact that the year 2000 is a leap year and any other 'troublesome' dates which may occur in the future. See clauses 6.2.1 and 6.2.2. With the passage of time this clause will become redundant, but clients should obtain specialist advice before deleting it altogether.
11     Published by the British Standard Institution, reference DISC PD 2000-1.

12 Insurance is often a topic which can involve protracted negotiations. If the sub-contractor is responsible for the design of any significant element of the development, professional indemnity insurance should be considered. If he is to install materials and goods, product liability insurance may be necessary. Warrantors often seek to include a provision whereby insurance cover is available at 'commercially reasonable rates'. Beneficiaries find this to be too subjective a test to be acceptable.

Insurers often cap liability for claims relating to contamination or pollution.

The required limit of indemnity and the amount of any excess are figures upon which the beneficiary should take professional advice. A commercial decision should then be taken in the light of the extent of cover that is in place.

The clause requires cover for each and every claim. Some warrantors seek to include a provision whereby the amount of the insurance cover is capped for any one year. Beneficiaries tend to reject this proposal.

A warrantor's liability under the provisions of the warranty should be contrasted with the amount of insurance cover that exists. Strictly, any shortfall would be a liability that remains with the warrantor.

This Form requires the sub-contractor to keep insurance on foot for 12 years from practical completion of the development as opposed to a period that runs from the making good of its defects. A sub-contractor's work may be completed early on in the undertaking of the project and it might be considered unreasonable for cover to be maintained for an extended period by virtue of a problem which was not of his making.

**[4531]**

13 The limitation period is 12 years following practical completion for the reason given in note 12 above.

14 Unless the parties agree otherwise, the benefits can be assigned freely without consent of the warrantor. If the number of assignments is to be limited, care should be taken in choosing the number. Two or three assignments appear to be acceptable in the market but particular circumstances may require a greater number.

15 Some commentators have suggested that this type of warranty could be regarded as a 'construction contract' for the purposes of the Housing Grants, Construction and Regeneration Act 1996 Pt II (11 Halsbury's Statutes (4th Edn) CONTRACT) which came into effect on 1st May 1998. The Act allows the parties to refer disputes to adjudication (Housing Grants, Construction and Regeneration Act 1996 s 108). If a contract does not comply with any one of the requirements of the Act, a statutory scheme will apply (Housing Grants, Construction and Regeneration Act 1996 s 108(5)) and this provides the procedures for the appointment of an adjudicator. Parties drafting or negotiating construction contracts will therefore have four choices:

(a) leave the contract silent and allow the statutory scheme to apply;

(b) incorporate one of the sets of rules which have been published by, for example, the Technology and Construction Solicitors' Association ('TeCSA') (formerly the Official Referees Solicitors' Association), the Centre for Dispute Resolution ('CEDR') or the Institution of Civil Engineers ('ICE'). This Form incorporates TeCSA's Adjudication Rules, but practitioners should be aware that there are others;

(c) incorporate the statutory scheme with amendments;

(d) draft their own provisions which meet the requirements of the Act. For an example, see the appointment of a professional, Form 131 clause 16 [4385] ante.

16 Ie the Scheme for Construction Contracts (England and Wales) Regulations 1998, SI 1998/649.

17 See vol 38(1) (2000 Reissue) SALE OF LAND Paragraph 230 [574] et seq.

18 Usually this documentation is executed as a deed so that consideration is unnecessary and any action for breach of contract is subject to a 12-year limitation period instead of the normal 6-year limit. See vol 5 (1994 Reissue) BUILDING AND ENGINEERING CONTRACTS Paragraph 140 [483].

**[4532]–[4550]**

# 137

## Deed of warranty by a professional in favour of third party beneficiaries[1]

THIS DEED is made the …… day of ………

BETWEEN:

(1) *(name)* [company number *(number)*[2]] [of *(address) or* whose registered office is at *(address)*] ('the Consultants')

(2) *(name)* [company number *(number)*] [of *(address) or* whose registered office is at *(address)*] ('the Beneficiary') which expression shall include its successors in title and assigns

## 1       Background

1.1       The Consultants were appointed by *(name)* [company number *(number)*] [of *(address) or* whose registered office is at *(address)*] ('the Building Owner') to act for the Building Owner in the capacity of *(insert discipline)* in connection with the development brief details of which are set out in the schedule below ('the Development') upon the terms and conditions contained in an Agreement dated *(date)* ('the Deed of Appointment') a copy of which is annexed[3]

1.2       [The Beneficiary has [acquired *or* taken an interest in *or* taken a lease of] [part of] the Development [more particularly known as *(specify)*][4]

          *or*

          The Beneficiary has agreed to provide loan facilities or other finance in respect of the [carrying out of the Development *or* acquisition of the Development when complete][5]

          *or*

          The Beneficiary is a company within the group of companies of which the Building Owner is a member[6]

          *or*

          The Beneficiary has entered into a joint venture with the Building Owner in respect of *(specify)*][7]

1.3       The Consultants have agreed to enter into this Deed in favour of the Beneficiary and its successors in title and assigns

                                                                                **[4551]**


## 2       Interpretation

In this Deed unless the context otherwise requires:

2.1       clause headings are inserted for convenience only and shall not affect the construction of this Deed and any references to a clause or schedule is to a clause of and schedule to this Deed

2.2       words denoting the singular number include the plural and vice versa

2.3       references to persons include references to bodies corporate and unincorporate


## 3       Exercise of skill care and diligence

The Consultants warrant and undertake to the Beneficiary that in respect of all matters which lie within the scope of their professional responsibilities in relation to the Development:

3.1       they have exercised and will continue to exercise all the reasonable skill care and diligence to be expected of properly qualified and competent consultants experienced in carrying out work of a similar size scope complexity and purpose as the Development in the provision of their duties under the Deed of Appointment

3.2       they shall owe a duty of care to the Beneficiary in respect of such matters and the Beneficiary shall be deemed to have relied exclusively upon the Consultants' professional skill and judgment in respect of such matters

3.3       they have performed and shall continue properly and diligently to perform all of their duties and obligations under the Deed of Appointment


## 4       Copyright and licence to use the Materials

4.1       The Consultants grant to the Beneficiary an irrevocable royalty free non-exclusive licence to use and reproduce all of the Materials as defined in the Deed of Appointment (whether in existence or to be prepared in the future) and any works designs or inventions of the Consultants incorporated or referred to in them for any purposes connected with the Development

4.2     The licence carries the right for the Beneficiary to grant sub-licences and is transferable without the prior consent of the Consultants

4.3     The Consultants will not be liable for the use of any of the Materials by the beneficiary of the licence or sub-licence for any purpose other than that for which they were prepared by or on behalf of the Consultants

[4552]

## 5     Prohibited Materials

The Consultants further warrant to the Beneficiary that:

5.1     they have not specified and will not specify any goods materials products or substances for use in the Development which are not in accordance with the relevant British and European Standards and Codes of Practice or which are generally known or suspected within the construction or engineering industries at the time of use to be deleterious to health and safety or to the durability of the Development in the particular circumstances in which they are used ('Prohibited Materials')[8]

5.2     without prejudice to the generality of the foregoing they have exercised and will continue to exercise all reasonable skill care and diligence to see so far as is consistent with their duties under the Deed of Appointment that no Prohibited Materials have been specified for use in the Development by any other consultant involved with the Development

## 6     Variation of deed of appointment

The Consultants undertake to the Beneficiary not to vary or depart from the terms of the Deed of Appointment without the prior written consent of the Beneficiary and agree that any variation or departure made without such consent shall not be binding on the Beneficiary or affect or prejudice the Beneficiary's rights under this Deed or under the Deed of Appointment or in any other way

## 7     Indemnity insurance[9]

7.1     The Consultants warrant to the Beneficiary that they have and that they will maintain insurance cover in respect of all claims for negligence with a limit of indemnity of not less that £... and an excess of not more than £... for each and every event unlimited in number (or in the case of claims for pollution or contamination with not less than such limit of indemnity in the aggregate for any and all claims notified in the year of insurance) for a period of 12 years from the date of practical completion of the Development and under a policy or policies issued by a reputable insurance company carrying on business in the United Kingdom

7.2     On request the Consultants shall produce for inspection by the Beneficiary documentary evidence that the insurance required under this clause 7 is being maintained

7.3     If the Consultants fail to comply with this clause 7 they shall repay to the Beneficiary on demand any money the Beneficiary reasonably spends to effect insurance against any risk or amount with respect to which such default has occurred

7.4     The Consultants have prior to the date of this Deed notified their insurers of the terms of this Deed and will disclose the terms to any new insurers before changing insurers

                                                                                        **[4553]**

## 8     Indemnity

[Save that the Sub-contractor shall owe the Beneficiary no greater duty than it owes to the Contractor under the Sub-contract the *or* The] Sub-contractor further undertakes to indemnify the Beneficiary from and against the consequences of any breach by the Sub-contractor of any of the warranties covenants and undertakings contained in this Deed

## 9     Concurrent liabilities

The obligations of the Consultants under or pursuant to this Deed shall be in addition to and without prejudice to any other present or future liability of the Consultants to the Beneficiary including any liability in negligence provided always that the Consultants shall owe no greater liability to the Beneficiary under the terms of this Deed than they owe to the Building Owner under the Deed of Appointment

## 10    Continuing effect

Notwithstanding the completion of the Development or any part of it this Deed shall continue to have effect

## 11    Limitation period

The liability of the Consultants under this Deed shall cease 12 years after the date of practical completion of the Development save so far as concerns any matter in respect of which proceedings (whether by way of action adjudication or otherwise) shall have been commenced before the expiry of the period of 12 years

## 12    Assignment

The Beneficiary and its successors in title shall be entitled to assign by way of absolute legal assignment and/or charge the benefit of this Deed and/or any of the present or future rights interests and benefits of the Beneficiary to any third party at any time during the period of 12 years from the date of Practical Completion of the Development [on *(number)* occasions only without the consent of the Consultants and thereafter only with the consent of the Consultants such consent not to be unreasonably withheld or delayed][10]

                                                                                        **[4554]**

## 13    Further warranty deeds

The Consultants covenant that if required by the Beneficiary they will enter into further deeds of warranty with all and each of such persons who shall acquire or agree to acquire an interest in the whole or any part of the Development. Each such deed of warranty shall be in the same form as this Deed mutatis mutandis save for this clause

## 14    Disputes[11]

14.1    If any dispute or difference as to the construction of this Deed or any matter or thing of whatsoever nature arising under it or in connection with it shall arise it shall be determined in the Courts of England and Wales or by adjudication and not in arbitration

14.2    The parties' right to refer a dispute arising under this Deed to adjudication shall be in accordance with this clause 14

14.3    The Technology and Construction Solicitors' Association's Adjudication Rules shall apply if a dispute or difference is required to be referred to adjudication. Therefore it is agreed that the provisions of Part I of the Schedule to the Scheme for Construction Contracts (England and Wales) Regulations 1998[12] shall not apply

## [15    Third party rights[13]

A person who is not a party to this Deed has no rights under the Contracts (Rights of Third Parties) Act 1999 to enforce any terms of this Deed]

## 16    Law and jurisdiction

This Deed shall be governed by and construed in accordance with English Law and the parties submit to the [non-exclusive] jurisdiction of the English courts

## 17    Notices

17.1    All notices or other communications under or in respect of this Deed to either party shall be deemed to be duly given or made when delivered (in the case of personal delivery or letter) or when despatched (in the case of facsimile) to the party addressed to it at the address appearing below (or at such address as the party may after the date of this Agreement specify for this purpose to the other):

17.1.1    In the case of the Consultants:
17.1.1.1    Address: *(address)*
17.1.1.2    Facsimile number: *(number)*

17.1.2    In the case of the Beneficiary:
17.1.2.1    Address: *(address)*
17.1.2.2    Facsimile number: *(number)*

17.2    A written notice includes a notice by facsimile. A notice or other communication received on a non-working day or after business hours in the place of receipt shall be deemed to be given or made on the next following working day in that place

**[4555]**

## [18    Determination *(for insertion only where the beneficiary is a lender)*

The Consultants covenant and agree with the Lender that they will not exercise or seek to exercise any right they may now or at any time hereafter have under the Deed of Appointment or serve notice to determine their appointment under the Deed of Appointment or discontinue the performance of any of their obligations or duties thereunder without first giving to the Lender not less than 28 days' prior written notice of the Consultants' intention specifying the ground or grounds for the purported determination of their appointment and notwithstanding any provision of the Deed of Appointment (unless the Consultants' appointment is determined by the Building Owner) the Consultants' appointment under the Deed of Appointment shall not otherwise determine]

IN WITNESS etc[14]

## THE SCHEDULE
### The Development
*(insert description)*

*(signatures (and common seals) of the parties)*
*(signatures of witnesses)*
**[4556]**

1  No stamp duty. As to collateral warranties generally see vol 38(1) (2000 Reissue) SALE OF LAND Paragraph 225 [548] et seq.

2  If any party is a company it is desirable to include the company registration number before the address of the registered office. This avoids any problems arising when a company has been wound up and a new company formed with the same name, or when the name of a company is changed, or if companies swap names eg on a reconstruction of a group of companies.

3  The Deed of Appointment must be annexed, as reference is made to its terms in various clauses of this Form.

4  Identify the transaction which has taken place which allows the beneficiary to obtain the warranty.

5  Identify the transaction which has taken place which allows the beneficiary to obtain the warranty.

6  Identify the transaction which has taken place which allows the beneficiary to obtain the warranty.

7  Identify the transaction which has taken place which allows the beneficiary to obtain the warranty.

8  Alternatively, if the prohibited materials are listed in the consultant's appointment, an identical list should be included in the warranty. See Form 134 note 7 [4494] ante as to the risks of inserting a list.

9  Indemnity insurance is often a topic which can involve protracted negotiations. Warrantors often seek to include a provision whereby insurance cover is available at 'commercially reasonable rates'. Beneficiaries find this to be too subjective a test to be acceptable.

Insurers often cap liability for claims relating to contamination or pollution.

The required limit of indemnity and the amount of any excess are figures upon which the beneficiary should take professional advice. A commercial decision should then be taken in the light of the extent of cover that is in place.

The clause requires cover for each and every claim. Some warrantors seek to include a provision whereby the amount of the insurance cover is capped for any one year. Beneficiaries tend to reject this proposal.

A warrantor's liability under the provisions of the warranty should be contrasted with the amount of insurance cover that exists. Strictly, any shortfall would be a liability that remains with the warrantor.

10  Unless the parties agree otherwise, the benefits can be assigned freely without consent of the warrantor. If the number of assignments is to be limited, care should be taken in choosing the number. Two or three assignments appear to be acceptable in the market but particular circumstances may require a greater number. Practitioners should appreciate the difference between the availability of a warranty itself and the ability to assign its benefits to third parties. If a development is to be multi-let a developer will wish to ensure that professionals will be providing warranties to first purchasers and tenants. See Form 131 clause 14 [4383] ante.

11  Some commentators have suggested that this type of warranty could be regarded as a 'construction contract' for the purposes of the Housing Grants, Construction and Regeneration Act 1996 Pt II (11 Halsbury's Statutes (4th Edn) CONTRACT) which came into effect on 1st May 1998. The Act allows the parties to refer disputes to adjudication (Housing Grants, Construction and Regeneration Act 1996 s 108). If a contract does not comply with any one of the requirements of the Act, a statutory scheme will apply (Housing Grants, Construction and Regeneration Act 1996 s 108(5)) and this provides the procedures for the appointment of an adjudicator. Parties drafting or negotiating construction contracts will therefore have four choices:

(a)  leave the contract silent and allow the statutory scheme to apply;

(b)  incorporate one of the sets of rules which have been published by, for example, the Technology and Construction Solicitors' Association ('TeCSA'), (formerly the Official Referees Solicitors' Association), the Centre for Dispute Resolution ('CEDR') or the Institution of Civil Engineers ('ICE'). This Form incorporates TeCSA's Adjudication Rules but practitioners should be aware that there are others;

(c)  incorporate the statutory scheme with amendments;

(d)  draft their own provisions which meet the requirements of the Act. For an example, see Form 131 clause 16 [4385] and schedule 7 [4427] ante.

12  Ie the Scheme for Construction Contracts (England and Wales) Regulations 1998, SI 1998/649.

13  See vol 38(1) (2000 Reissue) SALE OF LAND Paragraph 230 [574] et seq.

14  Usually this documentation is executed as a deed so that consideration is unnecessary and any action for breach of contract is subject to a 12-year limitation period instead of the normal 6-year limit. See vol 5 (1994 Reissue) BUILDING AND ENGINEERING CONTRACTS Paragraph 140 [483].

**[4557]**

## 138

### Deed of novation of a professional's appointment to a substitute client

THIS DEED is dated the ... day of ......

BETWEEN:

(1)    *(name)* [company number *(number)*[1]] [of *(address) or* whose registered office is at *(address)*] ('the Client')

(2)    *(name)* [company number *(number)*] [of *(address) or* whose registered office is at *(address)*] ('the Consultant')

(3)    *(name)* [company number *(number)*] [of *(address) or* whose registered office is at *(address)*] ('the Substitute Client')

## 1    Background

1.1    By an Agreement ('the Consultancy Agreement') dated *(date)* made between the Client and the Consultant a copy of which is annexed the Client appointed the Consultant to act as *(insert discipline)* in relation to *(insert brief description of the development)*

1.2    It has been agreed between the Client and the Substitute Client that the Substitute Client shall assume the rights and obligations of the Client under the Consultancy Agreement

1.3    This Deed of Novation is supplemental to the Consultancy Agreement

## 2    Novation

The Consultant consents to the substitution of the Substitute Client for the Client under the Consultancy Agreement

## 3    Release by Client

The Client releases and discharges the Consultant from further performance of the Consultant's obligations under the Consultancy Agreement and from all claims and demands whatsoever arising out of or in respect of the Consultancy Agreement whether arising prior to on or subsequent to the date of this Deed but without prejudice to the provisions of clause 5 or to the provisions of the collateral warranty to be provided to the Client by the Consultant pursuant to the Consultancy Agreement

[4558]

## 4    Release by Consultant

The Consultant releases and discharges the Client from further performance of the Client's obligations under the Consultancy Agreement and from all claims and demands whatsoever arising out of or in respect of the Consultancy Agreement whether arising prior to on or subsequent to the date of this Deed

## 5    Acceptance of liability by Substitute Client

The Substitute Client accepts the liabilities of the Client under the Consultancy Agreement and agrees to perform all the duties and to discharge all the obligations of the Client under it and to be bound by all its terms and conditions in every way as if it were named in the Consultancy Agreement as a party to it from the start in place of the Client. Without limiting the generality of the foregoing the Substitute Client acknowledges and agrees that it will receive and accept responsibility for negotiating and settling all claims and demands whatsoever against the Client arising out of or in respect of the Consultancy Agreement whether arising prior to on or subsequent to the date of this Deed

## 6    Acceptance of liability by Consultant

6.1    The Consultant agrees to perform all his duties and to discharge all his obligations under the Consultancy Agreement and to be bound by all its terms and conditions in favour of the Substitute Client in every way as if the Substitute Client were named in the Consultancy Agreement as a party to it from the start in place of the Client

6.2    Without limiting the generality of the foregoing the Consultant acknowledges and agrees that the Substitute Client shall have the right to enforce the Consultancy Agreement and pursue all claims and demands (future or existing) by the Client whatsoever arising out of or in respect of the Consultancy Agreement whether arising prior to on or subsequent to the date of this Deed

6.3    Nothing in this Deed shall operate to extend or increase the liability of the Consultant beyond that which would have existed but for this Deed and without limiting the generality of the foregoing it is expressly agreed that nothing in this Deed shall operate to enable any claims to be brought against the Consultant which but for this Deed would be statute barred if made by the Client

**[4559]**

## 7    Acknowledgement of payment

The Consultant acknowledges that up to the date of this Deed he has been paid the sum of £… exclusive of VAT by the Client

## 8    The Consultancy Agreement in force

The terms and conditions of this Deed represent the entire agreement between the parties relating to the novation of the Consultancy Agreement and except as specifically amended by this Deed all the terms and conditions of the Consultancy Agreement remain in full force and effect

## 9    No discharge of Consultant's liability

Nothing in this Deed shall operate to discharge the Consultant from any liability in respect of duties performed prior to the execution of this Deed

## [10    Third Party Rights[2]

A person who is not a party to this Deed has no rights under the Contracts (Rights of Third Parties) Act 1999 to enforce any terms of this Deed]

IN WITNESS etc[3]

*(signatures (and common seals) of the parties)*
*(signatures of witnesses)*

1    If any party is a company it is desirable to include the company registration number before the address of the registered office. This avoids any problems arising when a company has been wound up and a new company formed with the same name, or when the name of a company is changed, or if companies swap names eg on a reconstruction of a group of companies.

2    See vol 38(1) (2000 Reissue) SALE OF LAND Paragraph 230 [574] et seq.

3    Usually this documentation is executed as a deed so that consideration is unnecessary and any action for breach of contract is subject to a 12-year limitation period instead of the normal 6-year limit. See vol 5 (1994 Reissue) BUILDING AND ENGINEERING CONTRACTS Paragraph 140 [483].

**[4560]**

# 139

## Deed of assignment of a warranty[1]

THIS DEED OF ASSIGNMENT is made the ...... day of .........

BETWEEN:

(1)      *(name)* [company number *(number)*[2]] [of *(address) or* whose registered office is at *(address)*] ('the Assignor') and

(2)      *(name)* [company number *(number)*] [of *(address) or* whose registered office is at *(address)*] ('the Assignee')

NOW IT IS AGREED as follows:

## 1    Background

1.1      The Assignor has the benefit of [a warranty ('the Warranty') *or* warranties ('the Warranties')] obtained in connection with a development known as *(specify)* ('the Development') brief details of which are set out in the schedule below

1.2      [The Assignee] has by an agreement made between *(parties)* agreed to [purchase *or* take a lease of *or* provide funds for] [the whole *or* part] of the Development [more particularly known as *(description)*]

1.3      The Assignor has agreed to assign the benefit of its interest in the [Warranty *or* Warranties] to the Assignee

## 2    Assignment

The Assignor with limited title guarantee assigns to the Assignee absolutely the whole of the rights title and benefit which the Assignor may now have or become entitled to under the [Warranty *or* Warranties]

IN WITNESS etc[3]

### THE SCHEDULE
### The [Warranty *or* Warranties]

| Capacity in which employed | Name and address of warrantor | Date of warranty deed | Parties |
|---|---|---|---|

*(insert relevant details of the professionals, building contractor and any specialist sub-contractors)*

*(signatures (and common seals) of the parties)*
*(signatures of witnesses)*
**[4561]**

---

1    No stamp duty. As to assignment of rights generally, see vol 38(1) (2000 Reissue) SALE OF LAND Paragraph 222 [543].

2    If any party is a company it is desirable to include the company registration number before the address of the registered office. This avoids any problems arising when a company has been wound up and a new company formed with the same name, or when the name of a company is changed, or if companies swap names eg on a reconstruction of a group of companies.

3    Usually this documentation is executed as a deed so that consideration is unnecessary and any action for breach of contract is subject to a 12-year limitation period instead of the normal 6-year limit. See vol 5 (1994 Reissue) BUILDING AND ENGINEERING CONTRACTS Paragraph 140 [483].

**[4562]–[4580]**

# PART 11: ADDITIONAL AND ALTERNATIVE CONTRACT CLAUSES

## Forms and Precedents

### A: BUILDING SAFETY

### 140

#### Building consents and notices

0.1    The Seller will hand over to the Buyer on completion copies of all Building Regulations Consents and Fire Certificates that relate to the Premises

0.2    The Seller warrants that no abatement notice has been served in respect of the premises under Section 80 of the Environmental Protection Act 1990

**[4581]**

### B: ASSIGNMENT OF COLLATERAL WARRANTIES

### 141

#### Collateral warranties: condition providing for rights against contractors or professionals to be assigned—long form[1]

0.1    The Seller shall execute and deliver to the Buyer on completion of the sale and purchase of the Property an assignment ('the Assignment') of all rights of the Seller against third parties in respect of any defects of construction and/or design becoming manifest in or upon the Property

**[4582]**

0.2    In the Assignment the Seller shall:

    0.2.1    assign to the Buyer:

        0.2.1.1    all (if any) rights of the Seller in contract or tort or otherwise against all professional persons employed by the Seller in connection with the design of the Property and the supervision of its construction and the building contractor employed by the Seller to construct the Property and all specialist sub-contractors employed in connection with the construction and the suppliers and/or manufacturers of all materials plant and equipment incorporated into the Property in respect of any defects of construction and/or design becoming manifest in or upon the Property and

0.2.1.2    all rights of the Seller (if any) against other third parties in contract tort or otherwise in respect of the defects

0.2.2    in consideration of £1 to be paid to the Seller by the Buyer on the Contractual Completion Date[2]:

0.2.2.1    irrevocably appoint the Buyer to be his attorney in his name to enforce the rights assigned to the Buyer in any lawful manner

0.2.2.2    authorise the Buyer to retain for his own benefit all money received as a result of the enforcement of the rights or any of them and

0.2.2.3    undertake to ratify all proper acts and deeds of the Buyer in the course of the exercise of the power conferred upon the Buyer as the attorney of the Seller

0.3    In the Assignment the Buyer shall covenant fully and effectually to indemnify and keep so indemnified the Seller from and against all costs claims and other expenses whatsoever incurred or arising from anything done in the exercise or purported exercise of the power of attorney conferred upon the Buyer by the Seller[3]

0.4    The Buyer shall execute and deliver to the Seller on the date of completion of the sale and purchase of the Property a duplicate of the Assignment

[0.5    The Assignment and its duplicate shall be deeds and shall expressly be executed as deeds][4]

**[4583]**

1   For forms of collateral warranty deeds see Forms 134 [4484]–137 [4551] post. For an alternative clause see vol 38(1) (2000 Reissue) SALE OF LAND Form 57 clause 21 [2145]. This version should be used only where the contract for the sale and purchase is to be entered into before all the details to be inserted in the schedule to the assignment are available, or there is some other reason why the form of the assignment cannot then be finalised.

2   The consideration should be paid so that the power then being granted for valuable consideration and being expressed to be irrevocable cannot, in favour of a buyer, be revoked by anything done by the donor of the power without the donee's concurrence, or by the donor's death, disability, bankruptcy or liquidation, even where the buyer has express notice of a purported revocation, or of the donor's death, disability or liquidation: see the Powers of Attorney Act 1971 s 4(1) (1 Halsbury's Statutes (4th Edn) AGENCY).

3   Consideration should always be given to whether a surety or guarantor of the buyer's liability under this clause is desirable.

4   It is essential to note on the face of a document that it is a deed if it is to be one: see the Law of Property (Miscellaneous Provisions) Act 1989 s 1(2)(a) (37 Halsbury's Statutes (4th Edn) REAL PROPERTY).

**[4584]**

# C: CONFIDENTIALITY

# 142

### Condition providing for confidentiality of an agreement for sale[1]

The Seller and the Buyer agree that except where such disclosure is required in order to comply with the requirements of any statutory or other competent authority neither of them shall disclose to any third person any details of this agreement and that they shall respectively use all reasonable endeavours to prevent the publication or disclosure of any such details

1    As to confidentiality clauses generally see vol 38(1) (2000 Reissue) SALE OF LAND Paragraph 281 [691] et seq and for other forms of confidentiality agreement see vol 4(3) (1997 Reissue) BOILERPLATE CLAUSES Form 34 [340]. Since 3 December 1990 when registers of title became open to public inspection, it has not been possible to keep the existence of an agreement for sale secure from public knowledge if it is protected by entry of a notice or caution.

[4585]

# D: ENVIRONMENTAL MATTERS

## 143

### Drainage

0.1    The Seller warrants that no effluent or other solid or liquid matter has been discharged into [the drains and sewers serving the Property *or* any watercourses from the Property] without first obtaining the necessary consent required by [the Water Industry Act 1991 *or* the Water Resources Act 1991]

0.2    Where a consent has been obtained for the discharge of effluent or other solid or liquid matter the Seller warrants that all conditions of that/those consent(s) have been complied with

0.3    The Seller will hand over to the Buyer on completion copies of all consents obtained under the [Water Industry Act 1991 *or* Water Resources Act 1991] that relate to discharges from the Property

[4586]

## 144

### General environmental warranties[1]

The Seller warrants that all regulatory requirements *(specify which regulatory requirements)* relating to the Property [have been complied with *or* will have been complied with by completion] in particular:

0.1    that all approvals authorisations consents licences permissions and registrations [have been obtained *or* will have been obtained by completion] and are [up to date *or* will be up to date at completion] and

0.2    that all notices and/or orders issued by the regulatory authorities [have been complied with *or* will have been complied with by completion] to the satisfaction of the regulatory authorities and

0.3    that all approvals authorisations consents licences permissions and registrations which are capable of assignment or transfer will be assigned or transferred to the Buyer on completion.

1    For full environmental warranties see vol 38(1) (2000 Reissue) SALE OF LAND Form 57 schedule 13 [2171].

[4587]

# 145

## Environmental management

The Seller warrants that it has attained BS EN ISO 14001[1] and has:

0.1      complied with all requirements of the International Standard

0.2      complied with the requirements of the [local authority] as to *(specify what: eg transport contributions)*

0.3      complied with the following codes of practice/non-regulatory guidance: *(specify)*

1       ISO 14001 is published by the British Standards Institution.

**[4588]**

# 146

## Fire precautions

The Seller warrants that [he *or* it] has complied with all the requirements of the fire authority[1] in respect of the Property

1       Where a fire certificate is not in force the above will be adequate. However, where there is one in force the certificate will be required: see Form 140 [4581] ante. As to fire certificates generally see vol 38(1) (2000 Reissue) SALE OF LAND Paragraph 74 [170] et seq.

**[4589]**

# 147

## Processes

The Seller warrants that the terms of the [waste management licence *or* applicable licence] held by [him *or* it] in respect of *(specify process or waste)* have been fully complied with

**[4590]**

# E: REVERSIONS AND GROUND RENT

*For forms of clauses relating to apportionment of rents where a rent review is in progress, recovery of arrears of rent, service charge expenditure, rent deposits, pending rent reviews under leases subject to which the property is sold, leases renewals, assignment of reserve and sinking funds and landlord release see vol 38(1) (2000 Reissue) SALE OF LAND Form 57 schedule 5 [2148].*

# 148

## Sale of property subject to a lease

The Property is sold subject to and with the benefit of a lease dated *(date)* made between *(parties)* [and the Buyer having been supplied with a copy of it shall raise no objection or requisition in relation to it]

**[4591]**

# 149

## Sale of property subject to an existing lease or tenancy with provision for apportionment

0.1    The Property is sold subject to and with the benefit of [a [lease *or* tenancy agreement] dated *(date)* made between *(parties)* ('the Lease') *or* the unwritten tenancy of *(name)* who has been in occupation since *(date)*]

[0.2   The Buyer having been supplied with a copy of the Lease buys with full knowledge of it and shall not raise any enquiry or requisition on it]

[0.3   The rent shall be apportioned from [the date of actual completion to the next rent day and the Seller shall allow the apportioned sum to the Buyer *or* the last rent day to the date of actual completion and the Buyer shall pay the apportioned sum on completion in addition to the Purchase Price][1]

---

1    The first alternative wording should be used where the rent is paid in advance and the second alternative where the rent is paid in arrear.

[4592]

# 150

## Details of leases contained in a schedule

The Property is sold subject to and with the benefit of the leases short particulars of which are set out in the *(number)* schedule[1]

---

1    The schedule should contain details of the date and parties to each lease, the property concerned and the current rent. If the property comprises or includes a building which contains more than one flat (which may include rooms separately occupied as part of a flat) and whether or not it also includes other property such as shops or offices, the provisions of the Landlord and Tenant Act 1987 (23 Halsbury's Statutes (4th Edn) LANDLORD AND TENANT) may apply. This Act confers on tenants of flats certain rights, including a pre-emption right if the landlord wishes to sell. There are provisions for the service of notices, and also provisions enabling tenants to buy out a buyer where the seller landlord has not followed the procedures.

[4593]

# 151

## Sale of a furnished flat subject to an existing tenancy[1]

0.1    The Property is sold subject to and with the benefit of a tenancy agreement dated *(date)* and made between *(parties)* ('the Tenancy Agreement')

0.2    The Tenancy Agreement included the right to use certain items of furnishings listed in an inventory signed by the parties to it ('the Furnishings') and an obligation that if any of the Furnishings were lost or destroyed the Tenant should replace them

0.3    [The sale includes *or* The Buyer shall in addition to the purchase of the Property buy at the price of £...][2] the Furnishings and the right to their replacement

0.4    The Buyer having inspected the Property acknowledges that the items listed in the [*(number)*] schedule[3] to this Agreement represent the Furnishings or the present replacements of them now subject to the Tenancy Agreement

0.5     On the grant of the Tenancy Agreement the Tenant paid a deposit to the Seller as security against non-payment of rent and loss of or damage to the Furnishings and the Buyer shall indemnify the Seller against any liability to refund that deposit[4]

1     Complications can be caused if ownership of a flat is separated from ownership of its contents, and this Form assumes that the sale includes both.

2     If the furnishings are valuable it may be desirable to apportion the price for stamp duty and capital gains tax purposes.

3     If possible an up-to-date inventory should be drawn up and preferably agreed with the tenant.

4     The obligation to repay the deposit is personal to the original parties and therefore the seller remains liable to the tenant notwithstanding the assignment of the reversion: *Hua Chiao Commercial Bank Ltd v Chiaphua Industries Ltd* [1987] AC 99, [1987] 1 All ER 1110, PC.

**[4594]**

# 152

## Sale of property subject to a verbal agreement to grant a lease[1]

0.1     The Property is sold subject to the rights of *(name)* ('the Tenant') as tenant under a verbal agreement made on or about *(date)* to grant him a lease for *(number)* years at a rent of £… [on the terms that he make certain improvements]

0.2     The Tenant has taken occupation and paid rent [and carried out the improvements] and the sale is subject to such rights as he may have[2]

1     As to agreements for lease generally see 27(1) Halsbury's Laws (4th Edn Reissue) para 50 et seq.

2     The rights of a tenant in occupation of registered land are binding against the proprietor of the land as overriding interests under the Land Registration Act 1925 s 70(1)(g) (37 Halsbury's Statutes (4th Edn) REAL PROPERTY).

**[4595]**

# 153

## Sale of property subject to a lease for which the mortgagee's consent was not obtained

0.1     The Property is subject to a tenancy agreement dated *(date)* made between *(grantor)* ('the Grantor') (1) and *(tenant)* ('the Tenant') (2) ('the Lease') but at the time of the grant of the Lease the interest of the Grantor was subject to a mortgage in favour of *(mortgagee)* which excluded the mortgagor's power of leasing under the Law of Property Act 1925 Section 99[1]

0.2     The Buyer shall take the Property subject to the Lease and shall indemnify the Seller against all claims and demands by the Tenant or arising out of the Lease

1     Ie the Law of Property Act 1925 s 99 as amended by the Agricultural Tenancies Act 1995 s 31 (37 Halsbury's Statutes (4th Edn) REAL PROPERTY). This section cannot be excluded in the case of a mortgage of:

    (1)    agricultural land made after 1 March 1948 and before 1 September 1995 or

    (2)    an agricultural holding made on or after 1 September to which the Agricultural Tenancies Act 1995 s 4 (1 Halsbury's Statutes (4th Edn) AGRICULTURE) applies: Law of Property 1925 s 99(13A) as inserted by the Agricultural Tenancies Act 1995 s 31.

Where the power of leasing is excluded a lease made without the mortgagee's consent is not binding on the mortgagee but is binding between the mortgagor and the tenant: *Lows v Telford* (1876) 1 App Cas 414, HL. On a sale by the mortgagor the lease is validated in the moment of time between redemption of the mortgage and completion of the sale. As against the mortgagee the tenant has no rights, but the seller remains liable to the tenant if the mortgagee takes possession.

**[4596]**

# 154

### Buyer not to object to the absence of a written tenancy agreement[1]

0.1     The Property is sold subject to the tenancy of *(name)* who went into occupation on or about *(date)* but the terms of the tenancy have never been recorded in writing

0.2     The Buyer has been given such information as the Seller has about the terms of letting and shall not raise any objection or requisition in relation to the tenancy

1     Subject to certain specific provisions in relation to agricultural tenancies (see vol 2(1) (1996 Reissue) AGRICULTURAL TENANCIES), business tenancies (see vols 22(1)–(4) (1996 and 1997 Reissues) LANDLORD AND TENANT) and assured tenancies (see vol 23 LANDLORD AND TENANT) a lease may be made orally if it is to take effect in possession for a term not exceeding 3 years, is at the best rent reasonably obtainable without taking a fine and is not of an incorporeal hereditament: Law of Property Act 1925 s 54(2) (37 Halsbury's Statutes (4th Edn) REAL PROPERTY). Unwritten tenancies of all kinds are very common. A contract to grant a lease must be made in writing and must comply with the provisions of the Law of Property (Miscellaneous Provisions) Act 1989 s 2 as amended by the Trusts of Land and Appointment of Trustees Act 1996 s 25(2), Sch 4 (37 Halsbury's Statutes (4th Edn) REAL PROPERTY): see vol 35 (1997 Reissue) SALE OF LAND Paragraph 200 [257] et seq.

[4597]

# 155

### Subsisting tenancy between seller and buyer to continue[1]

The [Lease *or* Tenancy] between the Seller and Buyer shall continue in full force and effect until the Buyer has paid the Purchase Price in full under this Agreement

1     This Form is intended for use with vol 36 (1997 Reissue) SALE OF LAND Form 103 [1819]. The purpose of this clause is to prevent the relationship of landlord and tenant being brought to an end inadvertently, eg by the existence of the contract for sale of the freehold to the tenant, which could give rise to difficulties if the tenant subsequently defaulted on completion: see eg *Cockwell v Romford Sanitary Steam Laundry Ltd* [1939] 4 All ER 370, CA.

[4598]

# 156

### Sale of a possessory title to a ground rent where there is a lease in existence

0.1     The Property is sold subject to a lease dated *(date)* made between *(parties)* ('the Lease')

0.2     The Buyer shall not require any documentary title to the reversion expectant on the Lease but shall accept a statutory declaration by [the Seller that he [and his predecessors as owners of the *(name)* Estate] [has *or* have] been in undisputed receipt of the rent for upwards of [12] years *or (name of agent)* agent to the *(name of estate)* Estate that he [and his firm] [has *or* have] collected the rent on behalf of the Seller [and his predecessors as owners of the *(name)* Estate] for upwards of [12] years]

[4599]

## 157

### Sale of a possessory title to a ground rent where no lease can be found[1]

0.1     The Property is sold subject to the rights of occupation of *(name of occupier)* who [and whose predecessors in title] [has *or* have] been in occupation of the Property for upwards of [12] years paying a [yearly] rent of £...

0.2     The Buyer shall take such title as the Seller can offer supported by a statutory declaration by [the Seller that he [and his predecessors as owners of the *(name)* Estate] [has *or* have] been in undisputed receipt of the rent for upwards of [12] years *or (name of agent)* agent to the *(name)* Estate that he [and his firm] [has *or* have] collected the rent on behalf of the Seller [and his predecessors as owners of the *(name)* Estate] for upwards of [12] years] and by a letter from *(name of occupier)* confirming that he does not claim to be the owner of the fee simple but has always regarded the Seller as the person entitled to the rents

**[4600]**

1       It is often the case that properties have been occupied, sometimes for centuries, in return for a fixed payment to a local landowner. There can be many explanations for this, eg a freehold estate subject to a rentcharge, a yearly tenancy whose rent has never been reviewed, or even some form of ancient freehold tenure reserving a rent of assize. The rents vary from a few pence to a few pounds and are rarely worth litigation so that in many cases it is impossible to determine the true situation. As inflation reduces the value of the rents these interests disappear and the occupier in due course obtains a possessory title.

In relation to the kind of long lease where records tend to have gone missing long ago (if they ever existed in documentary form), these were typically for hundreds of years, if not for a thousand years or more. This had in many cases to do with the 'rotten boroughs' arrangements where local landowners created long leases in order not to enfranchise citizens in an era when voting rights were accorded only to freeholders. In such cases, unless the conditions exist under which the leases can be enlarged by the current leasehold owner under the Law of Property Act 1925 s 153 (37 Halsbury's Statutes (4th Edn) REAL PROPERTY), the leases continue despite non-payment of rent. Otherwise, whilst the landlord can lose the right to recover rent that has been unpaid for more than the relevant limitation period, the tenant cannot obtain the freehold by adverse possession against the landlord until there has been the requisite possession after the term of the lease has expired.

**[4601]**

## 158

### Buyer to take the property in its present state of repair[1]

The Buyer [shall purchase the Property with notice of its present condition and] shall in the transfer indemnify the Seller against all liability for past or subsisting breaches of [repairing] covenants whether express or implied

1       This Form may be used if the lease contains covenants on the part of the landlord which have not been fully complied with, eg repairing covenants whether contained in the lease or implied by statute. The tenant may have claims against both the person who was landlord at the time of the breach and the landlord for the time being if the breach is continuing.

**[4602]**

## 159

### Assignment of rights arising from a breach of covenant

The Seller shall in the transfer specifically assign to the Buyer all subsisting rights arising out of breach of any covenant in the Lease whether relating to matters arising exclusively before the date of completion or being continuing breaches

**[4603]**

# 160

## Assignment of the benefit of a guarantee[1]

The Seller shall [on completion *or* in the transfer] assign to the Buyer the benefit of the guarantee contained in [the Lease *or* a licence to assign] dated *(date)* made between *(parties)*

1    Normally the benefit of a guarantee touches and concerns the land and therefore passes to a buyer of the reversion without express assignment: *P & A Swift Investments v Combined English Stores Group plc* [1989] AC 632, [1988] 2 All ER 885. A form of this type may, therefore, be considered superfluous, but a cautious buyer may require it.

**[4604]**

# 161

## Assignment of the benefit of covenants by sureties etc—full form[1]

The Seller and the Buyer shall execute in duplicate a deed (expressed to be supplemental to the assurance of the Property to the Buyer) in which:
0.1    the Seller will:
    0.1.1    with [full *or* limited] title guarantee assign to the Buyer the benefit of and right to enforce the covenants on the part of [the *or* each] [surety *or* guarantor] named in the [sub-][under]lease[s] subject to and with the benefit of which the Property is agreed to be sold contained in [the *or* those] [sub-][under]lease[s]
    0.1.2    irrevocably appoint the Buyer the attorney of the Seller in the name of the Seller to enforce the covenants and guarantees
    0.1.3    authorise the Buyer to retain for his absolute benefit all money recovered by the Buyer as the attorney of the Seller pursuant to such supplemental deed and
    0.1.4    undertake to ratify all things properly done by the Buyer as the attorney of the Seller pursuant to such supplemental deed
0.2    the Buyer shall covenant to keep the Seller fully and effectually indemnified from and against all costs claims demands damages and losses and any other expenses arising from anything done or purported to be done by the Buyer as the attorney of the Seller pursuant to such supplemental deed

1    In *Kumar v Dunning* [1989] QB 193, [1987] 2 All ER 801, CA, it was stated that a covenant by a surety, guaranteeing performance of tenants' covenants which touch and concern the land, itself touches and concerns the land and is enforceable by an assignee of the reversion. The covenant in that case related not only to payment of rent but also to repair, insurance and user of the premises. All such covenants by a tenant in favour of the landlord touch and concern the land, ie the landlord's reversion. Consequently, it is necessary to have an express assignment only where the covenant by the surety extends to covenants by the tenant which do not touch and concern the land.

**[4605]**

# 162

## Assignment of the benefit of covenants by sureties etc—short form referring to an annexed draft[1]

There shall be executed in duplicate by the Seller and the Buyer and delivered on the Completion Date a deed (expressed to be supplemental to the assurance of the Property to the Buyer) in the form of the annexed draft deed marked *(insert details of identifying mark)*

1    See Form 161 note 1 [4605] ante.

**[4606]**

# 163

### Transfer of a service charge account[1]

The Seller shall on completion [transfer *or* allow] to the Buyer the amount of the balance in the service charge account [and will assign to the Buyer the right to recover all arrears of service charge]

1      This Form is intended for guidance only. The wording required will depend on the circumstances of each case. Service charge accounts can be substantial, particularly if a sinking fund for major repairs has built up over several years, and the tax position on the fund and any interest earned will need to be considered. The accounting year of the service charge is unlikely to end with the completion date and unless the whole of the cost of services is recoverable from the tenants provision may be needed for apportionments. For another Form see vol 38(1) (2000 Reissue) SALE OF LAND Form 57 schedule 5 para 3 [2150].

**[4607]**

# 164

### Collection of unpaid rent due on completion[1]

If the rent due on the last rent day falling on or before the date of actual completion has not been paid by that date the Buyer will pay in addition to the purchase price a sum equal to the outstanding rent and the Seller will assign to the Buyer the right to recover that rent from the tenant

1      Arrears of rent are always a problem. If the tenant is habitually slow the buyer will not want to pay to the seller a sum which he may only be able to recover with difficulty. An alternative is to preserve the seller's right to recover the rent and provide that the buyer shall, at the seller's cost, give all reasonable assistance including forfeiting the lease. However, the buyer will probably not be willing to do that. For a fuller form see vol 38(1) (2000 Reissue) SALE OF LAND Form 57 schedule 5, paragraph 2 [2149].

**[4608**

# 165

### Assignment of arrears of rent of a tenanted property[1]

0.1      If at the date of completion the tenant shall be in arrears with his rent the Buyer shall pay to the Seller or as the Seller may direct the full amount of such arrears due on the date of actual completion and the Seller will if required by the Buyer assign or obtain the assignment to the Buyer of the arrears due from the tenant

0.2      The costs of preparing arranging and executing the assignment shall be borne by the Buyer

1      For a fuller form see vol 38(1) (2000 Reissue) SALE OF LAND Form 57 schedule 5, paragragh 2 [2149].

**[4609]**

# 166

## Buyer to indemnify the seller against future breach of landlord's obligations[1]

The Buyer shall in a deed (expressed to be supplemental to the assurance of the Property to the Buyer) to be executed by the Buyer and delivered to the Seller on the Completion Date covenant with the Seller:

0.1     fully and effectually to indemnify and keep so indemnified the Seller [and his estate and effects] in respect of any obligations of the Seller relating to the [tenancy *or* tenancies] the future breach non-observance or non-performance of which would expose the Seller to liability notwithstanding completion[2]

[0.2     not during the subsistence of [any of] the [tenancy *or* tenancies] to grant any lease tenancy licence or other occupational interest in respect of the Property or any part of the Property upon terms which are in breach of or may result in the breach of [any of] the [tenancy *or* tenancies] and

0.3     not to allow any person to grant any lease tenancy licence or occupational interest in respect of the Property or any part of the Property which if granted by the Buyer would be in breach of the covenant by the Buyer contained in sub-clause 2 of this clause][3]

**[4610]**

---

1     This clause is intended to protect a seller selling property subject to existing tenancies where, by application of the doctrine of privity of contract, the seller remains liable to tenants for the due performance of obligations entered into by the seller, notwithstanding the sale of the property. It is most likely to be useful where the seller covenanted to provide services, eg to insure, to carry out some or all repairs, to provide the services of specified staff and the like, or where the seller covenanted to restrict competitive trading.

    An example of a situation in which the seller could be exposed in the absence of a deed such as provided for by this clause would arise if the seller owned a parade of, say, three shops and in the lease of one of them, covenanted with the tenant that he would not allow either of the other two shops to be used as a newsagents or tobacconists. A prudent landlord will provide in such a lease that the observance of the restrictive covenant is to be dependent upon the registration of a land charge, notice or caution by the tenant within a short specified period after the date of the grant of the lease. If the effectiveness of the restriction is not made dependent upon such registration, and if the tenant fails to register accordingly, the seller may, by oversight, sell one of the other shops free from the restriction and if subsequently the shop sold is used as a newsagents or tobacconists, whilst the restriction is not binding on the buyer of that shop from the landlord, the tenant of the shop having the benefit of the restriction will be able to claim damages from the landlord: see *Wright v Dean* [1948] Ch 686, [1948] 2 All ER 415.

    The landlord is not able to claim an indemnity from the buyer of the shop sold because the buyer of that shop has purchased it without notice of the restriction.

    Where the only continuing obligation of the seller is for quiet enjoyment, it is generally considered that sub-clauses 2 and 3 of this clause are unnecessary.

2     The modern practice is to provide for a specific indemnity.

3     This sub-clause creates a restrictive covenant. To be effective, it must be protected (in the case of unregistered land) by the registration of a Class D(ii) land charge under the Land Charges Act 1972 s 2(5)(ii) (37 Halsbury's Statutes (4th Edn) REAL PROPERTY), against the buyer on the completion of the sale, pursuant to a priority notice which should be registered between exchange of contracts and completion. Where the buyer's title to the property will be registered, by the Land Registration Rules 1925, SR&O 1925/1093 r 40 the restriction is bound to be entered in the register of the buyer's title provided the deed is disclosed with the application for first registration as it should be by virtue of the applicant's obligation to lodge all deeds and documents relating to the property (see SR&O 1925/1093 r 20 as amended by SI 1997/3037) and the statements made in the application form. The covenantee may lodge a caution against first registration to protect his position once the deed has been executed.

**[4611]–[4650]**

# INDEX

*References are to the numbers in square brackets which appear on the right hand side of the text*

**RESIDENTIAL DEVELOPMENT—** *Cont*
  estate, sale of plots on—*Cont*
    steps in preparation for—*Cont*
      instructions, taking, [3961]
      Land Registry, [3969]
      local Land Charge search, [3970]
      mortgagee consents, [3969]
      National House Building Council Scheme, [3975] [3976]
      plot disposals, method of, [3966]
      plot sale record, [3970]
      post office postal numbers, [3970]
      roads and sewers, [3971]–[3973]
      site inspection, [3962]
      structural guarantee schemes, [3974]–[3978]
      unadopted amenity areas, [3967]
      Zurich Municipal building guarantees, [3977] [3978]
  pre-contract information—
    access, [4002]
    adverse rights, [4004]
    boundaries, [4001]
    disputes and notice, [4004]
    guarantees, [4002]
    land registration, [4005]
    local searches, [4005]
    planning, [4003]
    services, [4003]
    shared facilities, [4004]
    specification, [4004]

**ROAD.** *See* HIGHWAY

**SALE AGREEMENT (COMMERCIAL PROPERTY)**
  additional consideration based on residual land value, agreement for—
    agreement, [3293]
    ascertainment of consideration—
      further consideration, [3298]
      residual land value, [3299]
    buyer obligations, [3295]
    cut-off period, [3296]

**SALE AGREEMENT (COMMERCIAL PROPERTY)—** *Cont*
  additional consideration based on residual land value, agreement for—*Cont*
    deed of variation, [3294]
    further consideration, [3294]
    joint and several liability, [3296]
    receipt, [3296]
    restrictive covenant—
      seller's right of re-entry, [3332] [3333]
      use of property for other than agricultural purposes, preventing, [3331]–[3333]
  conditional—
    inter-relation of, [3011]
    supplementary precedents, [3004]
  purchase price, ascertainment of—
    adjustment according to rents reserved on subsequent letting of vacant space, [3261]–[3264]
    adjustment by reference to indexation, [3270]–[3271]
    open market value basis, on, [3257]–[3259]
    residential density, according to, [3267]–[3268]
    residual land value, by, [3251]–[3254]
  single freehold commercial property with vacant possession, for, conditional on obtaining planning permission—
    buyer, drafted in favour of—
      agreement for sale, [3128]
      assignment and sub-sale, restriction on, [3137]
      completion, [3131]
      conditions of sale and documents, incorporation, [3137]
      deposit, [3128]
      disclaimer, [3135]
      encumbrances, [3133] [3134]
      governing law, [3138]
      guarantee, [3138] [3142] [3143]
      insolvency of buyer, [3138]